Juniper Networks® Field Guide and Reference

Juniper Networks® Field Guide and Reference

Aviva Garrett, Gary Drenan, Cris Morris
and Juniper Networks®

Addison-Wesley

Boston • San Francisco • New York • Toronto • Montreal
London • Munich • Paris • Madrid
Capetown • Sydney • Tokyo • Singapore • Mexico City

The publisher offers discounts on this book when ordered in quantity for bulk purchases and special sales. For more information, please contact:

U.S. Corporate and Government Sales
(800) 382-3419
corpsales@pearsontechgroup.com

For sales outside the U.S., please contact:

International Sales
(317) 581-3793
international@pearsontechgroup.com

Visit Addison-Wesley on the Web: www.awprofessional.com

Library of Congress Cataloging-in-Publication Data

Garrett, Aviva

Juniper Networks field guide and reference / Garrett, Aviva; Drenan, Gary; Morris, Cris.

p. cm

Includes bibliographical references and index.

ISBN 0-321-12244-5 (alk. paper)

1. Routers (Computer networks) 2. Computer Networks--Equipment and supplies. 3. Juniper Networks, Inc. I. Drenan, Gary. II. Morris, Cris. III. Title.

TK5105.543.G37 2003

004.6--dc21 2002027720

ISBN 0-321-12244-5
Text printed on recycled paper
1 2 3 4 5 6 7 8 9 10—MA—0605040302
First printing, September 2002

Brief Contents

Contents

List of Figures

List of Tables

Introduction

When I wrote the first Juniper Networks software manual in the early summer of 1997, it was about 250 pages. When we shipped JUNOS Release 3.2 in March 1999, the JUNOS manual was just shy of 1,000 pages. I was dismayed at the prospect of having the manual be in two volumes and asked the development engineers to stop writing code. Of course, they didn't honor my request. At the time of this writing, the JUNOS documentation set is 5,700 pages in 13 separate volumes. Similarly, the hardware documentation set has grown from a single 120-page manual to more than 250 pages of documentation for each of six platforms.

When our long-time publishing consultant, Patrick Ames, suggested that we might want to create a small field guide for installing, configuring, and operating Juniper Networks routers, I thought it would be nice to return to a world in which we could document the product in under 1,000 pages. We created a small team of technical documentation writers and editors—Gary Drenan, Cris Morris, Patrick Ames, and myself—and together we sifted the contents of all the JUNOS and hardware documentation, extracting the material that we felt was essential for understanding the mission of Juniper Networks and for understanding our hardware and software products. (We felt this was a more prudent method than simply removing all the vowels or deleting all the verbs.)

This book is the result of our extracting and condensing process. We begin with a brief overview of Juniper Networks the company, describing our markets, services, and offerings. While much of this information exists on the Web site—and we recommend you get the most updated material there—we felt that the book should provide some background about the company itself.

Chapter 2, "JUNOS Internet Software Overview," presents the big-picture view of the JUNOS software. This chapter is short not by design, but because the JUNOS architecture has always been straightforward, clear, and succinct. In Chapter 3, "Juniper Network Router Overview," our senior hardware writer Gary Drenan has worked diligently not only to review all the components and specifications of both the M-series and new T-series routers, but also to collect and collate it in one place. In creating Chapter 4, "Router Installation and

Basic JUNOS Setup," Gary has similarly collected everything about installation, from unpacking the crate to getting the router up and running in the network.

Chapters 4 through 12 are concerned with configuring the router and describing the feature set of the JUNOS Internet software. Beginning with Chapter 5, "CLI and System Management," our senior editor Cris Morris efficiently describes how to work with the software. The following chapters detail interfaces and class of service (in Chapter 6) and IPSec (in Chapter 7). Chapters 8 through 10 get to the heart of IP networking, discussing routing policy and firewall filters, routing and routing protocols, and IPv6, respectively.

Chapter 11 looks at MPLS applications, Chapter 12 at virtual private networks (VPNs), and Chapter 13 contains a useful, tabular summary of all the critical JUNOS Internet software monitoring commands (I suspect these might turn out to be the most dog-eared pages of your field guide). Chapter 13 provides sample configurations that come directly from the Juniper Networks testing labs. Finally, we conclude with a glossary of the many Juniper Networks–specific acronyms and terms so you don't have to try to memorize them all.

While we have tried to summarize the Juniper Networks hardware and software features in this field guide, there will undoubtedly be places where the information is insufficient for your needs. Please refer to the Appendix in this book that lists additional resources. Also remember that you can always find a full and complete discussion in the Juniper Networks technical product documentation.

The *Juniper Networks Field Guide and Reference* has been edited and reviewed by myself and the core team at Juniper Networks that has been working on this project. However, it represents the work of dozens if not hundreds of Juniper Networks employees over the past five years to write, refine, review, edit, and test the Juniper Networks IP networking technology. While we cannot acknowledge everyone, we would like to acknowledge a few of the key contributors.

First and foremost my fellow editors and I would like to thank the writers, editors, and production and tools contributors to the technical documentation effort over the years: Pat Adams, Dirk Bergstrom, Renu Bhargava, Barbara Bissinger, Faith Bradford, John Chan, Barbara Dahl, Brenda DePaolis, Nancy Edmonds, Betsy Fitch, Stella Hackell, Ed Harper, Jim Hayes, Richard Hendricks, Betsy Herbert, Margaret Jones, Joshua Kim, Jenna Kinghorn, Elizabeth Lichtenberg,

Ken Liou, Barbara Matsumura, Donice Mitchell, Eva Moore, Pam Muraca, Rene Partyka, Frank Reade, Liz Rodgers, Regina Roman, Sonia Saruba, Albert Statti, Cathy Steinberg, Alan Twhigg, Ellen Turner, Carrie Unger, and Merisha Wazna.

Second, we would like to thank and acknowledge the members of the development engineering, system test, and mechanical and compliance groups at Juniper Networks, as well as the members of the product management team. I apologize for thanking them as a group, but I fear I would forget many names if I attempted to list them all. For help in the development of this book, I would like to thank Sachin Vasudeva and his team for providing the sample configurations.

Third, we would like to thank our customers—early adopters, beta customers, and regular customers—for providing us ongoing feedback and input about our documentation. We would especially like to thank Andrew Partan, Guy Davies, and Randy Bush, as well as John Heasley, Dorian Kim, Jared Mauch, Peter Schoenmaker, Sara Ruhmann, and other members of the Verio network design team.

Finally, I would like to thank Peter Wexler, my first manager at Juniper Networks, for having faith in me and allowing me to create a world-class technical publications group to partner with our peers in engineering. I would also like to thank my husband, David, and my daughter, Sage, for patiently supporting me through the startup years at the company.

Cris Morris would like to personally thank his wife, Laura, for her patience and encouragement.

Gary Drenan would like to personally thank his mother, for, among many things, providing a strong foundation in the English language that has served him well as a writer; Cindy and Arandi, for their constant friendship; and Nicolai, for his invaluable guidance in developing Gary's life and career.

Our joint appreciation goes to Karen Gettman, Emily Frey, Kim Dawley, John Fuller, and Tyrrell Albaugh at Addison-Wesley, and to their many competent and thorough editors and publishing personnel.

If you would like to give us your feedback or errata about this field guide, please send us e-mail at tech-doc@juniper.net.

Aviva Garrett
September 2002

Book Conventions

We've used a few common conventions within this field guide to help you work with Juniper Networks information and content.

We use marginalia to call attention to references and key topics. These can generally be one of four usages:

- A cross-reference within this book.
- A cross-reference to the Juniper Networks documentation. Some are explicit, and some might seem vague depending on the reference itself. For references that seem vague, we suggest using the comprehensive index manual or the book's index to help you find exactly what you need. The documentation undergoes constant change, so we try to provide references that will not go out of date quickly.
- A cross-reference to other publications such as RFCs.
- A key idea, concept, or note worthy of calling attention to itself in the margin. Sometimes you'll also find the same information stressed within the text body.

Router and router component labels are shown in a sans serif font, as when `Ethernet` is the label for the Ethernet management port on a router.

Statements, commands, filenames, directory names, IP addresses, and configuration hierarchy levels are also shown in a sans serif font, as in the following example in which *stub* is a statement name and *[edit protocols osfp area area-id]* is a configuration hierarchy level:

> To configure a stub area, include the `stub` management at the `[edit protocols ospf area` *`area-id`*`]` hierarchy level.

Options, which are variable terms for which you substitute appropriate values, are shown in italics, as in the following example in which *area-id* is an option:

```
area area-id;
```

In examples, text that you type literally is shown in bold. In the following example, you type the word *show*:

```
[edit protocols ospf area area-id]
cli# show
stub <default-metric metric >
```

Optional portions of a configuration statement are enclosed in angle brackets. In the following example, the "`default-metric` *`metric`*" portion of the statement is optional:

```
stub <default-metric metric>;
```

CHAPTER

1

Juniper Networks

Juniper Networks develops and sells Internet Protocol (IP) infrastructure systems to more than 500 service providers and carriers worldwide. The company is known for its purpose-built approach to product design that has helped service providers develop and exploit intelligent IP networks.

To contact Juniper Networks by phone, call 888-JUNIPER (888-586-4737) or 408-745-2000.

Shares of Juniper Networks publicly trade on Nasdaq under the symbol JNPR. The corporate headquarters are located in Sunnyvale, California, with sales, service, and educational offices located around the world.

Juniper Networks routers are designed around purpose-built application-specific integrated circuits (ASICs), which have the capability to process packets across all interfaces without affecting performance. Juniper Networks platforms support more than 75 network interface types. The routers are compact with high port density, saving scarce space in equipment racks and boosting power efficiency.

All Juniper Networks routers run JUNOS software, which provides full manageability and interoperability with other vendors' equipment and applications. All Juniper Networks routers support IPv4 and IPv6, and a robust set of protocols, including BGP, MPLS, IS-IS, OSPF, MSDP, PIM, MBGP, DVMRP, and RIP. The routers support such features as MPLS traffic engineering and the Virtual Router Redundancy Protocol (VRRP) to minimize congestion and increase reliability. Juniper Networks provides carrier-class fault tolerance, which is the highest level of system reliability, equivalent to less than five minutes of unscheduled equipment downtime annually.

By nature of their design, Juniper Networks routers and JUNOS software are inherently secure. The JUNOS software is stable and robust, and the router hardware and JUNOS software provide features to protect against attacks, thus minimizing router vulnerabilities.

For additional phone numbers, street addresses, and worldwide corporate offices, see www.juniper.net.

Juniper Networks outsources all manufacturing for faster time to market, faster production volume, and lower total product costs. The company sells products and services through a direct sales force, specialized value-added resellers, and global distributors. It offers a customer services portfolio for service providers and carriers that includes standard support through telephone and the Web, plus options for onsite support and hardware replacement.

Juniper Networks Markets

Juniper Networks offers service providers and carriers a range of IP services to accelerate the carrier transition to IP in four specific markets: backbone core, edge, mobile, and cable. The following descriptions of these markets are herewith abbreviated from the *Juniper Networks 2001 Annual Report.*

Backbone Core

The core of service provider networks needs to provide a unique combination of speed and intelligence to scale network offerings on demand at the edge of the network. Core users are service providers and carriers provisioning and deploying scalable IP infrastructure for quickly creating premium IP services. These value-added services are delivered to enterprises, governments, and regional providers that resell the services. Growth in the network edge business fuels the need for more backbone core capacity and shared software functionality to enable new IP services. The need is for scalable solutions with a common set of features and services to minimize capital expenses and reduce operational costs.

Edge

The edge is where service providers depend on the New Public Network for value-added IP services that give their customers connections to resilient IP services and dedicated access. Stress on edge and dedicated access infrastructure stems from growth in multilayer enterprise VPN offerings, consumer broadband connections, and other concurrent class-differentiated services, including access from mobile networks.

Mobile

Legacy Frame Relay and cell relay networks need IP overlays to scale new, concurrent voice, video, or data services on 2.5G and 3G wireless networks. Mobile operators require a new gateway platform—a scalable, wireless Internet router—to interface hundreds of thousands of wireless connections with the edge of a mobile network.

Cable

Cable market multiservice operators (MSOs) enhance the value of hybrid fiber–coax networks through a unique combination of scalable IP voice, video, and data services. Consumer users depend on MSOs to provide scalable access to these IP services through two-way interactive cable modems. MSOs need to upgrade both the legacy routing and asymmetric cable head-end portions of their networks to provision two-way IP services at scale. These cable operators require infrastructure that efficiently facilitates software control and management of multimedia IP services from multiple service operators over the same network.

Customer Services

A portfolio of customer services is available from Juniper Networks, some of them freely available to the public at www.juniper.net. Most services, however, are incorporated in sales service agreements designed to help and assist the Juniper Networks customer. The support services plan for maintenance and hardware delivery needs has several levels of support. Education and training services offer programs for product and technology training, and a certification program to enable engineers and others to validate product competence. The advanced professional services program provides supplemental consulting, design, and project management resources. Onsite residence is available.

Support Services Packages

Several support packages are available from Juniper Networks to ensure maximum uptime. Other levels of service are part of specific or customized service agreements that are best handled by contacting a Juniper Networks sales representative.

Core Support Package. This service package provides access to the Juniper Networks Technical Assistance Center (JTAC) and to the Customer Support Center (CSC).

Next-day Hardware Replacement. This service includes the Core Support Package plus the delivery of covered replacement hardware on the next business day.

Same-day Hardware Replacement. It includes the Core Support Package features, plus the delivery of covered replacement hardware within four hours of your request on the same day.

Same-day Onsite Technician. With this service, Juniper Networks sends a skilled technician to install replacement parts. It includes all Core Support Package features, plus the delivery of covered replacement hardware within four hours of your request.

Premier Support. When a predetermined level of support is reached, customers are automatically enrolled in the Premier Support Program and receive a designated JTAC Technical Support Engineer and a backup engineer allocated to their account.

Professional services consultants are available to help develop a plan to apply these advanced services where they are most needed, such as network design, project management, and even customized network workshops. Dedicated seats are also reserved for select staff in Juniper Networks standard technical product training courses.

Juniper Networks Technical Assistance Center (JTAC)

The Juniper Networks Technical Assistance Center (JTAC) is available for all levels of service agreement. All levels of supports allow an unlimited number of calls and cases, as well as availability 24 hours a day, 7 days a week, 365 days a year. JTAC support also provides unlimited access to JTAC engineers through the Internet and phone. The engineers help troubleshoot and diagnose any network anomaly.

Escalation Management

To ensure quick response, automatic escalation alerts to senior management are triggered on priority issues. A priority management system is used for each case opened with the JTAC. A Juniper Networks engineer and the customer designated representative jointly set the priority.

Customer Support Center (CSC)

Access to the online Customer Support Center (CSC), which includes the ability to download major, minor, and maintenance JUNOS Internet software upgrades, is part of all support packages. The CSC provides secure Web-based access to key technical information, such as frequently asked questions (FAQs), field alerts, problem reports, technical notes, release notes, and product documentation. The Juniper.net Case Manager enables customers to create, search, view, and change their technical support cases (see "Juniper.net" on page 7).

Education Services

Juniper Networks technical education courses are designed to teach the technical detail and capabilities required to ensure a network is operating at peak performance. Courses are offered at Juniper Networks Knowledge Centers.

Courses are also conducted by authorized instructors at Juniper Networks Authorized Education Centers. These strategic education partners use only Juniper Networks–authorized instructors and Juniper Networks–developed courseware. They must maintain the same strict quality standards that we require of our own instructors and training organizations.

To register for a course at one of the Juniper Networks Knowledge Centers, go to www.juniper.net/training.

While there are no official course prerequisites, attendees of all Juniper Networks technical education courses are expected to have general familiarity with TCP/IP basics, link-state routing protocols, operation of BGP4 and its mandatory attributes, and general interdomain routing issues. Although not required, familiarity with the command-line interface of a routing platform or UNIX is helpful. Classes are posted on www.juniper.net or the Juniper Networks Authorized Education Center's Web site.

Occasionally, Juniper Networks delivers open enrollment courses at locations other than its Knowledge Centers. See www.juniper.net for course availability. Courses can also be taught at your site.

Technical Certification

The JNTCP consists of four certification programs: Certified Internet Associate (CIA), Certified Internet Specialist (CIS), Certified Internet Professional (CIP), and Certified Internet Expert (CIE).

The Juniper Networks Technical Certification Program (JNTCP) allows participants to demonstrate, through a combination of paper-based proficiency tests and hands-on configuration and debugging tests, competence with Juniper Networks technology. Anyone experienced with Juniper Networks products and platforms can qualify for the certification process. Non-Juniper Networks certification, such as from Cisco Systems, is not applicable toward the successful completion of the exams.

Juniper Networks Certified Internet Experts (JNCIE) receive full-time Technical Assistance Center access, an engraved crystal plaque with their name and certification status, and a reproducible Juniper Networks Certification logo to use on business cards, personal Web pages, and printed documents.

Professional Services

Professional services consultants are available both short-term and long-term to supplement staff in planning, analyzing, designing, implementing, operating, and managing networks. They assist with network planning, modeling, and design; network optimization and enhancement; routing policy and configuration design; project implementation and management; and custom design workshops. Resident engineers are available on a quarterly or yearly basis as onsite resources for operational, design, and planning assistance.

Juniper.net

The Juniper Networks Web site (www.juniper.net) is a central repository for company information and technical support solutions. It provides solutions-oriented and technology literature, including technical documentation, application notes, interoperability test papers, white papers, and technology notes. Also on the Juniper.net Web site are sales contacts, sales programs, and new and noteworthy educational and training course information. Software downloads are available to customers with annual service agreements. You can also find the Case Manager, a resource for creating, tracking, and editing support cases.

Technical Documentation

Current Juniper Networks technical documentation is available on www.juniper.net. The JUNOS Internet software guides and references, and JUNOScript API guides and references are available in HTML and PDF formats. Enterprise MIBs are also available in a downloadable text format. Hardware guides for all Juniper Networks hardware platforms, including the M-series and T-series routers, and for all physical interface cards (PICs) are also available.

Most Juniper Networks documentation is also available in the ToGo document format, which can be read by devices running the Palm OS, and in Microsoft Reader eBook format.

The general public can purchase official Juniper Network print documentation from Vervante.com. Individual titles and complete sets can be ordered in any quantity and shipped around the world. Juniper.net has direct links to this print-on-demand service.

JUNOScript API Software Download

The JUNOScript application programming interface (API) is an Extensible Markup Language (XML) application that Juniper Networks routers use to exchange information with client applications. XML is a metalanguage for defining how to mark the organizational structures and individual elements in a data set or document with tags that describe the function of the structures and elements.

Juniper.net provides a set of Perl modules whose external interface, JUNOS::Device, helps in the development of custom Perl applications for configuring and monitoring routers. JUNOS::Device provides an object interface that client applications can use to communicate with the JUNOScript server on a router. The JUNOScript server is bundled with the standard JUNOS Internet software in JUNOS Releases 4.3 and later.

Accompanying the JUNOS::Device module are several sample Perl scripts that illustrate how to use the module to perform various functions, including requesting status information and parsing the JUNOScript server's response, configuring a router, and converting JUNOScript data for storage in and retrieval from a relational database. Readme files on Juniper.net provide instructions about installing the latest JUNOScript Perl module, sample scripts, and required Perl modules.

Other packages available on Juniper.net contain the XML document type definitions (DTDs) for JUNOScript operational responses. Applications can validate XML data returned by the JUNOScript API using these DTDs.

Case Manager

The Case Manager is a support tool that allows customers and partners to open noncritical support cases and to view and edit all technical support cases on Juniper.net. The Web service provides an alternative method of monitoring cases other than calling a support engineer. The service is exclusively offered to customers and partners with service agreements.

For critical cases that need immediate attention, call the Juniper Networks Technical Assistance Center at 1-888-314-JTAC (Canada and USA) or 408-745-2121 (outside of USA).

A username and password are provided when you purchase a service agreement. Further password assistance is available on Juniper.net. You can query your account information by case ID and condition (open, closed, all). Each function in the Case Manager has an associated help screen. The process can be monitored at the user's discretion.

Internet and E-mail Contact Information

Use the e-mail addresses listed in Table 1.1 to reach the appropriate department at Juniper Networks.

Table 1.1 *Internet and E-mail Contact Addresses*

Category	Topic	E-mail Address or URL
General and Corporate	Juniper Networks, the company and current products and services	www.juniper.net
	Juniper Networks investments or investing in Juniper Networks	investor-relations@juniper.net
	Employment opportunities	jobs@juniper.net (US) jobs-emea@juniper.net (non-US) http://www.juniper.net/jobs
	Juniper.net Web site	webmaster@juniper.net
	Regular press updates	http://www.juniper.net/news/presscenter/news_subscribe.html
	Juniper Networks Industry Analyst Center	analyst-relations@juniper.net
	Juniper Networks community involvement	community-relations@juniper.net
Technical Support	Product or technology questions from existing customers	support@juniper.net
	Professional Services	prosvcs@juniper.net
Discussion List	Juniper-nsp is an open customer e-mail list for discussing Juniper Networks products and technology	http://puck.nether.net/lists/juniper-nsp/
Sales	To have a Juniper Networks sales representative contact you, complete this form	www.juniper.net/products/sales.html
	Service contracts	contracts@juniper.net
	Product repair and returns	logistics@juniper.net
	Reseller marketing	partner-marketing@juniper.net

Table 1.1 *Internet and E-mail Contact Addresses*

Category	Topic	E-mail Address or URL
Education and Training	Training	training@juniper.net
	Certification program	certification@juniper.net
Publications	Technical documentation feedback and errata	techpubs-comments@juniper.net
	Juniper Networks Book Initiative (JNBI)	book-publishing@juniper.net

CHAPTER

2

JUNOS Internet Software Overview

The JUNOS Internet software provides IP routing protocol software—as well as software for interface, network, and chassis management—specifically designed for the large production networks typically supported by Internet service providers (ISPs). The JUNOS Internet software runs on all Juniper Networks M-series and T-series routers and routing nodes.

Architecturally, the router is composed of two components as shown in Figure 2.1:

- Packet Forwarding Engine—Forwards packets through the router. The Packet Forwarding Engine is a high-performance switch that is capable of forwarding 40 million packets per second for any packet size. The Packet Forwarding Engine forwards packets between input and output interfaces. The function of the Packet Forwarding Engine can be understood by following the flow of a packet through the router—first into a PIC, then through the switching fabric, and finally out another PIC for transmission on a network link. When a packet arrives on an input interface, a media-specific PIC performs all media-specific functions such as framing and checksum verification.
- Routing Engine—Performs routing updates and system management. The Routing Engine consists of routing-protocol software processes running inside a protected memory environment on a general-purpose computer platform. The Routing Engine has a direct 100-Mbps connection to the Packet Forwarding Engine.

See "Router Architecture" on page 28.

Because this architecture separates control operations such as routing updates and system management from packet forwarding, the router can deliver superior performance and highly reliable Internet operation.

The Routing Engine handles all the routing protocol processes and other software processes that control the router's interfaces, a few of the chassis components, system management, and user access to the router. These routing and software processes run on top of a kernel that interacts with the Packet Forwarding Engine. Following are the features of the Routing Engine:

- Process routing protocol packets—All routing protocol packets from the network are directed to the Routing Engine, and therefore do not delay the Packet Forwarding Engine unnecessarily.

Figure 2.1 *Juniper Networks Router Architecture*

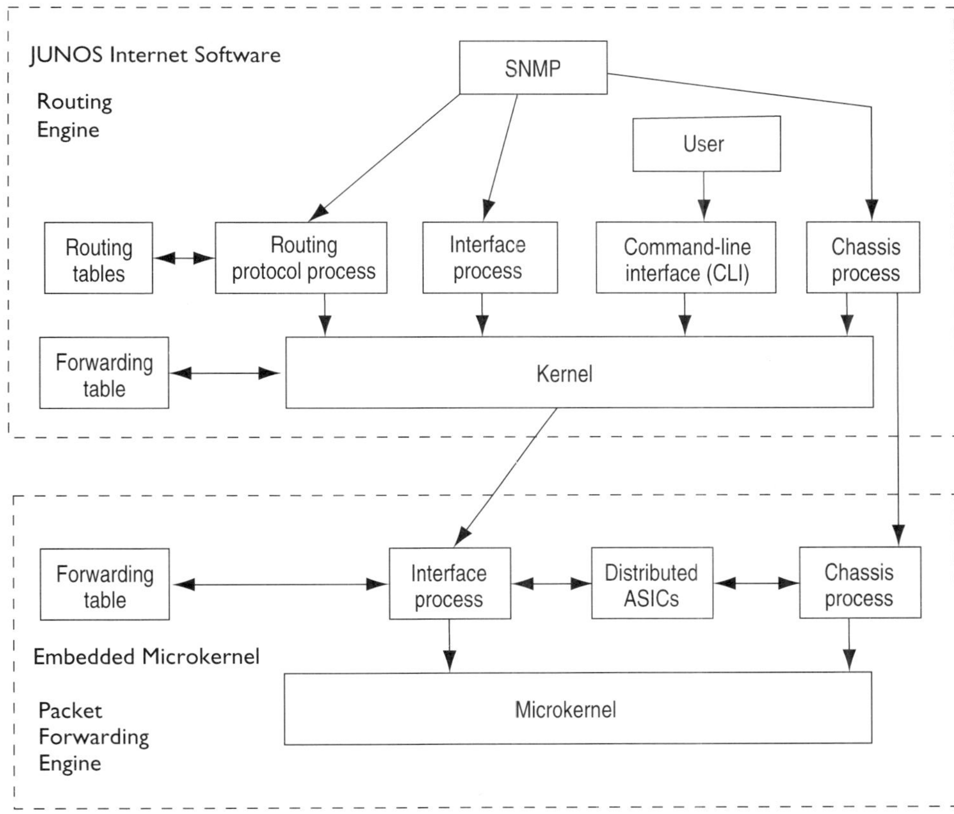

- Software modularity—By dividing software functions into separate processes, a failure of one process has little or no effect on the other software processes.
- In-depth Internet functionality—Each routing protocol is implemented with a complete set of Internet features and provides full flexibility for advertising, filtering, and modifying routes. Routing policies are set according to route parameters, such as prefix, prefix length, and BGP attributes.
- Scalability—The JUNOS routing tables are designed to hold all the routes in the network. Additionally, the JUNOS software can efficiently support large numbers of interfaces and virtual circuits.

- Management interfaces—System management is possible with a command-line interface (CLI), a craft interface, SNMP, and JUNOScript.
- Storage and change management—Configuration files, system images, and microcode can be held and maintained in one primary and two secondary storage systems, permitting local or remote upgrades.
- Monitoring efficiency and flexibility—Alarms can be generated and packets can be counted without adversely affecting packet forwarding performance.

The Routing Engine constructs and maintains one or more routing tables. From the routing tables, the Routing Engine derives a table of active routes, called the *forwarding table*, which is copied into the Packet Forwarding Engine. The forwarding table in the Packet Forwarding Engine can be updated without interrupting the router's forwarding.

JUNOS Processes

The Routing Engine software consists of several software processes that control router functionality and a kernel that provides the communication among all the processes (see Figure 2.1). It consists of software processes that support Internet routing protocols, control the router's interfaces and the router chassis itself, and allow router system management. All these processes run on top of a kernel that enables communication among all the processes and has a direct link to the Packet Forwarding Engine software. You use the JUNOS software to configure the routing protocols that should run on the router and to configure properties of the router's interfaces. Then, you use the JUNOS software to monitor the router and to troubleshoot protocol and network connectivity problems.

The Routing Engine kernel provides the underlying infrastructure for all JUNOS software processes. In addition, it provides the link between the routing tables and the Routing Engine's forwarding table. It is also responsible for all communication with the Packet Forwarding Engine, which includes keeping the Packet Forwarding Engine's copy of the forwarding table synchronized with the master copy in the Routing Engine.

Routing Protocol Process

The routing protocol process (RPD) controls the routing protocols that run on the router. It starts all configured routing protocols and handles all routing messages. It maintains one or more routing tables, which consolidate the routing information learned from all routing protocols into common tables. From this routing information, the routing protocol process determines the active routes to network destinations and installs them into the Routing Engine's forwarding table. Finally, it implements routing policy, which allows you to control the routing information that is transferred between the routing protocols and the routing table. Using routing policy, you can filter routing information so that only some of it is transferred, and you also can set properties associated with the routes.

JUNOS software implements full IP routing functionality, providing support for IP Version 4 (IPv4) and IP Version 6 (IPv6). The routing protocols are fully interoperable with existing IP routing protocols, and they have been developed to provide the scalability and control necessary for the Internet core.

JUNOS software provides the following routing and MPLS applications protocols:

- Unicast routing protocols
  - IS-IS—Intermediate System-to-Intermediate System
  - OSPF—Open Shortest Path First
  - RIP—Routing Information Protocol
  - ICMP—Internet Control Message Protocol
  - BGP—Border Gateway Protocol
- Multicast routing protocols
  - DVMRP—Distance Vector Multicast Routing Protocol
  - PIM—Protocol-Independent Multicast (sparse mode, dense mode, sparse-dense mode)
  - MSDP—Multicast Source Discovery Protocol
  - IGMP—Internet Group Management Protocol
  - SAP/SDP—Session Announcement Protocol and Session Description Protocol

- MPLS applications protocols
  - MPLS—Multiprotocol Label Switching
  - RSVP—Resource Reservation Protocol
  - LDP—Label Distribution Protocol
  - CCC—circuit cross-connect

A major function of the routing protocol process is to maintain the Routing Engine's routing tables and from these tables to determine the active routes to network destinations. The routing protocol process then installs these routes into the Routing Engine's forwarding table. The JUNOS kernel then copies this forwarding table to the Packet Forwarding Engine.

The routing protocol process maintains multiple routing tables. By default, it maintains the following three routing tables. You can configure additional routing tables to suit your requirements.

With each routing table, the routing protocol process uses the collected routing information to determine active routes to network destinations.

- Unicast routing table—Stores routing information for all unicast routing protocols running on the router. IS-IS, OSPF, RIP, and BGP all store their routing information in this routing table. You can configure additional routes, such as static routes, to be included in this routing table. IS-IS, OSPF, RIP, and BGP use the routes in this routing table when advertising routing information to their neighbors.
- Multicast routing table (cache)—Stores routing information for all the running multicast protocols. DVMRP and PIM both store their routing information in this routing table, and you can configure additional routes to be included in this routing table.
- MPLS routing table—Stores MPLS path and label information.

For unicast routes, the routing protocol process determines active routes by choosing the most preferred route, which is the route with the lowest preference value. By default, the route's preference value is simply a function of how the routing protocol process learned about the route. You can modify the default preference value using routing policy and with software configuration parameters.

For multicast traffic, the routing protocol process determines active routes based on traffic flow and other parameters specified by the multicast routing protocol algorithms. The routing protocol process then installs one or more active routes to each network destination into the Routing Engine's forwarding table.

By default, all routing protocols place their routes into the routing table. When advertising routes, the routing protocols by default advertise only a limited set of routes from the routing table. Specifically, each routing protocol exports only the active routes that were learned by that protocol. In addition, the Interior Gateway Protocols (IGPs) IS-IS, OSPF, and RIP export the direct (interface) routes for the interfaces on which the protocol is explicitly configured.

You can control the routes that a protocol places into each table and the routes from that table that the protocol advertises. You do this by defining one or more routing policies and then applying them to the specific routing protocol.

Routing policies applied when the routing protocol places routes into the routing table are referred to as *import policies* because the routes are being imported into the routing table. Those applied when the routing protocol is advertising routes that are in the routing table are referred to as *export policies* because the routes are being exported from the routing table. In other words, the terms *import* and *export* are used with respect to the routing table.

Routing policies allow you to control (filter) which routes a routing protocol imports into the routing table and which routes a routing protocol exports from the routing table. Routing policy also allows you to set the information associated with a route as it is being imported into or exported from the routing table. Filtering imported routes allows you to control the routes used to determine active routes. Filtering routes being exported from the routing table allows you to control the routes that a protocol advertises to its neighbors.

You implement routing policy by defining policies and then applying them to specific protocols. A policy specifies the conditions to use to match a route and the action to perform on the route when a match occurs. For example, when a routing table imports routing information from a routing protocol, a routing policy might modify the route's preference, mark the route with a color to identify it and allow it to be manipulated at a later time, or prevent the route from even being installed in a routing table. When exporting routes from a routing table into a routing protocol, a policy might assign metric values, modify the BGP community information, tag the route with additional information, or prevent the route from being exported altogether. You also can define policies for redistributing the routes learned from one protocol into another protocol.

Interface Process

The JUNOS interface process (dcd) allows you to configure and control the physical interface devices and logical interfaces present in a router. You can configure various interface properties such as the interface location (that is, which slot a Flexible PIC Concentrator [FPC] is installed in and which location on the FPC the Physical Interface Card [PIC] is installed in), the interface encapsulation, and interface-specific properties. You can configure the interfaces that currently are present in the router, as well as interfaces that currently are not present but that you might be adding at a future time.

The JUNOS interface process communicates, through the JUNOS kernel, with the interface process in the Packet Forwarding Engine, thus enabling the JUNOS software to track the status and condition of the router's interfaces.

Chassis Process

The JUNOS chassis process (chassisd) allows you to configure and control the properties of the router, including conditions that trigger alarms and clock sources. The chassis process communicates directly with a chassis process in the JUNOS kernel.

SNMP and MIB II Processes

The JUNOS software supports the Simple Network Management Protocol (SNMP), which helps administrators monitor the state of a router. The software supports SNMP Version 1 and Version 2 (also known as Version 2c, or v2c). The JUNOS implementation of SNMP does not include any of the security features that were originally included in the IETF SNMP drafts but were later dropped because of the inability to standardize on a particular method. The SNMP software is controlled by the JUNOS SNMP and MIB II processes, which consist of an SNMP master agent and various subagents.

Management Process

Within the JUNOS software, the management process (mgd), a process-controlling process, starts and monitors all the other software processes. It also starts the command-line interface (CLI), which is the primary tool you use to control and monitor the JUNOS Internet software. This management process starts all the software processes and the CLI when the router boots. If a software process terminates, the management process attempts to restart it.

Supported Networking Standards

To access Internet RFCs and drafts, go to the IETF Web site: http://www.ietf.org.

The JUNOS Internet software supports Internet RFCs and drafts; ISO standards; SDH and SONET standards; and ATM, Ethernet, Frame Relay, and T3 standards. Table 2.1, Table 2.2, and Table 2.3 list the networking standards supported by JUNOS software as of Release 5.4.

Table 2.1 *Supported Internet RFCs and Drafts*

Category	Title
ATM	RFC 1483, *Multiprotocol Encapsulation over ATM Adaptation Layer 5* (routed Protocol Data Units only)
	RFC 2225, *Classical IP and ARP over ATM* (responses only)
BGP	RFC 1771, *A Border Gateway Protocol 4 (BGP-4)*
	RFC 1772, *Application of the Border Gateway Protocol in the Internet*
	RFC 1966, *BGP Route Reflection—An Alternative to Full-Mesh IBGP*
	RFC 1997, *BGP Communities Attribute*
	RFC 2270, *Using a Dedicated AS for Sites Homed to a Single Provider*
	RFC 2283, *Multiprotocol Extensions for BGP-4*
	RFC 2385, *Protection of BGP Sessions via the TCP MD5 Signature Option*
	RFC 2439, *BGP Route Flap Damping*
	RFC 3065, *Autonomous System Confederations for BGP*
	Internet draft draft-ietf-ppvpn-rfc2547bis-00.txt, *BGP/MPLS VPNs*
	Internet draft draft-ietf-idr-cap-neg-01, *Capabilities Negotiation with BGP4*
CHAP	RFC 1994, *PPP Challenge Handshake Authentication Protocol (CHAP)*
Frame Relay	RFC 1490, *Multiprotocol Interconnect over Frame Relay*

Table 2.1 *Supported Internet RFCs and Drafts*

Category	Title
GRE and IP-IP Encapsulation	RFC 1701, *Generic Routing Encapsulation (GRE)*
	RFC 1702, *Generic Routing Encapsulation over IPv4 Networks*
	RFC 2003, *IP Encapsulation within IP*
IP Multicast	RFC 1112, *Host Extensions for IP Multicasting* (defines IGMP Version 1)
	RFC 2236, *Internet Group Management Protocol, Version 2*
	RFC 2327, *SDP: Session Description Protocol*
	RFC 2362, *Protocol Independent Multicast-Sparse Mode (PIM-SM): Protocol Specification*
	RFC 2365, *Administratively Scoped IP Multicast*
	Internet draft draft-ietf-mboned-anycast-rp-05.txt, *Anycast RP Mechanism using PIM and MSDP*
	Internet draft draft-ietf-idmr-dvmrp-v3-07.txt, *Distance Vector Multicast Routing Protocol*
	Internet draft draft-ietf-idmr-igmp-v3-07.txt (only SAP, Versions 0 and 1), *Internet Group Management Protocol,* Version 3
	Internet draft draft-ietf-msdp-spec-01.txt, *Multicast Source Discovery Protocol (MSDP)*
	Internet Draft draft-ietf-idmr-pim-sm-specv2-00.txt, *Protocol Independent Multicast-Sparse Mode (PIM-SM): Protocol Specification*
	Internet draft draft-ietf-pim-v2-dm-03.txt, *Protocol Independent Multicast-Version 2 Dense Mode Specification*
	Internet draft draft-ietf-mmusic-sap-00.txt, *SAP: Session Announcement Protocol*
IPSec and IKE	RFC 2085, *HMAC-MD5 IP Authentication with Replay Prevention*
	RFC 2401, *Security Architecture for the Internet Protocol*
	RFC 2402, *IP Authentication Header* (except for ES PIC)
	RFC 2403, *The Use of HMAC-MD5-96 within ESP and AH*
	RFC 2404, *The Use of HMAC-SHA-1-96 within ESP and AH*
	RFC 2405, *The ESP DES-CBC Cipher Algorithm with Explicit IV*
	RFC 2406, *IP Encapsulation Security Payload*
	RFC 2407, *The Internet IP Security Domain of Interpretation for ISAKMP*
	RFC 2408, *Internet Security Association and Key Management Protocol (ISAKMP)*
	RFC 2409, *Internet Key Exchange*
	RFC 2410, *The NULL Encryption Algorithm and Its Use with IPSec*
	RFC 2412, *The OAKLEY Key Determination Protocol*

Table 2.1 *Supported Internet RFCs and Drafts*

Category	Title
IPv6	ISO/IEC 10589, *Information technology, Telecommunications and information exchange between systems, Intermediate system to intermediate system intradomain routing information exchange protocol for use in conjunction with the protocol for providing the connectionless-mode network service (ISO 8473)*
	RFC 1157, *A Simple Network Management Protocol (SNMP)*
	RFC 1213, *Management Information Base for Network Management of TCP/IP-Based Internets: MIB-II*
	RFC 1215, *A Convention for Defining Traps for Use with SNMP*
	RFC 1195, *Use of OSI IS-IS for Routing in TCP/IP and Dual Environments*
	RFC 1771, *A Border Gateway Protocol 4 (BGP-4)*
	RFC 1772, *Application of the Border Gateway Protocol in the Internet*
	RFC 1901, *Introduction to Community-based SNMPv2*
	RFC 1902, *Structure of Management Information for Version 2 of the Simple Network Management Protocol (SNMPv2)*
	RFC 1905, *Protocol Operations for Version 2 of the Simple Network Management Protocol (SNMPv2)*
	RFC 1965, *Autonomous System Confederations for BGP*
	RFC 1966, *BGP Route Reflection: An Alternative to Full-Mesh IBGP*
	RFC 1997, *BGP Communities Attribute*
	RFC 2080, *RIPng for IPv6*
	RFC 2081, *RIPng Protocol Applicability Statement*
	RFC 2270, *Using a Dedicated AS for Sites Homed to a Single Provider*
	RFC 2283, *Multiprotocol Extensions for BGP-4*
	RFC 2373, *IP Version 6 Addressing Architecture*
	RFC 2385, *Protection of BGP Sessions via the TCP MD5 Signature Option*
	RFC 2439, *BGP Route Flap Damping*
	RFC 2545, *Use of BGP-4 Multiprotocol Extensions for IPv6 Inter-Domain Routing*
	RFC 2460, *Internet Protocol, Version 6 (IPv6) Specification*
	RFC 2461, *Neighbor Discovery for IP Version 6 (IPv6)*
	RFC 2578, *Structure of Management Information Version 2 (SMIv2)*
	RFC 2763, *Dynamic Hostname Exchange Mechanism for IS-IS*
	RFC 2893, *Transition Mechanisms for IPv6 Hosts and Routers*
	IETF draft draft-ietf-isis-ipv6-02.txt, *Routing IPv6 with IS-IS*
	IETF draft draft-ietf-idr-cap-neg-01.txt, *Capabilities Negotiation with BGP4*
	IETF draft draft-ramachandra-bgp-ext-communities-09.txt, *BGP Extended Communities Attribute*

Table 2.1 *Supported Internet RFCs and Drafts*

Category	Title
IS-IS	RFC 1195, *Use of OSI IS-IS for Routing in TCP/IP and Dual Environments*
	RFC 2104, *HMAC: Keyed-Hashing for Message Authentication*
	RFC 2763, *Dynamic Hostname Exchange Mechanism for IS-IS*
	RFC 2966, *Domain-wide Prefix Distribution with Two-Level IS-IS*
	RFC 2973, *IS-IS Mesh Groups*
	Internet draft draft-ietf-isis-traffic-02.txt , *IS-IS Extensions for Traffic Engineering*
	Internet draft draft draft-ietf-isis-3way-03.txt, *Three-Way Handshake for IS-IS Point-to-Point Adjacencies*
LDP	Internet draft draft-ietf-mpls-ldp-06.txt, *Label Distribution Protocol (LDP)—Version 1 Functional Specification*
MIBs	IEEE, 802.3ad, *Aggregation of Multiple Link Segments* (only the objects `dot3adAggMACAddress, dot3adAggAggregateOrIndividual, dot3adAggPortListPorts, and dot3adTablesLastChanged`)
	RFC 1157, *A Simple Network Management Protocol (SNMP)*
	RFC 1213, *Management Information Base for Network Management of TCP/IP-based Internets: MIB-II.* (except for `ipRouteTable`, which has been replaced by `ipCidrRouteTable` (RFC 2096)
	RFC 1215, *Convention for Defining Traps for Use with the SNMP* (only MIB II SNMP version 1 traps and version 2 notifications)
	RFC 1657, *Definitions of Managed Objects for the Fourth Version of the Border Gateway Protocol (BGP-4) using SMIv2*
	RFC 1850, *OSPF Version 2 Management Information Base* (except for the `ospfOriginateNewLsas` and `ospfRxNewLsas` objects, the Host Table, and the traps `ospfOriginateLSA`, `ospfLsdbOverflow`, and `ospfLsdbApproachingOverflow`)
	RFC 1901, *Introduction to Community-based SNMPv2*
	RFC 1902, *Structure of Management Information for Version 2 of the Simple Network Management Protocol (SNMPv2)*
	RFC 1905, *Protocol Operations for Version 2 of the Simple Network Management Protocol (SNMPv2)*
	RFC 1907, *Management Information Base for Version 2 of the Simple Network Management Protocol (SNMPv2)*
	RFC 2011, *SNMPv2 Management Information Base for the Internet Protocol Using SMIv2*
	RFC 2012, *SNMPv2 Management Information Base for the Transmission Control Protocol Using SMIv2*
	RFC 2013, *SNMPv2 Management Information Base for the User Datagram Protocol Using SMIv2*

Table 2.1 *Supported Internet RFCs and Drafts*

Category	Title
MIBs (continued)	RFC 2096, *IP Forwarding Table MIB*
	RFC 2115, *Management Information Base for Frame Relay DTEs Using SMIv2*
	RFC 2233, *The Interfaces Group MIB-II using SMIv2* (except `ifRcvAddressTable`)
	RFC 2287, *Definitions of System-Level Managed Objects for Applications* (only `sysApplInstallPkgTable`, `sysApplInstallElmtTable`, `sysApplElmtRunTable`, and `sysApplMapTable`)
	RFC 2465, *Management Information Base for IP Version 6: Textual Conventions and General Group* (except IPv6 or ICMPv6 statistics)
	RFC 2495, *Definitions of Managed Objects for the DS1, E1, DS2, and E2 Interface Types* (except for `dsx1FarEndConfigTable`, `dsx1FarEndCurrentTable`, `dsx1FarEndIntervalTable`, `dsx1FarEndTotalTable`, and `dsx1FracTable`)
	RFC 2496, *Definitions of Managed Objects for the DS3/E3 Interface Type* (except `dsx3FarEndConfigTable`, `dsx3FarEndCurrentTable`, `dsx3FarEndIntervalTable`, `dsx3FarEndTotalTable`, and `dsx3FracTable`)
	RFC 2515, *Definitions of Managed Objects for ATM Management*
	RFC 2558, *Definitions of Managed Objects for the SONET/SDH Interface Type*
	RFC 2665, *Definitions of Managed Objects for the Ethernet-like Interface Types*
	RFC 2790, *Host Resources MIB* (only the objects of the `hrSystem` and `hrSWInstalled` groups)
	RFC 2819, *Remote Network Monitoring Management Information Base* (the `etherStatsTable` for Ethernet interfaces only)
	RFC 2925, *Definitions of Managed Objects for Remote Ping, Traceroute, and Lookup Operations* (only the objects `pingCtlTable`, `pingResultsTable`, `pingProbeHistoryTable`, and `pingMaxConcurrentRequests`)
	RFC 2932, *IPv4 Multicast Routing MIB*
	IANAiftype Textual Convention MIB, Internet Assigned Numbers Authority (referenced by RFC 2233, available at ftp://ftp.isi.edu/mib/ianaiftype.mib)
	Internet draft draft-ietf-idmr-igmp-mib-13.txt, *Internet Group Management Protocol (IGMP) MIB*
	Internet Draft draft-ietf-idmr-pim-mib-09.txt, *Protocol Independent Multicast (PIM) MIB*

Table 2.1 *Supported Internet RFCs and Drafts*

Category	Title
MPLS	RFC 2205, *Resource Reservation Protocol (RSVP)—Version 1 Functional Specification*
	RFC 2209, *Resource Reservation Protocol (RSVP)—Version 1 Message Processing Rules*
	RFC 2210, *The Use of RSVP with IETF Integrated Services*
	RFC 2211, *Specification of the Controlled-load Network Element Service*
	RFC 2215, *General Characterization Parameters for Integrated Service Network Elements*
	RFC 2216, *Network Element Service Specification Template*
	RFC 2702, *Requirements for Traffic Engineering over MPLS*
	RFC 2961, *RSVP Refresh Overhead Reduction Extensions*
	Internet Draft draft-ietf-ppvpn-rfc2547bis-00.txt, *BGP/MPLS VPNs*
	Internet Draft draft-ietf-mpls-rsvp-lsp-tunnel-05.txt, *Extensions to RSVP for LSP Tunnels*
	Internet Draft draft-ietf-mpls-icmp-01.txt, *ICMP Extensions for Multiprotocol Label Switching*
	Internet Draft draft-kompella-ppvpn-l2vpn-00.txt, *MPLS-based Layer 2 VPNs*
	Internet Draft draft-ietf-mpls-label-encaps-07.txt, *MPLS Label Stack Encoding*
	Internet Draft draft-martini-l2circuit-trans-mpls-07.txt, *Transport of Layer 2 Frames over MPLS*
OSPF	RFC 1587, *The OSPF NSSA Option*
	RFC 2328, *OSPF Version 2*
	Internet Draft draft-katz-yeung-ospf-traffic-01.txt, *Traffic Engineering Extensions to OSPF*
PPP	RFC 1332, *The PPP Internet Protocol Control Protocol (IPCP)*
	RFC 1661, *The Point-to-Point Protocol (PPP)*
	RFC 1662, *PPP in HDLC-like Framing*
	RFC 2615, *PPP over SONET/SDH*
RIP	RFC 1058, *Routing Information Protocol*
	RFC 2453, *RIP Version 2*

Table 2.1 *Supported Internet RFCs and Drafts*

Category	Title
RSVP	RFC 2205, *Resource ReSerVation Protocol (RSVP), Version 1, Functional Specification*
	RFC 2209, *Resource ReSerVation Protocol (RSVP), Version 1, Message Processing Rules*
	RFC 2210, *The Use of RSVP with IETF Integrated Services*
	RFC 2211, *Specification of the Controlled-Load Network Element Service*
	RFC 2212, *Specification of Guaranteed Quality of Service*
	RFC 2215, *General Characterization Parameters for Integrated Service Network Elements*
	RFC 2216, *Network Element Service Specification Template*
	RFC 2747, *RSVP Cryptographic Authentication*
	Internet draft draft-ietf-mpls-rsvp-lsp-tunnel-05.txt, *Extensions to RSVP for LSP Tunnels*
	Internet draft draft-ietf-rsvp-refresh-reduct-05.txt, *RSVP Refresh Reduction Extensions*
TCP and IPv4	RFC 768, *User Datagram Protocol*
	RFC 791, *Internet Protocol*
	RFC 792, *Internet Control Message Protocol*
	RFC 793, *Transmission Control Protocol*
	RFC 826, *Ethernet Address Resolution Protocol*
	RFC 854, *Telnet Protocol Specification*
	RFC 862, *Echo Protocol*
	RFC 863, *Discard Protocol*
	RFC 896, *Congestion Control in IP/TCP Internetworks*
	RFC 919, *Broadcasting Internet Datagrams*
	RFC 922, *Broadcasting Internet Datagrams in the Presence of Subnets*
	RFC 959, *File Transfer Protocol*
	RFC 1027, *Using ARP to Implement Transparent Subnet Gateways*
	RFC 1042, *Standard for the Transmission of IP Datagrams over IEEE 802 Networks*
	RFC 1157, *Simple Network Management Protocol (SNMP)*
	RFC 1166, *Internet Numbers*
	RFC 1195, *Use of OSI IS-IS for Routing in TCP/IP and Dual Environments*
	RFC 1256, *ICMP Router Discovery Messages*
	RFC 1305, *Network Time Protocol (Version 3) Specification, Implementation, and Analysis*
	RFC 1519, *Classless Inter-Domain Routing (CIDR): An Address Assignment and Aggregation Strategy*
	RFC 1812, *Requirements for IP Version 4 Routers*
	RFC 2338, *Virtual Router Redundancy Protocol*

Table 2.2 *Supported ISO Standards*

Category	Title
IS-IS	ISO/IEC 10589, *Information technology, Telecommunications and information exchange between systems, Intermediate system to intermediate system intradomain routing information exchange protocol for use in conjunction with the protocol for providing the connectionless-mode network service (ISO 8473)*

Table 2.3 *Supported SDH and SONET Standards*

Category	Title
SDH and SONET	ANSI T1.105, *Synchronous Optical Network (SONET) Basic Description Including Multiplex Structures, Rates, and Formats*
	ANSI T1.105.02, *Synchronous Optical Network (SONET) Payload Mappings*
	ANSI T1.105.06, *SONET: Physical Layer Specifications*
	GR-253-CORE, *SONET Transport Systems: Common Generic Criteria*
	GR-499-CORE, *Transport System Generic Requirements (TSGR): Common Requirements*
	GR-1377-CORE, *SONET OC-192 Transport System Generic Criteria*
	ITU-T Recommendation G.691, *Optical interfaces for single channel SDH systems with optical amplifiers and STM-64 systems*
	ITU-T Recommendation G.707 (1996), *Network node interface for the synchronous digital hierarchy (SDH)*
	ITU-T Recommendation G.783 (1994), *Characteristics of Synchronous Digital Hierarchy (SDH) equipment functional blocks*
	ITU-T Recommendation G.813 (1996), *Timing characteristics of SDH equipment slave clocks (SEC)*
	ITU-T Recommendation G.825 (1993), *The control of jitter and wander within digital networks which are based on the Synchronous Digital Hierarchy (SDH)*
	ITU-T Recommendation G.826 (1999), *Error performance parameters and objectives for international, constant bit rate digital paths at or above the primary rate*
	ITU-T Recommendation G.831 (1993), *Management capabilities of transport networks based on Synchronous Digital Hierarchy (SDH)*
	ITU-T Recommendation G.957 (1995), *Optical interfaces for equipment and systems relating to the synchronous digital hierarchy*
	ITU-T Recommendation G.958 (1994), *Digital line systems based on the Synchronous Digital Hierarchy for use on optical fibre cables*
	ITU-T Recommendation I.432 (1993), *B-ISDN User-Network Interface Physical layer specification*

CHAPTER

3

Juniper Networks Router Overview

The Juniper Networks line of routers includes the M-series routers and the new T-series router and routing node. Each platform is a complete routing system that supports a variety of high-speed interfaces (including SONET/SDH, Ethernet, and ATM) for large networks and network applications. All Juniper Networks routers share common JUNOS Internet software, features, and technology for compatibility across all platforms.

Application-specific integrated circuits (ASICs) form a definitive part of the router design and enable the router to achieve data forwarding rates that match current fiber-optic capacity. All M-series routers use the Internet Processor II ASIC, which performs the route lookup function and several types of packet processing, such as filtering, class of service, policing, rate limiting, and sampling. The T-series router routing node uses the new T-series Internet Processor for route lookups and notification forwarding.

Router Architecture

Each router consists of two major architectural components: the Routing Engine and the Packet Forwarding Engine.

In each Juniper Networks router, the router architecture cleanly separates routing and control functions from packet forwarding operations, eliminating bottlenecks and permitting the router to maintain a high level of performance. Each router consists of two major architectural components: the Routing Engine, which provides Layer 3 routing services and network management, and the Packet Forwarding Engine, which provides Layer 2 and Layer 3 packet switching, route lookups, and packet forwarding.

The Routing Engine and Packet Forwarding Engine perform their primary tasks independently, while constantly communicating through a high-speed internal link. This arrangement provides streamlined forwarding and routing control and the capability to run Internet-scale networks at high speeds. Figure 3.1 illustrates the relationship between the Routing Engine and the Packet Forwarding Engine.

For more information about the Routing Engine, see "Routing Engine" on page 37.

The Routing Engine consists of an Intel-based PCI platform running JUNOS Internet software. The Routing Engine maintains the routing tables used by the router and controls the routing protocols that run on the router. For more information about the JUNOS Internet software that runs on the Routing Engine, see Chapter 2, "JUNOS Internet Software Overview."

Figure 3.1 *Router Architecture*

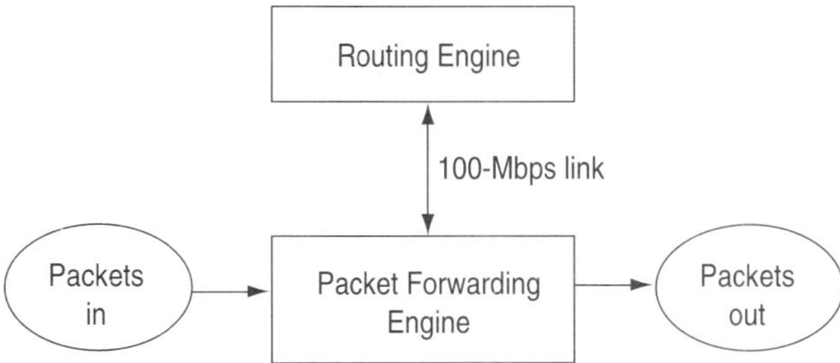

The Routing Engine constructs and maintains one or more routing tables. From the routing tables, the Routing Engine derives a table of active routes, called the forwarding table, which is then copied into the Packet Forwarding Engine. The design of the Internet Processor II and T-series Internet Processor ASICs allows the forwarding table in the Packet Forwarding Engine to be updated without interrupting forwarding performance (see Figure 3.2).

Figure 3.2 *Control Packet Handling: Routing and Forwarding Table Updates*

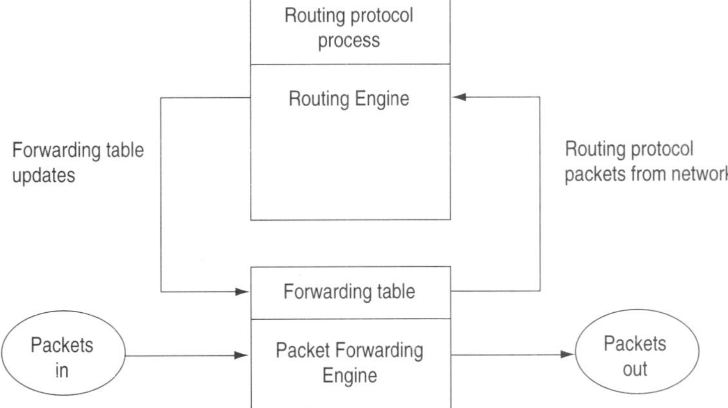

The Packet Forwarding Engine uses ASICs to perform Layer 2 and Layer 3 packet switching, route lookups, and packet forwarding. On M-series routers, the Packet Forwarding Engine includes the router midplane (on an M40 router, the backplane), Flexible PIC Concentrators (FPCs), Physical Interface Cards (PICs), and other components, unique to each router, that handle forwarding decisions.

Packets enter the router through incoming PIC interfaces, which contain controllers that perform media-specific processing. The PICs pass the packets to the FPCs, where they are divided into cells and distributed to the router's shared memory. The Packet Forwarding Engine performs route lookups, forwards the notification to the destination port, reassembles the cells into packets, and sends them to the destination port on the outgoing PIC. The PIC performs encapsulation and other media-specific processing, and sends the packets out to the network.

Figure 3.3 illustrates the flow of data packets through an M-series router, using the M40e router architecture as an example. In this example, a packet enters through the incoming PIC, which parses and de-encapsulates the packet, then passes it to the FPC. On the FPC, the Packet Director ASIC distributes packets among the I/O Manager ASICs, where each is divided into cells and sent across the midplane to the SFMs.

When cells arrive at an SFM, the Distributed Buffer Manager ASIC writes them into packet buffer memory, which is distributed evenly across the router's FPCs. The Distributed Buffer Manager ASIC also extracts information needed for route lookups and passes the information to the Internet Processor II ASIC. The Internet Processor II performs the lookup in the full forwarding table, finding the outgoing interface and specific next hop for each packet. The forwarding table can forward all unicast packets that do not have options and multicast packets that have not been previously cached. Other packets are sent to the Routing Engine for resolution.

After the Internet Processor II ASIC has determined the next hop, it notifies a second Distributed Buffer Manager ASIC, which forwards the notification to the outgoing FPC. A pointer to the packet is queued at the outgoing port. When the packet pointer reaches the front of the queue and is ready for transmission, the cells are read from packet buffer memory and reassembled into the packet, which is passed to the outgoing PIC interface. The PIC performs media-specific processing and sends the packet to the network.

Figure 3.3 *Data Flow through an M40e Router*

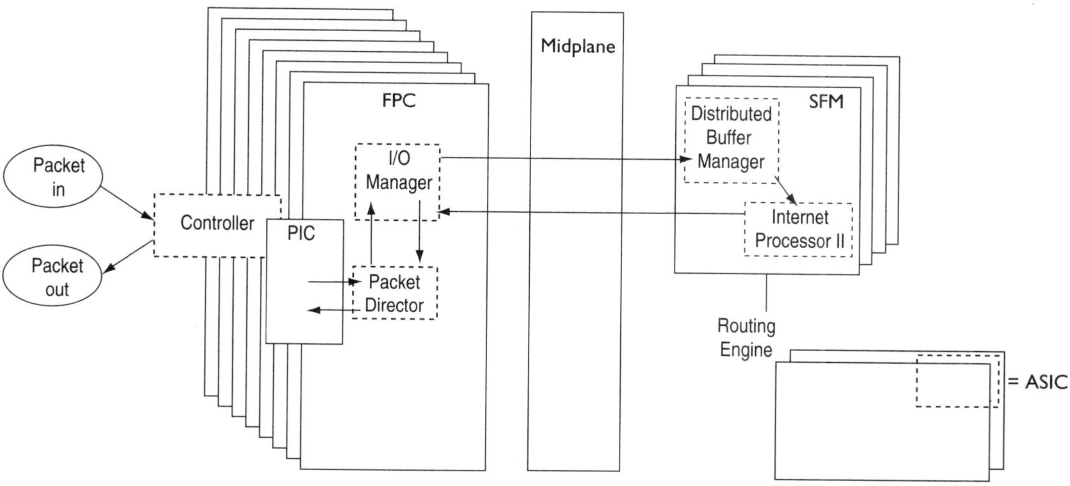

The T-series routing node features multiple Packet Forwarding Engines, up to a maximum of 16. On the T-series routing node, the Packet Forwarding Engines are contained on the FPCs. Each FPC has one or two Packet Forwarding Engines, each with its own memory buffer. Each Packet Forwarding Engine maintains a high-speed link to the Routing Engine.

Figure 3.4 shows the data flow through a T640 routing node. Packets enter through an incoming PIC and are passed to the Packet Forwarding Engine on the originating FPC. The Layer 2/Layer 3 Packet Processing ASIC parses the packets and divides them into cells. The network-facing–Switch Fabric ASIC places the lookup key in a notification and passes it to the T-series Internet Processor. The Switch Fabric ASIC also passes the data cells to the Queuing and Memory Interface ASICs for buffering on the FPC. The T-series Internet Processor ASIC performs the route lookup and forwards the notification to the Queuing and Memory Interface ASIC.

The Queuing and Memory Interface ASIC sends the notification to the switch-fabric–facing Switch Interface ASIC, which sends bandwidth requests through the switch fabric to the destination port and issues read requests to the Queuing and Memory Interface ASIC to begin reading data cells out of memory. The Switch Interface ASIC on the destination FPC sends bandwidth grants through the switch fabric to the originating Switch Interface ASIC. Upon receipt of each grant, the originating Switch Interface ASIC sends a cell through the switch fabric to the destination Packet Forwarding Engine.

On the destination Packet Forwarding Engine, the switch-fabric–facing Switch Interface ASIC receives the data cells, places the lookup key in a notification, and forwards the notification to the T-series Internet Processor. The T-series Internet Processor performs the route lookup and forwards the notification to the Queuing and Memory Interface ASIC, which forwards it to the network-facing Switch Interface ASIC. The Switch Interface ASIC sends requests to the Queuing and Memory Interface ASIC to read the data cells out of memory and passes the cells to the Layer2/Layer 3 Packet Processing ASIC, which reassembles the cells into packets, performs the necessary Layer 2 encapsulation, and sends the packets to the outgoing PIC. The PIC passes the packets into the network.

Figure 3.4 *Data Flow through a T640 Routing Node*

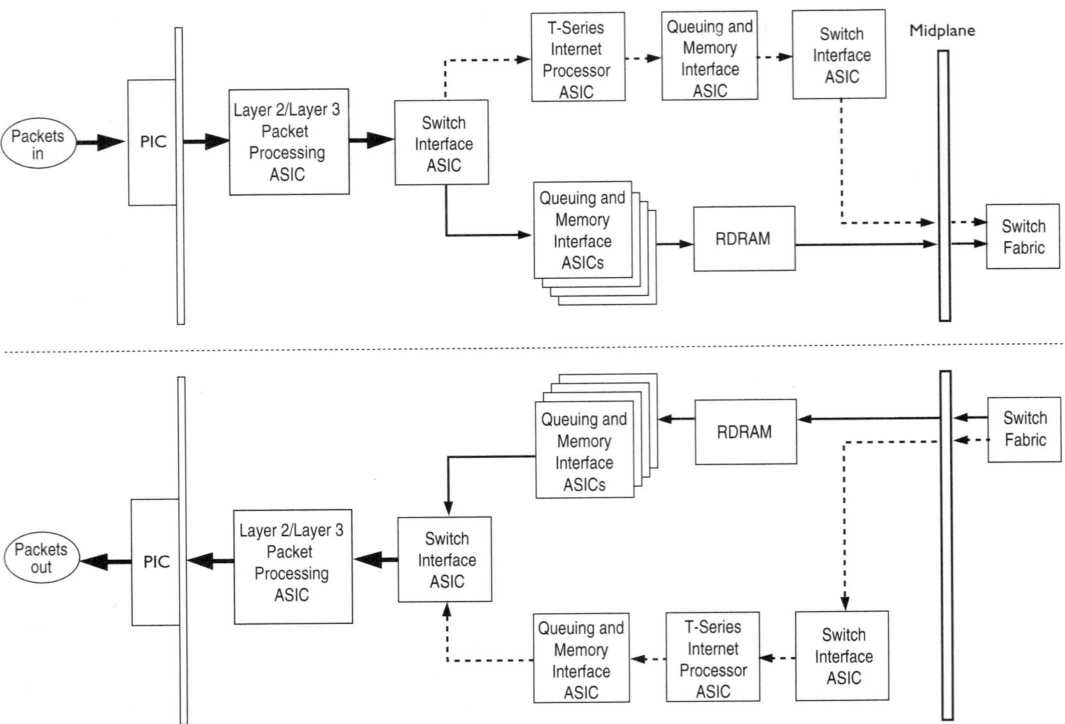

Hardware Components

Each Juniper Networks router consists of a chassis and a set of components, including FPCs, PICs, Routing Engines, power supplies, cooling system, and cable management system. Many of the components are field replaceable units. Each major component is discussed in this section.

Chassis

Chassis dimensions for each router are listed in the physical specifications table for each router.

Each Juniper Networks router features a rigid sheet metal chassis that houses all the router components. The chassis are designed to install into a variety of racks, including standard 19-inch equipment racks, telco center-mount racks, and four-post racks and cabinets. See Table 3.1 for the maximum number of each router that can be installed into a rack. Each chassis includes mounting ears or support posts to facilitate rack mounting, and one or more points for connecting an electrostatic discharge (ESD) wrist strap for use when servicing the router.

Table 3.1 *Maximum Number of Routers Per Rack*

Router	Maximum in Standard Rack
T640	2
T320	3
M160	2
M40e	2
M40	2
M20	5
M5 and M10	14

Each chassis includes a midplane (called the backplane on an M40 router). The major functions of the midplane include transferring data packets to and from the FPCs, distributing power to router components, and providing signal connectivity to the router components for monitoring and control of the system.

Flexible PIC Concentrators

The Flexible PIC Concentrators (FPCs) house the PICs used in the router and connect them to other router components. FPCs install into the front of the router in either a vertical or horizontal orientation, depending on the router. A compatible FPC can be installed into any available FPC slot, regardless of the PICs it contains. If a slot is not occupied by an FPC, a blank FPC panel must be installed to shield the empty slot and to allow cooling air to circulate properly through the FPC card cage. Some routers support more than one type of FPC. The FPCs for each router are unique to that router.

Physical Interface Cards

Juniper Networks routers use Physical Interface Cards (PICs) to connect to a wide variety of network media. (See Table 3.2 for a list of PIC interfaces as of the time of publication.) PICs receive incoming packets from the network and transmit outgoing packets to the network, performing framing and line-speed signaling for their specific media type. Before transmitting outgoing data packets, the PICs encapsulate the packets received from the FPCs. Each PIC is equipped with an ASIC that performs control functions specific to the PIC's media type.

Table 3.2 *PIC Media Types*

Media Type	Ports	Slots	Connectors	JUNOS Interface Name
ATM DS-3 ATM E3 ATM OC-3 ATM OC-12	4 4 2 1	Single Single Single Single	SC duplex	at
Channelized DS-3 Channelized E1 Channelized OC-12 Channelized STM-1 Multichannel DS-3	4 10 1 1 2	Single Single Single Single Single	Posilock to BNC RJ-48 SC duplex SC duplex Posilock to BNC	–
DS–3	4	Single	Posilock to BNC	ds
E1	4	Single	RJ-48 or BNC	e1

Table 3.2 *PIC Media Types*

Media Type	Ports	Slots	Connectors	JUNOS Interface Name
E3	4	Single	Posilock to BNC	e3
Fast Ethernet	4 8 12 48	Single Single Single Single	RJ-45	fe
Gigabit Ethernet 10 Gigabit Ethernet	1 2 4 4 1	Single Single Quad Single Quad	SC duplex SC duplex SC duplex SC duplex SC duplex	ge
ES Monitoring Services Multilink Services Tunnel Services	– – – –	Single Single Single Single	– – – –	es – ml gr or ip
SONET/SDH OC-3c SONET/SDH OC-12c SONET/SDH OC-12c SONET/SDH OC-48c SONEC-SDH OC-48c SONET/SDH OC-48c SONET/SDH OC-192c SONET/SDH OC-192c	4 1 4 1 1 4 1 1	Single Single Single Quad Single Single Quad Single	SC duplex	so
T1	4	Single	RJ-48	t1

PICs install into the FPCs (on the M5 and M10 routers, into the FEB). Each FPC can accept up to four PICs. (Table 3.3 lists the number and type of PICs currently supported on each router.) The PICs for each router are unique to that router.

Table 3.3 *PICs Supported on Each Router*

PICs Supported	T640 Routing Node	T320 Router	M160 Router	M40e Router	M20 and M40 Routers	M5 and M10 Routers
ATM DS-3			4 per FPC		4 per FPC	M5–4, M10–8
ATM E3			4 per FPC		4 per FPC	M5–4, M10–8
ATM OC-3			4 per FPC	4 per FPC	4 per FPC	M5–4, M10–8
ATM OC-12			4 per FPC	4 per FPC	4 per FPC	M5–4, M10–8
Channelized DS-3			4 per FPC	4 per FPC	4 per FPC	M5–4, M10–8
Channelized E1			4 per FPC		4 per FPC	M5–4, M10–8
Channelized OC-12			4 per FPC	4 per FPC	4 per FPC	M5–4, M10–8
Channelized STM-1			4 per FPC	4 per FPC	4 per FPC	M5–4, M10–8
Multichannel DS-3			4 per FPC	4 per FPC	4 per FPC	M5–4, M10–8
DS–3			4 per FPC	4 per FPC	4 per FPC	M5–4, M10–8
E1			4 per FPC	4 per FPC	4 per FPC	M5–4, M10–8
E3			4 per FPC	4 per FPC	4 per FPC	M5–4, M10–8
Fast Ethernet			4 per FPC	4 per FPC	4 per FPC	M5–4, M10–8
Gigabit Ethernet	4 per FPC	4 per FPC	4 per FPC	4 per FPC	4 per FPC 1 per FPC	M5–4, M10–8 M5–1, M10–2
10 Gigabit Ethernet	4 per FPC	4 per FPC	1 per FPC			
ES			4 per FPC	4 per FPC	4 per FPC	M5–4, M10–8
Monitoring Services			4 per FPC			
Multilink Services				4 per FPC	4 per FPC	M5–4, M10–8
Tunnel Services	4 per FPC	4 per FPC		4 per FPC	4 per FPC	M5–4, M10–8
SONET/SDH OC-3c			4 per FPC	4 per FPC	4 per FPC	M5–4, M10–8
SONET/SDH OC-12c	4 per FPC	4 per FPC	4 per FPC	4 per FPC	4 per FPC	M5–4, M10–8
SONET/SDH OC-48c	4 per FPC	4 per FPC	4 per FPC	4 per FPC	4 per FPC	M5–1, M10–2
SONET/SDH OC-192c	4 per FPC	4 per FPC	1 per FPC			
T1			4 per FPC	4 per FPC	4 per FPC	M5–4, M10–8

Routing Engine

The Routing Engine consists of an Intel-based PCI platform running the JUNOS software. The Routing Engine maintains the routing tables used by the router in which it is installed and controls the routing protocols on the router. The T640 routing node, T-320, and the M160, M40e, and M20 routers support up to two Routing Engines, while the M40, M10, and M5 routers support a single Routing Engine.

The Routing Engine maintains the routing tables used by the router in which it is installed and controls the routing protocols on the router.

Each Routing Engine consists of a CPU; SDRAM for storage of the routing and forwarding tables and other processes; a compact flash disk (on some M40 routers, a floppy disk) for primary storage of software images, configuration files, and microcode; a hard disk for secondary storage; a PC card slot for storage of software upgrades; and interfaces for out-of-band management access.

Power Supplies

Each Juniper Networks router has two load-sharing power supplies. A single power supply can provide full power for as long as the router is operational. The power supplies are redundant: if one power supply is removed or fails, the other power supply automatically assumes the entire electrical load.

The power supplies are connected to the router midplane (on an M40 router, the backplane), which distributes the different output voltages throughout the router and its components. Some routers can operate using either AC or DC power; others operate with DC power only. For information about the type of power used by each router, see the "Electrical Specifications" table for each router.

Cooling System

Each Juniper Networks router features a cooling system designed to keep all router components within recommended operating temperature limits. If one component of the cooling system fails or is removed, the system adjusts the speed of the remaining components automatically to keep the temperature within the acceptable range. The cooling system for each router is unique and can consist of fans, impellers, and air filters. For information about the cooling system components of each router, see the "Major Hardware Components" table for each router.

Cable Management System

Each Juniper Networks router includes a cable management system designed to maintain the proper bend radius for optical cables and to keep installed cables organized and securely in place. The cable management system evenly distributes the weight of the optical cables so that no individual cable is subjected to undue stress.

Field-Replaceable Units

Components that can be replaced at the customer site are called *field-replaceable units* (FRUs). FRUs can be replaced with minimal loss of performance or router downtime. Most of the components previously discussed in this section—including the FPCs, PICs, Routing Engine, power supplies, and cooling system components—are FRUs.

There are three types of FRUs: hot-insertable and hot-removable FRUs, which can be removed and replaced without powering down the router or disrupting router functions; hot-pluggable FRUs, which can be removed and replaced without powering down the router, but whose removal does cause an interruption to router performance; and FRUs whose removal requires powering down the router. For a list of which components are FRUs for each Juniper Networks router, see "Major Hardware Components" table for each router.

T640 Internet Routing Node

Figure 3.5 *T640 Internet Routing Node Chassis and Components*

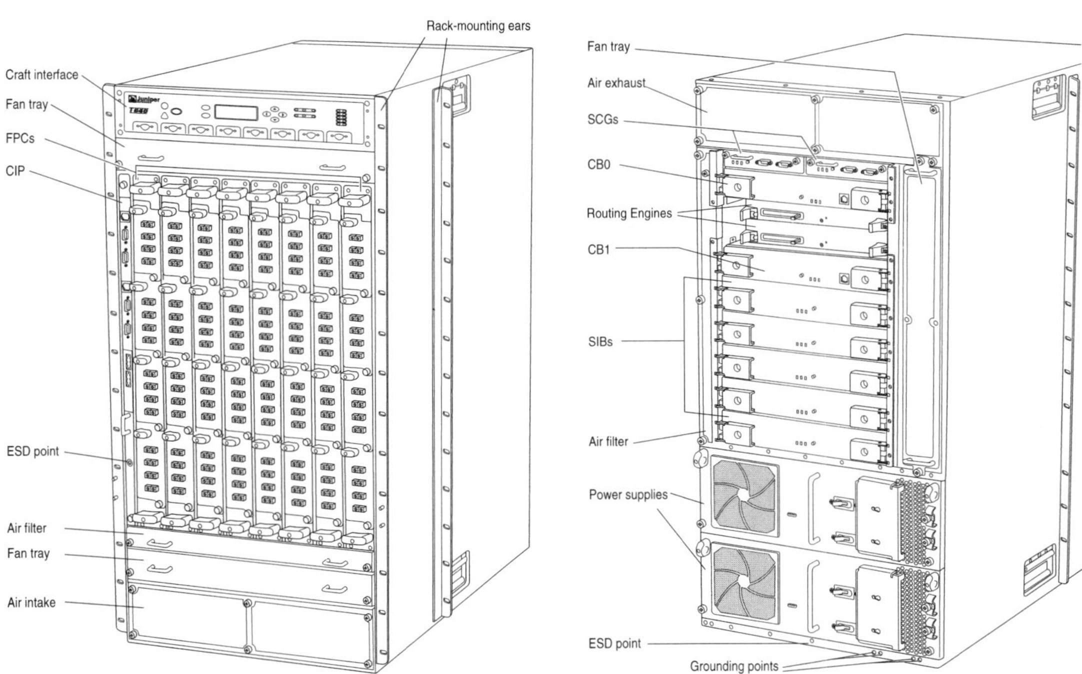

The T640 Internet routing node (see Figure 3.5) has a maximum aggregate throughput of 320 Gbps, full duplex. It utilizes the latest ASIC architecture to support high-bandwidth interfaces. It accepts up to eight FPCs and offers a high level of redundancy so that no single point of failure can cause the entire system to fail.

Table 3.4 shows the physical specifications of the T640 Internet routing node, and Table 3.5 gives an overview of the major hardware components of the routing node

Table 3.4 *T640 Internet Routing Node Physical Specifications*

Category	Value
Chassis dimensions	37.45 in. (95.6 cm) high x 17.4 in. (44.3 cm) wide x 31 in. (78.7 cm) deep
Routing node weight	205 lb (93 kg) empty chassis 435 lb (197 kg) minimum configuration 565 lb (256 kg) maximum configuration
Required clearances	24 in. (61 cm) front and rear; 6 in. (15.2 cm) each side

Table 3.5 *T640 Internet Routing Node Major Hardware Components*

Component	Quantity	Function	Redundant	FRU	Offline button
Chassis (including midplane)	1	Houses all router components	–	–	–
Switch Interface Boards (SIBs)	5	Performs packet switching	Yes	Hot-removable Hot-insertable	Yes
Flexible PIC Concentrators (FPCs)	1–8	Contain Packet Forwarding Engines, connect PICs to router components	–	Hot-removable Hot-insertable	Yes
Physical Interface Cards (PICs)	1–4 per FPC	Provides interfaces to network media	–	Hot-removable Hot-insertable	Yes
Routing Engine	1–2	Maintains routing protocols, routing tables	Yes	Hot-pluggable	–
Control Board (CB)	1–2	Performs control and monitoring functions	Yes	Hot-pluggable	Yes
SONET Clock Generators (SCGs)	2	Provides 19.44–MHz Stratum 3 clock	Yes	Hot-pluggable	Yes
Power supplies	2	Distributes voltages to components	Yes	Hot-removable Hot-insertable	–
Cooling system	2 front and 1 rear fan tray; air filters	Cools router components	Yes	Hot-removable Hot-insertable	–

Table 3.5 *T640 Internet Routing Node Major Hardware Components*

Component	Quantity	Function	Redundant	FRU	Offline button
Craft interface	1	Displays status and troubleshooting information, provides control functions	–	–	–
Connector Interface Panel (CIP)	1	Provides interfaces to Routing Engine ports and alarm relay devices	–	Hot-pluggable	–

The chassis includes two front support posts to attach the routing node to a front-mount or four-post rack or a cabinet, two mounting ears for center-rack mounting, and two ESD points, one at the front and one at the rear. The midplane is located in the center of the chassis and forms the rear of the FPC card cage. The FPCs install into the midplane from the front of the chassis, and the SIBs, Routing Engines, CBs, and SCGs install into the midplane from the rear of the chassis. The power supplies and cooling system components also connect to the midplane.

The SIBs (see Figure 3.6) provide the switching function to the destination FPC. Five SIBs are installed in the rear of the routing node. The SIBs create the switch fabric for the routing node, providing up to 640 million packets per second (Mpps) of forwarding.

Figure 3.6 *T640 SIB*

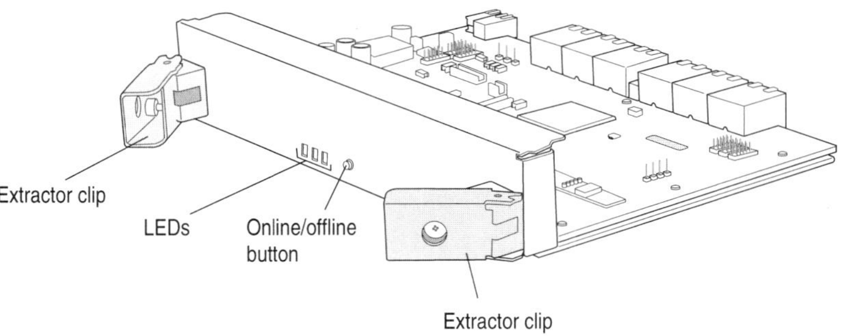

The FPCs (see Figure 3.7) install vertically in the front of the chassis. The FPCs are numbered left to right from 0 through 7. Each FPC accepts up to four PICs. An FPC can be installed into any FPC slot on the routing node, regardless of which PICs it contains.

Each FPC contains one or two Packet Forwarding Engines. The Packet Forwarding Engines receive incoming packets from the PICs installed on the FPC and forward them through the switch planes to the destination port. Each FPC contains data memory, which is managed by the Queuing and Memory Interface ASICs on the board and a processor subsystem (PMB). Two LEDs located on the craft interface above the FPC display the status of the FPC. An FPC online/offline button, located between the LEDs, is used to take the FPC offline and bring it online.

FPCs are hot-removable and hot-insertable. When you bring an FPC online, the Routing Engine downloads the FPC software, the FPC runs its diagnostics, and the PICs in the FPC are enabled. No interruption occurs to the routing functions.

Figure 3.7 *T640 FPCs*

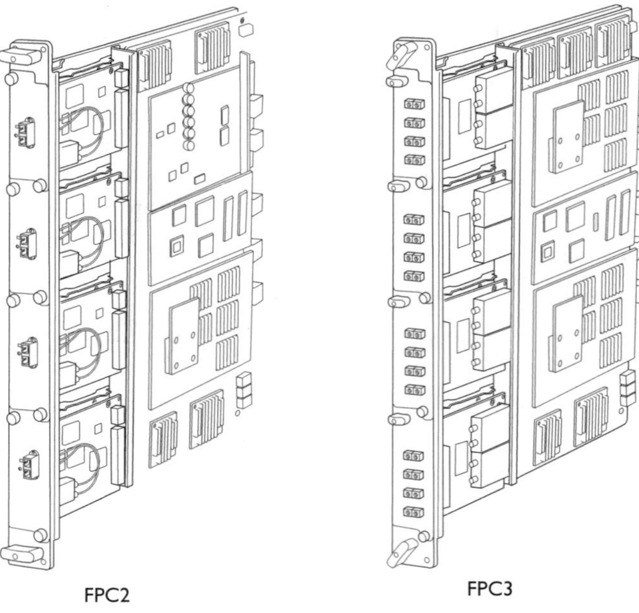

The routing node supports two types of FPC: FPC2, rated at 10 Gbps full duplex, which supports PICs also used in the M160 router, and FPC3, rated at 40 Gbps full duplex, which supports higher-speed PICs. The routing node can operate with any combination of FPC2s and FPC3s installed. The installation and removal of the two FPC types are identical. The two types of FPC can be visually distinguished by the ejectors on the PICs installed in the FPC. PICs compatible with an FPC3 have a plastic ejector handle at the top of their faceplate, and PICs compatible with an FPC2 have captive screws at the top and bottom of their faceplate. In this guide, both types are referred to simply as "FPC" except where the differences between the two are discussed.

The T640 routing node can have one or two host subsystems, which provide the routing and system management functions of the routing node. Each host subsystem consists of a Routing Engine and a CB installed in adjacent slots. Each host subsystem functions as a unit; the Routing Engine requires the corresponding CB to operate, and vice versa. Each host subsystem has three LEDs, located on the craft interface, that display its status.

For more information about the Routing Engines, see "Routing Engine" on page 37.

The T640 routing node can have one or two Routing Engines. The Routing Engines install into the upper rear of the chassis. If two Routing Engines are installed, one functions as master and the other as backup. If the master Routing Engine fails or is removed, the backup restarts and becomes master. The Routing Engines are hot-pluggable.

The LEDs that report Routing Engine status are located on the craft interface, rather than on the Routing Engine faceplate.

Each CB works with its adjacent Routing Engine to provide control and monitoring functions for the routing node (see Figure 3.8). These include determining Routing Engine mastership, controlling power, reset and SONET clocking for the other routing node components, monitoring and controlling fan speed, and monitoring system status.

The CBs install into the upper rear of the chassis. If two CBs are installed, one functions as master and the other as backup. If the master CB fails or is removed, the backup restarts and becomes master. The CBs are hot-pluggable.

Each CB contains an Ethernet switch for intermodule communication; a bus to the Routing Engines; a processor subsystem (the SPMB); and three LEDs, located on the CB faceplate, that display the status of the CB.

Figure 3.8 *T640 CB*

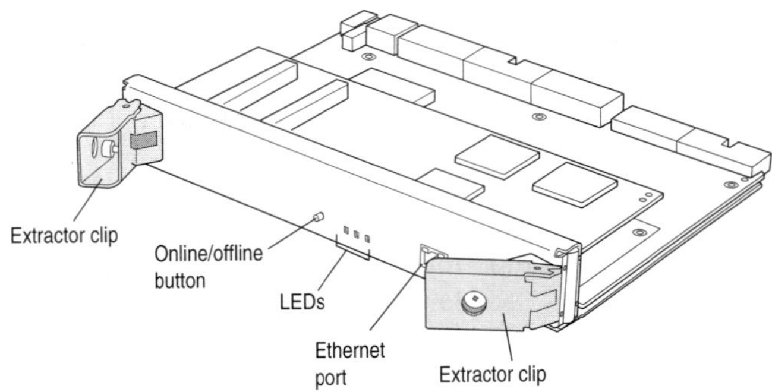

The SCGs provide a 19.44-MHz Stratum 3 clock signal for the SONET/SDH interfaces. They can also select a clock signal from any FPC or from external clock inputs.

The routing node has two SCGs. The SCGs provide the clock signal for the SONET/SDH interfaces on the routing node (see Figure 3.9). They can also select a clock signal from any FPC or from the external clock inputs. The SCGs install into the upper rear of the chassis. The SCGs are hot-pluggable.

Each SCG contains a 19.44-MHz Stratum 3 clock; two external clock inputs; and three LEDs, located on the SCG faceplate, that display the status of the SCG.

Figure 3.9 *T640 SCG*

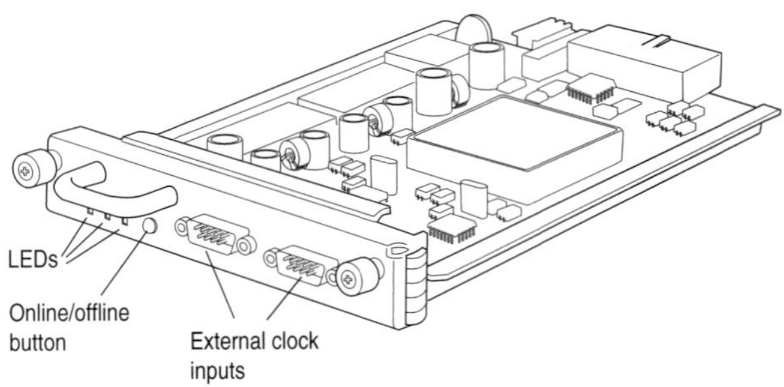

The craft interface allows you to view status and troubleshooting information at a glance and to perform many system control functions.

The craft interface (see Figure 3.10) allows you to view status and troubleshooting information and to perform many system control functions. The craft interface is located on the front of the routing node above the FPCs and contains alarm LEDs and a lamp test button, an LCD display, LEDs for the host subsystems, SIBs, FPCs, and FPC online/offline buttons.The craft interface is hot-insertable and hot-removable.

Figure 3.10 *T640 Craft Interface*

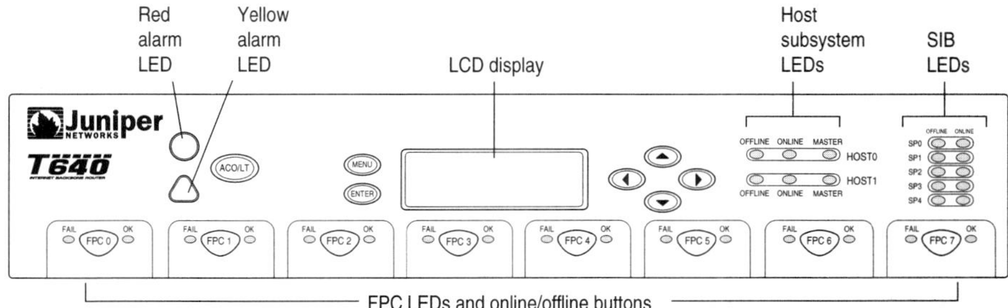

The CIP, located at the left side of the FPC card cage, consists of Ethernet, console, and auxiliary connectors for the Routing Engine ports, and alarm relay contacts (see Figure 3.11). The front electrostatic discharge point is located near the bottom of the CIP. The CIP is hot-pluggable.

Figure 3.11 *T640 CIP*

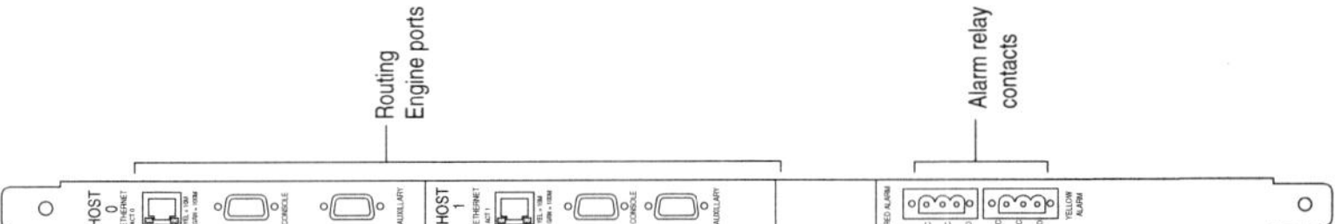

The routing node has two load-sharing DC power supplies, located at the lower rear of the chassis. The power supplies connect to the midplane, which distributes the output voltages produced by the power supplies to the routing node components, depending on their voltage requirements (see Table 3.6). Each power supply has two inputs, each with its own 80-A circuit breaker and each requiring a dedicated DC power source.

The power supplies are redundant. If one power supply fails or is removed, the second power supply instantly assumes the entire electrical load and can provide full power for as long as the routing node is operational.

Power supplies are hot-removable and hot-insertable. The routing node supports DC power only. Each power supply is cooled by its own internal cooling system.

Table 3.6 *T640 Power Supply Electrical Specifications*

Item	Specification
Maximum input power	6500 W
DC input voltage	Nominal –48 VDC, –60 VDC Operating range: –42 to –72 VDC
Input DC current rating	68 A @ –48 VDC (nominal) for each input 152 A @ –48 VDC (nominal) system current rating

The routing node cooling system consists of two front fan trays, one rear fan tray, front and rear air filters, and an air filter on each power supply. The cooling system components work together to keep all routing node components within the acceptable temperature range. All fan trays and filters are hot-insertable and hot-removable. The two front fan trays are interchangeable. The front and rear fan trays are not interchangeable.

The host subsystem monitors the temperature of the routing node components. When the routing node is operating normally, the fans function at lower than full speed. If a fan fails, the speed of the remaining fans is automatically adjusted to keep the temperature within the acceptable range. Figure 3.12 shows the air flow through the routing node and the location of the cooling system components.

Figure 3.12 *Air Flow through the T640 Chassis*

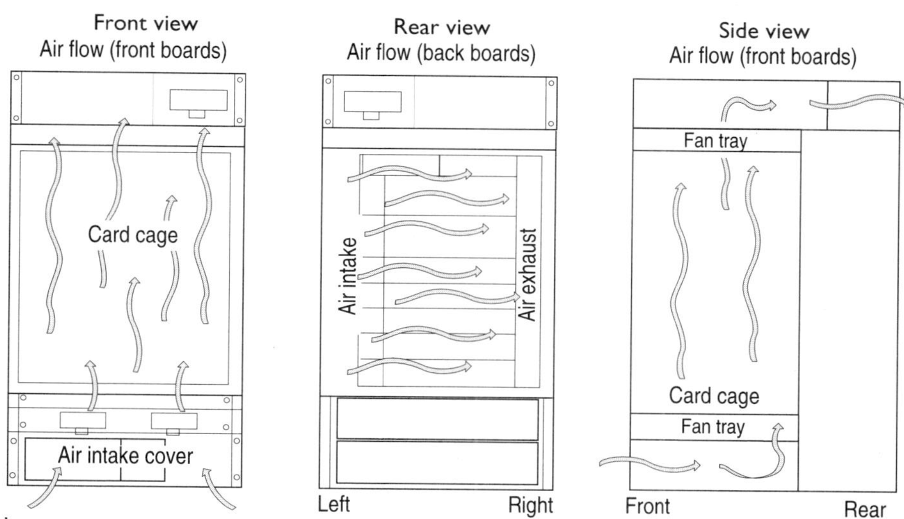

The routing node's cable management system consists of a row of nine semicircular plastic bobbins mounted on the front of the routing node below the FPC card cage. The PIC cables wrap around the bobbins, keeping the cables organized and securely in place. The curvature of the bobbins also helps maintain the proper bend radius for optical PIC cables.

The routing node has LEDs that display the status of various routing node components. Table 3.7 lists the LEDs on the craft interface and the individual routing node components.

Table 3.7 *T640 Internet Routing Node LEDs*

Component	LED	Location
SIBs	Green OK Amber FAIL Green Active	SIB faceplate
	Green OK Red FAIL	Craft interface
FPCs	Green OK Red FAIL	Craft interface
PICs	Tricolor: red, green, amber	PIC faceplate
SCGs	Green OK Amber FAIL Blue MASTER	PCG faceplate
Host module	Green OK Red FAIL Green MASTER	Craft interface
CB	Green OK Amber FAIL Blue MASTER	CB faceplate
Power supplies	Green CB ON Amber CB TRIP Amber OVER TEMP Blue DC OK	Power supply faceplate
Alarm LEDs		
Red alarm	Large, circular red	Craft interface
Yellow alarm	Large, triangular amber	Craft interface
Ethernet LEDs		
10-Mbps link	Yellow	CIP
100-Mbps link	Green	CIP

T320 Internet Router

Figure 3.13 *T320 Internet Router Chassis and Components*

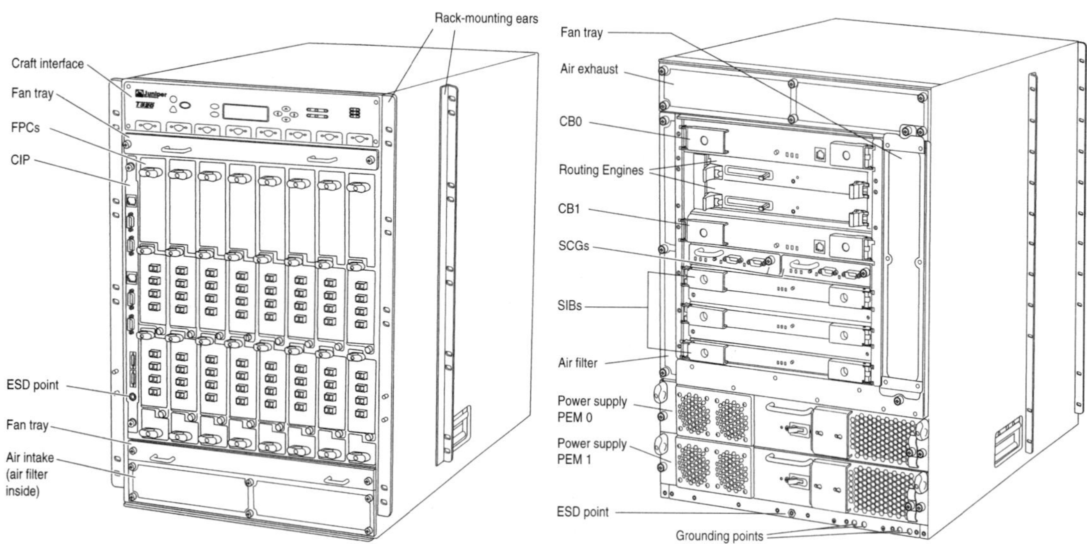

The T320 Internet router (see Figure 3.13) has a maximum aggregate throughput of 160 Gbps, full duplex. It utilizes the latest ASIC architecture to support high-bandwidth interfaces. It accepts up to eight FPCs and offers a high level of redundancy so that no single point of failure can cause the entire system to fail.

Table 3.8 shows the physical specifications of the T320 Internet router, and Table 3.9 gives an overview of the major hardware components of the router.

Table 3.8 *T320 Internet Router Physical Specifications*

Category	Value
Chassis dimensions	25.13 in. (63.82 cm) high x 17.43 in. (44.3 cm) wide x 31 in. (78.7 cm) deep Total depth (including cable management system): 35.5 in. (90.2 cm)
Router weight	131.4 lb (59.6 kg) empty chassis 272.1 lb (123.4 kg) minimum configuration 369.9 lb (167.8 kg) maximum configuration
Required clearances	24 in. (61 cm) front and rear; 6 in. (15.2 cm) each side

Table 3.9 *T320 Internet Router Major Hardware Components*

Component	Quantity	Function	Redundant	FRU	Offline button
Chassis (including midplane)	1	Houses all router components	–	–	–
Switch Interface Boards (SIBs)	3	Performs packet switching	Yes	Hot-removable Hot-insertable	Yes
Flexible PIC Concentrators (FPCs)	1–8	Contain Packet Forwarding Engines, connect PICs to router components	–	Hot-removable Hot-insertable	Yes
Physical Interface Cards (PICs)	1–2 per FPC	Provides interfaces to network media	–	Hot-removable Hot-insertable	Yes
Routing Engine	1–2	Maintains routing protocols, routing tables	Yes	Hot-pluggable	–
Control Board (CB)	1–2	Performs control and monitoring functions	Yes	Hot-pluggable	Yes
SONET Clock Generators (SCGs)	2	Provides 19.44–MHz Stratum 3 clock	Yes	Hot-pluggable	Yes
Power supplies	2	Distributes required voltages to components	Yes	Hot-removable Hot-insertable	–
Cooling system	2 front and 1 rear fan tray; air filters	Cools router components	Yes	Hot-removable Hot-insertable	–
Craft interface	1	Displays status and troubleshooting information, provides control functions	–	–	–
Connector Interface Panel (CIP)	1	Provides interfaces to Routing Engine ports and alarm relay devices	–	Hot-pluggable	–

The chassis includes two front support posts to attach the router to a front-mount or four-post rack or a cabinet, two mounting ears for center-rack mounting, and two ESD points, one at the front and one at the rear. The midplane is located in the center of the chassis and forms the rear of the FPC card cage. The FPCs install into the midplane from the front of the chassis, and the SIBs, Routing Engines, CBs, and SCGs install into the midplane from the rear of the chassis. The power supplies and cooling system components also connect to the midplane.

The Switch Interface Boards (SIBs) (see Figure 3.14) provide the switching function to the destination FPC. Three SIBs are installed in the rear of the chassis. The SIBs create the switch fabric for the router, providing up to 320 million packets per second (Mpps) of forwarding.

Figure 3.14 *T320 SIB*

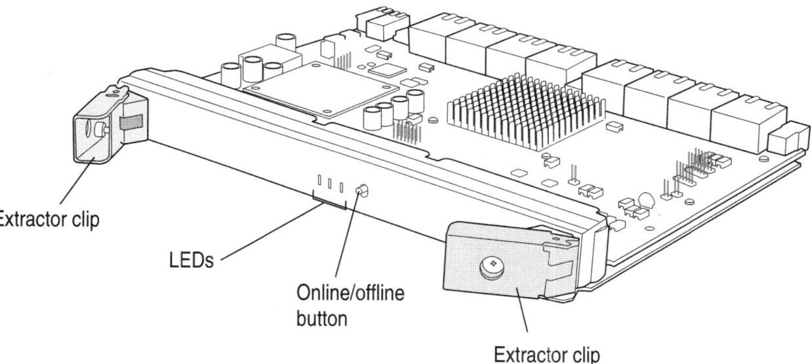

The Flexible PIC Concentrators (FPCs) install vertically in the front of the chassis. The FPCs are numbered left to right from 0 through 7. Each FPC accepts up to two PICs. An FPC can be installed into any FPC slot on the router, regardless of which PICs it contains.

Each FPC contains one Packet Forwarding Engine. The Packet Forwarding Engines receive incoming packets from the PICs installed on the FPC and forward them through the switch planes to the destination port. Each FPC contains data memory which is managed by the Queuing and Memory Interface ASICs on the board and a processor subsystem (PMB). Two LEDs located on the craft interface above the

FPC display the status of the FPC. An FPC online/offline button, located between the LEDs, is used to take the FPC offline and bring it online.

FPCs are hot-removable and hot-insertable. When you bring an FPC online, the Routing Engine downloads the FPC software, the FPC runs its diagnostics, and the PICs in the FPC are enabled. No interruption occurs to the routing functions.

Figure 3.15 *T320 FPCs*

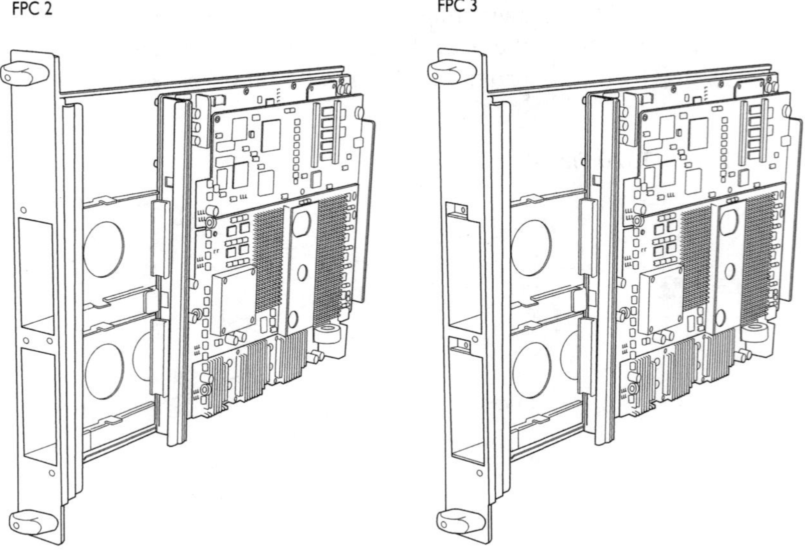

The T320 router supports two types of FPC: FPC2, rated at 10 Gbps full duplex, which supports PICs also used in the M160 router, and FPC3, rated at 20 Gbps full duplex, which supports higher-speed PICs. The router can operate with any combination of FPC2s and FPC3s installed. The installation and removal of the two FPC types is identical. The two types of FPC can be visually distinguished by the ejectors on the PICs installed in the FPC. PICs compatible with an FPC3 have a plastic ejector handle at the top of their faceplate, and PICs compatible with an FPC2 have captive screws at the top and bottom of their faceplate. In this guide, both types are referred to simply as "FPC" except where the differences between the two are discussed.

The T320 router can have one or two host subsystems, which provide the routing and system management functions of the router. Each host subsystem consists of a Routing Engine and a Control Board (CB) installed in adjacent slots. Each host subsystem functions as a unit; the Routing Engine requires the corresponding CB to operate, and vice versa. Each host subsystem has three LEDs, located on the craft interface, that display its status.

For more information about the Routing Engines, see "Routing Engine" on page 37.

The T320 router can have one or two Routing Engines. The Routing Engines install into the upper rear of the chassis. If two Routing Engines are installed, one functions as master and the other as backup. If the master Routing Engine fails or is removed, the backup restarts and becomes master. The Routing Engines are hot-pluggable.

The LEDs that report Routing Engine status are located on the craft interface, rather than on the Routing Engine faceplate.

Each CB works with its adjacent Routing Engine to provide control and monitoring functions for the router (see Figure 3.16). These include determining Routing Engine mastership, controlling power, reset and SONET clocking for the other router components, monitoring and controlling fan speed, and monitoring system status.

The CBs install into the upper rear of the chassis. If two CBs are installed, one functions as master and the other as backup. If the master CB fails or is removed, the backup restarts and becomes master. The CBs are hot-pluggable.

Figure 3.16 *T320 CB*

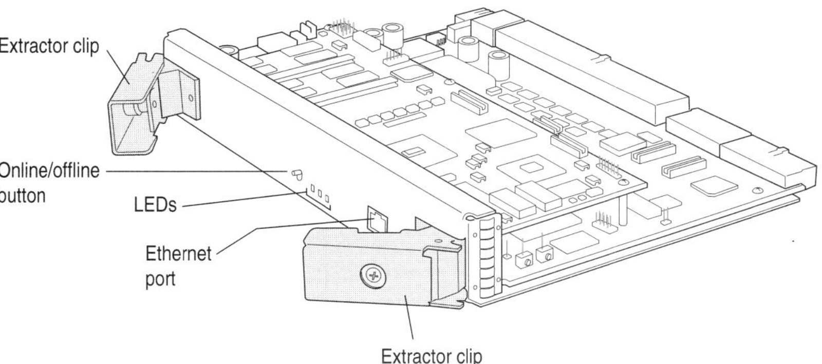

Each CB contains an Ethernet switch for intermodule communication; a bus to the Routing Engines; a processor subsystem (the SPMB); and three LEDs, located on the CB faceplate, that display the status of the CB.

The SCGs provide a 19.44-MHz Stratum 3 clock signal for the SONET/SDH interfaces. They can also select a clock signal from any FPC, or from external clock inputs.

The router has two SONET Clock Generators (SCGs). The SCGs provide the clock signal for the SONET/SDH interfaces on the router (see Figure 3.17). They can also select a clock signal from any FPC or from the external clock inputs. The SCGs install into the upper rear of the chassis. The SCGs are hot-pluggable. Each SCG contains a 19.44-MHz Stratum 3 clock; two external clock inputs; and three LEDs, located on the SCG faceplate, that display the status of the SCG.

Figure 3.17 *T320 SCG*

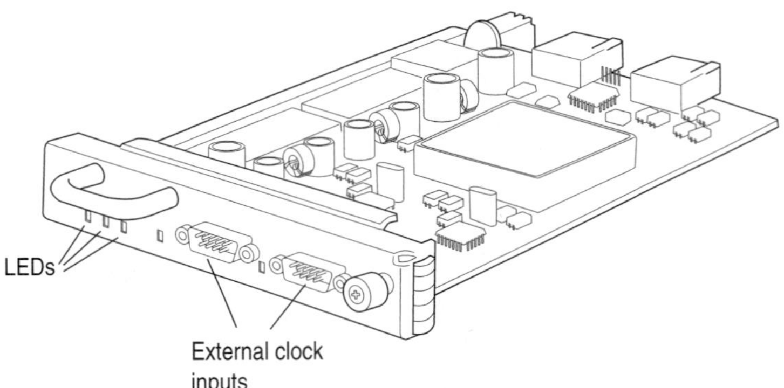

The craft interface allows you to view status and troubleshooting information at a glance and to perform many system control functions.

The craft interface (see Figure 3.18) allows you to view status and troubleshooting information at a glance and to perform many system control functions. The craft interface is located on the front of the router above the FPCs and contains alarm LEDs, a lamp test button, an LCD display, LEDs for the host subsystems, SIBs, FPCs, and FPC online/offline buttons.The craft interface is hot-insertable and hot-removable.

Figure 3.18 *T320 Craft Interface*

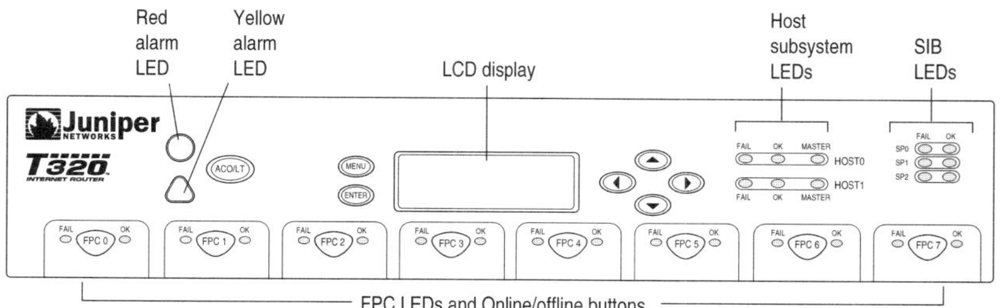

The Connector Interface Panel (CIP), located at the left side of the FPC card cage, consists of Ethernet, console, and auxiliary connectors for the Routing Engine ports, and alarm relay contacts (see Figure 3.19). The front electrostatic discharge point is located near the bottom of the CIP. The CIP is hot-pluggable.

Figure 3.19 *T320 CIP*

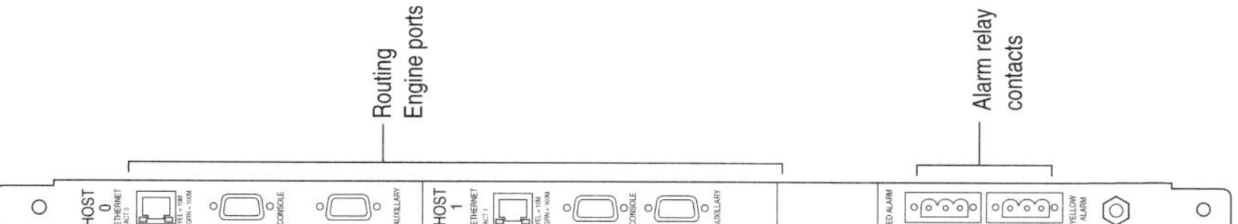

The router has two load-sharing DC power supplies, located at the lower rear of the chassis. The power supplies connect to the midplane, which distributes the output voltages produced by the power supplies to the router components, depending on their voltage requirements (see Table 3.10). Each power supply has two inputs, each with its own 80-A circuit breaker and each requiring a dedicated DC power source.

The power supplies are redundant. If one power supply fails or is removed, the second power supply instantly assumes the entire electrical load and can provide full power for as long as the router is operational.

Power supplies are hot-removable and hot-insertable. The router supports DC power only. Each power supply is cooled by its own internal cooling system.

Table 3.10 *T320 Power Supply Electrical Specifications*

Item	Specification
Maximum input power	3200 W
DC input voltage	Nominal –48 VDC, –60 VDC Operating range: –42 to –72 VDC
Input DC current rating	60 A @ –48 to –60 VDC to (nominal) 60 A @ –48 VDC (nominal) system current rating

The router cooling system consists of two front fan trays, one rear fan tray, front and rear air filters, and an air filter on each power supply. The cooling system components work together to keep all router components within the acceptable temperature range. All fan trays and filters are hot-insertable and hot-removable. The two front fan trays are interchangeable. The front and rear fan trays are not interchangeable.

The host subsystem monitors the temperature of the router components. When the router is operating normally, the fans function at lower than full speed. If a fan fails, the speed of the remaining fans is automatically adjusted to keep the temperature within the acceptable range. Figure 3.20 shows the air flow through the router and the location of the cooling system components.

Figure 3.20 *Air Flow through the T320 Chassis*

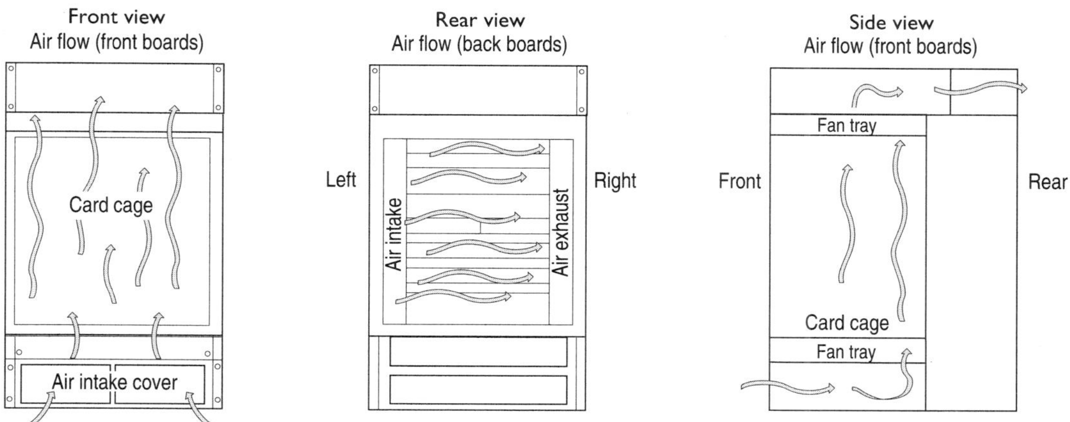

The router's cable management system consists of a row of nine semicircular plastic bobbins mounted on the front of the router below the FPC card cage. The PIC cables wrap around the bobbins, keeping the cables organized and securely in place. The curvature of the bobbins also helps maintain the proper bend radius for optical PIC cables.

The router has LEDs that display the status of various router components. Table 3.11 lists the LEDs on the craft interface and the individual router components.

Table 3.11 *T320 Internet Router LEDs*

Component	LED	Location
SIBs	Green OK Amber FAIL Green Active	SIB faceplate
	Green OK Red FAIL	Craft interface
FPCs	Green OK Red FAIL	Craft interface
PICs	Tricolor: red, green, amber	PIC faceplate
SCGs	Green OK Amber FAIL Blue MASTER	PCG faceplate
Host module	Green OK Red FAIL Green MASTER	Craft interface
CB	Green OK Amber FAIL Blue MASTER	CB faceplate
Power supplies	Green CB ON Amber CB TRIP Amber OVER TEMP Blue DC OK	Power supply faceplate
Alarm LEDs		
Red alarm	Large, circular red	Craft interface
Yellow alarm	Large, triangular amber	Craft interface
Ethernet LEDs		
10-Mbps link	Yellow	CIP
100-Mbps link	Green	CIP

M160 Internet Router

Figure 3.21 *M160 Internet Router Chassis and Components*

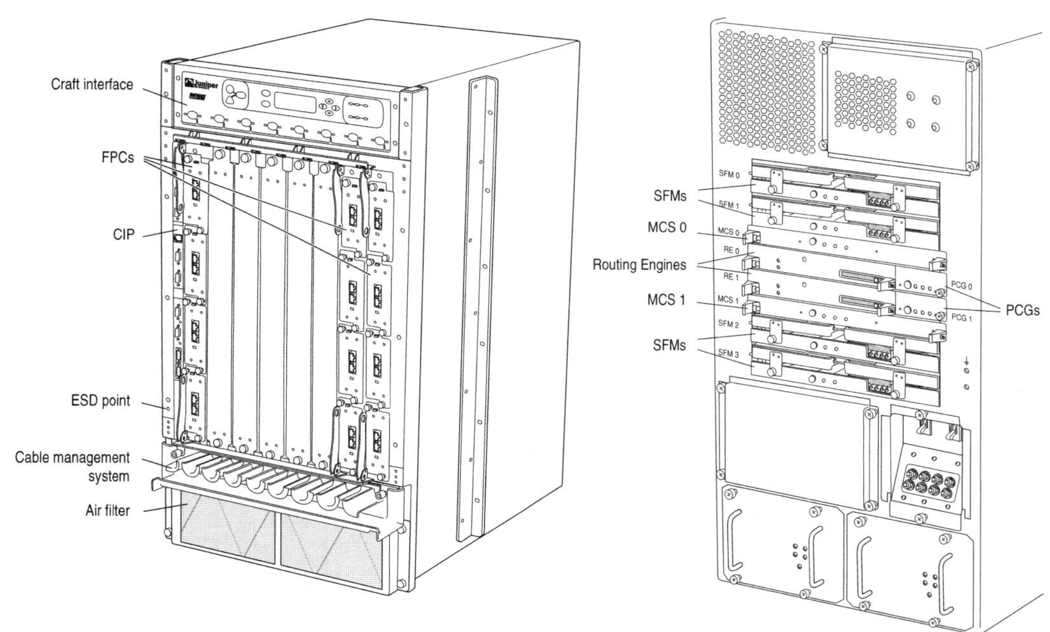

The M160 Internet router (see Figure 3.21) has a maximum aggregate throughput of 160 Gbps. It accepts up to eight FPCs and offers a high level of redundancy so that no single point of failure can cause the entire system to fail. Table 3.12 shows the physical specifications of the M160 router and Table 3.13 gives an overview of the major hardware components of the router.

Table 3.12 *M160 Internet Router Physical Specifications*

Category	Value
Chassis dimensions	35 in. (88.9 cm) high x 19 in. (48.3 cm) wide x 29 in. (73.6 cm) deep
Router weight	113.5 lb (51.5 kg) empty chassis 190 lb (86 kg) minimum configuration 370.5 lb (168 kg) maximum configuration
Required clearances	24 in. (61 cm) front and rear; 6 in. (15.2 cm) each side

Table 3.13 *M160 Internet Router Major Hardware Components*

Component	Quantity	Function	Redundant	FRU	Offline button
Chassis (including midplane)	1	Houses router components	–	–	–
Switching and Forwarding Modules (SFMs)	1–4	Performs packet switching, forwarding, route lookup	Yes	Hot-removable Hot-insertable	Yes
Flexible PIC Concentrators (FPCs)	1–8	Connects PICs to other components	–	Hot-removable Hot-insertable	Yes
Physical Interface Cards (PICs)	1–4 per FPC	Interfaces to network media	–	Hot-removable Hot-insertable	Yes
Routing Engine	1-2	Maintains routing protocols, routing tables	Yes	Hot-pluggable	–
Miscellaneous Control Subsystem (MCS)	1-2	Performs system control and monitoring	Yes	Hot-pluggable	Yes
PFE Clock Generators (PCGs)	2	Provides 125-MHz system clock	Yes	Hot-pluggable	Yes
Power supplies	2	Distributes voltages to components	Yes	Hot-removable Hot-insertable	–
Cooling system	3 impellers; 1 fan tray	Cools router components	Yes	Hot-removable Hot-insertable	–
Craft interface	1	Displays status and troubleshooting information, provides control functions	–	–	
Connector Interface Panel (CIP)	1	Provides interfaces to Routing Engine ports, BITS sources, and alarm relay devices	–	–	–

The router chassis includes two front support posts to attach the router to a front-mount rack, two mounting ears for center-rack mounting, and two ESD points, one at the front and one at the rear. The midplane is located in the center of the chassis and forms the rear of the FPC card cage. The FPCs install into the midplane from the front of the chassis, and the SFMs, Routing Engines, MCSs, and PCGs install into the midplane from the rear of the chassis. The power supplies and cooling system components also connect to the midplane.

Up to four interconnected SFMs can be installed in the router, providing a total of 160 million packets per second (Mpps) of forwarding.

The Switching and Forwarding Modules (SFMs) (see Figure 3.22) provide route lookup, filtering, and switching to the destination FPC. Up to four interconnected SFMs can be installed in the router, providing a total of 160 Mpps of forwarding.

The SFM is a two-board system; its components include Distributed Buffer Manager ASICs, which send packets to the output buffer and forward notification to the I/O Manager ASICs on the FPCs, the Internet Processor II ASIC, which performs route lookups, 8MB of parity-protected SSRAM, a processor subsystem that handles exception packets and management of the SFM, two LEDs, and an online/offline button for removing and installing the SFM.

Figure 3.22 *M160 SFM*

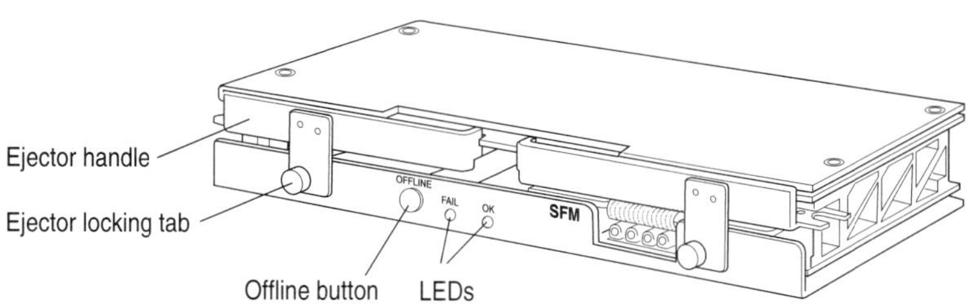

The FPCs install vertically into the midplane from the front of the chassis. The FPCs are numbered left to right, from 0 through 7. Each FPC accepts up to four PICs.

The FPCs connect the PICs to the rest of the router so that incoming packets can be forwarded across the midplane to the appropriate destination port. FPCs contain shared memory, which is managed by the Distributed Buffer Manager ASIC on each SFM, for storing data packets received by the PICs. The I/O Manager ASIC on each FPC divides incoming data packets from the PICs into cells, which are stored in a shared memory buffer, and reassembles them into data packets when they are ready for transmission.

The components of the FPC include the I/O Manager ASICs, which parse Layer 2 and Layer 3 data and perform encapsulation and segmentation; the Packet Director ASICs, which distribute incoming packets to the I/O Manager ASICs and direct outgoing packets from the I/O Manager ASIC to the PICs; 32-MB SDRAM DIMMs, which form the shared memory buffer for the router; parity-protected SSRAM, which stores data structures used by the I/O Manager ASICs, a processor subsystem; two LEDs; and an offline button, located on the craft interface, for removing and installing the FPC.

> The router supports two types of FPC: FPC1 and FPC2. The router can operate with any combination of FPC1s and FPC2s installed.

The router supports two types of FPC: FPC1, which supports PICs including single-port OC-12 and Gigabit Ethernet, and FPC2, which supports higher-speed PICs including OC-48 and Tunnel Services. The router can operate with any combination of FPC1s and FPC2s installed. The installation and removal of the two FPC types are identical. PICs that can be inserted on an FPC2 are distinguished by having an offline button on their faceplate. The FPC1 has built-in offline buttons for the PICs it holds (see Figure 3.23). In this guide, both the FPC1 and FPC2 are referred to simply as "FPC" except where the differences between the two are being discussed.

FPCs are hot-insertable and hot-removable. When you bring an FPC online, the Routing Engine downloads the FPC software, the FPC runs its diagnostics, and the PICs on the FPC slot are enabled. No interruption occurs to the routing functions.

Figure 3.23 *M160 FPCs*

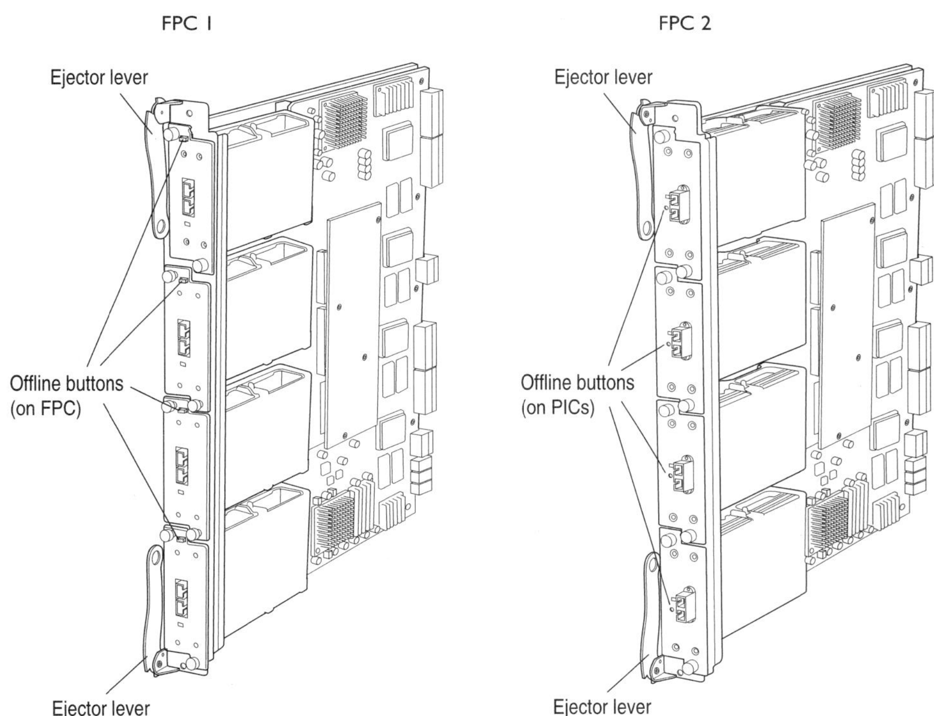

The router has two PCGs, located in the rear of the chassis to the right of the Routing Engine slots (see Figure 3.24). The PCGs supply the 125-MHz system clock to the Packet Forwarding Engine components.

The PCGs both send clock signals to the Packet Forwarding Engine modules, along with a signal indicating which is the master clock source. The master Routing Engine controls which PCG is master and which is backup.

The components of each PCG include a 125-MHz system clock generator, three LEDs, and an online/offline button for removing and installing the PCG.

Figure 3.24 *M160 PCG*

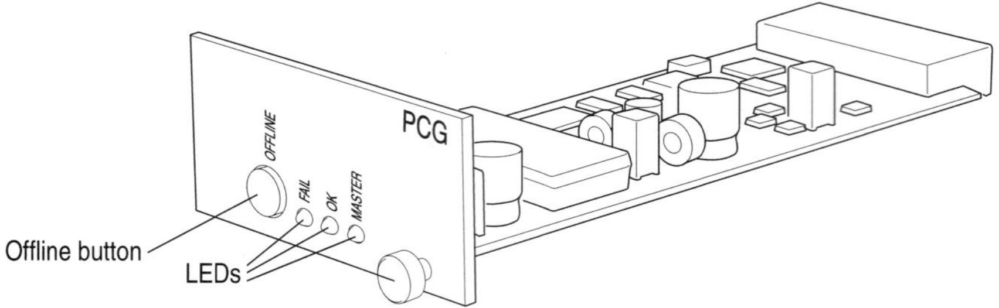

The router can have one or two host modules. The host modules provide the routing and system management functions of the router, and provide the clock source for SONET/SDH interfaces.

The Routing Engine and MCS function as a unit to provide the routing and system management functions of the router.

Each host module consists of a Routing Engine and an MCS installing in adjacent slots. For each host module, the Routing Engine and MCS function as a unit, each component requiring the other to operate; if the adjacent component is not present, a Routing Engine or MCS will not operate, even if physically installed in the router.

The M160 router can have one or two Routing Engines. The Routing Engines install into the upper rear of the chassis. If two Routing Engines are installed, one functions as master and the other as backup. If the master Routing Engine fails or is removed, the backup restarts and becomes master. The Routing Engines are hot-pluggable.

The Miscellaneous Control Subsystem (MCS) works with the Routing Engine installed in the adjacent slot to provide control and monitoring functions for router components and to provide SONET clocking for the router (see Figure 3.25). The MCS installs into the rear of the chassis, in the slot adjacent to the Routing Engine with which it forms the host module.

The router can be equipped with up to two MCSs for redundancy. If two MCSs are installed, one functions as the master MCS and the other as backup. If the master MCS fails or is removed, the backup restarts and becomes the master MCS.

The functions of the MCS include monitoring and controlling of router components; controlling the powerup sequence of router components at startup; powering down of components when their offline buttons are pressed; controlling mastership (in a router with redundant Routing Engine, MCS, or PCG modules); controlling FPC resets, providing the clock source for SONET/SDH interfaces; and monitoring the SONET clock, the SONET reference clocks from the FPCs, and the system clocks from the PCGs.

The components of each MCS include an interface to the Routing Engine, high-speed switch for intermodule communication, a 19.44-MHz Stratum 3 reference clock for SONET/SDH PICs, three LEDs, and an online/offline button for removing and installing the MCS.

Figure 3.25 *M160 MCS*

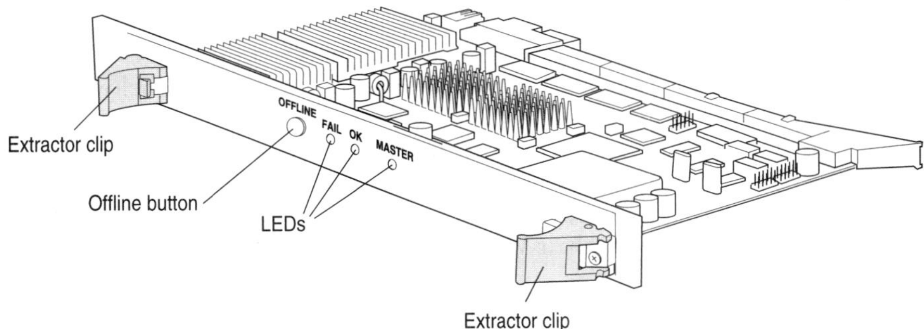

The craft interface (see Figure 3.26) is located on the front of the chassis above the FPC card cage, and contains the alarm LEDs and alarm cutoff button, LCD display and navigation buttons, host module LEDs, and FPC LEDs and online/offline buttons.

Figure 3.26 *M160 Craft Interface*

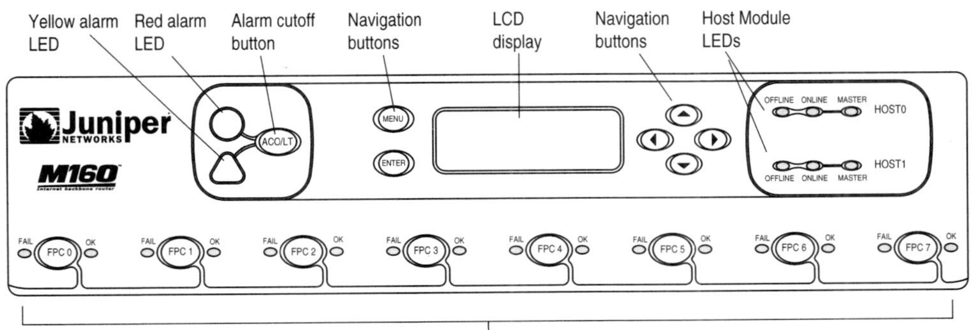

Figure 3.27 *M160 CIP*

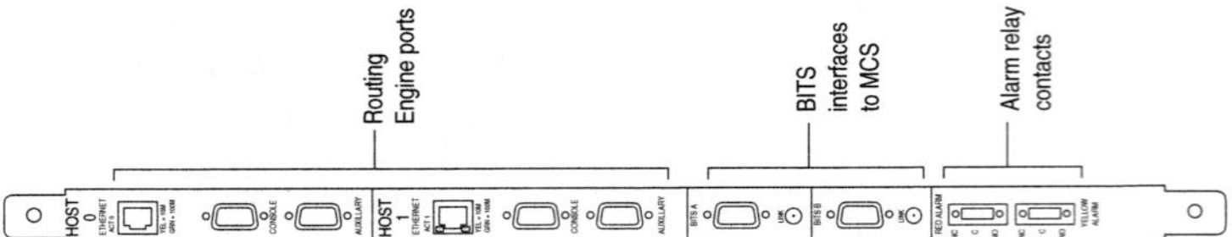

The CIP, located at the left side of the FPC card cage (see Figure 3.27) consists of connectors for the Routing Engines, BITS interfaces for the MCS, and alarm relay contacts to connect the router to external alarm display devices.

The router has two load-sharing DC power supplies, of either the original or enhanced type (see Table 3.14). The power supplies are located at the lower rear of the chassis, below the rear lower impeller and the router's on-board circuit breaker box. The power supplies connect to the midplane, which delivers the power input from the circuit breaker box and distributes the different output voltages produced by the power supplies to the router's components, depending on their voltage requirements.

The router supports DC power supplies only. Power supplies are hot-removable and hot-insertable. Each power supply has handles to facilitate removal from the chassis.

Table 3.14 *M160 Power Supply Electrical Specifications*

Item	Original Power Supply Specification	Enhanced Power Supply Specification
Power supply	2600 W maximum output; nonisolated	3200 W maximum output; nonisolated
DC input voltage	Nominal: –48 VDC, –60 VDC Operating range: –42 to –72 VDC	Nominal: –48 VDC, –60 VDC Operating range: –42 to –72 VDC
Input DC current rating	65 A @ –48 V	80 A @ –48 V
Output voltages	+48 V @ 8 A (cooling system), +8 V @ 6 A (bias), –48 V @ 60 A	+48 V @ 8 A (cooling system), +8 V @ 6 A (bias), –48 V @ 75 A

Power must be connected from two DC sources for load sharing, one for each circuit breaker, for proper operation of the router.

The power cables from the DC power source connect to the circuit breaker box, which is located on the rear of the chassis above the right power supply. The circuit breaker box provides one circuit breaker for each power supply. Power must be connected from two DC sources for load sharing, one for each circuit breaker, for proper operation of the router.

Power cables are attached to the terminal studs on the circuit breaker box by cable lugs and washers. A grounding cable is attached to separate grounding points on the chassis above the circuit breaker box by bolts and washers.

The router has fuses for the FPCs, SFMs, MCS, and PCGs. The fuses are located in a fuse box on the rear of the midplane. To access the fuses, you remove the rear lower impeller assembly. The router uses Cooper Bussman brand GMT-type fuses. The fuse locations are also shown on a table attached to the midplane below the fuse box.

The M160 router has two separate cooling subsystems, one for the front and one for the rear.

The M160 router has two separate cooling subsystems, one for the front and one for the rear. The front cooling subsystem consists of an upper impeller and a lower fan tray, which cool the FPCs, the PICs, and the midplane. The rear cooling subsystem consists of a pair of impellers, which cool the SFMs, the host module, the PCGs, and the power supplies. The air intake for both cooling subsystems is located on the front of the chassis, below the FPC card cage. An air filter in front of the air intake prevents dust and other particles from entering the cooling system.

The MCS monitors the temperature of the router's components. When the router is operating normally, the impellers and fans function at lower than full speed. If an impeller or fan fails or is removed, the temperature increases and the speed of the remaining impellers and fans is automatically adjusted to keep the temperature within the acceptable range. Figure 3.28 shows air flow through the chassis and the location of the cooling system components.

Figure 3.28 *Air Flow through the M160 Router*

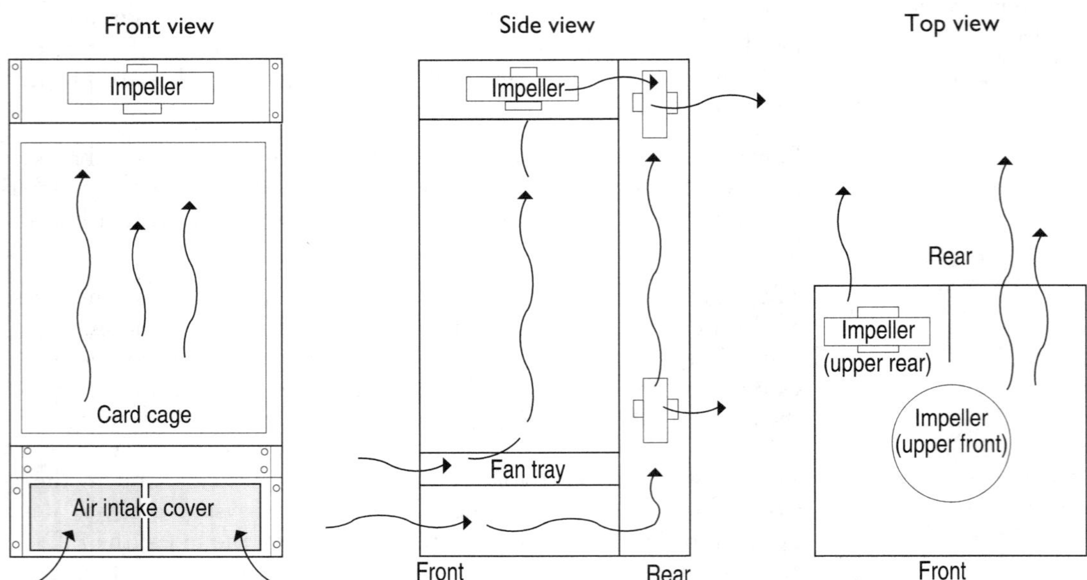

The M160 router's cable management system consists of a row of nine semicircular plastic bobbins, mounted on the front of the chassis below the FPC card cage. The PIC cables wrap around the bobbins, keeping the cables organized and securely in place. The curvature of the bobbins also maintains the proper bend radius for optical PIC cables.

The router has LEDs that display the status of various router components. Table 3.15 lists the LEDs on the craft interface and the individual router components.

Table 3.15 *M160 and M40e Internet Router LEDs*

Component	LED	Location
SFMs	Green OK Red FAIL	SFM faceplate
FPCs	Green OK Red FAIL	Craft interface
PICs	Tricolor: red, green, amber	PIC faceplate
PCGs	Blue MASTER Green OK Red FAIL	PCG faceplate
Host module	Green MASTER Green ONLINE Red OFFLINE	Craft interface
MCS	Blue MASTER Green OK Amber FAIL	MCS faceplate
Power supplies	Green CB ON Blue OUTPUT OK Amber NO AIRFLOW Amber CB OFF	Power supply faceplate
Alarm LEDs		
Red alarm	Large, circular red	Craft interface
Yellow alarm	Large, triangular amber	Craft interface
Ethernet LEDs		
10-Mbps link	Yellow	CIP
100-Mbps link	Green	CIP

M40e Internet Router

Figure 3.29 *M40e Internet Router Chassis and Components*

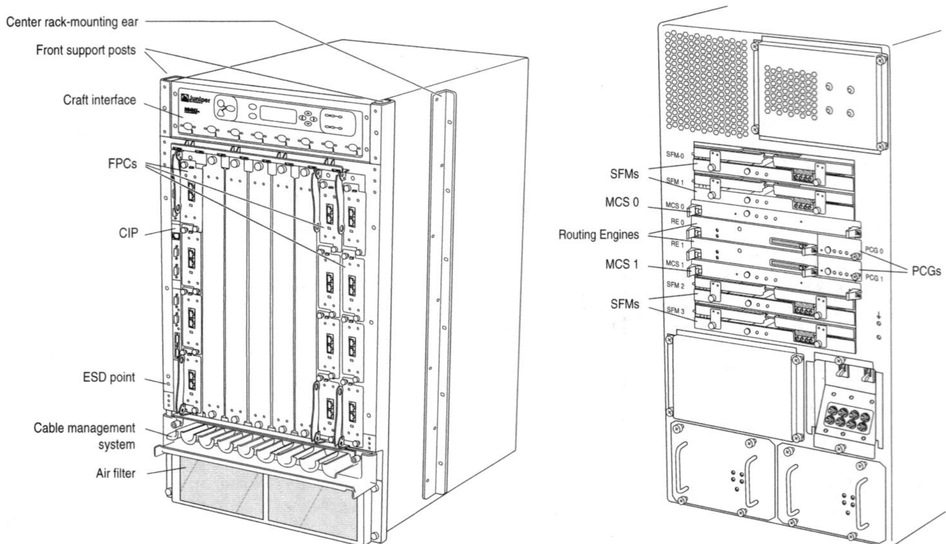

The M40e router (see Figure 3.29) shares the same chassis, and many of the same components, with the M160 router, but accepts both AC and DC power supplies and has a maximum of two SFMs instead of four. The FPCs for the M40e and M160 routers are not interchangeable. Many of the M40e components, including the SFMs, PCGs, Routing Engine, MCS, CIP, cooling system, and cable management system are identical in structure and function to those in the M160 router.

Table 3.12 lists the M40e router's physical specifications, and Table 3.13 describes the router's major hardware components.

The M40e shares the same chassis, and many of the same components, as the M160 router.

The M40e router chassis includes two front support posts to attach the router to a front-mount rack, two center-mounting ears for center-rack mounting, and ESD points, one at the front and one at the rear.

The midplane is located in the center of the chassis and forms the rear of the FPC card cage. It performs the functions of data transfer, power distribution, and signal connectivity.

Table 3.16 *M40e Internet Router Physical Specifications*

Category	Value
Chassis dimensions	35 in. (88.9 cm) high x 19 in. (48.3 cm) wide x 29 in. (73.6 cm) deep
Router weight	113.5 lb (51.5 kg) empty chassis 190 lb (86 kg) minimum configuration 370.5 lb (168 kg) maximum configuration
Required clearances	24 in. (61 cm) front and rear; 6 in. (15.2 cm) on each side

The SFMs perform the route lookup, filtering, and switching functions. Each SFM can process 40 Mpps. The M40e router can operate with one or two SFMs; only one SFM is active at a time, with the optional second SFM in standby mode.

Removing the standby SFM has no effect on router function. If the active SFM fails or is removed from the chassis, the effect depends on the number of SFMs installed: If only one SFM is installed, forwarding halts until the SFM is replaced and functioning again. If two SFMs are installed, forwarding halts until the standby SFM boots and becomes active.

The M40e router supports two types of FPC: M40e-FPC1 and M40e-FPC2. The router can operate with any combination of the two types installed.

The M40e router can accommodate up to eight FPCs, which install vertically into the front of the chassis. The FPCs install into the FPC slots, which are numbered left to right from 0 through 7. Each FPC accommodates either one or up to four PICs, depending on the type of FPC and PIC. For more information, see Table 3.3 on page 36.

An FPC can be installed into any FPC slot regardless of the PICs it contains, and any combination of slots can be used. Any slot not occupied by an FPC must have a blank FPC panel to maintain proper airflow through the router. FPCs for the M40e router and M160 router are not interchangeable.

Table 3.17 *M40e Internet Router Major Hardware Components*

Component	Quantity	Function	Redundant	FRU	Offline button
Chassis (including midplane)	1	Houses router components	–	–	–
Switching and Forwarding Modules (SFMs)	1–2	Performs packet switching forwarding, route lookup	Yes	Hot-removable Hot-insertable	Yes
Flexible PIC Concentrators (FPCs)	1–8	Connects PICs to other components	–	Hot-removable Hot-insertable	Yes
Physical Interface Cards (PICs)	1–4 per FPC	Interfaces to network media	–	Hot-removable Hot-insertable	Yes
Routing Engine	1–2	Maintains routing protocols, routing tables	Yes	Hot-pluggable	–
Miscellaneous Control Subsystem (MCS)	1–2	Performs system control and monitoring	Yes	Hot-pluggable	Yes
PFE Clock Generators (PCGs)	2	Provides 125-MHz system clock	Yes	Hot-pluggable	Yes
Power supplies	2	Distributes voltages to components	Yes	Hot-removable Hot-insertable	–
Cooling system	3 impellers; 1 fan tray	Cools router components	Yes	Hot-removable Hot-insertable	–
Craft interface	1	Displays status and troubleshooting information, provides control functions	–	–	–
Connector Interface Panel (CIP)	1	Provides interfaces to Routing Engine ports, BITS sources, and alarm relay devices	–	–	

The M40e router has two PCGs, located in the rear of the chassis, which supply the 125-MHz system clock to the Packet Forwarding Engine components. The master Routing Engine controls which PCG is master and which is backup.

Each PCG consists of a clock generator, three LEDs, which display the status of the PCG, and an online/offline button for removing and installing the PCG.

The Routing Engine and MCS work together to monitor and control system functions.

The M40e router can have one or two host modules; if two are installed, both are powered on, but one is active (master) and the other is in standby mode. The host modules construct routing tables, perform system management functions, and generate the clock signal for SONET/SDH interfaces. Each host module consists of a Routing Engine and an adjacent MCS.

The router can have one or two Routing Engines. The Routing Engines install into the upper rear of the chassis. If two Routing Engines are installed, one functions as master and the other as backup. If the master Routing Engine fails or is removed, the backup restarts and becomes master. The Routing Engines are hot-pluggable.

The router can have one or two MCSs, located in the rear of the chassis in the slots adjacent to the Routing Engines. The MCSs work with the Routing Engines to monitor and control system functions. The router can have up to two MCSs for redundancy. If two are installed, one acts as master and the other as backup. If the master MCS fails or is removed, the backup restarts and becomes master.

Each MCS consists of an interface to the Routing Engine, a high-speed switch for intermodule communication, a 19.44-MHz Stratum 3 clock for SONET/SDH interfaces, three LEDs, and an online/offline button.

The craft interface provides status and troubleshooting information at a glance and has buttons for deactivating alarms and for removing and installing the FPCs. The craft interface is located on the front of the chassis above the FPC card cage.

The M160 CIP is discussed on page 66.

The CIP, located at the left side of the FPC card cage, houses connections for the Routing Engine ports, BITS interfaces for the MCS, and alarm relay contacts to connect the router to external alarm display devices. It is identical in structure and function to the CIP on the M160 router.

The router has two load-sharing power supplies, located at the lower rear of the chassis. The router can use either AC or DC power, but the two types cannot be mixed in a single router. The power supplies connect to the midplane, which distributes power to router components according to their individual voltage requirements. An AC-powered router can use only 220 VAC power (nominal range 200 to 240 VAC), not 110 VAC power (nominal range 100–120 VAC).

Each AC power supply has one LED, which indicates power supply status, and a self-test button, for use by qualified service personnel only. Table 3.18 lists electrical specifications for the AC power supply.

Table 3.18 *M40e AC Power Supply Electrical Specifications*

Item	Specification
Power output	2900 WDC maximum output; isolated
AC input voltage	Nominal: 200 to 240 VAC Operating range: 187 to 264 VAC
AC input line frequency	47 to 63 Hz
AC input current rating	16 A
Output voltages	+48 V @ 7.3 A (cooling system), +8 V @ 6 A (bias), –50 V @ 50 A isolated

Each DC power supply has three LEDs, which indicate power supply status, and a self-test button, for use by qualified service personnel only. Table 3.19 lists electrical specifications for the DC power supply.

Table 3.19 *M40e DC Power Supply Electrical Specifications*

Item	Specification
Power output	3000 W maximum output; nonisolated
DC input voltage	Nominal: –48 VDC, –60 VDC Operating range: –42 to –72 VDC
Input DC current rating	80 A @ –48 V
Output voltages	+48 V @ 8.3 A (cooling system), +8.3 V @ 6 A (bias), –48 V to –60 V@ 75 A

The M40e router has separate front and rear cooling subsystems. The front cooling system consists of an upper impeller and a lower fan tray, which cool the FPCs, the PICs, and the midplane. The rear cooling system consists of a pair of impellers, which cool the SFMs, the host modules, the PCGs, and the power supplies. The air intake for both cooling systems, located on the front of the chassis, includes an air filter.

The MCS monitors the temperature of the router's components. If a fan or impeller fails or is removed, the MCS adjusts the speed of the remaining fans and impellers to keep the temperature within the acceptable range.

The M40e router's cable management system, consists of nine semicircular plastic bobbins, mounted on the front of the chassis below the FPC card cage. The function of the cable management system is identical to that on the M160 router.

The LEDs on the M40e router components are identical to those on the M160 router. For a description of the LED locations and meanings see Table 3.15, "M160 and M40e Internet Router LEDs," on page 69.

M40 Internet Router

Figure 3.30 *M40 Internet Router Chassis and Components*

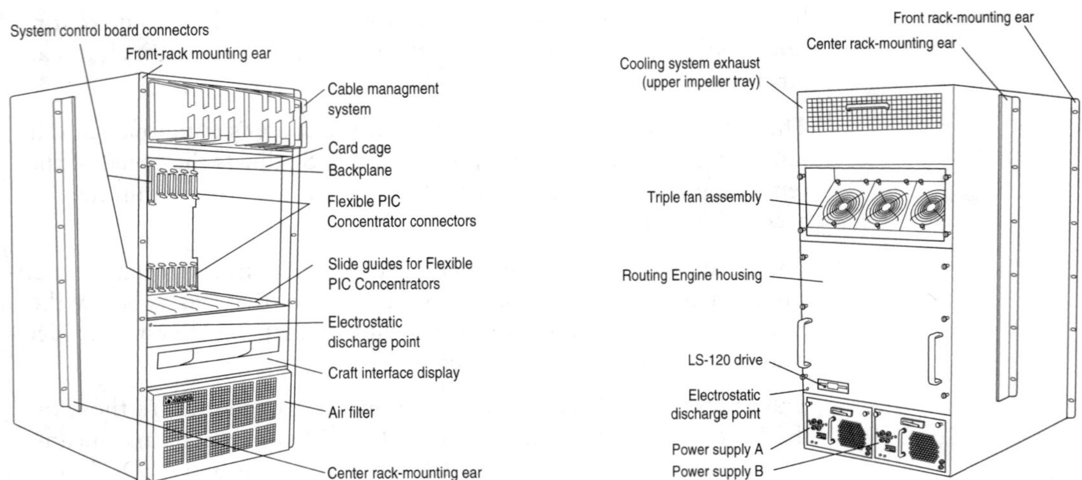

The M40 Internet router (see Figure 3.30) has a maximum aggregate throughput of 12 Gbps. It accepts up to eight FPCs. Table 3.20 shows the physical specifications of the M40 router, and Table 3.21 gives an overview of the major hardware components of the router.

Table 3.20 *M40 Router Physical Specifications*

Category	Value
Chassis dimensions	35 in. (89 cm) high x 19 in. (48.3 cm) wide x 23.5 in. (60 cm) deep
Router weight	180 lb (81 kg) minimum configuration 280 lb (127 kg) maximum configuration
Required clearances	19 in. (48 cm) front and rear; 6 in. (15.2 cm) each side

Table 3.21 *M40 Internet Router Major Hardware Components*

Component	Quantity	Function	Redundant	FRU	Online/ offline Button
Chassis (including backplane)	1	Houses router components	–	–	–
Flexible PIC Concentrators (FPCs)	1–8	Connects PICs to other components, houses shared memory	–	Hot-removable Hot-insertable	Yes
System Control Board (SCB)	1	Performs route lookups, monitors system, transfers control packets	–	Hot-pluggable	–
Physical Interface Cards (PICs)	1–4 per FPC	Interfaces to network media	–	From removed FPC	Yes
Routing Engine	1	Maintains routing protocols, routing tables	–	Hot-pluggable	–
Power supplies	2 AC or 2 DC	Distributes voltages to components	Yes	Hot-removable Hot-insertable	–
Cooling system	2 impeller trays and 1 fan assembly (3 fans)	Cools router components	Yes	Hot-removable Hot-insertable	–
Craft interface	1	Displays status and troubleshooting information, provides control functions	–	Hot-removable Hot-insertable	–

The router chassis includes two front-mounting metal ears, two center-mounting ears, and two ESD points, one front and one rear. The backplane forms the rear of the FPC card cage. The SCB and the FPCs install into the front of the chassis. The backplane contains a temperature sensor and is cooled by three fans.

Up to eight FPCs install vertically into the backplane from the front of the chassis, four on either side of the SCB. An FPC can be installed into any FPC slot. Each FPC accepts up to four PICs. The FPCs connect the PICs to the rest of the router so that incoming packets can be forwarded across the backplane to the destination port. The FPCs contain shared memory, which is managed by the Distributed Buffer Manager ASIC on the backplane, for storing data packets received by the PICs. The I/O Manager ASIC on each FPC breaks incoming data packets from the PICs into cells, which are stored in the shared memory buffer, and reassembles them into data packets when they are ready for transmission.

When you remove an FPC and install a new one, the backplane flushes the entire system memory pool before the new card is brought online, a process that takes about 200 milliseconds. When you install an FPC into a running system, the Routing Engine downloads the FPC software, the FPC runs its diagnostics, and the PICs on the FPC slot are enabled. Routing functions continue uninterrupted.

For information about the PICs used in the router, see "Physical Interface Cards" on page 34.

The SCB occupies the center slot of the FPC card cage. The SCB is a component of the Packet Forwarding Engine, and performs route lookups, monitoring of system components, transfer of exception and control packets, and control of FPC resets.

The components of the SCB include a PowerPC processor, which processes control packets; the Internet Processor ASIC, which performs route lookups; four slots of SSRAM for the forwarding tables; a 19.44-MHz Stratum 3 reference clock for SONET/SDH PICs; and two pairs of LEDs.

The M40 router has a single Routing Engine. The Routing Engine installs into the housing on the rear of the router. For more information, see "Routing Engine" on page 37.

The craft interface, located on the lower impeller tray on the front of the chassis, allows you to view status and troubleshooting information at a glance and to perform many system control functions (see Figure 3.31). The craft interface contains the system LEDs and buttons, LCD display, alarm relay contacts, and Routing Engine ports.

The M40 router has two redundant power supplies. A single power supply can provide full power (up to 1500 W) for as long as the system is operational. Redundancy is necessary only in case of power supply failure or removal.

The power supplies install at the lower rear of the chassis. The power supplies connect to the backplane, which distributes the different output voltages produced by the power supplies throughout the system and its components. Each power supply contains an integrated fan that cools the power assembly.

Figure 3.31 *M40 Craft Interface*

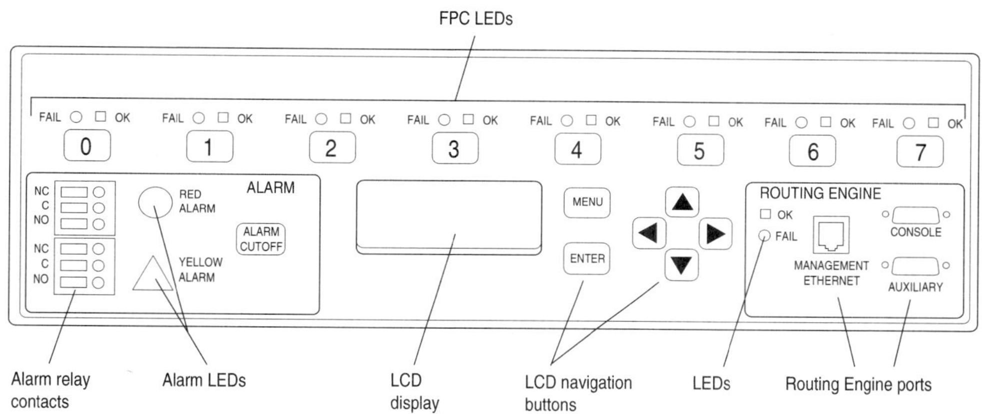

The M40 router supports both AC and DC power supplies. Table 3.22 lists the specifications for both types. You cannot mix both types of power supply in a single router. Both types are field-replaceable and hot-removable and hot-insertable. Each power supply has a handle for removing the unit from the chassis. Both types have a safety interlock lever that prevents the unit from being removed until the power is cut off.

Table 3.22 *M40 Router Power Supply Specifications*

Item	**AC Specification**	**DC Specification**
Maximum power consumption	1664 W	1664 W
Input voltage	180 through 264 VAC operating range	–38 through –75 VDC operating range
Input line frequency	50 through 60 Hz, autoranging	–
Input current rating	8 A @ 208 V	35 A @ 48 V
Output voltages	+3.3 V; +5 V; +2.5 V; +12 V; +24 V	+3.3 V; +5 V; +2.5 V; +12 V; +24 V
Power and grounding cords and cables	Country-specific; see *M40 Router Hardware Guide*	4 AWG wire cables with dual 1/4–20 UNC terminal studs @ 15.86 mm (0.625 in.)

The M40 router cooling system consists of three separate subsystems: one for the Packet Forwarding Engine, one for the Routing Engine and the backplane, and one for each power supply.

The M40 router cooling system consists of three separate subsystems: two pairs of redundant impellers that cool the Packet Forwarding Engine; three load-sharing fans that cool the backplane and the Routing Engine; and a built-in fan on each power supply. Each cooling subsystem maintains a separate air flow, and each is monitored independently for temperature control. An air filter at the lower front of the chassis covers all three air intakes.

Figure 3.32 shows the air flow through the router and the location of the cooling system components. As the impellers draw air into the front of the card cage through an air filter that covers the air intake vent, they force the exhaust from the rear of the chassis through vents located in the upper impeller tray. The air is channelled past the Packet Forwarding Engine components, keeping them cool.

The fans are load-sharing. If one fan is removed or fails, the other two fans can assume the entire load. The backplane temperature sensor detects temperatures above the acceptable range. A fan failure or excessive temperature condition triggers alarm LEDs on the craft interface and activates alarm relay contacts. Each fan is hot-insertable and hot-removable.

Figure 3.32 *Air Flow through the M40 Chassis*

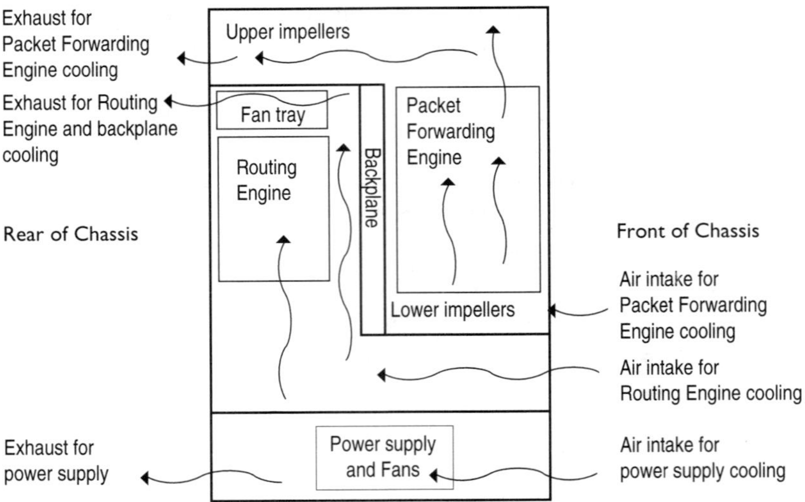

Each power supply has its own integrated fan, which cools the power supply. The fan blows air out the exhaust vent at the rear of the chassis, drawing air in through an air filter that covers the air intake vent at the front of the chassis.

The cable management system is attached to the chassis and consists of a row of staggered metal hooks, each draped with a rounded plastic shield. This row of hooks is shielded by a removable cable management system cover.

The router has LEDs that display the status of various router components. Table 3.23 lists the LEDs on the craft interface and the individual router components.

Table 3.23 *M40 Router LEDs*

Component	LED	Location
FPCs	Green OK Red FAIL	Craft interface
PICs	Tricolor: red, green, amber	PIC faceplate
SCB	Green ACTIVE Red FAIL Green RUN Amber STAT1 Amber FAIL	SCB faceplate
Routing Engine	Green OK Red FAIL	Craft interface
Power supplies	Green OK Red FAIL	Power supply faceplate
Alarm LEDs		
Red alarm	Large, circular red	Craft interface
Yellow alarm	Large, triangular amber	Craft interface

M20 Internet Router

Figure 3.33 *M20 Internet Router Chassis and Components*

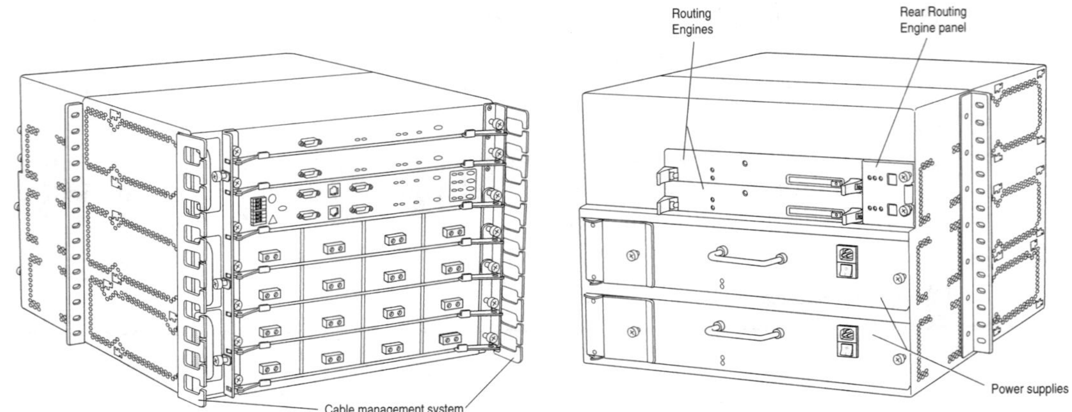

The M20 Internet router (see Figure 3.33) has a maximum aggregate bandwidth of 20 Gbps. It accepts up to four FPCs. Table 3.24 shows the physical specifications of the M20 router, and Table 3.25 gives an overview of the major hardware components of the router.

Table 3.24 *M20 Router Physical Specifications*

Category	Value
Dimensions	14 in. (36 cm) high x 19 in. (48.3 cm) wide x 21 in. (54 cm) deep
Router weight	80 lb (36 kg) minimum configuration 134 lb (61 kg) maximum configuration
Required clearances	19 in. (48 cm) front and rear; 6 in. (15.2 cm) on each side

Table 3.25 *M20 Internet Router Major Hardware Components*

Component	Quantity	Function	Redundant	FRU	Online/offline Button
Chassis (including midplane)	1	Houses router components	–	–	–
Flexible PIC Concentrators (FPCs)	1–4	Connects PICs to other components, houses shared memory	–	Hot-removable Hot-insertable	Yes
System and Switch Boards (SSBs)	1–2	Performs route lookups, manages shared memory, transfers control packets	–	Hot-pluggable	–
Physical Interface Cards (PICs)	1–4 per FPC	Interfaces to network media	–	From removed FPC	Yes
Routing Engines	1–2	Maintains routing protocols, routing tables	–	Hot-pluggable	Yes
Power supplies	2 AC or 2 DC	Distributes voltages to components	Yes	Hot-removable Hot-insertable	–
Cooling system	3 fan trays and 1 rear Routing Engine fan	Cools router components	Yes	Hot-removable Hot-insertable	–
Craft interface	1	Displays status and troubleshooting information, provides control functions	–	Hot-removable Hot-insertable	–

The router chassis includes two front-mounting metal ears, two optional rack-mounting ears for telco center-rack mounting, two optional front-mounting brackets, and two ESD points. The midplane forms the back of the card cage. The FPCs, SSB, and craft interface install into the midplane from the front of the chassis. Power supplies and the Routing Engine plug into the midplane from the back of the chassis. Fan trays plug into the midplane from both the front and rear of the chassis.

The M20 router can have up to four FPCs, which install horizontally in the front of the chassis (see Figure 3.34). The FPCs connect the PICs to the rest of the router so that incoming packets can be forwarded across the midplane to the appropriate destination port. FPCs contain shared memory, which is managed by the Distributed Buffer Manager ASIC on the SSB, for storing data packets. The I/O Manager ASIC on each FPC divides incoming data packets from the PICs into cells, which are stored in a shared memory buffer, and reassembles them into data packets when they are ready for transmission.

For information about the PICs used in the router, see "Physical Interface Cards" on page 34.

FPCs are hot-insertable and hot-removable. When you bring an FPC online, the midplane flushes the entire system memory pool before the new card is brought online, a process that takes about 200 milliseconds. Then the Routing Engine downloads the FPC software, the FPC runs its diagnostics, and the PICs on the FPC slot are enabled. No interruption occurs to the routing functions.

The components of each FPC include two SDRAM modules used as shared memory by the Distributed Buffer Manager ASIC on the SSB, an SSRAM module, and a DRAM module used by the PowerPC processor. Each FPC has two LEDs, located on the craft interface, that indicate its status.

Figure 3.34 *M20 FPCs in the Chassis*

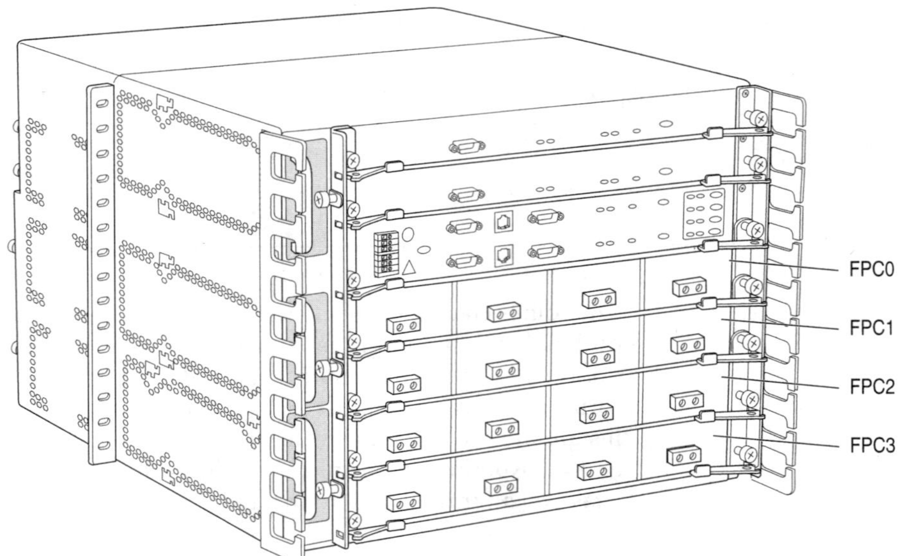

The System and Switch Board (SSB) (see Figure 3.35) occupies the top slot of the card cage, installing into the midplane from the front of the chassis. The SSB houses the Internet Processor II ASIC and the Distributed Buffer Manager ASICs. The SSB communicates with the Routing Engine using a high-speed internal link to transfer routing table data and nondata packets.

The SSB contains processing components, including a 200-MHz CPU, Internet Processor II ASIC, and Distributed Buffer Manager ASICs; storage components, including four slots of 2-MB RAM for forwarding tables associated with the ASICs, and 64-MB DRAM for the microkernel; system interfaces, including a 19.44-MHz Stratum 3 reference clock for SONET/SDH PICs; and two LEDs.

Figure 3.35 *M20 SSB*

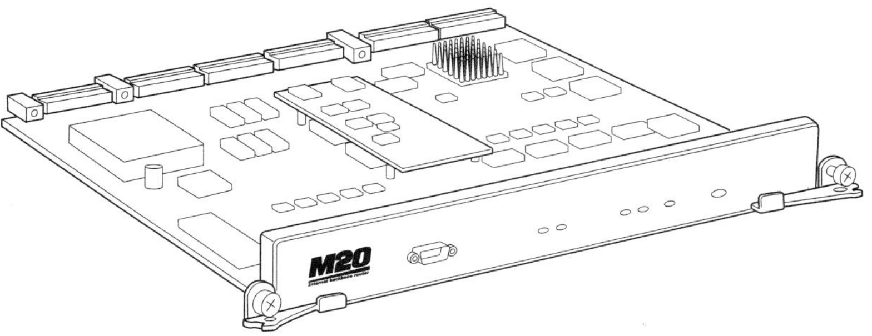

For more information, see "Routing Engine" on page 37.

The M20 router has one or two Routing Engines. The Routing Engines install into the rear of the chassis above the power supplies. There is also a Routing Engine panel on the rear of the router that has LEDs indicating each Routing Engine's status and offline switches for removing the Routing Engines.

The craft interface (see Figure 3.36) is located below the SSB on the front of the chassis, and contains the alarm relay contacts, alarm LEDs, alarm cutoff button, Routing Engine ports, link and activity status lights, Routing Engine LEDs, and FPC online/offline buttons.

Figure 3.36 *M20 Craft Interface*

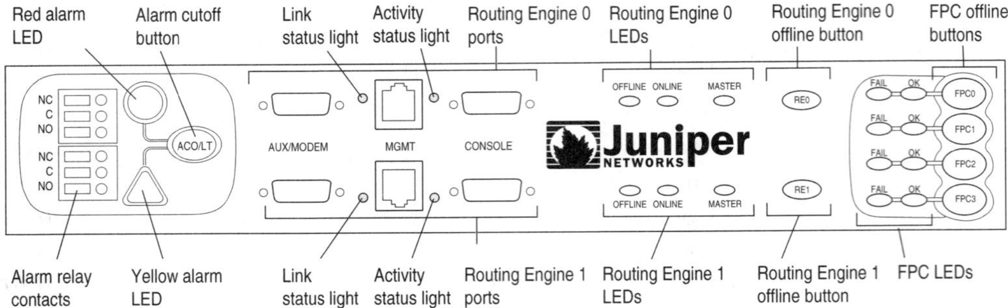

The router has two redundant load-sharing power supplies. A single power supply can provide full power (up to 750 W) for as long as the system is operational. Redundancy is necessary only in case of power supply failure or removal.

The power supplies install into slots on the lower rear of the chassis. The power supplies are internally connected to the midplane, which distributes the different output voltages produced by the power supplies throughout the system and its components. Each power supply contains an integrated fan that cools the power assembly.

The router supports both AC and DC power supplies. Table 3.26 lists the specifications for both types. You cannot mix both types in a single router. An enable control signal on the output connector ensures that the power supply is fully seated into the router midplane before the power supply can be turned on. The enable pin prevents a user-accessible energy hazard, so there is no interlocking mechanism. The enable pin disables the voltage at the output connector if the power supply is not turned off before removal.

Table 3.26 *M20 Router Power Supply Specifications*

Item	AC Specification	DC Specification
Maximum power consumption	750 W	750 W
Input voltage	90 through 264 VAC operating range	–40 through –72 VCD operating range
Input line frequency	47–63 Hz, autoranging	—
Input current rating	13 A @ 90 V	24 A @ –48 V (typical)

Table 3.26 *M20 Router Power Supply Specifications*

Item	AC Specification	DC Specification
Output voltages	+3.3 V, +5 V, + 2.5 V, +12 V, +24 V	+3.3 V, +5 V, + 2.5 V, +12 V, +24 V
Power and grounding cords and cables	Country specific; see *M20 Internet Router Hardware Guide*	4 or 6 AWG wire cables with dual hole 20 UNC terminal studs @ 15.86 mm (0.625 in.) centers

AC power supply cords are country-specific. The AC inlet is oriented to allow a standard right-angle power cord to exit to the right of the power supply. A power cord latching mechanism is provided for the use of straight power cords. The DC power supply uses a cable lug and locking washers to attach the cables to the supply.

The M20 router cooling system consists of three front fan trays, located on the left front side of the chassis, that cool the FPCs and the SSB; one rear fan tray, located immediately to the right of the Routing Engine, that cools the Routing Engine; and a fan built into each power supply that cools the power supply. Each front fan tray contains three fans. The rear fan tray contains two fans. Both front and rear fan trays are hot-swappable. The four fan trays work together to provide side-to-side cooling (see Figure 3.37).

Figure 3.37 *Air Flow through the M20 Chassis*

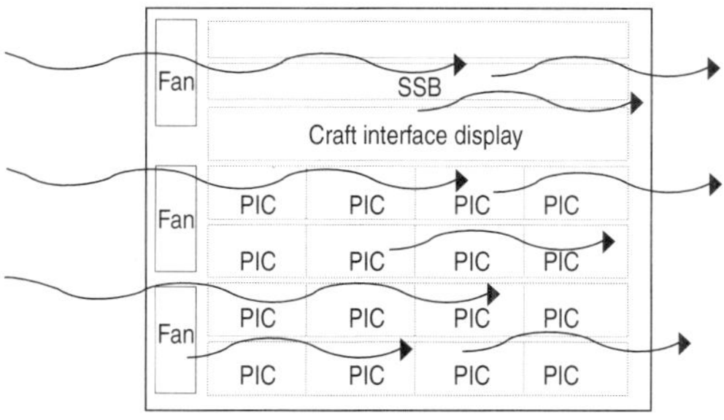

The cable management system is attached to the chassis and consists of a row of staggered metal hooks, each draped with a rounded plastic shield.

The router has LEDs that display the status of various router components. Table 3.27 lists the LEDs on the craft interface and the individual router components.

Table 3.27 *M20 Internet Router LEDs*

Component	LED	Location
FPCs	Green OK Red FAIL	Craft interface
PICs	Tricolor: Red, green, amber	PIC faceplate
SSBs	Blue MASTER Green ONLINE Amber OFFLINE 2 Green STATUS	SSB faceplate
Routing Engines	Blue MASTER Green ONLINE Amber OFFLINE	Craft interface and Routing Engine panel
Power supplies	Green OK Red FAIL	Power supply faceplate
Alarm LEDs		
Red alarm	Large, circular red	Craft interface
Yellow alarm	Large, triangular amber	Craft interface

M5 and M10 Internet Routers

Figure 3.38 *M5 and M10 Internet Routers Chassis and Components*

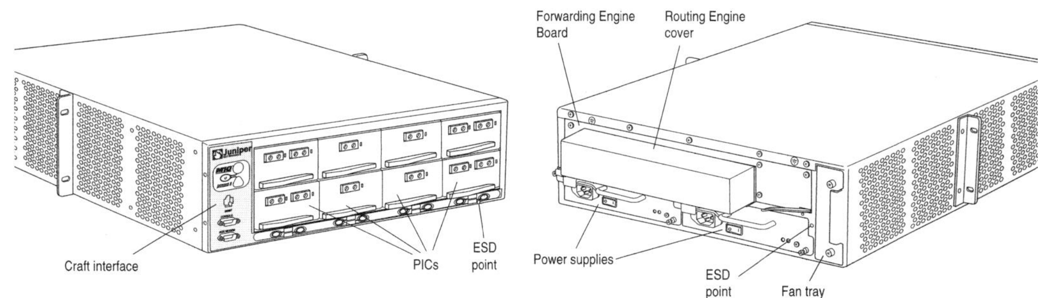

The M5 and M10 Internet routers (see Figure 3.38) have a maximum aggregate bandwidth of 6.4 Gbps full duplex. Table 3.28 shows the physical specifications of the M5 and M10 routers, and Table 3.29 gives an overview of the major hardware components of the routers.

Table 3.28 *M5 and M10 Routers Physical Specifications*

Category	Value
Chassis dimensions	5.25 in. (13.3 cm) high x 17.4 in. (44.2 cm) wide x 24 in. (61 cm) deep
Router weight	57 lb (25.8 kg) minimum configuration 61 lb (27.6 kg) maximum configuration, M5 router 65 lb (29.5 kg) maximum configuration, M10 router
Required clearances	24 in. (61 cm) front and rear; 6 in. (15.2 cm) each side

Table 3.29 *M5 and M10 Routers Major Hardware Components*

Component	Quantity	Function	Redundant	FRU	Online/offline Button
Chassis	1	Houses all router components	–	–	–
Forwarding Engine Board (FEB)	1	Connects PICs to router components, houses shared memory	–	Requires router shutdown	–

Table 3.29 *M5 and M10 Routers Major Hardware Components*

Component	Quantity	Function	Redundant	FRU	Online/offline Button
Physical Interface Cards (PICs)	M5 router: 1–4, M10 router: 1—8	Interfaces to network media	Yes	Hot-removable Hot-insertable	Yes
Routing Engine	1	Maintains routing protocols, routing tables	–	Requires router shutdown	–
Power supplies	2 AC or 2 DC	Distributes voltages to components	Yes	Hot-removable Hot-insertable	–
Cooling system	1 fan tray	Cools router components	Yes	Hot-removable Hot-insertable	–
Craft interface	1	Displays status and allows you to take PICs offline	–	–	–

The router chassis includes two metal ears, which can be used for either front-mounting or center-mounting, and two ESD points for use when servicing the router.

The M5 and M10 routers have one Routing Engine. For more information, see “Routing Engine” on page 37.

The FEB is located on the rear of the router above the power supplies (see Figure 3.39). It provides route lookup, filtering, and switching to the destination port. The FEB performs the function of the FPCs on other Juniper Networks routers. It communicates with the Routing Engine using a high-speed internal link that transfers routing table data from the Routing Engine to the forwarding table in the Internet Processor II ASIC. This link is also used to transfer routing link-state updates and other packets destined for the router from the FEB to the Routing Engine. The FEB is field-replaceable, but is not hot-removable or hot-pluggable. You must power down the router before removing or replacing the FEB.

For information about the PICs used in the router, see "Physical Interface Cards" on page 34.

The FEB contains processing components, including a 266-MHz CPU and supporting logic, Internet Processor II ASIC, Distributed Buffer Manager ASICs, and I/O Manager ASICs with corresponding SRAM; storage components, including four banks of 2-MB SRAM for forwarding tables associated with the ASICs, and 64-MB DRAM for the microkernel; and system interfaces, including a 19.44-MHz reference clock for SONET/SDH PICs. The FEB also contains either 64-MB (on the M5 router) or 128-MB (on the M10 router) SDRAM, used as shared memory by the Distributed Buffer Manager ASIC.

Figure 3.39 *M5 and M10 FEB*

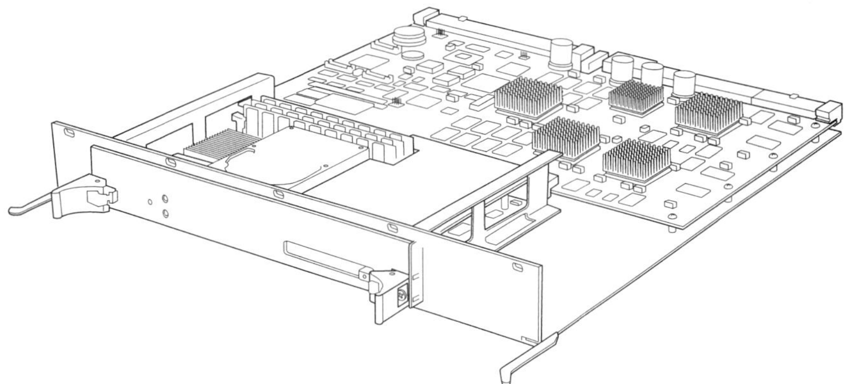

The craft interface (see Figure 3.40) allows you to view alarm status information and to perform some system control functions. The craft interface is located on the left front of the chassis, extending across the front below the PIC slots. The craft interface contains the alarm LEDs and lamp test button, Routing Engine ports, link and activity status lights, and PIC online/offline buttons.

Figure 3.40 *M10 Craft Interface*

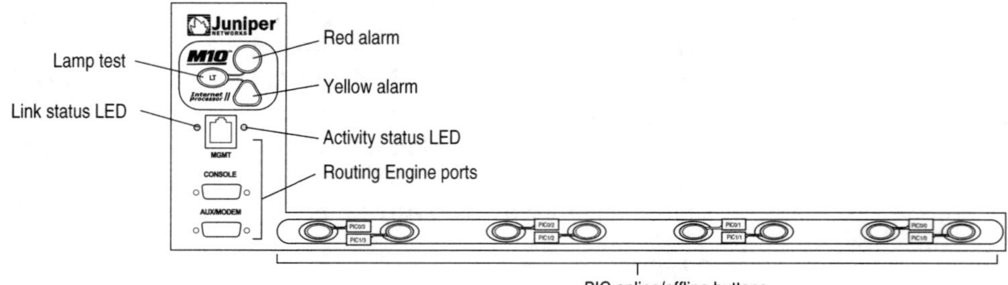

The router has two redundant, load-sharing power supplies, located at the lower rear of the chassis. The power supplies connect to the midplane, which distributes the output voltages produced by the power supplies to the router components.

A single power supply can provide full power (up to 434 W) for as long as the router is operational. Redundancy is necessary only if one of the power supplies fails or is removed.

Power supplies are hot-removable and hot-insertable, but you must turn off the power to the individual power supply before removing it from the chassis. Each power supply has a handle to facilitate removal from the chassis. When one power supply fails or is switched off, the other power supply immediately and automatically assumes the entire electrical load.

The router supports both AC and DC power supplies. Table 3.30 lists the specifications for both types. You cannot mix both types in a single router. An enable control signal on the output connector ensures that the power supply is fully seated into the router midplane before the power supply can be turned on. The enable pin prevents a user-accessible energy hazard, so there is no interlocking mechanism. The enable pin disables the voltage at the output connector if the power supply is not turned off before removal.

Table 3.30 *M5 and M10 Routers Power Supply Specifications*

Item	AC Specification	DC Specification
Maximum power consumption	434 W	434 W
Input voltage	101 through 264 VAC operating range	-42.5 through -72 VDC operating range
Input line frequency	47–63 Hz, autoranging	—
Input current rating	8 A @ 100 VAC, 4 A @ 240 VAC	13.5 A @ -48 VDC (typical)
Output voltages	+1.5 V, +2.5 V, + 3.3 V, +5 V, +12 V	+1.5 V, +2.5 V, + 3.3 V, +5 V, +12 V
Power and grounding cords and cables	Country specific; see *M5 and M10 Internet Router Hardware Guide*	12 wire cables attaching to quick-connect terminals; grounding cable attaches to single-hole cable lugs

The AC inlet is oriented to allow a standard right-angle power cord to exit to the right of the power supply. A power cord latching mechanism is provided for the use of straight power cords. DC power supply cables are 12-AWG, single-strand-count wire cable, with two leads. The cables connect to the input and return quick connect terminals on each DC power supply.

The M5 and M10 router cooling system consists of a fan tray, located along the left side of the chassis, that provides side-to-side cooling (see Figure 3.41). The fan tray is a single unit containing four fans. It is hot-removable and hot-insertable, and connects directly to the router midplane.

The M5 and M10 router cable management system consists of two vertical pieces, each with a pair of metal hooks draped in a plastic shield, that attach to each side of the front of the chassis. The cable management system is designed to maintain the proper bend radius for optical cables and to keep installed cables organized and securely in place.

Figure 3.41 *Air Flow through the M5 and M10 Chassis*

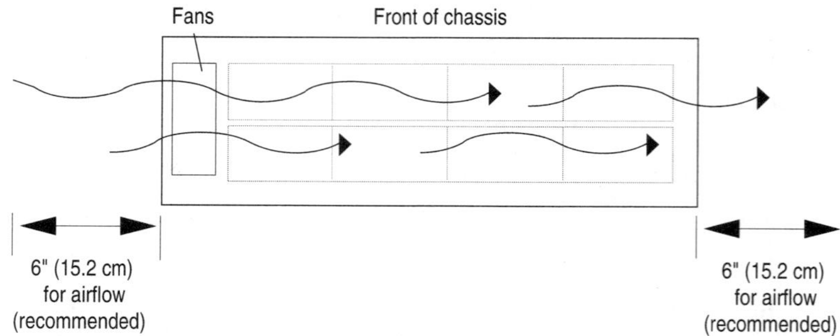

The router has LEDs that display the status of various router components. Table 3.31 lists the LEDs on the craft interface and the individual router components.

Table 3.31 *M5 and M10 Routers LEDs*

Component	**LED**	**Location**
PICs	1 LED per port, with 4 states: Red – Green – Amber – Off	PIC faceplate
Power supplies	Blue OUTPUT OK	Power supply faceplate
Alarm LEDs		
Red alarm	Large, circular red	Craft interface
Yellow alarm	Large, triangular amber	Craft interface

CHAPTER

4

Router Installation and Basic JUNOS Setup

Installing a Juniper Networks router involves preparing the site and following the procedures to physically install the router and make it ready to add to the network. This chapter describes site preparation required before installing a Juniper Networks router, router installation and initial configuration, software installation and upgrade procedures, and basic JUNOS setup procedures.

Preparing for Installation

For more information about preparing the site for a specific router, see the Juniper Networks hardware guide for that router.

Before installing a Juniper Networks router, several steps must be taken to prepare the installation site. These include installing the rack that will house the router; ensuring adequate clearance for router air flow and maintenance access; providing appropriate cables for power, grounding, and network connections; and calculating the router's power budget and power margin.

Rack Requirements

Juniper Networks routers can be installed into several types of racks, including standard 19-inch equipment racks, telco four-post racks, and center-mount racks. The rack used must be tall enough to hold the router or routers, and strong enough to support the combined weight of the installed equipment. There must be enough space around the router and the rack for proper airflow and to allow servicing of the router. Table 4.1 shows the size and weight of each router and the amount of clearance required.

Table 4.1 *Router Physical Specifications and Clearance Requirements*

	T640	T320	M160/M40e	M40	M20	M5/M10
Chassis Dimensions						
Height	37.5 in. (95 cm)	37.5 in. (95 cm)	35 in. (89 cm)	35 in. (89 cm)	14 in. (36 cm)	5.25 in. (13.3 cm)
Width	17.4 in. (44.3 cm)	17.4 in. (44.3 cm)	17.5 in. (44.4 cm)	19 in. (48 cm)	19 in. (48 cm)	17.4 in. (44.2 cm)
Depth	31 in. (78.7 cm)	31 in. (78.7 cm)	19.2 in. (48.8 cm)	23.5 in. (60 cm)	21 in. (54 cm)	24 in. (61 cm)

Table 4.1 *Router Physical Specifications and Clearance Requirements*

	T640	T320	M160/M40e	M40	M20	M5/M10
Weight						
Minimum configuration	435 lb (197 kg)	272.1 lb (123.4 kg)	190 lb (86 kg)	180 lb (81 kg)	80 lb (36 kg)	57 lb (26 kg)
Maximum configuration	565 lb (256 kg)	369.9 lb (167.8 kg)	370.5 lb (168 kg)	280 lb (127 kg)	134 lb (61 kg)	M5 router: 61 lb (28 kg) M10 router: 65 lb (29. 5 kg)
Required Clearance						
Front and back	24 in. (61 cm)	24 in. (61 cm)	24 in. (61 cm)	19 in. (50 cm)	19 in. (50 cm)	24 in. (61 cm) front; 19 in. (50 cm) rear
Sides	6 in. (16 cm)	6 in. (16 cm)	6 in. (16 cm)	6 in. (16 cm)	6 in. (16 cm)	6 in. (16 cm)

Power and Grounding Cable Requirements

The proper cables are required to connect the router to the power source and to earth ground. Table 4.2 lists the AC power cable requirements for those routers using AC power, and Figure 4.1 shows the AC plug types. Table 4.3 lists the DC power and grounding cable requirements.

Table 4.2 *AC Power Cord Requirements*

	M40e	M40	M20	M5/M10
Power cord	8-ft (2.5-m) cords with suitable plugs	4 or 6 AWG wire	4 or 6 AWG wire	12 AWG wire
Voltage capacity				
Australia	240 VAC, 50 Hz			
Europe	220 or 230 VAC, 50 Hz	230 VAC, 50 Hz		
Italy	230 VAC, 50 Hz	220 VAC, 50 Hz		230 VAC, 50 Hz
North America	208 VAC, 60 Hz 240 VAC, 50 Hz			120 VAC, 50 Hz
Cable connector type	IEC 320 C19			IEC 320 C13W

Figure 4.1 *AC Plug Types*

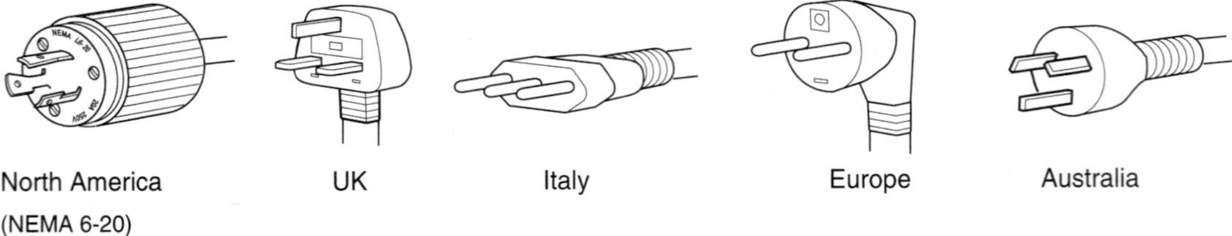

Table 4.3 *DC Power and Grounding Cable Specifications*

	T640	T320	M160/M40e	M40	M20	M5/M10
Required power and grounding cables	4 AWG (16 mm^2), 90°C (194°F) braided wire	6 AWG (13.3 mm2), 90°C (194°F) braided wire cables	4 AWG (16 mm^2) wire	4 or 6 AWG wire	4 or 6 AWG wire	12 AWG wire
Power cable connector type	Dual-hole lug, sized to fit 1/4-20 UNC terminal studs at 15.86-mm (0.625-in.) center line					Quick connect terminals
Grounding cable connector type	Dual-hole lug, sized to fit 1/4-20 UNC terminal studs at 15.86-mm (0.625-in.) center line					Cable lug on power supply faceplate

When planning the wiring for a site, distance limitations for signaling, radio frequency interference, and electromagnetic interference must be taken into consideration. If wires are installed improperly, they can emit radio interference. In addition, potential damage from lightning strikes increases if wires exceed recommended distances, or if wires pass between buildings. The electromagnetic pulse (EMP) caused by lightning can damage unshielded conductors and destroy electronic devices.

Network Cable Requirements

Appropriate cables of the proper type and length are required for each network interface connection, and for the management device connections. Table 4.4 lists the cable requirements for each type of connection.

Table 4.4 *Network Cable Specifications*

Cable Type	Cable Specification	Supplied with Router	Maximum Length	Connector Type
Single-mode interface (fiber)	SC-SC duplex	No	Short reach: 1.25 mi (2 km)	SC
	LC (for 4-port OC-48/STM-16 PIC on the T640 routing node)	No	Short reach: 1.25 mi (2 km)	LC
Multimode interface (fiber)	SC-SC duplex	No	Intermediate reach: 9.3 mi (15 km)	SC
Routing Engine `CONSOLE` and `AUXILIARY` ports	RS-232 serial	One 6-foot length with DB-9/DB-9 connectors	6 ft (1.83 m)	DB-9 male
Routing Engine `ETHERNET` port	Category 5 or equivalent, suitable for 100BaseT operation	One 15-foot length with RJ-45/RJ-45 connectors	328 ft (100 m)	RJ-45

Site Wiring Guidelines

Proper site wiring involves consideration of distance limitations for signaling, radio frequency interference (RFI), and electromagnetic interference (EMI).

Using twisted-pair cable with a good distribution of grounding conductors, and keeping cable lengths within recommended distances, minimizes the risk of RFI. If recommended distances are exceeded, a high-quality twisted-pair cable with one ground conductor for each data signal, when applicable, is recommended.

Strong EMI could destroy the signal drivers and receivers in the router and could conduct power surges over the lines into the equipment, resulting in an electrical hazard. To minimize the risk of damage from EMI, it is important to provide a properly grounded and shielded environment and to use electrical surge suppression devices.

Fiber-Optic Connection Guidelines

Fiber-optic interfaces use one of two types of fiber connection: multimode or single-mode. *Multimode fiber* is large enough in diameter to allow rays of light to internally reflect or bounce off the inner walls of the fiber. Light sources on interfaces with multimode optics are typically LEDs, which are not coherent light sources. An LED sprays varying wavelengths of light into multimode fiber, which reflects the light at different angles. Light rays travel in jagged lines through a multimode fiber, causing signal dispersion. When light traveling in the fiber core radiates into the fiber cladding, higher-order mode loss (HOL) results. All these factors limit the transmission distance of multimode fiber compared to single-mode fiber. Multimode fiber has an approximate maximum transmission distance of up to 1.5 miles (2 kilometers). Significant signal loss, causing unreliable transmission, can occur at greater distances.

Keep fiber-optic cable connectors clean using an appropriate fiber-cleaning device.

Single-mode fiber is so small in diameter that there is not enough room for the rays of light passing through it to reflect internally through more than one layer. Light sources on interfaces with single-mode optics are lasers, which generate light rays in a single wavelength and which travel in a straight line, directly through the single-mode fiber. Single-mode transmission is useful for longer distances and is capable of higher bandwidth than multimode fiber. However, it is more expensive.

The maximum distance between transponders is determined by fiber loss, chromatic dispersion, transmitter power, and receiver sensitivity. Table 4.6 on page 103 lists the factors that contribute to link loss.

Attenuation and Dispersion

A functional optical data link depends on modulated light reaching the receiver with enough power to be correctly demodulated. *Attenuation* is the reduction in power of the light signal as it is transmitted. Attenuation is caused by passive media components, such as cables, cable splices, and connectors. While attenuation is significantly lower for optical fiber than for other media, it still occurs in both multimode and single-mode transmission. An efficient optical data link must have enough light available to overcome attenuation.

Dispersion is the spreading of the signal in time. The following two types of dispersion can affect an optical data link:

- Chromatic dispersion—The spreading of the signal in time resulting from the different speeds of light rays
- Modal dispersion—The spreading of the signal in time resulting from the different propagation modes in the fiber

For multimode transmission, modal dispersion, rather than chromatic dispersion or attenuation, usually limits the maximum bit rate and link length. For single-mode transmission, modal dispersion is not a factor. However, at higher bit rates and over longer distances, chromatic dispersion, rather than modal dispersion, limits maximum link length.

An efficient optical data link must have enough light to exceed the minimum power that the receiver requires to operate within its specifications. In addition, the total dispersion must be less than the limits specified in Telecordia GR-253-CORE Section 4.3 and ITU G.957 for the corresponding type of link.

When chromatic dispersion is at the maximum allowed, its effect can be considered as a power penalty in the power budget. The optical power budget must allow for the sum of component attenuation, power penalties (including those from dispersion), and a safety margin for unexpected losses.

Power Budget and Power Margin

The power budget (P_B) is the maximum possible amount of power that can be transmitted over the link. It is calculated as a worst-case analysis to provide a margin of error, although all the parts of an actual system do not operate at the worst-case levels. The worst-case estimate of power budget (P_B) is calculated assuming minimum transmitter power (P_T) and minimum receiver sensitivity (P_R). Table 4.5 lists equations for calculating the power budget for SONET/SDH PIC interfaces.

Table 4.5 *Sample Power Budget Calculation for SONET/SDH PIC Interfaces*

PIC Interface	Power Budget Equation
Multimode	P_B = PT - PR P_B = -15 dBm - (-28 dBm) P_B = 13 dB
Single-mode (OC-12)	P_B = PT - PR P_B = -15 dBm - (-28 dBm) P_B = 13 dB
Single-mode (OC-48)	P_B = PT - PR P_B = -5 dBm - (-18 dBm) P_B = 13 dB

The power budget is used to calculate the power margin (P_M), which estimates the amount of power available for the link after subtracting attenuation or link loss (LL) from the power budget. A worst-case estimate of P_M assumes maximum LL:

$$P_M = P_B - LL$$

A P_M greater than zero indicates that the power budget is sufficient to operate the receiver. Table 4.6 lists the factors that contribute to link loss and estimates the link-loss value attributable to those factors.

The following example calculates a multimode power margin with the length of multimode link at 2 kilometers, with 5 connectors, 2 splices, a higher-order loss, and a clock recovery module:

$$P_M = P_B - LL$$
$$P_M = 13\ dB - 2\ km\ (1.0\ dB/km) - 5\ (0.5\ dB) - 2\ (0.5\ dB) - 0.5\ dB\ (HOL) - 1\ dB\ (CRM)$$
$$P_M = 13\ dB - 2\ dB - 2.5\ dB - 1\ dB - 0.5\ dB - 1\ dB$$
$$P_M = 6\ dB$$

The following example calculates the single-mode fiber power budget for two sites that are 8 kilometers apart, connected with single-mode SONET cable with 7 connectors:

$$P_M = P_B - LL$$
$$P_M = 13\ dB - 8\ km\ (0.5\ dB/km) - 7\ (0.5\ dB)$$
$$P_M = 13\ dB - 4\ dB - 3.5\ dB$$
$$P_M = 5.5\ dB$$

The calculated value of 5.5 dB indicates that this link has sufficient power for transmission and does not exceed the maximum receiver input power.

Table 4.6 *Link-Loss Estimation*

Link-Loss Factor	Estimate of Link-Loss Value
Higher-order mode losses	Single-mode—None Multimode—0.5 dB
Modal and chromatic dispersion	Single-mode—None Multimode—Product of bandwidth and distance must be less than 500 MHz/km
Connector	0.5 dB
Splice	0.5 dB
Fiber attenuation	Single-mode—0.5 dB/km Multimode—1 dB/km

Unpacking the Router

Each router comes packaged in a shipping crate (M5 and M10 routers, because of their smaller size and weight, come packaged in a cardboard box). Before unpacking the router, move the shipping crate as close to the installation site as possible.

To unpack the router from the shipping crate (see Figure 4.2):

1. Twist the locking tabs holding the front, top, and sides of the shipping crate onto the pallet and remove them from the pallet.
2. Remove the packing materials, the accessory box, and the quick start installation poster from on top of the router.
3. Verify the parts received against the packing list. Use a socket wrench to remove the bolts securing the chassis to the pallet. Store the brackets and bolts in the accessory box.
4. Save the shipping crate, packing materials, and pallet in case the router must be moved or shipped later.

Figure 4.2 *Unpacking a Router from the Shipping Crate*

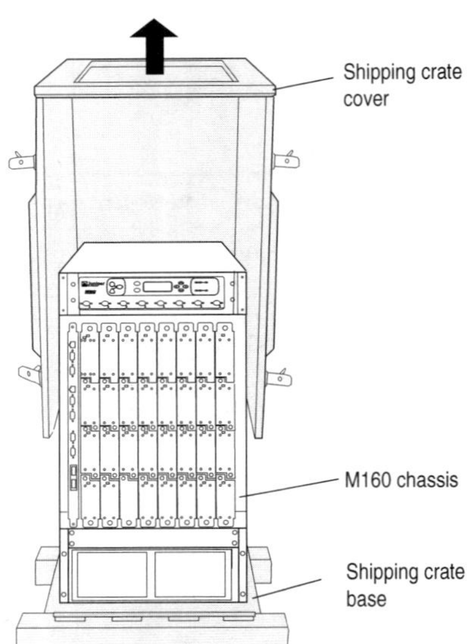

To unpack an M5 or M10 router from the shipping box (see Figure 4.3):

1. Position the shipping box with the arrows facing up.
2. Open the top flaps of the box.
3. Lift out the packing material, the accessory kit, and the quick start installation poster.
4. Lift the router out of the box.
5. Verify the parts received against the packing list.
6. Save the shipping box and packing materials in case the router must be moved or shipped later.

Figure 4.3 *Unpacking an M5 or M10 Router from the Shipping Box*

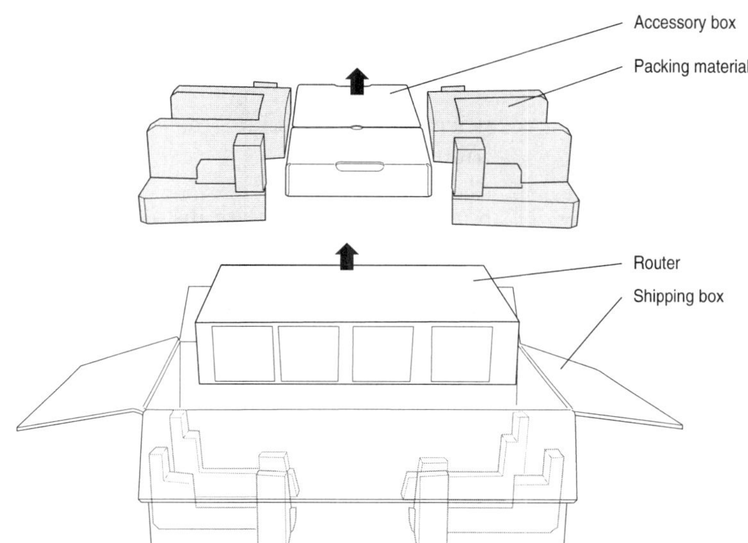

Installing the Router

Before installing the router, prepare the site as described in "Preparing for Installation" on page 96, and unpack the router as close to the installation site as possible, as described in "Unpacking the Router" on page 103.

Tools and parts required for installation include a mechanical lift (recommended for the T640 routing node and T320, M160, M40, and M20 routers; required for a T640 routing node in an upper rack position), Phillips screwdrivers (numbers 1 and 2), flat-blade screwdrivers (3/16-inch and 1/4-inch), 9/16-inch socket wrench, 7/16-inch open-end or socket wrench (if the router is being front-mounted), wire cutters, pliers, electrostatic discharge wrist strap, electrostatic bags for components being removed, and an antistatic mat located on a flat, stable surface.

All routers can be installed into a center-mount, front-mount, or four-post rack or a cabinet. The holes in the mounting ears are spaced at 5.25 and at 7 inches (for a T640 routing node, only at 5.25 inches). The rack must be large enough to hold the router and strong enough to support the combined weight of all installed equipment.

Installing the Chassis into a Rack Using a Lift

Because of their large size and weight, Juniper Networks strongly recommends using a lift to install the router. M5 and M10 routers, because of their smaller size and weight, can be installed manually. Before installing the router, make sure that the rack is properly secured to the building in its permanent location and that there is sufficient space around the rack for proper airflow and for servicing the router.

For detailed instructions about installing the mounting hardware for each router, see the Juniper Networks hardware guide for that router.

Some routers come with installation handles, a mounting shelf, or other mounting hardware used to secure the router in the rack. Install the mounting hardware onto the rack, and attach the installation handle to the router, before proceeding to install the router.

To install a router using a lift (see Figure 4.4):

1. Load the router securely onto the lift.
2. Use the lift to position the router in the rack at the correct height.
3. Align the bottom mounting holes on the chassis mounting ears with the holes in the rack.
4. Install a mounting screw (provided) into each of the two aligned holes.
5. Moving up the sides of the router, install screws in every open hole on the mounting ears.
6. Move the lift away from the rack.

Figure 4.4 *Installing a T640 Routing Node Using a Lift*

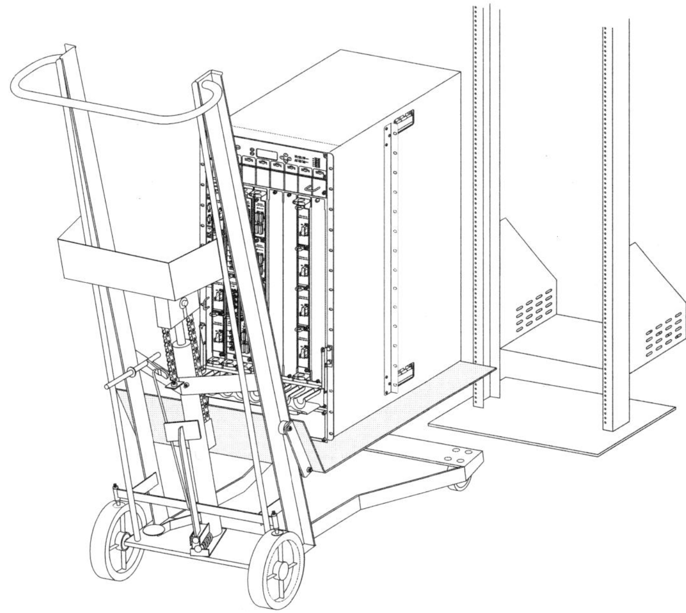

Manually Installing the Chassis into a Rack

Before manually installing a router, remove components from the chassis so that the router is light enough to lift (for the weight of each router, see Table 4.1). Table 4.7 lists the components that must be removed from each router before installing it in the rack.

For detailed instructions about removing router components, see the Juniper Networks hardware guide for that router.

When removing router components, slide each component evenly out of the chassis so that it does not become stuck or damaged. Label each component so that it can be reinstalled in the correct location, and immediately store each removed component in an electrostatic bag or place it on an antistatic mat. Do not stack removed components; lay each one on a flat surface.

After the components are removed, the router chassis can be installed in the rack. Table 4.8 lists the number of people required to lift each router into the rack.

Table 4.7 *Components Removed for Manual Installation*

	T640	T320	M160 and M40e	M40	M20	M5/M10
Front of chassis	FPCs Front fan trays Cable manager	FPCs Front fan trays Cable manager	FPCs Fan tray Upper impeller assembly	FPCs SCB Cable manager Air filter Impeller tray	FPCs SSB Fan trays	No components need to be removed
Rear of chassis	SCGs CBs SIBs Power supplies	SCGs CBs SIBs Power supplies	Impeller assemblies Routing Engines MCSs SFMs Power supplies	Impeller tray Routing Engine Fan tray Power supplies	Routing Engine Fan tray Power supplies	

Table 4.8 *Number of People Required for Manual Installation*

	T640	T320	M160 and M40e	M40	M20	M5 and M10
People required to install	4	3	3	2	2	2

To lift the chassis into the rack (see Figure 4.5):

The installation process for T-series platforms is more complex than for the M-series routers. For more information, see the *T640 Internet Routing Node Hardware Guide* or the *T320 Internet Router Hardware Guide.*

1. Make sure that the shelf or other mounting hardware is installed in the proper position. If the router includes an installation handle, make sure that it is securely attached to the router.
2. Align the bottom mounting holes on the chassis mounting ears with the holes in the rack.
3. Install one of the provided mounting screws into each of the two aligned holes.
4. Moving up the sides of the router, install screws in every open hole on the mounting ears.

Figure 4.5 *Installing a Chassis Manually*

After installing the chassis in the rack, reinstall the removed components into the chassis. When reinstalling components, slide them evenly into the chassis so that they do not become stuck or damaged.

Some routers (including the T640 routing node and the M160 and M40e routers) include a cover that covers some or all of the rear components. Make sure that the rear component cover is installed and that all empty slots are covered with a blank panel before booting and operating the router.

Connecting Management Consoles and PIC Cables

After the components are reinstalled into the chassis, the router can be connected to an external management device, and the PICs can be connected to the network.

To connect a management console:

1. Turn off the power switch on the console.
2. Plug the female end of the RS-232 serial connector into the Console port (see Figure 4.6). On some routers, this port is located on the craft interface. On some routers, it is on the CIP.
3. Tighten the screws on the connector.

Figure 4.6 *Console and Auxiliary Port Connector*

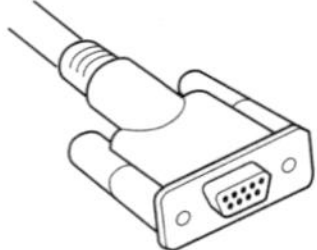

WARNING Do not look directly into the PIC transceivers or into the ends of fiber-optic cables. Fiber-optic cables contain laser light sources that can damage your eyes.

To connect the router to a network for out-of-band management:

1. Plug one of the Ethernet cable connectors into the Ethernet port (see Figure 4.7). On some routers, this port is located on the craft interface. On some routers, it is on the CIP.
2. Plug the other end into the networking device.

Figure 4.7 *Ethernet Port Connector*

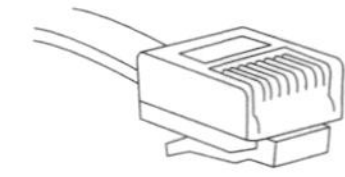

To connect the PIC cables (see Figure 4.8):

1. Identify the appropriate cable to be connected to each PIC.
2. Insert the appropriate cable connector into the PIC cable receptacle.

3. Drape the cables over the bobbins of the cable management system to protect them from bending past their recommended bend radius.

Figure 4.8 *Fiber-Optic Cable Connector*

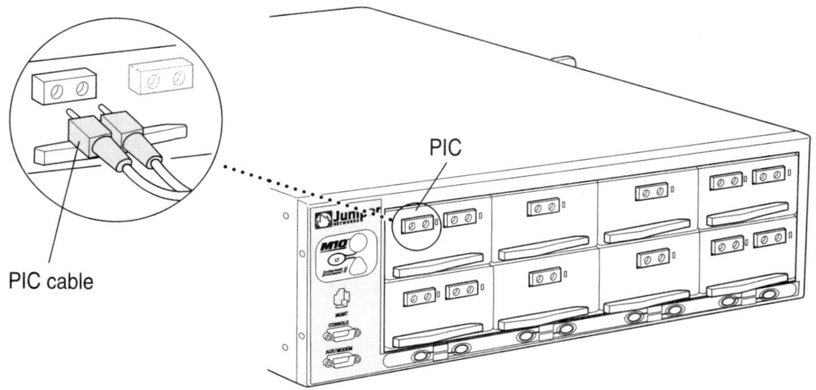

Connecting Power and Ground

When the management devices and PIC cables are connected, connect the power and grounding cables. The M40e, M40, M20, M10, and M5 routers can use either AC or DC power; the T640 routing node, T320 router, and M160 router operate using only DC power. The procedures for connecting AC-powered and DC-powered routers are different.

To connect AC-powered routers (see Figure 4.9):

1. Locate the AC power cable and verify that the cable is the correct type for the site.
2. Plug the AC power cable into the receptacle on the AC power supply.
3. Plug the other end of the power cable into the AC power source receptacle.
4. If the router has two power supplies, repeat Steps 1 through 3 for the second power supply.

Figure 4.9 *Connect the AC Power Cord to an M20 Router*

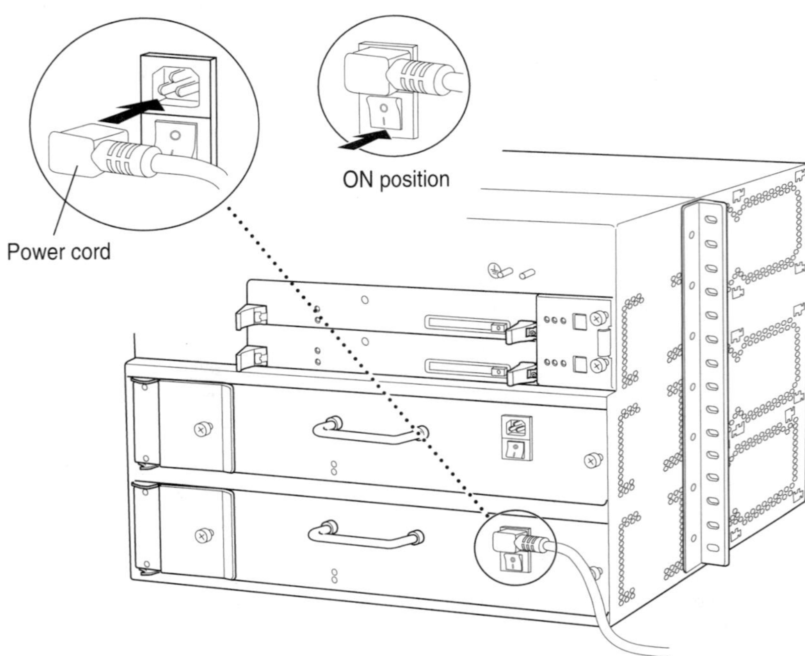

To connect DC-powered routers always connect the router to ground before connecting it to the power source. The terminals for the DC power cables on the T640 routing node, T320, M40, M20, M10, and M5 routers are located on the power supply faceplates. On the M160 and M40e routers, the terminals are located on the circuit breaker box on the lower right of the chassis.

To connect DC-powered routers (see Figure 4.10):

1. Make sure that the voltage across the DC power source cables is 0 V and that the cable leads will not become active during installation.
2. Place the grounding cable lug over the grounding points on the chassis. The grounding cable should already be attached to a proper earth ground for both DC power sources.

3. Secure the grounding cable lug to the grounding points with the washers, then with the bolts.
4. Remove the clear plastic cover from the power supply faceplate or circuit breaker box.
5. Attach the power cable lugs for both DC power sources to the terminal studs:
   - Connect the positive (+) cable lugs to the RTN (return) terminals.
   - Connect the negative (–) cable lugs to the –48V (input) terminals.
6. Secure the power cable lugs to the terminal studs with the washers, then with the bolts. Verify that the power cabling and the grounding cabling are correct.
7. Replace the clear plastic cover.

Figure 4.10 *Connect DC Power to an M40e or M160 Router*

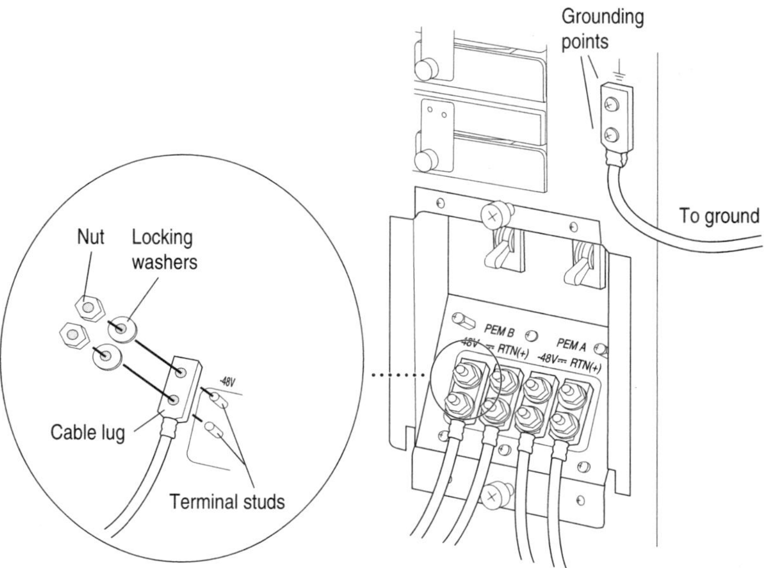

Initial Powerup

After the router is connected to power and ground, power up the router and initially configure the software.

To power up the router:

1. Make sure that the power supplies are securely installed into the router and that all power and ground cables are properly connected.
2. Turn on the power to the management device connected to the router through either the console or Ethernet management port.
3. Turn on one of the power supplies (on an M160 or M40e router, the circuit breakers) and observe the LEDs on the power supply faceplate. The LEDs startup sequence varies for each router.
4. Turn on the second power supply (or circuit breaker) and observe the LEDs on the faceplate.
5. On the management device, monitor the startup process to verify that the router has booted properly.

Initially Configuring the Software

The JUNOS Internet software is configured through a hierarchy of configuration statements that define the desired software properties. All properties of the JUNOS Internet software, including interfaces, general routing information, routing protocols, and user access, as well as several system hardware properties, can be configured. First a candidate configuration is created, then it is committed, to be evaluated and activated by the JUNOS Internet software.

For a detailed description of the initial software configuration steps and configuring the software, see the JUNOS *Getting Started* technical documentation.

The software can be configured in one of two ways: by creating a configuration for the router interactively, working in the command-line interface (CLI) on the router, or by loading an ASCII file that contains a router configuration created earlier, either on this system or on another system. In the second case, the configuration can either be activated and run as is, or it can be edited using the CLI before being activated.

When the router is initially booted, the system prompts for the minimal information needed to configure the router, including the router's name, domain name, and Internet address of at least one interface on the router. After the router finishes booting initially, the user booting the router logs in as the user "root" (with no password) and configures a password for the user "root."

After this initial minimal configuration is completed, all other properties of the software can be configured. If the software is configured interactively using the CLI, configuration statements can be entered to create a candidate configuration that contains a hierarchy of statements. At any given hierarchy level, statements can generally be entered in any order. While configuring the software, all or portions of the candidate configuration can be displayed, and statements can be inserted or deleted. Any changes affect only the candidate configuration, not the active configuration that is running on the router.

The configuration hierarchy logically groups related functions together, which results in configuration statements that have a regular, consistent syntax. For example, routing protocols, routing policies, interfaces, and Simple Network Management Protocol (SNMP) management are each configured in their own portion of the configuration hierarchy.

At each level of the configuration hierarchy, a list of the statements available at that level, along with a short description of the statements' functions, can be displayed. The CLI features command completion, which allows typing a partial statement name followed by a space or tab to have the CLI complete the statement name if it is unambiguous or otherwise provide a list of possible completions. More than one user can edit a router configuration simultaneously. All changes made by all users are visible to everyone editing the configuration.

A configuration is edited by working in a copy of the current configuration to create a candidate configuration. The changes made to the candidate configuration are visible in the CLI immediately, so if multiple users are editing the configuration at the same time, all users can see all changes.

When the candidate configuration is committed, the changes take effect. At this point, the candidate file is checked for proper syntax, activated, and marked as the current operational software configuration file. If multiple users are editing the configuration and the candidate configuration is committed, all changes made by all the users take effect.

The router can be configured from a console attached to the console port on the CIP or by using Telnet over a network connected to the Ethernet port.

The CLI always maintains a copy of the previously committed version of the software configuration. A user can inactivate the current configuration and return to the previous configuration using the CLI.

Candidate configurations can be saved to a file on the router. They are saved as plain text files.

To initially configure the software:

1. Power up the router as described in "Initial Powerup" on page 114.
2. Log in as the "root" user. There is no password.
3. Start the CLI:

```
root# cli
root@>
```

4. Enter configuration mode:

```
cli> configure
[edit]
root@#
```

5. Configure the name of the router. If the name includes spaces, enclose the name in quotation marks (" ").

```
[edit]
root@# set system host-name host-name
```

6. Configure the router's domain name:

```
[edit]
root@# set system domain-name domain-name
```

7. Configure the IP address and prefix length for the router's Ethernet interface:

```
[edit]
root@# set interfaces fxp0 unit 0 family inet
address address/prefix-length
```

8. Configure the IP address of a backup router, which is used only while the routing protocols are not running:

```
[edit]
root@# set system backup-router address
```

9. Configure the IP address of a DNS server:

```
[edit]
root@# set system name-server address
```

10. Set the root password, entering either a clear-text password, an encrypted password, or an SSH public key string (DSA or RSA):

```
[edit]
root@# set system root-authentication plain-text-
password
New password: type password
Retype new password: retype password
or
[edit]
root@# set system root-authentication encrypted-
password encrypted-password
or
[edit]
root@# set system root-authentication ssh-rsa key
```

11. Optionally, display the configuration statements to verify that the configuration is correct:

```
[edit]
root@ show
system {
  host-name host-name;
  domain-name domain.name;
  backup-router address;
  name-server {
    address;
  }
  interfaces {
    fxp0 {
      unit 0 {
        family inet {
          address address;
        }
      }
    }
  }
}
```

12. Commit the configuration to activate it on the router:

```
[edit]
root@# commit
```

For a detailed description of the initial software configuration steps and configuring the software, see the JUNOS *Getting Started* technical documentation.

13. Optionally, configure additional properties by adding the necessary configuration statement. Then commit the changes to activate them on the router:

```
[edit]
root@host-name# commit
```

14. After the router is configured, exit configuration mode:

```
[edit]
root@host-name# exit
root@host-name>
```

The router is now connected to the network, but not fully configured. It must be completely configured before using the router to pass traffic. Information about configuring the software is presented in the following chapters.

Installing the Software

Each router comes with JUNOS software installed on it. When the router is powered on, all software starts automatically. The software is then configured, and the router is ready to participate in the network.

The software is installed on the router's flash drive and hard drive. A copy of the software also is provided on a removable PC card (or, on some M40 routers, an LS-120 floppy disk), which can be inserted into the router's card slot (for the LS-120, the floppy drive). Normally, when the router is powered on, it runs the copy of the software that is installed on the flash drive.

The router software can be upgraded as new features are added or software problems are fixed. Software can be upgraded by downloading images onto the router or onto another system on the network, then installing them on the router's flash and hard drives. The software can also be copied onto the removable media. If the software on the flash, hard disk, or removable media becomes damaged, the software can be reinstalled onto those devices.

The JUNOS software comprises collections of files called *packages*. Each JUNOS software release consists of the following packages: the base package (jbase), which contains additions to the operating system; the kernel and network tools package (jkernel), which contains the operating system; the routing package (jroute), which contains the software that runs on the Routing Engine; the Packet Forwarding Engine package (jpfe); the crypto package (jcrypto), which contains security software (in the domestic version only); and the documentation package (jdocs), which contains the documentation for the software.

These software packages are provided as a single unit, called a *bundle* (jbundle). The bundle can be used to upgrade all the packages at once, or packages can be upgraded individually. When upgrading to a new major release, the bundle must be used to upgrade all the software to the new level.

Two sets of JUNOS software packages are provided, one for customers in the United States and Canada and another for customers in other parts of the world. The worldwide version does not include any capabilities that provide encryption of data leaving the router. Otherwise, the two packages are identical.

A JUNOS software release has a name in the following format: junos-`m.nZnumber.m.n` is two integers that represent the software release number; *`m`* denotes the major release number. *`Z`* is a capital letter that indicates the type of software release. In most cases, it is an `R`, to indicate that this is released software. The letters `A` (for alpha-level software), `B` (for beta-level software), or `I` (a capital letter I; for internal, test) are used for prerelease versions of the software. `number` represents the version of the major software release. An example of a software release name is: junos-5.3R1.

A software package has a name in the following format: *`package-`*`name-release`.tgz. `package-name` is the name of the package. `release` is the software release number; for example, 5.4R1 or 5.2R2.3. Examples of package names are `jroute-5.4R1.tgz`, `jkernel-5.4R1.tgz`, `jpfe-5.4R1.tgz`, and `jinstall-5.4R1.tgz`.

Table 4.9 lists the storage media (flash drives, hard drives, and removable media) device names which are displayed when the router boots.

The router typically boots from the flash disk. (It is also possible to

Table 4.9 *Release 5.x Device Names*

Device	CPV5000	Teknor
Flash drive	`ad0`	`ad0`
Hard drive	`ad2`	`ad1`
Removable media	`afd0`	`ad4`

boot the router from the hard drive or the removable media.) These disks are referred to as the *boot devices*. The disk from which the router boots is called the *primary boot device*, and the other disk is the *alternate boot device*. The primary boot device is generally the flash disk, and the alternate boot device is generally the hard disk.

Normally, the router boots from the flash disk. If it fails, it attempts to boot from the hard drive, which is the alternate boot device.

If a PC card (or floppy disk) is installed when the router boots, the router attempts to boot from the image on the card or disk. If the router fails, it next tries the flash disk and finally the hard disk.

If the router boots from an alternative medium, the JUNOS software displays a message indicating this when logging in to the router. For example, the following message shows that the software booted from the hard disk (`/dev/ad2`):

```
login: username
Password: password
Last login: date on terminal

--- JUNOS 5.3R1 built date
---
--- NOTICE: System is running on alternate media device (/
dev/ad2).
```

Upgrading Software Packages

Normally, you use the bundle to upgrade all the software packages at the same time. They can also be upgraded individually. When upgrading to a new release, use the bundle; do not upgrade the packages individually.

To determine which packages are running on the router and to get information about these packages, use the `show version` command at the top level of the CLI.

To upgrade all software packages:

1. Download the software packages you need from the Juniper Networks Support Web site (http://www.juniper.net/support/).

   To download the software packages, you must have a service contract and an access account. If you need help obtaining an account, contact your Juniper Networks sales representative or go to http://www.juniper.net/pwassistance.htm.

2. Back up the currently running and active file system so that it can be recovered to a known, stable environment in case something goes wrong with the upgrade:

```
user@host> request system snapshot
```

CAUTION Juniper Networks recommends upgrading all software packages out of band using the console or `fxp0` interface, because inband connections can be lost during the upgrade process.

The root file system is backed up to `/altroot`, and `/config` is backed up to `/altconfig`. The root and `/config` file systems are on the router's flash drive, and the `/altroot` and `/altconfig` file systems are on the router's hard drive.

After the `request system snapshot` command is issued, the previous version of the software cannot be recovered, because the running and backup copies of the software are identical.

3. Copy each software package to the router. Juniper Networks recommends copying them to the `/var/tmp` directory, a large file system on the rotating medium (hard disk):

```
user@host> file copy ftp://
username:prompt@ftp.hostname.net/
     filename /var/tmp/filename
```

4. Delete the existing software packages and add the new ones:

```
user@host> request system software add /var/tmp/
jbundle-package-name
```

```
Installing package '/var/tmp/jbundle-package-name' ...
Auto-deleting old jroute...
Auto-deleting old jdocs...
Auto-deleting old jpfe...
Auto-deleting old jkernel...
Adding JUNOS base software release-number...
Adding jkernel...
Adding jpfe...
Adding jdocs...
Adding jroute...
NOTICE: uncommitted changes have been saved in /var/
db/config/juniper.conf.pre-install
Saving package file in /var/sw/pkg/jbundle-package-
name ...
```

`package-name` is the full URL to the file. `release-number` is the major software release number; for example, 5.4R1.

5. Reboot the router to start the new software:

```
user@host> request system reboot
```

6. After the new software version is successfully running, issue the `request system snapshot` command to back up the new software:

```
user@host> request system snapshot
```

The root file system is backed up to `/altroot`, and `/config` is backed up to `/altconfig`. The root and `/config` file systems are on the router's flash drive, and the `/altroot` and `/altconfig` file systems are on the router's hard drive.

Upgrading Individual Software Packages

To upgrade an individual JUNOS software package:

1. Download the necessary software packages from the Juniper Networks Support Web site, http://www.juniper.net/support/.

A service contract and an access account are required to download the software. Customers can create an account by completing a registration form on the Juniper Networks Web site at https://www.juniper.net/registration/Register.jsp, or by calling Juniper Networks support at 1-888-314-JTAC (from within the United States); 1-408-745-2121 (from outside the United States).

CAUTION Juniper Networks recommends upgrading all individual software packages out of band using the console or `fxp0` interface, because inband connections can be lost during the upgrade process.

---

2. Back up the currently running and active file system so that it can be recovered in case something goes wrong with the upgrade:

   ```
   user@host> request system snapshot
   ```

   The root file system is backed up to `/altroot`, and `/config` is backed up to `/altconfig`. The root and `/config` file systems are on the router's flash drive, and the `/altroot` and `/altconfig` file systems are on the router's hard drive.

3. Copy each software package to the router. Juniper Networks recommends copying them to the `/var/tmp` directory, which is on the rotating media (hard disk) and is a large file system.

   ```
   user@host> file copy ftp://
   username:prompt@ftp.hostname.net/
     filename /var/tmp/filename
   ```

4. Delete the old package and add the new package:

   ```
   user@host> request system software add /var/tmp/
   package-name
   Checking available free disk space...11200k available,
   6076k suggested.
   ```

   package-name is the full URL to the file.

   The system might display the following message:

   ```
   pkg_delete: couldn't entirely delete package
   ```

This message indicates that someone manually deleted or changed an item that was in a package. No action is required; the package is still properly deleted.

If more than one package is being upgraded at the same time, add `jbase` first and the routing software package `jroute` last. If all packages are being upgraded at once using this procedure, add them in the following order:

```
user@host> request system software add /var/tmp/
jbase
user@host> request system software add /var/tmp/
jkernel
user@host> request system software add /var/tmp/jpfe
user@host> request system software add /var/tmp/
jdocs
user@host> request system software add /var/tmp/
jroute
user@host> request system software add /var/tmp/
jcrypto
```

5. Reboot the router to start the new software:

```
user@host> request system reboot
```

6. After the software has been upgraded or downgraded and is successfully running, issue the `request system snapshot` command to back up the new software:

```
user@host> request system snapshot
```

The root file system is backed up to `/altroot`, and `/config` is backed up to `/altconfig`. The root and `/config` file systems are on the router's flash drive, and the `/altroot` and `/altconfig` file systems are on the router's hard drive.

Basic Software Setup

After the router is installed and operational and the software is configured, several basic setup procedures should be performed. These include configuring user accounts so that various users can access the router, configuring login classes to allow different levels of access, configuring user authentication to validate users, and configuring the time zone and network time protocols.

Configuring User Accounts

Users can access the router without accounts if RADIUS or TACACS+ servers are configured, as described in "Configuring User Authentication" on page 132.

User accounts provide one way for users to access the router. For each account, the login name for the user and, optionally, information that identifies the user are defined. After an account is created, the software creates a home directory for the user.

To create user accounts, include the `user` statement at the `[edit system login]` hierarchy level:

```
[edit system]
login {
  user user-name {
    full-name complete-name;
    uid uid-value;
    class class-name;
    authentication {
      (encrypted-password "password" | plain-text-
password);
      ssh-rsa "public-key";
      ssh-dsa "public-key";
    }
  }
}
```

The following properties can be defined for each account:

- Username—(Optional) Name that identifies the user. It must be unique within the router. Do not include spaces, colons, or commas in the username.
- User's full name—(Optional) If the full name contains spaces, enclose it in quotation marks. Do not include colons or commas.
- User identifier (UID)—(Optional) Numeric identifier that is associated with the user account name. The identifier must be in the range 100 through 64,000 and must be unique within the router. If a UID is not assigned to a username, the software assigns one when the configuration is committed, preferring the lowest available number.
- User's access privilege—(Required) One of the login classes defined in the `class` statement at the `[edit system login]` hierarchy level or one of the default classes listed in Table 4.10 on page 128.

- Authentication method or methods and passwords that the user can use to access the router—(Optional) The authentication method used can be an ssh or an MD5 password, or a plain-text password that the JUNOS software encrypts using MD5-style encryption before entering it in the password database. For each method, the user's password can be specified. If the `plain-text-password` option is used, the user is prompted to enter and confirm the password:

```
[edit system]
user@host# set root-authentication plain-text-
password
New password: type password here
Retype new password: retype password here
```

For ssh authentication, the contents of an ssh keys file can be copied into the configuration. To load an ssh key file, include the `load-key-file` statement in the *root-authentication* statement. This option loads RSA (ssh version 1) and DSA (ssh version 2) public keys. A user's authentication can also be configured to use ssh-rsa and ssh-dsa keys.

If the ssh keys file is loaded, the contents of the file are copied into the configuration immediately after the `load-key-file` statement is entered. To view the ssh keys entries, use the configuration mode `show` command. An account for the user `root` is always present in the configuration.

```
[edit system]
user@host# set root-authentication load-key-file my-
host:.ssh/identity.pub
.file.19692                    |           0 KB |    0.3 kB/s
| ETA: 00:00:00 | 100%
[edit system]
user@host# show
root-authentication {
ssh-
rsa "1024 35 97276382040842510554682267572498642416303
222074049625283903820386901415845349641700196106083587
229615634757849182736033612764418742659468932077391083
448101268312595772262546166799927831612350043866091586
628382248974673260566119218148953981396556156378621194
032768780653816960202749164163735913269396344008443
boojum@juniper.net"; # SECRET-DATA
}
```

Configuring Login Classes

User access to the router is configured by defining login classes. All users who log in to the router must be in a login class. Any number of login classes can be defined. The properties defined in a login class include user access privileges, commands, and statements users can and cannot specify, and how long a login session can be idle before it times out and the user is logged off.

To define a login class and its access privileges, include the `class` statement:

```
[edit system login]
class class-name {
  allow-commands "regular-expression";
  deny-commands "regular-expression";
  idle-timeout minutes;
  permissions [ permissions ];
}
```

Use *`class-name`* to name the login class. The software contains a few predefined login classes, which cannot be modified.

Predefined login class names cannot be modified.

If the `set` command is issued on a predefined class name, the JUNOS software appends `-local` to the login class name. The following message is also displayed:

```
warning: '<classname>' is a predefined class name;
changing to '<classname>-local'
```

The `rename` or `copy` commands cannot be used on a predefined login class. Doing so results in the following message:

```
error: target '<classname>' is a predefined class
```

Configuring Access Privilege Levels

Each top-level CLI command and each configuration statement has an access privilege level associated with it. Users can execute only those commands and configure and view only those statements for which they have access privileges. The access privileges for each login class are defined by one or more *permission bits*.

To configure access privilege levels, include the `permissions` statement:

```
[edit system login class]
permissions [ permissions ];
```

In *permissions*, specify one or more of the permission bits listed in Table 4.10. The default permission bits are listed in Table 4.11. Permission bits are not cumulative, so for each class list all the bits needed, including `view` to display information and `configure` to enter configuration mode. Two forms for the permissions control the individual parts of the configuration:

- "Plain" form—Provides read-only capability for that permission type. An example is `interface`.
- Form that ends in `-control`—Provides read and write capability for that permission type. An example is `interface-control`.

Table 4.10 *Login Class Permission Bits*

Permission Bit	Description
`admin`	Can view user account information in configuration mode and with the `show configuration` command.
`admin-control`	Can view user accounts and configure them (at the `[edit system login]` hierarchy level).
`all`	Has all permissions.
`clear`	Can clear (delete) information learned from the network that is stored in various network databases (using the `clear` commands).
`configure`	Can enter configuration mode (using the `configure` command) and commit configurations (using the `commit` command).
`control`	Can perform all control-level operations (all operations configured with the `-control` permission bits).
`edit`	Can edit all portions of a configuration, can load a configuration from an ASCII file, and can commit new and modified configurations (using all the commands in configuration mode).
`field`	Reserved for field (debugging) support.
`firewall`	Can view the firewall filter configuration in configuration mode.
`firewall-control`	Can view and configure firewall filter information (at the `[edit firewall]` hierarchy level).
`floppy`	Can read from and write to the removable media.
`interface`	Can view the interface configuration in configuration mode and with the `show configuration` operational mode command.
`interface-control`	Can view interface configuration information and configure interfaces (at the `[edit interfaces]` hierarchy level).

Table 4.10 *Login Class Permission Bits*

Permission Bit	Description
maintenance	Can perform system maintenance, including starting a local shell on the router and becoming the superuser in the shell (by issuing the su root command), and can halt and reboot the router (using the request system commands).
network	Can access the network by entering the ping, ssh, telnet, and traceroute commands.
reset	Can restart software processes using the restart command and can configure whether software processes are enabled or disabled (at the [edit system processes] hierarchy level).
rollback	Can use the rollback command to return to a previously committed configuration other than the most recently committed one.
routing	Can view general routing, routing protocol, and routing policy configuration information in configuration and operational modes.
routing-control	Can view general routing, routing protocol, and routing policy configuration information and configure general routing (at the [edit routing-options] hierarchy level), routing protocols (at the [edit protocols] hierarchy level), and routing policy (at the [edit policy-options] hierarchy level).
secret	Can view passwords and other authentication keys in the configuration.
secret-control	Can view passwords and other authentication keys in the configuration and can modify them in configuration mode.
shell	Can start a local shell on the router by entering the start shell command.
snmp	Can view SNMP configuration information in configuration and operational modes.
snmp-control	Can view SNMP configuration information and configure SNMP (at the [edit snmp] hierarchy level).
system	Can view system-level information in configuration and operational modes.
system-control	Can view system-level configuration information and configure it (at the [edit system] hierarchy level).
trace	Can view trace file settings in configuration and operational modes.
trace-control	Can view trace file settings and configure trace file properties.
view	Can use various commands to display current systemwide, routing table, and protocol-specific values and statistics.

Table 4.11 *Default System Login Classes*

Login Class	Permission Bits Set
`operator`	`clear`, `network`, `reset`, `trace`, `view`
`read-only`	`view`
`super-user`	`all`
`unauthorized`	None

Denying or Allowing Individual Commands

By default, all top-level CLI commands have associated access privilege levels. Users can execute only those commands and view only those statements for which they have access privileges. For each login class, individual commands normally associated with a given privilege level can be explicitly denied or allowed (using operational mode commands). One `deny-commands` and one `allow-commands` statement can be included in each login class.

To explicitly deny a command that would otherwise be permitted, include the `deny-commands` statement:

```
[edit system login class class-name]
deny-commands regular-expression;
```

To explicitly allow additional commands that would otherwise be denied, include the `allow-commands` statement:

```
[edit system login class class-name]
allow-commands regular-expression;
```

If the *`regular-expression`* contains any spaces, operators, or wildcard characters, enclose it in quotation marks. Regular expressions are not case-sensitive.

Extended regular expressions are used to specify which commands are denied or allowed. These regular expressions can be specified in the `allow-commands` and `deny-commands` statements at the `[edit system login class]` hierarchy level or as JUNOS-specific attributes in the RADIUS authentication server's configuration. If regular expressions are received during RADIUS authentication, they override any regular expressions configured on the local router.

Command regular expressions implement the extended (modern) regular expressions as defined in POSIX 1003.2. Table 4.12 lists common regular expression operators.

Table 4.12 *Common Regular Expression Operators*

Operator	Match Conditions
|	One of the two terms on either side of the pipe.
^	At the beginning of an expression, used to denote where the command begins, where there might be some ambiguity.
$	Character at the end of a command. Used to denote a command that must be matched exactly up to that point. For example, `allow-commands "show interfaces $"` means that the user cannot issue `show interfaces detail` or `show interfaces extensive`.
[ ]	Range of letters or digits. To separate the start and end of a range, use a hyphen (-).
( )	A group of commands, indicating an expression to be evaluated; the result is then evaluated as part of the overall expression.

Configuring the Timeout Value for Idle Login Sessions

An idle login session is one in which the CLI operational mode prompt is displayed but there is no input from the keyboard. By default, a login session remains established until a user logs out of the router, even if that session is idle. To close idle sessions automatically, a time limit can be configured for each login class. If a session established by a user in that class remains idle for the configured time limit, the session automatically closes.

To define the timeout value for idle login sessions, include the `idle-timeout` statement. Specify the number of minutes that a session can be idle before it is automatically closed.

```
[edit system login class class-name]
idle-timeout minutes;
```

If a timeout value has been configured, the CLI displays messages similar to the following starting 5 minutes before timing out the user:

```
user@host# Session will be closed in 5 minutes if there is
no activity.
Warning: session will be closed in 1 minute if there is no
activity
Warning: session will be closed in 10 seconds if there is
no activity
Idle timeout exceeded: closing session
```

The session closes after the specified time has elapsed except if the user is running Telnet or monitoring interfaces using the `monitor interface` or `monitor traffic` command.

Configuring User Authentication

The router can be configured to use RADIUS or TACACS+ authentication, or both, to validate users who attempt to access the router. If both authentication methods are used, the preference of which authentication method the router will use first can also be configured.

User authentication can be configured by configuring RADIUS authentication, TACACS+ authentication, template accounts for RADIUS and TACACS+ authentication, and the authentication order.

RADIUS Authentication

To use RADIUS authentication on the router, configure information about one or more RADIUS servers on the network by including the `radius-server` statement:

```
[edit system]
radius-server server-address {
  port number;
  secret password;
  retry number;
  timeout seconds;
}
```

In *server-address*, specify the address of the RADIUS server.

A port number on which to contact the RADIUS server can be specified. By default, port number `1812` is used (as specified in RFC 2138).

A password must be specified in the `secret` statement. Passwords can contain spaces. The secret used by the local router must match that used by the server.

To configure multiple RADIUS servers, include multiple `radius-server` statements.

To configure a set of users that share a single account for authorization purposes, create a template user. To do this, include the `user` statement at the `[edit system login]` hierarchy level, as described in "Creating Template Accounts for RADIUS and TACACS+ Authentication" on page 135.

Optionally, the amount of time that the local router waits to receive a response from a RADIUS server (in the `timeout` statement) and the number of times that the router attempts to contact a RADIUS authentication server (in the `retry` statement) can be specified. By default, the router waits 3 seconds. The value can be in the range of 1 through 90 seconds. By default, the router retries connecting to the server 3 times. This value can be in the range of 1 through 10 times.

The JUNOS software supports the configuration of Juniper Networks-specific RADIUS attributes. These attributes are known as vendor-specific attributes and are described in RFC 2138, *Remote Authentication Dial-In User Service (RADIUS)*. The Juniper Networks-specific attributes are encapsulated in a RADIUS vendor-specific attribute with the vendor ID set to the Juniper Networks ID number, 2636. Table 4.13 lists the configurable Juniper Networks-specific RADIUS attributes.

Table 4.13 *Juniper Networks–Specific RADIUS Attributes*

Name	Description	Type	Length	String
`Juniper-Local-User-Name`	Indicates the name of the user template used by this user when logging in to a device. This attribute is used only in Access-Accept packets.	1	≥3	One or more octets containing printable ASCII characters.
`Juniper-Allow-Commands`	Contains an extended regular expression that allows the user to run commands in addition to the commands authorized by the user's login class permission bits. This attribute is used only in Access-Accept packets.	2	≥3	One or more octets containing printable ASCII characters, in the form of an extended regular expression.
`Juniper-Deny-Commands`	Contains an extended regular expression that denies the user permission to run commands authorized by the user's login class permission bits. This attribute is used only in Access-Accept packets.	3	≥3	One or more octets containing printable ASCII characters, in the form of an extended regular expression.

TACACS+ Authentication

To use TACACS+ authentication on the router, configure information about one or more TACACS+ servers on the network by including the `tacplus-server` statement:

```
[edit system]
tacplus-server server-address {
  secret password;
  single-connection;
  timeout seconds;
}
```

In *server-address*, specify the address of the TACACS+ server.

A secret (password) that the local router passes to the TACACS+ client (in the `secret` statement) must be specified. Secrets can contain spaces. The secret used by the local router must match that used by the server.

Optionally, specify the length of time that the local router waits to receive a response from a TACACS+ server (in the `timeout` statement). By default, the router waits 3 seconds. The value can be in the range of 1 through 90 seconds.

Optionally, the software can maintain one open TCP connection to the server for multiple requests, rather than opening a connection for each connection attempt, thus optimizing attempts to connect to a TACACS+ server. To do this, include the `single-connection` statement. Early versions of the TACACS+ server do not support a single TCP connection. If the `single-connection` statement is configured and the server does not support it, the JUNOS software will be unable to communicate with that TACACS+ server.

To configure multiple TACACS+ servers, include multiple `tacplus-server` statements.

> To configure a set of users that share a single account for authorization purposes, create a template user. To do this, include the `user` statement at the `[edit system login]` hierarchy level, as described in "Creating Template Accounts for RADIUS and TACACS+ Authentication" on page 135.

The TACACS+ attributes listed in Table 4.14 are specific to Juniper Networks. They are specified in the TACACS+ server configuration file on a per-user basis. The JUNOS software retrieves these attributes through an authorization request of the TACACS+ server after authenticating a user. These attributes do not need to be configured to run JUNOS software with TACACS+. To configure these attributes, include a `service` statement in the TACACS+ server configuration file of the following form in a user or group statement:

```
service = junos-exec {
    local-user-name = <username-local-to-router>
    allow-commands = "<allow-commands-regexp>"
    deny-commands = "<deny-commands-regexp>"
}
```

Table 4.14 *Juniper Networks-Specific TACACS+ Attributes*

Name	Description	Length	String
`local-user-name`	Indicates the name of the user template used by this user when logging into a device.	≥3	One or more octets containing printable ASCII characters.
`allow-commands`	Contains an extended regular expression that allows the user to run commands in addition to those commands authorized by the user's login class permission bits.	≥3	One or more octets containing printable ASCII characters, in the form of an extended regular expression.
`deny-commands`	Contains an extended regular expression that denies the user permission to run commands authorized by the user's login class permission bits.	≥3	One or more octets containing printable ASCII characters, in the form of an extended regular expression.

Creating Template Accounts for RADIUS and TACACS+ Authentication

When local password authentication is used, a local user account must be created for every user who wants to access the system. However, when using RADIUS or TACACS+ authentication, single accounts can be created (for authorization purposes) that are shared by a set of users. These accounts are created using the remote and local user template accounts. When a user is using a template account, the CLI username is the login name; however, the privileges, file ownership, and effective user ID are inherited from the template account.

By default, the JUNOS software uses the remote template account when the authenticated user does not exist locally on the router, the authenticated user's record in the authentication server specifies local user, or local user is specified as a user that does not exist locally on the router.

To configure a remote template account, include the username *`remote`* and specify the privileges you want to provide to these remote users:

```
[edit system login]
user remote {
  full-name "All remote users";
  uid uid-value;
  class class-name;
}
```

To configure different access privileges for users who share the remote template account, include the `allow-commands` and `deny-commands` commands on the authentication server configuration file.

Local User Template Accounts

Local user template accounts are used when different types of templates are needed. Each template can define a different set of permissions appropriate for the group of users who use that template. These templates are defined locally on the router and referenced by the TACACS+ and RADIUS authentication servers.

When local user templates are configured and a user logs in, the JUNOS software issues a request to the authentication server to authenticate the user's login name. If a user is authenticated, the server returns the local username to the JUNOS software, which then determines whether a local username is specified for that login name (`local-username` for TACACS+, `Juniper-Local-User` for RADIUS). If so, the JUNOS software selects the appropriate local user template locally configured on the router. If a local user template does not exist for the authenticated user, the router defaults to the remote template.

To configure different access privileges for users who share the local user template account, include the `allow-commands` and `deny-commands` commands in the authentication server configuration file.

To configure the local user template, include the local username and specify the privileges to provide to these local users:

```
[edit system login]
user local-user-name {
  full-name "local user account";
  uid uid-value;
  class class-name;
}
```

Configuring the Authentication Order

If the router is configured to be both a RADIUS and TACACS+ client (by including the `radius-server` and `tacplus-server` statements), the order in which the software tries the different authentication methods when verifying that a user can access the router can be configured. For each login attempt, the JUNOS software tries the authentication methods in order, starting with the first one, until the password matches.

To configure the authentication order, include the `authentication-order` statement:

```
[edit system]
authentication-order [ authentication-methods ];
```

Specify one or more of the following in the preferred order, from first tried to last tried:

- `radius`—Verify the user using RADIUS authentication services.
- `tacplus`—Verify the user using TACACS+ authentication services.
- `password`—Verify the user using the password configured for the user with the `authentication` statement.

If the `authentication-order` statement is not included, users are verified based on their configured passwords.

Configuring Time

The default local time zone on the router is UTC (Coordinated Universal Time, formerly known as Greenwich Mean Time). To modify the local time zone, include the `time-zone` statement:

For information about available time zones, see the JUNOS Internet software technical documentation.

```
[edit system]
time-zone time-zone;
```

Specify the *`time-zone`* using the continent/country/zone primary name. For the time zone change to take effect for all processes running on the router, the router must be rebooted.

Configuring the Network Time Protocol

The Network Time Protocol (NTP) provides mechanisms to synchronize time and coordinate time distribution in a large, diverse network. NTP uses a returnable-time design in which a distributed subnet of time servers operating in a self-organizing, hierarchical master-slave configuration synchronizes local clocks within the subnet and to national time standards by means of wire or radio. The servers also can redistribute reference time using local routing algorithms and time daemons.

NTP is defined in RFC 1305, *Network Time Protocol (Version 3) Specification, Implementation, and Analysis.*

To configure NTP on the router, include the ntp statement:

```
[edit system]
ntp {
  authentication-key number type type value password;
  boot-server address;
  broadcast <address> <key key-number> <version value>
<ttl value>;
  broadcast-client;
  multicast-client <address>;
  peer address <key key-number> <version value> <prefer>;
  server address <key key-number> <version value>
<prefer>;
  trusted-key [ key-numbers ];
}
```

When configuring NTP, time servers are not actively configured. Rather, all clients also act as servers. An NTP server is not believed unless it, in turn, is synchronized to another NTP server—which itself must be synchronized to something upstream, eventually terminating in a high-precision clock.

If the time difference between the local router clock and the NTP server clock is more than 128 milliseconds, but less than 128 seconds, the clocks are slowly stepped into synchronization. However, if the difference is more than 128 seconds, the clocks are not synchronized. The time must be set on the local router so that the difference is less than 128 seconds to start the synchronization process. On the local router, the date and time must be set using the `set date` command. To set the time automatically, include the `boot-server` statement.

When the router is booted, it issues an `ntpdate` request, which polls a network server to determine the local date and time. A server that the router uses to determine the time when the router boots must be specified. Otherwise, NTP is not able to synchronize to a time server if the server's time appears to be very far off the local router's time.

To configure the NTP boot server, include the `boot-server` statement, specifying the address of an NTP server. Do not specify a hostname.

```
[edit system ntp]
boot-server address;
```

For NTP, the system on the network that acts as the authoritative time source (or time server) and how time is synchronized between systems on the network can be configured. To do this, the router is configured to operate in one of the following modes:

- Client mode—In this mode, the local router can be synchronized to the remote system, but the remote system can never be synchronized to the local router.
- Symmetric active mode—In this mode, the local router and the remote system can synchronize each other. This mode is used in a network in which either the local router or the remote system might be a better source of time.
- Broadcast mode—In this mode, the local router sends periodic broadcast messages to a client population at the specified broadcast or multicast address. Normally, this mode is used only when the local router is operating as a transmitter.

Symmetric active mode can be initiated by either the local or remote system. Only one system needs to be configured to do so. This means that the local system can synchronize to any system that offers symmetric active mode without any configuration whatsoever.

NOTE Juniper Networks strongly recommends configuring authentication to ensure that the local system synchronizes only to known time servers.

Configure the Router to Operate in Client Mode

To configure the local router to operate in client mode, include the `server` statement:

```
[edit system ntp]
server address <key key-number> <version value> <prefer>;
```

Specify the address of the system acting as the time server. An address, not a hostname, must be specified.

To include an authentication key in all messages sent to the time server, include the `key` option. The key corresponds to the key number specified in the `authentication-key` statement as described in "Configuring NTP Authentication Keys" on page 141.

By default, the router sends NTP version 3 packets to the time server. To set the NTP version level to 1 or 2, include the `version` option.

If more than one time server is configured, one server can be marked as being preferred by including the `prefer` option.

Configure the Router to Operate in Symmetric Active Mode

To configure the local router to operate in symmetric active mode, include the `peer` statement:

```
[edit system ntp]
peer address <key key-number> <version value> <prefer>;
```

Specify the address of the remote system. An address must be specified, not a hostname.

To include an authentication key in all messages sent to the remote system, include the `key` option. The key corresponds to the key number specified in the `authentication-key` statement as described in the section "Configuring NTP Authentication Keys" on page 141.

By default, the router sends NTP version 3 packets to the remote system. To set the NTP version level to 1 or 2, include the `version` option.

If more than one remote system is configured, include the `prefer` option to mark one system as being preferred.

Configure the Router to Operate in Broadcast Mode

To configure the local router to operate in broadcast mode, include the `broadcast` statement:

```
[edit system ntp]
broadcast address <key key-number> <version value> <ttl
value>;
```

Specify the broadcast address on one of the local networks or a multicast address assigned to NTP. An address must be specified, not a hostname. The multicast address must be `224.0.1.1`.

To include an authentication key in all messages sent to the remote system, include the `key` option. The key corresponds to the key number specified in the `authentication-key` statement as described in the section "Configuring NTP Authentication Keys" on page 141.

By default, the router sends NTP version 3 packets to the remote system. To set the NTP version level to 1 or 2, include the `version` option.

Configuring NTP Authentication Keys

Time synchronization can be authenticated to ensure that the local router obtains its time services only from known sources. By default, network time synchronization is unauthenticated. The router synchronizes to whatever system appears to have the most accurate time. Juniper Networks strongly recommends configuring authentication of network time services.

To authenticate other time servers, include the `trusted-key` statement. Only time servers transmitting network time packets that contain one of the specified key numbers and whose key matches the value configured for that key number are eligible to be synchronized to. Other systems can synchronize to the local router without being authenticated.

```
[edit system ntp]
trusted-key [ key-numbers ];
```

Each key can be any 32-bit unsigned integer except 0. Include the `key` option in the `peer`, `server`, or `broadcast` statements to transmit the specified authentication key when transmitting packets. The key is necessary if the remote system has authentication enabled so that it can synchronize to the local system.

To define the authentication keys, include the `authentication-key` statement:

```
[edit system ntp]
authentication-key key-number type type value password;
```

`number` is the key number, *`type`* is the authentication type (either MD5 or DES), and *`password`* is the password for this key. The key number, type, and password must match on all systems using that particular key for authentication.

Configuring the Router to Listen for Broadcast Messages

When NTP is being used, the local router can be configured to listen for broadcast messages on the local network to discover other servers on the same subnet by including the `broadcast-client` statement:

```
[edit system ntp]
broadcast-client;
```

When the router hears a broadcast message for the first time, it measures the nominal network delay using a brief client-server exchange with the remote server. Then, it enters *broadcast client* mode, in which it listens for, and synchronizes to, succeeding broadcast messages.

To avoid accidental or malicious disruption in this mode, both the local and remote systems must use authentication and the same trusted key and key identifier.

Configuring the Router to Listen for Multicast Messages

When using NTP, the local router can be configured to listen for multicast messages on the local network to discover other servers on the same subnet by including the `multicast-client`:

```
[edit system ntp]
multicast-client <address>;
```

When the router hears a multicast message for the first time, it measures the nominal network delay using a brief client-server exchange with the remote server. Then, it enters *multicast client* mode, in which it listens for, and synchronizes to, succeeding multicast messages.

One or more IP addresses can be specified. An address must be specified, not a hostname. If an address is specified, the router joins those multicast groups. If no address is specified, the software uses `224.0.1.1`.

To avoid accidental or malicious disruption in this mode, both the local and remote systems must use authentication and the same trusted key and key identifier.

CHAPTER

5

CLI and System Management

The command-line interface (CLI) is the interface to the software that you use when you log in to the router. The CLI, which automatically starts after the router finishes booting, provides commands that you use to configure, monitor, and troubleshoot the router.

You can also use the JUNOScript API to access the router. This API is an XML application that Juniper Networks routers use to exchange information with client applications. It defines tags for describing the components and configuration of routers. For more information, see the JUNOScript technical documentation.

The CLI has two modes: operational and configuration. In operational mode, you monitor and troubleshoot the software, network connectivity, and the router by entering commands. In configuration mode, you configure the JUNOS software by creating a hierarchy of configuration statements. When you have finished entering the configuration statements, you commit them, which activates the configuration on the router.

The CLI commands and statements are organized hierarchically, with commands or statements that perform a similar function grouped together under the same level. For example, all commands that display information about the system and the system software are grouped under the `show` command, and all commands that display information about the routing table are grouped under the `show route` command. Figure 5.1 illustrates a portion of the `show` command hierarchy.

Figure 5.1 *CLI Command Hierarchy Example*

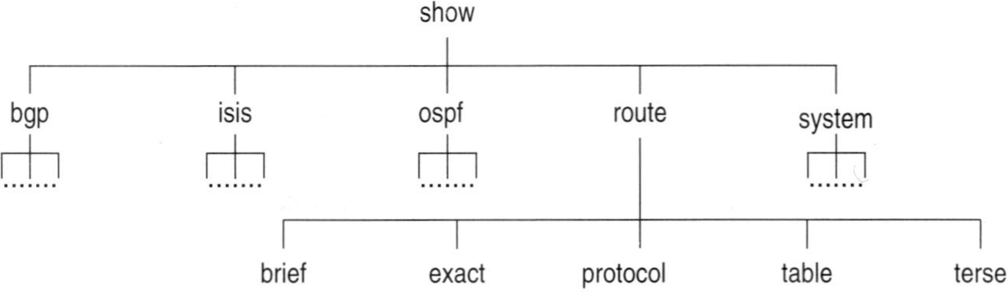

Using the CLI

In the CLI, you type commands on a single line, and they are executed when you press the `Enter` key. The CLI provides context-sensitive help at every level of the command hierarchy. The help information tells you which commands are available at the current level in the hierarchy and provides a brief description of each. To get help while in the CLI, type `?`. You do not need to press `Enter` after typing the question mark.

You do not have to remember or type the full command or option name for the CLI to recognize it. To display all possible command or option completions, type the partial command followed immediately by a question mark.

To complete a command or option that you have partially typed, press the `tab` key or the spacebar. If the partially typed letters begin a string that uniquely identifies a command, the complete command name appears. Otherwise, the possible completions are displayed.

Command completion also applies to other strings, such as filenames and usernames. To display all possible values, type a partial string followed immediately by a question mark. To complete these strings, press the `tab` key.

When you commit a configuration, the JUNOS software checks the configuration you are committing. If there are no problems, a message indicates that the configuration was accepted. If there are problems, a message indicates where the errors are.

In the top-level CLI commands and in configuration mode, if you type an invalid string—for example, the name of a command or statement that does not exist—you see the message "syntax error" or "unknown command." A caret (^) indicates where the error is.

The CLI provides emacs-style keyboard sequences to help you work on the CLI, as shown in Table 5.1.

Table 5.1 *CLI Keyboard Sequences*

Category	Action	Keyboard Sequence
Move the cursor.	Move the cursor back one character.	`Ctrl-b`
	Move the cursor back one word.	`Esc-b` or `Alt-b`
	Move the cursor forward one character.	`Ctrl-f`
	Move the cursor forward one word.	`Esc-f` or `Alt-f`
	Move the cursor to the beginning of the command line.	`Ctrl-a`
	Move the cursor to the end of the command line.	`Ctrl-e`
Delete characters.	Delete the character before the cursor.	`Ctrl-h`, `Delete`, or `Backspace`
	Delete the character at the cursor.	`Ctrl-d`
	Delete all characters from the cursor to the end of the command line.	`Ctrl-k`
	Delete all characters on the command line.	`Ctrl-u` or `Ctrl-x`
	Delete the word before the cursor.	`Ctrl-w`, `Esc-Backspace`, or `Alt-Backspace`
	Delete the word after the cursor.	`Esc-d` or `Alt-d`
Insert recently deleted text.	Insert the most recently deleted text at the cursor.	`Ctrl-y`
Redraw the screen.	Redraw the current line.	`Ctrl-l`
Display previous command lines.	Scroll backward through the list of recently executed commands.	`Ctrl-p`
	Scroll forward through the list of recently executed commands.	`Ctrl-n`
	Search the CLI history in reverse order for lines matching the search string.	`Ctrl-r`
	Search the CLI history by typing some text at the prompt, followed by the keyboard sequence. The CLI attempts to expand the text into the most recent word in the history for which the text is a prefix.	`Esc-/`
Repeat keyboard sequences.	Specify the number of times to execute a keyboard sequence. *`number`* can be from 1 through 9.	`Esc-`*`number sequence`* or `Alt-`*`number sequence`*

CLI Screen Output

When you issue commands in operational mode, or when you issue the `show` command in configuration mode, the output appears on the screen. If the output is too long to display on one screen, it is displayed on several screens using a UNIX-like "more" interface as shown in Table 5.2.

Table 5.2 *"More" Prompt Keyboard Sequences*

Category	Action	Keyboard Sequence
Get help.	Display information about the keyboard sequences you can display at the `---More---` prompt.	`h`
Scroll down.	Scroll down one line.	`Enter`, `Return`, `k`, `Ctrl-m`, `Ctrl-n`, or down arrow
	Scroll down one-half screen.	`tab`, `d`, *`Ctrl-d`*, or *`Ctrl-x`*
	Scroll down one whole screen.	Space or *`Ctrl-f`*
	Scroll down to the bottom of the output.	`Ctrl-e` or `G`
	Display the output all at once instead of one screen at a time. (Same as specifying the `| no-more` command.)	`N`
Scroll up.	Display the previous line of output.	`j`, `Ctrl-h`, `Ctrl-p`, or up arrow
	Scroll up one-half screen.	`u` or `Ctrl-u`
	Scroll up one whole screen.	`b` or `Ctrl-b`
	Scroll up to the top of the output.	`Ctrl-a` or `g`
Search.	Search forward for a string.	`/`*`string`*
	Search backward for a string.	`?`*`string`*
	Repeat the previous search for a string.	`n`
	Search for a text string. You are prompted for the string to match. (Same as specifying the `| match` *`string`* command.)	`m` or `M`
	Search, ignoring a text string. You are prompted for the string to not match. (Same as specifying the `| except` *`string`* command.)	`e` or `E`

Table 5.2 *"More" Prompt Keyboard Sequences*

Category	Action	Keyboard Sequence
Interrupt or end output, redraw the output, and save the output to a file.	Interrupt the display of output.	`Ctrl-C`, `q`, `Q`, or `Ctrl-k`
	Do not redisplay the CLI prompt immediately after displaying the output, but remain at the `---More---` prompt. (Same as specifying the `| hold` command.)	`H`
	Clear any match conditions and display the complete output.	`c` or `C`
	Redraw the output on the screen.	`Ctrl-l`
	Save the command output to a file. You are prompted for a filename. (Same as specifying the `| save` *`filename`* command.)	`s` or `S`

Filtering Screen Output

For operational and configuration commands that display output, such as the `show` commands, you can filter the output (see Table 5.3). When you display help about these commands, one of the options listed is `|` , called a *pipe*, which allows you to filter the command output. Table 5.4 lists common regular expression operators that you can specify when searching for a string in the output.

Table 5.3 *Filtering the Command Output*

Action	Command
Place command output in a file.	`user@host>` *`command`* `| save` *`filename`*
Search for a string in the output.	Match a regular expression: `user@host>` *`command`* `| match` *`regular-expression`* Ignore text that matches a regular expression: `user@host>` *`command`* `| except` *`regular-expression`*

Table 5.3 *Filtering the Command Output*

<table>
<tr><th>Action</th><th>Command</th></tr>
<tr><td>Compare configuration changes with a prior version.</td><td>user@host# show | compare [filename | rollback n]
filename is the full path to a configuration file. n is the index into the list of previously committed configurations.
Statements that are only in the candidate configuration are prefixed with a plus sign (+). Statements that are only in the comparison file are prefixed with a minus sign (–). Statements that are unchanged are prefixed with a single blank space ( ).</td></tr>
<tr><td>Count the number of lines in the output.</td><td>user@host> command | count</td></tr>
<tr><td>Display all output at once.</td><td>user@host> command | no-more</td></tr>
<tr><td>Retain the output after the last screen.</td><td>user@host> command | hold</td></tr>
<tr><td>Display additional information about the configuration.</td><td>user@host> show <<i>hierarchy</i>-level> | display detail</td></tr>
<tr><td>Filter command output multiple times.</td><td>user@host> command | match regular-expression | except regular-expression | match other-regular-expression | find regular-expression | hold</td></tr>
</table>

Table 5.4 *Common Regular Expression Operators*

<table>
<tr><th>Operator</th><th>Match...</th></tr>
<tr><td>|</td><td>One of the two terms on either side of the pipe.</td></tr>
<tr><td>^</td><td>At the beginning of an expression, denotes where the command begins.</td></tr>
<tr><td>$</td><td>Character at the end of a command. Used to denote a command that must be matched exactly up to that point. For example, allow-commands "show interfaces $" means that the user cannot issue show interfaces detail or show interfaces extensive.</td></tr>
<tr><td>[ ]</td><td>Range of letters or digits. To separate the start and end of a range, use a hyphen (-).</td></tr>
<tr><td>( )</td><td>A group of commands, indicating an expression to be evaluated; the result is then evaluated as part of the overall expression.</td></tr>
</table>

CLI Operational Mode

The CLI operational mode provides commands to monitor the router and the network and to perform system-level operations. When you log in to the router and the CLI starts, you are at the top level of operational mode. In operational mode, the prompt is a >. Table 5.5 describes these top-level operational mode CLI commands.

Table 5.5 *Top-Level Operational Mode CLI Commands*

Category	Command	Description
Control the CLI environment.	`set`	Configure the CLI display screen.
Monitor and troubleshoot.	`clear`	Clear statistics and protocol database information.
	`mtrace`	Trace multicast routes.
	`monitor`	Perform real-time debugging of various software components, including the routing protocols and interfaces.
	`ping`	Determine the reachability of a remote network host.
	`show`	Display the current configuration and information about interfaces, routing protocols, routing tables, routing policy filters, and the chassis.
	`test`	Test the configuration and application of policy filters and AS path regular expressions.
	`traceroute`	Trace the route to a remote network host.
Connect to other network systems.	`ssh`	Open a secure shell connection.
	`telnet`	Opens Telnet sessions to another host on the network.
Copy files.	`file copy`	Copy files from one location on the router to another, from the router to a remote system, or from a remote system to the router.
Restart software processes.	`restart`	Restart the JUNOS software processes.
Install and manage software and system-level operations.	`request`	Perform system-level operations, including stopping and rebooting the router and loading JUNOS software images.

Table 5.5 *Top-Level Operational Mode CLI Commands*

Category	Command	Description
Exit the CLI.	`start` `quit`	Exit the CLI and start a UNIX shell. Exit the CLI.
Configure the router.	`configure`	Enter configuration mode.

Setting the Date and Time

To set the date and time on the router, use the `set date` operational mode command:

```
user@host> set date YYYYMMDDhhmm.ss
```

YYYY is the four-digit year, *MM* is the two-digit month, *DD* is the two-digit date, *hh* is the two-digit hour, *mm* is the two-digit minute, and *ss* is the two-digit second.

If the NTP server is unable to synchronize the current date and time on the router, a system log message similar to the following appears:

```
"time error %.0f over %d seconds; set clock manually".
```

To set the date and time from all NTP servers configured at the `[edit system ntp server]` hierarchy level to determine the correct time, use the `set date ntp` command:

```
user@host> set date ntp
```

Displaying CLI Command History

To display a list of recently issued commands, use the `show cli history` operational mode command. By default, this command displays the last 100 commands issued in the CLI. If you specify a number with the command, it displays that number of recent commands.

```
user@host> show cli history
  03-03 01:00:50 -- show cli history
  03-03 01:01:12 -- show interfaces terse
  03-03 01:01:22 -- show interfaces lo0
  03-03 01:01:44 -- show bgp next-hop-database
  03-03 01:01:51 -- show cli history
```

Monitoring Who Uses the CLI

Depending on how you configure the JUNOS software, multiple users can log in to the router, use the CLI, and configure or modify the software configuration. The JUNOS software provides a general `syslog`-like mechanism to log system operations, such as when users log in to the router and when they issue CLI commands. To configure system logging, include the `syslog` statement in the configuration.

Controlling the CLI Environment

To configure the CLI environment, use the `set` operational mode CLI command:

```
user@host> set cli ?
Possible completions:
  complete-on-spaceToggle word completion on space
  idle-timeout    Set the cli maximum idle time
  prompt          Set the cli command prompt string
  restart-on-upgradeSet cli to prompt for restart after a
software upgrade
  screen-length   Set number of lines on screen
  screen-width    Set number of characters on a line
  terminal        Set terminal type
```

When you log in to the router using ssh, or log in from the console when its terminal type is already configured, the terminal type, screen length, and screen width are already set, so you do not need to change them from the CLI. Table 5.6 describes the various ways you can control the CLI environment.

Table 5.6 *Controlling the CLI Environment*

Description	Command	Comment
Terminal type	`set cli terminal terminal-type`	Terminal type can be `ansi`, `vt100`, `small-xterm`, or `xterm`.
Screen length	`set cli screen-length length`	Default screen length is 24 lines. Setting the length to 0 lines disables the display of output one screen at a time.
Screen width	`set cli screen-width width`	Default width is 80 columns.

Table 5.6 *Controlling the CLI Environment*

Description	Command	Comment
Prompt	`set cli prompt string`	Default prompt is `user@host>`. If the prompt string contains spaces, enclose the string in quotation marks (" ").
Maximum time an individual session can be idle before the user is logged off the router	`set cli idle-timeout timeout`	By default, an individual CLI session never times out after extended times, unless the `idle-timeout` statement has been included in the user's login class configuration. `timeout` can be 0 through 100,000 minutes. Setting `timeout` to 0 disables the timeout.
Prompt after upgrade	Disable the prompt for an individual session: `set cli restart-on-upgrade off`	By default, the CLI prompts to restart after a software upgrade.To re-enable the prompt, use the `set cli restart-on-upgrade on` command.
Command completion	Have the CLI allow only a tab to complete a command: `set cli complete-on-space off`	By default, press the spacebar or `tab` key to have the CLI complete a command.To re-enable the use of both spaces and tabs for command completion, use the `set cli complete-on-space on` command.
Display current settings	`show cli`	

CLI Configuration Mode

To configure the router, including the routing protocols, router interfaces, network management, and user access, you enter a separate mode called *configuration mode*. Do this by issuing the `configure` operational mode command. Table 5.7 describes the commands available in configuration mode.

In configuration mode, the prompt is a `#`. The portion of the prompt in braces, `[edit]`, is a *banner* that shows your location in the statement hierarchy. When you first enter configuration mode, you always are at the top level of the hierarchy, which is indicated by the `[edit]` banner.

Table 5.7 *Configuration Mode Commands*

Command	Description
activate	Remove the inactive: tag from a statement, effectively adding the statement or identifier back to the configuration. Statements or identifiers that have been activated take effect when you next issue the commit command.
annotate	Add comments to a configuration. You can add comments only at the current hierarchy level.
commit	Commit the set of changes to the database and cause the changes to take operational effect.
copy	Make a copy of an existing statement in the configuration.
deactivate	Add the inactive: tag to a statement, effectively commenting out the statement or identifier from the configuration. Statements or identifiers marked as inactive do not take effect when you issue the commit command.
delete	Delete a statement or identifier. All subordinate statements and identifiers contained within the specified statement path are deleted with it.
edit	Move inside the specified statement hierarchy. If the statement does not exist, it is created.
exit	Exit the current level of the statement hierarchy, returning to the level prior to the last edit command, or exit from configuration mode. The quit and exit commands are synonyms.
help	Display help about available configuration statements.
insert	Insert an identifier into an existing hierarchy.
load	Load a configuration from an ASCII configuration file or from terminal input.
quit	Exit the current level of the statement hierarchy, returning to the level prior to the last edit command, or exit from configuration mode. The quit and exit commands are synonyms.
rename	Rename an existing configuration statement or identifier.
rollback	Return to a previously committed configuration.
run	Run a CLI operational mode command without exiting from configuration mode.
save	Save the configuration to an ASCII file.
set	Create a statement hierarchy and set identifier values. This is similar to edit except that your current level in the hierarchy does not change.
show	Display the current configuration.
status	Display the users currently editing the configuration.
top	Return to the top level of configuration command mode, which is indicated by the [edit] banner.
up	Move up one level in the statement hierarchy.

Configuration Statements and Identifiers

You configure all router properties by including *statements* in the configuration. A statement consists of a keyword, which is fixed text, and, optionally, an *identifier*. An identifier is an identifying name that you define, such as the name of an interface or a username, and that allows you and the CLI to discriminate among a collection of statements. Table 5.8 shows the statements available at the top level of configuration mode (that is, the trunk of the hierarchy tree).

Table 5.8 *Top-Level Configuration Mode Statements*

Statement	Configures...
`accounting-options`	Accounting statistics data collection for interfaces and firewall filters
`chassis`	Properties of the router chassis, including the clock source, conditions that activate alarms, and SONET/SDH framing and concatenation properties
`class-of-service`	Class-of-service parameters
`firewall`	Filters that select packets based on their contents.
`forwarding-options`	Forwarding options, including traffic sampling options
`groups`	Configuration groups
`interfaces`	Interface information, such as encapsulation, interfaces, virtual channel identifiers (VCIs), and data link channel identifiers (DLCIs)
`policy-options`	Routing policies, which allow you to filter and set properties in incoming and outgoing routes
`protocols`	Routing protocols, including BGP, IS-IS, OSPF, RIP, MPLS, LDP, and RSVP
`routing-instances`	Multiple routing instances
`routing-options`	Protocol-independent routing options, such as static routes, autonomous system numbers, confederation members, and global tracing (debugging) operations to log
`snmp`	SNMP community strings, interfaces, traps, and notifications
`system`	Systemwide properties, including the host name, domain name, DNS server, user logins and permissions, mappings between host names and addresses, and software processes

How the Configuration Is Stored

When you edit a configuration, you work in a copy of the current configuration to create a *candidate* configuration. The changes you make to the candidate configuration are visible in the CLI immediately, so if multiple users are editing the configuration at the same time, all users can see all changes.

To have a candidate configuration take effect, you *commit* the changes. At this point, the candidate file is checked for proper syntax, activated, and marked as the current, operational software configuration file. If multiple users are editing the configuration, when you commit the candidate configuration, all changes made by all the users take effect.

In addition to saving the current configuration, the CLI saves the current operational version and the previous nine versions of committed configurations. The currently operational JUNOS software configuration is stored in the file `juniper.conf`, and the last three committed configurations are stored in the files `juniper.conf.1`, `juniper.conf.2`, and `juniper.conf.3`. These four files are located in the directory `/config`, which is on the router's flash drive. The remaining six previous versions of committed configurations are stored in the directory `/var/db/config` on the hard disk.

Figure 5.2 illustrates the various router configuration states and the configuration mode commands you use to load, commit, copy, save, or roll back the configuration.

Figure 5.2 *Commands for Storing and Modifying the Router Configuration*

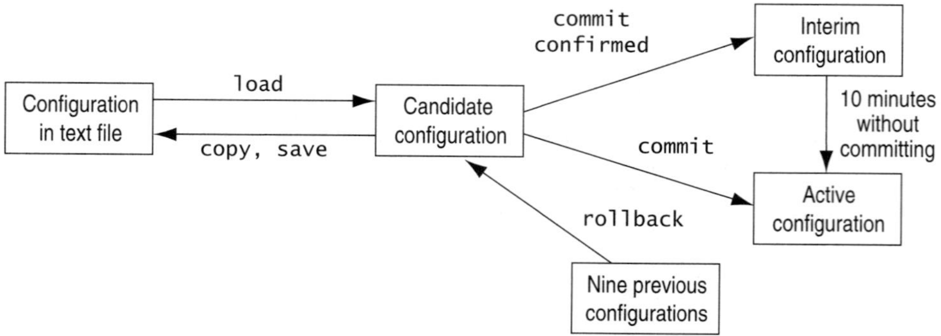

How the CLI Performs Type-Checking

The CLI expects to receive specific types of input and performs type-checking to verify that the data you entered is in the correct format. For example, for a statement in which you must specify an IP address, the CLI checks that you entered an address in a valid format. If you have not, an error message indicates what you were expected to type. Table 5.9 lists the data types the CLI checks.

Table 5.9 *CLI Configuration Input Types*

Data Type	Format	Examples
Physical interface name (used in the `[edit interfaces]` hierarchy)	*type-fpc/pic/port*	**Correct:** so-0/0/1 **Incorrect:** so-0
Full interface name	*type-fpc/pic/port<:channel>.logical*	**Correct:** so-0/0/1.0 **Incorrect:** so-0/0/1
Full or abbreviated interface name (used in places other than the `[edit interfaces]` hierarchy)	*type-<fpc</pic/port>><<:channel>.logical>*	**Correct:** so, so-1, so-1/2/3:4.5
IP address	0x*hex-bytes* *octet<.octet<.octet.<octet>>>*	**Correct:** 1.2.3.4, 0x01020304, 128.8.1, 128.8 **Sample translations:** 1.2.3 becomes 1.2.3.0 0x01020304 becomes 1.2.3.4 0x010203 becomes 0.1.2.3
IP address (destination prefix) and prefix length	0x*hex-bytes</length>* *octet<.octet<.octet.<octet>>></length>*	**Correct:** 10/8, 128.8/16, 1.2.3.4/32, 1.2.3.4 **Sample translations:** 1.2.3 becomes 1.2.3.0/32 0x01020304 becomes 1.2.3.4/32 0x010203 becomes 0.1.2.3/32 default becomes 0.0.0.0/0
ISO address	*hex-nibble<hex-nibble ...>*	**Correct:** 47.1234.2345.3456.00, 47123423453456.00, 47.12.34.23.45.34.56.00 **Sample translations:** 47123456 becomes 47.1234.56 47.12.34.56 becomes 47.1234.56 4712.3456 becomes 47.1234.56

Table 5.9 *CLI Configuration Input Types*

Data Type	Format	Examples
OSPF area identifier (ID)	`0x`*hex-bytes* *octet*<.*octet*<.*octet*.<*octet*>>> *decimal-number*	**Correct:** 54, 0.0.0.54, 0x01020304, 1.2.3.4 **Sample translations:** 54 becomes 0.0.0.54 257 becomes 0.0.1.1 128.8 becomes 128.8.0.0 0x010203 becomes 0.1.2.3

Entering and Exiting Configuration Mode

If many users enter configuration mode at the same time, everyone can make configuration changes and commit all changes. If one user enters configuration mode when another user is also in configuration mode, a message indicates who the user is and what portion of the configuration he or she is viewing or editing:

```
user@host> configure
Entering configuration mode
Current configuration users:
  root terminal p3 (pid 1088) on since 1999-05-13 01:03:27
EDT
    [edit interfaces so-3/0/0 unit 0 family inet]
The configuration has been changed but not committed
```

If, when you enter configuration mode, the configuration contains changes that have not been committed, a message appears:

```
user@host> configure
Entering configuration mode
The configuration has been changed but not committed
```

If, while in configuration mode, you try to make a change while the configuration is locked by another user, a message indicates that the configuration database is locked, who the user is, and what portion of the configuration the user is viewing or editing:

```
user@host# set system host-name ipswitch
error: configuration database locked by:
  user2 terminal d0 (pid 1828) on since 19:47:58 EDT, idle
00:02:11
    exclusive [edit protocols]
```

If you enter configuration mode with the `configure exclusive` command, you lock the candidate configuration for as long as you remain in configuration mode, allowing you to make changes without interference from other users. If another user is also in configuration mode, and has the configuration locked, a message indicates who the user is and what portion of the configuration the user is viewing or editing:

```
user@host> configure exclusive
Entering configuration mode
Users currently editing the configuration:
  root terminal p3 (pid 1088) on since 2000-10-30 19:47:58
EDT, idle 00:00:44
  exclusive [edit interfaces so-3/0/0 unit 0 family inet]
```

To exit configuration mode, use the `exit configuration-mode` configuration mode command from any level or use the `exit` command from the top level. If you try to exit from configuration mode using the `exit` command and the configuration contains changes that have not been committed, you see a message and prompt:

```
[edit]
user@host# exit
The configuration has been changed but not committed
Exit with uncommitted changes? [yes,no] (yes) <Enter>
Exiting configuration mode
user@host>
```

To exit with uncommitted changes without having to respond to a prompt, use the `exit configuration-mode` command.

Moving among Levels of the Hierarchy

To move down through an existing configuration command hierarchy, or to create a hierarchy and move down to that level, use the `edit` configuration mode command, specifying the hierarchy level at which you want to be. To move up the hierarchy, use the `exit` configuration mode command. This command is, in effect, the opposite of the `edit` command.

To move up the hierarchy one level at a time, use the `up` configuration mode command.

To move directly to the top level, use the `top` configuration mode command.

Displaying the Current Configuration

To display the configuration at the current hierarchy level or at the specified level, use the `show` configuration mode command.

```
user@host> show <statement-path>
```

The configuration statements appear in a fixed order. The CLI indents each level in the hierarchy to indicate each statement's relative position in the hierarchy and generally sets off each level with braces, using an open brace at the beginning of each hierarchy level and a closing brace at the end. If the statement at a hierarchy level is empty, the braces are not printed. Each leaf statement ends with a semicolon. If the hierarchy does not extend as far as a leaf statement, the last statement in the hierarchy ends with a semicolon. Interfaces appear alphabetically by type, and then in numerical order by slot number, PIC number, and port number.

You also can use the CLI operational mode `show configuration` command to display the last committed current configuration, which is the configuration currently running on the router:

```
user@host> show configuration
```

To display the users currently editing the configuration, use the `status` configuration mode command:

```
user@host# status
Current configuration users:
  user terminal p0 (pid 518) on since 2002-03-12 18:24:27
PST
      [edit protocols]
```

The system displays who is editing the configuration (`user`), how the user is logged in (`terminal p0`), the date and time the user logged in (`2002-03-12 18:24:27 PST`), and what level of the hierarchy the user is editing (`[edit protocols]`).

Creating and Modifying the Configuration

To configure the router or to modify an existing router configuration, you add statements to the configuration. For each statement hierarchy, you create the hierarchy starting with a statement at the top level and continuing with statements that move progressively lower in the hierarchy.

To create the hierarchy, you use two configuration mode commands:

- `set`—Creates a statement hierarchy and sets identifier values. After you issue a `set` command, you remain at the same level in the hierarchy. The `set` command has the following syntax:

  ```
  set <statement-path> statement <identifier>
  ```

  statement-path is the hierarchy to the configuration statement and the statement itself. If you have already moved to the statement's hierarchy level, you omit this. *statement* is the configuration statement itself. *identifier* is a string that identifies an instance of a statement.

- `edit`—Moves to a particular hierarchy level. If that hierarchy level does not exist, the `edit` command creates it and then moves to it. The `edit` command has the following syntax:

  ```
  edit <statement-path> statement <identifier>
  ```

Removing a Statement

To delete a statement or identifier, use the `delete` configuration mode command. Deleting a statement or an identifier effectively "unconfigures" the functionality associated with that statement or identifier, returning that functionality to its default condition. When you delete a statement, the statement and all its subordinate statements and identifiers are removed from the configuration.

```
delete <statement-path> <identifier>
```

To delete the entire hierarchy starting at the current hierarchy level, do not specify a statement or an identifier in the `delete` command:

```
[edit]
user@host# delete
Delete everything under this level? [yes, no] (no) ?
  Possible completions:
    no    Don't delete everything under this level
    yes   Delete everything under this level
Delete everything under this level? [yes, no] (no)
```

Copying a Statement

To make a copy of an existing statement in the configuration, use the `copy` configuration mode command. Copying a statement duplicates that statement and the entire hierarchy of statements configured under that statement.

```
copy existing-statement to new-statement
```

Renaming an Identifier

You can rename an identifier in the configuration either by deleting the identifier (using the `delete` command) and then adding the renamed identifier (using the `set` and `edit` commands) or by using the `rename` configuration mode command:

```
rename <statement-path> identifier1 to identifier2
```

Inserting a New Identifier

When configuring the router, you can enter most statements and identifiers in any order. However, there are a few cases where the statement order matters because the configuration statements create a sequence that is analyzed in order. For example, in a routing policy or firewall filter, you define terms that are analyzed sequentially. Also, when you create a named path in dynamic Multiprotocol Label Switching (MPLS), you define an ordered list of the transit routers in the path, starting with the first transit router and ending with the last.

To modify a portion of the configuration in which the statement order matters, use the `insert` configuration mode command:

```
insert <statement-path> identifier1 (before | after)
identifier2
```

If you do not use the `insert` command, but instead simply configure the identifier, it is placed at the end of the list of similar identifiers.

Deactivating and Reactivating Statements and Identifiers

In a configuration, you can deactivate statements and identifiers so that they do not take effect when you issue the `commit` command. Any deactivated statements and identifiers are marked with the `inactive:` tag. They remain in the configuration, but are not activated when you issue a `commit` command.

To deactivate a statement or identifier, use the `deactivate` configuration mode command:

```
deactivate (statement | identifier)
```

To reactivate a statement or identifier, use the `activate` configuration mode command:

```
activate (statement | identifier)
```

In some portions of the configuration hierarchy, you can include a `disable` statement to disable functionality. One example is disabling an interface by including the `disable` statement at the `[edit interface interface-name]` hierarchy level. When you deactivate a statement, that specific object or property is completely ignored and is not applied at all when you issue a `commit` command. When you disable a functionality, it is activated when you issue a `commit` command but is treated as though it is down or administratively disabled.

Running Operational Mode CLI Commands from Configuration Mode

To display the output of an operational mode `show` or other command while configuring the software, you can execute a single operational mode command by issuing the `run` configuration mode command and specifying the operational mode command:

```
[edit]
user@host# run operational-mode-command
```

Displaying Configuration Mode Command History

To display a list of the recent commands you issued while in configuration mode, use the `run show cli history` command. By default, this command displays the last 100 commands issued in the CLI.

```
user@host# run show cli history
  12:40:08 -- show
  12:40:17 -- edit protocols
  12:40:27 -- set isis
  12:40:29 -- edit isis
  12:40:40 -- run show cli history
```

Verifying and Committing a Configuration

To verify that the syntax of a configuration is correct, use the `commit check` configuration mode command:

```
user@host# commit check
configuration check succeeds
```

If there are any errors, a message indicates the location.

To save software configuration changes to the configuration database and activate the configuration on the router, use the `commit` configuration mode command:

```
user@host# commit
commit complete
```

You can issue the `commit` command from any hierarchy level.

The configuration is checked for syntax errors. If the syntax is correct, the configuration is activated and becomes the current, operational router configuration. If the configuration contains syntax errors, a message indicates the location of the error and the configuration is not activated. You must correct the error before recommitting the configuration.

To save software configuration changes, activate the configuration on the router, and exit configuration mode, use the `commit and-quit` configuration mode command. This command succeeds only if the configuration contains no errors.

```
[edit]
user@host# commit and-quit
commit complete
exiting configuration mode
user@host>
```

To commit the current candidate configuration but require an explicit confirmation for the commit to become permanent, use the `commit confirmed` configuration mode command. This is useful for verifying that a configuration change works correctly and does not prevent management access to the router.

```
user@host# commit confirmed
commit complete
```

To keep the new configuration active, enter a `commit` or `commit check` command within 10 minutes of the `commit confirmed` command. If the commit is not confirmed, the JUNOS software automatically rolls back to the previous configuration.

Like the `commit` command, the `commit confirmed` command verifies the configuration syntax and reports any errors. If there are no errors, the configuration is activated and begins running on the router. Figure 5.3 illustrates how the `commit confirmed` command works.

Figure 5.3 *Confirm a Configuration*

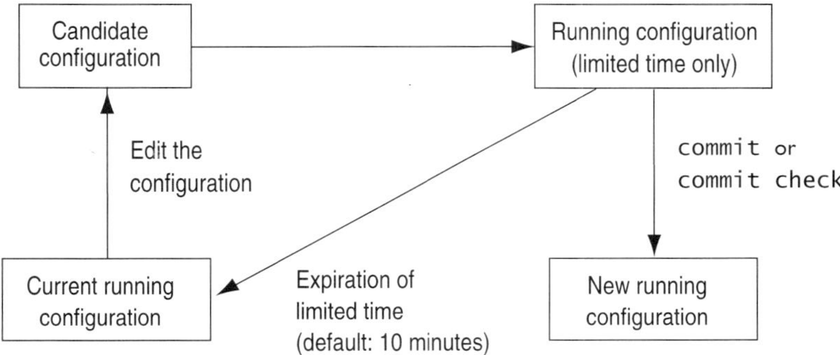

To change the amount of time before you have to confirm the new configuration, specify the number of minutes when you issue the `commit` command:

```
[edit]
user@host# commit confirmed minutes
commit complete
```

Saving a Configuration to a File

To save the configuration to a text (ASCII) file so that you can edit it with a text editor of your choice, use the save configuration mode command. By default, the configuration is saved to that file in your home directory, which is on the flash disk.

```
[edit]
user@host# save filename
```

Loading a Configuration

To create a file containing the router configuration, copy it to the local router, and then load it into the CLI. After you have loaded the file, you can commit it to activate the configuration on the router, or you can edit the configuration interactively using the CLI and commit it at a later time.

You can also create a configuration while typing at the terminal and then load it. Loading a configuration from the terminal is generally useful when you are cutting existing portions of the configuration and pasting them elsewhere in the configuration.

To load an existing configuration file that is located on the router, use the following version of the `load` configuration mode command:

```
[edit]
user@host# load (replace | merge | override) filename
```

To load a configuration from the terminal, use the following version of the `load` configuration mode command:

```
[edit]
user@host# load (replace | merge | override) terminal
[Type ^D to end input]
```

To replace an entire configuration, specify the `override` option. An override operation discards the current candidate configuration and loads the configuration in *`filename`* or the one that you type at the terminal.

To combine the current configuration and the configuration in *`filename`* or the one that you type at the terminal, specify the `merge` option. If the existing configuration and the incoming configuration contain conflicting statements, the statements in the incoming configuration override those in the existing configuration.

To replace portions of a configuration, specify the `replace` option. For this operation to work, you must include `replace:` tags in the file or configuration you type at the terminal. The software searches for the `replace:` tags, deletes the existing statements of the same name, if any, and replaces them with the incoming configuration. If there is no existing statement of the same name, the `replace` operation adds to the configuration the statements marked with the `replace:` tag.

If, in an override or merge operation, you specify a file or type text that contains `replace:` tags, the `replace:` tags are ignored, and the override or merge operation is performed.

To copy a configuration file from another network system to the local router, you can use the `ssh` and `telnet` commands.

If you are performing a `replace` operation and the file you specify or text you type does not contain any `replace:` tags, the replace operation is effectively equivalent to a `merge` operation. This might be useful if you are running automated scripts and cannot know in advance whether the scripts need to perform a replace or a merge operation. The scripts can use the `replace` operation to cover either case.

Figures 5.4, 5.5, and 5.6 compare the effect of the `load override`, `load replace`, and `load merge` commands.

Figure 5.4 *Load a Configuration from a File Using Load Override*

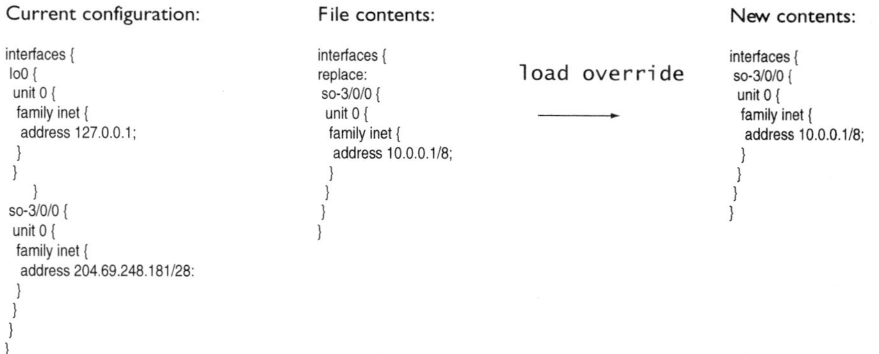

Figure 5.5 *Load a Configuration from a File Using Load Replace*

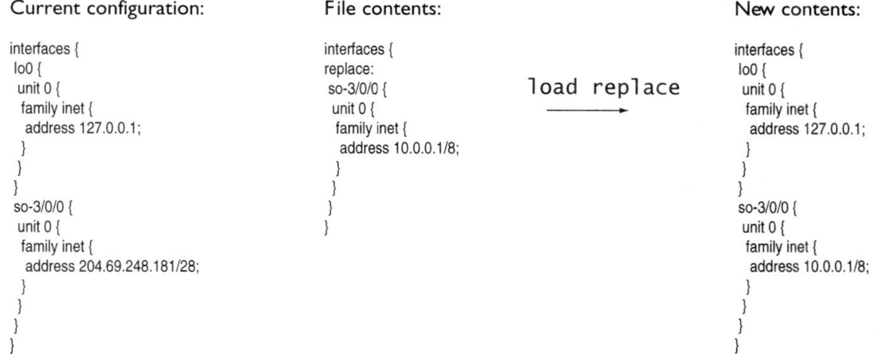

Figure 5.6 *Load a Configuration from a File Using Load Merge*

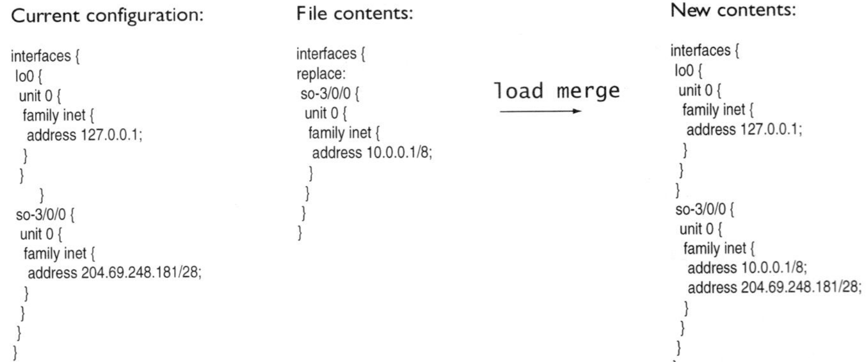

Returning to a Previously Committed Configuration

To return to the most recently committed configuration and load it into configuration mode without activating it, use the `rollback` configuration mode command:

```
[edit]
user@host# rollback
load complete
```

To activate the configuration that you loaded, use the `commit` command:

```
[edit]
user@host# rollback
load complete
[edit]
user@host# commit
```

To return to a configuration prior to the most recently committed one, include the number in the `rollback` command. *`number`* can be a number in the range 0 through 9. The most recently saved configuration is number 0 (which is the default configuration to which the system returns), and the oldest saved configuration is number 9.

```
[edit]
user@host# rollback number
load complete
```

For more information about configuration versions, see "Configuration Statements and Identifiers" on page 155.

To display previous configurations, including rollback number, date, time, the name of the user who committed changes, and the method of commit, use the `rollback ?` command.

```
[edit]
user@host# rollback ?
Possible completions:
<[Enter]> Execute this command
<number> Numeric argument
0 2001-02-27 12:52:10 PST by abc via cli
1 2001-02-26 14:47:42 PST by cde via cli
2 2001-02-14 21:55:45 PST by fgh via cli
3 2001-02-10 16:11:30 PST by hij via cli
4 2001-02-10 16:02:35 PST by klm via cli
| Pipe through a command
[edit]
```

Getting Help

In configuration mode, you can use the `help` command to display help based on a text string contained in a statement name. This command displays help for statements at the current hierarchy level and below.

```
help string
```

You can also display help based on a text string contained in a statement name using the `help topic` and `help reference` commands. The `help topic` command displays usage guidelines for the statement, whereas the `help reference` command displays summary information about the statement.

```
help topic string
help reference string
```

If you do not type an option for a statement that requires one, a message indicates the type of information expected. In this example, you need to type an area number to complete the command:

```
[edit]
user@host# set protocols ospf area<Enter>

syntax error, expecting <identifier>.
```

In this example, you need to type a value for the hello interval to complete the command:

```
[edit]
user@host# set protocols ospf area 45 interface so-0/0/0
        hello-interval<Enter>

syntax error, expecting <data>
```

If you have omitted a required statement at a particular hierarchy level, when you attempt to move from that hierarchy level or when you issue the show command in configuration mode, a message indicates which statement is missing. For example:

```
[edit protocols pim interface so-0/0/0]
user@host# top
Warning: missing mandatory statement: 'mode'
[edit]
user@host# show
protocols {
  pim {
    interface so-0/0/0 {
      priority 4;
      version 2;
      # Warning: missing mandatory statement(s): 'mode'
    }
  }
}
```

Adding Comments in a Configuration

You can include comments in a configuration to describe any statement in the configuration. You can add comments interactively in the configuration mode and by editing the text configuration file. When you add comments in configuration mode, they are associated with a statement at the current level. Each statement can have one single-line comment associated with it. Before you can associate a comment with a statement, the statement must exist. The comment is placed on the line preceding the statement.

To add comments to a configuration, use the annotate configuration mode command:

```
annotate statement "comment-string"
```

statement is the configuration statement to which you are attaching the comment; it must be at the current hierarchy level. *comment-string* is the text of the comment. The comment text can be any length, and you must type it on a single line. If the comment contains spaces, you must enclose it in quotation marks.

To delete an existing comment, specify an empty comment string:

```
annotate statement ""
```

When you edit the text configuration file to add comments, they can be one or more lines and must precede the statement they are associated with. You can format the comments in the following ways:

- Start the comment with a `/*` and end it with a `*/`. The comment text can be on a single line or can span multiple lines.
- Start the comment with a `#` and end it with a new line (carriage return).

If you add comments with the `annotate` command, you can view them within the configuration by using the `show` configuration mode command or the `show configuration` operational mode command.

System Management with SNMP

Simple Network Management Protocol (SNMP) enables the monitoring of network devices from a central location. The SNMP agent exchanges network management information with SNMP manager software running on a network management system (NMS), or host. The agent responds to requests for information and actions from the manager. The agent also controls access to the agent's management information base (MIB), the collection of objects that can be viewed or changed by the SNMP manager.

The SNMP manager collects information on network connectivity, activity, and events by polling managed devices. Communication between the agent and the manager occurs in one of the following forms:

- Get, GetBulk, and GetNext requests—The manager requests information from the agent; the agent returns the information in a Get response message.
- Set requests—The manager changes the value of a MIB object controlled by the agent; the agent indicates status in a Set response message.
- Traps notification—The agent sends traps to notify the manager of significant events that occur on the network device.

Management Information Base

A management information base, or MIB, is a hierarchy of information used to define managed objects in a network device. The MIB structure is based on a tree structure, which defines a grouping of objects into related sets. Each object in the MIB is associated with an object identifier (OID), which names the object. The "leaf" in the tree structure is the actual managed object instance, which represents a resource, event, or activity that occurs in your network device.

MIBs are either standard or enterprise-specific. Standard MIBs are created by the IETF and documented in various RFCs. Depending on the vendor, many standard MIBs are delivered with the NMS software. You can also download the standard MIBs from the IETF Web site, http://www.ietf.org, and compile them into your NMS if necessary.

For the contents of Juniper Networks enterprise MIBs, see the JUNOS technical documentation *Network Management.*

Enterprise MIBs are developed and supported by a specific equipment manufacturer. If your network contains devices that have enterprise MIBs, you must obtain them from the manufacturer and compile them into your network management software. Table 5.10 lists the enterprise MIBs supported in JUNOS 5.4.

Table 5.10 *JUNOS Enterprise MIBs*

MIB	Description
Chassis	Environmental monitoring (power supply state, board voltages, fans, temperatures, air flow) and inventory support for the chassis, SCB, SSB, SFM, FPCs, and PICs
MPLS	Support for the JUNOS MPLS implementation
Extensions to the interface MIB (RFC 1213)	Support for Juniper Networks PICs
Alarm	Juniper Networks outer chassis alarm
Firewall	Accessibility to firewall filter counters through SNMP queries; routers must have the Internet Processor II ASIC to perform firewall monitoring
Destination class usage	Monitoring of packet counts based on the ingress and egress points for traffic transiting your networks
Extensions to ping MIB (RFC 2925)	Support for the JUNOS `ping` command implementation
Extensions to traceroute MIB	Support for the JUNOS `traceroute` command implementation
ATM	Support for JUNOS ATM implementation
IPv6 and ICMPv6	Support for JUNOS implementation of IPv6 and ICMPv6
IPv4	Support for JUNOS implementation of IPv4
Extensions to RMON events and alarms MIB	Support for JUNOS implementation of RMON events and alarms
Extensions to LDP traps MIB	Support for JUNOS implementation of LDP traps. LDP traps support IPv4 standards only
CoS	Support for JUNOS CoS implementation
Reverse-path forwarding	Support for JUNOS RPF implementation
Source class usage	Support for JUNOS implementation of source class usage

SNMP Traps

You can also download the standard traps from the IETF Web site, http://www.ietf.org.

Traps report significant events occurring on a network device, most often errors or failures. SNMP traps are defined in either standard or enterprise MIBs. Standard traps are created by the IETF and documented in various RFCs. The standard traps are compiled into the network management software. Enterprise traps are developed and supported by a specific equipment manufacturer. If your network contains devices that have enterprise traps, you must obtain them from the manufacturer and compile them into your network management software. Table 5.11 and Table 5.12 summarize the SNMP traps supported by the JUNOS software.

For SNMP version 1, the JUNOS software supports the traps listed in Table 5.11 and Table 5.12. If you need SNMP version 1 traps for BGP and OSPF, you must translate into SMI version 1 format the BGP and OSPF SMI version 2 trap definitions from RFC 1657 (*Definitions of Managed Objects for the Fourth Version of the Border Gateway Protocol [BGP-4] using SMIv2*) and RFC 1850 (*OSPF Version 2 Management Information Base*). If you need SNMP version 2 traps for BGP and OSPF, you do not need to reformat the SMI version 2 trap definitions in RFCs 1657 and 1850; you use the definitions as they are documented in the RFCs.

Table 5.11 *Supported SNMP Version 1 Standard Traps*

Trap Name	Enterprise ID	Generic Trap Number	Specific Trap Number	Trap Category
Cold start	1.3.6.1.4.1.2636	0	0	Startup
Warm start	1.3.6.1.4.1.2636	1	0	Startup
Link down	1.3.6.1.4.1.2636	2	0	Link
Link up	1.3.6.1.4.1.2636	3	0	Link
Authentication failure	1.3.6.1.4.1.2636	4	0	Authentication
BGP established	1.3.6.1.2.1.15.7	6	1	Routing
BGP backward transition	1.3.6.1.2.1.15.7	6	2	Routing
OSPF virtual interface state change	1.3.6.1.2.1.14.16.2	6	1	Routing
OSPF neighbor state change	1.3.6.1.2.1.14.16.2	6	2	Routing

Table 5.11 *Supported SNMP Version 1 Standard Traps*

Trap Name	Enterprise ID	Generic Trap Number	Specific Trap Number	Trap Category
OSPF virtual neighbor state change	1.3.6.1.2.1.14.16.2	6	3	Routing
OSPF interface configuration error	1.3.6.1.2.1.14.16.2	6	4	Routing
OSPF virtual interface configuration error	1.3.6.1.2.1.14.16.2	6	5	Routing
OSPF interface authentication error	1.3.6.1.2.1.14.16.2	6	6	Routing
OSPF virtual interface authentication error	1.3.6.1.2.1.14.16.2	6	7	Routing
OSPF interface receiving bad packet	1.3.6.1.2.1.14.16.2	6	8	Routing
OSPF virtual interface receiving bad packet	1.3.6.1.2.1.14.16.2	6	9	Routing
OSPF transmit packet retransmitted	1.3.6.1.2.1.14.16.2	6	10	Routing
OSPF virtual interface transmit packet retransmitted	1.3.6.1.2.1.14.16.2	6	11	Routing
OSPF originating LSA (currently not supported)	1.3.6.1.2.1.14.16.2	6	12	Routing
OSPF maximum aged LSA	1.3.6.1.2.1.14.16.2	6	13	Routing
OSPF LSDB overflow (currently not supported)	1.3.6.1.2.1.14.16.2	6	14	Routing
OSPF LSDB approaching overflow (currently not supported)	1.3.6.1.2.1.14.16.2	6	15	Routing
OSPF interface state change	1.3.6.1.2.1.14.16.2	6	16	Routing
Ping probe failed	1.3.6.1.2.1.80.0	6	1	Remote-operations
Ping test failed	1.3.6.1.2.1.80.0	6	2	Remote-operations
Ping test completed	1.3.6.1.2.1.80.0	6	3	Remote-operations
Redundancy switchover	1.3.6.1.4.1.2636.4.1	6	4	Chassis

Table 5.12 *Supported SNMP Version 1 Enterprise Traps*

Trap Name	Enterprise ID	Generic Trap Number	Specific Trap Number	Trap Category
Power failure	1.3.6.1.4.1.2636.4.1	6	1	Chassis
Fan failure	1.3.6.1.4.1.2636.4.1	6	2	Chassis
Overtemperature	1.3.6.1.4.1.2636.4.1	6	3	Chassis
MPLS LSP up	1.3.6.1.4.1.2636.3.2.4	6	1	Routing
MPLS LSP down	1.3.6.1.4.1.2636.3.2.4	6	2	Routing
MPLS LSP change	1.3.6.1.4.1.2636.3.2.4	6	3	Routing

JUNOS SNMP Agent Features

The JUNOS SNMP agent software consists of an SNMP master agent that delegates all SNMP requests to subagents. Each subagent is responsible for the support of a specific set of MIBs. The JUNOS software supports SNMP version 1 and version 2c. SNMP version 1 is the initial implementation of SNMP that defines architecture and framework for SNMP. SNMP version 2c is the revised protocol, with improvements to performance and manager-to-manager communications. Specifically, SNMP version 2c implements community strings, which act as passwords when determining who, what, and how the SNMP clients can access the data in SNMP agent. The community string is contained in SNMP `Get`, `GetBulk`, `GetNext`, and `Set` requests. The agent might require a different community string for `Get`, `GetBulk`, and `GetNext` (read-only access) than for `Set` (read-write access). The JUNOS SNMP implementation supports `Set` requests only with the ping MIB. To use `Set` requests with the ping MIB, you must create a MIB view that includes the ping MIB subtree and include the `view` statement at the `[edit snmp community]` hierarchy level.

The JUNOS implementation of SNMP supports the IPv6 objects defined in RFC 2465, with the exception of `ipv6IfStatsTable`. The Juniper IPv6 MIB supports additional IPv6 and ICMPv6 statistics. The JUNOS SNMP agent software accepts IPv4 and IPv6 addresses for transport over IPv4 and IPv6.

System Logging for SNMP Traps

For more information about syslog severity levels, see the JUNOS technical documentation *Getting Started*.

When a trap condition occurs, whether the SNMP agent sends a trap to an NMS or not, the trap is logged if the system logging is configured to log an event with that syslog severity level. Table 5.13 lists the syslog severity levels for the SNMP traps supported by the JUNOS software. These levels cannot be changed.

Table 5.13 *System Logging Severity Levels for SNMP Traps*

Trap Type	Trap Name	Severity Level
Standard Traps	Cold start	critical
	Warm start	error
	Link down	warning
	Link up	info
	Authentication failure	notice
Enterprise Traps	Power failure	critical
	Fan failure	critical
	Over temperature	alert

Configuring SNMP

To configure SNMP, you include statements at the [edit snmp] hierarchy level of the configuration:

```
snmp {
  community community-name {
    authorization authorization;
    clients {
      address restrict;
    }
    view view-name;
  }
  contact contact;
  description description;
  interface [interface-name];
  location location;
  traceoptions {
    file files number size size;
    flag flag;
  }
```

```
    trap-group group-name {
      categories category;
      targets {
        address;
      }
      version version;
    }
    trap-options {
      agent-address outgoing-interface;
      source-address address;
    }
    view view-name;
      oid object-identifier (include | exclude);
    }
  }
```

By default, SNMP is disabled.

To configure the minimum requirements for SNMP, include the following statements. The community defined here as `public` grants read access to all MIB data to any client.

```
[edit]
snmp {
  community public;
}
```

Configuring System Information

You can specify an administrative contact, the location of each system being managed, and a description for each system being managed by SNMP. To configure a contact name, include the `contact` statement:

```
[edit snmp]
contact contact;
```

To configure a system location, include the `location` statement:

```
[edit snmp]
location location;
```

To configure a description, include the `description` statement:

```
[edit snmp]
description description;
```

Configuring the SNMP Community String

The SNMP community string defines the relationship between an SNMP server system and the client systems. This string acts like a password to control the clients' access to the server. To configure a community string, include the `community` statement:

If the community name contains spaces, enclose it in quotation marks (" ").

```
[edit snmp]
community name {
  authorization authorization;
  clients {
    default restrict;
    address restrict;
  }
  view view-name;
}
```

The default authorization level for a community is `read-only`. To allow `Set` requests within a community, you need to define that community as `authorization read-write`. (The JUNOS SNMP implementation supports `Set` requests only with the ping MIB.) For `Set` requests, you also need to include which specific MIB objects are accessible with read-write privileges using the `view` statement. The default view includes all supported MIB objects that are accessible with read-only privileges; no MIB objects are accessible with read-write privileges.

The `clients` statement lists the IP addresses of the `clients` (community members) that are allowed to use this community. If no `clients` statement is present, all clients are allowed. For the address, you must specify an address, not a hostname. Include the `default restrict` statement to deny access to all SNMP clients for which access is not explicitly granted. We recommend that you always include the `default restrict` statement to limit SNMP client access to the local router.

Configuring SNMP Trap Options

Some carriers have more than one trap receiver that forwards traps to a central NMS. This allows for more than one path for SNMP traps from a router to the central NMS through different trap receivers. A router can be configured to send the same copy of each SNMP trap to each trap receiver configured in the trap group.

By default, the source address in the IP header of each SNMP trap packet is set to the address of the outgoing interface. When a trap receiver forwards the packet to the central NMS, the source address is preserved. The central NMS, looking only at the source address of each SNMP trap packet, assumes that each SNMP trap comes from a different source. In reality, the SNMP traps came from the same router, but each left the router through a different outgoing interface.

SNMP trap options allow the NMS to recognize duplicate traps and to distinguish version 1 SNMP traps based on the outgoing interface.

Using SNMP trap options, you can set the source address of each SNMP trap packet sent by the router to a single address regardless of the outgoing interface. In addition, you can set the agent address of the SNMP version 1 traps.

You can configure the source address and the agent address of trap packets. The agent address is available only in the SNMP version 1 trap packets (see RFC 1157). Currently, the only value that can be specified for the source address is `lo0`, which indicates that the source address of the SNMP trap packets is set to the lowest loopback address configured at the `lo0`interface.

To enable and configure the source address of SNMP traps, include the `source-address` statement:

```
[edit snmp]
trap-options {
  source-address address;
}
```

To configure the loopback address, include the `address` statement:

```
[edit interfaces]
lo0 {
  unit 0 {
    family inet {
      address ip-address;
    }
  }
}
```

By default, the agent address for SNMP traps is disabled. To set the agent address, include the `agent-address` statement. Currently, the only option available is the address of the outgoing interface.

```
[edit snmp]
trap-options {
  agent-address outgoing-interface;
}
```

You can create and name a group of one or more types of SNMP trap and then define which systems receive the group of SNMP traps. The trap group must be configured for SNMP traps to be sent. To create an SNMP trap group, include the `trap-group` statement:

```
[edit snmp]
trap-group group-name {
  categories category;
  targets {
    address;
  }
  version version;
}
```

The trap group name can be any string and is embedded in SNMP trap notification packets as one variable binding (varbind) known as the community name. Each trap group you define must have a name and one or more targets, which are the systems that receive the SNMP traps. Specify the targets by address, not by hostname. Specify the types of traps the trap group can receive in the `categories` statement.

For information about which traps belong to which category, see the JUNOS *Network Management* technical documentation.

The `version` statement specifies the SNMP version of the traps sent to targets of the trap group. If you specify version 1 only, SNMP version 1 traps are sent. If you specify version 2 only, SNMP version 2 traps are sent. If all is specified, both an SNMP version 1 and an SNMP version 2 trap are sent for every trap condition.

Configuring the Interfaces on Which SNMP Requests Are Accepted

By default, all router interfaces have SNMP access privileges. To limit the access through certain interfaces only, include the `interface` statement. Specify the names of any logical or physical interfaces that should have SNMP access privileges. Any SNMP requests entering the router from interfaces not listed are discarded.

```
[edit snmp]
interface [interface-names];
```

Configuring MIB Views

By default, an SNMP community grants read access and denies write access to all supported MIB objects (even communities configured as `authorization read-write`). To restrict or grant read or write access to a set of MIB objects, you must configure a MIB view and associate the views with a community. To configure MIB views, include the `view` statement:

```
[edit snmp]
view view-name {
  oid object-identifier (include | exclude);
}
```

The `view` statement defines a MIB view and identifies a group of MIB objects. Each MIB object of a view has a common OID prefix. Each object identifier represents a subtree of the MIB object hierarchy.

To associate a MIB view with a community, include the `view` statement:

```
[edit snmp community community-name]
view view-name;
```

Tracing SNMP Activity

To trace SNMP activity, include the `traceoptions` statement:

```
[edit snmp]
traceoptions {
  file files number size size;
  flag flag;
}
```

The output of the tracing operations is placed into log files in the `/var/log` directory. Each of these log files is named after the SNMP agent that generates it. Currently, the following log files are created in the `/var/log` directory when the `traceoptions` statement is used:

- `chassisd`
- `craftd`
- `ilmid`
- `mib2d`
- `rmopd`
- `serviced`
- `snmpd`

You can use the `file` statement to control log file generation. The `size` statement limits the size (in kilobytes) of each log file before it is closed, compressed, and a new file opened in its place. The `file` statement limits the total number of log files archived for each SNMP agent.

You can specify one or more of the following values for the `flag` option:

- `all`—All SNMP events
- `interface-stats`—Physical and logical interface statistics
- `pdu`—SNMP request and response packets
- `protocol-timeouts`—SNMP response timeouts
- `routing-socket`—Routing socket calls
- `subagent`—Subagent restarts
- `timer`—Internal timer events
- `varbind-error`—Variable-binding errors

CHAPTER 6

Interfaces and Class of Service

Routers typically contain several types of interfaces suited to various functions. For the interfaces on a router to function, you must configure them, specifying properties such as the interface location (that is, which slot the FPC is installed in and which location on the FPC the PIC is installed in), the interface type (such as SONET or ATM), encapsulation, and interface-specific properties.

You can configure the interfaces that are currently present in the router, and you can also configure interfaces that you might be adding in the future. When the hardware corresponding to a configured interface is installed in the router, the JUNOS software detects its presence and applies the appropriate configuration to it.

JUNOS Interface Terminology

The router has two types of interfaces, *permanent interfaces*, which are always present in the router, and *transient interfaces*, which can be inserted into and removed from the router depending on your network configuration needs.

Each router has two permanent interfaces. The *management Ethernet interface* provides an out-of-band method for connecting to the router. You can connect to the management interface over the network using utilities such as ssh and Telnet. SNMP can use the management interface to gather statistics from the router. The *internal Ethernet interface* connects the Routing Engine (the portion of the router running the JUNOS Internet routing software) to the System Control Board (SCB), the System and Switch Board (SSB), the Forwarding Engine Board (FEB), or the System and Forwarding Module (SFM), depending on router model, which is part of the Packet Forwarding Engine. The router uses this interface as the main communications link between the JUNOS software and the components of the Packet Forwarding Engine.

Each router also has two serial ports, labeled *console* and *auxiliary*, for connecting tty-type terminals to the router using standard PC-type tty cables. Although these ports are not network interfaces, they do provide access to the router.

The router contains slots for installing FPC boards, and almost all FPCs can accommodate up to four PICs, which provide the actual physical interfaces to the network. These physical interfaces are the router's transient interfaces. They are referred to as transient because you can hot-swap an FPC or its PICs at any time. You can insert any FPC into any of the router's slots, and you can generally place any combination of PICs in any location on an FPC. You must configure each of the transient interfaces based on the slot in which the FPC is installed, the location in which the PIC is installed, and for some PICs, the port to which you are connecting. You can configure the interfaces on PICs that are already installed in the router as well as interfaces on PICs that you plan to install later. The JUNOS software detects which interfaces are actually present, so when the software activates its configuration, it activates only present interfaces and retains the configuration information for the interfaces that are not present. When the JUNOS software detects that an FPC containing PICs has been inserted into the router, the software activates the configuration for those interfaces.

Table 6.1 lists the interface types supported by the JUNOS software and each interface's software name.

Table 6.1 *Interface Types Supported by the JUNOS Software*

Interface Groups	Interface Type	Interface Name in Configuration
ATM	ATM	`at`
Channelized	Channelized DS-3 to DS-0 Channelized DS-3 to DS-1 Channelized E1 Channelized OC3 to T1 Channelized OC-12 to DS-3 Channelized STM-1 to E1	

DS-3, T1, T3, E1, E3	DS-3
	E1
	E3
	T1
	T3
		`ds`
		`e1`
		`e3`
		`t1`
		`t3`

Ethernet	Aggregated Ethernet
	Fast Ethernet
	Gigabit Ethernet
	10 Gigabit Ethernet
	Internal Ethernet
	Management Ethernet
		`ae`
		`fe`
		`ge`
		`ge`
		`fxp`
		`fxp`

Multilink	Frame Relay PPP	`ml` `ml`

Table 6.1 *Interface Types Supported by the JUNOS Software*

Interface Groups	Interface Type	Interface Name in Configuration
SONET/SDH	Aggregated SONET/SDH SONET/SDH	`as` `so`

Other	Encryption
	GRE tunnel
	IP-IP tunnel
	Loopback
		`es`
		`gr`
		`ip`
		`lo`

When you configure an interface, you give it a name that effectively specifies the properties for a physical interface descriptor. In most cases, the physical interface descriptor corresponds to a single physical device and consists of the interface name, which defines the media type, the slot in which the FPC is located, the location on the FPC in which the PIC is installed, the PIC port, and, optionally, the interface's channel and logical unit numbers. The interface name is represented by a physical part, a logical part, and a channel part in the following format:

```
physical<:channel>.logical
```

The physical part of an interface name identifies the physical device, which corresponds to a single physical network connector. This part of the interface name has the following format:

```
type-fpc/pic/port
```

`fpc` identifies the number of the FPC card on which the physical interface is located. `pic` identifies the number of the PIC card on which the physical interface is located. `port` identifies a specific port on a PIC.

Each physical interface descriptor can contain one or more logical interface descriptors. These allow you to map one or more logical (or virtual) interfaces to a single physical device. The logical unit part of the interface name corresponds to the logical unit number, which can be a number in the range 0 through 16,384.

The channel identifier part of the interface name is required only on channelized interfaces. Channel 0 identifies the first channelized interface. A nonconcatenated (that is, channelized) SONET/SDH OC-48 interface has four OC-12 channels, numbered 0 through 3. A Channelized OC-12 interface has twelve DS-3 channels, numbered 0 through 11.

There is a separator of some kind between each element of an interface name. In the physical part of the name, a hyphen (-) separates the media type from the FPC number, and a slash separates the FPC, PIC, and port numbers. In the virtual part of the name, a period (.) separates the channel and logical unit numbers. A colon (:) separates the physical and virtual parts of the interface name.

Configuring Interfaces on the Router

From the point of view of the JUNOS software, interface properties belong to the following groups:

- Physical interface properties, which are properties of the media type that apply to the interface device itself. You configure physical interface properties at the `[edit interfaces` *`interface-name`*`]` hierarchy level.
- Logical interface properties, which include the protocol family and other properties that vary by PIC and encapsulation type, including the IP address of the interface, whether the interface supports multicast traffic, DLCIs, VCIs and VPIs, and traffic shaping. You configure logical interface properties at the `[edit interfaces` *`interface-name`* `unit` *`logical-unit-number`*`]` hierarchy level.
- Family interface properties, which define the protocols supported on the interface. You configure these properties at the `[edit interfaces` *`interface-name`* `unit` *`logical-unit-number`* `family` *`family`*`]` hierarchy level.
- Address interface properties, which configure the IP and other addresses associated with the interface. You configure these properties at the `[edit interfaces` *`interface-name`* `unit` *`logical-unit-number`* `address` *`address`*`]` hierarchy level.

This section describes some of the more important physical, logical, family, and address interface properties. The remainder of this chapter describes how to configure the interfaces corresponding to specific PIC types.

Configuring Physical Interface Properties

For each network media type, the software driver for that media sets reasonable default values for general interface properties, such as the interface's MTU size, receive and transmit leaky bucket properties, link operational mode, and clock source. To modify any of the default general interface properties, include one or more of the following statements:

```
[edit interfaces interface-name]
access-profile name;
clocking clock-source;
dce;
disable;
description text;
encapsulation type;
hold-time up milliseconds down milliseconds;
keepalives <down-count number> <interval seconds>
  <up-count number>;
link-mode mode;
mac mac-address;
mtu bytes;
no-keepalives;
no-traps;
ppp-options {
  chap {
    access-profile name;
    local-name name;
    passive;
  }
}
receive-bucket {
  overflow (tag | discard);
  rate percentage;
  threshold number;
}
speed (10m | 100m);
transmit-bucket {
  overflow (discard);
  rate percentage;
  threshold number;
}
```

To configure the interface name, specify it:

```
[edit interfaces]
interface-name {
  ...
}
```

You can include a text description of each physical interface in the configuration file. Any descriptive text you include is displayed in the output of the `show interfaces` commands but has no impact on the interface's configuration. To add a text description, include the `description` statement:

```
[edit interfaces interface-name]
description text;
```

The default media MTU size used on a physical interface depends on the encapsulation being used on that interface. Table 6.2, Table 6.3, and Table 6.4 list the media MTU size by interface type, whereas Table 6.5 lists the encapsulation overhead by encapsulation type. Note that the physical MTU for Ethernet interfaces does not include the 4-byte FCS field of the Ethernet frame.

Table 6.2 *Media MTU Sizes by Interface Type for M5, M10, M20, and M40 Routers*

Interface Type	Default Media MTU (Bytes)	Maximum MTU (Bytes)	Default IP Protocol MTU (Bytes)
ATM	4,482	9,192	4,470
E1/T1	1,504	9,192	1,500
E3/T3	4,474	9,192	4,470
Fast Ethernet	1,514	9,192	1,500 (IPv4) 1,497 (ISO)
Gigabit Ethernet	1,514	9,192	1,500 (IPv4) 1,497 (ISO)
SONET/SDH	4,474	9,192	4,470

Table 6.3 *Media MTU Sizes by Interface Type for M40e and M160 Routers*

Interface Type	Default Media MTU (Bytes)	Maximum MTU (Bytes)	Default IP Protocol MTU (Bytes)
ATM	4,482	9,192	4,470
E1/T1	1,504	4,500	1,500
E3/T3	4,474	4,500	4,470
Fast Ethernet	1,514	4,500	1,500 (IPv4) 1,497 (ISO)

Table 6.3 *Media MTU Sizes by Interface Type for M40e and M160 Routers*

Interface Type	Default Media MTU (Bytes)	Maximum MTU (Bytes)	Default IP Protocol MTU (Bytes)
Gigabit Ethernet	1,514	9,192 (1- or 2-port PICs) 4,500 (4-port PICs)	1,500 (IPv4) 1,497 (ISO)
SONET/SDH	4,474	4,500	4,470

Table 6.4 *Media MTU Sizes by Interface Type for T-series Platforms*

Interface Type	Default Media MTU (Bytes)	Maximum MTU (Bytes)	Default IP Protocol MTU (Bytes)
48-port Fast Ethernet	1,514	1,532	1,500 (IPv4) 1,497 (ISO)
Gigabit Ethernet	1,514		1,500 (IPv4) 1,497 (ISO)
1- or 2-port		9,192	
4-port		4,500	
10-gigabit		9,192	
SONET/SDH	4,474	9,192	4,470

Table 6.5 *Encapsulation Overhead by Encapsulation Type*

Interface Encapsulation	Encapsulation Overhead (Bytes)
ATM PVC	12
Cisco HDLC	4
Ethernet Version 2	14
Ethernet 802.3	17
802.1Q/Ethernet Version 2	18
802.1Q/Ethernet 802.3	21
Ethernet SNAP	22
802.1Q/Ethernet SNAP	26
Frame Relay	4
Point-to-Point Protocol	4

The default media MTU is calculated as follows:

Default media MTU = Default IP MTU + encapsulation overhead

When you are configuring point-to-point connections, the MTU sizes on both sides of the connections must be the same. Also, when you are configuring point-to-multipoint connections, all interfaces in the subnet must use the same MTU size. The actual frames transmitted also contain cyclic redundancy check (CRC) bits, which are not part of the media MTU. For example, the media MTU for a Gigabit Ethernet interface is specified as 1,500 bytes, but the largest possible frame size is actually 1,504 bytes; you need to consider the extra bits in calculations of MTUs for interoperability.

To modify the default media MTU size for a physical interface, include the `mtu` statement:

```
[edit interfaces interface-name]
mtu bytes;
```

For more information about protocol MTUs, see page 205.

If you change the size of the media MTU, you must ensure that the size is equal to or greater than the sum of the protocol MTU and the encapsulation overhead. You configure the protocol MTU by including the `mtu` statement at the `[edit interfaces interface-name unit logical-unit-number family family]` hierarchy level.

Point-to-Point Protocol (PPP) encapsulation is the default encapsulation type for physical interfaces. You need not configure encapsulation for any physical interfaces that support PPP encapsulation. If you do not configure encapsulation, PPP is used by default. For physical interfaces that do not support PPP encapsulation, you must configure an encapsulation to use for packets transmitted on the interface. You can optionally configure an encapsulation on a logical interface, which is the encapsulation used within certain packet types.

The physical interface encapsulation can be one of the following:

Defined in RFC 1331, *The Point-to-Point Protocol (PPP) for the Transmission of Multiprotocol Datagrams over Point-to-Point Links.*

- Point-to-Point Protocol (PPP)—PPP is the default encapsulation type for physical interfaces. E1, E3, SONET, T1, and T3 interfaces can use PPP encapsulation. Two related versions are supported:
  - Circuit cross-connect (CCC) version (`ppp-ccc`)—The logical interfaces do not require an `encapsulation` statement, but they cannot have families.

- Translational cross-connect (TCC) version (`ppp-tcc`)—Similar to CCC and having the same configuration restrictions, but used for circuits with different media on either side of the connection.

- ATM cell relay—Connects two remote virtual circuits or ATM physical interfaces with a label-switched path (LSP). Traffic on the circuit is ATM cells.

Defined in RFC 1483, *Multiprotocol Encapsulation over ATM Adaptation Layer 5.*

- ATM PVC—When you configure physical ATM interfaces with ATM PVC encapsulation, you can configure the logical interfaces with any ATM encapsulation.
- Cisco HDLC—E1, E3, SONET, T1, and T3 interfaces can use Cisco HDLC encapsulation. Two related versions are supported:
  - CCC version (`cisco-hdlc-ccc`)—The logical interfaces do not require an `encapsulation` statement, but they cannot have families.
  - TCC version (`cisco-hdlc-tcc`)—Similar to CCC and having the same configuration restrictions, but used for circuits with different media on either side of the connection.
- Ethernet circuit cross-connect (CCC)—Untagged Ethernet interfaces can use Ethernet CCC encapsulation. This encapsulation type is supported only on the four-port Fast Ethernet PIC.

Defined in RFC 1490, *Multiprotocol Interconnect over Frame Relay.*

- Frame Relay—E1, E3, SONET, T1, and T3 interfaces can use Frame Relay encapsulation. Two related versions are supported:
  - CCC version (`frame-relay-ccc`)—The same as standard Frame Relay for DLCIs 0 through 511. DLCIs 512 through 1,022 are dedicated to CCC, and the logical interface must also use Frame Relay CCC encapsulation.
  - TCC version (`frame-relay-tcc`)—Similar to Frame Relay CCC and having the same configuration restrictions, but used for circuits with different media on either side of the connection.
- VLAN circuit cross-connect (CCC)—Ethernet interfaces with Virtual Local Area Network (VLAN) tagging enabled can use VLAN CCC encapsulation.

To configure the encapsulation on a physical interface, include the `encapsulation` statement:

```
[edit interfaces interface-name]
encapsulation (atm-ccc-cell-relay | atm-pvc | cisco-hdlc |
    cisco-hdlc-ccc | cisco-hdlc-tcc | ethernet-ccc |
    frame-relay | frame-relay-ccc | frame-relay-tcc | ppp
    | ppp-ccc | ppp-tcc | vlan-ccc);
```

When you configure a point-to-point encapsulation (such as PPP or Cisco HDLC) on a physical interface, the physical interface can have only one logical interface (that is, only one `unit` statement) associated with it. When you configure a multipoint encapsulation (such as Frame Relay), the physical interface can have multiple logical units, and the units can be either point-to-point or multipoint.

Ethernet interfaces in VLAN mode can have multiple logical interfaces, but in CCC mode VLAN IDs from 0 through 511 are reserved for normal VLANs, and VLAN IDs from 512 through 4,095 are reserved for CCC VLANs.

When you configure a TCC encapsulation, some modifications are needed to handle VPN connections over unlike Layer 2 links and terminate the Layer 2 protocol locally. The router performs the following media-specific changes:

- ATM—Operation, Administration, and Maintenance (OAM) and Interim Local Management Interface (ILMI) processing is terminated at the router. Cell relay is not supported. The JUNOS software strips all ATM encapsulation data from incoming frames before forwarding them. For output, the next hop is changed to ATM encapsulation.
- Cisco HDLC TCC—Keepalive processing is terminated on the router. The JUNOS software strips all Cisco HDLC encapsulation data from incoming frames before forwarding them. For output, the next hop is changed to Cisco HDLC encapsulation.
- Frame Relay TCC—All Local Management Interface (LMI) processing is terminated on the router. The JUNOS software strips all Frame Relay encapsulation data from incoming frames before forwarding them. For output, the next hop is changed to Frame Relay encapsulation.
- PPP TCC—Both Link Control Protocol (LCP) and Network Control Protocol (NCP) are terminated on the router. Internet Protocol Control Protocol (IPCP) IP address negotiation is not supported. The JUNOS software strips all PPP encapsulation data

from incoming frames before forwarding them. For output, the next hop is changed to PPP encapsulation.

The ATM encapsulations are defined in RFC 1483, *Multiprotocol Encapsulation over ATM Adaptation Layer 5.*

Generally, you configure an interface's encapsulation at the `[edit interfaces interface-name]` hierarchy level. However, for some encapsulation types, such as Frame Relay, ATM, and Ethernet VLAN, you also can configure the encapsulation type that is used inside the Frame Relay, ATM, or VLAN circuit itself. To do this, include the `encapsulation` statement when configuring the logical interface:

```
[edit interfaces interface-name unit logical-unit-number]
encapsulation (atm-ccc-cell-relay | atm-nlpid | atm-cisco-
    nlpid | atm-snap | atm-vc-mux | atm-ccc-vc-mux |
    frame-relay-ccc | multilink-framerelay | multilink-ppp
    | vlan-ccc);
```

With the `atm-nlpid`, `atm-cisco-nlpid`, and `atm-vc-mux` encapsulations, you can configure the family `inet` only. With the circuit cross-connect (CCC) encapsulations, you cannot configure a family on the logical interface. A logical interface cannot have `frame-relay-ccc` encapsulation unless the physical device also has `frame-relay-ccc` encapsulation. In addition, you must assign this logical interface a DLCI in the range 512 through 1,022 and configure it as point-to-point.

A logical interface cannot have `vlan-ccc` encapsulation unless the physical device also has `vlan-ccc` encapsulation. You must also assign this logical interface a VLAN ID in the range 512 through 1,023; if the VLAN ID is 511 or lower, it is subject to the normal destination filter lookups in addition to source address filtering.

You can create an ATM cell relay circuit by configuring an entire ATM physical device or an individual virtual circuit (VC). When you configure an entire device, only cell relay encapsulation is allowed on the logical interfaces; you control the number and location of VCs using the `atm-options` statement. Allowed VCs on both ingress and egress ATM interfaces should be the same. You can define a maximum of 4,090 VCs per interface.

If you are dedicating the entire device to a cell relay circuit, include the `allow_any_vci` statement under `unit 0` as shown in the following example. After you enter this statement, you cannot configure other logical interfaces in the same physical interface.

```
[edit interfaces at-1/2/0]
encapsulation atm-ccc-cell-relay;
```

```
atm-options {
  vpi 0 maximum-vcs 256;
}
unit 0 {
  point-to-point;
  encapsulation atm-ccc-cell-relay;
  allow_any_vci;
}
```

Alternatively, to configure an individual VC on a specific logical interface, include statements similar to the following example:

```
[edit interfaces at-1/1/0]
encapsulation atm-ccc-cell-relay;
atm-options {
  vpi 0 maximum-vcs 256;
}
unit 120 {
  encapsulation atm-ccc-cell-relay;
  vci 0.120;
}
```

When you use ATM CCC cell relay encapsulation, you must configure both the physical and logical encapsulation with `atm-ccc-cell-relay` encapsulation. You cannot mix different logical encapsulation types on an interface that you have configured with ATM CCC cell relay physical encapsulation.

You can configure interfaces to support PPP Challenge Handshake Authentication Protocol (CHAP), as defined in RFC 1994. When CHAP is enabled, an interface with PPP encapsulation can authenticate its peer and can be authenticated by its peer. By default, PPP CHAP is disabled. If CHAP is not explicitly enabled, the interface makes no CHAP challenges and denies all incoming CHAP challenges. To enable CHAP on links with PPP encapsulation, you must create a global mapping of link names and authentication data associated with those links, and you must create a per-interface configuration.

See RFC 1994, *PPP Challenge Handshake Authentication Protocol (CHAP).*

To create a global mapping of link names and authentication data, you configure access profiles using statements in the `access` hierarchy; The per-interface configuration includes a reference to an access profile. When a given interface receives CHAP challenges and responses, the named access profile in the packet is used to look up the shared secret.

To configure PPP CHAP on an interface with PPP encapsulation, include the chap statement:

```
[edit interfaces interface-name ppp-options]
chap {
  access-profile name;
  local-name name;
  passive;
}
```

The CHAP authentication method depends on a "secret" known only to the authenticator and that peer. The secret is not sent over the link. An access profile is a map between peer names (or "clients") and the secrets associated with their respective links. When an interface receives CHAP challenges and responses, the value of the access profile is extracted from the packets. This value is the identity of the peer for a given interface. To assign an access profile to an interface, include the access-profile statement:

```
[edit interfaces interface-name ppp-options chap]
access-profile name;
```

You can configure the value sent in CHAP challenge and response packets on a per-interface basis. By default, each interface uses the router's system hostname as the name sent in CHAP challenge and response packets. To configure the name sent in CHAP challenge and response packets, include the local-name statement:

```
[edit interfaces interface-name ppp-options chap]
local-name name;
```

By default, when the chap statement is configured, the interface always challenges its peer and responds to challenges from its peer. You can configure the interface not to challenge its peer, and only respond when challenged. To configure the interface not to challenge its peer, include the passive statement:

```
[edit interfaces interface-name ppp-options chap]
passive;
```

By default, SNMP notifications are sent when the interface or connection state changes. To disable this notification on the physical interface, include the no-traps statement:

```
[edit interfaces interface-name]
no-traps;
```

Configuring Logical Interface Properties

To configure logical interface properties, include the `unit` statement and one or more of the statements in its hierarchy:

```
[edit interfaces interface-name]
unit logical-unit-number {
  access-profile name;
  disable;
  dlci dlci-identifier;
  drop-timeout milliseconds;
  encapsulation type;
  fragment-threshold bytes;
  inverse-arp;
  mrru bytes;
  multicast-dlci dlci-identifier;
  multicast-vci vpi-identifier.vci-identifier;
  multipoint;
  no-traps;
  oam-liveness {
    up-count cells;
    down-count cells;
  }
  oam-period (disable | seconds);
  point-to-point;
  shaping {
    (cbr rate | vbr peak rate sustained rate burst length);
    queue-length number;
  }
  short-sequence;
  tunnel {
    source source-address;
    destination destination-address;
    routing-instance {
    destination routing-instance-name;
    }
    ttl number;
  }
  vci vpi-identifier.vci-identifier;
  vlan-id number;
}
```

Each logical interface must have a logical unit number. The logical unit number corresponds to the logical unit part of the interface name. PPP and Cisco HDLC encapsulations support only a single logical interface, whose logical unit number must be 0. Frame Relay and ATM encapsulations support multiple logical interfaces, so you can configure one or more logical unit numbers. You specify the logical unit number in the `unit` statement. The logical unit number can range from 0 through 16,384.

```
[edit interfaces]
interface-name {
  unit 0 {
    ...
  }
}
```

By default, all interfaces are assumed to be point-to-point connections. You must ensure that the MTU sizes on both sides of the connection are the same. Optionally, you can explicitly configure an interface to be a point-to-point connection by including the `point-to-point` statement:

```
[edit interfaces interface-name unit logical-unit-number]
point-to-point;
```

To configure an interface to be a multipoint connection, include the `multipoint` statement:

```
[edit interfaces interface-name unit logical-unit-number]
multipoint;
```

By default, SNMP notifications are sent when the state of an interface or a connection changes. To disable these notifications on the logical interface, include the `no-traps` statement:

```
[edit interfaces interface-name unit logical-unit-number]
no-traps;
```

Configuring Family and Address Interface Properties

For each logical interface, you must configure one or more protocol families, and you can configure interface address properties. To do this, include one or more of the following statements:

```
[edit interfaces interface-name unit logical-unit-number]
family family {
  bundle ml-fpc/pic/port;
  destination-class-usage;
  filter {
    input filter-name;
    output filter-name;
    group filter-group-number;
  }
```

```
  ipsec-sa sa-name;
  mtu bytes;
  multicasts-only;
  no-redirects;
  primary;
  address address {
    arp ip-address (mac | multicast-mac) mac-address
<publish>;
    destination destination-address;
    broadcast address;
    multipoint-destination destination-address (dlci dlci-
identifier | vci vci-identifier);
    multipoint-destination destination-address {
      inverse-arp;
      oam-liveness {
        up-count cells;
        down-count cells;
      }
      oam-period seconds;
      shaping {
        (cbr rate | vbr peak rate sustained rate burst
length);
        queue-length number;
      }
      vci vpi-identifier.vci-identifier;
    }
    preferred;
    primary;
    vrrp-group group-number {
      virtual-address [addresses];
      priority number;
      (accept-data | no-accept-data);
      advertise-interval seconds;
      authentication-type authentication;
      authentication-key key;
      (preempt | no-preempt);
      track {
        interface interface-name priority-cost cost;
      }
    }
  }
}
```

To configure the logical interface's protocol family, include the `family` statement, specifying the selected family. To configure more than one protocol family on a logical interface, include multiple `family` statements. Following is the minimum configuration:

```
[edit interfaces interface-name unit logical-unit-number]
family family {
```

```
    mtu size;
    multicasts-only;
    no-redirects;
    primary;
    address address {
      destination address;
      broadcast address;
      primary;
      preferred;
    }
  }
```

For each logical interface, you can configure one or more of the following protocol families to run on the interface:

- `inet`—IP (Internet Protocol). You must configure this protocol family for the logical interface to support IP protocol traffic, including OSPF, BGP, and ICMP.
- `iso`—ISO. You must configure this protocol family for the logical interface to support IS-IS traffic.
- `mlfr`—Multilink Frame Relay (MLFR). You must configure this protocol (or MLPPP) for the logical interface to support multilink bundling.
- `multilink-ppp`—Multilink Point-to-Point Protocol (MLPPP). You must configure this protocol (or MLFR) for the logical interface to support multilink bundling.
- `mpls`—Multiprotocol Label Switching (MPLS). You must configure this protocol family for the logical interface to participate in an MPLS path.
- `tnp`—Trivial Network Protocol (TNP). This protocol is used to communicate between the Routing Engine and the System Control Board (SCB), System and Switch Board (SSB), Forwarding Engine Board (FEB), or System and Forwarding Module (SFM), depending on router model, in the router's Packet Forwarding Engine. The JUNOS software automatically configures this protocol family on the router's internal interfaces.

You assign an address to an interface by specifying the address in the `address` statement when configuring the protocol family. For the `inet` family, you configure the interface's IP address. For the `iso` family, you configure an address for the loopback interface. For the `mpls` and `tnp` families, you never configure an address. The JUNOS software also supports IS-IS addresses on interfaces other than `lo0`, such as ATM, Fast Ethernet, SONET/SDH, T1, and T3 interfaces. This can be useful when you are running multiple instances of IS-IS.

To configure the address of the remote side of the connection (for point-to-point interfaces only), include the `destination` statement.

To configure the broadcast address for the interface's subnet, include the `broadcast` statement. This statement applies only to Ethernet interfaces, such as the management interface `fxp0`, the Fast Ethernet interface, and the Gigabit Ethernet interface.

The router has a default address and a primary interface, and interfaces have primary and preferred addresses. The *default address* of the router is used as the source address on unnumbered interfaces. The routing protocol process tries to pick the default address as the router ID, which is used by protocols, including OSPF and IBGP. The *primary interface* for the router is the interface that packets go out when no interface name is specified and when the destination address does not imply a particular outgoing interface. An interface's *primary address* is used by default as the local address for broadcast and multicast packets sourced locally and sent out the interface. An interface's *preferred address* is the default local address used for packets sourced by the local router to destinations on the subnet.

The default address of the router is chosen using the following sequence:

1. The primary address on the loopback interface `lo0` that is not `127.0.0.1` is used.
2. Otherwise, the primary address on the primary interface is used.

The *primary interface* for the router has the following characteristics:

- It is the interface that packets go out when you type a command such as `ping 255.255.255.255`—that is, a command that does not include an interface name (there is no `interface` *`type`*`-0/0/0.0` statement) and where the destination address does not imply any particular outgoing interface.
- It is the interface on which multicast applications running locally on the router, such as SAP, do group joins by default.
- It is the interface from which the default local address is derived for packets sourced out an unnumbered interface if there are no non-`127` addresses configured on the loopback interface, `lo0`.

By default, the multicast-capable interface with the lowest index address is chosen as the primary interface. If there is no such interface, the point-to-point interface with the lowest index address is chosen. Otherwise, any interface with an address could be picked. In practice, this means that the `fxp0` interface is picked by default. To configure a different interface to be the primary interface, include the `primary` statement:

```
[edit interfaces interface-name unit logical-unit-number
family family]
primary;
```

The *primary address* on an interface is the address that is used by default as the local address for broadcast and multicast packets sourced locally and sent out the interface. For example, the local address in the packets sent by a `ping interface so-0/0/0.0 255.255.255.255` command is the primary address on interface `so-0/0/0.0`. The primary address also can be useful for selecting the local address used for packets sent out unnumbered interfaces when multiple non-`127` addresses are configured on the loopback interface, `lo0`. By default, the primary address on an interface is selected as the numerically lowest local address configured on the interface. To set a different primary address, include the `primary` statement:

```
[edit interfaces interface-name unit logical-unit-number
family family address address]
primary;
```

The *preferred address* on an interface is the default local address used for packets sourced by the local router to destinations on the subnet. By default, the numerically lowest local address is chosen. For example, if the addresses `128.100.1.1/24`, `128.100.1.2/24`, and `128.100.1.3/24` are configured on the same interface, the preferred address on the subnet (by default, `128.100.1.1`) would be used as a local address when you issue a `ping 128.100.1.5` command. To set a different preferred address for the subnet, include the `preferred` statement:

```
[edit interfaces interface-name unit logical-unit-number
family family address address]
preferred;
```

When you need to conserve IP addresses, you can configure unnumbered interfaces. To do this, configure the protocol family, but do not include the `address` statement:

```
[edit interfaces interface-name unit logical-unit-number]
family family;
```

When configuring unnumbered interfaces, you must ensure that a source address is configured on some interface in the router. This address is the default address. We recommend that you do this by assigning an address to the loopback interface (lo0). If you configure an address (other than a martian) on the lo0 interface, that address is always the default address, which is preferable because the loopback interface is independent of any physical interfaces and therefore is always accessible.

For each interface, you can configure an interface-specific MTU by including the `mtu` statement at the `[edit interfaces interface-name]` hierarchy level. To modify this MTU for a particular protocol family, include the `mtu` statement:

```
[edit interfaces interface-name unit logical-unit-number
family family]
mtu mtu;
```

For more information about MTUs, see Tables 6.2, 6.3, and 6.4 beginning on page 191.

The default protocol MTU is 4,470 bytes for ATM PVC, Cisco HDLC, Frame Relay, and PPP encapsulations. For Ethernet encapsulation on IPv4, the default protocol MTU is 1,500 bytes. For Ethernet encapsulation on ISO, the default protocol MTU is 1,497 bytes. When you initially configure an interface, the protocol MTU is calculated automatically. However, if you subsequently change the media MTU, the protocol MTU on existing address families does not automatically adjust. If you increase the size of the protocol MTU, you must ensure that the size of the media MTU is equal to or greater than the sum of the protocol MTU and the encapsulation overhead. If you reduce the media MTU size, but there are already one or more address families configured and active on the interface, you must also reduce the protocol MTU size. (You configure the media MTU by including the `mtu` statement at the `[edit interfaces interface-name]` hierarchy level.)

For Ethernet encapsulation when the family is `mpls`, the default protocol MTU is 1,488 bytes. MPLS packets are 1,500 bytes and have 4 to 12 bytes of overhead. The maximum number of DCLIs is determined by the MTU on the interface. If you have keepalives enabled, the maximum number of DLCIs is 1,000, with the MTU set to 5,012. The actual frames transmitted also contain cyclic redundancy check (CRC) bits, which are not part of the MTU. For example, the default protocol MTU for a Gigabit Ethernet interface is specified as 1,500 bytes, but the largest possible frame size is actually 1,504 bytes; you need to consider the extra bits in calculations of MTUs for interoperability.

By default, the interface sends protocol redirect messages. To disable the sending of these messages on an interface, include the `no-redirects` statement:

```
[edit interfaces interface-name unit logical-unit-number
family family]
no-redirects;
```

To disable the sending of protocol redirect messages for the entire router, include the `no-redirects` statement at the `[edit system]` hierarchy level.

See Chapter 8, "Routing Policy and Firewall Filters," on page 301.

To apply firewall filters to an interface, include the `filter` statement. In the `group` statement, specify the interface group number to associate with the filter. In the `input` statement, list the name of one firewall filter to be evaluated when packets are received on the interface. In the `output` statement, list the name of one firewall filter to be evaluated when packets are transmitted on the interface. You can use the same filter one or more times. If you apply the filter to the `lo0` interface, it is applied to packets received or transmitted by the Routing Engine.

```
[edit interfaces interfaces interface-name unit logical-
unit-number]
family inet {
  filter {
    group group-number;
    input filter-name;
    output filter-name;
  }
}
```

When applying a firewall filter, you can define an interface to be part of an *interface group*. Packets received on that interface are tagged as being part of the group. You can then match these packets using the `interface-group` match statement. To define the interface to be part of an interface group, include the `group` statement:

```
[edit interfaces interface-name unit logical-unit-number]
family inet {
  filter {
    group group-number;
  }
}
```

You can maintain packet counts based on the entry and exit points for traffic passing through your network. The entry point is identified by the input interface. Exit points are identified by destination prefixes grouped into one or more disjoint sets defined as a *destination class*. You can set up one counter per interface per destination class, up to a maximum of 16 counters per interface. You can configure multiple destination classes, up to a global limit of 16 destination classes in a configuration. To configure destination-class usage, your router must be equipped with the Internet Processor II ASIC. To enable packet counting on an interface, include the `destination-class-usage` statement:

```
[edit interfaces interface-name unit logical-unit-number
family inet]
destination-class-usage;
```

See "Configuring Routing Policy," on page 326.

After you enable accounting on an interface, the software maintains packet counters for that interface. You must then configure the `destination-class` attribute in a policy action statement, which must be included in a forwarding-table export policy.

To use IPSec security services, you create a security association (SA) between hosts. An SA is a simplex connection that allows two hosts to communicate with each other securely by means of IPSec. You can configure two types of SAs:

- Manual—Requires no negotiation; all values, including the keys, are static and specified in the configuration. As a result, each peer must have the same configured options for communication to take place.
- Dynamic—Specifies proposals to be negotiated with the tunnel peer. The keys are generated as part of the negotiation and therefore do not need to be specified in the configuration. The dynamic SA includes one or more `proposal` statements, which allow you to prioritize a list of protocols and algorithms to be negotiated with the peer.

To configure an SA for IPSec, include the `security-association` statement:

```
[edit security ipsec]
security-association name;
```

To configure encryption interfaces, you associate the security profile with the interface by including the `ipsec-sa` *sa-name* statement:

```
[edit interfaces es-fpc/pic/port unit logical-unit-number
family inet]
ipsec-sa sa-name;
```

Configuring ATM Interfaces

Asynchronous Transfer Mode (ATM) is a network protocol designed to facilitate the simultaneous handling of various types of traffic streams (voice, data, video) at very high speeds over the same physical connection. ATM relies on the concepts of virtual paths and virtual circuits. A virtual path, represented by a specific virtual path identifier (VPI), establishes a route between two devices in a network. Each VPI can contain multiple virtual circuits, each represented by a virtual circuit identifier (VCI).

For ATM physical interfaces, you can configure two ATM-specific physical device properties: the maximum number of virtual circuits (VCs) allowed on a virtual path (VP) and communication with directly attached ATM switches. You configure these properties by including the `atm-options` statement:

```
[edit interfaces interface-name]
atm-options {
  vpi vpi-identifier maximum-vcs maximum-vcs;
  ilmi;
}
```

You configure the maximum number of virtual circuits allowed on a virtual path so that sufficient memory on the ATM PIC can be allocated for each VC. When configuring ATM interfaces on the router, you must include this statement. To configure the largest numbered VCs on a VP, include the `vpi` statement. The VP identifier can be a value from 0 through 255. You can configure a maximum number of 4,090 VCs per ATM interface; the largest value you can configure is 4,089.

You configure communication to directly attached ATM switches to enable querying of the IP addresses and port numbers of the switches. To configure communication between the router and its directly attached ATM switches, include the `ilmi` statement.

When you are using ATM encapsulation on an interface, you must map each logical interface to a VCI. You can optionally map logical interfaces to a VPI. An ATM interface can be a point-to-point interface or a point-to-multipoint (also called a multipoint nonbroadcast multiaccess [NBMA] connection).

To configure a VCI and a VPI on a point-to-point ATM interface, include the `vci` statement. For each VCI, you configure the VCI and VPI identifiers. The default VPI identifier is 0. The VCI identifier cannot exceed the highest numbered VC configured for the interface with the `vpi` statement. When you are configuring point-to-point connections, the MTU sizes on both sides of the connections must be the same.

```
[edit interfaces interface-name unit logical-unit-number]
vci vpi-identifier.vci-identifier;
```

To configure a point-to-multipoint (NBMA) ATM connection, include the `multipoint-destination` statement:

```
[edit interfaces interface-name unit logical-unit-number
family inet address address]
multipoint-destination destination-address vci vpi-
    identifier.vci-identifier;
```

`address` is the interface's address. The address must include the destination prefix (for example, `/24`). For each destination, include one `multipoint-destination` statement. *`destination-address`* is the address of the remote side of the connection, and *`vci-identifier`* and *`vpi-identifier`* are the VCI and optional VPI identifiers for the connection. For point-to-multipoint connections, all interfaces in the subnet must use the same MTU size.

By default, ATM connections assume unicast traffic. If your ATM switch performs multicast replication, you can configure the connection to support multicast traffic by including the `multicast-vci` statement. You can configure multicast support only on point-to-multipoint ATM connections.

```
[edit interfaces interface-name unit logical-unit-number]
multicast-vci vpi-identifier.vci-identifier;
```

You can configure ATM interfaces to support inverse ATM ARP, as described in RFC 2225.

When inverse ATM ARP is enabled, the router responds to received inverse ATM ARP requests by providing IP address information to the requesting ATM device. To configure a VC to respond to inverse ATM

ARP requests, include the `inverse-arp` statement. You must configure ATM LLC-SNAP encapsulation on the logical interface to support inverse ARP. The other ATM encapsulation types are disallowed.

```
[edit interfaces interface-name unit logical-unit-number]
or
[edit interfaces interface-name unit logical-unit-number
family inet address address multipoint-destination
destination]
inverse-arp;
```

When using an ATM encapsulation, you can configure a traffic-shaping profile that defines bandwidth utilization, which consists of either a constant rate or a peak cell rate with sustained cell rate, and burst tolerance; and maximum queue length. These values are used in the generic ATM cell-rate algorithm, which is a leaky bucket algorithm that defines the short-term burst rate for ATM cells, the maximum number of cells that can be included in a burst, and the long-term sustained ATM cell traffic rate. Each individual VC has its own independent shaping parameters.

By default, the bandwidth utilization is unlimited; that is, unspecified bit rate (UBR) is used. Also, by default, buffer usage by VCs is unregulated. To define limits to bandwidth utilization on a point-to-point interface or to limit buffer use, include the `shaping` statement. For point-to-point interfaces, include the `shaping` statement at the `[edit interfaces` *`interface-name`* `unit` *`logical-unit-number`*`]` hierarchy level; for virtual circuits that are part of a point-to-multipoint interface, include it at the `[edit interfaces` *`interface-name`* `unit` *`logical-unit-number`* `family` *`family`* `address` *`address`*`]` hierarchy level.

```
shaping {
  (cbr rate | vbr peak rate sustained rate burst length);
  queue-length number;
}
```

For traffic that does not need to periodically burst to a higher rate, you can specify a constant bit rate (CBR) by including the `cbr` statement at the `[edit interfaces` *`interface-name`* `unit` *`logical-unit-number`* `shaping]` or `[edit interfaces` *`interface-name`* `unit` *`logical-unit-number`* `family` *`family`* `address` *`address`* `multipoint-destination` *`destination-address`* `shaping]` hierarchy level:

```
cbr rate;
```

To define variable bandwidth utilization (VBR), include the `vbr` statement at the `[edit interfaces interface-name unit logical-unit-number shaping]` or `[edit interfaces interface-name unit logical-unit-number family family address address multipoint-destination destination-address shaping]` hierarchy level:

```
vbr peak rate sustained rate burst length;
```

When configuring VBR, you can define the peak rate, which is the top rate at which traffic can burst, the sustained rate, which is the normal traffic rate averaged over time, and the burst length, which is the maximum number of cells that a burst of traffic can contain and can be a value from 1 through 255 cells.

With an ATM encapsulation, you can configure the OAM F5 loopback cell period on virtual circuits, which is the interval at which OAM F5 loopback cells are transmitted. By default, no OAM F5 loopback cells are sent. To send OAM F5 loopback cells on a point-to-point interface, include the `oam-period` statement at the `[edit interfaces interface-name unit logical-unit-number]` hierarchy level; to send them on a virtual circuit that is part of a point-to-multipoint interface, include the statement at the `[edit interfaces interface-name unit logical-unit-number family family address address]` hierarchy level. The period can range from 1 through 900 seconds.

```
oam-period (disable | seconds);
```

With an ATM encapsulation, you can configure the OAM F5 loopback cell threshold on VCs, which is the minimum number of consecutive OAM F5 loopback cells received before declaring that a VC is up or lost before declaring that a VC is down. By default, when five consecutive OAM F5 loopback cells are received, the VC is considered to be up, and when five consecutive cells are lost, the VC is considered to be down. To modify these values on a point-to-point interface, include the `oam-liveness` statement at the `[edit interfaces interface-name unit logical-unit-number]` hierarchy level, and to modify it on a virtual circuit that is part of a point-to-multipoint interface, include the `oam-liveness` statement at the `[edit interfaces interface-name unit logical-unit-number family family address address]` hierarchy level. The cell count can be a value from 1 through 255 cells.

```
oam-liveness {
  up-count cells;
  down-count cells;
}
```

See RFC 1483, *Multiprotocol Encapsulation over ATM Adaptation Layer 5*.

For an ATM interface, the physical interface encapsulation can be ATM PVC, and ATM cell relay, which connects two remote virtual circuits or ATM physical interfaces with a label-switched path (LSP). For ATM PVC encapsulation, you can configure the logical interfaces with any ATM encapsulation. To configure the encapsulation on a physical interface, include the following `encapsulation` statement:

```
[edit interfaces interface-name]
encapsulation (atm-ccc-cell-relay | atm-pvc | cisco-hdlc |
cisco-hdlc-ccc | frame-relay | frame-relay-ccc | ppp |
ppp-ccc |vlan-ccc);
```

For ATM encapsulations, you also can configure the encapsulation type that is used inside the ATM cell itself by including the following `encapsulation` statement:

```
[edit interfaces interface-name unit logical-unit-number]
encapsulation (atm-ccc-cell-relay | atm-nlpid | atm-cisco-
nlpid | atm-snap | atm-vc-mux | atm-ccc-vc-mux | frame-
relay-ccc | vlan-ccc);
```

To configure ATM E3 and T3 interfaces, include the following statements:

```
[edit interfaces at-fpc/pic/port]
e3-options {
  atm-encapsulation (plcp | direct);
  buildout <distance> (ft | m);
  framing (g.751 | g.832);
  loopback (local | remote);
  (payload-scrambler | no-payload-scrambler);
}
t3-options {
  atm-encapsulation (plcp | direct);
  buildout <distance> (ft | m);
  (cbit-parity | no-cbit-parity);
  loopback (local | remote);
  (payload-scrambler | no-payload-scrambler);
}
```

See "Configuring E1 and E3 Interfaces," on page 214 and "Configuring T1 and T3 Interfaces," on page 256.

Some of the options and default values vary from those for the E3 and T3 interfaces:

- `atm-encapsulation`–PLCP is the default value. The E3 `line-format` option `g.832` supports `direct` ATM encapsulation only.
- `buildout`—The default value is 10 feet. *`distance`* can be any integer value, followed by a unit specifier of `ft` or `m`. The range is 0 through 255 feet for E3 traffic or 0 through 450 feet for T3 traffic.
- `cbit-parity`—The default option is to enable C-bit parity.
- `framing`—There is no default option for E3 interfaces; T3 interfaces use the `cbit-parity` statement in place of `framing`.
- `loopback`—The default is no loopback.
- `payload-scrambler`—The default is to enable payload scrambling.

See "Configuring SONET/SDH Interfaces," on page 240.

In addition, the ATM E3 and T3 PICs support the `clocking` statement at the interface level, similar to the SONET PICs.

You must configure all the ports on an ATM E3 or T3 PIC with the same framing and encapsulation. Otherwise, all ports on the PIC are set to the slowest framing and encapsulating configuration. For ATM T3, this is PLCP and for ATM E3, this is G.751 PLCP.

When configuring ATM SONET/SDH interfaces, you also can include the following statements in the `sonet-options` statement to set SONET/SDH parameters on ATM interfaces:

```
[edit interfaces at-fpc/pic/port]
sonet-options {
  aps {
    advertise-interval milliseconds;
    authentication-key key;
    force;
    hold-time milliseconds;
    lockout;
    neighbor address;
    paired-group group-name;
    protect-circuit group-name;
    request;
    revert-time seconds;
    working-circuit group-name;
  }
  bytes {
    e1-quiet value;
```

```
    f1 value;
    f2 value;
    s1 value;
    z3 value;
    z4 value;
  }
  fcs (32 | 16);
  loopback (local | remote);
  path-trace trace-string;
  (payload-scrambler | no-payload-scrambler);
  rfc-2615;
  (z0-increment | no-z0-increment);
}
```

Configuring E1 and E3 Interfaces

E1 is a standard WAN digital communication format designed to operate over copper facilities at a rate of 2.048 Mbps. E3 is a high-speed WAN digital communication technique designed to operate over copper facilities at a rate of 34.368 Mbps. Both are widely used outside North America. E1 is a basic time division multiplexing scheme used to carry digital circuits, and E3 is the time division multiplexing scheme used to carry 16 E1 circuits.

To configure E1-specific physical interface properties, include the `e1-options` statement:

```
[edit interfaces interface-name]
e1-options {
  bert-error-rate rate;
  bert-period seconds;
  fcs (32 | 16);
  framing (g704 | g704-no-crc4 | unframed);
  idle-cycle-flag (flags | ones);
  loopback (local | remote);
  start-end-flag (shared | filler);
  timeslots time-slot-number;
}
```

To configure E3-specific physical interface properties, include the `e3-options` statement:

```
[edit interfaces interface-name]
e3-options {
  bert-algorithm algorithm;
  bert-error-rate rate;
  bert-period seconds;
```

```
    compatibility-mode (digital-link | kentrox | larscom)
      <subrate value>;
    fcs (32 | 16);
    idle-cycle-flag value;
    loopback (local | remote);
    (payload-scrambler | no-payload-scrambler);
    start-end-flag value;
  }
```

You can configure an E1 or E3 interface to execute a bit error rate test (BERT) when the interface receives a request to run this test. You specify the duration of the test and the error rate to include in the bit stream by including the `bert-period` and `bert-error-rate` statements. For E3 interfaces, you specify the pattern to send in the bit stream by including the `bert-algorithm` statement:

```
[edit interfaces interface-name e1-options] or
[edit interfaces interface-name e3-options]
bert-algorithm algorithm;
bert-error-rate rate;
bert-period seconds;
```

For E3 interfaces, *algorithm* is the pattern to send in the bit stream. The algorithm for the E1 BERT procedure is `pseudo-2e15-o151` (pattern is $2^{15}-1$, as defined in the CCITT/ITU O.151 standard). *rate* is the bit error rate. This can be an integer in the range 0 through 7, which corresponds to a bit error rate in the range 10^{-0} (that is, 0, which corresponds to no errors) to 10^{-7} (that is, 1 error per 10 million bits). The default is 0. *seconds* is the duration of the BERT procedure, in seconds. The test can last from 1 to 240 seconds; the default is 10 seconds.

To configure an E3 interface so that it is compatible with the channel service unit (CSU) at the remote end of the line, include the `compatibility` statement:

```
[edit interfaces interface-name e3-options]
compatibility-mode (digital-link | kentrox | larscom)
   <subrate value>;
```

You can configure the interface to be compatible with a Digital Link, Kentrox, or Larscom CSU. The subrate of an E3 interface must exactly match that of the remote CSU. To specify the subrate, include the `subrate` option in the `compatibility-mode` statement. For Digital Link CSUs only, you can specify the subrate *value* as the data rate you configured on the CSU in the format `xkb` or `x.xMb`. For a list of specific rate values, use the command completion feature in the CLI. The range is 358 kbps through 33.7 Mbps. Kentrox and Larscom CSUs do not support E3 subrate.

By default, E1 and E3 interfaces support a 16-bit checksum. You can configure a 32-bit checksum, which provides more reliable packet verification. However, some older equipment might not support 32-bit checksums. To configure a 32-bit checksum, include the `fcs 32` statement:

```
[edit interfaces interface-name e1-options] or
[edit interfaces interface-name e3-options]
fcs 32;
```

E3 HDLC payload scrambling, which is disabled by default, provides better link stability. Both sides of a connection must either use or not use scrambling. To configure scrambling on the interface, include the `payload-scrambler` statement:

```
[edit interfaces interface-name e3-options]
payload-scrambler;
```

By default, E1 and E3 interfaces transmit the value 0x7E in the idle cycles. To have the interface transmit the value 0xFF (all ones) instead, include the `idle-cycle-flag` statement, specifying the `ones` option:

```
[edit interfaces interface-name e1-options] or
[edit interfaces interface-name e3-options]
idle-cycle-flag ones;
```

By default, E1 and E3 interfaces wait two idle cycles between sending start and end flags. To configure the interface to share the transmission of start and end flags, include the `start-end-flag` statement, specifying the `shared` option.

```
[edit interfaces interface-name e1-options] or
[edit interfaces interface-name e3-options]
start-end-flag shared;
```

You can configure loopback capability between the local E1 or E3 interface and the remote channel service unit (CSU), as shown in Figure 6.1. You can configure the loopback to be local or remote. With local loopback, the E1 or E3 interface can transmit packets to the CSU but receives its own transmission back again and ignores data from the CSU. With remote loopback, packets sent from the CSU are received by the E1 or E3 interface but also are immediately retransmitted to the CSU.

Figure 6.1 *Remote and Local E1 Loopback*

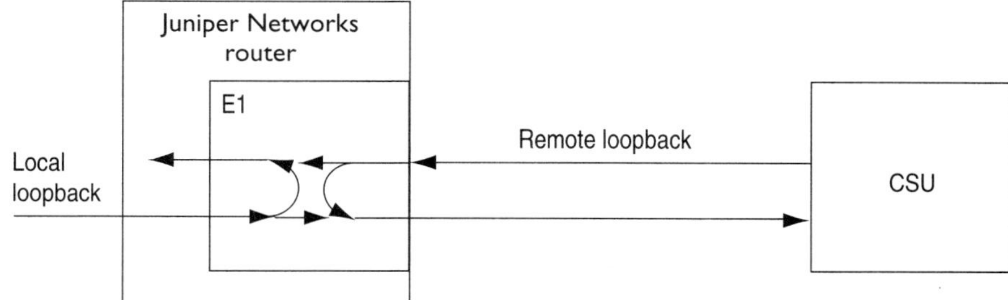

To configure loopback capability on an E1 or E3 interface, include the `loopback` statement:

```
[edit interfaces interface-name e1-options] or
[edit interfaces interface-name e3-options]
loopback (local | remote);
```

Packets can be looped on either the local router or the remote CSU. To turn off loopback, remove the `loopback` statement from the configuration.

On an E1 interface, to configure the number of time slots allocated to the interface, include the `timeslots` statement:

```
[edit interfaces interface-name e1-options]
timeslots time-slot-number;
```

The slot number can be in the range 1 through 32. E1 interfaces have 32 time slots. You can designate any combination of time slots for usage. The default is to use all the time slots.

Configuring Encryption Interfaces

> IPSec is discussed in detail in Chapter 7, "IP Security (IPSec)," on page 287.

The Internet Protocol security architecture (IPSec) provides a security suite for the IPv4 and IPv6 network layers. The suite provides functionality such as authentication of origin, data integrity, confidentiality, replay protection, and nonrepudiation of source. It also defines mechanisms for key generation and exchange, management of security associations, and support for digital certificates. IPSec defines a security association (SA) and key management framework that can be used with any network layer protocol. The SA specifies what protection policy to apply to traffic between two IP-layer entities.

To configure IPSec, your router must have an ES PIC.

Secure traffic travels through tunnel interfaces between remote hosts. You configure each IPSec tunnel as a logical interface on the ES PIC. To specify the source and destination addresses, include the `tunnel` statement:

```
[edit interfaces]
es-fpc/pic/port {
  unit logical-unit-number {
    tunnel {
      source address;
      destination address;
    }
  }
}
```

IPSec runs in two modes: transport and tunnel. The ES PIC supports tunnel mode only.

A security association is the set of properties that define the protocols for encrypting the Internet traffic. To configure encryption interfaces, specify the security association (SA) name associated with the interface by including the `ipsec-sa` statement:

```
[edit interfaces es-fpc/pic/port unit logical-unit-number
family inet]
ipsec-sa sa-name;
```

You use firewall filters to configure traffic to flow through an IPsec tunnel. To configure inbound and outbound traffic for an IPsec tunnel, include the `filter` statement:

```
[edit firewall]
filter inbound-decrypt-filter;
filter outbound-encrypt-filter;
```

To ensure outbound traffic is transmitted on the appropriate interface, include the `filter` and `output` statements:

```
[edit interfaces interface-name unit logical-unit-number
family inet]
filter {
  output outbound-encrypt-filter;
}
```

See Chapter 8, "Routing Policy and Firewall Filters," on page 301.

To ensure that inbound traffic is received on the appropriate interface, include the `filter` and `input` statements:

```
[edit interfaces]
interfaces interface-name {
  unit logical-unit-number {
    family inet {
      filter {
        input inbound-decrypt-filter;
      }
    }
  }
}
```

The protocol MTU value for encryption interfaces must always be less than the default interface MTU value of 3,900 bytes; the configuration fails to commit if you select a greater value. To set the MTU value, include the `mtu` statement:

```
[edit interfaces interface-name unit logical-unit-number
family inet]
mtu bytes;
```

Configuring Ethernet Interfaces

Ethernet was developed in the early 1970s at the Xerox Palo Alto Research Center as a data-link control layer protocol for interconnecting computers. It was first widely used at 10 Mbps over coaxial cables and later over unshielded twisted pairs using 10BaseT. More recently, 100BaseTX (Fast Ethernet, 100 Mbps), Gigabit Ethernet (1 Gbps), and 10 Gigabit Ethernet have become available.

Juniper Networks routers support Fast Ethernet, Gigabit Ethernet, and 10 Gigabit Ethernet interfaces; a management Ethernet interface, which is an out-of-band management interface within the router; an internal Ethernet interface, which connects the Routing Engine to the Packet Forwarding Engine; and, an aggregated Ethernet interface, a logical linkage of Fast Ethernet or Gigabit Ethernet physical connections.

Configuring Ethernet Physical Interface Properties

To configure Fast Ethernet-specific physical interface properties, include the `fastether-options` statement:

```
[edit interfaces interface-name]
link-mode (full-duplex | half-duplex);
speed (10m | 100m)
fastether-options {
  802.3ad aex;
  (flow-control | no-flow-control);
  ingress-rate-limit rate;
  (loopback | no-loopback);
  source-address-filter {
    mac-address;
  }
  (source-filtering | no-source-filtering);
}
```

To configure Gigabit Ethernet-specific physical interface properties, include the `gigether-options` statement:

```
[edit interfaces interface-name]
gigether-options {
  802.3ad aex;
  (flow-control | no-flow-control);
  (loopback | no-loopback);
  source-address-filter {
    mac-address;
  }
  (source-filtering | no-source-filtering);
}
```

To configure aggregated Ethernet-specific physical interface properties, include the `aggregated-ether-options` statement:

```
[edit interfaces interface-name]
aggregated-ether-options {
  (flow-control | no-flow-control);
  (loopback | no-loopback);
  minimum-links number;
  source-address-filter {
    mac-address;
  }
  (source-filtering | no-source-filtering);
}
```

On Fast Ethernet and Gigabit Ethernet interfaces, you can associate a physical interface with an aggregated Ethernet interface. Specify the interface instance number *x* to complete the link association; *x* can range from 0 through 15, for a total of 16 aggregated interfaces, by including the `802.3ad` statement:

```
802.3ad aex;
```

On aggregated Ethernet interfaces, you can configure the minimum number of links that must be up for the bundle as a whole to be labeled up by including the `minimum-links` statement. The default minimum is 1, and the number can be a value from 1 through 8.

```
[edit interfaces interface-name aggregated-ether-options]
minimum-links number;
```

On aggregated Ethernet, Fast Ethernet, and Gigabit Ethernet interfaces, you can enable source address filtering, which blocks all incoming packets to that interface. To enable the filtering, include the `source-filtering` statement:

```
[edit interfaces interface-name aggregated-ether-options]
or
[edit interfaces interface-name fastether-options] or
[edit interfaces interface-name gigether-options]
source-filtering;
```

When source address filtering is enabled, you can configure the interface to receive packets from specific MAC addresses by specifying the MAC addresses in the `source-address-filter` statement. Specify the MAC address as *nn*:*nn*:*nn*:*nn*:*nn*:*nn* or *nnnn*.*nnnn*.*nnnn*, where *n* is a hexadecimal number.

```
[edit interfaces interface-name aggregated-ether-options]
or
[edit interfaces interface-name fastether-options] or
[edit interfaces interface-name gigether-options]
source-address-filter {
  mac-address;
  <additional mac-address;>
}
```

By default, local aggregated Ethernet, Fast Ethernet, or Gigabit Ethernet interfaces connect to a remote system. To place an interface in loopback mode, include the `loopback` statement:

```
[edit interfaces interface-name aggregated-ether-options]
or
[edit interfaces interface-name fastether-options] or
[edit interfaces interface-name gigether-options]
loopback;
```

By default, the router imposes flow control to regulate the amount of traffic sent out a Fast Ethernet or Gigabit Ethernet interface. This is useful if the remote side of the connection is a Fast Ethernet or Gigabit Ethernet switch. To disable flow control if you want the router to permit unrestricted traffic, include the `no-flow-control` statement:

```
[edit interfaces interface-name aggregated-ether-options]
or
[edit interfaces interface-name fastether-options] or
[edit interfaces interface-name gigether-options]
no-flow-control;
```

By default, the router's management Ethernet interface, `fxp0`, autonegotiates whether to operate in full-duplex or half-duplex mode. Fast Ethernet interfaces can operate in either full-duplex or half-duplex mode, and all other interfaces can operate only in full-duplex mode. For Gigabit Ethernet, the link partner must also be set to full duplex. To explicitly configure an Ethernet interface to operate in either full-duplex or half-duplex mode, include the `link-mode` statement:

```
[edit interfaces interface-name]
link-mode (full-duplex | half-duplex);
```

On Fast Ethernet 12-port and 48-port PIC interfaces and the management Ethernet interface (`fxp0`) only, you can explicitly set the interface speed to either 10 Mbps or 100 Mbps by including the `speed` statement:

```
[edit interfaces interface-name]
speed (10m | 100m);
```

On Fast Ethernet 8-port, 12-port, and 48-port PIC interfaces only, you can apply port-based rate limiting to the ingress traffic that arrives at the PIC by including the `ingress-rate-limit` statement. *rate* can range in value from 1 through 100 Mbps.

```
[edit interfaces interface-name fastether-options]
ingress-rate-limit rate;
```

Configuring 802.1Q VLANs

For Ethernet, Fast Ethernet, and Gigabit Ethernet interfaces, the JUNOS software supports a subset of the IEEE 802.1Q standard for channelizing an Ethernet interface into multiple logical interfaces, allowing many hosts to be connected to the same Gigabit Ethernet switch, but preventing them from being in the same routing or broadcast domain. The software supports receiving and forwarding routed Ethernet frames with 802.1Q Virtual Local Area Network (VLAN) tags and supports running VRRP over 802.1Q-tagged interfaces. To configure the router to receive and forward frames with 802.1Q VLAN tags, include the `vlan-tagging` statement:

```
[edit interfaces interface-name]
vlan-tagging;
```

Gigabit Ethernet interfaces can be partitioned; you can assign up to 4,095 different logical interfaces, one for each VLAN, but you are limited to a maximum of 1,024 VLANs on any single Gigabit Ethernet port. You can configure any VLAN ID in the range from 0 through 4,094. Fast Ethernet interfaces can also be partitioned, with a maximum of 1,024 logical interfaces for the four-port Fast Ethernet PIC and 16 logical interfaces for the M40e and M160 Fast Ethernet 48-port PIC.

To bind a VLAN ID to a logical interface, include the `vlan-id` statement:

```
[edit interfaces interface-name unit logical-unit-number]
vlan-id number;
```

Ethernet interfaces with VLAN tagging enabled can use VLAN circuit cross-connect (CCC) encapsulation. To configure the encapsulation on a physical interface, include the `encapsulation vlan-ccc` statement:

```
[edit interfaces interface-name]
encapsulation vlan-ccc;
```

Ethernet interfaces in VLAN mode can have multiple logical interfaces, but in CCC mode VLAN IDs from 0 through 511 are reserved for normal VLANs, and VLAN IDs from 512 through 4,095 are reserved for CCC VLANs.

In general, you configure an interface's encapsulation at the `[edit interfaces interface-name]` hierarchy level. However, for some encapsulation types, including Ethernet VLAN-CCC, you also can configure the encapsulation type that is used inside the VLAN circuit itself. To do this, include the following `encapsulation` statement:

```
[edit interfaces interface-name unit logical-unit-number]
encapsulation vlan-ccc;
```

You cannot configure a logical interface with an encapsulation of `vlan-ccc` unless you also configure the physical device with the same encapsulation. The logical interface must also have a VLAN ID in the range from 512 through 4,095; if the VLAN ID is 511 or lower, it is subject to the normal destination filter lookups in addition to source address filtering.

Configuring Static ARP Table Entries

For Ethernet, Fast Ethernet, and Gigabit Ethernet interfaces, you can configure static ARP table entries, defining mappings between IP and MAC addresses. To do this, include the `arp` statement:

```
[edit interfaces interface-name unit logical-unit-number
family inet address address]
arp ip-address (mac | multicast-mac) mac-address
    <publish>;
```

The IP address that you specify must be part of the subnet defined in the enclosing `address` statement. To associate a multicast MAC address with a unicast IP address, include the `multicast-mac` statement. Specify the MAC address as six hexadecimal bytes in one of the following formats: *nnnn.nnnn.nnnn* or *nn:nn:nn:nn:nn:nn*. For example, `0011.2233.4455` or `00:11:22:33:44:55`. If you include the `publish` option, the router replies to ARP requests for the specified IP address. The JUNOS software does not support proxy ARP.

Configuring VRRP

For Ethernet, Fast Ethernet, and Gigabit Ethernet interfaces, you can configure the Virtual Router Redundancy Protocol (VRRP). VRRP allows hosts on a LAN to make use of redundant routers on that LAN without requiring more than the static configuration of a single default router on the hosts. The VRRP routers share the IP address corresponding to the default router configured on the hosts. At any time, one of the VRRP routers is the master (active), and the others are backups. If the master fails, one of the backup routers becomes the new master, thus always providing a virtual default router and allowing traffic on the LAN to be routed without relying on a single router.

VRRP is defined in RFC 2338, *Virtual Router Redundancy Protocol.*

To configure basic VRRP support, configure VRRP groups on an interface by including the following statements:

```
[edit interfaces interface-name unit logical-unit-number
family inet address address]
vrrp-group group-number {
  virtual-address [ addresses ];
  priority number;
}
```

An interface can be a member of one or more VRRP groups. For each group, you must configure the following:

- Group number—Identifies the VRRP group. It can be a value from 0 through 255. If you also enable MAC source address filtering on the interface, you must include the virtual MAC address in the list of source MAC addresses that you specify in the `source-address-filter` statement. MAC addresses ranging from `00:00:5E:00:01:00` through `00:00:5E:00:01:FF` are reserved for VRRP, as defined in RFC 2338. The VRRP group number must be the decimal equivalent of the last hexadecimal byte of the virtual MAC address.
- Addresses of one or more virtual routers that are members of the VRRP group—Virtual IP addresses associated with the virtual router in the VRRP group. Normally, you configure only one virtual IP address per group. The virtual IP addresses must be the same for all routers in the VRRP group. In the addresses, specify the address only. Do not include a prefix length.

If you configure a virtual IP address to be the same as the interface's address (the address configured with the `address` statement), the interface becomes the master virtual router for the group. In this case, you must configure the priority to be 255, and you must configure preemption by including the `preempt` statement. If you have multiple VRRP groups on an interface, the interface can be the master virtual router for only one of the groups.

If the virtual IP address you choose is not the same as the interface's address, you must ensure that this address does not appear anywhere else in the router's configuration. Check that you do not use this address for other interfaces, for the IP address of a tunnel, or for the IP address of static ARP entries.

- Priority for this router to become the master virtual router—Value used to elect the master virtual router in the VRRP group. It can be a number from 1 through 255. The default value for backup routers is 100. A larger value indicates a higher priority. The router with the highest priority within the group becomes the master router.

Within a single VRRP group, the master and backup routers cannot be the same router.

All VRRP protocol exchanges can be authenticated to guarantee that only trusted routers participate in the AS's routing. By default, VRRP authentication is disabled. You can configure simple authentication, which uses a text password included in the transmitted packet, or the MD5 algorithm, which creates the authentication data field in the IP authentication header that is used to encapsulate the VRRP protocol data unit (PDU). Each VRRP group must use the same method: To enable authentication and specify an authentication method, include the `authentication-type` statement:

```
[edit interfaces interface-name unit logical-unit-number
family inet address address vrrp-group group-number]
authentication-type authentication;
```

`authentication` can be `none`, `simple`, or `md5`. The authentication type must be the same for all routers in the VRRP group. If you include the `authentication-type` statement to select an authentication method, you can configure a key (password) on each interface by including the `authentication-key` statement. The key is an ASCII string. For simple

authentication, it can be 1 through 8 characters long. For MD5 authentication, it can be 1 through 16 characters long. If you include spaces, enclose all characters in quotation marks (" "). The key must be the same for all routers in the VRRP group.

```
[edit interfaces interface-name unit logical-unit-number
family inet address address vrrp-group group-number]
authentication-key key;
```

By default, the master router sends VRRP advertisement packets every second to all members of the VRRP group. These packets indicate that the master router is still operational. If the master router fails or becomes unreachable, the backup router with the highest priority value becomes the new master router. To modify the time between the sending of VRRP advertisement packets, include the `advertise-interval` statement. The interval can range from 1 through 255 seconds. The interval must be the same for all routers in the VRRP group.

```
[edit interfaces interface-name unit logical-unit-number
family inet address address vrrp-group group-number]
advertise-interval seconds;
```

By default, a higher priority backup router preempts a lower priority master router. To explicitly allow the master router to be preempted, include the `preempt` statement:

```
[edit interfaces interface-name unit logical-unit-number
family inet address address vrrp-group group-number]
preempt;
```

To prohibit a higher priority backup router from preempting a lower priority master router, include the `no-preempt` statement. The router that owns the IP addresses associated with the virtual router always preempts, independent of the setting of this statement.

```
[edit interfaces interface-name unit logical-unit-number
family inet address address vrrp-group group-number]
no-preempt;
```

See "Configuring VRRP," on page 224.

VRRP can track whether an interface is up or down and dynamically change the priority of the VRRP group based on the state of the tracked interface, which might trigger a new master router election. When interface tracking is enabled, you cannot configure a priority of 255, thereby designating the master router. For each VRRP group, 1 through 10 interfaces can be tracked. To configure an interface to be tracked, include the `track` statement. The priority cost is the value to be subtracted from the configured VRRP priority when the tracked interface is down, forcing a new master router election. The cost can range from 1 through 254. The sum of the costs for all tracked interfaces or routes must be less than or equal to the configured priority of the VRRP group.

```
[edit interfaces interface-name unit logical-unit-number
family inet address address vrrp-group group-number]
track {
  interface interface-name priority-cost cost;
}
```

To trace VRRP operations, include the `traceoptions` statement. By default, VRRP logs the error, DCD configuration, and routing socket events in a file in the `/var/log` directory. By default, this file is named `/var/log/vrrpd`. The default file size is 1 MB, and three files are created before the first one gets overwritten. To change the configuration of the logging file, include the `file` statement:

```
[edit protocols vrrp traceoptions]
file {
  filename filename;
  files number;
  size size;
  (world-readable | no-world-readable);
}
flag flag;
```

For more information about tracing and global tracing options, see the JUNOS technical documentation.

You can specify the following VRRP tracing flags:

- `all`—VRRP operations
- `database`—Database changes
- `general`—General events
- `interfaces`—Interface changes
- `normal`—Normal events
- `packets`—All packets sent and received
- `state`—State transitions
- `timer`—Timer events

Configuring the Management Ethernet Interface

The router's management Ethernet interface, `fxp0`, is an out-of-band management interface. You must configure an IP address and prefix length for this interface, which you commonly do when you first install the software. You must configure the management Ethernet interface for the router to function.

```
[edit]
interfaces {
  fxp0 {
    unit 0 {
      family inet {
        address/prefix-length;
      }
    }
  }
}
```

Configuring the Internal Ethernet Interface

The router's internal Ethernet interface, `fxp1`, connects the Routing Engine with the System Control Board (SCB), System and Switch Board (SSB), Forwarding Engine Board (FEB), or Switching and Forwarding Module (SFM), depending on router model, in the Packet Forwarding Engine. The router software automatically configures this interface. Do not modify or remove the configuration for the internal Ethernet interface that the software automatically configures. If you do, the router will stop functioning.

```
user@host> show configuration
...
interfaces {
...
  fxp1 {
    unit 0 {
      family tnp {
        address 1;
      }
    }
  }
}
```

Configuring Aggregated Ethernet Interfaces

Link aggregation of Ethernet interfaces is defined in the IEEE 802.3ad standard. The JUNOS implementation of 802.3ad balances traffic across the member links within an aggregated Ethernet bundle based on the Layer 3 information carried in the packet. This implementation uses the same load balancing algorithm as for per-packet load balancing. You configure an aggregated Ethernet virtual link by specifying the link number as a physical device and then associating a set of ports that have the same speed and are in full-duplex mode. The physical interfaces can be either Fast Ethernet or Gigabit Ethernet devices but must not intermix within the same aggregated link.

To specify aggregated Ethernet interfaces, include the `vlan-tagging` statement at the `[edit interfaces aex]` hierarchy level and also include the `vlan-id` statement:

```
[edit interfaces]
aex {
  vlan-tagging;
  unit 0 {
    vlan-id identifier;
    family inet {
      address address;
    }
  }
}
```

Configuring Frame Relay

Frame Relay does not require private and permanently connected wide-area network facilities, unlike some older WAN protocols.

The Frame Relay protocol allows network designers to reduce costs by using shared facilities that are managed by a Frame Relay service provider. Users pay fixed charges for the local connections from each site in the Frame Relay network to the first point of presence (POP) in which the provider maintains a Frame Relay switch. The portion of the network between the end point switches is shared by all the customers of the service provider, and individual Data Link Connection Identifiers (DLCIs) are assigned to ensure each customer receives only their own traffic. Users contract with their providers for a specific minimum portion of the shared bandwidth Committed Information Rate (CIR) and for a maximum allowable peak rate, Burst Information Rate (BIR). Depending on the terms of the contract, traffic exceeding the CIR can be marked as eligible for discard, in the event of network congestion, or a best effort term can apply up to the BIR rate.

Point-to-Point Protocol (PPP) encapsulation is the default encapsulation type for physical interfaces. You need not configure encapsulation for any physical interfaces that support PPP encapsulation. If you do not configure encapsulation, PPP is used by default. For physical interfaces that do not support PPP encapsulation, you must configure an encapsulation to use for packets transmitted on the interface. You can optionally configure an encapsulation on a logical interface, which is the encapsulation used within certain packet types.

Frame Relay encapsulation is defined in RFC 1490, *Multiprotocol Interconnect over Frame Relay*.

For Frame Relay interfaces, you configure Frame Relay encapsulation on the physical interface. SONET and T3 interfaces can use Frame Relay encapsulation. To configure Frame Relay encapsulation on a physical interface, include the `encapsulation` statement, specifying the `frame-relay` option:

```
[edit interfaces interface-name]
encapsulation frame-relay;
```

When you configure a multipoint encapsulation (such as Frame Relay), the physical interface can have multiple logical units, and the units can be either point to point or multipoint. When you are using Frame Relay encapsulation, you must disable keepalives to ensure that the interface sends LMI requests. If keepalives are not disabled, LMI requests are not sent.

Generally, you configure an interface's encapsulation at the `[edit interfaces interface-name]` hierarchy level. However, for Frame Relay encapsulation, you can also configure the encapsulation type that is used inside the Frame Relay packet itself. To do this, include the `encapsulation` statement, specifying the `frame-relay-ccc` option:

```
[edit interfaces interface-name unit logical-unit-number]
encapsulation frame-relay-ccc;
```

For more information about MTUs, see Table 6.2, Table 6.3, and Table 6.4 beginning on page 191.

For Frame Relay interfaces, the default media MTU is 4,482 bytes. To modify the default media MTU size for a physical interface, include the `mtu` statement:

```
[edit interfaces interface-name]
mtu bytes;
```

If you change the size of the media MTU, you must ensure that the size is equal to or greater than the sum of the protocol MTU and the encapsulation overhead. You configure the protocol MTU by including the `mtu` statement at the `[edit interfaces interface-name unit logical-unit-number family family]` hierarchy level:

```
[edit interfaces interface-name unit logical-unit-number
family family]
mtu mtu;
```

By default, physical interfaces configured with Cisco HDLC or PPP encapsulation send keepalive packets at 10-second intervals. The Frame Relay term for keepalives is Local Management Interface (LMI) packets; note that the JUNOS software supports both ANSI T1.617 Annex D LMIs and ITU Q933 Annex A LMIs. To disable the sending of keepalives on a physical interface, include the `no-keepalives` statement:

```
[edit interfaces interface-name]
no-keepalives;
```

On interfaces configured with Frame Relay connections, you can tune the keepalive settings by using the `lmi` statement. A Frame Relay interface can be either data circuit-terminating equipment (DCE) or data terminal equipment (DTE) (the default JUNOS configuration). DTE acts as a master, requesting status from the DCE part of the link. By default, the JUNOS software uses ANSI T1.617 Annex D LMIs. To change to ITU Q933 Annex A LMIs, include the `lmi-type itu` statement:

```
[edit interfaces interface-name lmi]
lmi-type itu;
```

To configure Frame Relay keepalive parameters, include the `lmi` statement:

```
[edit interfaces interface-name]
lmi {
  lmi-type (ansi | itu);
  n391dte number;
  n392dce number;
  n392dte number;
  n393dce number;
  n393dte number;
  t391dte seconds;
  t392dce seconds;
}
```

You can set the following parameters:

- `n391dte`—DTE full status polling interval. The DTE sends a status inquiry to the DCE at the interval specified by the `t391dte` statement. The value specifies the frequency at which these inquiries expect a full status report; for example, a `n391dte` value of 10 would specify a full status report in response to every tenth inquiry. The intermediate inquiries ask for a keepalive exchange only. The range is 1 through 255, with a default value of 6.
- `n392dce`—DCE error threshold, which is the number of errors required to bring down the link, within the event-count specified by the `n393dce` statement. The range is 1 through 10, with a default value of 3.
- `n392dte`—DTE error threshold, which is the number of errors required to bring down the link, within the event-count specified by the `n393dte` statement. The range is 1 through 10, with a default value of 3.
- `n393dce`—DCE monitored event-count. The range is 1 through 10, with a default value of 4.
- `n393dte`—DTE monitored event-count. The range is 1 through 10, with a default value of 4.
- `t391dte`—DTE keepalive timer, which is the period at which the DTE sends out a keepalive response request to the DCE and updates status depending on the DTE error threshold value. The range is 5 through 30 seconds, with a default value of 10 seconds.
- `t392dce`—DCE keepalive timer, which is the period at which the DCE checks for keepalive responses from the DTE and updates status depending on the DCE error threshold value. The range is 5 through 30 seconds, with a default value of 15 seconds.

Frame Relay interfaces support inverse Frame Relay ARP, as described in RFC 2390. When inverse Frame Relay ARP is enabled, the router responds to received inverse Frame Relay ARP requests by providing IP address information to the requesting router on the other end of the Frame PVC (permanent virtual circuit). The router does not initiate inverse Frame Relay ARP requests. By default, inverse Frame Relay ARP is disabled. To configure a router to respond to inverse Frame Relay ARP requests, include the `inverse-arp` statement. You must also configure Frame Relay encapsulation on the logical interface to support inverse ARP.

```
[edit interfaces interface-name unit logical-unit-number]
inverse-arp;
```

By default, when you configure an interface with Frame Relay encapsulation, the router is assumed to be a DTE. That is, the router is assumed to be at a terminal point on the network. To configure the router to be a DCE, include the `dce` statement. When you configure the router to be a DCE, keepalives are disabled by default.

```
[edit interfaces interface-name]
dce;
```

When you are using Frame Relay encapsulation on an interface, each logical interface corresponds to one or more permanent virtual circuits (PVCs) or switched virtual circuits (SVCs). For each PVC or SVC, you must configure one data-link connection identifier (DLCI). A Frame Relay interface can be a point-to-point interface or a point-to-multipoint (also called a multipoint nonbroadcast multiaccess [NBMA]) connection.

To configure a point-to-point Frame Relay connection, include the `dlci` statement:

```
[edit interfaces interface-name unit logical-unit-number]
dlci dlci-identifier;
```

`dlci-identifier` is the DLCI identifier, which is a number from 1 through 1,022. Numbers 1 through 15 are reserved. A point-to-point interface can have one DLCI. When you are configuring point-to-point connections, the MTU sizes on both sides of the connection must be the same.

To configure a point-to-multipoint Frame Relay connection (also called a multipoint NBMA connection), include the `multipoint-destination` statement:

```
[edit interfaces interface-name unit logical-unit-number]
address address {
  multipoint-destination destination-address dlci dlci-
identifier;
}
```

address is the interface's address. For each destination, include one `multipoint-destination` statement. *destination-address* is the address of the remote side of the connection, and *dlci-identifier* is the DLCI identifier for the connection. When you are configuring point-to-multipoint connections, all interfaces in the subnet must use the same MTU size. If keepalives are enabled, causing the interface to send LMI messages during idle times, the number of possible DLCI configurations is limited by the MTU selected for the interface.

By default, Frame Relay connections assume unicast traffic. If your Frame Relay switch performs multicast replication, you can configure the connection to support multicast traffic by including the `multicast-dlci` statement:

```
[edit interfaces interface-name unit logical-unit-number]
multicast-dlci dlci-identifier;
```

dlci-identifier is the DLCI identifier, which is a number from 1 through 1,022 that defines the Frame Relay DLCI over which the switch is expecting to receive multicast packets for replication. You can configure multicast support only on point-to-multipoint Frame Relay connections.

Configuring the Loopback Interface

On the router, you can configure one physical loopback interface, `lo0`, and one or more addresses on the interface. To do this, include the following statements:

```
[edit interfaces]
lo0 {
  unit 0 {
    family inet {
      loopback-address;
      <loopback-address2>;
      ...
    }
  }
}
```

When specifying the loopback address, do not include a destination prefix. Also, do not specify a loopback address on any unit number other than unit 0.

Configuring Multilink Interfaces

The standards for MLPPP and MLFR FRF.15 are defined in RFC 1990, *The PPP Multilink Protocol (MP)*, and in FRF.15, *End-to-End Multilink Frame Relay Implementation Agreement.*

The Multilink Protocol (MP) enables you to split, recombine, and sequence datagrams across multiple logical data links. The goal of multilink operation is to coordinate multiple independent links between a fixed pair of systems, providing a virtual link with greater bandwidth than any of the members. The physical connections must be E1 or T1 interfaces. The Multilink Protocol includes two encapsulation types: Multilink Point-to-Point Protocol (MLPPP) and Multilink Frame Relay (MLFR). The JUNOS software supports both MLPPP and MLFR (FRF.15 only).

Each Multilink Services PIC can support a number of multilink *bundles*. A multilink bundle can contain up to eight individual *links*, such as T1 or E1 physical interfaces. Each link is associated with a logical unit number that you configure. You must configure a link before it can join a bundle. Each bundle should consist solely of one type of link; Juniper Networks recommends not mixing T1 and E1 physical interfaces within a bundle.

Multilink Services PICs are available in three versions, as shown in Table 6.6. The PIC hardware is identical, except for different faceplates that enable you to identify which version you are installing. The software limits the unit numbers and maximum number of physical interfaces you assign to the PIC. You can install a maximum of four Multilink Services PICs per router.

Table 6.6 *Multilink Services PIC Capacities*

PIC Capacity	Unit Numbers	Maximum Number of T1 Interfaces	Maximum Number of E1 Interfaces
4-bundle PIC	0 through 3	32 links	32 links
32-bundle PIC	0 through 31	256 links	219 links
128-bundle PIC	0 through 127	292 links	219 links

A single PIC can support an aggregate bandwidth of 450 Mbps. You can configure a larger number of links, but the Multilink Services PIC can reliably process only 450 Mbps of traffic. A higher rate of traffic might degrade performance.

Configuring Multilink Properties

By default, the drop timeout value is disabled. You can configure a drop timeout value to provide a recovery mechanism if individual links in the multilink bundle drop one or more packets. Make sure that the value you set is larger than the expected differential delay across the links, although drop timeout is not a differential delay tolerance setting and does not limit the overall latency. To configure the drop timeout value, include the `drop-timeout` statement. *milliseconds* is the duration of the drop timer; its range is 1 through 127 milliseconds. Values less than 5 milliseconds are not recommended; a value of 0 disables the timer.

```
[edit interfaces ml-fpc/pic/port unit logical-unit-number]
drop-timeout milliseconds;
```

By default, the encapsulation on multilink interfaces is MLPPP. MLPPP and Multilink Frame Relay (MLFR) are the encapsulation types used to transmit packets within the multilink interface. To configure multilink encapsulation, include the `encapsulation` statement. You must also configure the T1 or E1 physical interface with the same encapsulation type.

```
[edit interfaces ml-fpc/pic/port unit logical-unit-number]
encapsulation (multilink-ppp | multilink-framerelay);
```

By default, the fragmentation threshold parameter is disabled. For MLPPP interfaces only, you can configure a fragmentation threshold to set a maximum size for packet payloads transmitted across the individual links within the multilink circuit. The software splits any incoming packet that exceeds the fragmentation threshold into smaller units suitable for the circuit size; it reassembles the fragments at the other end, but does not affect the output traffic stream. The threshold value affects the payload only; it does not affect the MLPPP header. To configure a fragmentation threshold value, include the `fragment-threshold` statement, specifying the maximum fragment size, beyond which the software automatically subdivides packet payloads; its range is 128 through 16,320 bytes. Any value you set must be a multiple of 64 bytes. The default value of 0 results in no fragmentation.

```
[edit interfaces ml-fpc/pic/port unit logical-unit-number]
fragment-threshold bytes;
```

To set the minimum number of links that must be up for the multilink bundle as a whole to be labeled up, include the `minimum-links` statement. *number* can be a value from 1 through 8. The default is 1.

```
minimum-links number;
```

The maximum received reconstructed unit (MRRU) is similar to a maximum transmission unit (MTU), but applies only to multilink bundles; it is the maximum packet size that the multilink interface can process. By default, the MRRU is set to 1,500 bytes; you can configure a different MRRU value if the peer equipment allows. The MRRU includes the original payload plus the 2-byte PPP header, but not the additional MLPPP or MLFR header applied while the individual multilink packets are traversing separate links in the bundle. To configure a different MRRU value, include the `mrru` statement. *bytes* is the MRRU size; its range is 1,500 through 4,500 bytes.

```
[edit interfaces ml-fpc/pic/port unit logical-unit-number]
mrru bytes;
```

For MLPPP, the sequence header format is set to 24 bits by default. You can configure an alternative value of 12 bits, but 24 bits is considered the more robust value for most networks. To configure a different sequence header value, include the `short-sequence` statement. For MLFR, the sequence header format is set to 24 bits by default. This is the only valid option.

```
[edit interfaces ml-fpc/pic/port unit logical-unit-number]
short-sequence;
```

Configuring Physical and Logical Multilink Interfaces

To complete a multilink interface configuration, you configure both the physical interface, either a T1 or E1, and the multilink bundle, which is a logical connection (see Figure 6.2). The physical interface is usually connected to networks capable of supporting MLPPP or MLFR.

Using the topology in Figure 6.2 as an example, configure a multilink bundle over a T1 connection (for which you have already configured the T1 physical interface) with the following additional configuration statements:

Figure 6.2 *Multilink Interface Configuration*

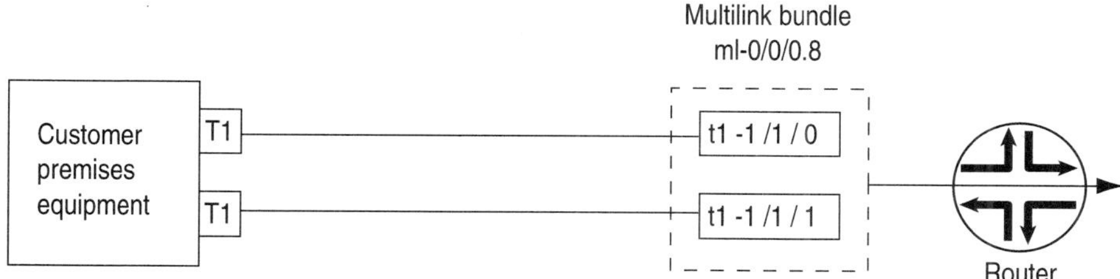

1. To configure a physical T1 link for MLPPP, include the following statements:

```
[edit interfaces t1-fpc/pic/port]
unit 0 {
  family mlppp {
    bundle ml-fpc/pic/port;
  }
}
```

You do not need to configure an IP address on this link.

If the MLPPP bundle is interoperating with Cisco IOS, the IOS configuration must include the `ppp multilink fragment-delay` command within the `interface multilink#` configuration group. The time should be 500 milliseconds.

```
interface Multilink#
ppp multilink fragment-delay milliseconds
```

To configure a physical T1 link for MLFR, include the following statements:

```
[edit interfaces t1-fpc/pic/port]
unit 0 {
  dlci dlci-identifier;
  encapsulation multilink-framerelay;
  family mlfr {
    bundle ml-fpc/pic/port;
  }
}
```

You do not need to configure an IP address on this link.

2. To configure the logical address for the MLPPP bundle, include the `address` and `destination` statements:

```
[edit interfaces ml-fpc/pic/port unit logical-unit-number]
  family inet {
    address address {
      destination address;
    }
  }
}
```

When you add statements such as MRRU to the configuration and commit, the T1 interface becomes part of the multilink bundle.

To configure the logical address for the MLFR bundle, include the `address` and `destination` statements:

```
[edit interfaces ml-fpc/pic/port unit logical-unit-number]
  encapsulation multilink-framerelay;
  family inet {
    address address {
      destination address;
    }
  }
}
```

For MLPPP and MLFR links, you must specify the address as `/32` or `/30`. Other subnet designations are treated as mismatches.

Configuring SONET/SDH Interfaces

Synchronous Digital Hierarchy (SDH) is a CCITT standard for a hierarchy of optical transmission rates. Synchronous Optical Network (SONET) is an American standard that is largely equivalent to SDH. Both are widely used methods for very high speed transmission of voice and data signals across the numerous worldwide fiber-optic networks.

Configuring SONET/SDH Physical Interface Properties

To configure SONET/SDH physical interface properties, include the `sonet-options` statement:

```
[edit interfaces so-fpc/pic/port]
sonet-options {
  aggregate asx;
  aps {
    advertise-interval milliseconds;
    authentication-key key;
    force;
    hold-time milliseconds;
    lockout;
    neighbor address;
    paired-group group-name;
    protect-circuit group-name;
    request;
    revert-time seconds;
    working-circuit group-name;
  }
  bytes {
    e1-quiet value;
    f1 value;
    f2 value;
    s1 value;
    z3 value;
    z4 value;
  }
  fcs (32 | 16);
  loopback (local | remote);
  path-trace trace-string;
  (payload-scrambler | no-payload-scrambler);
  rfc-2615;
  (z0-increment | no-z0-increment);
}
```

To configure values in SONET header bytes, include the `bytes` statement. You can configure the following SONET header bytes:

- `e1-quiet`—Default idle byte sent on the orderwire SONET overhead bytes. The router does not support the orderwire channel, and hence sends this byte continuously. For the E1-quiet byte, *value* can be in the range 0 through 255. The default value is 0x7F.
- `f1`, `f2`, `z3`, `z4`—SONET overhead bytes. For these bytes, *value* can be in the range 0 through 255. The default value is 0x00.
- `s1`—Synchronization message SONET overhead byte. This byte is normally controlled as a side effect of the system reference clock configuration and the state of the external clock coming from an interface if the system reference clocks have been configured to use an external reference. For the S1 byte, *value* can be in the range 0 through 255.

On SONET OC-48 interfaces that you configure for channelized (multiplexed) mode (by including the `no-concatenate` statement at the `[edit chassis fpc` *`slot-number`* `pic` *`pic-number`*`]` hierarchy level), the `bytes e1-quiet` and `bytes f1` options have no effect. The `bytes f2`, `bytes z3`, `bytes z4`, and `path-trace` options work correctly on channel 0 and work in the transmit direction only on channels 1, 2, and 3. Table 6.7 lists the JUNOS software framing bytes.

Table 6.7 *SONET/SDH Framing Bytes for Specific Speeds*

OH	STM-4	STM-16	STM-64	OC-12	OC-48	OC-192
A1	F6	F6	F6	F6	F6	F6
A2	28	28	28	28	28	28
J0/Z0	01/CC	01/CC	01/CC	—	—	—
C1	—	—	—	1.12	1.48	1.192
H1/H2	6A0A	6A0A	6A0A	620A	620A	620A
Concatenated mode	93FF	93FF	93FF	93FF	93FF	93FF

The use of J0 for framing has been deprecated. For DS-3 channels on a Channelized OC-12 interface, the `bytes e1-quiet, bytes f1, bytes f2, bytes z3,` and `bytes z4` statements have no effect. The `bytes s1` statement is supported only for channel 0; it is ignored if configured on channels 1 through 11. The `bytes s1` value configured on channel 0 applies to all channels on the interface.

When configured in SDH framing mode, SONET/SDH interfaces on a Juniper Networks router might not interoperate with some older versions of ADMs or regenerators that require an incrementing STM ID. To resolve this incompatibility, you can explicitly configure an incrementing STM ID rather than a static one in the SDH overhead by including the `z0-increment` statement. You should include this statement only for SDH mode; do not use it for SONET mode.

```
[edit interfaces so-fpc/pic/port sonet-options]
z0-increment;
```

By default, SONET interfaces use a 16-bit frame checksum. You can configure a 32-bit checksum, which provides more reliable packet verification. However, some older equipment may not support 32-bit checksums. To configure a 32-bit checksum, include the `fcs` 32-statement:

```
[edit interfaces so-fpc/pic/port sonet-options]
fcs 32;
```

To configure loopback capability on a SONET interface, include the `loopback` statement. Packets can be looped on either the local or the remote router.

```
[edit interfaces so-fpc/pic/port sonet-options]
loopback (local | remote);
```

The SONET path trace identifier is a text string that identifies the circuit. To configure a path trace identifier, include the `path-trace` statement. If the string contains spaces, enclose it in quotation marks. The common convention is to use the circuit identifier as the path trace identifier. If you do not configure an identifier, the JUNOS software uses the system and interface names. The local system's path trace identifier is displayed when you issue a `show interfaces` command on the remote system. For DS-3 channels on a Channelized OC-12 interface, you can configure a unique path trace for each of the 12 channels. Each path trace can be up to 16 bytes.

```
[edit interfaces so-fpc/pic/port sonet-options]
path-trace trace-string;
```

SONET HDLC payload scrambling, which is enabled by default, provides better link stability. Both sides of a connection must either use or not use scrambling. To disable HDLC payload scrambling, include the `no-payload-scrambler` statement:

```
[edit interfaces so-fpc/pic/port sonet-options]
no-payload-scrambler;
```

RFC 2615 requires certain C2 header byte and frame checksum (FCS) settings that vary from the default values configured in accordance with RFC 1619. The newer values are optimized for stronger error detection, especially when combined with payload scrambling at higher bit rate links. Table 6.8 shows the older (RFC 1619) and newer (RFC 2615) values, together with the Juniper Networks default values.

Table 6.8 *SONET Default Settings*

	RFC 1619	Default	RFC 2615
SONET C2 header byte	0XCF	0XCF	0X16
Frame checksum (bit)	16	16	32
Payload scrambling	–	Enabled	Enabled

To enable support for the RFC 2615 features, include the `rfc-2615` statement:

```
[edit interfaces so-fpc/pic/port sonet-options]
rfc-2615;
```

Configuring APS

Automatic Protection Switching (APS) is used by SONET add/drop multiplexers (ADMs) to protect against circuit failures. The JUNOS implementation of APS allows you to protect against circuit failures between an ADM and one or more routers and between multiple interfaces in the same router. When a circuit or router fails, a backup immediately takes over. The JUNOS software supports APS 1+1 switching, bidirectional only, and either revertive or nonrevertive mode. The JUNOS software does not transmit identical data on the working and protect circuits, as the APS specification requires for 1+1 switching, but this causes no operational impact.

With APS, you configure two circuits, a *working circuit* and a *protect circuit*. Normally, traffic is carried on the working circuit (that is, the working circuit is the active circuit), and the protect circuit is disabled. If the working circuit fails or degrades, or if the working router fails, the ADM and the protect router switch the traffic to the protect circuit, and the protect circuit becomes the active circuit.

To configure APS, you configure a *working* and a *protect* circuit, as shown in Figure 6.3. To protect against a router failure, you connect two routers to the ADM, configuring one of them as the working router and the second as the protect router. To protect against a PIC or an FPC failure, you connect one router to the ADM through both the working and protect circuits, configuring one of the PICs or FPCs as the working circuit and the second as the protect circuit.

Figure 6.3 *APS Configuration Topologies*

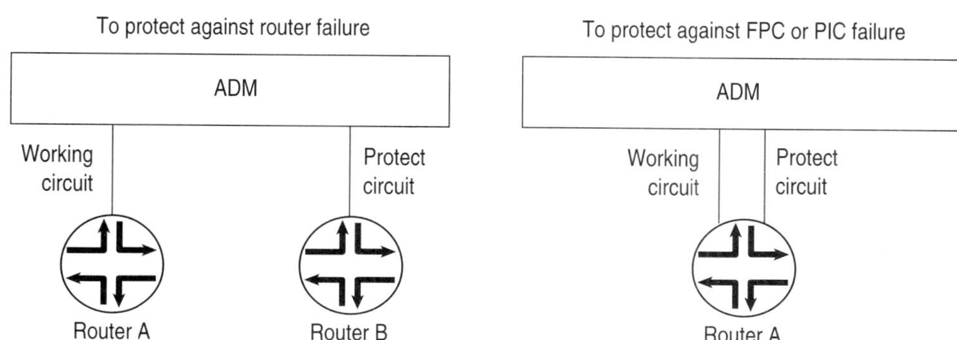

To set up a basic APS configuration, configure one interface to be the working circuit and a second to be the protect circuit. If you are using APS to protect against router failure, configure one interface on each router. If you are using APS to protect against FPC failure, configure two interfaces on the router, one on each FPC. For each working–protect circuit pair, configure the following:

- Group name—Creates the association between the two circuits. Configure the same group name for both the working and protect routers.
- Authentication key—You configure this on both interfaces. Configure the same key for both the working and protect routers.
- Address of the other interface on the other router—If you are configuring one router to be the working router and a second to be the protect router, you must configure the address of the remote interface. You configure this on one or both of the interfaces. The address you specify for the neighbor must never be routed through the interface on which APS is configured, or instability will result. APS neighbor only applies to inter-router configurations. Juniper Networks strongly recommends that you directly connect the working and protect routers and that you configure the interface address of this shared network as the neighbor address.

The working and protect configurations on the routers must match the circuit configurations on the ADM; that is, the working router must be connected to the ADM's working circuit, and the protect router must be connected to the protect circuit.

To set up a basic APS configuration, include the following statements:

On the working router/circuit:

```
[edit interfaces so-fpc/pic/port sonet-options]
aps {
  working-circuit group-name;
  authentication-key key;
  neighbor address; # Include only if protect circuit
    is on a different router
}
```

On the protect router/circuit:

```
aps {
  protect-circuit group-name;
  authentication-key key;
  neighbor address;# Include only if working circuit
    is on a different router
}
```

When there are multiple reasons to switch between the working and protect circuits, a priority scheme is used to decide which circuit to use. The routers and the ADM might automatically switch traffic between the working and protect circuits because of circuit and router failures. You can also choose to switch traffic manually between the working and protect circuits. There are three priority levels of manual configuration, listed here in order from lowest to highest priority:

A router failure is considered to be equivalent to a signal failure on a circuit.

- Request (also known as manual switch)—Overridden by signal failures, signal degradations, or any higher-priority reasons.
- Force (also known as forced switch)—Overrides manual switches, signal failures, and signal degradation.
- Lockout (also known as lockout of protection)—Do not switch between the working and protect circuits.

To perform a manual switch, include the `request` statement. This statement is honored only if there are no higher-priority reasons to switch.

```
[edit interfaces so-fpc/pic/port sonet-options aps]
request (protect | working);
```

When the working circuit is operating in nonrevertive mode, use the `request working` statement to switch the circuit manually to being the working circuit or to override the revert timer.

To perform a forced switch, include the `force` statement. This statement is honored only if there are no higher-priority reasons to switch. This configuration can be overridden by a signal failure on the protect circuit, thus causing a switch to the working circuit.

```
[edit interfaces so-fpc/pic/port sonet-options aps]
force (protect | working);
```

To configure a lockout of protection, forcing the use of the working circuit and locking out the protect circuit regardless of anything else, include the `lockout` statement:

```
[edit interfaces so-fpc/pic/port sonet-options aps]
lockout;
```

By default, APS is nonrevertive, which means that if the protect circuit becomes active, traffic is not switched back to the working circuit unless the protect circuit fails or you manually configure a switch to the working circuit. In revertive mode, traffic is automatically switched back to the working circuit. You should configure the ADM and routers consistently with regard to revertive or nonrevertive mode. To configure revertive mode, include the `revert-time` statement, specifying the amount of time to wait after the working circuit has again become functional before making the working circuit active again:

```
[edit interfaces so-fpc/pic/port sonet-options aps]
revert-time seconds;
```

If you are using nonrevertive APS, you can use the `request working` statement to switch the circuit manually to being the working circuit or to override the revert timer (configured with the `revert-time` statement).

The protect and working routers periodically send packets to their neighbors to advertise that they are operational. By default, these advertisement packets are sent every 1,000 milliseconds. A router considers its neighbor to be operational for a period, called the *hold time*, that is, by default, three times the advertisement interval. If the protect router does not receive an advertisement packet from the working router within the hold time configured on the protect router, the protect router assumes that the working router has failed and becomes active. APS is symmetric; either side of a circuit can time out the other side (for example, when detecting a crash of the other). Under normal circumstances, the failure of the protect router does not cause any changes because the traffic is already moving on the working router. However, if you had configured `request protect` and the protect router failed, the working router would enable its interface. To modify the advertisement interval, include the `advertise-interval` statement:

```
[edit interfaces so-fpc/pic/port sonet-options aps]
advertise-interval milliseconds;
```

The advertisement intervals and hold times on the protect and working routers can be different.

To modify the hold time, include the `hold-time` statement:

```
[edit interfaces so-fpc/pic/port sonet-options aps]
hold-time milliseconds;
```

When two routers are connected to a single ADM, they can back up each other on two different pairs of circuits. This arrangement provides load balancing between the routers if one of the working circuits fails. Figure 6.4 illustrates load sharing between circuits on two routers. Router A has a working circuit "Start" and a protect circuit "Up," and Router B has a working circuit "Up" and a protect circuit "Start." Under normal circumstances, Router A carries the "Start" circuit traffic, and Router B carries the "Up" circuit traffic. If the working circuit "Start" were to fail, Router B would end up carrying all the traffic for both the "Start" and "Up" circuits. To balance the load between the circuits, you pair the two circuits. In this case, you pair the "Start" and "Up" circuits. Then, if the working circuit "Start" fails, the two routers automatically switch the "Up" traffic from the working to the protect circuit so that each router is still carrying only one circuit's worth of traffic. That is, the working circuit on Router A would be "Up," and the working circuit on Router B would be "Start."

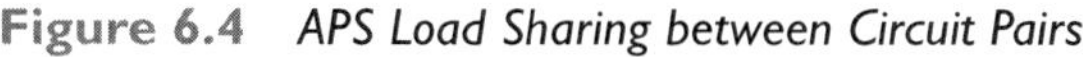

Figure 6.4 *APS Load Sharing between Circuit Pairs*

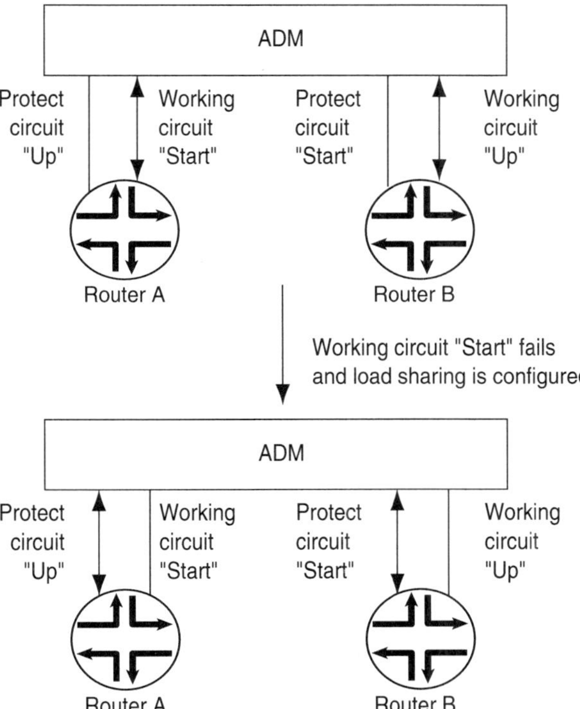

To configure load sharing between two working–protect circuit pairs, include the `paired-circuit` statement when configuring one of the circuits on one of the routers. In this statement, the *`group-name`* is the name of the group you assigned to one of the circuits with the `working-circuit` and `protect-circuit` statements. The software automatically configures the remainder of the load-sharing setup based on the group name.

```
[edit interfaces so-fpc/pic/port sonet-options aps]
paired-group group-name;
```

Configuring the Media MTU

The default media MTU size used on a physical interface depends on the encapsulation being used on that interface. To modify the default media MTU size for a physical interface, include the mtu statement:

See Table 6.2 and Table 6.3 on page 191.

```
[edit interfaces interface-name]
mtu bytes;
```

If you change the size of the media MTU, you must ensure that the size is equal to or greater than the sum of the protocol MTU and the encapsulation overhead. You configure the protocol MTU by including the mtu statement at the [edit interfaces *interface-name* unit *logical-unit-number* family *family*] hierarchy level.

Configuring the Clock Source

For interfaces such as SONET that can use different clock sources, you can configure the source of the transmit clock on each interface. The source can be internal (also called *line timing* or normal) or external (also called *loop timing*). The default source is internal, which means that each interface uses the router's internal Stratum 3 clock.

For DS-3 channels on a Channelized OC-12 interface, the clocking statement is supported only for channel 0; it is ignored if included in the configuration of channels 1 through 11. The clock source configured for channel 0 applies to all channels on the Channelized OC-12 interface. The individual DS-3 channels use a gapped 45-MHz clock as the transmit clock.

To configure loop timing on an interface, include the clocking external statement:

```
[edit interfaces interface-name]
clocking external;
```

To explicitly configure line timing on an interface, include the clocking internal statement:

```
[edit interfaces interface-name]
clocking internal;
```

Configuring Receive and Transmit Leaky Bucket Properties

Congestion control is particularly difficult in high-speed networks with high volumes of traffic. When congestion occurs in such a network, it is usually too late to react. You can avoid congestion by regulating the flow of packets into your network. Smoother flows prevent bursts of packets from arriving at (or being transmitted from) the same interface and causing congestion. For all interface types except ATM, Fast Ethernet, and Gigabit Ethernet, you can configure leaky bucket properties, which allow you to limit the amount of traffic received on and transmitted by a particular interface. You effectively specify what percentage of the interface's total capacity can be used to receive or transmit packets. You might want to set leaky bucket properties to limit the traffic flow from a link that is known to transmit high volumes of traffic.

The leaky bucket is used at the host–network interface to allow packets into the network at a constant rate. Packets might be generated in a bursty manner, but after they pass through the leaky bucket, they enter the network evenly spaced. In some cases, you might want to allow short bursts of packets to enter the network without smoothing them out. By controlling the number of packets that can accumulate in the bucket, a threshold property can control burstiness. The maximum number of packets entering the network in *t* time units is *threshold* + *rate* * *t*.

By default, leaky buckets are disabled, and the interface can receive and transmit packets at the maximum line rate. For each DS-3 channel on a Channelized OC-12 interface, you can configure unique receive and transmit buckets.

To configure leaky bucket properties, include one or both of the `receive-bucket` and `transmit-bucket` statements:

```
[edit interfaces interface-name]
receive-bucket {
  overflow (tag | discard);
  rate percentage;
  threshold number;
}
transmit-buckets {
  overflow (discard);
  rate percentage;
  threshold number;
}
```

In the `rate` statement, specify the percentage of the interface line rate that is available to receive or transmit packets. The percentage can be a value from 0 (none of the interface line rate is available) to 100 (the maximum interface line rate is available). For example, when you set the line rate to 33, the interface receives or transmits at one-third of the maximum line rate.

In the `threshold` statement, specify the bucket threshold, which controls the burstiness of the leaky bucket mechanism. The larger the value, the more bursty the traffic, which means that over a very short amount of time the interface can receive or transmit close to line rate, but the average over a longer time is at the configured bucket rate. The threshold can be a value from 0 through 16,777,215 bytes. For ease of entry, you can enter *`number`* either as a complete decimal number or as a decimal number followed by the abbreviation `k` (1,000) or `m` (1,000,000). For example, the entry `threshold 2m` corresponds to a threshold of 2,000,000 bytes.

In the `overflow` statement, specify how to handle packets that exceed the threshold:

- `tag`—(`receive-bucket` statement only) Tag, count, and process received packets that exceed the threshold.
- `discard`—Discard received packets that exceed the threshold. No counting is done.

Damping Interface Transitions

By default, when an interface changes from being up to being down, or from down to up, this transition is advertised immediately to the router software and hardware. In some situations, for example, when an interface is connected to an ADM or WDM, or to protect against SONET framer holes, you might want to damp interface transitions, thereby not advertising the interface's transition until a certain period of time has transpired. When you have damped interface transitions and the interface goes from up to down, the interface is not advertised to the rest of the system as being down until it has remained down for the hold-time period. Similarly, when an interface goes from down to up, it is not advertised as being up until it has remained up for the hold-time period.

To damp interface transitions, include the `hold-time` statement. The time can be a value from 0 through 65,534 milliseconds. The time value that you specify is rounded up to the nearest whole second. The default value is 0, which means that interface transitions are not damped.

```
[edit interfaces interface-name]
hold-time up milliseconds down milliseconds;
```

Configuring Interface Encapsulation

Point-to-Point Protocol (PPP) encapsulation is the default encapsulation type for physical interfaces. You need not configure encapsulation for any physical interfaces that support PPP encapsulation.

For SONET/SDH interfaces, the physical interface encapsulation can be one of the following:

PPP encapsulation is defined in RFC 1331, *The Point-to-Point Protocol (PPP) for the Transmission of Multiprotocol Datagrams over Point-to-Point Links.*

- Point-to-Point Protocol (PPP) includes two related versions, circuit cross-connect (CCC) (`ppp-ccc`) and translational cross-connect (TCC) (`ppp-tcc`).
- Cisco HDLC includes two related versions, CCC (`cisco-hdlc-ccc`) and TCC (`cisco-hdlc-tcc`).

Defined in RFC 1490, *Multiprotocol Interconnect over Frame Relay.*

- Frame Relay, including Frame Relay encapsulation. Two related versions are supported: CCC (`frame-relay-ccc`) and TCC (`frame-relay-tcc`).

To configure the encapsulation on a physical interface, include the `encapsulation` statement:

```
[edit interfaces interface-name]
encapsulation (cisco-hdlc | cisco-hdlc-ccc | cisco-hdlc-
   tcc | frame-relay | frame-relay-ccc | frame-relay-tcc |
   ppp | ppp-ccc | ppp-tcc);
```

For Frame Relay encapsulation, you also can configure the encapsulation type that is used inside the Frame Relay packet itself by including the following `encapsulation` statement, specifying the `frame-relay-ccc` option:

```
[edit interfaces interface-name unit logical-unit-number]
encapsulation frame-relay-ccc;
```

Configuring Aggregated SONET/SDH Interfaces

The JUNOS software enables link aggregation of SONET/SDH interfaces; this is similar to Ethernet link aggregation, but is not defined in a public standard. You configure an aggregated SONET/SDH virtual link by specifying the link number as a physical device and then associating a set of physical interfaces that have the same speed. By default, no aggregated SONET/SDH interfaces are created. To define the number of aggregated SONET/SDH interfaces, include the `device-count` statement. The maximum number of aggregated interfaces is 16, and the assigned number can range from 0 through 15.

```
[edit chassis aggregated-devices sonet]
device-count number;
```

To configure aggregated SONET/SDH interfaces, assign a number for the aggregated SONET/SDH interface `asx` at the `[edit interfaces]` hierarchy level:

```
[edit interfaces]
asx {
  ...
}
```

You also need to specify the constituent physical interfaces by including the `aggregate` statement at the `[edit interfaces interface-name sonet-options]` hierarchy level. You can optionally specify other physical properties that apply specifically to the aggregated SONET interfaces.

To remove the configuration statements related to `asx` and set the aggregated SONET/SDH interface to down state, delete the interface from the configuration. However, the aggregated SONET/SDH interface is not deleted until you delete the `chassis aggregated-devices sonet device-count` configuration statement.

To associate a physical interface with an aggregated SONET link, include the `aggregate` statement:

```
[edit interfaces interface-name sonet-options]
aggregate asx;
```

`x` is the interface instance number and can range from 0 through 15, for a total of 16 aggregated interfaces. You should not mix SONET and SDH mode on the same aggregated interface. The interface instance you specify must match the one you configured as `asx` at the `[edit interfaces]` hierarchy level.

When you configure the `aggregate` statement, the only other statement allowed under the `sonet-options` hierarchy is `loopback`. You can combine like interfaces only, so each physical interface in the aggregate must be the same speed.

You can set the required link speed for all interfaces included in the bundle. All interfaces that make up a bundle must be the same speed. If you include in the aggregated SONET interface an individual link that has a speed different from the speed you specify in the `link-speed` parameter, an error message is logged. To set the required link speed, include the `link-speed` statement:

```
[edit interfaces interface-name aggregated-sonet-options]
link-speed speed;
```

speed can be one of the following values:

- `oc3`—For OC-3c or STM-1c
- `oc12`—For OC-12c or STM-4c
- `oc48`—For OC-48c or STM-16c
- `oc192`—For OC-192c or STM-64c

On aggregated SONET interfaces, you can set the minimum number of links that must be up for the bundle as a whole to be labeled up by including the `minimum-links` statement. By default, the minimum number is 1. *number* can be a value from 1 through 8.

```
[edit interfaces interface-name aggregated-sonet-options]
minimum-links number;
```

For information about defining the filter, see Chapter 8, "Routing Policy and Firewall Filters," on page 301.

To set up firewall filters or sampling on aggregated SONET interfaces, you must configure the `asx` interface with these properties. The filters function in the same manner as on other interfaces. To configure a filter, include the `filter` statement:

```
[edit interfaces]
asx {
  unit 0 {
    family inet {
      address address {
```

```
              destination address;
            }
            filter {
              input input-filter-name;
              output output-filter-name;
            }
          }
        }
      }
```

Configuring T1 and T3 Interfaces

T1 is the basic physical layer protocol used by the Digital Signal level 1 (DS-1) multiplexing method in North America. A T1 interface operates at a bit rate of 1.544 Mbps and can support 24 DS-0 channels. T3 is the physical layer protocol used by the Digital Signal level 3 (DS-3) multiplexing method in North America. A T3 interface operates at a bit rate of 44.736 Mbps. The JUNOS software supports payload scrambling and subrate operation on each physical T3 interface. DS-1 and DS-3 standards supported include ANSI TI.107, TI.102; GR 499-core, GR 253-core; Bellcore TR-TSY-000009 (DS-3 only); AT&T Pub 54014; and, ITU G.751, G.703, G823 (DS-3 only).

To configure T1-specific physical interface properties, include the `t1-options` statement:

```
[edit interfaces interface-name]
t1-options {
  bert-error-rate rate;
  bert-period seconds;
  buildout (0-133 | 133-266 | 266-399 | 399-532 | 532-
      655);
  byte-encoding (nx64 | nx56);
  fcs (32 | 16);
  framing (sf | esf);
  idle-cycle-flag (flags | ones);
  invert-data;
  line-encoding (ami | b8zs);
  loopback (local | remote);
  start-end-flag (shared | filler);
  timeslots time-slot-number;
}
```

To configure T3-specific physical interface properties, include the `t3-options` statement:

```
[edit interfaces interface-name]
```

```
t3-options {
  bert-algorithm algorithm;
  bert-error-rate rate;
  bert-period seconds;
  (cbit-parity | no-cbit-parity);
  compatibility-mode (digital-link | kentrox | larscom)
   <subrate value>;
  fcs (32 | 16);
  (feac-loop-respond | no-feac-loop-respond);
  idle-cycle-flag value;
  (long-buildout | no-long-buildout);
  loopback (local | remote);
  (payload-scrambler | no-payload-scrambler);
  start-end-flag value;
}
```

You can configure a T1 or T3 interface to execute a bit error rate test (BERT) when the interface receives a request to run this test. You specify the duration of the test and the error rate to include in the bit stream by including the `bert-period` and `bert-error-rate` statements. For T3 interfaces, you specify the pattern to send in the bit stream by including the `bert-algorithm` statement.

```
[edit interfaces interface-name t1-options] or
[edit interfaces interface-name t3-options]
bert-algorithm algorithm;
bert-error-rate rate;
bert-period seconds;
```

For T3 interfaces, *`algorithm`* is the pattern to send in the bit stream. The algorithm for the T1 BERT procedure is `pseudo-2e15-o151` (pattern is 2^{15}–1, as defined in the CCITT/ITU O.151 standard). *`rate`* is the bit error rate. This can be an integer in the range 0 through 7, which corresponds to a bit error rate in the range 10^{-0} (that is, 0, which corresponds to no errors) to 10^{-7} (that is, 1 error per 10 million bits). The default is 0. *`seconds`* is the duration of the BERT procedure, in seconds. The test can last from 1 to 240 seconds; the default is 10 seconds.

A T1 interface has five possible setting ranges for the T1 line buildout: 0-133, 133-266, 266-399, 399-532, or 532-655 feet. By default, the T1 interface uses the shortest setting (0-133). To have the interface drive a line at one of the longer distance ranges, include the `buildout` statement:

```
[edit interfaces interface-name t1-options]
buildout 532-655;
```

By default, T1 interfaces use a byte encoding of 8 bits per byte (nx64). You can configure an alternative byte encoding of 7 bits per byte (nx56). To have the interface use an encoding of 7 bits per byte, include the byte-encoding statement, specifying the nx56 option:

```
[edit interfaces interface-name t1-options]
byte-encoding nx56;
```

To configure a T3 interface so that it is compatible with the channel service unit (CSU) at the remote end of the line, include the compatibility statement:

```
[edit interfaces interface-name t3-options]
compatibility-mode (digital-link | kentrox | larscom)
    <subrate value>;
```

You can configure the interface to be compatible with a Digital Link, Kentrox, or Larscom CSU. The subrate of a T3 interface must exactly match that of the remote CSU. To specify the subrate, include the subrate option in the compatibility-mode statement:

- For Digital Link CSUs, specify the subrate *value* as the data rate you configured on the CSU in the format *x*kb or *x.x*Mb. For a list of specific rate values, use the command completion feature in the CLI. The range is 301 kbps through 44.2 Mbps.
- Kentrox CSUs do not support subrate.
- For Larscom CSUs, specify the subrate *value* as a number from 1 through 14 that exactly matches the value configured on the CSU.

On T3 interfaces, C-bit parity mode controls the type of framing that is present on the transmitted T3 signal. When C-bit parity mode is enabled, the C-bit positions are used for the FEBE, FEAC, terminal data link, path parity, and mode indicator bits, as defined in ANSI T1.107a-1989. When C-bit parity mode is disabled, the basic T3 framing mode (M13) is used. By default, C-bit parity mode is enabled. To disable C-bit parity mode and use M13 framing for your T3 link, include the no-cbit-parity statement:

```
[edit interfaces interface-name t3-options]
no-cbit-parity;
```

The T3 far-end alarm and control (FEAC) signal is used to send alarm or status information from the far-end terminal back to the near-end terminal and to initiate T3 loopbacks at the far-end terminal from the near-end terminal. To allow the remote CSU to place the local router into loopback, you must configure the router to respond to the CSU's FEAC request by including the `feac-loop-respond` statement:

```
[edit interfaces interface-name t3-options]
feac-loop-respond;
```

By default, the router does not respond to FEAC requests. If you have configured remote or local loopback with the T3 `loopback` statement, the router does not respond to FEAC requests from the CSU even if you have included the `feac-loop-respond` statement in the configuration. To have the router respond, you must delete the `loopback` statement from the configuration.

By default, T1 and T3 interfaces use a 16-bit frame checksum. You can configure a 32-bit checksum, which provides more reliable packet verification. However, some older equipment might not support 32-bit checksums. To configure a 32-bit checksum, include the `fcs 32` statement:

```
[edit interfaces interface-name t1-options] or
[edit interfaces interface-name t3-options]
fcs 32;
```

By default, T1 interfaces use extended super frame (ESF) framing format. You can configure SF (super frame) as an alternative. To have the interface use the SF framing format, include the `framing` statement, specifying the `sf` option:

```
[edit interfaces interface-name t1-options]
framing sf;
```

By default, data inversion is disabled on T1 interfaces. To enable data inversion at the HDLC level, include the `invert-data` statement. When you enable data inversion, all data bits in the data stream are transmitted inverted; that is, zeros are transmitted as ones and ones as zeroes. Data inversion is normally used only in AMI mode to guarantee ones' density in the transmitted stream.

```
[edit interfaces interface-name t1-options]
invert-data;
```

A T3 interface has two settings for the T3 line buildout: a short setting, which is less than 225 feet (about 68 meters), and a long setting, which is greater than 225 feet. By default, the interface uses the short setting. The `long-buildout` and `no-long-buildout` statements apply only to copper-cable–based T3 interfaces. You cannot configure a line buildout for a DS-3 channel on a Channelized OC-12 interface, which runs over fiber-optic cable. If you configure this statement on a Channelized OC-12 interface, it is ignored. To have the interface drive a line that is longer than 255 feet, include the `long-buildout` statement:

```
[edit interfaces interface-name t3-options]
long-buildout;
```

By default, T1 interfaces use B8ZS line encoding. To configure AMI line encoding, include the `line-encoding` statement, specifying the `ami` option:

```
[edit interfaces interface-name t1-options]
line-encoding ami;
```

When setting the line encoding parameter, you must set the same value for paired ports. Ports 0 and 1 must share the same value, and likewise ports 2 and 3 must share the same value, but ports 0 and 1 can have a different value from that of ports 2 and 3.

You can configure loopback capability between the local T1 or T3 interface and the remote channel service unit (CSU), as shown in Figure 6.5. You can configure the loopback to be local or remote. With local loopback, the T1 or T3 interface can transmit packets to the CSU, but receives its own transmission back again and ignores data from the CSU. With remote loopback, packets sent from the CSU are received by the T1 or T3 interface but also are immediately retransmitted to the CSU.

Figure 6.5 *Remote and Local T1 Loopback*

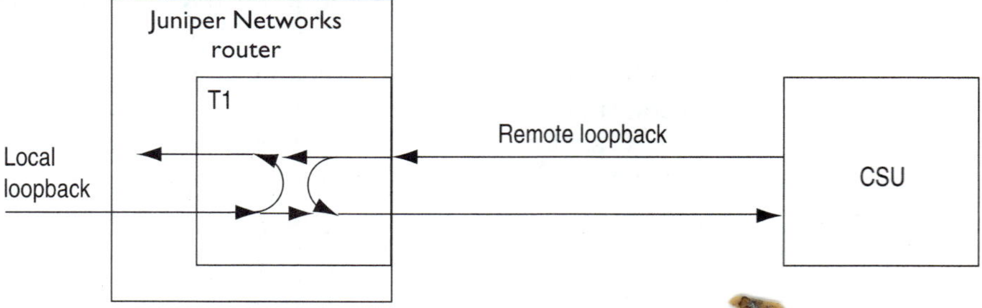

To configure loopback capability on a T1 or T3 interface, include the `loopback` statement:

```
[edit interfaces interface-name t1-options] or
[edit interfaces interface-name t3-options]
loopback (local | remote);
```

Packets can be looped on either the local router or the remote CSU. To turn off loopback, remove the `loopback` statement from the configuration.

T3 HDLC payload scrambling, which is disabled by default, provides better link stability. Both sides of a connection must either use or not use scrambling. On a Channelized OC-12 interface, the SONET `payload-scrambler` statement is ignored. To configure scrambling on the DS-3 channels on the interface, you can include the `t3-options payload-scrambler` statement:

```
[edit interfaces interface-name t3-options]
payload-scrambler;
```

By default, a T1 or T3 interface transmits the value 0x7E in the idle cycles. To have the interface transmit the value 0xFF (all ones) instead, include the `idle-cycle-flag` statement, specifying the `ones` option:

```
[edit interfaces interface-name t1-options] or
[edit interfaces interface-name t3-options]
idle-cycle-flag ones;
```

By default, a T1 or T3 interface waits two idle cycles between sending start and end flags. To configure the interface to share the transmission of start and end flags, include the `start-end-flag` statement, specifying the `shared` option:

```
[edit interfaces interface-name t1-options]
start-end-flag shared;
```

To configure the number of time slots allocated to a T1 interface, include the `timeslots` statement. The slot number can be in the range 1 through 24 for T1 interfaces. There are 24 time slots on a T1 interface. You can designate any combination of time slots for usage.

```
[edit interfaces interface-name t1-options]
timeslots timeslot-number;
```

Configuring Tunnel Interfaces

By encapsulating arbitrary packets inside a transport protocol, tunneling provides a private, secure path through an otherwise public network. Tunnels connect discontinuous subnetworks and enable encryption interfaces, virtual private networks (VPNs), and Multiprotocol Label Switching (MPLS). If you have a Tunnel PIC installed in your router, you can configure unicast and multicast tunnels.

The JUNOS software supports the following tunnel encapsulations:

- Generic route encapsulation (GRE)
- IP over IP (IP-IP)
- Virtual Private Network (VPN)
- PIM encapsulation

Configuring a Unicast Tunnel

To configure a bidirectional unicast tunnel, configure the `gr` interface (to use GRE encapsulation) or the `ip` interface (to use IP-IP encapsulation) and include the `tunnel` statement:

```
[edit interfaces]
gr-fpc/pic/port or ip-fpc/pic/port {
  unit logical-unit-number {
    tunnel {
      source address;
      destination address;
      routing-instance {
        destination routing-instance-name;
      }
      ttl number;
    }
    family family {
      address address {
        destination address;
      }
    }
  }
}
```

You can configure multiple logical units for each GRE or IP-IP interface, and you can configure only one tunnel per unit.

Each tunnel interface must be a point-to-point interface. Point to point is the default interface connection type, so you do not need to include the `point-to-point` statement when configuring the logical interface.

You must specify the tunnel's destination and source addresses. The remaining statements are optional.

To set the TTL field that is included in the encapsulating header, include the `ttl` statement. If you explicitly configure a TTL value for the tunnel, you must configure it to be one larger than the number of hops in the tunnel. For example, if the tunnel has seven hops, you must configure a TTL value of 8.

You must configure at least one family on the logical interface. To enable MPLS over GRE tunnel interfaces, you must include the `family mpls` statement in the GRE interface configuration. In addition, you must configure the `protocols` statements to enable RSVP, MPLS, and LSPs over GRE tunnels.

Configuring a Multicast Tunnel

To configure a multicast tunnel for interfaces that carry IPv4 or IPv6 traffic, include the `multicasts-only` statement:

```
[edit interfaces interface-name unit logical-unit-number family inet] or
[edit interfaces interface-name unit logical-unit-number family inet6]
multicasts-only;
```

Multicast tunnels filter all unicast packets; if an incoming packet is not destined for a `224/8` or greater prefix, the packet is dropped and a counter is incremented. You can configure multicast tunnels on GRE, IP-IP, PIM, and multicast tunnel is (MT) only.

Configuring a VPN Tunnel for Route Table Lookup

To configure tunnel interfaces to facilitate route table lookups for VPNs, you specify a tunnel's end point IP addresses and associate them with a routing instance that belongs to a particular routing table. This enables the software to search in the appropriate routing table for the route prefix, because the same prefix can appear in multiple routing tables. To configure the destination VPN, include the routing-instance statement:

For more information, see Chapter 12, "Layer 2 and Layer 3 VPNs," on page 613.

```
[edit interfaces]
gr-fpc/pic/port {
  unit logical-unit-number {
    tunnel {
      source address;
      destination address;
      routing-instance {
        destination routing-instance-name;
      }
    }
  }
}
```

Configuring a VPN Tunnel for VRF Table Lookup

To configure a VPN tunnel interface to facilitate VPN routing and forwarding (VRF) table lookup based on MPLS labels, specify a VPN tunnel interface name and associate it with a routing instance that belongs to a particular routing table. To specify a VPN tunnel interface name, configure the vt interface and include the family inet and family mpls statements:

```
[edit interfaces]
vt-fpc/pic/port {
  unit 0 {
    family inet;
    family mpls;
  }
  unit 1 {
    family inet;
  }
}
```

To associate the VPN tunnel with a routing instance, configure the VPN tunnel interface, vt, within the routing instance. For a VPN tunnel interface, none of the statements in the tunnel configuration block are valid.

```
[edit routing-instances]
interface vt-fpc/pic/port;
```

Configuring PIM Tunnels

PIM tunnels are unidirectional tunnels that are enabled automatically on routers that have a tunnel PIC and on which you enable PIM sparse mode. You do not need to configure the tunnel interface. In PIM sparse mode, the first-hop router encapsulates packets destined for the rendezvous point (RP) router. The packets are encapsulated with a unicast header and are forwarded through a unicast tunnel to the RP. The RP then decapsulates the packets and transmits them through its multicast tree. To perform the encapsulation and decapsulation, the first-hop and RP routers, respectively, must contain Tunnel Services PICs.

The JUNOS software creates two interfaces to handle PIM tunnels:

- `pe`—Encapsulates packets destined for the RP. This interface is present on the first-hop router.
- `pd`—Deencapsulates packets at the RP. This interface is present on the RP.

Configuring Channelized Interfaces

Channelized interfaces enable you to configure a number of individual channels that subdivide the bandwidth of a larger interface and minimize the number of PICs that an installation requires.

Configuring Channelized DS-3 to DS-0 Interfaces

To configure Channelized DS-3 to DS-0 interface properties, include the `t3-options`, `t1-options`, or `ds0-options` statement. To specify options for the T3 side of the connection, include the `t3-options` statement. These statements are supported only for channel 0; they are ignored if configured on other channels.

```
[edit interfaces interface-name]
t3-options {
  bert-algorithm algorithm;
  bert-error-rate rate;
  bert-period seconds;
  (cbit-parity | no-cbit-parity);
  (feac-loop-respond | no-feac-loop-respond);
  loopback (local | remote);
}
```

To specify options for each of the T1 channels, include the `t1-options` statement:

```
[edit interfaces interface-name]
t1-options {
  byte-encoding (nx64 | nx56);
  fcs (32 | 16);
  framing (sf | esf);
  idle-cycle-flag (flags | ones);
  invert-data;
  loopback (local | remote);
  start-end-flag (shared | filler);
  timeslots time-slot-number;
}
```

To specify options for each of the DS-0 channels, include the `ds0-options` statement:

```
[edit interfaces interface-name]
ds0-options {
  byte-encoding (nx64 | nx56);
  fcs (32 | 16);
  idle-cycle-flag (flags | ones);
  invert-data;
  start-end-flag (shared | filler);
}
```

You can configure 28 T1 channels per T3 interface. Each T1 link can have up to eight DS-0 channel groups, and each channel group can hold any combination of DS-0 time slots. To specify the T1 link and DS-0 channel group number in the interface name, use colons (:) as separators. The software uses the following rules to apply the interface options:

- To configure the T3 options, set the T1 link to 0 and channel group to 0:

  ```
  ds-0/0/0:0:0.
  ```

- To configure the `t1-options`, set channel group to 0; the T1 link can be any value:

  ```
  ds-0/0/0:x:0
  ```

- There are no restrictions on configuring the DS-0 options.
- If you delete a configuration you previously committed for channel group 0, the options return to default values.

To configure the channel groups and time slots for a Channelized DS-3 to DS-0 interface, include the `channel-group` and `timeslots` statements. If you commit the interface name but do not include the `[edit chassis]` configuration, the Channelized DS-3 to DS-0 PIC behaves like a Channelized DS-3 to DS-1 PIC: none of the DS-0 functionality is accessible. Table 6.9 shows the ranges for each of the quantities in the following configuration:

```
[edit chassis fpc slot-number pic pic-number ct3 port
port-number t1 link-number]
channel-group group-number timeslots time-slot-number;
```

Table 6.9 *Ranges for Channelized DS-3 to DS-0 Configuration*

Item	Option	Range
FPC slot	*slot-number*	0 through 7
PIC slot	*pic-number*	0 through 3
Port	*port-number*	0 through 1
T1 link	*link-number*	0 through 27
DS-0 channel group	*group-number*	0 through 7
Time slot	*time-slot-number*	1 through 24

Bandwidth limitations restrict the interface to a maximum of 128 channel groups per T3 port, rather than the theoretical maximum of 224 (8 times 28).

There are 24 time slots on a T1 interface. You can designate any combination of time slots for use, but you can use each time slot number on only one channel group within the same T1 link.

Configuring Channelized DS-3 to DS-1 Interfaces

To configure Channelized DS-3 to DS-1 interface properties, include both the `t1-options` and `t3-options` statements. To specify options for the T3 side of the connection, include the `t3-options` statement. These statements are supported only for channel 0; they are ignored if configured on other channels.

For information about configuring these statements, see "Configuring T1 and T3 Interfaces," on page 256.

```
[edit interfaces interface-name]
t3-options {
  bert-algorithm algorithm;
  bert-error-rate rate;
  bert-period seconds;
  (cbit-parity | no-cbit-parity);
  (feac-loop-respond | no-feac-loop-respond);
  loopback (local | remote);
}
```

To specify options for each of the T1 channels, include the `t1-options` statement:

```
[edit interfaces interface-name]
t1-options {
  byte-encoding (nx64 | nx56);
  fcs (32 | 16);
  framing (sf | esf);
  idle-cycle-flag (flags | ones);
  loopback (local | remote);
  start-end-flag (shared | filler);
  timeslots time-slot-number;
}
```

You can configure 28 T1 channels per T3 interface, and each interface can have logical interfaces. To specify the channel number, include it after the colon (:) in the interface name.

Configuring Channelized E1 Interfaces

To configure Channelized E1 interface properties, include the `e1-options` statement:

For information about configuring these statements, see "Configuring E1 and E3 Interfaces," on page 214.

```
[edit interfaces interface-name]
e1-options {
  fcs (32 | 16);
  framing (g704 | g704-no-crc4 | unframed);
  idle-cycle-flag (flags | ones);
  loopback (local | remote);
  start-end-flag (shared | filler);
}
```

To specify options for each of the DS-0 channels, include the `ds0-options` statement:

```
[edit interfaces interface-name]
ds0-options {
```

```
        byte-encoding (nx64 | nx56);
        fcs (32 | 16);
        idle-cycle-flag (flags | ones);
        loopback (local | remote);
        start-end-flag (shared | filler);
    }
```

Each Channelized E1 PIC has 10 E1 ports that you can channelize to the *N*xDS-0 level. Each E1 interface has 32 time slots (DS-0), in which time slot 0 is reserved. You can combine one or more of these DS-0 time slots (channels) to create a channel group (*N*xDS-0). There can be a maximum of 24 channel groups per E1 interface. Thus, you can configure a maximum of 240 channel groups per PIC (10 ports times 24 channel groups per port).

To specify the DS-0 channel group number in the interface name, include a colon (:) as a separator. The software applies the interface options you configure according to the following rules:

- To configure the E1 options, you must set channel group *x* to 0; that is, `ds-0/0/0:0`.
- There are no restrictions on configuring the DS-0 options.
- If you delete a configuration you previously committed for channel group 0, the options return to default values.

To configure the channel groups and time slots for a Channelized E1 interface, include the `channel-group` and `timeslots` statements. If you commit the interface name but do not include the `[edit chassis]` configuration, the Channelized E1 PIC behaves like a standard E1 PIC: none of the DS-0 functionality is accessible. Table 6.10 shows the ranges for each of the quantities in the following configuration:

```
[edit chassis]
fpc slot-number {
  pic pic-number {
    ce1 {
      e1 link-number {
        channel-group group-number timeslots time-slot-number;
      }
    }
  }
}
```

The theoretical maximum number of channel groups possible per PIC is 240 (10 times 24). This is within the maximum bandwidth available.

Table 6.10 *Ranges for Channelized E1 Configuration*

Item	Option	Range
FPC slot	*slot-number*	0 through 7
PIC slot	*pic-number*	0 through 3
E1 link	*link-number*	0 through 9
DS-0 channel group	*group-number*	0 through 23
Time slot	*time-slot-number*	0 through 31 (with time slot 0 reserved)

There are 32 time slots on an E1 interface. You can configure any combination of time slots. However, time slot 0 is reserved. For channelized fractional E1 interfaces only, when you include the `time slots` statement at the `[edit interfaces` *`interface-name`* `e1-options]` hierarchy level, time slot 1 is reserved, so you must allocate time slots in the range of 2 through 32. Alternatively, you can configure time slots by including the `channel-group` and `timeslots` statements at the `[edit chassis]` hierarchy level, in which case you can allocate time slots in the range of 1 through 31.

Configuring Channelized OC-12 Interfaces

To configure Channelized OC-12 interface properties, include the `sonet-options` and `t3-options` statements. For more information, see "Configuring SONET/SDH Interfaces," on page 240 and "Configuring T1 and T3 Interfaces," on page 256.

Configuring Channelized OC-3 and STM-1 Interfaces

There are two types of channelized optical PICs: Channelized OC-3 to T1 and Channelized STM-1 to E1. To configure the interface properties for these PICs, include the `e1-options` or `t1-options` statement and the `sonet-options` statement for both sides of the connection.

To specify options for each of the E1 channels on the Channelized STM-1 to E1 PIC, include the `e1-options` statement:

For information about configuring these statements, see "Configuring E1 and E3 Interfaces," on page 214.

```
[edit interfaces interface-name]
e1-options {
  bert-error-rate;
  bert-period;
  fcs (32 | 16);
  framing (g704 | g704-no-crc4 | unframed);
  idle-cycle-flag (flags | ones);
  loopback (local | remote);
  start-end-flag (shared | filler);
  timeslots time-slot-number;
}
```

To specify options for the SONET/SDH side of the connection, include the `sonet-options` statement:

For information about configuring these statements, see "Configuring SONET/SDH Interfaces," on page 240.

```
[edit interfaces interface-name]
sonet-options {
  bytes {
    e1-quiet value;
    f1 value;
    f2 value;
    s1 value;
    z3 value;
    z4 value;
  }
  loopback (local | remote);
}
```

To specify options for each of the T1 channels on the Channelized OC-3 to T1 PIC, include the `t1-options` statement:

For information about configuring these statements, see "Configuring T1 and T3 Interfaces," on page 256.

```
[edit interfaces interface-name]
t1-options {
  byte-encoding (nx64 | nx56);
  fcs (32 | 16);
  framing (sf | esf);
  idle-cycle-flag (flags | ones);
  loopback (local | remote);
  start-end-flag (shared | filler);
  timeslots time-slot-number;
}
```

You can configure up to 63 E1 channels per single-port Channelized STM-1 to E1 PIC. To specify the channel number, include it after the colon (`:`) in the interface name. You can configure up to 84 T1 channels per single-port Channelized OC-3 to T1 PIC. To specify the channel number, include it after the colon (`:`) in the interface name.

By default, virtual tributary mapping uses KLM mode. To configure virtual tributary mapping to use ITU-T mode, include the `vtmapping` statement, specifying the `itu-t` option:

```
[edit chassis fpc slot-number pic pic-number]
vtmapping itu-t;
```

Configuring Class of Service (CoS)

For interfaces that carry IPv4, IPv6, or MPLS traffic, you can configure class-of-service (CoS) features to provide multiple classes of service for different applications. On the router, you can configure multiple forwarding classes for transmitting packets, define which packets are placed into each output queue, schedule the transmission service level for each queue, and manage congestion using a Random Early Detection (RED) algorithm.

To configure CoS properties, include the following statements:

```
[edit]
class-of-service {
  classifiers {
    type classifier-name {
      import (classifier-name | default);
      forwarding-class class-name {
        loss-priority (low | high) code-points [ alias | bits
];
      }
    }
  }
  code-point-aliases {
    (dscp | exp | ieee-802.1 | inet-precedence) {
      alias-name bits;
    }
  }
  drop-profiles {
    profile-name {
      fill-level percentage drop-probability percentage;
      interpolate {
        drop-probability value;
        fill-level value;
      }
    }
  }
  forwarding-classes {
    queue queue-number class-name;
  }
  forwarding-policy {
    next-hop-map map-name {
      forwarding-class class-name {
```

```
          next-hop [ next-hop-name ];
        }
      }
      class class-name {
        classification-override {
          forwarding-class class-name;
        }
      }
    }
    interfaces
      interface-name {
        scheduler-map map-name;
        unit logical-unit-number {
          classifiers {
            (dscp | exp | ieee-802.1 | inet-precedence)
(classifier-name | default);
          }
          forwarding-class class-name;
          rewrite-rules {
            (dscp | exp | inet-precedence) (rewrite-name |
default);
          }
        }
      }
    }
    rewrite-rules {
      (dscp | exp | inet-precedence) rewrite-name {
        import (rewrite-name | default);
        forwarding-class class-name {
          loss-priority (low | high) code-point (alias | bits);
        }
      }
    }
    scheduler-maps {
      map-name {
        forwarding-class class-name scheduler scheduler-name;
      }
    }
    schedulers {
      scheduler-name {
        transmit-rate (rate | percent percentage | remainder)
<exact>;
        maximum-buffer-delay (milliseconds | percent percentage
| remainder);
        priority (low | high);
        drop-profile-map loss-priority (low | high) protocol
(non-tcp | tcp | any)
          drop-profile profile-name;
      }
    }
}
```

Table 6.11 lists the RFCs that define the standards supported by certain aspects of the JUNOS CoS software.

Table 6.11 *CoS Standards Supported by JUNOS Software*

Standard	Title
RFC 2474	*Definition of the Differentiated Services Field (DS Field) in the IPv4 and IPv6 Headers*
RFC 2597	*Assured Forwarding PHB Group*
RFC 2598	*An Expedited Forwarding PHB* (see also draft-ietf-diffserv-rfc2598bis-01.txt)

The JUNOS software supports only two loss priorities and, by default, supports only one assured forwarding (AF) class, although you can configure more at the expense of other class types. Only IEEE 802.1p Layer 2 classification propagation mechanisms are currently supported. RFC 2983, *Diffserv and Tunnels*, is not supported.

Defining Code-Point Aliases

A *code-point alias* is a name you assign to a set of DiffServ code-point (DSCP) bits. When you configure classes and define classifiers, you can refer to the code points by these alias names. You can configure user-defined classifiers in terms of alias names. If the value of an alias changes, it alters the behavior of any classifier that references that alias. Table 6.12, Table 6.13, Table 6.14, and Table 6.15 list the default mappings between the bit values and standard aliases. For example, it is widely accepted that the alias for DSCP 101110 is expedited forwarding (ef).

To define a code-point alias, include the `code-point-aliases` statement:

```
[edit class-of-service]
code-point-aliases {
  (dscp | exp | ieee-802.1 | inet-precedence) {
    alias-name bits;
  }
}
```

Table 6.12 *Default DSCP Mappings for DiffServ Code Points*

DiffServ Code Designator	Mapping
ef	101110
af11	001010
af12	001100
af13	001110
af21	010010
af22	010100
af23	010110
af31	011010
af32	011100
af33	011110
af41	100010
af42	100100
af43	100110
be	000000
cs1	001000
cs2	010000
cs3	011000
cs4	100000
cs5	101000

Table 6.13 *Default DSCP Mappings for MPLS EXP Code Points*

DiffServ Code Designator	Mapping
be	000
be1	001
ef	010
ef1	011
af11	100
af12	101

Table 6.13 *Default DSCP Mappings for MPLS EXP Code Points*

DiffServ Code Designator	Mapping
nc1/cs6	110
nc2/cs7	111

Table 6.14 *Default DSCP Mappings for IEEE 802.1 Code Points*

DiffServ Code Designator	Mapping
be	000
be1	001
ef	010
ef1	011
af11	100
af12	101
nc1/cs6	110
nc2/cs7	111

Table 6.15 *Default DSCP Mappings for Legacy IP Precedence Code Points*

DiffServ Code Designator	Mapping
ef	101110
be	000
be1	001
ef	010
ef1	011
af11	100
af12	101
nc1/cs6	110
nc2/cs7	111

Configuring Forwarding Classes

Forwarding classes control how packets are assigned to output queues. To assign each forwarding class to an internal queue number, include the `forwarding-classes` statement:

```
[edit class-of-service]
forwarding-classes {
  queue queue-number class-name;
}
```

The default CoS configuration is based on queue number. The name of the forwarding class that shows up when the default configuration is displayed is the forwarding class currently associated with that queue. Following is the default configuration for forwarding classes:

```
[edit class-of-service]
forwarding-classes {
  queue 0 best-effort;
  queue 1 expedited-forwarding;
  queue 2 assured-forwarding;
  queue 3 network-control;
}
```

If you reassign the forwarding-class names, the forwarding-class name `best-effort` appears in the locations in the configuration previously occupied by `network-control`, as follows:

```
forwarding-classes {
  queue 0 network-control;
  queue 1 assured-forwarding;
  queue 2 expedited-forwarding;
  queue 3 best-effort;
}
```

In the current default configuration, only IP precedence classifiers are associated with interfaces, the only classes designated are best effort and network control, and schedulers are not defined for the `expedited-forwarding` or `assured-forwarding` classes. You must make a conscious effort to classify packets to the `expedited-forwarding` or `assured-forwarding` class and define schedulers for these classes.

If classifiers fail to classify a packet, it always receives the default classification, to the class associated with queue 0.

The number of queues depends on the hardware in the chassis. CoS configurations are inherently contingent on the number of queues on the system. Only two classes, `best-effort` and `network-control`, are actually referenced in the default configuration. The default configuration works on any platform.

CoS configurations that specify more queues than the platform can support are not accepted. The commit fails with a detailed message that states the total number of queues available.

Classifying Packets by Behavior Aggregate Class

The simplest way to classify a packet is to use behavior aggregate classification. The DSCP or IP precedence bits of the IP header convey the behavior aggregate class information. The information might also be found in the MPLS EXP bits or IEEE 802.1p CoS bits. Table 6.16 lists the default system classification scheme for the well-known DSCPs. Note that all af classes other than af11, af12, and af13 are mapped to `best-effort`, because RFC 2597 prohibits a node from aggregating classes. In effect, mapping to `best-effort` implies that the node does not support that class.

Table 6.16 *Default Behavior Aggregate Classification*

DSCP	Forwarding Class	PLP
ef	`expedited-forwarding`	Low
af11	`assured-forwarding`	Low
af12	`assured-forwarding`	High
af13	`assured-forwarding`	High
af21	`best-effort`	Low
af22	`best-effort`	Low
af23	`best-effort`	Low
af31	`best-effort`	Low
af32	`best-effort`	Low
af33	`best-effort`	Low
af41	`best-effort`	Low
af42	`best-effort`	Low

Table 6.16 *Default Behavior Aggregate Classification*

DSCP	Forwarding Class	PLP
af43	`best-effort`	Low
be	`best-effort`	Low
cs1	`best-effort`	Low
cs2	`best-effort`	Low
cs3	`best-effort`	Low
cs4	`best-effort`	Low
cs5	`best-effort`	Low
nc1/cs6	`network-control`	Low
nc2/cs7	`network-control`	Low
Other	`best-effort`	Low

To define new classifiers for all code-point types, include the `classifiers` statement:

```
[edit class-of-service]
classifiers {
  (dscp | exp | ieee-802.1 | inet-precedence) classifier-
      name {
    import [classifier-name | default];
    forwarding-class class-name {
      loss-priority (low | high) code-points [alias |
        bits];
    }
  }
}
```

To assign the classification map to a logical interface, include the `forwarding-class` statement in the following configuration. The `dscp` classifier classifies all incoming IPv4 packets, while the `exp` classifier handles MPLS packet classification.

```
[edit class-of-service interfaces interface-name unit
logical-unit-number]
forwarding-class class-name;
classifiers {
  (dscp | exp | ieee-802.1 | inet-precedence) (classifier-
      name | default);
}
```

Configuring Scheduling Policy Maps

You use scheduling policy maps to configure the forwarding classes that represent packet queues and associate them with physical interfaces. A *scheduler* configuration block specifies the buffer size, bandwidth, and priority for a queue. It also specifies the RED drop profile for packets that fall within specification and out of specification. To configure schedulers, include the `schedulers` statement:

```
[edit class-of-service]
schedulers {
  scheduler-name {
    transmit-rate (rate | percent percentage | remainder)
      <exact>;
    maximum-buffer-delay (time | percent percentage |
      remainder);
    priority (low | high);
    drop-profile-map loss-priority (low | high) protocol
      (non-tcp | tcp | any)
      drop-profile profile-name;
  }
}
```

After you define a scheduler, include it in a *scheduler map* to map a given forwarding class to a scheduler configuration:

```
[edit class-of-service]
scheduler-maps {
  map-name {
    forwarding-class class-name scheduler scheduler-name;
  }
}
```

Then associate the *`map-name`* with an output interface:

```
[edit class-of-service]
interfaces {
  interface-name {
    scheduler-map map-name;
  }
}
```

You must configure each forwarding class in turn. The following is the default set of schedulers and scheduler maps:

```
[edit class-of-service]
schedulers {
  network-control {
    transmit-rate percent 5;
```

```
      maximum-buffer-delay percent 5;
      priority low;
      drop-profile-map loss-priority low protocol-type any
        drop-profile passive;
      drop-profile-map loss-priority high protocol-type any
        drop-profile aggressive;
    }
    best-effort {
      transmit-rate percent 95;
      maximum-buffer-delay 95;
      priority low;
      drop-profile-map loss-priority low protocol-type any
        drop-profile passive;
      drop-profile-map loss-priority high protocol-type any
        drop-profile aggressive;
    }
  }
  scheduler-map default {
    forwarding-class best-effort scheduler best-effort;
    forwarding-class network-control scheduler network-
        control;
  }
```

Configuring RED Drop Profiles

RED drop profiles are associated with the forwarding classes and loss priorities from the scheduler map you configured on the interface. To configure the drop profiles themselves, include the `drop-profiles` statement:

```
[edit class-of-service]
drop-profiles {
  profile-name {
    fill-level percentage drop-probability percentage;
    interpolate {
      fill-level value;
      drop-probability value;
    }
  }
}
```

Include either the `interpolate` statement and its options, or the fill-level and drop-probability percentage values. These two alternatives enable you to configure either each individual drop probability at up to 64 fill-level/drop-probability paired values, or a profile represented as a series of line segments. If you include the `interpolate` statement, you can specify more than 64 pairs, but the system generates only 64 discrete entries.

The line segments are defined in terms of the following graphical model: in the first quadrant, the x axis represents the fill level, and the y axis represents the drop probability. The initial line segment spans from the origin (0,0) to the point (<l1>, <p1>); a second line runs from (<l1>, <p1>) to (<l2>, <p2>) and so forth, until a final line segment connects (100, 100). The system automatically constructs a drop profile containing 64 fill levels at drop probabilities that approximate the calculated line segments. Figure 6.6 shows sample line graphs contrasting use of the segment percentages (on the left) and interpolated values (on the right).

Figure 6.6 *Segmented and Interpolated Drop Profiles*

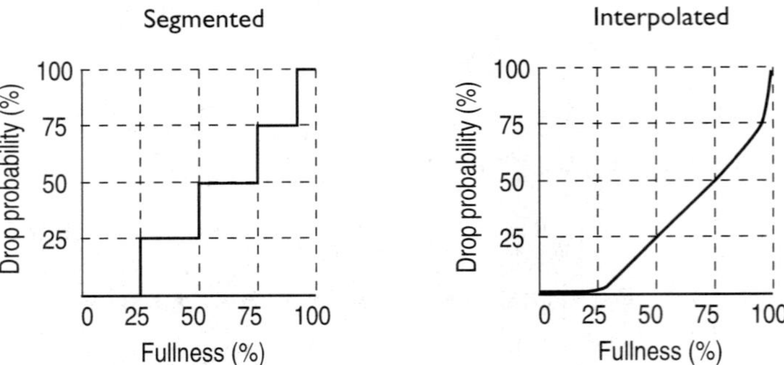

The JUNOS software supports two packet loss priority (PLP) designations, low and high. The packet loss priority is used to determine the RED drop profile when queuing a packet. You can set it by configuring a classifier or policer.

Rewriting Packet Header Information

You can rewrite the packet header bits because the logical interface transmits the packet along with the forwarding class and PLP information associated with the packet. The rewrite-rules configurations define the mappings. Table 6.17 lists the default mappings.

Table 6.17 *Default Packet Header Rewrite Mappings*

Map to DSCP/EXP/ IEEE/IP	Map from Forwarding Class	PLP Value
ef	`expedited-forwarding`	Low
ef	`expedited-forwarding`	High
af11	`assured-forwarding`	Low
af12 (DSCP/EXP)	`assured-forwarding`	High
be	`best-effort`	Low
be	`best-effort`	High
nc1/cs6	`network-control`	Low
nc2/cs7	`network-control`	High

To configure a rewrite-rules mapping and associate it with the appropriate forwarding class and code-point alias or bit set, include the `rewrite-rules` statement:

```
[edit class-of-service]
rewrite-rules {
  (dscp | exp | inet-precedence) rewrite-name {
    import (rewrite-name | default);
    forwarding-class class-name {
      loss-priority (low | high) code-point alias | bits;
    }
  }
}
```

To assign the rewrite-rules configuration to the output logical interface, include the following statements:

```
[edit class-of-service]
interfaces {
  interface-name {
    unit logical-unit-number {
      rewrite-rules {
        (dscp | exp | inet-precedence) rewrite-rule-name;
      }
    }
  }
}
```

Configuring CoS-Based Forwarding

CoS-based forwarding enables you to control next-hop selection based on a packet's class of service and, in particular, the value of the IP packet's precedence bits. For example, you might want to specify a particular interface or next hop to carry high-priority traffic while all best-effort traffic takes some other path. When a routing protocol discovers equal cost paths, it can pick a path at random or load-share across the paths either through hash selection or round robin. CoS-based forwarding allows path selection based on class. You can apply CoS-based forwarding only to a defined set of routes. To do this, include the `cos-next-hop-map` statement in a policy `then` statement. To apply a CoS next-hop map, include the `forwarding-policy` statement:

See Chapter 8, "Routing Policy and Firewall Filters," on page 301.

```
[edit class-of-service]
forwarding-policy {
  next-hop-map map-name {
    forwarding-class class-name {
      next-hop [ next-hop-name ];
    }
  }
}
```

The JUNOS software applies the CoS next-hop map to the set of next hops previously defined; the next hops themselves can be located across any outgoing interfaces on the router.

Finally, apply the route filter to routes exported to the forwarding engine. This configuration instructs the routing process to insert routes to the forwarding engine matching `my-cos-forwarding` with the associated next-hop CoS-based forwarding rules.

```
routing-options {
  forwarding-table {
    export my-cos-forwarding;
  }
}
```

The following rules are used to apply a configuration to a route:

- If the route is a single next-hop route, all traffic goes to that route; that is, no CoS-based forwarding takes effect.

- For each next hop, associate the proper forwarding class. If a next hop appears in the route but not in the `cos-next-hop` map, it does not appear in the forwarding table entry.
- The default forwarding class is used if all forwarding classes are not specified in the next-hop map. If the default is not specified, one is chosen randomly.

For IPv4 or IPv6 packets, you can override the incoming classification, assigning them to the same forwarding class based on their input interface, input precedence bits, or destination address. You do so by defining a policy class when configuring CoS properties and referencing this class when configuring a routing policy. When you override the classification of incoming packets, any mappings you configured for associated precedence bits or incoming interfaces to output transmission queues are ignored. Also, if the packet loss priority bit was set in the packet by the incoming interface, the packet-loss priority bit is cleared. To override the input packet classification, do the following:

1. Define the policy class by including the `class` statement. *`class-name`* is a name that identifies the class.

```
[edit class-of-service]
forwarding-policy {
  class class-name {
    classification-override {
      forwarding-class class-name;
    }
  }
}
```

2. Associate the policy class with a routing policy by including it in a `policy-statement` statement. Specify the destination prefixes in the `route-filter` statement and the CoS policy class name in the `then` statement.

```
[edit policy-options]
policy-statement policy-name {
  term term-name {
    from {
      route-filter destination-prefix match-type <class
        class-name>;
    }
    then class class-name;
  }
}
```

3. Apply the policy by including the `export` statement:

```
[edit routing-options]
forwarding-table {
  export policy-name;
}
```

CHAPTER

7

IP Security (IPSec)

The Internet Protocol Security (IPSec) architecture provides a security suite for the IPv4 and IPv6 network layers. The suite provides such functionality as authentication of origin, data integrity, confidentiality, replay protection, and nonrepudiation of source. In addition to IPSec, the JUNOS software also supports the Internet Key Exchange (IKE), which defines mechanisms for key generation and exchange, and manages security associations (SAs). IPSec also defines a security association and key management framework that can be used with any network layer protocol. The SA specifies what protection policy to apply to traffic between two IP-layer entities. IPSec provides secure tunnels between two peers.

To use IPSec security services, you create SAs between hosts. An SA is a simplex connection that allows two hosts to communicate with each other securely by means of IPSec. There are two types of SAs:

- Manual SAs—Require no negotiation; all values, including the keys, are static and specified in the configuration. Manual SAs statically define the security parameter index values, algorithms, and keys to be used and require matching configurations on both end points of the tunnel. As a result, each peer must have the same configured options for communication to take place.
- Dynamic SAs—Require configuration. With dynamic SAs, you configure IKE first and then the SA. IKE creates dynamic security associations; it negotiates SAs for IPSec. The IKE configuration defines the algorithms and keys used to establish the secure IKE connection with the peer security gateway. This secure connection is then used to dynamically agree on keys and other data used by the dynamic IPSec SA. The IKE SA is negotiated first and then used to protect the negotiations that determine the dynamic IPSec SAs.

The JUNOS implementation of IPSec supports two types of security: host to host and gateway to gateway. Host-to-host security protects BGP sessions with other routers. Any SA to be used with BGP must be configured manually and use transport mode. Static values must be configured on both ends of the security association. To apply host protection, you configure manual SAs in transport mode and then reference the SA by name at the `[edit protocols bgp]` hierarchy level to protect a session with a given peer.

Gateway-to-gateway security protects traffic traveling between two security gateways. It is most often used to encrypt virtual private network (VPN) traffic. Because of the high speeds of the transit interfaces, this functionality requires an ES PIC. To enable gateway-to-gateway protection, you must configure IKE (for dynamic SAs only), an SA, an ES PIC, and traffic parameters.

IKE is a key management protocol that creates dynamic SAs; it negotiates SAs for IPSec. An IKE configuration defines the algorithms and keys used to establish a secure connection with a peer security gateway. IKE negotiates and manages IKE and IPSec parameters, authenticates secure key exchange, provides mutual peer authentication by means of shared secrets (not passwords) and public keys, and provides identity protection (in main mode). IKE occurs over two phases. In the first phase, it negotiates security attributes and establishes shared secrets to form the bidirectional IKE SA. In the second phase, inbound and outbound IPSec SAs are established. The IKE SA secures the exchanges in the second phase. IKE also generates keying material, provides Perfect Forward Secrecy (PFS), and exchanges identities.

To configure security services, include the following statements:

```
[edit security]
ike {
  numerous global IKE statements
  proposal ike-proposal-name {
    authentication-algorithm (md5 | sha1);
    authentication-method pre-shared-keys;
    dh-group (group1 | group2);
    encryption-algorithm (3des-cbc | des-cbc);
    lifetime-seconds seconds;
  }
  policy ike-peer-address {
    mode (aggressive | main);
    proposal [ike-proposal-names];
    pre-shared-key (ascii-text key | hexadecimal key);
  }
}
ipsec {
  numerous global ipsec statements
  proposal ipsec-proposal-name {
    authentication-algorithm (hmac-md5-96 | hmac-sha1-96);
    encryption-algorithm (3des-cbc | des-cbc);
    lifetime-seconds seconds;
    protocol esp;
  }
  policy ipsec-policy-name {
    perfect-forward-secrecy {
```

```
          keys (group1 | group2);
        }
        proposal [ipsec-proposal-names];
      }
      security-association name {
        mode (tunnel | transport);
        replay-window-size (32 | 64);
        manual {
          direction (inbound | outbound | bi-directional) {
            authentication {
              algorithm (hmac-md5-96 | hmac-sha1-96);
              key (ascii-text key | hexadecimal key);
            }
            encryption {
              algorithm (des-cbc | 3des-cbc);
              key (ascii-text key | hexadecimal key);
            }
            protocol (esp | ah);
            spi spi-value;
          }
        }
        dynamic ipsec-policy policy-name;
      }
    }
```

The following is the minimum configuration for manual SAs:

```
[edit security ipsec]
security-association name {
  manual {
    direction (inbound | outbound | bi-directional) {
      authentication {
        algorithm (hmac-md5-96 | hmac-sha1-96);
        key (ascii-text key | hexadecimal key);
      }
      encryption {
        algorithm (des-cbc | 3des-cbc);
        key (ascii-text key | hexadecimal key);
      }
      protocol (esp | ah);
      spi spi-value;
    }
  }
}
```

The following is the minimum configuration for dynamic SAs:

```
[edit security]
ike {
  proposal ike-proposal-name {
    authentication-algorithm (md5 | sha1);
    authentication-method pre-shared-keys;
    dh-group (group1 | group2);
    encryption-algorithm (3des-cbc | des-cbc);
  }
  policy ike-peer-address {
    proposal [ike-proposal-names];
    pre-shared-key (ascii-text key | hexadecimal key);
  }
}
ipsec {
  policy ipsec-policy-name {
    proposal [ipsec-proposal-names];
  }
  proposal ipsec-proposal-name {
    authentication-algorithm (hmac-md5-96 | hmac-sha1-96);
    encryption-algorithm (3des-cbc | des-cbc);
    protocol esp;
  }
  security-association name {
    dynamic ipsec-policy policy-name;
  }
}
```

Configuring IPSec Global and Proposal Properties

To define global IPSec properties, which apply to all IPSec proposals, include one or more of the following statements:

```
[edit security ipsec]
authentication-algorithm (hmac-md5-96 | hmac-sha1-96);
encryption-algorithm (3des-cbc | des-cbc);
lifetime-seconds seconds;
protocol esp;
```

To define IPSec proposal-specific properties, include one or more of the following statements:

```
[edit security ipsec proposal ipsec-proposal-name]
authentication-algorithm (hmac-md5-96 | hmac-sha1-96);
encryption-algorithm (3des-cbc | des-cbc);
lifetime-seconds seconds;
protocol esp;
```

Configuring Security Associations

To configure an SA for IPSec, include the `security-association` statement, specifying a security association name:

```
[edit security ipsec]
security-association name;
```

IPSec runs in two modes: transport and tunnel. By default, tunnel mode is enabled. Tunnel mode protects connections between security gateways. Tunnel mode requires the ES PIC. To configure transport mode, include the `mode` statement, specifying the `transport` option. In transport mode, the JUNOS software does not support AH and encapsulating security payload (ESP) header bundles.

```
[edit security ipsec security-association name]
mode transport;
```

To set the replay window size to protect the receiver against replay attacks by rejecting old or duplicate packets, include the `replay-window-size` statement:

```
[edit security ipsec security-association name]
replay-window-size (32 | 64);
```

Manual SAs require no negotiation; all values, including the keys, are static and specified in the configuration. As a result, each peer must have the same configured options for communication to take place. To configure the manual IPSec security association, include the `manual` statement:

```
[edit security ipsec security-association name]
manual {
  direction (inbound | outbound | bi-directional) {
    authentication {
      algorithm (hmac-md5-96 | hmac-sha1-96);
      key (ascii-text key | hexadecimal key);
    }
    encryption {
      algorithm (des-cbc | 3des-cbc);
      key (ascii-text key | hexadecimal key);
    }
    spi spi-value;
    protocol (esp | ah);
  }
}
```

The `direction` statement sets inbound and outbound IPSec processing. To define different algorithms, keys, or security parameter index (SPI) values for each direction, configure the `inbound` and `outbound` options. To have the same attributes in both directions, use the `bidirectional` option.

IPSec uses two protocols to protect IP traffic: encapsulation security header (ESP) and authentication header (AH). For transport mode SAs, both ESP and AH are supported. To configure the IPSec protocol, include the `protocol` statement.

An SPI is an arbitrary value that uniquely identifies which SA to use at the receiving host. The sending host uses the SPI to identify and select which SA to use to secure every packet. The receiving host uses the SPI to identify and select the encryption algorithm and key used to decrypt packets. Each manual SA must have a unique SPI and protocol combination. To configure the SPI, include the `spi` statement.

To configure an authentication algorithm, include the `authentication` statement. The algorithm can be one of the following:

- `hmac-md5-96`—Hash algorithm that authenticates packet data. It produces a 128-bit authenticator value and 96-bit digest.
- `hmac-sha1-96`—Hash algorithm that authenticates packet data. It produces a 160-bit authenticator value and a 96-bit digest.

The key can be one of the following:

- `ascii-text`—ASCII text key. With the `hmac-md5-96` option, the key contains 16 ASCII characters. With the `hmac-sha1-96` option, the key contains 20 ASCII characters.
- `hexadecimal`—Hexadecimal key. With the `hmac-md5-96` option, the key contains 32 hexadecimal characters. With the `hmac-sha1-96` option, the key contains 40 hexadecimal characters.

To configure IPSec encryption, include the `encryption` statement. The algorithm can be one of the following:

- `des-cbc`—Encryption algorithm that has a block size of 8 bytes; its key size is 64 bits long.

For a list of DES weak and semi-weak keys, see RFC 2409, *Internet Key Exchange*.

- `3des-cbc`—Encryption algorithm that has a block size of 24 bytes; its key size is 192 bits long. For `3des-cbc`, the first 8 bytes must not be the same as the second 8 bytes, and the second 8 bytes must not be the same as the third 8 bytes.

The key can be one of the following:

- ascii-text–ASCII text key. With the des-cbc option, the key contains 8 ASCII characters. With the 3des-cbc option, the key contains 24 ASCII characters.
- hexadecimal—Hexadecimal key. With the des-cbc option, the key contains 16 hexadecimal characters. With the 3des-cbc option, the key contains 48 hexadecimal characters.

You cannot configure encryption when you use the AH protocol.

Configuring Dynamic Security Associations

You configure dynamic SAs with a set of proposals negotiated by the security gateways. The keys are generated as part of the negotiation and therefore do not need to be specified in the configuration. The dynamic SA includes one or more proposals, which allow you to prioritize a list of protocols and algorithms to be negotiated with the peer.

To enable a dynamic SA, configure IKE proposals and IKE policies associated with these proposals, configure IPSec proposals and an IPSec policy associated with these proposals, and associate an SA with an IPSec policy. To associate an SA with an IPSec policy, include the dynamic statement:

```
[edit security ipsec security-association name]
dynamic ipsec-policy policy-name;
```

Configuring IKE

To use dynamic SAs, you must configure IKE. To define global IKE properties, which apply to all IKE proposals, include one or more of the following statements:

```
[edit security ike]
authentication-algorithm (md5 | sha1);
authentication-method pre-shared-keys;
dh-group (group1 | group2);
encryption-algorithm (3des-cbc | des-cbc);
lifetime-seconds seconds;
```

To define proposal-specific properties, include one or more of the following statements:

```
[edit security ike proposal ike-proposal-name]
authentication-algorithm (md5 | sha1);
authentication-method pre-shared-keys;
dh-group (group1 | group2);
encryption-algorithm (3des-cbc | des-cbc);
lifetime-seconds seconds;
```

You can configure one or more IKE proposals. Each proposal is a list of IKE attributes to protect the IKE connection between the IKE host and its peer. To configure an IKE proposal, include the `proposal` statement:

```
[edit security ike]
proposal ike-proposal-name;
```

To configure an IKE authentication algorithm, include the `authentication-algorithm` statement:

```
authentication-algorithm (md5 | sha1);
```

The authentication algorithm can be one of the following:

- `md5`—Produces a 128-bit digest
- `sha1`—Produces a 160-bit digest

To configure an IKE authentication method, include the `authentication-method` statement and specify `pre-shared-keys`.

```
authentication-method pre-shared-keys;
```

Diffie-Hellman is a public-key cryptography scheme that allows two parties to establish a shared secret over an insecure communications channel. It is also used within IKE to establish session keys. To configure an IKE Diffie-Hellman group, include the `dh-group` statement:

```
dh-group (group1 | group2);
```

The group can be one of the following:

- `group1`—IKE uses the 768-bit Diffie-Hellman prime modulus group when performing the new Diffie-Hellman exchange.
- `group2`—IKE uses the 1,024-bit Diffie-Hellman prime modulus group when performing the new Diffie-Hellman exchange. `group2` provides more security but requires more processing time.

To configure an IKE encryption algorithm, include the `encryption-algorithm` statement:

```
encryption-algorithm (3des-cbc | des-cbc);
```

The encryption algorithm can be one of the following:

- `3des-cbc`—Block size is 24 bytes, and key length is 192 bits
- `des-cbc`—Block size is 8 bytes, and key length is 48 bits

An IKE SA has a lifetime. When the SA expires, it is replaced by a new SA (and SPI) or terminated. To configure IKE lifetime, include the `lifetime-seconds` statement and specify the number of seconds (180 through 4,294,967,295);

```
lifetime-seconds seconds;
```

An IKE policy defines a combination of security parameters (IKE proposals) to be used during IKE negotiation. It defines a peer address, the preshared key for the given peer, and the proposals needed for that connection. During the IKE negotiation, IKE looks for an IKE policy that is the same on both peers. The peer that initiates the negotiation sends all its policies to the remote peer, and the remote peer tries to find a match.

A match is made when both policies from the two peers have a proposal that contains the same configured attributes. If the lifetimes are not identical, the shorter lifetime between the two policies (from the host and peer) is used. The configured preshared key must also match its peer.

You can create multiple, prioritized proposals at each peer to ensure that at least one proposal will match a remote peer's proposal. First, you configure one or more IKE proposals; then you associate these proposals with an IKE policy. You can also prioritize a list of proposals used by IKE in the `policy` statement by listing the proposals you want to use, from first to last.

To configure an IKE policy, include the `policy` statement. The IKE policy peer address must be an IPSec tunnel destination address.

```
[edit security ike]
policy ike-peer-address [ ike-proposal ];
```

IKE policy has two modes: aggressive and main. By default, main mode is enabled. Main mode uses six messages, in three exchanges, to establish the IKE SA. (These three steps are IKE SA negotiation, a Diffie-Hellman exchange, and authentication of the peer.) Main mode also allows a peer to hide its identity. Aggressive mode also establishes an authenticated IKE SA and keys. However, aggressive mode uses half the number of messages, has less negotiation power, and does not provide identity protection. The peer can use the aggressive or main mode to start IKE negotiation; the remote peer accepts the mode sent by the peer. To configure IKE policy mode, include the `mode` statement:

```
[edit security ike policy ike-peer-address]
mode (aggressive | main);
```

The IKE policy proposal is a list of one or more proposals associated with an IKE policy. To configure an IKE policy proposal, include the `proposal` statement:

```
[edit security ike policy ike-peer-address]
proposal [ ike-proposal-names ];
```

IKE policy preshared keys authenticate peers. You must manually configure a preshared key, which must match that of its peer. The preshared key can be an ASCII text (alphanumeric) key or a hexadecimal key. To configure an IKE policy preshared key, include the `pre-shared-key` statement:

```
[edit security ike policy ike-peer-address]
pre-shared-key (ascii-text key | hexadecimal key);
```

Configuring an IPSec Proposal

An IPSec proposal lists protocols and algorithms (security services) to be negotiated with the remote IPSec peer. To configure an IPSec proposal, include the `proposal` statement:

```
[edit security ipsec]
proposal ike-proposal-name {
  authentication-algorithm (md5 | sha1);
  authentication-method pre-shared-keys;
  dh-group (group1 | group2);
  encryption-algorithm (3des-cbc | des-cbc);
  lifetime-seconds seconds;
}
```

To configure an IPSec authentication algorithm, include the `authentication-algorithm` statement. The authentication algorithm can be one of the following:

- `hmac-md5-96`—Hash algorithm that authenticates packet data, producing a 128-bit digest
- `hmac-sha1-96`—Hash algorithm that authenticates packet data, producing a 160-bit digest

To configure an IPSec encryption algorithm, include the `encryption-algorithm` statement. The encryption algorithm can be one of the following:

- `3des-cbc`—Block size is 24 bytes, and key length is 192 bits
- `des-cbc`—Block size is 8 bytes, and key length is 48 bits

The IPSec lifetime option sets the lifetime of an IPSec SA. When the SA expires, it is replaced by a new SA (and SPI) or terminated. If you do not configure a lifetime and a lifetime is not sent by a responder, it defaults to 28,800 seconds. To configure the IPSec lifetime, include the `lifetime-seconds` statement.

Configuring an IPSec Policy

An IPSec policy defines a combination of security parameters (IPSec proposals) used during IPSec negotiation. It defines Perfect Forward Secrecy (PFS) and the proposals needed for the connection. During the IPSec negotiation, IPSec looks for an IPSec proposal that is the same on both peers. The peer that initiates the negotiation sends all its policies to the remote peer, and the remote peer tries to find a match.

A match is made when both policies from the two peers have a proposal that contains the same configured attributes. If the lifetimes are not identical, the shorter lifetime between the two policies (from the host and peer) is used.

You can create multiple, prioritized IPSec proposals at each peer to ensure that at least one proposal will match a remote peer's proposal. First, you configure one or more IPSec proposals first; then you associate these proposals with an IPSec policy. You can then prioritize a list of proposals used by IPSec in the `policy` statement by listing the proposals you want to use, from first to last.

To configure an IPSec policy, include the `policy` statement and specify the policy name and one or more proposals you want to associate with this policy:

```
[edit security ipsec]
policy ipsec-policy-name;
```

Perfect Forward Secrecy (PFS) provides additional security by means of a Diffie-Hellman shared secret value. With PFS, if one key is compromised, previous and subsequent keys are secure because they are not derived from previous keys. To configure PFS, include the `perfect-forward-secrecy` statement.

```
[edit security ipsec]
perfect-forward-secrecy {
    keys (group1 | group2);
}
```

The key can be one of the following:

- `group1`—IKE uses the 768-bit Diffie-Hellman prime modulus group when performing the new Diffie-Hellman exchange.
- `group2`—IKE uses the 1,024-bit Diffie-Hellman prime modulus group when performing the new Diffie-Hellman exchange. `group2` provides more security than `group1`, but requires more processing time.

CHAPTER

8

Routing Policy and Firewall Filters

The JUNOS Internet software provides a *policy framework*, which is a collection of JUNOS policies that allows you to control flows of routing information and packets. The policy framework is composed of routing policy, which allows you to control the routing information or change between the routing protocols and the routing tables and between the routing tables and the forwarding table and firewall filter policy, which allows you to control packets transiting the router to a network destination and packets destined for and sent by the router.

NOTE The term *firewall filter policy* is used here to emphasize that a firewall filter is a policy and shares some fundamental similarities with a routing policy. However, when referring to a firewall filter policy in the remainder of this book, the term *firewall filter* is used.

The JUNOS policies affect the following router flows:

- Flow of routing information between the routing protocols and the routing tables and between the routing tables and the forwarding table. The Routing Engine handles this flow. *Routing information* is the information about routes learned by the routing protocols from a router's neighbors. This information is stored in routing tables and is subsequently advertised by the routing protocols to the router's neighbors. Routing policies allow you to control the flow of this information.
- Flow of data packets in and out of the router physical interfaces. The Packet Forwarding Engine handles this flow. *Data packets* are chunks of data that transit the router as they are being forwarded from a source to a destination. When a router receives a data packet on an interface, the router determines where to forward the packet by looking in the forwarding table for the best route to a destination. The router then forwards the data packet toward its destination through the appropriate interface. Firewall filters allow you to control the flow of these data packets.
- Flow of local packets from the router physical interfaces and to the Routing Engine. The Routing Engine handles this flow. *Local packets* are chunks of data that are destined for or sent by the router. Local packets usually contain routing protocol data, data for IP services such as telnet or secure shell (ssh), and data for administrative protocols such as the Internet Control Message Protocol (ICMP). When the Routing Engine receives a local

packet, it forwards the packet to the appropriate daemon or to the kernel, which are both part of the Routing Engine, or to the Packet Forwarding Engine. Firewall filters allow you to control the flow of these local packets.

Figure 8.1 illustrates the flows of routing information and packets through the router. Although the flows are very different from each other, they are also interdependent. Routing policies determine which routes are placed in the forwarding table. The forwarding table in turn has an integral role in determining the appropriate physical interface through which to forward a packet.

Figure 8.1 *Flows of Routing Information and Packets*

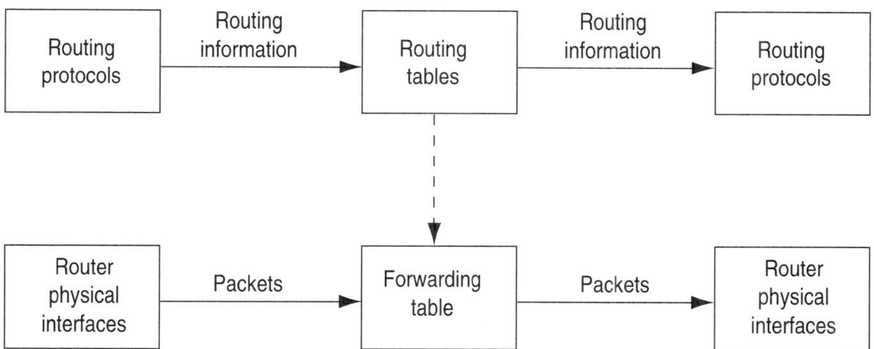

You can configure routing policies to control which routes the routing protocols place in the routing tables and to control which routes the routing protocols advertise from the routing tables (see Figure 8.2). The routing protocols advertise active routes only from the routing tables. (An *active route* is a route that is chosen from all routes in the routing table to reach a destination.)

For more information about the active route selection process, see "How the Active Route Is Determined," on page 376.

You can also use routing policies to change specific route characteristics, which allow you to control which route is selected as the active route to reach a destination, to effect changes to the default BGP route flap-damping values, to perform per-packet load balancing, and to enable class of service (CoS).

Figure 8.2 *Routing Policies to Control Routing Information Flow*

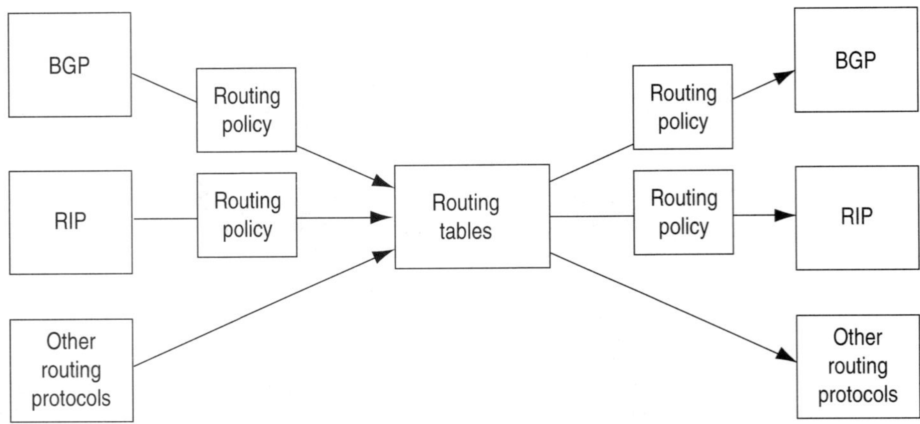

Firewall filters provide a means of protecting your router from excessive traffic transiting the router to a network destination or destined for the Routing Engine. Firewall filters that control local packets can also protect your router from external aggressions such as denial-of-service (DoS) attacks. You can configure firewall filters to control which data packets are accepted on and transmitted from the physical interfaces and which local packets are transmitted from the physical interfaces to the Routing Engine (see Figure 8.3).

Figure 8.3 *Firewall Filters to Control Packet Flow*

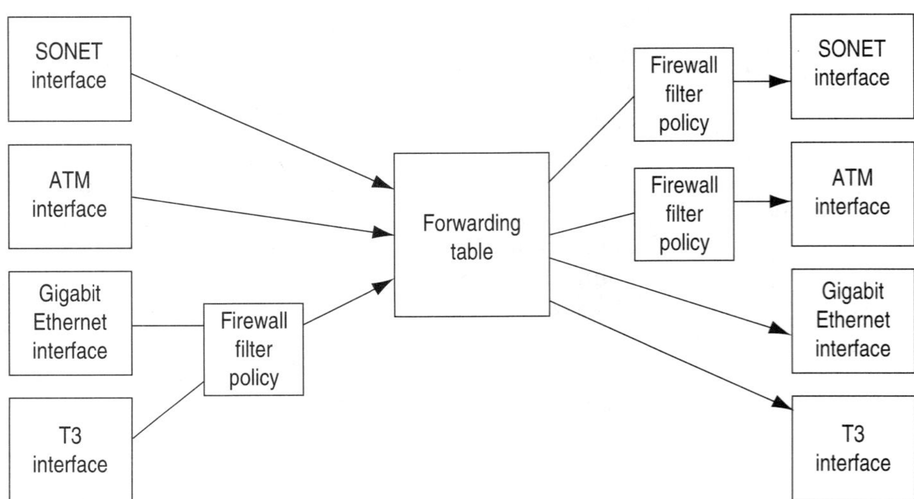

Policy Terminology

A *policy* is a mechanism in the JUNOS policy framework that allows you to configure criteria against which something can be compared and an action that is performed if the criteria are met.

All policies provide two points at which you can control routing information or packets through the router (see Figure 8.4). These *control points* allow you to control routing information before and after it is placed in the routing table, data packets before and after a forwarding table lookup, and local packets before and after they are received by the Routing Engine. (Figure 8.4 appears to depict only one control point, but because of the bidirectional flow of the local packets, two control points actually exist.)

Figure 8.4 *Policy Control Points*

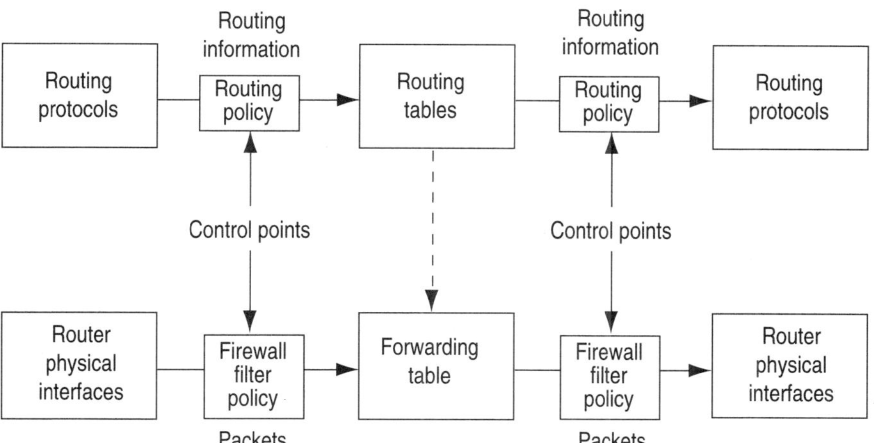

Because there are two control points, you can configure policies that control the routing information or data packets before and after their interaction with their respective tables and local packets before and after their interaction with the Routing Engine. *Import routing policies* control the routing information that is placed in the routing tables, while *export routing policies* control the routing information that is advertised from the routing tables. *Input firewall filters* control packets that are received on a router interface, while *output firewall filters* control packets that are transmitted from a router interface.

All policies consist of the following configurable components:

- Match conditions—Criteria against which a route or packets are compared. You can configure one or more criteria. If all criteria match, one or more actions are applied.
- Actions—What happens if all criteria match. You can configure one or more actions.
- Terms—Named structures in which match conditions and actions are defined. You can define one or more terms.

The policy framework software evaluates each incoming and outgoing route or packet against the match conditions in a term. If the criteria in the match conditions are met, the defined action is taken. In general, the policy framework software compares the route or packet against the match conditions in the first term in the policy, then goes on to the next term, and so on. Therefore, the order in which you arrange terms in a policy is relevant. However, the order of match conditions within a term is not relevant because a route or packet must match all match conditions in a term for an action to be taken.

If an incoming or outgoing route or packet arrives and an explicitly configured policy related to the route or to the interface upon which the packet arrives is not configured, the action specified by the default policy is taken. A *default policy* is a rule or a set of rules that determine whether the route is placed in or advertised from the routing table, or whether the packet is accepted into or transmitted from the router interface. All policies also have default actions in case a policy does not specify a match condition, a match occurs, but a policy does not specify an action, a match does not occur with a term in a policy and subsequent terms in the same policy exist, or a match does not occur by the end of a policy.

All policies share a two-step configuration process:

- Define the policy—Define the policy components, including criteria against which routes or packets are compared and actions that are performed if the criteria are met.
- Apply the policy—Apply the policy to whatever moves the routing information or packets through the router, for example, the routing protocol or router interface.

The JUNOS policy architecture is simple and straightforward. However, the actual implementation of each policy adds layers of complexity to the respective policies as well as power and flexibility to your router's capabilities. Configuring a policy has a major impact on the flow of routing information or packets within and through the router. For example, you can configure a routing policy that does not allow routes associated with a particular customer to be placed in the routing table. As a result of this routing policy, the customer routes are not used to forward data packets to various destinations, and the routes are not advertised by the routing protocol to neighbors. Before configuring a policy, determine what you want to accomplish with it and thoroughly understand how to achieve your goal using the various match conditions and actions. Also, make sure that you understand the default policies and actions for the policy you are configuring.

Comparison of Routing Policies and Firewall Filters

Although routing policies and firewall filters share a common architecture, several differences exist. The fundamental difference between the policies is their purpose, and because of this, the implementation details, and, consequently, the configuration methods for each are very different. Table 8.1 compares the implementation details for routing policies and firewall filters, highlighting the similarities and differences between the two policies.

Table 8.1 *Policy Implementation Details*

Policy Architecture	Routing Policy Implementation	Firewall Filter Implementation
Control points	Control routing information that is placed in the routing table with an import routing policy and advertised from the routing table with an export routing policy.	Control packets that are accepted on a router interface with an input firewall filter and that are forwarded from an interface with an output firewall filter.

Table 8.1 *Policy Implementation Details*

Policy Architecture	Routing Policy Implementation	Firewall Filter Implementation
Configuration tasks: ■ Define policy ■ Apply policy	Define a policy that contains terms, match conditions, and actions. Apply one or more export or import policies to a routing protocol. You can also apply a *policy expression*, which uses Boolean logical operators with multiple import or export policies. You can also apply one or more export policies to the forwarding table.	Define a policy that contains terms, match conditions, and actions. Apply one input or output firewall filter to a physical interface or physical interface group to filter data packets received by or forwarded to a physical interface (on routers with an Internet Processor II ASIC only). You can also apply one input or output firewall filter to the router's loopback interface, which is the interface to the Routing Engine (on all routers). Doing this allows you to filter local packets received by or forwarded from the Routing Engine.
Terms	Configure as many terms as desired in a policy. Define a name for each term. Terms are evaluated in the order in which you specify them in a policy. Evaluation of a policy ends after a packet matches the criteria in a term and the defined or default policy action of accept or reject is taken. The route is not evaluated against subsequent terms in the same policy or subsequent policies.	Configure as many terms as desired in a firewall filter. Define a name for each term. Terms are evaluated in the order in which you specify them in a firewall filter. Evaluation of a firewall filter ends after a packet matches the criteria in a term and the defined or default action is taken. The packet is not evaluated against subsequent terms in the firewall filter.
Match conditions	Specify zero or more criteria that a route must match. You can specify criteria based on source, destination, or properties of a route. You can also specify the following match conditions, which require more configuration: ■ Autonomous system (AS) path expression—A combination of AS numbers and regular expression operators. ■ Community—A group of destinations that share a common property. ■ Prefix list—A named list of prefixes. ■ Route list—A list of destination prefixes. ■ Subroutine—A routing policy that is called repeatedly from other routing policies.	Specify zero or more criteria that a packet must match. You must match various fields in the packet's header. The fields are grouped into the following categories: ■ Numeric values, such as port and protocol numbers. ■ Prefix values, such as IP source and destination prefixes. ■ Bit-field values, that is, if particular bits in the fields are or are not set, such as IP options, TCP flags, and IP fragmentation fields. You can specify the fields using Boolean logical operators.

Table 8.1 *Policy Implementation Details*

Policy Architecture	Routing Policy Implementation	Firewall Filter Implementation
Actions	Specify zero or one action to take if a route matches all criteria. You can specify the following actions: ■ Accept—Accept the route into the routing table and propagate it. After this action is taken, the evaluation of subsequent terms and policies ends. ■ Reject—Do not accept the route into the routing table, and do not propagate it. After this action is taken, the evaluation of subsequent terms and policies ends. In addition to the actions described above, you can also specify zero or more of the following types of actions: ■ Next term—Evaluate the next term in the routing policy. ■ Next policy—Evaluate the next routing policy. ■ Actions that manipulate characteristics associated with a route as the routing protocol places it in the routing table or advertises it from the routing table. ■ Trace action, which logs route matches.	Specify zero or one action to take if a packet matches all criteria. (Juniper Networks recommends that you always explicitly configure an action.) You can specify the following actions: ■ Accept—Accept a packet. ■ Discard—Discard a packet silently, without sending an ICMP message. ■ Reject—Discard a packet and send an ICMP destination unreachable message. ■ Routing instance—Specify a routing table to which packets are forwarded. In addition to zero or one of the actions described above, you can also specify zero or more action modifiers. You can specify the following action modifiers: ■ Count—Add packet to a count total. ■ Forwarding class—Set the packet forwarding class to a specified value from 0 through 3. ■ IPSec security association—Used with the source and destination address match conditions, specify an IP Security (IPSec) security association (SA) for the packet. ■ Log—Store the header information of a packet on the Routing Engine. ■ Loss priority—Set the packet loss priority (PLP) bit to a specified value, 0 or 1. ■ Policer—Apply rate-limiting procedures to the traffic. ■ Sample—Sample the packet traffic. ■ Syslog—Log an alert for the packet.

Table 8.1 *Policy Implementation Details*

Policy Architecture	Routing Policy Implementation	Firewall Filter Implementation
Default policies and actions	If an incoming or outgoing route arrives and a policy related to the route is not explicitly configured, the action specified by the default policy for the associated routing protocol is taken. The following default actions exist for routing policies: ■ If a policy does not specify a match condition, all routes evaluated against the policy match. ■ If a match occurs but the policy does not specify an accept, reject, next term, or next policy action, one of the following occurs: ▪ The next term, if present, is evaluated. ▪ If no other terms are present, the next policy is evaluated. ▪ If no other policies are present, the action specified by the default policy is taken. ■ If a match does not occur with a term in a policy and subsequent terms in the same policy exist, the next term is evaluated. ■ If a match does not occur with any terms in a policy and subsequent policies exist, the next policy is evaluated. ■ If a match does not occur by the end of a policy and no other policies exist, the accept or reject action specified by the default policy is taken.	If an incoming or outgoing packet arrives on an interface and a firewall filter is not configured for the interface, the default policy is taken (the packet is accepted). The following default actions exist for firewall filters: ■ If a firewall filter does not specify a match condition, all packets are considered to match. ■ If a match occurs but the firewall filter does not specify an action, the packet is accepted. ■ If a match occurs, the defined or default action is taken, and the evaluation ends. Subsequent terms in the firewall filter are not evaluated. ■ If a match does not occur with a term in a firewall filter and subsequent terms in the same filter exist, the next term is evaluated. ■ If a match does not occur by the end of a firewall filter, the packet is discarded.

Routing Policy Framework

All routing protocols store their routing information in routing tables. From these tables, the routing protocols calculate the best route to each destination and place these routes in a forwarding table. These routes are then used to forward routing protocol traffic toward a destination, and they can be advertised to neighbors using one or more routing protocols. In general, the routing protocols place all their routes in the routing table and advertise a limited set of routes from the routing table. The general rules for handling the routing information between the routing protocols and the routing table are known as the *routing policy framework*.

Instead of referring to the multiple routing tables that the JUNOS software maintains, this discussion assumes the `inet.0` routing table unless explicitly stated otherwise. By default, the JUNOS software stores unicast Internet Protocol Version 4 (IPv4) routes in the `inet.0` routing table.

A *routing policy* is a mechanism in the JUNOS software that allows you to modify the routing policy framework to suit your needs.

The routing policy framework is composed of default rules for each routing protocol that determine which routes the protocol places in the routing table and advertises from the routing table. The default rules for each routing protocol are known as *default routing policies*. You can create routing policies to preempt the default policies, which are always present. A *routing policy* is a mechanism in the JUNOS software that allows you to modify the routing policy framework to suit your needs. You can create and implement your own routing policies to control which routes a routing protocol places in the routing table, control which active routes a routing protocol advertises from the routing table, or manipulate the route characteristics as a routing protocol places it in the routing table or advertises it from the routing table.

You might want to preempt the default routing policies in the routing policy framework by creating your own routing policies in the following circumstances:

- To not have a protocol to import all routes into the routing table. If the routing table does not learn about certain routes, they can never be used to forward packets, and they can never be redistributed into other routing protocols.
- To not have a routing protocol export all the active routes learned by that protocol.

- To have a routing protocol announce active routes learned from another routing protocol, which is sometimes called *route redistribution.*
- To manipulate route characteristics, such as the preference value, AS path, or the community. You can manipulate the route characteristics to control which route is selected as the active route to reach a destination. In general, the active route is also advertised to a router's neighbors.
- To change the default BGP route flap-damping parameters.
- To perform per-packet load balancing.
- To enable class of service (CoS).

You can manipulate the route characteristics to control which route is selected as the active route to reach a destination. The active route is placed in the forwarding table and used to forward traffic toward the route's destination. In general, the active route is also advertised to a router's neighbors. To create a routing policy, you must define the policy and apply it. You define the policy by specifying the criteria that a route must match and the actions to perform if a match occurs. You then apply the policy to a routing protocol or to the forwarding table.

To better understand the routing policy framework, it is necessary to define two terms that explain how routes move between the routing protocols and the routing table (see Figure 8.5):

- When the Routing Engine places the routes of a routing protocol into the routing table, it is *importing* routes into the routing table.
- When the Routing Engine uses active routes from the routing table to send a protocol advertisement, it is *exporting* routes from the routing table.

The process of moving routes between a routing protocol and the routing table always is described *from the point of view of the routing table*. That is, routes are *imported into* a routing table from a routing protocol, and they are *exported from* a routing table to a routing protocol. Remember this distinction when working with routing policies.

Figure 8.5 *Importing and Exporting Routes*

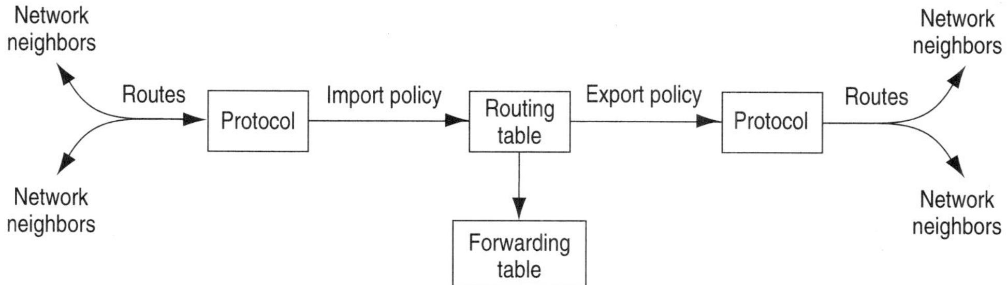

When evaluating routes for export, the Routing Engine uses only active routes from the routing table. In other words, an export policy does not evaluate all routes; it evaluates only those routes that a routing protocol is allowed to advertise to a neighbor.

Table 8.2 lists the routing protocols from which the routing table can import routes and to which routing protocols the routing table can export routes. This table also lists direct and explicitly configured routes, which for the purposes of this table are considered a pseudoprotocol. An *explicitly configured route* is a route that you have configured. *Direct routes* are not explicitly configured; they are created as a result of IP addresses being configured on an interface. Explicitly configured routes include aggregate, generated, local, and static routes. An *aggregate route* is a route that distills groups of routes with common addresses into one route. A *generated route* is a route used when the routing table has no information about how to reach a particular destination. A *local route* is an IP address assigned to a router interface. A s*tatic route* is a nonchanging route to a destination.

The policy framework software treats direct and explicitly configured routes as if they are learned through routing protocols; therefore, they can be imported into the routing table. Routes cannot be exported from the routing table to the pseudoprotocol because this protocol is not a real routing protocol. However, aggregate, direct, generated, and static routes can be exported from the routing table to routing protocols, whereas local routes cannot.

For information about the default routing policies for each routing protocol, see Table 8.4. For information about the import and export routing policies supported for each routing protocol and the level at which you can apply these policies, see Table 8.6 on page 320.

Table 8.2 *Protocols the Routing Table Can Import from and Export to*

Protocol	Import	Export
Border Gateway Protocol (BGP)	Yes	Yes
Distance Vector Multicast Routing Protocol (DVMRP)	Yes	Yes
Intermediate System to Intermediate System (IS-IS)	Yes	Yes
Label Distribution Protocol (LDP)	Yes	Yes
Multiprotocol Label Switching (MPLS)	Yes	No
Open Shortest Path First (OSPF)	Yes	Yes
Protocol-Independent Multicast (PIM) dense mode	Yes	Yes
PIM sparse mode	Yes	Yes

Pseudo protocols:
■ Direct routes
■ Explicitly configured routes
  ▪ Aggregate routes
  ▪ Generated routes
  ▪ Local routes
  ▪ Static routes
	Yes	No

Routing Information Protocol (RIP) and Routing Information Protocol Next-Generation (RIPng)	Yes	Yes

Table 8.3 lists the routing tables affected by default and user-defined routing policies and the types of routes that each routing table stores.

Table 8.3 *Routing Tables Affected by Routing Policies*

Routing Table	Type of Routes Stored
`inet.0`	Unicast IPv4 routes
`instance-name``.inet.0`	Unicast IPv4 routes for a particular routing instance
`inet.1`	Multicast IPv4 routes

Table 8.3 *Routing Tables Affected by Routing Policies*

Routing Table	Type of Routes Stored
`inet.2`	Unicast IPv4 routes for multicast reverse-path forwarding (RPF) lookup
`inet.3`	MPLS routes
`mpls.0`	MPLS routes for label-switched path (LSP) next hops
`inet6.0`	Unicast IPv6 routes

Table 8.4 summarizes the default routing policies for each routing protocol that imports and exports routes. The actions in the default routing policies are taken if you have not explicitly configured a routing policy.

Table 8.4 *Default Routing Policies*

Importing or Exporting Protocol	Default Import Policy	Default Export Policy
BGP	Import all BGP IPv4 routes learned from configured neighbors into the `inet.0` routing table. Import all BGP IPv6 routes learned from configured neighbors into the `inet6.0` routing table.	Export active BGP routes.
DVMRP	Import all DVMRP routes into the `inet.1` routing table.	Export active DVMRP routes.
IS-IS	Import all IS-IS routes into the `inet.0` and `inet6.0` routing tables. (You cannot override or change this default policy.)	Export active IS-IS routes. Export direct (interface) routes for the interfaces on which IS-IS is explicitly configured.
LDP	Import all LDP routes into the `inet.3` routing table.	Export active LDP routes.
MPLS	Import all MPLS routes into the `inet.3` routing table.	Export active MPLS routes.
OSPF	Import all OSPF routes into the `inet.0` routing table. (You cannot override or change this default policy.)	Export active OSPF routes. Export direct (interface) routes for the interfaces on which OSPF is explicitly configured.

Table 8.4 Default Routing Policies

Importing or Exporting Protocol	Default Import Policy	Default Export Policy
PIM dense mode	Import all PIM dense mode routes into the `inet.1` routing table.	Export active PIM dense mode routes.
PIM sparse mode	Import all PIM sparse mode routes into the `inet.1` routing table.	Export active PIM sparse mode routes.

Pseudoprotocol:
■ Direct routes
■ Explicitly configured routes:
  ▪ Aggregate routes
  ▪ Generated routes
  ▪ Static routes
	Import all direct and explicitly configured routes into the `inet.0` routing table.	Does not export any routes. The pseudoprotocol cannot export any routes from the routing table because it is not a routing protocol.
		Routing protocols can export these or any routes from the routing table.

RIP	Import all RIP routes learned from configured neighbors into the `inet.0` routing table.	Does not export any routes. To export RIP routes, you must configure an export policy for RIP.
RIPng	Import all RIPng routes learned from configured neighbors into the `inet6.0` routing table.	Does not export any routes. To export RIPng routes, you must configure an export policy for RIPng.

When multiple routes for a destination exist in the routing table, the protocol selects an active route, and that route is placed in the appropriate routing table. For equal-cost routes, the JUNOS software places multiple next hops in the appropriate routing table. When a protocol is exporting routes from the routing table, it exports active routes only (applies to actions specified by both default and user-defined export policies).

You cannot change the default import policy for the link-state protocols IS-IS and OSPF. As link-state protocols, IS-IS and OSPF exchange routes between systems within an autonomous system (AS). All routers and systems within an AS must share the same link-state database, which includes routes to reachable prefixes and the metrics associated with the prefixes. If an import policy were configured and applied to IS-IS or OSPF, some routes might not be learned or advertised, or the metrics for learned routes might be altered, which would make a consistent link-state database impossible.

The following default actions are taken if one of the following situations arises during policy evaluation:

- If a policy does not specify a match condition, all routes evaluated against the policy match.
- If a match occurs but the policy does not specify an accept, reject, next term, or next policy action, one of the following occurs:
  - The next term, if present, is evaluated.
  - If no other terms are present, the next policy is evaluated.
  - If no other policies are present, the action specified by the default policy is taken.
- If a match does not occur with a term in a policy and subsequent terms in the same policy exist, the next term is evaluated.
- If a match does not occur with any terms in a policy and subsequent policies exist, the next policy is evaluated.
- If a match does not occur by the end of a policy or all policies, the accept or reject action specified by the default policy is taken.

When you configure routing policy, you use *import routing policies* to control which routes routing protocols place in the routing table and *export routing policies* to control which routes a routing protocol advertises from the routing table to its neighbors (see Figure 8.6).

Figure 8.6 *Import and Export Routing Policies*

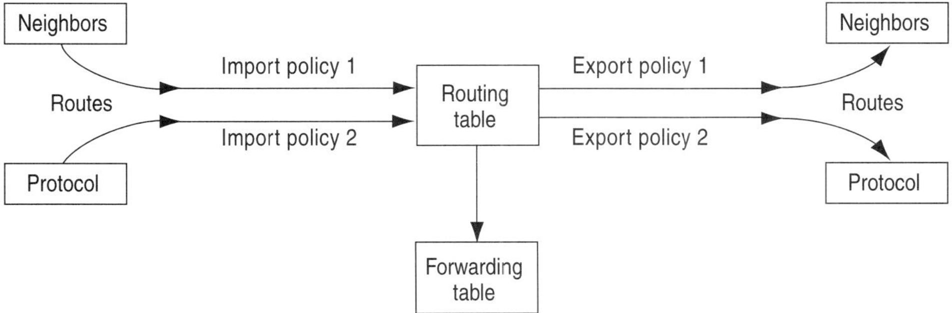

To define a routing policy, you create a *term* that specifies *match conditions*, which are criteria that a route must match, and *actions*, which is what to do if a route matches the conditions. The actions can specify whether to accept or reject the route, control how a series of policies is evaluated, and manipulate the characteristics associated with a route. You define match conditions and actions within a *term*. After defining a routing policy, you then apply it to a routing protocol or to the forwarding table.

Routing policy match conditions fall into two categories: standard and extended (see Table 8.5). In general, the standard match conditions include criteria that are defined within a routing policy and are less complex than the extended match conditions, and the extended match conditions include criteria that are defined separately from the routing policy (AS path regular expressions, communities, and prefix lists) and are more complex than standard match conditions. Some match conditions, including communities, prefix lists, and AS path regular expressions, are defined separately from the routing policy and are given names. You then reference the name of the match condition in the definition of the routing policy itself. Named match conditions allow you to reuse match conditions in other routing policies and read configurations that include complex match conditions with more ease.

Table 8.5 *Match Conditions*

Match Condition	Category	When to Use	Notes
AS path regular expression—Combination of AS numbers and regular expression operators	Extended	(BGP only) Match a route based on its AS path.	—
Community—Group of destinations that share a common property (community information is included as a path attribute in BGP update messages)	Extended	Match a group of destinations that share a common property. Use a routing policy to define a community that specifies a group of destinations you want to match and one or more actions that you want taken on this community.	Actions can be performed on the entire group. You can create multiple communities associated with one particular destination. You can create match conditions using regular expressions.
Prefix list—Named list of IP addresses	Extended	Match a route based on prefix information. You can specify an exact match of a particular route only.	You can specify a common action only for all prefixes in the list.
Route list—List of destination prefixes	Extended	Match a route based on prefix information. You can specify an exact match of a particular route or a less precise match.	You can specify an action for each prefix in the route list or a common action for all prefixes in the route list.

Table 8.5 *Match Conditions*

Match Condition	Category	When to Use	Notes
Standard—Collection of criteria that can match a route	Standard	Match a route based on one of the following criteria: area ID, color, external route, family, instance (routing), interface name, level number, local preference, metric, neighbor address, next-hop address, origin, preference, protocol, routing table name, or tag. For the protocol criterion, you can specify one of the following: BGP, direct, DVMRP, IS-IS, local, MPLS, OSPF, PIM dense mode, PIM sparse mode, RIP, RIPng, static, and aggregate.	—
Subroutine—Routing policy that is called repeatedly from another routing policy.	Extended	Use an effective routing policy in other routing policies.	The subroutine action influences but does not necessarily determine the final action.

An *action* is what the policy framework software performs if a route matches all criteria defined in a match condition. You can configure one or more actions in a term. The policy framework software supports flow control actions, which affect whether to accept or reject the route or whether to evaluate the next term or routing policy, actions that manipulate route characteristics, and trace action, which logs route matches.

A *term* is a named structure in which match conditions and actions are defined. You can define one or more terms. In general, the policy framework software compares a route against the match conditions in the first term in the first routing policy, then goes on to the next term and the next policy if present, and so on until an explicitly configured or default action of accept or reject is taken. Therefore, the order in which you arrange terms in a policy is relevant. The order of match conditions in a term is not relevant because a route must match all match conditions in a term for an action to be taken.

After defining a routing policy, you can apply it to routing protocols, to a pseudoprotocol (explicitly created routes, which include aggregate and generated routes), and to the forwarding table. Table 8.6 summarizes the import and export policy support for each routing protocol. You can apply an import policy to aggregate and generated routes, but you cannot apply an export policy to these routes. These routes cannot be exported from the routing table to the pseudoprotocol, because this protocol is not a real routing protocol. However, aggregate and generated routes can be exported from the routing table to routing protocols.

Table 8.6 *Apply Routing Policies to Protocols*

Protocol	Import Policy	Export Policy	Supported Levels
BGP	Yes	Yes	Import: global, group, peer Export: global, group, peer
DVMRP	Yes	Yes	Global
IS-IS	No	Yes	Export: global
LDP	Yes	Yes	Global
MPLS	No	No	—
OSPF	No	Yes	Export: global
PIM dense mode	Yes	Yes	Global
PIM sparse mode	Yes	Yes	Global
Pseudoprotocol—Explicitly configured routes, including aggregate routes and generated routes	Yes	No	Import: global
RIP and RIPng	Yes	Yes	Import: global, neighbor Export: group

For BGP only, you can also apply import and export policies at group and peer levels as well as at the global level. A peer import or export policy overrides a group import or export policy. A group import or export policy overrides a global import or export policy.

For RIP and RIPng only, you can apply import policies at the global and neighbor levels and export policies at a group level.

You can apply export policies to routes being exported from the routing table into the forwarding table for per-packet load balancing and CoS.

Figure 8.7 shows how a single routing policy is evaluated. This routing policy consists of multiple terms. Each term consists of match conditions and actions to apply to matching routes. Each route is evaluated against the policy as follows:

Figure 8.7 *Routing Policy Evaluation*

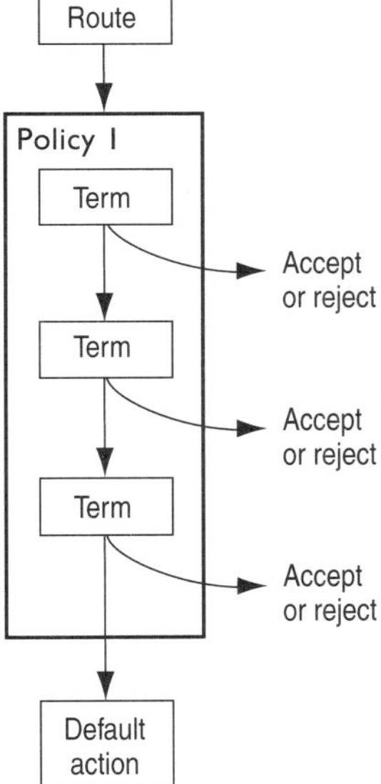

1. The route is evaluated against the first term. If it matches, the specified action is taken. If the action is to accept or reject the route, that action is taken and the evaluation of the route ends. If the next term action is specified, if an action is not specified, or if the route does not match, the evaluation continues as described in Step 2. If the next policy action is specified, any accept or reject action specified in this term is skipped, all remaining terms in this policy are skipped, all other actions are taken, and the evaluation continues as described in Step 3.

2. The route is evaluated against the second term. If it matches, the specified action is taken. If the action is to accept or reject the route, that action is taken and the evaluation of the route ends. If the next term action is specified, if an action is not specified, or if the route does not match, the evaluation continues in a similar manner against the last term. If the next policy action is specified, any accept or reject action specified in this term is skipped, all remaining terms in this policy are skipped, all other actions are taken, and the evaluation continues as described in Step 3.

3. If the route matches no terms in the routing policy or the next policy action is specified, the accept or reject action specified by the default policy is taken.

Figure 8.8 shows how a chain of routing policies is evaluated. These routing policies consist of multiple terms. Each term consists of match conditions and actions to apply to matching routes. Each route is evaluated against the policies as follows:

1. The route is evaluated against the first term in the first routing policy. If it matches, the specified action is taken. If the action is to accept or reject the route, that action is taken and the evaluation of the route ends. If the next term action is specified, if an action is not specified, or if the route does not match, the evaluation continues as described in Step 2. If the next policy action is specified, any accept or reject action specified in this term is skipped, all remaining terms in this policy are skipped, all other actions are taken, and the evaluation continues as described in Step 3.

2. The route is evaluated against the second term in the first routing policy. If it matches, the specified action is taken. If the action is to accept or reject the route, that action is taken and the evaluation of the route ends. If the next term action is specified, if an action is not specified, or if the route does not match, the evaluation continues in a similar manner against the last term in the first routing policy. If the next policy action is specified, any accept or reject action specified in this term is skipped, all remaining terms in this policy are skipped, all other actions are taken, and the evaluation continues as described in Step 3.

3. If the route does not match a term or matches a term with a next policy action in the first routing policy, it is evaluated against the first term in the second routing policy.

4. The evaluation continues until the route matches a term with an accept or reject action defined or until there are no more routing policies to evaluate. If there are no more routing policies, the accept or reject action specified by the default policy is taken.

Figure 8.8 *Routing Policy Chain Evaluation*

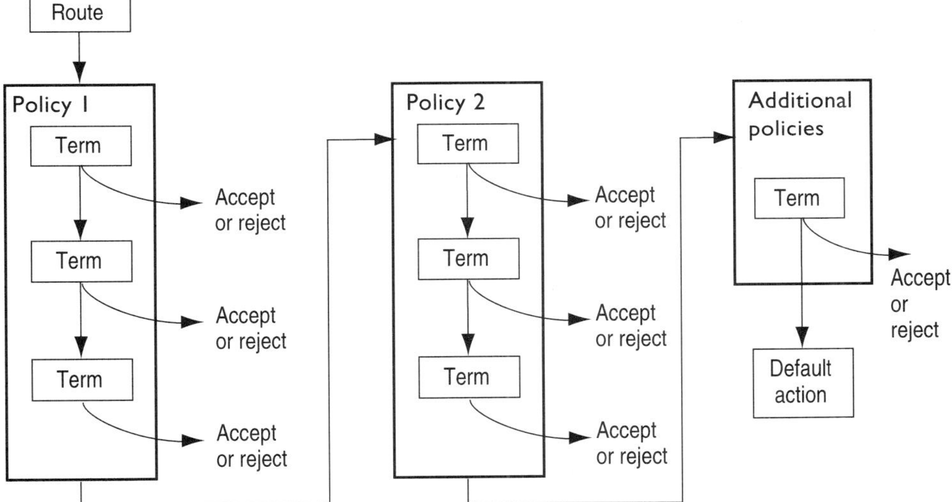

Figure 8.9 on page 325 shows how a subroutine is evaluated. The subroutine is included in the first term of the first routing policy in a chain. Each route is evaluated against the subroutine as follows:

1. The route is evaluated against the first term in the first routing policy. If the route does not match all match conditions specified before the subroutine, the subroutine is skipped and the next term in the routing policy is evaluated (see Step 2). If the route matches all match conditions specified before the subroutine, the route is evaluated against the subroutine. If the route matches the match conditions in any of the subroutine terms, two levels of evaluation occur in the following order:

a. The actions in the subroutine term are evaluated. If one of the actions is accept, evaluation of the subroutine ends and a Boolean value of TRUE is returned to the calling policy. If one of the actions is reject, evaluation of the subroutine ends and FALSE is returned to the calling policy. If one of the actions is meant to manipulate route characteristics, the characteristic is changed regardless of whether accept, reject, or neither action is specified.

   If the subroutine does not specify the accept or reject actions, it uses the accept or reject action specified by the default policy and the values of TRUE or FALSE are returned to the calling policy as described above.

b. The calling policy's subroutine match condition is evaluated. During this part of the evaluation, TRUE equals a match and FALSE equals no match. If the subroutine returned TRUE to the calling policy, then the evaluation of the calling policy continues. If the subroutine returned FALSE to the calling policy, then the evaluation of the current term ends and the next term is evaluated.

2. The route is evaluated against the second term in the first routing policy. If a term defines multiple match conditions, including a subroutine, and a route does not match a condition specified before the subroutine, the evaluation of the term ends and the subroutine is not called and evaluated. In this situation, an action specified in the subroutine that manipulates a route's characteristics is not implemented. If you specify a policy chain as a subroutine, the entire chain acts as a single subroutine. That is, as with other chains, the action specified by the default policy is taken only when the entire chain does not accept or reject a route.

Figure 8.9 *Routing Policy Subroutine Evaluation*

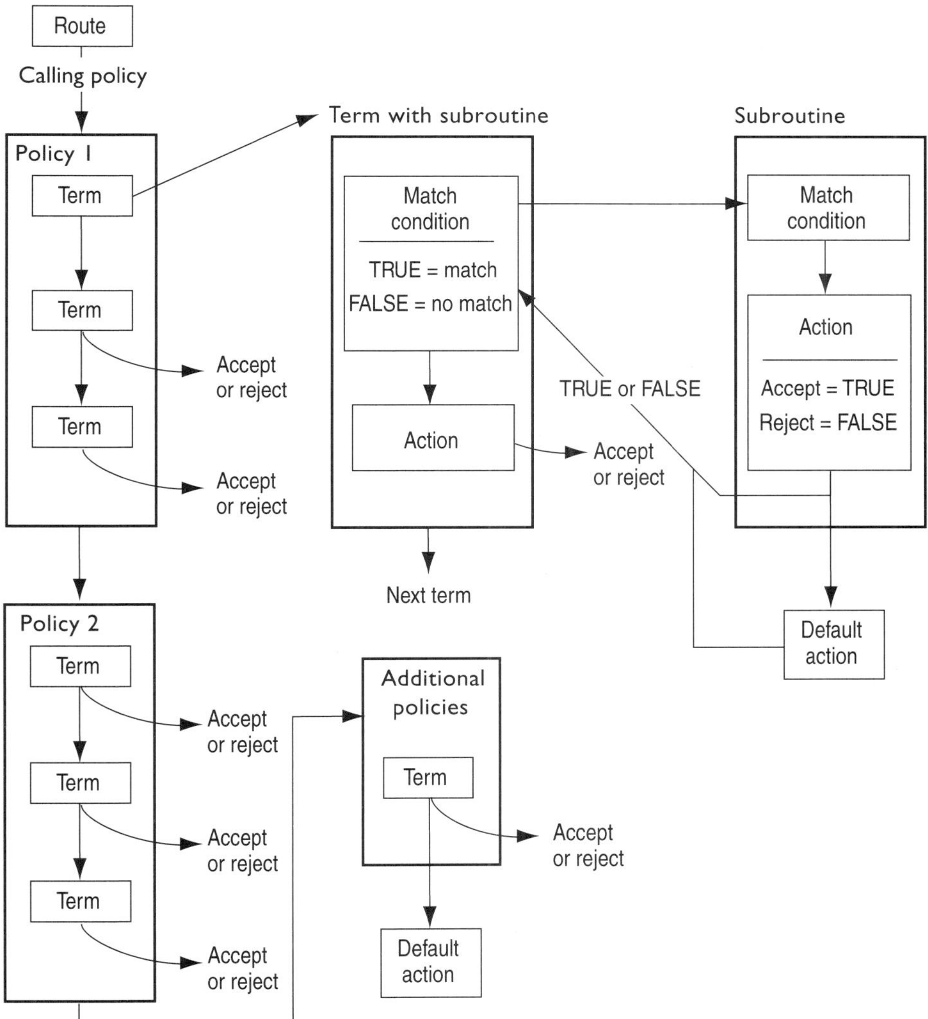

Configuring Routing Policy

To configure routing policy, you first define the policy, then apply it to a routing protocol or the forwarding table.

Defining Routing Policies

To define a routing policy, include the `policy-statement` statement. Each routing policy name must be unique within a configuration.

```
[edit policy-options]
policy-statement policy-name {
  term term-name {
    from {
      match-conditions;
      policy subroutine-policy-name;
      prefix-list name;
      route-filter destination-prefix match-type <actions>;
      source-address-filter destination-prefix match-type
        <actions>;
    }
    to {
      match-conditions;
      policy subroutine-policy-name;
    }
    then actions;
    prefix-list name {
    ip-addresses;
  }
}
```

Each policy term can consist of two statements, `from` and `to`, that define match conditions. In the `from` statement, define the criteria that an incoming route must match. You can specify one or more match conditions. If you specify more than one, they all must match the route for a match to occur. The `from` statement is optional. If you omit it and the `to` statement, all routes are considered to match. In export policies, omitting the `from` statement in a routing policy term might lead to unexpected results. In the `to` statement, define the criteria that an outgoing route must match. You can specify one or more match conditions. If you specify more than one, they all must match the route for a match to occur. You can specify most of the same match conditions in the `to` statement as in the `from` statement. In most cases, specifying a match condition in the `to` statement produces the same result as specifying the same match condition in the `from` statement. The `to` statement is optional. If you omit both it and the `from` statement, all routes are considered to match.

All conditions in the `from` and `to` statements must match for the action to be taken. The match conditions are effectively a logical AND operation. Table 8.7 describes the match conditions for incoming and outgoing routes. This table indicates whether the match condition is standard or extended. In general, the extended match conditions include criteria that are defined separately from the routing policy (AS path regular expressions, communities, and prefix lists) and are more complex than standard match conditions.

Table 8.7 *Routing Policy Match Conditions*

Match Condition	**Match Condition Category**	`from` **Statement Description**	`to` **Statement Description**
`area` *`area-id`*	Standard	(OSPF only) Area identifier. In a `from` statement used with an `export` policy, match a route learned from the specified OSPF area when exporting OSPF routes into other protocols.	
`as-path` *`name`*	Extended	(BGP only) Name of an AS path regular expression.	
`color` *`preference`* `color2` *`preference`*	Standard	Color value, for preference values (`color` and `color2`) that are finer-grained than those specified in the `preference` and `preference2` match conditions. The color value can be a number in the range 0 through 4,294,967,295 (2^{32} –1), with a lower number indicating a more-preferred route. For more information about preference values, see Table 9.1, "Default Route Preference Values," on page 379.	
`community [`*`names`*`]`	Extended	Name of one or more communities. If you list more than one name, only one name needs to match for a match to occur. The community matching is effectively a logical OR operation.	
`external [type` *`metric-type`*`]`	Standard	(OSPF only) External routes, including routes exported from one level to another. `type` is an optional keyword. *`metric`* can either be 1 or 2. When you do not specify `type`, this condition matches all external routes. When you specify `type`, this condition matches only OSPF routes with the specified OSPF metric type.	
`family` *`family-name`*	Standard	Name of an address family. *`family-name`* can be either `inet` or `inet6`. Match the address family (IPv4 or IPv6) of the route.	

Table 8.7 *Routing Policy Match Conditions*

Match Condition	Match Condition Category	`from` Statement Description	`to` Statement Description
`instance` *`instance-name`*	Standard	Routing instance or instances specified by name. Match a route learned from one of the specified instances.	Routing instance or instances specified by name. Match a route to be advertised over one of the specified instances.
`interface` *`interface-name`*	Standard	Router interface or interfaces specified by name or IP address. Do not use this qualifier with protocols that are not interface specific, such as IBGP. Match a route learned from one of the specified interfaces. Direct routes match routes configured on the specified interface.	Router interface or interfaces specified by name or IP address. Do not use this qualifier with protocols that are not interface specific, such as IBGP. Match a route to be advertised from one of the specified interfaces.
`level` *`level`*	Standard	(IS-IS only) IS-IS level. Match a route learned from a specified level.	(IS-IS only) IS-IS level. Match a route to be advertised to a specified level.
`local-preference` *`value`*	Standard	(BGP only) BGP local preference (`LOCAL_PREF`) attribute. The value can be a number in the range 0 through 4,294,967,295 (2^{32} –1).	
`metric` *`metric`* `metric2` *`metric`* `metric3` *`metric`* `metric4` *`metric`*	Standard	Metric value. You can specify up to four metric values, starting with `metric` (for the first metric value) and continuing with `metric2`, `metric3`, and `metric4`. (BGP only) `metric` corresponds to the MED, and `metric2` corresponds to the IGP metric if the BGP next hop runs back through another route.	
`neighbor` *`address`*	Standard	Neighbor (peer) address or addresses. For BGP, the address can be a directly connected or indirectly connected peer. For all other protocols, the address is the neighbor from which the advertisement is received.	Neighbor (peer) address or addresses. For BGP import policies, specifying `to neighbor` produces the same result as specifying `from neighbor`. For BGP export policies, specifying the `neighbor` match condition has no effect and is ignored. For all other protocols, the `to` statement matches the neighbor to which the advertisement is sent.
`next-hop` *`address`*	Standard	Next-hop address or addresses specified in the routing information for a particular route.	

Table 8.7 *Routing Policy Match Conditions*

Match Condition	Match Condition Category	`from` Statement Description	`to` Statement Description
`origin` *`value`*	Standard	(BGP only) BGP origin attribute, which is the origin of the AS path information. The value can be one of the following: ■ `egp`—Path information originated in another AS. ■ `igp`—Path information originated within the local AS. ■ `incomplete`—Path information was learned by some other means.	
`policy [` *`policy-name`* `]`	Extended	Name of a policy to evaluate as a subroutine.	
`preference` *`preference`* `preference2` *`preference`*	Standard	Preference value. You can specify a primary preference value (`preference`) and a secondary preference value (`preference2`). The value can be a number in the range 0 through 4,294,967,295 ($2^{32}-1$), with a lower number indicating a more-preferred route. To specify even finer-grained preference values, see the `color` and `color2` match conditions in this table. For more information about preference values, see Table 9.1, "Default Route Preference Values," on page 379.	
`prefix-list` *`name`* *`ip-addresses`*	Extended	Named list of IP addresses. You can specify an exact match with incoming routes.	You cannot specify this match condition.
`protocol` *`protocol`*	Standard	Name of the protocol from which the route was learned or to which the route is being advertised. It can be one of the following: `aggregate`, `bgp`, `direct`, `dvmrp`, `isis`, `local`, `ospf`, `pim-dense`, `pim-sparse`, `rip`, `ripng`, or `static`.	
`rib` *`routing-table`*	Standard	Name of a routing table. It can be one of the following: ■ `inet.0`—Unicast IPv4 routes. ■ *`instance-name`*`.inet.0`—Unicast IPv4 routes for a particular routing instance. ■ `inet.1`—Multicast IPv4 routes. ■ `inet.2`—Unicast IPv4 routes for multicast reverse-path forwarding (RPF) lookup. ■ `inet.3`—MPLS routes. ■ `mpls.0`—MPLS routes for label-switched path (LSP) next hops. ■ `inet6.0`—Unicast IPv6 routes.	

Table 8.7 *Routing Policy Match Conditions*

Match Condition	Match Condition Category	`from` Statement Description	`to` Statement Description
`route-filter` *`destination-prefix`* *`match-type`* *`<actions>`*	Extended	List of destination prefixes. When specifying a destination prefix, you can specify an exact match with a specific route or a less precise match using match types. You can configure either a common action that applies to the entire list or an action associated with each prefix.	You cannot specify this match condition.
`source-address-filter` *`destination-prefix`* *`match-type`* *`<actions>`*	Extended	List of multicast source addresses. When specifying a source address, you can specify an exact match with a specific route or a less precise match using match types. You can configure either a common action that applies to the entire list or an action associated with each prefix.	You cannot specify this match condition.
`tag` *`string`* `tag2` *`string`*	Standard	You can specify two tag strings: `tag` (for the first string) and `tag2`. These values are local to the router and can be set on configured routes or by using an import routing policy.	

Each policy term can include a `then` statement, which defines the actions to take if a route matches all the conditions in the `from` and `to` statements. If a term does not have `from` and `to` statements, all routes are considered to match and the actions apply to them all. The `then` statement is optional. You can specify one or more actions. There are three types of actions: flow control actions (see Table 8.8), which affect whether to accept or reject the route and whether to evaluate the next term or routing policy, actions that manipulate route characteristics (see Table 8.9), and trace action, which logs route matches.

If you do not include a `then` statement, the next term in the routing policy, if one is present, is evaluated; if there are no more terms in the routing policy, the next routing policy, if one is present, is evaluated; or if there are no more terms or routing policies, the accept or reject action specified by the default policy is taken.

Table 8.8 *Flow Control Actions*

Flow Control Action	Description
`accept`	Accept the route and propagate it. After a route is accepted, no other terms in the routing policy and no other routing policies are evaluated.
`reject`	Reject the route and do not propagate it. After a route is rejected, no other terms in the routing policy and no other routing policies are evaluated.
`next term`	Skip to and evaluate the next term in the same routing policy. Any accept or reject action specified in the `then` statement is skipped. Any actions in the `then` statement that manipulate route characteristics are applied to the route. `next term` is the default control action if a match occurs and if you do not specify a flow control action.
`next policy`	Skip to and evaluate the next routing policy. Any accept or reject action specified in the `then` statement is skipped. Any actions in the `then` statement that manipulate route characteristics are applied to the route. `next policy` is the default control action if a match occurs, if you do not specify a flow control action, and if there are no further terms in the current routing policy.

Table 8.9 *Actions That Manipulate Route Characteristics*

Action	Description
`as-path-prepend` *`as-path`*	(BGP only) Affix one or more AS numbers at the beginning of the AS path. To specify more than one AS number, include the numbers in quotation marks. The AS numbers are added after the local AS number has been added to the path. This action adds AS numbers to AS sequences only, not AS sets. If the existing AS path begins with a confederation sequence or set, the affixed AS numbers are placed within a confederation sequence. Otherwise, the affixed AS numbers are placed with a nonconfederation sequence.
`as-path-expand last-as count` *`n`*	(BGP only) Extract the last AS number in the existing AS path and affix that AS number to the beginning of the AS path *n* times, where *n* is from 1 through 32. The AS number is added before the local AS number has been added to the path. This action adds AS numbers to AS sequences only. AS sets are ignored. If the existing AS path begins with a confederation sequence or set, the affixed AS numbers are placed within a confederation sequence. Otherwise, the affixed AS numbers are placed with a nonconfederation sequence. This option is typically used in EBGP export policies.
`class` *`class-name`*	(CoS only) Apply parameters to routes installed into the routing table. For more information about CoS, see Chapter 6, "Interfaces and Class of Service," on page 185.

Table 8.9 *Actions That Manipulate Route Characteristics*

Action	Description
`color` *`preference`* `color2` *`preference`*	Set the preference value to a specific value. The `color` and `color2` preference values are even finer-grained than those specified in the `preference` and `preference2` actions. The color value can be a number in the range 0 through 4,294,967,295 (2^{32} –1), with a lower number indicating a more-preferred route. If you set the preference with the `color` action, the value is internal to the JUNOS software and is not transitive. For more information about preference values, see Table 9.1, "Default Route Preference Values," on page 379.
`color (add | subtract) number color2 (add | subtract) number`	Change the color preference value by the specified amount. If an addition operation results in a value that is greater than 4,294,967,295 (2^{32} –1), the value is set to 2^{32} –1. If a subtraction operation results in a value less than 0, the value is set to 0. If no attribute value is set before the addition or subtraction operation, the attribute value defaults to 0. If you perform an addition to an attribute with a value of 0, that number becomes the constant value.
`community (+ | add) [ names ]`	(BGP only) Add communities to the set of communities in the route.
`community (- | delete) [ names ]`	(BGP only) Delete communities from the set of communities in the route.
`community (= | set) [ names ]`	(BGP only) Set the communities in the route, replacing any communities that were in the route.
`damping name`	(BGP only) Apply route-damping parameters to the route. These parameters override the default damping parameters. This action is useful only in an import policy, because the damping parameters affect the state of routes in the routing table. To apply damping parameters, you must enable BGP flap damping as described in "Configuring Route Flap Damping," on page 406, and you must create a named list of parameters.
`destination-class destination-class-name`	Maintain packet counts for a route passing through your network based on the ingress and egress points. To configure, group destination prefixes by configuring a routing policy. Enable packet counting on one or more interfaces by including the `destination-class-usage` statement at the `[edit interfaces interface-name unit logical-unit-number family inet]` hierarchy level, then apply that routing policy to the forwarding table with the corresponding destination class.
`external type metric`	Set the external metric type for routes exported by OSPF. You must specify the keyword `type`.
`install-nexthop lsp lsp-name`	Choose which, among a set of equal-cost label-switched path (LSP) next hops, are installed in the forwarding table. To choose, use the export policy for the forwarding table to specify the LSP next hop to be used for the desired routes.
`load-balance per-packet`	(For export to the forwarding table only) Install all next-hop addresses into the forwarding table and have the forwarding table perform per-packet load balancing.
`local-preference value`	(BGP only) Set the BGP local preference (`LOCAL_PREF`) attribute. The preference value can be a number in the range 0 through 4,294,967,295.

Table 8.9 *Actions That Manipulate Route Characteristics*

Action	Description
`local-preference (add | subtract) number`	Change the local preference value by the specified amount. If an addition operation results in a value that is greater than 4,294,967,295 ($2^{32}-1$), the value is set to $2^{32}-1$. If a subtraction operation results in a value less than 0, the value is set to 0. If no attribute value is set before the addition or subtraction operation, the attribute value defaults to 0. If you perform an addition to an attribute with a value of 0, that number becomes the constant value. For BGP, if the attribute value is not known, the local preference attribute value is initialized to 100 before the routing policy is applied.
`metric metric metric2 metric metric3 metric metric4 metric`	Set the metric. You can specify up to four metric values, starting with `metric` (for the first metric value) and continuing with `metric2`, `metric3`, and `metric4`. (BGP only) `metric` corresponds to the multiple exit discriminator (MED), and `metric2` corresponds to the IGP metric if the BGP next hop recourses through another router.
`metric (add | subtract) number metric2 (add | subtract) number metric3 (add | subtract) number metric4 (add | subtract) number`	Change the metric value by the specified amount. If an addition operation results in a value that is greater than 4,294,967,295 ($2^{32}-1$), the value is set to $2^{32}-1$. If a subtraction operation results in a value less than 0, the value is set to 0. If no attribute value is set before the addition or subtraction operation, the attribute value defaults to 0. If you perform an addition to an attribute with a value of 0, that number becomes the constant value.
`metric (igp | minimum-igp) site-offset`	(BGP only) Change the MED value by the specified negative or positive offset. This action is useful only in an EBGP export policy.
`next-hop (address | peer-address)`	Set the next hop. When the advertising protocol is BGP, you can set the next hop only when any third-party next hop can be advertised; that is, when using IBGP or EBGP confederations. If you specify *address* as `self`, the next-hop address is replaced by one of the local router's addresses. The advertising protocol determines which address to use. When the advertising protocol is BGP, this address is set to the local IP address used for the BGP adjacency. A router cannot install routes with itself as the next hop. If you specify `peer-address`, the next-hop address is replaced by the peer's IP address. This option is only valid in import policies. Primarily used by BGP to enforce using the peer's IP address for advertised routes, this option is only meaningful when the next hop is the advertising router or another directly connected router.
`origin` *value*	(BGP only) Set the BGP origin attribute to one of the following values: ■ `igp`—Path information originated within the local AS. ■ `egp`—Path information originated in another AS. ■ `incomplete`—Path information was learned by some other means.

Table 8.9 *Actions That Manipulate Route Characteristics*

Action	Description
`preference` *`preference`* `preference2` *`preference`*	Set the preference value. You can specify a primary preference value (`preference`) and a secondary preference value (`preference2`). The preference value can be a number in the range 0 through 4,294,967,295 ($2^{32}-1$), with a lower number indicating a more-preferred route. To specify even finer-grained preference values, see the `color` and `color2` actions in this table. If you set the preference with the `preference` action, the new preference remains associated with the route. The new preference is internal to the JUNOS software and is not transitive. For more information about preference values, see the Table 9.1, "Default Route Preference Values," on page 379.
`preference (add | subtract)` *`number`* `preference2 (add | subtract)` *`number`*	Change the preference value by the specified amount. If an addition operation results in a value that is greater than 4,294,967,295 ($2^{32}-1$), the value is set to $2^{32}-1$. If a subtraction operation results in a value less than 0, the value is set to 0. If no attribute value is set before the addition or subtraction operation, the attribute value defaults to 0. If you perform an addition to an attribute with a value of 0, that number becomes the constant value.
`tag` *`tag`* `tag2` *`tag`*	You can specify two tag strings: `tag` (for the first string) and `tag2`. These values are local to the router. For OSPF only, the `tag` and `tag2` actions set the 32-bit tag field in OSPF external LSA packets.
`tag (add | subtract)` *`number`* `tag2 (add | subtract)` *`number`*	Change the tag value by the specified amount. If an addition operation results in a value that is greater than 4,294,967,295 ($2^{32}-1$), the value is set to $2^{32}-1$. If a subtraction operation results in a value less than 0, the value is set to 0. If no attribute value is set before the addition or subtraction operation, the attribute value defaults to 0. If you perform an addition to an attribute with a value of 0, that number becomes the constant value.

Applying Routing Policies

For a routing policy to take effect, you must apply it to either a routing protocol or the forwarding table. To apply a routing policy to a routing protocol, include the `import` and `export` statements:

```
[edit protocols protocol-name]
import policy-name;
export policy-name;
```

In the `import` statement, list the name of the routing policy to be evaluated when routes are imported into the routing table from the routing protocol. In the `export` statement, list the name of the routing policy to be evaluated when routes are being exported from the routing table into a dynamic routing protocol. Only active routes are exported from the routing table.

To apply multiple routing policies (chains) to a routing protocol, include the `import` and `export` statements at the `[edit protocols` *`protocol-name`*`]` hierarchy level:

```
[edit protocols protocol-name]
import [ policy-name policy-name ... ]
export [ policy-name policy-name ... ]
```

In the `import` statement, list the names of multiple routing policies to be evaluated when routes are imported into the routing table from the routing protocol. In the `export` statement, list the names of multiple routing policies to be evaluated when routes are being exported from the routing table into a dynamic routing protocol. Only active routes are exported from the routing table.

The policy framework software evaluates the routing policies sequentially, from left to right. If an action specified in one of the policies manipulates a route characteristic, the policy framework software carries the new route characteristic forward during the evaluation of the remaining policies. For example, if the action specified in the first policy of a chain sets a route's metric to 500, this route matches the criterion of `metric 500` defined in the next policy.

The policy framework software can evaluate routing policies using *policy expressions*, which use Boolean logical operators with policies. The logical operators establish rules by which the policies are evaluated. During evaluation of a routing policy in a policy expression, the policy actions of accept, reject, or next policy are converted to the value of TRUE or FALSE. This value is then evaluated against the logic of the specified logical operator to produce output of either TRUE or FALSE. The output is then converted back to a flow control action of accept, reject, or next policy. The result of the policy expression is applied in the same manner as it would be applied to a single policy; that is, the route is accepted or rejected and the evaluation ends, or the next policy is evaluated. Table 8.10 summarizes the policy actions and their corresponding TRUE and FALSE values and flow control action values. Table 8.11 describes the logical operators. You can place a policy expression anywhere in the `import` or `export` statements and in the `from policy` statement, enclosing the expression in parentheses.

Table 8.10 *Policy Action Conversion Values*

Policy Action	Conversion Value	Flow Control Action Conversion Value
accept	TRUE	accept
reject	FALSE	reject
next policy	TRUE	next policy

Table 8.11 *Policy Expression Logical Operators*

Logical Operator	Policy Expression Logic	How Logical Operator Affects Policy Expression Evaluation
&& (Logical AND)	Logical AND requires that all values must be TRUE to produce output of TRUE. Routing policy value of TRUE and TRUE produces output of TRUE. Value of TRUE and FALSE produces output of FALSE. Value of FALSE and FALSE produces output of FALSE.	If the first routing policy returns the value of TRUE, the next policy is evaluated. If the first policy returns the value of FALSE, the evaluation of the expression ends and subsequent policies in the expression are not evaluated.
|| (Logical OR)	Logical OR requires that at least one value must be TRUE to produce output of TRUE. Routing policy value of TRUE and FALSE produces output of TRUE. Value of TRUE and TRUE produces output of TRUE. Value of FALSE and FALSE produces output of FALSE.	If the first routing policy returns the value of TRUE, the evaluation of the expression ends and subsequent policies in the expression are not evaluated. If the first policy returns the value of FALSE, the next policy is evaluated.
! (Logical NOT)	Logical NOT reverses value of TRUE to FALSE and of FALSE to TRUE. Also reverses the actions of accept and next policy to reject, and reject to accept.	If used with the logical AND operator and the first routing policy value of FALSE is reversed to TRUE, the next policy is evaluated. If the value of TRUE is reversed to FALSE, the evaluation of the expression ends and subsequent policies in the expression are not evaluated. If used with the logical OR operator and the first routing policy value of FALSE is reversed to TRUE, the evaluation of the expression ends and subsequent policies in the expression are not evaluated. If the value of TRUE is reversed to FALSE, the next policy is evaluated. If used with a policy and the flow control action is accept or next policy, these actions are reversed to reject. If the flow control action is `reject`, this action is reversed to `accept`.

The policy framework software evaluates a policy expression as follows:

1. The software evaluates a route against the first routing policy in a policy expression and converts the specified or default action to a value of TRUE or FALSE.

2. The software takes the value of TRUE or FALSE and evaluates it against the logical operator used in the policy expression. Based on the logical operator used, the software determines whether to evaluate the next routing policy, if one is present.

   The policy framework software uses a method of shortcut evaluation. When a result is certain, the software stops evaluating subsequent routing policies in the policy expression. For example, if the policy expression specifies logical AND and the evaluation of the first routing policy returns the value of FALSE, the software determines that the output will be FALSE no matter what the value of the unevaluated routing policies are. Therefore, the software does not evaluate the subsequent routing policies in this policy expression.

3. The software performs the same tasks described in Steps 1 and 2 for each subsequent routing policy in the policy expression, if they are present and if the software has determined that it is appropriate to evaluate them.

4. After evaluating the last routing policy, if it is appropriate, the software evaluates the value of TRUE or FALSE obtained from each routing policy evaluation. Based on the logical operator used, it calculates an output of TRUE or FALSE.

5. The software converts the output of TRUE or FALSE back to an action, and the action is performed.

   In cases where each policy in the expression returned a value of TRUE, the software converts the output of TRUE back to the flow control action specified in the last policy. For example, if the policy expression `(policy1 && policy2)` is specified and `policy1` specifies `accept` and `policy2` specifies `next term`, the `next term` action is performed.

If an action specified in one of the policies manipulates a route characteristic, the policy framework software carries the new route characteristic forward during the evaluation of the remaining policies. For example, if the action specified in the first policy of a policy expression sets a route's metric to 500, this route matches the criteria of `metric 500` defined in the next policy. However, if a route characteristic manipulation action is specified in a policy located in the middle or the end of a policy expression, it is possible, because of the shortcut evaluation, that the policy is never evaluated and the manipulation of the route characteristic never occurs.

Applying Routing Policies to the Forwarding Table

To apply an export routing policy to the forwarding table for per-packet load balancing and CoS, include the `forwarding-table` statement:

```
[edit routing-options]
forwarding-table {
  export [ policy-name ];
}
```

Configuring AS Path Regular Expressions

A BGP *AS path* is a path to a destination. To define a match condition based on all or portions of the AS path, first define the AS path in the `as-path` statement:

```
[edit policy-options]
as-path name regular-expression;
```

Then, name the AS path regular expression in a routing policy, including the `as-path` match condition in the `from` statement:

```
[edit policy-options]
policy-statement policy-name {
  term term-name {
    from {
      as-path names;
    }
  }
}
```

The regular expression, which is used to match all or portions of the AS path, consists of two components, which you specify in the following format:

```
term <operator>
```

The term identifies an AS. You can specify it in one of the following ways:

- AS number—The entire AS number composes one `term`. You cannot reference individual characters within an AS number, which differs from regular expressions as defined in POSIX 1003.2.
- Wildcard character—Matches any single AS number. The wildcard character is a period (.). You can specify multiple wildcard characters.
- AS path—A single AS number or a group of AS numbers enclosed in parentheses. Grouping the regular expression in this way allows you to perform a common operation on the group as a whole and to give the group precedence. The grouped path can itself include operators.

You can specify one or more term–operator pairs in a single regular expression.

The optional operator defines pattern matching operations to apply to the term. You define the operations using regular expressions. Table 8.12 lists the regular expression operators supported for AS paths. You place operators immediately after `term` with no intervening space, except for the pipe (|) and dash (–) operators, which you place between two terms, and parentheses, with which you enclose terms.

Table 8.12 *AS Path and Community Attribute and Regular Expressions Operators*

Operator	Match
{*m*, *n*}	At least *m* and at most *n* repetitions of `term`. Both *m* and *n* must be positive integers, and *m* must be smaller than *n*.
{*m*}	Exactly *m* repetitions of `term`. *m* must be a positive integer.
{*m*,}	*m* or more repetitions of `term`. *m* must be a positive integer.
*	Zero or more repetitions of `term`. This is equivalent to {0,}.
+	One or more repetitions of `term`. This is equivalent to {1,}.
?	Zero or one repetition of `term`. This is equivalent to {0,1}.
|	One of the two terms on either side of the pipe.
–	Between a starting and ending range, inclusive.
^	Character at the beginning of an AS path regular expression. This character is added implicitly; therefore, the use of it is optional.
$	Character at the end of an AS path regular expression. This character is added implicitly; therefore, its use is optional.

Table 8.12 *AS Path and Community Attribute and Regular Expressions Operators*

Operator	Match
( )	A group of terms that are enclosed in the parentheses. If enclosed in quotation marks with no intervening space ("()"), indicates a null. Intervening space between the parentheses and the terms is ignored.
[ ]	Set of characters. One character from the set can match. To specify the start and end of a range, use a dash (–).

AS path regular expressions implement the extended (modern) regular expressions as defined in POSIX 1003.2 They are identical to the UNIX regular expressions with the following exceptions:

- The basic unit of matching in an AS path regular expression is the AS number, not an individual character.
- A regular expression matches a route only if the AS path in the route exactly matches *`regular-expression`*. The equivalent UNIX regular expression is `^`*`regular-expression`*`$`. For example, the AS path regular expression `1234` is equivalent to the UNIX regular expression `^1234$`.
- You can specify a regular expression using wildcard operators.

Configuring Communities

A *BGP community* is a group of destinations that share a common property. Community information is included as a path attribute in BGP update messages and identifies community members and allows you to perform actions on a group without having to elaborate on each member. You can define match conditions based on a BGP community, which this section describes. You can assign community tags to non-BGP routes through configuration (for static, aggregate, or generated routes) or an import routing policy. These tags can then be matched when BGP exports the routes.

To create a named community and define the community members, include the `community` statement:

```
[edit policy-options]
community name members [ community-ids ];
```

Then, name the community in a routing policy, including the `community` condition in the `from` statement. If you include the names of multiple communities, only one community need match for a match to occur.

```
[edit policy-options]
policy-statement policy-name {
  term term-name {
    from {
      community names;
    }
  }
}
```

name identifies the community or communities. It can contain letters, numbers, and hyphens (-), and can be up to 255 characters long. To include spaces in the name, enclose the entire name in quotation marks (double quotes).

Specify the community identifier in the following format:

```
as-number:community-value
```

The AS number of the community member can be a value from 1 through 65,534. The community value can be a number from 0 through 65,535. You can specify these numbers in one of the following ways:

- AS number.
- Asterisk (*)—A wildcard character that matches all AS numbers. (In the definition of the community attribute, the asterisk also functions as described in Table 8.12.)
- Period (.)—A wildcard character that matches any single digit in an AS number.
- Group of numbers—A single AS or community number or a group of numbers enclosed in parentheses. Grouping the numbers in this way allows you to perform a common operation on the group as a whole and to give the group precedence. The grouped numbers can themselves include regular expression operators.

You also can specify the community identifier as one of the following well-known community names, which are defined in RFC 1997:

- `no-advertise`—Routes in this community name must not be advertised to other BGP peers.
- `no-export`—Routes in this community must not be advertised outside a BGP confederation boundary.
- `no-export-subconfed`—Routes in this community must not be advertised to external BGP peers, including peers in other members' ASs inside a BGP confederation.

When specifying community identifiers, you can use UNIX-style regular expressions to specify the AS number and the member identifier. A regular expression consists of two components, which you specify in the following format:

```
term<operator>
```

`term` identifies the string to match. *`operator`* defines pattern-matching operations to apply to the term. Table 8.12 lists the regular expression operators supported for the community attribute. You place an operator immediately after *`term`* with no intervening space, except for the pipe (|) and dash (–) operators, which you place between two terms, and parentheses, with which you enclose terms.

Community regular expressions are identical to the UNIX regular expressions. Both implement the extended (or modern) regular expressions as defined in POSIX 1003.2. Community regular expressions evaluate the string specified in the *`term`* on a character-by-character basis. For example, if you specify 1234:5678 as the *`term`*, the regular expressions see nine discrete characters, including the colon (:), instead of two sets of numbers (1234 and 5678) separated by a colon.

By default, communities are sent to BGP peers. To suppress the advertisement of communities to a neighbor, remove all communities by defining a wildcard set of communities (here, the community is named `wild`) and then specifying the `community delete` action. When the result of an export policy is an empty set of communities, the community attribute is not sent.

```
[edit policy-options]
community wild members "*:*";
policy-statement policy-name {
  term term-name {
    then community delete wild;
  }
}
```

To configure extended communities, define the community and then reference it in the `from` statement:

```
[edit policy-options]
community name members [ community-ids ];
policy-statement policy-name {
  term term-name {
    from {
      community name;
    }
  }
}
```

The community identifier is the type of extended community in the following format:

```
type:administrator:assigned-number
```

`type` is the type of extended community and can be either a `target`, `origin`, or `domain-id` community. The `target` community identifies the destination to which the route is going. The `origin` community identifies where the route originated. The `domain-id` community identifies the OSPF domain from which the route originated. *`administrator`* is the administrator. It is either an AS number or an IPv4 address prefix, depending on the type of extended community. *`assigned-number`* identifies the local provider. Note that regular expressions are not supported for extended communities.

The policy framework software evaluates communities as follows:

- Each route is evaluated against each named community in a routing policy `from` statement. If a route matches one of the named communities in the `from` statement, the evaluation of the current term continues. If a route does not match, the evaluation of the current term ends.
- The route is evaluated against each member of a named community. The evaluation of all members must be successful for the named community evaluation to be successful.

- Each member in a named community is either a literal community value or a regular expression (applies to community attributes only). Each member is evaluated against each community on the route. (Communities are an unordered property on a route. For example, `1:2 3:4` is the same as `3:4 1:2`.) Only one community from the route must match for the member evaluation to be successful.
- Community regular expressions evaluate the string specified in the *term* on a character-by-character basis. For example, if you specify 1234:5678 as the *term*, the regular expressions see nine discrete characters, including the colon (:), instead of two sets of numbers (1234 and 5678) separated by a colon. For example:

```
[edit]
policy-options {
  policy-statement one {
    from {
      community [ comm-one comm-two ];
    }
  }
  community members comm-one [ 1:2 "^4:(5|6)$" ];
  community members comm-two [ 7:8 9:10 ];
}
```

  To match routing policy `one`, the route must match either `comm-one` or `comm-two`. To match `comm-one`, the route must have a community that matches `1:2` and a community that matches `4:5` or `4:6`. To match `comm-two`, the route must have a community that matches `7:8` and a community that matches `9:10`.

Configuring Prefix Lists and Route Lists

A *prefix list* is a named list of IP addresses. You can specify an exact match with incoming routes and apply a common action to all matching prefixes in the list. A *route list* is a collection of destination prefixes on which a common policy action is performed. In a prefix, you can specify an exact match with a particular route or a less precise match.

A prefix list functions similarly to a route list that contains multiple instances of the `exact` match type only. While some functional similarities exist between these two extended match conditions, so do some important differences, which are summarized in Table 8.13.

Table 8.13 *Prefix List and Route List Differences*

Feature	Prefix List	Route Lists
Match types	Does not support match types. The specified prefixes must be matched exactly.	Supports several match types. For more information, see Table 8.14 on page 347.
Action	Can specify action in a `then` statement only. This action is applied to all prefixes in the list.	Can specify action that is applied to a particular prefix in a `route-filter` match condition in a `from` statement or to all prefixes in the list using a `then` statement.

To create a named prefix list, include the `prefix-list` statement, specifying one or more addresses:

```
[edit policy-options]
prefix-list name {
  ip-addresses;
}
```

To include a prefix list in a routing policy, include the `prefix-list` match condition in the `from` statement, specifying the name of the prefix list:

```
[edit policy-options]
policy-statement policy-name {
  term term-name {
    from {
      prefix-list name;
    }
    then actions;
  }
}
```

During prefix list evaluation, the policy framework software performs a *longest-match lookup*, which means that the software searches for the prefix in the list with the longest length. (Because the policy framework software scans a list looking for the longest prefix, the order in which you specify the prefixes, from top to bottom, does not matter.) The software then compares a route's source address to the longest prefix. If a match occurs, the evaluation of the current term continues. If a match does not occur, the evaluation of the current term ends. If you specify multiple prefixes in the prefix list, only one prefix need match for a match to occur.

Configuring Route Lists

To configure a route list, include one or more `route-filter` or `source-address-filter` options in the `from` statement:

```
[edit policy-options]
policy-statement policy-name {
  term term-name {
    from {
      route-filter destination-prefix match-type
        <actions>;
      source-address-filter destination-prefix match-type
        <actions>;
    }
    then actions;
  }
}
```

The `route-filter` statement is typically used to match prefixes of any type except for multicast source addresses. The `source-address-filter` option is typically used to match multicast source addresses in multiprotocol BGP (MBGP) and Multicast Source Discovery Protocol (MSDP) environments.

`destination-prefix` is the IPv4 or IPv6 prefix specified as *`prefix/prefix-length`*. *`match-type`* is the type of match to apply to the destination prefix (see Table 8.14). *`actions`* is the action to take if the destination prefix matches.

For a list of actions, see Table 8.8 and Table 8.9 on page 331.

If you specify actions in the `route-filter` or `source-address-filter` statement, they are taken immediately when a match occurs, and the `then` statement is not evaluated. If you specify actions in the `then` statement, they are taken when a match occurs and if an action is not specified in the `route-filter` or `source-address-filter` statement.

During route list evaluation, the policy framework software compares each route's source address with the destination prefixes in the route list. The policy framework software first performs a longest-match lookup, which considers the prefix and prefix length only and not the match type. The following sample route list illustrates this point:

```
route-filter 192.168.0.0/14 upto /24;
route-filter 192.168.0.0/15 exact;
```

Here, the longest prefix is `192.168.0.0/15`, which is based on prefix and prefix length only. Then, if the prefix of an incoming route matches the longest prefix, the software then examines the match type

Table 8.14 *Route List Match Types*

Match Type	Match If ...
`exact`	Route shares the same most-significant bits (described by *`prefix-length`*) and *`prefix-length`* is equal to the route's prefix length.
`longer`	Route shares the same most-significant bits (described by *`prefix-length`*) and *`prefix-length`* is greater than the route's prefix length.
`orlonger`	Route shares the same most-significant bits (described by *`prefix-length`*) and *`prefix-length`* is equal to or greater than the route's prefix length.
`prefix-length-range` *`prefix-length2-prefix-length3`*	Route shares the same most-significant bits (described by *`prefix-length`*) and the route's prefix length falls between *`prefix-length2-prefix-length3`*, inclusive. The `upto` and `prefix-length-range` match types are similar in that both specify the most significant bits and provide a range of prefix lengths that can match. The difference is that `upto` allows you to specify an upper limit only for the prefix length range, whereas `prefix-length-range` allows you to specify both lower and upper limits.
`through` *`destination-prefix`*	Matches all the following: ■ Route shares the same most-significant bits (described by *`prefix-length`*) of the first destination prefix. ■ Route shares the same most-significant bits (described by *`prefix-length`*) of the second destination prefix for the number of bits in the prefix length. ■ Number of bits in the route's prefix length is less than or equal to the number of bits in the second prefix. You do not use the `through` match type in most routing policy configurations.
`upto` *`prefix-length2`*	Route shares the same most-significant bits (described by *`prefix-length`*) and the route's prefix length falls between *`prefix-length`* and *`prefix-length2`*.

and action associated with the longest prefix. If a match occurs, the action specified with the prefix is taken. If an action is not specified with the prefix, the action in the `then` statement is taken. If neither action is specified, the software evaluates the next term or routing policy if present or takes the accept or reject action specified by the default policy. If you specify multiple prefixes in the route list, only one prefix need match for a match to occur. If a match does not occur, the software evaluates the next term or routing policy if present or takes the accept or reject action specified by the default policy.

The order in which you specify the prefixes typically does not matter, because the policy framework software scans the route list looking for the longest prefix during evaluation. An exception to this rule is when you use the same destination prefix multiple times in a list. Here, the order is important, because the list of identical prefixes is scanned from top to bottom and the first match type that matches the route applies. In the following example, different match types are specified for the same prefix. The route `0.0.0.0/0` would be rejected, the route `0.0.0.0/8` would be marked with `next-hop self`, and the route `0.0.0.0/25` would be rejected.

```
route-filter 0.0.0.0/0 upto /7 reject;
route-filter 0.0.0.0/0 upto /24 next-hop self;
route-filter 0.0.0.0/0 orlonger reject;
```

A common problem when defining a route list is including a shorter prefix that you want to match with a longer, similar prefix in the same list. For example, imagine that the prefix `192.168.254.0/24` is compared against the following route list:

```
route-filter 192.168.0.0/16 orlonger;
route-filter 192.168.254.0/23 exact;
```

Because of the longest-match lookup, the prefix `192.168.254.0/23` is determined to be the longest prefix. An exact match does not occur between `192.168.254.0/24` and `192.168.254.0/23 exact`, so the software concludes that the term does not match and goes on to the next term or routing policy if present or takes the accept or reject action specified by the default policy. The shorter prefix `192.168.0.0/16 orlonger` that you wanted to match is inadvertently ignored. One solution is to remove the prefix `192.168.0.0/16 orlonger` from the route list in this term and move it to a previous term in which it is the only prefix or the longest prefix in the list.

Configuring Subroutines

Using a routing policy called from another routing policy as a match condition makes the called policy a *subroutine*. To configure a subroutine, create the subroutine and specify its name using the `policy` match condition in the `from` or `to` statement of another routing policy:

```
[edit policy-options]
policy-statement subroutine-policy-name {
  term term-name {
    from {
      match-conditions;
      route-filter destination-prefix match-type <actions>;
      source-address-filter destination-prefix match-type
        <actions>;
```

```
        prefix-list name;
      }
      to {
        match-conditions;
      }
      then actions;
    }
  }
  policy-statement policy-name {
    term term-name {
      from {
        policy subroutine-policy-name;

      to {
        policy subroutine-policy-name;
      }
      then actions;
    }
  }
```

Do not evaluate a routing policy within itself. If you attempt to do so, no prefixes will ever match the routing policy.

The action specified in a subroutine is used to provide a match condition to the calling policy. If the subroutine specifies an action of accept, the calling policy considers the route to be a match. If the subroutine specifies an action of reject, the calling policy considers the route to not match. If the subroutine specifies an action that is meant to manipulate the route characteristics, the changes are made.

Configuring the AS Path Prepend Action

To *prepend*, or add, one or more AS numbers at the beginning of an AS path, specify the `as-path-prepend` action in the `then` statement. The AS numbers are added after the local AS number has been added to the path. Prepending an AS path makes a shorter AS path look longer and therefore less preferable to BGP.

```
[edit policy-options]
policy-statement name {
  term name {
    from {
      route-filter destination-prefix match-type <actions>;
    }
    then as-path-prepend "as-path";
  }
}
```

Configuring BGP Route Flap Damping

BGP flap damping is defined in RFC 2439, *BGP Route Flap Damping.*

BGP *route flapping* is the situation in which BGP systems send an excessive number of update messages to advertise network reachability information. BGP *flap damping* is a way to reduce the number of update messages sent between BGP peers, thereby reducing the load on these peers without adversely affecting the route convergence time. Flap damping reduces the number of update messages by marking routes as ineligible for selection as the active or preferable route. Doing this leads to some delay, or *suppression*, in the propagation of route information, but the result is increased network stability.

To apply the changes in BGP, see "Configuring Route Flap Damping," on page 406.

To effect changes to the default BGP flap damping values, include the following statements. Table 8.15 describes the damping parameters.

```
[edit policy-options]
damping name {
  disable;
  half-life minutes;
  max-suppress minutes;
  reuse number;
  suppress number;
}
policy-statement name {
  term name {
    from {
      ...
    }
    then damping name;
  }
}
```

Table 8.15 *Damping Parameters*

Damping Parameter	Description	Default	Possible Values
`half-life` *minutes*	Decay half-life, in minutes	15 minutes	1 through 45 minutes
`max-suppress` *minutes*	Maximum hold-down time, in minutes	60 minutes	1 through 720 minutes
`reuse` *number*	Reuse threshold	750 (unitless)	1 through 20,000 (unitless)
`suppress` *number*	Cutoff (suppression) threshold	3,000 (unitless)	1 through 20,000 (unitless)

Configuring Per-Packet Load Balancing

For the active route, when there are multiple equal-cost paths to the same destination, by default, the JUNOS software chooses in a random fashion one of the next-hop addresses to install into the forwarding table. Whenever the set of next hops for a destination changes in any way, the next-hop address is rechosen, also in a random fashion. You can configure the JUNOS software so that, for the active route, all next-hop addresses for a destination are installed in the forwarding table, a process called *per-packet load balancing*. You can use load balancing to spread traffic across multiple paths between routers.

On routers with the Internet Processor II ASIC, when per-packet load balancing is configured, traffic between routers with multiple paths is divided into individual traffic flows (up to 16 equal-cost load-balanced paths). Packets for each individual flow are kept on a single interface. To recognize individual flows in the transit traffic, the router examines the source IP address, destination IP address, and protocol.

The router recognizes packets that have all these parameters identical, and it ensures that these packets are sent out through the same interface. This prevents problems that might otherwise occur with packets arriving at their destination out of their original sequence.

For information on this action, see Table 8.9 on page 331.

To configure per-packet load balancing, you configure the `load-balance per-packet` action and apply the routing policy to the forwarding table by including the `export` statement at the `[edit routing-options forwarding-table]` hierarchy level.

Configuring Firewall Filters

To configure firewall filters, include the following statements:

```
[edit]
firewall {
  policer policer-name {
    if-exceeding {
      bandwidth-limit rate;
      burst-size-limit bytes;
    }
    then {
      policer-action;
    }
```

```
    }
    filter filter-name {
      accounting-profile name;
      interface-specific;
      policer policer-name {
        if-exceeding {
          bandwidth-limit rate;
          burst-size-limit bytes;
        }
        then {
          policer-action;
        }
      }
      term term-name {
        from {
          match-conditions;
        }
        then {
          actions;
          action-modifiers;
        }
      }
    }
  }
  interfaces {
    interface-name {
      unit logical-unit-number {
        family inet {
          filter {
            input filter-name;
            output filter-name;
          }
        }
      }
    }
  }
```

Policing does not use the filter match conditions. Instead, it uses the `if-exceeding` statement. For more information, see the JUNOS technical documentation: *Routing Policy.*

Firewall filter terms are evaluated in the order in which you specify them in the configuration. To reorder terms, use the configuration mode `insert` command. For example, the command `insert term up before term start` places the term `up` before the term `start`.

In the `then` statement of a firewall filter term, you specify the action to take if the packet matches the conditions in the `from` statement (see Table 8.16 and Table 8.17).

Table 8.16 *Firewall Filter Actions*

Action	Description
`accept`	Accept a packet. This is the default.
`discard`	Discard a packet silently, without sending an ICMP message. Discarded packets are not available for logging or sampling.
`reject` *<message-type>*	Discard a packet, sending an ICMP destination unreachable message. Rejected packets can be logged or sampled if you configure either of those action modifiers. You can specify one of the following message codes: `administratively-prohibited` (default), `bad-host-tos`, `bad-network-tos`, `host-prohibited`, `host-unknown`, `host-unreachable`, `network-prohibited`, `network-unknown`, `network-unreachable`, `port-unreachable`, `precedence-cutoff`, `precedence-violation`, `protocol-unreachable`, `source-host-isolated`, `source-route-failed`, or `tcp-reset`. If you specify `tcp-reset`, a TCP reset is returned if the packet is a TCP packet. Otherwise, nothing is returned.
`routing-instance` *routing-instance*	Specify a routing table to which packets are forwarded.

Table 8.17 *Firewall Filter Action Modifiers*

Action Modifier	Description
`count` *counter-name*	Increment a counter for this filter. The name can contain letters, numbers, and hyphens (-), and can be up to 24 characters long. A counter name is specific to the filter that uses it, so all interfaces that use the same filter count into the same counter.
`forwarding-class` *class-name*	Specify a particular forwarding class.
`ipsec-sa` *sa-name*	Specify an IPSec security association for the packet. Used with the `source-address` and `destination-address` match conditions.
`log`	Log the packet's header information in the Routing Engine. You can access this information from the CLI, but it is not available from network management.
`loss-priority` *priority*	Set the packet loss priority (PLP) to `any`, `low`, or `high`.
`policer` *policer-name*	Apply rate limits to the traffic using the named policer.
`sample`	Sample the traffic on the interface. Use this modifier only when traffic sampling is enabled.
`syslog`	Log an alert for this packet. The log can be sent to a server for storage and analysis.

When a firewall filter consists of a single term, the filter is evaluated as follows:

- If the packet matches all the conditions, the action in the `then` statement is taken.
- If the packet does not match all the conditions, it is discarded.

When a firewall filter consists of more than one term, the filter is evaluated sequentially:

- The packet is evaluated against the conditions in the `from` statement in the first term.
- If the packet matches, the action in the `then` statement is taken and the evaluation ends. Subsequent terms in the firewall filter are not evaluated.
- If the packet does not match, it is evaluated against the conditions in the `from` statement in the second term.

  This process continues until either the packet matches the `from` conditions in one of the subsequent terms or there are no more terms.

- If a packet passes through all the terms in the filter without matching any of them, it is discarded.

If a term does not contain a `from` statement, the packet is considered to match and the action in the term's `then` statement is taken. If a term does not contain a `then` statement or if you do not configure an action in the `then` statement, and if the packet matches the conditions in the term's `from` statement, the packet is accepted.

Each firewall filter has an implicit discard action at the end of the filter, which is equivalent to the following explicit filter term. Therefore, if a packet matches none of the terms in the filter, it is discarded.

```
term implicit-rule {
  then discard;
}
```

In the `from` statement in the `firewall filter` term, specify conditions that the packet must match for the action in the `then` statement to be taken. All conditions in the `from` statement must match for the action to be taken. The order in which you specify match conditions is not important, because a packet must match all conditions in a term.

If you specify no match conditions in a term, that term matches all packets.

An individual condition in a `from` statement can contain a list of values. For example, you can specify numeric ranges or multiple source or destination addresses. When a condition defines a list of values, a match occurs if one of the values in the list matches the packet.

Individual conditions in a `from` statement can be negated. When you negate a condition, you are defining an explicit mismatch. If a packet matches a negated condition, it is immediately considered not to match the `from` statement, and the next term in the filter is evaluated, if there is one; if there are no more terms, the packet is discarded.

Match conditions are grouped into the following categories depending on how you specify the condition:

- Numeric range
- Address filter
- Multiple match conditions
- Bit-field filter

Numeric range filter conditions match packet fields that can be identified by a numeric value, such as port and protocol numbers. For numeric range filter match conditions, you specify a keyword that identifies the condition and a single value or a range of values that a field in a packet must match. Table 8.18 describes the numeric range filter match conditions. You can specify the numeric range value in one of the following ways:

- Single number (for example, `source-port 25`)
- Range of numbers (for example, `source-port 1024-65535`)
- Text synonym for a single number (for example, `source-port smtp`)

Table 8.18 *Numeric Range Firewall Filter Match Conditions*

Match Condition	Description
keyword-except	Negate a match. For example, destination-port-except *number*.
destination-port *number*	TCP or UDP destination port field. You cannot specify both the port and destination-port match conditions in the same term. Normally, you specify this match in conjunction with the protocol match statement to determine which protocol is being used on the port. In place of the numeric value, you can specify one of the following text synonyms (the port numbers are also listed): afs (1483), bgp (179), biff (512), bootpc (68), bootps (67), cmd (514), cvspserver (2401), dhcp (67), domain (53), eklogin (2105), ekshell (2106), exec (512), finger (79), ftp (21), ftp-data (20), http (80), https (443), ident (113), imap (143), kerberos-sec (88), klogin (543), kpasswd (761), krb-prop (754), krbupdate (760), kshell (544), ldap (389), login (513), mobileip-agent (434), mobilip-mn (435), msdp (639), netbios-dgm (138), netbios-ns (137), netbios-ssn (139), nfsd (2049), nntp (119), ntalk (518), ntp (123), pop3 (110), pptp (1723), printer (515), radacct (1813), radius (1812), rip (520), rkinit (2108), smtp (25), snmp (161), snmptrap (162), snpp (444), socks (1080), ssh (22), sunrpc (111), syslog (514), tacacs-ds (65), talk (517), telnet (23), tftp (69), timed (525), who (513), xdmcp (177), zephyr-clt (2103), or zephyr-hm (2104).
dscp *number*	Differentiated Services code point (DSCP). The Diffserv protocol uses the ToS byte in the IP header. The most significant six bits of this byte form the DSCP. For more information, see Chapter 6, "Interfaces and Class of Service," on page 185. In place of the numeric value, you can specify one of the following text synonyms (the field values are also listed): The Expedited Forwarding RFC defines one code point: ef (46). The Assured Forwarding RFC defines four classes, with three drop precedences in each class, for a total of 12 code points: af11 (10), af12 (12), af13 (14); af21 (18), af22 (20), af23 (22); af31 (26), af32 (28), af33 (30); af41 (34), af42 (36), af43 (38).
fragment-offset *number*	Fragment offset field.

Table 8.18 *Numeric Range Firewall Filter Match Conditions*

Match Condition	Description
`icmp-code` *number*	ICMP code field. This value or keyword provides more specific information than the `icmp-type`. Because the value's meaning depends on the associated `icmp-type`, you must specify the `icmp-type` along with the `icmp-code`. In place of the numeric value, you can specify one of the following text synonyms (the field values are also listed). The keywords are grouped by the ICMP type with which they are associated: parameter-problem: `ip-header-bad` (0), `required-option-missing` (1); redirect: `redirect-for-host` (1), `redirect-for-network` (0), `redirect-for-tos-and-host` (3), `redirect-for-tos-and-net` (2); time-exceeded: `ttl-eq-zero-during-reassembly` (1), `ttl-eq-zero-during-transit` (0); unreachable: `communication-prohibited-by-filtering` (13), `destination-host-prohibited` (10), `destination-host-unknown` (7), `destination-network-prohibited` (9), `destination-network-unknown` (6), `fragmentation-needed` (4), `host-precedence-violation` (14), `host-unreachable` (1), `host-unreachable-for-TOS` (12), `network-unreachable` (0), `network-unreachable-for-TOS` (11), `port-unreachable` (3), `precedence-cutoff-in-effect` (15), `protocol-unreachable` (2), `source-host-isolated` (8), `source-route-failed` (5).
`icmp-type` *number*	ICMP packet type field. Normally, you specify this match in conjunction with the `protocol` match statement to determine which protocol is being used on the port. In place of the numeric value, you can specify one of the following text synonyms (the field values are also listed): `echo-reply` (0), `echo-request` (8), `info-reply` (16), `info-request` (15), `mask-request` (17), `mask-reply` (18), `parameter-problem` (12), `redirect` (5), `router-advertisement` (9), `router-solicit` (10), `source-quench` (4), `time-exceeded` (11), `timestamp` (13), `timestamp-reply` (14), or `unreachable` (3).
`interface-group` *group-number*	Interface group on which the packet was received. An interface group is a set of one or more logical interfaces. For information, see "Applying Firewall Filters to Interfaces," on page 361.
`packet-length` *bytes*	Length of the received packet, in bytes. The length refers only to the IP packet, including the packet header, and does not include any Layer 2 encapsulation overhead.
`port` *number*	TCP or UDP source or destination port field. You cannot specify both the `port` match and either the `destination-port` or `source-port` match conditions in the same term. Normally, you specify this match in conjunction with the `protocol` match statement to determine which protocol is being used on the port. In place of the numeric value, you can specify one of the text synonyms listed under `destination-port`.
`precedence` *ip-precedence-field*	IP precedence field. In place of the numeric field value, you can specify one of the following text synonyms (the field values are also listed): `critical-ecp` (0xa0), `flash` (0x60), `flash-override` (0x80), `immediate` (0x40), `internet-control` (0xc0), `net-control` (0xe0), `priority` (0x20), or `routine` (0x00).

Table 8.18 *Numeric Range Firewall Filter Match Conditions*

Match Condition	Description
`protocol` *number*	IP protocol field. In place of the numeric value, you can specify one of the following text synonyms (the field values are also listed): `egp` (8), `esp` (50), `gre` (47), `icmp` (1), `igmp` (2), `ipip` (4), `ipv6` (41), `ospf` (89), `pim` (103), `rsvp` (46), `tcp` (6), or `udp` (17).
`source-port` *number*	TCP or UDP source port field. You cannot specify the `port` and `source-port` match conditions in the same term. Normally, you specify this match in conjunction with the `protocol` match statement to determine which protocol is being used on the port. In place of the numeric field, you can specify one of the text synonyms listed under `destination-port`.

To specify multiple values in a single match condition, group the values within square brackets following the keyword (for example, `source-port [smtp ftp-data 25 1024-65535]`).

To exclude a numeric value, append the string `-except` to the match keyword.

Address filter conditions match prefix values in a packet, such as IP source and destination prefixes. For address filter match conditions, you specify a keyword that identifies the field and one or more prefixes of that type that a packet must match. Table 8.19 describes the address filter match conditions. You can specify the address as a single prefix (a match occurs if the value of the field matches the prefix) or as multiple prefixes (a match occurs if any one of the prefixes in the list matches the packet). To specify the address prefix, use the notation *prefix/prefix-length*. To exclude a prefix, specify the string `except` after the prefix. Because the prefixes are order-independent and use longest-match rules, shorter prefixes subsume longer ones as long as they are the same type (whether you specify `except` or not). This is because anything that would match the longer prefix would also match the shorter one.

Table 8.19 *Address Firewall Filter Match Conditions*

Match Condition	Description
`address` *prefix*	IP source or destination address field
`destination-address` *prefix*	IP destination address field
`destination-prefix-list` *prefix-list*	IP destination prefix list field

Table 8.19 *Address Firewall Filter Match Conditions*

Match Condition	Description
`prefix-list` *`prefix-list`*	IP source or destination prefix list field
`source-address` *`prefix`*	IP source address field
`source-prefix-list` *`prefix-list`*	IP source prefix list field

Bit-field filter conditions match packet fields if particular bits in those fields are or are not set. You can match the IP options, TCP flags, and IP fragmentation fields. For bit-field filter match conditions, you specify a keyword that identifies the field and tests to determine that the option is present in the field. Table 8.20 describes the bit-field match conditions. To specify the bit-field value to match, enclose the value in quotation marks (double quotes). Generally, you specify the bits being tested using keywords. Bit-field match keywords always map to a single bit value. You also can specify bit fields as hexadecimal or decimal numbers. To negate a match, precede the value with an exclamation point. To match multiple bit-field values, use the logical operators list in Table 8.21. The operators are listed in order, from highest precedence to lowest precedence. Operations are left-associative.When you specify a numeric value that has more than one bit set, the value is treated as a logical AND of the set bits. You can use text synonyms to specify some common bit-field matches. You specify these matches as a single keyword.

If you specify a port match condition or a match of the ICMP type or TCP flags field, there is no implied protocol match. If you use one of the following match conditions in a term, you should explicitly specify the protocol in the same term:

- `destination-port`—Specify the `protocol tcp` or `protocol udp` match condition in the same term.
- `icmp-code`—Specify the `protocol icmp` match condition in the same term.
- `icmp-type`—Specify the `protocol icmp` match condition in the same term.
- `port`—Specify the `protocol tcp` or `protocol udp` match condition in the same term.

Table 8.20 *Bit-Field Firewall Filter Match Conditions*

Match Condition	Description
Conditions with Variables	
`fragment-flags` *`number`*	IP fragmentation flags. In place of the numeric field value, you can specify one of the following keywords (the field values are also listed): `dont-fragment` (0x4000), `more-fragments` (0x2000), or `reserved` (0x8000).
`ip-options` *`number`*	IP options. In place of the numeric value, you can specify one of the following text synonyms (the field values are also listed): `loose-source-route` (131), `record-route` (7), `router-alert` (148), `strict-source-route` (137), or `timestamp` (68).
`tcp-flags` *`number`*	TCP flags. Normally, you specify this match in conjunction with the `protocol` match statement to determine which protocol is being used on the port. In place of the numeric value, you can specify one of the following text synonyms (the field values are also listed): `ack` (0x10), `fin` (0x01), `push` (0x08), `rst` (0x04), `syn` (0x02), or `urgent` (0x20).
Text Synonyms	
`first-fragment`	First fragment of a fragmented packet. This condition does not match unfragmented packets.
`is-fragment`	Matches if the packet is a fragment.
`tcp-established`	TCP packets other than the first packet of a connection. This is a synonym for "`(ack | rst)`". This condition does not implicitly check that the protocol is TCP. To check this, specify the `protocol tcp` match condition.
`tcp-initial`	First TCP packet of a connection. This is a synonym for "`(syn & !ack)`". This condition does not implicitly check that the protocol is TCP. To check this, specify the `protocol tcp` match condition.

Table 8.21 *Bit-Field Logical Operators*

Logical Operator	Description
`(...)`	Grouping
`!`	Negation
`&` or `+`	Logical AND
`|` or `,`	Logical OR

- `source-port`—Specify the `protocol tcp` or `protocol udp` match condition in the same term.
- `tcp-flags`—Specify the `protocol tcp` match condition in the same term.

When examining match conditions, the policy framework software tests only the specified field itself. It does not also test the IP header to determine that the packet is indeed an IP packet. If you do not explicitly specify the protocol when using the fields listed above, design your filters carefully to ensure that they are performing the expected matches.

Applying Firewall Filters to Interfaces

For a firewall filter to work, you must apply it to at least one interface:

```
[edit interfaces]
interfaces interface-name {
  unit logical-unit-number {
    family inet {
      filter {
        input filter-name;
        output filter-name;
      }
    }
  }
}
```

In the `input` statement, list the name of one firewall filter to be evaluated when packets are received on the interface. In the `output` statement, list the name of one firewall filter to be evaluated when packets are transmitted on the interface. You can apply only one input and one output firewall filter to each interface. You can use the same filter one or more times. Input or output filters applied to the loopback interface, `lo0`, affect only input or outbound traffic sent from the Routing Engine, respectively.

When you apply a firewall filter to multiple interfaces, you can name individual counters specific to each interface. These counters enable you to easily maintain statistics on the traffic transiting the different interfaces. Configuration of interface-specific counters also creates separate instances of any policers you have configured for the same interface. To configure interface-specific counters, include the `interface-specific` statement:

```
[edit firewall filter filter-name]
interface-specific;
```

When applying a firewall filter, you can define an interface to be part of an *interface group*. Packets received on that interface are tagged as being part of the group. You then can match these packets using the `interface-group` match statement. To define the interface to be part of an interface group, include the `group` statement:

```
[edit interfaces interface-name unit logical-unit-number
family inet filter]
group group-number;
```

Configuring Policing

Policing, or rate limiting, enables you to limit the amount of traffic that passes into or out of an interface. It is an essential component of filters designed to thwart DoS attacks. Policing applies two types of rate limits on the traffic: bandwidth, which is the number of bits per second permitted, on average, and maximum burst size. Policing uses a *token-bucket algorithm*, which enforces a limit on average bandwidth while allowing bursts up to a specified maximum value. It offers more flexibility than a *leaky bucket algorithm* in allowing a certain amount of bursty traffic before it starts discarding packets.

You define specific classes of traffic on an interface, to which you can apply a set of rate limits. To do this, you define *policers* within a filter statement. For example, to limit all ftp traffic from a particular source to certain rate limits configure the following:

1. Include one or more policer statements in the filter configuration; they must precede the term definitions. To avoid the time-consuming process of configuring a policer within each filter, you can also define a policer outside the filter; the policer can then be used as a template.
2. Reference the policers in the `then` clause of a term.
3. Add actions, such as accept or discard, or other action modifiers, such as count or log.

4. Apply the policers to an interface for them to be activated. You apply policers the same way you apply firewall filters.

The policer is applied to the packet first, and if the packet exceeds the defined limits, the actions of the `then` clause of the policer are applied. If the result of the policing action was not a discard, the remaining components of the `then` clause of the term are applied.

To specify the rate-limiting part of a policer, include an `if-exceeding` statement, specifying the bandwidth limit in bits per second and the burst size limit in bytes:

```
if-exceeding {
  bandwidth-limit rate;
  burst-size-limit bytes;
}
```

There is no absolute minimum value for the bandwidth limit, and the maximum value is 4.29 Gbps. Any value below 61,040 bps results in a minimum effective rate of 30,520 bps. The maximum value for the burst size limit is 100 MB. The preferred method for setting this limit is to multiply the bandwidth of the interface on which you are applying the filter by the amount of time you allow a burst of traffic at that bandwidth to occur: for example, 5 milliseconds. If you do not know the interface bandwidth, you can multiply the MTU of the traffic on the interface by 10 to obtain a value. If a packet does not exceed its rate limits, it is processed further without being affected. If the packet exceeds its limits, it can be discarded or marked for subsequent processing as specified in the `loss-priority` and `forwarding-class` statements.

To configure a policer action, include the following statements:

```
policer policer-name {
  then {
    policer-action;
  }
```

To simply discard a packet that exceeds the rate limits:

```
then {
  discard;
}
```

To set the loss priority equal to low:

```
then {
  loss-priority low;
}
```

To set the forwarding class:

```
then {
  forwarding-class class-name;
}
```

The possible values for `loss-priority` are `any`, `low`, and `high`, and *`class-name`* is any class name already configured for the forwarding class.

Configure Accounting

For more information, see the JUNOS *Getting Started* technical documentation.

Juniper Networks routers can collect various kinds of data about traffic passing through the router. You can set up one or more *accounting profiles* that specify some common characteristics of this data, including the fields used in the accounting records, the number of files that the router retains before discarding, the number of bytes per file, and the polling period that the system uses to record the data. You configure the profiles using statements at the `[edit accounting-options]` hierarchy level. You assign a unique accounting-profile name for each profile, and this name cross-references the information specified at the `[edit accounting-options]` hierarchy with `interfaces` or `firewall` configuration statements.

Configuring Filter-Based Forwarding

You can configure filters to classify packets based on source address and specify the forwarding path the packets take within the router. You can use this filter for applications to differentiate traffic from two clients that share a common access layer (for example, a Layer 2 switch) but are connected to different ISPs. When the filter is applied, the router can differentiate the two traffic streams and direct each to the appropriate network. Depending on the client's media type, the filter can use the source IP address to forward the traffic to the corresponding network through a tunnel. You can also configure filters to classify packets based on IP protocol type or IP precedence bits. You can forward packets based on input filters only; you cannot forward packets based on output filters. To direct traffic meeting defined match conditions to a specific routing table, include the `routing-instance` statement:

```
[edit firewall filter filter-name term term-name then]
routing-instance routing-instance;
```

See Chapter 9, "Routing and Routing Protocols," on page 373.

To implement filter-based forwarding, you must create a routing table group that adds interface routes to the routing instance created to direct traffic that meets defined match conditions to a specific routing table and to the default routing table `inet.0`. You create a routing table group to resolve the routes installed in the routing instance to directly connected next hops on that interface.

Configuring Traffic Sampling and Forwarding

On routers with an Internet Processor II ASIC, you can sample IP traffic based on particular input interfaces and various fields in the packet header. You can use traffic sampling to monitor any combination of specific logical interfaces, specific protocols on one or more interfaces, a range of addresses on a logical interface, or individual IP addresses. Information about the sampled packets is saved to files on the router's hard disk. The traffic sampling feature is not meant to capture all packets received by a router. Juniper Networks does not recommend excessive sampling (a rate greater than 1 in 1,000 packets), because it can increase the load on the processor. If you need to set a higher sampling rate to diagnose a particular problem or type of traffic received, we recommend that you revert to a lower sampling rate after the problem or troublesome traffic is discovered.

To configure traffic sampling, perform at least the following tasks:

1. Create a firewall filter:

```
[edit firewall]
filter filter-name {
  term term-name {
    then {
      sample;
      accept;
    }
  }
}
```

2. Apply the filter to the logical interfaces on which you want to sample traffic:

```
[edit interfaces]
interface-name {
  unit logical-unit-number {
    family inet {
      filter {
        input filter-name;
      }
      address address {
        destination destination-address;
      }
    }
  }
}
```

3. Enable sampling, specifying a nonzero sampling rate:

```
[edit forwarding-options]
sampling {
  input {
    family inet inet {
      rate number;
    }
  }
}
```

To configure other forwarding options, include one or more of the following statements:

```
[edit forwarding-options]
hash-key {
  family inet {
    layer-3;
    layer-4;
  }
  family mpls {
    label-1;
    label-2;
  }
}
sampling {
  disable;
  input {
    family inet {
      max-packets-per-second number;
      rate number;
      run-length number;
    }
  }
```

```
      output {
        cflowd host-name {
          aggregation {
            autonomous-system;
            destination-prefix;
            protocol-port;
            source-destination-prefix {
              caida-compliant;
            }
            source-prefix;
          }
          autonomous-system-type (origin | peer);
          (local-dump | no-local-dump);
          port port-number;
          version format;
        }
        file {
          filename filename;
          files number;
          size bytes;
          (stamp | no-stamp);
          (world-readable | no-world-readable);
        }
        port-mirroring {
          interface interface-name;
          next-hop address;
        }
      }
      traceoptions {
        file filename {
          files number;
          size bytes;
          (world-readable | no-world-readable);
        }
      }
    }
```

Configuring Per-Flow Load Balancing Information

You can specify what information the router uses for per-flow load balancing based on port data rather than based only on source and destination IP addresses. For aggregated Ethernet and aggregated SONET interfaces, you can load balance based on the MPLS label information. By default, the software ignores port data when determining flows. To enable per-flow load balancing, set the `load-balance per-packet` action in the routing policy configuration. To include port data in the flow determination, include the `family inet` statement:

```
[edit forwarding-options hash-key]
family inet {
  layer-3;
  layer-4;
}
```

By default, the router uses the following Layer 3 information in the packet header to load-balance: source IP address, destination IP address, and protocol. If you include both the `layer-3` and `layer-4` statements, the router uses the source IP address, destination IP address, protocol, source port number, destination port number, and incoming interface index to load balance. This is appropriate behavior for Transmission Control Protocol (TCP) and User Datagram Protocol (UDP) packets. For ICMP packets, the field location offset is the checksum field, which makes each ping packet a separate "flow." This can be problematic; for example, some `traceroute` implementations might use ICMP rather than UDP for the outgoing packets.

Configuring Traffic Sampling Output Files

To collect sampled packets in a file in the `/var/tmp` directory, include the `file` statement. Traffic sampling output is saved to an ASCII text file, with each line containing information for one sampled packet.

```
[edit forwarding-options sampling output]
  file {
    filename filename;
    files number;
    size bytes;
    (stamp | no-stamp);
    (world-readable | no-world-readable);
  }
}
```

Tracing Traffic Sampling Operations

Tracing operations track all traffic sampling operations and record them in a log file in the `/var/log` directory. By default, this file is named `/var/log/sampled`. The default file size is 128 KB, and 10 files are created before the first one gets overwritten. To trace traffic sampling operations, include the `file` statement:

```
[edit forwarding-options sampling traceoptions]
file filename {
  files number;
  size bytes;
  (world-readable | no-world-readable);
}
```

Configuring Flow Aggregation (cflowd)

You can collect an aggregate of sampled flows and send the aggregate to a specified host that runs the cflowd application available from CAIDA (http://www.caida.org). Using cflowd, you can obtain various types of byte and packet counts of flows through a router. The cflowd application collects the sampled flows over a period of 1 minute. At the end of the minute, the number of samples to be exported are divided over the period of another minute and are exported over the course of the same minute. By default, flow aggregation is disabled. To enable the collection of flow aggregates, include the `cflowd` statement, specifying the name or identifier of the host that collects the flow aggregates.

```
[edit forwarding-options sampling output]
cflowd host-name {
  aggregation {
    autonomous-system;
    destination-prefix;
    protocol-port;
    source-destination-prefix {
      caida-compliant;
    }
    source-prefix;
  }
  autonomous-system-type (origin | peer);
  (local-dump | no-local-dump);
  port port-number;
  version format;
}
```

You must also include the UDP port number on the host and the `version`, which gives the format of the exported cflowd aggregates. To collect cflowd records in a log file before exporting, include the `local-dump` statement. To specify aggregation of specific types of traffic, which conserves memory and bandwidth in enabling cflowd to export targeted flows rather than all the aggregated traffic, include the `aggregation` statement. The aggregation type can be one of the following:

- `autonomous-system`—Aggregate by AS number.
- `destination-prefix`—Aggregate by destination prefix only.
- `protocol-port`—Aggregate by protocol and port number; requires setting the separate `cflowd port` statement.
- `source-destination-prefix`—Aggregate by source and destination prefix.
- `source-prefix`—Aggregate by source prefix only.

Collection of sampled packets in a local ASCII file is not affected by the `cflowd` statement.

To collect the cflowd flows in a log file before they are exported, include the `local-dump` statement. By default, the flows are collected in `/var/log/sampled`. Note that you cannot configure both host (cflowd) sampling and port mirroring at the same time.

Configuring Port Mirroring

On routers containing an Internet Processor II ASIC, you can send a copy of an IPv4 packet from the router to an external host address or a packet analyzer for analysis, also known as *port mirroring*. Port mirroring is different from traffic sampling. In traffic sampling, a sampling key based on the IPv4 header is sent to the Routing Engine, and the key can be placed in a file or cflowd packets based on the key can be sent to a cflowd server. In port mirroring, the entire packet is copied and sent out through a next-hop interface. To configure port mirroring, configure traffic sampling on a logical interface by including the `input` statement at the `[edit forwarding-options sampling]` hierarchy level. Then specify the output interface to the analyzer and port-mirroring destination in the `port-mirroring` statement:

```
[edit forwarding-options sampling output]
port-mirroring {
  interface interface-name;
  next-hop address;
}
```

The following restrictions apply to port mirroring:

- You cannot configure both cflowd sampling and port mirroring in the same configuration.
- You cannot configure firewall filters on the port-mirroring interface.
- The interface you configure for port mirroring should not participate in any kind of routing activity.
- The destination address should not have a route to the ultimate traffic destination. For example, if the sampled IPv4 packets have a destination address of `190.68.9.10` and the port-mirrored traffic is sent to `190.68.20.15` for analysis, the device associated with the latter address should not know a route to `190.68.9.10`. Also, it should not send the sampled packets back to the source address.
- Only IPv4 traffic is supported.
- You can configure only one port-mirroring interface per router. If you include more than one interface in the `port-mirroring` statement, the previous one is overwritten.
- You must include a firewall filter with both the `accept` action and the `sample` action modifier on the inbound interface for port mirroring to work. Do not include the `discard` action or port mirroring does not work.

Chapter 9

Routing and Routing Protocols

The JUNOS routing protocol process supports a wide variety of routing protocols, including IS-IS, OSPF, RIP, BGP, PIM, MSDP, and DVMRP. The JUNOS software maintains two databases for routing information: the routing table, which contains all the routing information learned by all routing protocols, and the forwarding table, which contains the routes actually used to forward packets through the router. In addition, the interior gateway protocols (IGPs), IS-IS and OSPF, maintain link-state databases. This chapter explains the concepts, tables, and configurations used by the JUNOS routing protocol process.

Routing Protocols Concepts

Each IGP routing protocol maintains a database of the routing information it has learned from other routers running the same protocol and uses this information as defined and required by the protocol. IS-IS and OSPF use the routing information they received to maintain link-state databases, which they use to determine which adjacent neighbors are operational and to construct network topology maps. IS-IS and OSPF use the Dijkstra algorithm, and RIP uses the Bellman-Ford algorithm to determine the best route or routes (if there are multiple equal-cost routes) to reach each destination and installs these routes into the JUNOS software routing table.

The JUNOS software routing table is used by the routing protocol process (`rpd`) to maintain its database of routing information. In this table, the routing protocol process stores statically configured routes, directly connected interfaces (also called *direct routes* or *interface routes*), and all routing information learned from all routing protocols. The routing protocol process uses this collected routing information to select the *active route* to each destination, which is the route that actually is used to forward packets to that destination.

Each routing table is identified by a name, which consists of the protocol family followed by a period and small, nonnegative integer. The protocol family can be `inet` (Internet Protocol), `iso` (ISO), or `mpls` (MPLS). The following names are reserved for the default routing tables maintained by the JUNOS software:

- `inet.0`—Default unicast routing table
- `instance-name.inet.0`—Unicast routing table for a particular routing instance

- `inet.1`—Multicast forwarding cache
- `inet.2`—Unicast routes used for multicast reverse-path forwarding (RPF) lookup
- `inet.3`—MPLS routing table for path information
- `mpls.0`—MPLS routing table for label-switched path (LSP) next hops

The JUNOS software installs all active routes from the routing table into the forwarding table. The active routes are those used to forward packets to their destinations. The JUNOS kernel maintains a master copy of the forwarding table. It copies the forwarding table to the Packet Forwarding Engine, which is the part of the router responsible for forwarding packets.

The JUNOS routing protocol process is responsible for synchronizing the routing information between the routing and forwarding tables (see Figure 9.1). To do this, the routing protocol process calculates the active routes from all the routes in the routing table and installs them into the forwarding table. The routing protocol process then copies the forwarding table to the router's Packet Forwarding Engine, the part of the router that forwards packets.

Figure 9.1 *Synchronizing Routing Exchange between the Routing and Forwarding Tables*

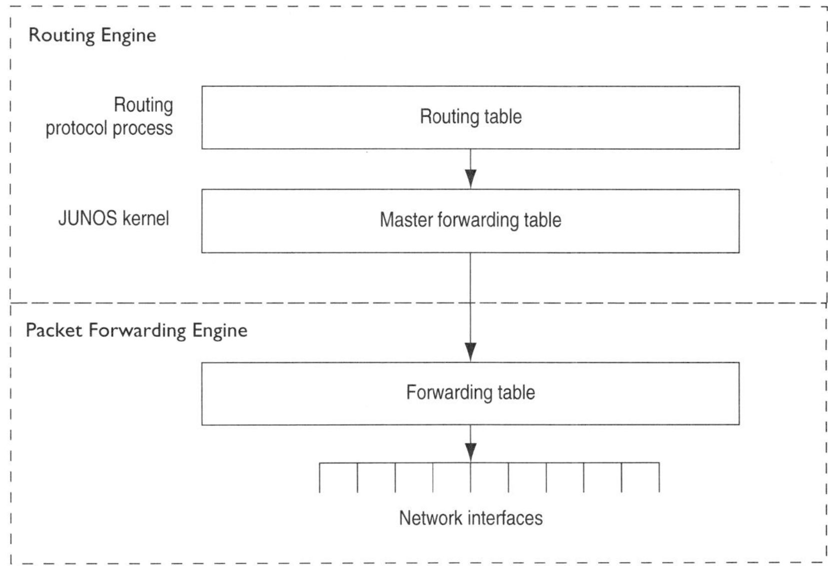

For unicast routes, the JUNOS routing protocol process uses the information in its routing table, along with the properties set in the configuration file, to choose an *active route* for each destination. While the JUNOS software might know of many routes to a destination, the active route is the preferred route to that destination and is the one that is installed in the forwarding table and used when actually routing packets.

The routing protocol process generally determines the active route by selecting the route with the lowest preference value. The preference is an arbitrary value in the range 0 through 255 that the software uses to rank routes received from different protocols, interfaces, or remote systems. When routes in the routing table are nearly identical, the routing protocol process prefers the route whose next hop has the lowest IP address.

The preference value is used to select routes to destinations in external ASs or routing domains; it has no effect on the selection of routes within an AS (that is, within an IGP). Routes within an AS are selected by the IGP and are based on that protocol's metric or cost value.

The JUNOS software provides support for alternate and tie-breaker preferences, and some of the routing protocols, including BGP and label switching, use these additional preferences. With these protocols, you can specify a primary route preference, `preference`, and a secondary preference, `preference2`, that are used as a tie breaker. You can also mark route preferences with additional route tie-breaker information by specifying a color, `color`, and a tie-breaker color, `color2`. The route preference is represented as a 4-byte value. When using the preference value to select an active route, the software first compares the primary route preference values, choosing the route with the lowest value. If there is a tie and if a secondary preference has been configured, the software compares the secondary preference values, choosing the route with the lowest value.

How the Active Route Is Determined

For each prefix in the routing table, the routing protocol process selects a single best path, called the *active route*. The algorithm for determining the active route is as follows:

1. Choose the path with the lowest preference value (routing protocol process preference). Routes that are not eligible to be used for forwarding (for example, because they were rejected by routing policy or because a next hop is inaccessible) have a preference of –1 and are never chosen.
2. For BGP, prefer the path with higher local preference. For non-BGP paths, choose the path with the lowest `preference2` value.
3. If the path includes an AS path:
   a. Prefer the route with a shorter AS path. Confederation sequences are considered to have a path length of 0, and AS and confederation sets are considered to have a path length of 1.
   b. Prefer the route with the lower origin code. Routes learned from an IGP have a lower origin code than those learned from an EGP, and both these have lower origin codes than incomplete routes (routes whose origin is unknown).
   c. Depending on whether nondeterministic routing table path selection behavior is configured, there are two possible cases:

      If nondeterministic routing table path selection behavior is not configured (that is, if the `path-selection cisco-nondeterministic` statement is not included in the BGP configuration), for paths with the same neighboring AS numbers at the front of the AS path, prefer the path with the lowest multiple exit discriminator (MED) metric. Confederation AS numbers are not considered when deciding what the neighbor AS number is. When you display the routes in the routing table using the `show route` command, they generally appear in order from most preferred to least preferred. Routes that share the same neighbor AS are grouped together in the command output. Within a group, the best route is listed first, and the other routes are marked with the `NotBest` flag in the `State` field of the `show route detail` command.

      To always compare MEDs whether the peer ASs of the compared routes are the same, use the `path-selection (always-compare-med)` statement.

If nondeterministic routing table path selection behavior is configured (that is, the `path-selection cisco-nondeterministic` statement is included in the BGP configuration), prefer the path with the lowest multiple exit discriminator (MED) metric. When you display the routes in the routing table using the `show route` command, they generally appear in order from most preferred to least preferred and are ordered with the best route first, followed by all other routes in order from newest to oldest.

In both cases, confederations are not considered when determining neighboring ASs. Also, in both cases, a missing metric is treated as if a MED were present but zero.

4. Prefer strictly internal paths, which include IGP routes and locally generated routes (static, direct, local, and so forth).
5. Prefer strictly external (EBGP) paths over external paths learned through interior sessions (IBGP).
6. For BGP, prefer the path whose next hop is resolved through the IGP route with the lowest metric.
7. Prefer paths from the higher routing table number. For example, `inet.3` is preferred to `inet.0`.
8. Prefer paths with a larger number of next hops.
9. For BGP, prefer the route with the lowest IP address value for the BGP router ID.
10. Prefer the path that was learned from the neighbor with the lowest peer IP address.

For information about controlling preference with routing policy, see Chapter 8, "Routing Policy and Firewall Filters," on page 301.

The IGPs compute equal-cost multipath next hops, and IBGP picks up these next hops. When multiple, equal-cost next hops are associated with a route, the routing protocol process installs only one of them in the forwarding path with each route, randomly selecting which next hop to install. For example, if there are three equal-cost paths to an exit router and 900 routes leaving through that router, each of the paths ends up with about 300 routes pointing at it. This mechanism provides load distribution among the paths while maintaining packet ordering per destination.

The routing protocol process assigns a default preference value to each route that the routing table receives (see Table 9.1). The default value depends on the source of the route. The preference is a value from 0 through 255, with a lower value indicating a more preferred route. In general, the narrower the scope of the statement, the higher precedence its preference value is given, but the smaller the set of routes it affects. To modify the default preference value for routes learned by routing protocols, you generally apply routing policy when configuring the individual routing protocols. You also can modify some preferences with other configuration statements, which are indicated in the table.

Table 9.1 *Default Route Preference Values*

How Route Is Learned	Default Preference	Statement to Modify Default Preference
Directly connected network	0	—
Static	5	`static` (see "Configuring Static, Aggregate, and Generated Routes," on page 382)
MPLS	7	MPLS `preference` (see Chapter 11, "MPLS Applications," on page 519)
OSPF internal route	10	OSPF `export` (see "Configuring OSPF," on page 441)
IS-IS Level 1 internal route	15	IS-IS `external-preference` and `preference` (see "Configuring IS-IS," on page 421)
IS-IS Level 2 internal route	18	IS-IS `external-preference` and `preference` (see "Configuring IS-IS," on page 421)
Redirects	30	—
RIP	100	RIP `preference` (see "Configuring RIP," on page 456)
Point-to-point interface	110	—
Generated or aggregate	130	`aggregate` and `generate` (see "Configuring Static, Aggregate, and Generated Routes," on page 382)
OSPF AS external routes	150	OSPF `external-preference` and `preference` (see "Configuring OSPF," on page 441)
IS-IS Level 1 external route	160	IS-IS `external-preference` and `preference` (see "Configuring IS-IS," on page 421)
IS-IS Level 2 external route	165	IS-IS `external-preference` and `preference` (see "Configuring IS-IS," on page 421)
BGP	170	BGP `preference`, `export`, and `import` (see "Configuring BGP," on page 398)

For equal-cost paths, load sharing is based on the BGP next hop. For example, if four prefixes all point to a next hop and there is more than one equal-cost path to that next hop, the routing protocol process randomizes the path chosen among the four prefixes. Also, for each prefix, the routing protocol process installs a single forwarding entry pointing along one of the paths. The routing software does not rerandomize the path taken as prefixes pointing to the next hop come and go, but it does rerandomize if the number of paths to the next-hop changes. Because a prefix is tied to a particular path, packet reordering should not happen. The degree of load sharing improves as the number of prefixes increases.

Creating Routing Tables

By default, the JUNOS software maintains three routing tables: one for unicast routes, one for multicast routes, and a third for Multiprotocol Label Switching (MPLS). You can configure additional routing tables to support situations where you need to separate out a particular group of routes or where you need greater flexibility in manipulating routing information. In general, most operations can be performed without resorting to the complexity of additional routing tables. However, creating additional routing tables has several specific uses, including importing interface routes into more than one routing table, applying different routing policies when exporting the same route to different peers, and providing greater flexibility with incongruent multicast topologies.

Creating routing tables is optional. If you do not create any, the JUNOS software uses its default routing tables, which are `inet.0` for unicast routes, `inet.1` for the multicast forwarding cache, and `inet.3` for Multiprotocol Label Switching (MPLS). If Multiprotocol Border Gateway Protocol (MBGP) is enabled, `inet.2` is used for subaddress family indicator (SAFI) 2 routes. If you configure a routing instance, the JUNOS software creates the default unicast routing table *`instance-name`*`.inet.0`.

To add static, aggregate, generated, or martian routes to only the default unicast routing table (`inet.0`), you do not have to create any routing tables because, by default, these routes are added to `inet.0`. You can add these routes just by including the `static`, `aggregate`, `generate`, and `martians` statements at the `[edit routing-options]` hierarchy level.

To explicitly create a routing table, include the `rib` statement:

```
[edit routing-options]
rib routing-table-name {
  static {
    defaults {
      static-options;
    }
    rib-group group-name;
    route destination-prefix {
      lsp-next-hop lsp-name {
        metric metric;
        preference preference;
      }
      next-hop;
      qualified-next-hop address {
        metric metric;
        preference preference;
      }
      static-options;
    }
  }
  aggregate {
    defaults {
      aggregate-options;
    }
    route destination-prefix {
      policy policy-name;
      aggregate-options;
    }
  }
  generate {
    defaults {
      generate-options;
    }
    route destination-prefix {
      policy policy-name;
      generate-options;
    }
  }
  martians {
    destination-prefix match-type <allow>;
  }
}
```

The routing table name includes the protocol family, optionally followed by a period and a number. The protocol family can be `inet` for the IP family or `iso` for the ISO protocol family. The number represents the routing instance. The first instance is 0.

Configuring Static, Aggregate, and Generated Routes

The router uses dynamic routes to learn how to reach network destinations. Dynamic routes are determined from the information exchanged by the routing protocols and, as the name implies, the routes might change as network conditions change and these changes are discovered by the routing protocols. You can configure static (nonchanging) routes to some network destinations. The router uses static routes when it does not have a route to a destination that has a better (lower) preference value, when it cannot determine the route to a destination, or when it is forwarding unroutable packets. A static route is installed in the routing table only when the route is active; that is, the list of next-hop routers configured for that route contains at least one next hop on an operational interface.

To configure static routes in the default routing table (`inet.0`), include the static statement at the `[edit routing-options]` hierarchy level. To configure static routes in one of the other routing tables, or to explicitly configure static routes in the default route table (`inet.0`), include the `static` statement at the `[edit routing-options rib` *`routing-table-name`*`]` hierarchy level.

```
static {
  defaults {
    static-options;
  }
  rib-group group-name;
  route destination-prefix {
    lsp-next-hop lsp-name {
      metric metric;
      preference preference;
    }
    next-hop;
    qualified-next-hop address {
      metric metric;
      preference preference;
    }
    static-options;
  }
}
```

Route aggregation allows you to combine groups of routes with common addresses into a single entry in the routing table. This decreases the size of the routing table as well as the number of route advertisements sent by the router. An aggregate route becomes active when it has one or more *contributing routes*. A contributing route is an active route that is a more specific match for the aggregate destination. For example, for the aggregate destination `128.100.0.0/16`, routes to `128.100.192.0/19` and `128.100.67.0/24` are contributing routes, but routes to `128.0.0.0./8`, `128.0.0.0/16`, and `128.100.0.0/16` are not.

A route can contribute only to a single aggregate route. However, an active aggregate route can recursively contribute to a less specific matching aggregate route. For example, an aggregate route to the destination `128.100.0.0/16` can contribute to an aggregate route to `128.96.0.0/13`.

When an aggregate route becomes active, it is installed in the routing table with the following information:

- Reject next hop—This means that if a more specific packet does not match a more specific route, the packet is rejected and an ICMP unreachable message is sent to the packet's originator.
- Metric value as configured with the `aggregate` statement.
- Preference value that results from the policy filter on the primary contributor, if a filter was specified—Otherwise, use the preference value as configured in the `aggregate` statement.
- AS path as configured in the `aggregate` statement, if any—Otherwise, the path is computed by aggregating the paths of all contributing routes.
- Community as configured in the `aggregate` statement, if any is specified.

You can configure only one aggregate route for each destination prefix.

To configure aggregate routes in the default routing table (`inet.0`), include the `aggregate` statement at the `[edit routing-options]` hierarchy level. To configure aggregate routes in one of the other routing tables, or to explicitly configure aggregate routes in the default routing table (`inet.0`), include the aggregate statement at the `[edit routing-options rib` *`routing-table-name`*`]` hierarchy level:

```
aggregate {
  defaults {
    aggregate-options;
  }
  route destination-prefix {
    policy policy-name;
    aggregate-options;
  }
}
```

Generated routes are used as the *route of last resort*. A packet is forwarded to the route of last resort when the routing tables have no information about how to reach that packet's destination. One use of these routes is to generate a default route to use if the routing table contains a route from a peer on a neighboring backbone. A generated route becomes active when it has one or more *contributing routes*. A contributing route is an active route that is a more specific match for the generated destination. For example, for the destination 128.100.0.0/16, routes to 128.100.192.0/19 and 128.100.67.0/24 are contributing routes, but routes to 128.0.0.0./8, 128.0.0.0/16, and 128.100.0.0/16 are not.

A route can contribute only to a single generated route. However, an active generated route can recursively contribute to a less specific matching generated route. For example, a generated route to the destination 128.100.0.0/16 can contribute to a generated route to 128.96.0.0/13.

By default, when generated routes are installed in the routing table, the next hop is chosen from the primary contributing route. You can configure only one generated route for each destination prefix.

To configure generated routes in the default routing table (inet.0), include the generate statement:

```
[edit routing-options]
generate {
  defaults {
    generate-options;
  }
  route destination-prefix {
    policy policy-name;
    generate-options;
  }
}
```

The static, aggregate, and generated statements consist of two parts:

- defaults—Specify global options. These are treated as global defaults and apply to all the static, aggregate, or generated routes you configure.
- route—Configure individual static, aggregate, or generated routes.

Specifying the Route's Destination

When you configure an individual static, aggregate, or generated route in the `route` part of the `static`, `aggregate`, or `generated` statement, specify the destination of the route (in `route` *`destination-prefix`*) in one of the following ways:

- *`network/masklen`*, where *`network`* is the network portion of the IP address, and *`masklen`* is the destination prefix length.
- `default` if this is the default route to the destination. This is equivalent to specifying an IP address of `0.0.0.0/0`.

Specifying Route Options

In the `defaults` and `route` parts of the `static`, `aggregate`, and `generated` statements, you can specify options that define additional information about routes that is included with the route when it is installed in the routing table. Options in the `defaults` part of the statement are treated as global defaults and apply to all configured routes. Options in the `route` part of the statement override any global options and apply to that destination only.

To configure static route options, include one or more of them in the `defaults` or `route` part of the `static` statement:

```
[edit routing-options]
static {
  defaults {
    (active | passive);
    as-path <as-path> <origin (egp | igp | incomplete)>
      <atomic-aggregate> <aggregator as-number in-address>;
    community [ community-ids ];
    (install | no-install);
    metric metric <type type>;
    (preference | preference2 | color | color2) preference
      <type type>;
    (readvertise | no-readvertise);
    (no-retain | retain);
    (tag | tag2) string;
  }
  route destination-prefix {
    (active | passive);
    as-path <as-path> <origin (egp | igp | incomplete)>
      <atomic-aggregate> <aggregator as-number in-address>;
    community [ community-ids ];
    (install | no-install);
    metric metric <type type>;
    (preference | preference2 | color | color2) preference
      <type type>;
    (readvertise | no-readvertise);
```

```
    (resolve | no-resolve);
    (no-retain | retain);
    (tag | tag2) string;
  }
}
```

To configure aggregate route options, include one or more of them in the `defaults` or `route` part of the `aggregate` statement:

```
[edit routing-options]
aggregate {
  (defaults | route) {
    (active | passive);
    as-path <as-path> <origin (egp | igp | incomplete)>
      <atomic-aggregate> <aggregator as-number in-address>;
    community [ community-ids ];
    discard;
    (full | brief);
    (metric | metric2 | metric3 | metric4) metric <type type>;
    (preference | preference2 | color | color2) preference
      <type type>;
    (tag | tag2) string;
  }
}
```

To configure generated route options, include one or more of them in the `defaults` or `route` part of the `generate` statement:

```
[edit routing-options]
generate {
  (defaults | route) {
    (active | passive);
    as-path <as-path> <origin (egp | igp | incomplete)>
      <atomic-aggregate>
      <aggregator as-number in-address>;
    community [ community-ids ];
    discard;
    (full | brief);
    (metric | metric2 | metric3 | metric4) metric <type type>;
    (preference | preference2 | color | color2) preference
      <type type>;
    (tag | tag2) string;
  }
}
```

To associate a metric value with a static route, include the metric statement. In the type option, specify the type of route. For OSPF, when routes are exported to OSPF, type 1 routes are advertised in type 1 externals, and routes of any other type are advertised in type 2 externals. If a qualified-next-hop metric value is configured, the type value overrides the route metric.

```
[edit routing-options static (defaults | route)]
metric metric <type type>;
```

For aggregate and generated routes, you can specify up to four metric values, starting with metric (for the first metric value) and continuing with metric2, metric3, and metric4 by including the following statement:

```
(metric | metric2 | metric3 | metric4) metric <type type>;
```

For more information about preferences, see "Routing Protocols Concepts," on page 374.

By default, static routes have a preference value of 5, and aggregate and generated routes have a preference value of 130. To modify the default preference value, specify a primary preference value (preference). You also can specify a secondary preference value (preference2) and colors, which are even finer-grained preference values (color and color2). To do this, include the following statement. The preference value can be a number in the range 1 through 255, with a lower number indicating a more preferred route.

```
(preference | preference2 | color | color2) preference
<type type>;
```

By default, no BGP community information is associated with static, aggregate, or generated routes. To associate community information with the routes, include the community statement. *community-ids* is one or more community or extended community identifiers.

```
community [ community-ids ];
```

Community identifiers are defined in RFC 1997: *BGP Communities Attribute.*

The format for community identifiers is *as-number*:*community-value*. *as-number* is the autonomous system (AS) number and can be a value in the range 1 through 65,534. *community-value* is the community identifier and can be a number in the range 0 through 65,535. You also can specify *community-ids* as one of the following well-known community names:

- no-export—Routes containing this community name are not advertised outside a BGP confederation boundary.

- `no-advertise`—Routes containing this community name are not advertised to other BGP peers.
- `no-export-subconfed`—Routes containing this community name are not advertised to external BGP peers, including peers in other members' ASs inside a BGP confederation.

The format for extended community identifiers is *`type`*:*`administrator`*:*`assigned-number`*. *`type`* is the type of extended community and can be either a `target`, `origin`, or `domain-id` community. The `target` community identifies the destination to which the route is going. The `origin` community identifies where the route originated. The `domain-id` community identifies the OSPF domain where the route originated. *`administrator`* is the administrator. It is either an AS number or an IPv4 address prefix, depending on the type of extended community. *`assigned-number`* identifies the local provider.

By default, no AS path information is associated with static, aggregate, or generated routes. To associate AS path information with the routes, include the `as-path` statement:

```
as-path <as-path> <origin (egp | igp | incomplete)>
<atomic-aggregate> <aggregator as-number in-address>;
```

`as-path` is the AS path to include with the route. It can include a combination of individual AS path numbers and AS sets. Enclose sets in brackets ([ ]). The first AS number in the path represents the AS immediately adjacent to the local AS. Each subsequent number represents an AS that is progressively farther from the local AS, heading toward the origin of the path. You also can specify the AS path using the BGP origin attribute, which indicates the origin of the AS path information:

- `igp`—Path information originated within the local AS
- `egp`—Path information originated in another AS
- `incomplete`—Path information learned by some other means

To attach the BGP ATOMIC_AGGREGATE path attribute to the route, specify the `atomic-aggregate` option. This path attribute indicates that the local system selected a less specific route rather than a more specific route. To attach the BGP AGGREGATOR path attribute to the route, specify the `aggregator` option. You must specify the last AS number that formed the route (encoded as two octets), followed by the IP address of the BGP system that formed the route.

By default, no OSPF tag strings are associated with static, aggregate, or generated routes. You can specify up to two OSPF tag strings by including the `tag` and `tag2` statement:

```
[edit routing-options static (defaults | route)]
(tag | tag2) string;
```

By default, all AS numbers from all contributing paths are included in the aggregate or generated route's path. To include only the longest common leading sequences from the contributing AS paths, include the `brief` statement when configuring the route. If doing this results in AS numbers being omitted from the aggregate or generated route, the BGP ATOMIC_ATTRIBUTE path attribute is included with the route.

```
brief;
```

To explicitly have all AS numbers from all contributing paths be included in the aggregate or generated route's path, include the `full` statement when configuring routes:

```
full;
```

By default, the JUNOS software installs all active static routes into the forwarding table. To configure the software not to install active static routes into the forwarding table, include the `no-install` statement:

```
[edit routing-options static (defaults | route)]
no-install;
```

Even if you configure a route so that it is not installed in the forwarding table, the route is still eligible to be exported from the routing table to other protocols. To explicitly install the routes into the forwarding table, include the `install` statement when configuring routes:

```
[edit routing-options static (defaults | route)]
install;
```

By default, statically configured routes are deleted from the forwarding table when the routing protocol process shuts down normally. To have a static route remain in the forwarding table, include the `retain` statement when configuring the route. Doing this greatly reduces the time required to restart a system that has a large number of routes in its routing table.

```
[edit routing-options static (defaults | route)]
retain;
```

By default, static, aggregate, and generated routes are removed from the routing and forwarding tables when they become inactive. To have the routes remain continually installed in the routing and forwarding tables, include the `passive` statement. Routes that have been configured to remain continually installed in the routing and forwarding tables are marked with `reject` next hops when they are inactive.

```
passive;
```

To explicitly remove static, aggregate, or generated routes when they become inactive, include the `active` statement:

```
active;
```

By default, static routes are eligible to be readvertised (that is, exported) by dynamic routing protocols. To mark a static route as being ineligible for readvertisement, include the `no-readvertise` statement:

```
[edit routing-options static (defaults | route)]
no-readvertise;
```

By default, static routes can point only to a directly connected next hop. To configure a route to a prefix that is not directly connected by resolving the route through the `inet.0` and `inet.3` routing tables, include the `resolve` statement:

```
[edit routing-options static (defaults | route)]
resolve;
```

Specifying the Next Hop of the Static Route

When you configure an individual static route in the `route` part of the `static` statement, specify how to reach the destination (in *`next-hop`*) in one of the following ways:

- `next-hop` *`address`*—IP address of the next hop to the destination, specified as:
  - IP address of the next hop
  - Interface name (for point-to-point interfaces only)
  - *`address/interface-name`* to specify an IP address on an operational interface

- `next-table` *`routing-table-name`*—Name of the next routing table to the destination.
- `reject`—Do not forward packets addressed to this destination. Instead, drop the packets, send ICMP unreachable messages to the packets' originators, and install a reject route for this destination into the routing table.
- `discard`—Do not forward packets addressed to this destination. Instead, drop the packets, do not send ICMP unreachable messages to the packets' originators, and install a reject route for this destination into the routing table.
- `receive`—Cause packets to the destination to be received by the local router.

Specifying an Independent Preference for a Static Route

You can configure multiple static routes with different preferences and metrics to the same destination. The static route with the best preference, metric, and reachable next hop is chosen as the active route. This feature allows you to specify preference and metric on a next-hop basis.

To specify an independent preference for a static route, include the following statements. The `preference` value can be in the range 1 through 255, with a lower number indicating a more preferred route. The `metric` value can be in the range 1 through 65,535.

```
[edit routing-options static route]
qualified-next-hop address {
  metric metric;
  preference preference;
}
```

The preference and metric configured by means of this statement apply only to the qualified next hops. The qualified-next-hop preference and metric override the route preference and metric (for that specific qualified next hop), similar to how the route preference overrides the default preference and metric (for that specific route).

Specifying an LSP as the Next Hop for a Static Route

Static routes can be configured with a next hop that is a label-switched path (LSP). This is useful when implementing filter-based forwarding. To specify an LSP as the next hop and assign an independent preference and metric to this next hop, include the following statements. The preference value can be a number in the range 1 through 255, with a lower number indicating a more preferred route. The metric value can be a number in the range 1 through 65,535.

```
[edit routing-options static route]
lsp-next-hop lsp-name {
  metric metric;
  preference preference;
}
```

Installing a Static Route into More Than One Routing Table

To install a static route into more than one routing table, instead of configuring the same static route for each routing table, use routing table groups. To create a routing table group, include the rib-group statement at one of the following hierarchy levels:

- [edit routing-options static]
- [edit routing-options rib *routing-table-name* static]
- [edit routing-instance *instance-name* routing-options static]
- [edit routing-instance instance-name routing-options rib *routing-table-name* static]

To install the routing table into a configured routing table group, include the import-rib statement at the [edit routing-options rib-groups] or [edit routing-options rib *routing-table-name* rib-groups] hierarchy level. The first routing table you list in the import-rib statement must be the one configured in the rib-group statement.

```
rib-group group-name {
  import-rib [ routing-table-names ]
}
```

Configuring a Default Static Route

To configure a default static route, include the next-hop address and retain statements:

```
[edit routing-options static route default]
next-hop address;
retain;
```

Propagating Static Routes into Routing Protocols

A common way to propagate static routes into the various routing protocols is to configure the routes so that the next-hop router is the loopback address (commonly, 127.0.0.1). However, configuring static routes in this way with the JUNOS software (by including a statement such as route *address/mask-length* next-hop 127.0.0.1) does not propagate the static routes, because the forwarding table ignores static routes whose next-hop router is the loopback address. To propagate static routes into the routing protocols, include the `discard` statement:

```
[edit routing-options rib inet6.0 static (defaults |
route)]
discard;
```

Specifying Policy with Aggregate and Generated Routes

You can associate a routing policy when configuring an aggregate or a generated route's destination prefix in the `routes` part of the aggregate or `generate` statement. Doing so provides the equivalent of an import routing policy filter for the destination prefix. That is, each potential contributor to a generated route, along with any generate options, is passed through the policy filter. The policy can accept or reject the route as a contributor to the route, and, if the contributor is accepted, the policy can modify the default preferences. The contributor with the numerically smallest prefix becomes the most preferred, or *primary*, contributor. A rejected contributor still can contribute to a less specific route. If you do not specify a policy filter, all candidate routes contribute to a route.

To associate a routing policy with an aggregate or a generated route, include the `policy` statement:

```
policy policy-name;
```

Configuring Martian Addresses

Martian addresses are host or network addresses about which all routing information is ignored. They commonly are sent by improperly configured systems on the network and have destination addresses that are obviously invalid.

In IPv4, the following are the default martian addresses:

- `0.0.0.0/8`
- `127.0.0.0/8`
- `128.0.0.0/16`
- `191.255.0.0/16`
- `192.0.0.0/24`

- 223.255.255.0/24
- 240.0.0.0/4

To add martian addresses to the list of default martian addresses in the default routing table (inet.0), include the martians statement at the [edit routing-options] hierarchy level. To add martian addresses to the list of default martian addresses in any other routing tables, or to explicitly add martian addresses to the list of default martian addresses in the default routing table (inet.0), include the martians statement:

```
[edit routing-options nb routing-table-name]
martians {
  destination-prefix match-type <allow>;
}
```

In *destination-prefix*, specify the routing destination in one of the following ways:

- *network/mask-length*—*network* is the network portion of the IP address, and *mask-length* is the destination prefix length.
- default—If this is the default route to the destination. This is equivalent to specifying the IP address 0.0.0.0/0.

For more information about match types, see Table 8.14, "Route List Match Types," on page 347.

In *match-type*, specify the type of match to apply to the destination prefix.

To delete a martian address from within a range of martian addresses, include the allow option in the martians statement. This option removes an exact prefix that is within a range of addresses that has been specified to be martian addresses. To delete a martian address from the default routing table (inet.0), include the martians statement at the [edit routing-options] hierarchy level. To delete a martian address from any other routing tables, or to explicitly delete a martian address from the default routing table (inet.0), include the martians statement at the [edit routing-options rib routing-table-name] hierarchy level.

BGP

The Border Gateway Protocol (BGP) is an exterior gateway protocol (EGP) that is used to exchange routing information among routers in different autonomous systems (ASs).

In BGP, routers are grouped into ASs. Each AS is a set of routers that is under a single technical administration and that normally uses a single interior gateway protocol (IGP) and a common set of metrics to propagate routing information within the set of routers. To other ASs, an AS appears to have a single, coherent interior routing plan and presents a consistent picture of what destinations are reachable through it.

BGP is a path-vector routing protocol that is used to exchange routing information among different ASs. BGP routing information includes the complete route to each destination, as well as additional information about the route. The route to each destination is called the *AS path*, and the additional route information is included in *path attributes*. BGP uses the AS path and the path attributes to completely determine the network topology. BGP uses the routing information to maintain a database of network reachability information, which it exchanges with other BGP systems. Once BGP understands the topology, it can detect and eliminate routing loops, and it can select among groups of routes to enforce administrative preferences and routing policy decisions.

BGP supports two types of exchanges of routing information: exchanges between different ASs and exchanges within a single AS. When used between ASs, BGP is called *external BGP* (EBGP), and BGP sessions perform *inter-AS routing*. When used within an AS, BGP is called *internal BGP* (IBGP), and BGP sessions perform *intra-AS routing*.

A BGP system shares network reachability information with adjacent BGP systems, which are referred to as *neighbors* or *peers*.

BGP systems are arranged into *groups*. In an IBGP group, all peers in the group—called *internal peers*—are in the same AS. Internal peers can be anywhere in the local AS and do not have to be directly connected. Internal groups use routes from an IGP to resolve forwarding addresses. They also propagate external routes among all other internal routers running internal BGP, computing the next hop by taking the BGP next hop received with the route and resolving it using information from one of the IGPs.

In an EBGP group, the peers in the group—called *external peers*—are in different ASs and normally share a subnet. In an external group, the next hop is computed with respect to the interface that is shared between the external peer and the local router.

BGP peers advertise routes to each other in update messages. The routes consist of a destination, described as an IP address prefix, and the AS path to the destination and path attributes. The AS path is a list of numbers of the ASs that a route passed through to reach the local router. The first number in the path is that of the last AS in the path—the AS closest to the local router. The last number in the path is the AS farthest from the local router, which is generally the origin of the path. Path attributes contain additional information about the AS path that is used in routing policy.

BGP stores its routes in the JUNOS routing table, including routing information learned from update messages received from peers, local routing information that the BGP system selects by applying local policies to routes received in update messages, and information that the BGP system selects to advertise to its BGP peers in the update messages it sends.

For each prefix in the routing table, the routing protocol process selects a single best path, called the *active path*. The algorithm for determining the active path is described in "How the Active Route Is Determined," on page 376.

Table 9.2 lists the BGP Version 4 standards and protocol extensions supported by the JUNOS software.

Table 9.2 *BGP Standards Supported by JUNOS Software*

Standard	Title
RFC 1771	*A Border Gateway Protocol 4 (BGP-4)*
RFC 1772	*Application of the Border Gateway Protocol in the Internet*
RFC 1966	*BGP Route Reflection: An Alternative to Full-Mesh IBGP*
RFC 1997	*BGP Communities Attribute*
RFC 2270	*Using a Dedicated AS for Sites Homed to a Single Provider*
RFC 2283	*Multiprotocol Extensions for BGP-4*
RFC 2385	*Protection of BGP Sessions via the TCP MD5 Signature Option*
RFC 2439	*BGP Route Flap Damping*
RFC 2796	*BGP Route Reflection*
RFC 3065	*Autonomous System Confederations for BGP*

Table 9.2 *BGP Standards Supported by JUNOS Software*

Standard	Title
IETF Draft draft-ietf-idr-cap-neg-01.txt	*Capabilities Negotiation with BGP4*
IETF Draft draft-ramachandra-bgp-ext-communities-04.txt	*BGP Extended Communities Attribute*

BGP Messages

BGP systems send four types of messages: open, update, keepalive, and notification. All BGP messages have the same fixed-size header, which contains a marker field indicating the total length of the message and a type field indicating the message type.

Open Messages

After a TCP connection is established between two BGP systems, they exchange BGP open messages to create a BGP connection between them. After the connection is established, the two systems can exchange BGP messages and data traffic. Open messages consist of the BGP header plus the following fields:

- Version—The current BGP version number is 4.
- Local AS number—You configure this with the `autonomous-system` statement at the `[edit routing-options]` hierarchy level.
- Hold time—Proposed hold-time value. You configure the local hold time with the BGP `hold-time` statement.
- BGP identifier—IP address of the BGP system. This address is determined when the system starts up and is the same for every local interface and every BGP peer. You can configure the BGP identifier with the `router-id` statement at the `[edit routing-options]` hierarchy level. By default, BGP uses the IP address of the first interface it finds in the router.
- Parameter field length and the parameter itself—These are optional fields.

Update Messages

BGP systems send update messages to exchange network reachability information. BGP systems use this information to construct a graph that describes the relationships among all known ASs. Update messages consist of the BGP header plus the following optional fields:

- Unfeasible routes length—Length of the field that lists the routes being withdrawn from service because they are no longer deemed reachable
- Withdrawn routes—IP address prefixes for the routes being withdrawn from service
- Total path attribute length—Length of the field that lists the path attributes for a feasible route to a destination
- Path attributes—Properties of the routes, including the path origin; the multiple exit discriminator (MED); the originating system's preference for the route; and information about aggregation, communities, confederations, and route reflection
- Network layer reachability information (NLRI)—IP address prefixes of feasible routes being advertised in the update message

Keepalive Messages

BGP systems exchange keepalive messages to determine whether a link or host has failed or is no longer available. Keepalive messages are exchanged often enough so that the hold timer does not expire. These messages consist only of the BGP header.

Notification Messages

BGP systems send notification messages when an error condition is detected. After the message is sent, the BGP session and the TCP connection between the BGP systems are closed. Notification messages consist of the BGP header plus the error code and subcode, and data that describes the error.

Configuring BGP

To configure BGP, include the following statements. To configure a BGP routing instance, include the statement at the `[edit routing-instances` *`routing-instance-name`* `routing-options]` hierarchy level.

For BGP to run on the router, you must define the local AS number, configure at least one group, and include information about at least one peer in the group (the peer's IP address and AS number).

```
protocols {
  bgp {
    numerous global BGP statements
    group group-name {
      peer-as autonomous-system;
      type type;
      allow [ prefix/prefix-length ];
      numerous group-specific statements
      neighbor address {
        numerous peer-specific statements
      }
    }
  }
}
routing-options {
  autonomous-system autonomous-system;
  confederation confederation-autonomous-system members [
    autonomous-systems ];
  router-id address;
}
```

When configuring BGP on an interface, you must also include the `family inet` statement at the `[edit interfaces interface-name unit logical-unit-number]` hierarchy level.

Each router running BGP must be configured with its AS number in the `autonomous-system` statement. This number is included in the local AS number field in BGP open messages.

To enable the local system to participate as a member of an AS confederation, you define the AS confederation identifier and specify the AS numbers that are members of the confederation in the `confederation` statement.

Each router running BGP must have a BGP identifier. This identifier is included in the BGP identifier field of open messages. You can explicitly assign a BGP identifier in the `router-id` statement. If you do not assign one, the IP address of the first interface encountered in the router is used.

You can configure many BGP properties at the global, group, and peer level (see Table 9.3). Global properties apply to all groups and peers and are configured at the `[edit protocols bgp]` hierarchy level. Group properties apply to the particular group and its peer, and they override global properties. Configure these properties at the `[edit protocols bgp group` *`group-name`*`]` hierarchy level. Peer properties apply to the particular peer, and they override global and group properties. Configure these properties at the `[edit protocols bgp group` *`group-name`* `neighbor` *`address`*`]` hierarchy level.

Table 9.3 *Global-, Group-, and Peer-Level BGP Configuration Statements*

Statement	Global	Group	Peer
`advertise-inactive;`	X	X	X
`allow [`*`network/mask-length`*`];`	—	X	—
`authentication-key` *`key`*`;`	X	X	X
`cluster` *`cluster-identifier`*`;`	X	X	X
`damping;`	X	X	X
`description` *`text-description`*`;`	X	X	X
`export [` *`policy-names`* `];`	X	X	X

family (inet| (inet6 | inet-vpn | l2-vpn) {
  (any | multicast | unicast) {
    prefix-limit {
      maximum *number*;
      teardown <*percentage*> <idle-timeout (forever | *time*
        -inminutes)>;
    }
    rib-group *group-name*;
  }
  labeled-unicast {
    prefix-limit {
      maximum *number*;
      teardown <*percentage*> <idle-timeout (forever | *time-in*
        -minutes)>;
    resolve-vpn;
    rib-group *group-name*;
  }
}
	X	X	X

`hold-time` *`seconds`*`;`	X	X	X
`import [` *`policy-names`* `];`	X	X	X
`keep (all | none);`	X	X	X
`local-address` *`address`*`;`	X	X	X
`local-as` *`autonomous-system`* `<private>;`	X	X	X

Table 9.3 *Global-, Group-, and Peer-Level BGP Configuration Statements*

<table>
<tr><th>Statement</th><th>Global</th><th>Group</th><th>Peer</th></tr>
<tr><td>local-preference local-preference;</td><td>X</td><td>X</td><td>X</td></tr>
<tr><td>log-updown;</td><td>X</td><td>X</td><td>X</td></tr>
<tr><td>metric-out (metric | minimum-igp <<i>offset</i>> | igp <<i>offset</i>>);</td><td>X</td><td>X</td><td>X</td></tr>
<tr><td>multihop <<i>ttl-value</i>>;</td><td>X</td><td>X</td><td>X</td></tr>
<tr><td>multipath;</td><td>—</td><td>X</td><td>X</td></tr>
<tr><td>neighbor address {
  peer-specific options;
}</td><td>—</td><td>X</td><td>—</td></tr>
<tr><td>no-aggregator-id;</td><td>X</td><td>X</td><td>X</td></tr>
<tr><td>no-client-reflect;</td><td>X</td><td>X</td><td>X</td></tr>
<tr><td>out-delay seconds;</td><td>X</td><td>X</td><td>X</td></tr>
<tr><td>passive;</td><td>X</td><td>X</td><td>X</td></tr>
<tr><td>path-selection (cisco-non-deterministic);</td><td>X</td><td>—</td><td>—</td></tr>
<tr><td>peer-as autonomous-system;</td><td>X</td><td>X</td><td>X</td></tr>
<tr><td>preference preference;</td><td>X</td><td>X</td><td>X</td></tr>
<tr><td>protocol protocol;</td><td>—</td><td>X</td><td>—</td></tr>
<tr><td>remove-private;</td><td>X</td><td>X</td><td>—</td></tr>
<tr><td>traceoptions {
file <i>name</i> <replace> <size <i>size</i>> <files <i>number</i>> <no-stamp>
<(world-readable | no-world-readable)>;
flag <i>flag</i> <<i>flag-modifier</i>> <disable>;
}</td><td></td><td></td><td></td></tr>
<tr><td>type type;</td><td>—</td><td>X</td><td>—</td></tr>
</table>

Defining BGP Groups and Peers

A BGP system must know which routers are its peers (neighbors). You define the peer relationships explicitly by configuring the neighboring routers that are the peers of the local BGP system. After peer relationships have been established, the BGP peers exchange update messages to advertise network reachability information.

You arrange BGP routers into groups of peers. Different peer groups must have different group types, AS numbers, or router reflector cluster identifiers. Each group must contain at least one peer.

To define a BGP group that recognizes only the specified BGP systems as peers, statically configure all the system's peers by including one or more `neighbor` statements. Include one `neighbor` statement for each peer. The peers on at least one side of each BGP connection must be configured statically.

```
[edit protocols bgp]
group group-name {
  peer-as autonomous-system;
  type type;
  neighbor address;
}
```

To define a BGP group in which the local system's peers are dynamic and change over time, include the `allow` statement. To recognize all BGP systems as peers, include the `allow all` statement. To recognize BGP systems within specified address ranges, specify a set of addresses in the `allow` *network/mask-length* statement.

```
[edit protocols bgp]
group group-name {
  peer-as autonomous-system;
  type type;
  (allow [prefix/prefix-length...] | allow all);
}
```

A BGP group can be an IBGP or EBGP. All peers in an IBGP group are in the same AS, whereas peers in an EBGP group are in different ASs and normally share a subnet. To configure an IBGP group, which allows intra-AS BGP routing, include the following form of the `type` statement:

```
[edit protocols bgp group group-name]
type internal;
```

To configure an EBGP group, which allows inter-AS BGP routing, include the following form of the `type` statement:

```
[edit protocols bgp group group-name]
type external;
```

When configuring a peer, you must specify the peer system's AS by including the `peer-as` statement, either globally, for all peers in a group, or for an individual peer. For EBGP, the peer is in another AS, so the AS number you specify in the `peer-as` statement must be different from the local router's AS number, which you specify in the `autonomous-system` statement. For IBGP, the peer is in the same AS, so the two AS numbers that you specify in the `autonomous-system` and `peer-as` statements must be the same.

```
peer-as autonomous-system;
```

To define group-specific properties, include one or more of the statements listed in Table 9.3 at the `[edit protocols bgp group group-name]` hierarchy level.

When you use the `neighbor` statement to configure BGP peers statically, you can also define peer-specific properties listed in Table 9.3 at the `[edit protocols bgp group group-name neighbor address]` hierarchy level.

Configuring Confederations

In standard IBGP implementations, all BGP systems within the AS are fully meshed so that any external routing information is redistributed among all routers within the AS. This type of implementation can present scaling issues when an AS has a large number of IBGP systems because of the amount of identical information that BGP systems must share with each other. BGP confederations provide one means of decreasing BGP control traffic, minimizing the number of update messages sent within the AS. BGP AS confederations split a single AS into multiple smaller ASs, referred to as *sub-ASs*.

Figure 9.2 illustrates an example confederation topology. For AS 32 to be a valid confederation, all routers in the AS must be members of the confederation. So, for example, Router B must have a confederation member AS number as well as a confederation AS number. Within a confederation, the links between the confederation member ASs must be EBGP links, not IBGP links.

To enable the local router to participate as a member of an AS confederation, define the AS confederation identifier and specify the AS numbers that are members of the confederation in the `confederation` statement:

```
[edit routing-options]
confederation confederation-autonomous-system
  members [ autonomous-systems ];
```

Figure 9.2 *Example: BGP Confederation Topology*

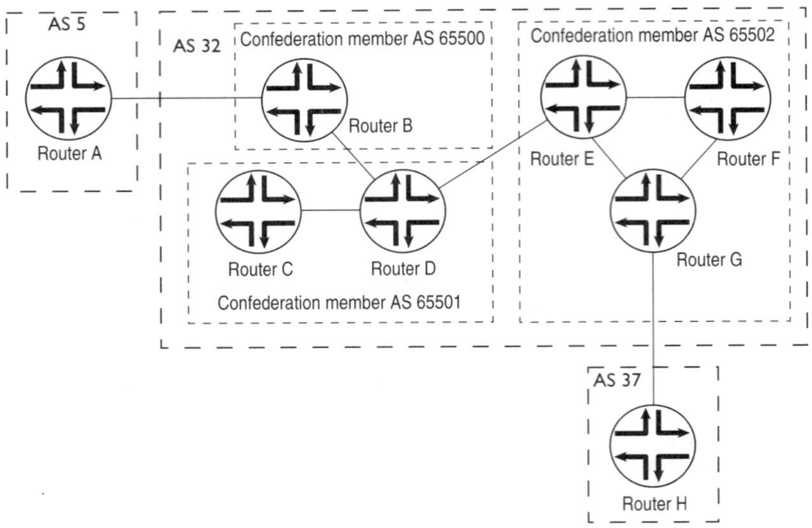

Configuring Route Reflection

Route reflection is a second method for decreasing BGP control traffic, minimizing the number of update messages sent within the AS. In route reflection, BGP systems are arranged in *clusters*. Each cluster consists of at least one system that acts as a *route reflector*, along with any number of *client peers*. BGP peers outside the cluster are called *nonclient peers*. The route reflector reflects (redistributes) routing information to each client peer (*intracluster reflection*) and to all nonclient peers (*intercluster reflection*). Because the route reflector redistributes routes within the cluster, the BGP systems within the cluster do not have to be fully meshed.

When the route reflector receives a route, it selects the best path. Then, if the route came from a nonclient peer, the route reflector sends the route to all client peers within the cluster. If the route came from a client peer, the route reflector sends it to all nonclient peers and to all client peers except the originator. In this process, none of the client peers sends routes to other client peers.

To configure route reflection, specify a cluster identifier only on the BGP systems that are to be the route reflectors. These systems then determine, from the network reachability information they receive, which BGP systems are part of its cluster and are client peers, and which BGP systems are outside the cluster and are nonclient peers.

To configure a router to be a route reflector, you must configure multiple IBGP groups, configure a cluster identifier (using the `cluster` statement) for groups that are members of the cluster, and configure all the groups with the same IBGP AS number.

To configure the route reflector, include the following statements in the configuration. The first `group` statement is for the group of nonclient peers of the local system that is acting as a route reflector. The second `group` statement is for the group of peers in the cluster; each peer is treated as a route reflector client by the local system. The peer AS numbers must be the same in both groups.

```
[edit protocols bgp]
group group-name {
  type internal;
  peer-as autonomous-system
  neighbor address1;
  neighbor address2;
}
group group-name {
  type internal;
  peer-as autonomous-system;
  cluster cluster-identifier;
  neighbor address3;
  neighbor address4;
}
```

By default, the route reflector performs intracluster reflection, because it assumes that all the client peers are not fully meshed. However, if the client peers are fully meshed, intracluster reflection results in the sending of redundant route advertisements. In this case, you can disable intracluster reflection by including the `no-client-reflect` statement:

```
[edit protocols bgp group group-name]
no-client-reflect;
```

Configuring Route Flap Damping

Route flapping describes the situation in which BGP systems send an excessive number of update messages to advertise network reachability information. *Flap damping* is a method of reducing the number of update messages sent between BGP peers, thereby reducing the load on these peers, without adversely affecting the route convergence time for stable routes.

By default, route flap damping is disabled. To enable it, include the `damping` statement:

```
damping;
```

Damping is applied to external peers and to peers at confederation boundaries. For finer control over which peers have damping enabled, include the `damping` statement at the group level.

By default, route flap damping uses the following parameters:

For information about flap damping and defining flap damping parameters, see "Configuring BGP Route Flap Damping," on page 350. For information about applying policy filters in BGP, see "Configuring BGP Routing Policy," on page 415.

- Decay half-life while reachable—15 minutes
- Maximum hold-down time—60 minutes
- Reuse threshold—750
- Cut-off threshold—3,000

To change the default parameters, define the flap damping parameters with the `damping` statement at the `[edit policy-options]` hierarchy level, then apply them using an `import` statement when configuring BGP.

Modifying the Hold-Time Value

The hold time is the maximum number of seconds allowed to elapse between the time that a BGP system receives successive keepalive or update messages from a peer. When establishing a BGP connection with the local router, a peer sends an open message, which contains a hold-time value. BGP on the local router uses the smaller of either the local hold-time value or the peer's hold-time value received in the open message as the hold time for the BGP connection between the two peers.

The hold time is three times the interval at which keepalive messages are sent. The default is 90 seconds. To modify the default on the local BGP system, include the `hold-time` statement:

```
hold-time seconds;
```

Configuring Authentication

All BGP protocol exchanges can be authenticated to guarantee that only trusted routers participate in the AS's routing. By default, authentication is disabled. You can configure MD5 authentication. The MD5 algorithm creates an encoded checksum that is included in the transmitted packet. The receiving router uses an authentication key (password) to verify the packet's MD5 checksum.

To configure authentication, include the `authentication-key` statement. The key (password) can be up to 255 characters long. Characters can include any ASCII strings. If you include spaces, enclose all characters in quotation marks (double quotes).

```
authentication-key key;
```

When configuring authentication for all peers in a group, you cannot include the `allow` statement in the configuration because BGP keys require a destination address.

Applying IPSec Security Association

IPSec can be applied to BGP traffic. IPSec is a protocol suite used for protecting IP traffic at the packet level. IPSec is based on security associations (SAs). A security association is a simplex connection that provides security services to the packets carried by the SA. After configuring the security association, you can apply the SA to BGP peers.

To apply a security association, include the `ipsec-sa` statement:

```
ipsec-sa ipsec-sa;
```

For more information, see Chapter 7, "IP Security (IPSec)," on page 287.

A more specific security association overrides a less general SA. For example, if a specific SA is applied to a specific peer, that SA overrides the SA applied to the whole peer group.

Opening a Peer Connection Passively

You can configure a router not to send open messages to a peer. After you configure the router to be passive, the router does not originate the TCP connection. However, when the router receives a connection from the peer and an open message, it replies with another BGP open message. Each router declares its own capabilities.

To configure the router so that it does not send open messages to a peer, include the `passive` statement:

```
passive;
```

Configuring the Local IP Address

You can explicitly specify the address of the local end of a BGP session. You generally do this to explicitly configure the system's IP address from BGP's point of view. Typically, an IP address is assigned to a loopback interface, and that IP address is configured here. This address is used to accept incoming connections to the peer and to establish connections to the remote peer. To assign a local address, include the `local-address` statement:

```
local-address address;
```

If you also include the `default-address-selection` statement at the `[edit system]` hierarchy level, the software chooses the system default address as the source for most locally generated IP packets. For protocols in which the local address is unconstrained by the protocol specification, for example IBGP and multihop EBGP, if you do not configure a specific local address when configuring the protocol, the local address is chosen using the same methods as other locally generated IP packets.

Configuring the Multiple Exit Discriminator

The BGP multiple exit discriminator (MED, or `MULTI_EXIT_DISC`) is an optional path attribute that can be included in BGP update messages. This attribute is used on EBGP links (that is, on inter-AS links) to select among multiple exit points to a neighboring AS. The MED attribute has a value that is referred to as a *metric*. If all other factors in determining an exit point are equal, the exit point with the lowest metric is preferred.

If a MED is received over an EBGP link, it is propagated over internal links to other BGP systems within the AS.

A MED metric is advertised with a route according to the following general rules:

- A more specific metric overrides a less specific metric. That is, a group-specific metric overrides a global BGP metric, and a peer-specific metric overrides a global BGP or group-specific metric.
- A metric defined with routing policy overrides a metric defined with the `metric-out` statement.
- If any metric is defined, it overrides a metric received in a route.
- If the received route does not have an associated MED metric, and if you do not explicitly configure a metric, no metric is advertised.

BGP update messages include a MED metric if the route was learned from BGP and already had a MED metric associated with it, or if you configure it.

To directly configure a MED metric to advertise in BGP update messages, include the `metric-out` statement:

```
metric-out (metric | minimum-igp <offset> | igp <offset>);
```

metric is the primary metric on all routes sent to peers. It can be a value in the range 0 through $2^{32} - 1$.

Specify `minimum-igp` to set the metric to the minimum metric value calculated in the IGP to get to the BGP next hop. If a newly calculated metric is greater than the minimum metric value, the metric value remains unchanged. If a newly calculated metric is lower, the metric value is lowered to that value.

Specify `igp` to set the metric to the most recent metric value calculated in the IGP to get to the BGP next hop.

Specify a value for *offset* to increase or decrease the metric that is used from the metric value calculated in the IGP. The metric value is offset by the value specified. The metric calculated in the IGP (by specifying either `igp` or `igp-minimum`) is increased if the *offset* value is positive. The metric calculated in the IGP (by specifying either `igp` or `igp-minimum`) is decreased if the *offset* value is negative. *offset* can be a value in the range -2^{31} through $2^{31} - 1$. Note that the adjusted metric can never go below 0 or above $2^{32} - 1$.

For more information about routing policy, see Chapter 8, "Routing Policy and Firewall Filters," on page 301.

To use routing policy to define a MED metric to advertise, define the routing policy with the `policy-statement` statement at the `[edit policy-options]` hierarchy level, then apply the filter using the `import` and `export` statements when configuring BGP. When defining the routing policy filter, include an action that specifies the desired metric value.

Controlling the Aggregator Path Attribute

The JUNOS implementation of BGP performs route aggregation, which is the process of combining the characteristics of different routes so that only a single route is advertised. Aggregation reduces the amount of information that BGP must store and exchange with other BGP systems. BGP adds the aggregator path attribute to BGP update messages. This attribute contains the local system's AS number and IP address (router ID).

To prevent different routers within an AS from creating aggregate routes that contain different AS paths, set the IP address in the aggregator path attribute to 0 by including the `no-aggregator-id` statement:

```
no-aggregator-id;
```

Choosing the Protocol Used to Determine the Next Hop

By default, BGP uses the active routes determined from all IGPs when resolving routes to next hops. To limit the IGPs that BGP uses, include the `protocol` statement, specifying the protocol as `isis` or `ospf`:

```
protocol protocol;
```

Configuring an EBGP Multihop Session

If an EBGP peer is more than one hop away from the local router, you must specify the next hop to the peer so that the two systems can establish a BGP session. This type of session is called a *multihop* BGP session. To configure a multihop session, include the `multihop` statement:

```
multihop <ttl-value>;
```

To configure the maximum value for the TTL in the IP header of BGP packets, specify *ttl-value*. If you do not specify a TTL value, the system's default maximum TTL value is used.

Configuring the BGP Local Preference

IBGP sessions use a metric called the *local preference*, which is carried in IBGP update packets in the path attribute `LOCAL_PREF`. This metric indicates the degree of preference for an external route. The route with the highest local preference value is preferred.

The `LOCAL_PREF` path attribute is always advertised to IBGP peers and to neighboring confederations. It is never advertised to EBGP peers. The default behavior is not to modify the `LOCAL_PREF` path attribute if it is present. The `LOCAL_PREF` path attribute is applied to exported routes only.

By default, if a received route contains a `LOCAL_PREF` path attribute value, the value is not modified. If a BGP route is received without a `LOCAL_PREF` attribute, the route is handled locally (that is, it is stored in the routing table and advertised by BGP) as if it were received with a `LOCAL_PREF` value of 100. A non-BGP route that is advertised by BGP is advertised with a `LOCAL_PREF` value of 100 by default.

To change the local preference metric advertised in the path attribute, include the `local-preference` statement, specifying a value from 0 through 4,294,967,295 ($2^{32} - 1$):

```
local-preference local-preference;
```

Controlling Route Preference

When the JUNOS software determines a route's preference to become the active route, it selects the route with the lowest preference as the active route and installs this route into the forwarding table. By default, the routing software assigns a preference of 170 to routes that originated from BGP. Of all the routing protocols, BGP has the highest default preference value, which means that routes learned by BGP are the least likely to become the active route.

For information about route preferences, see Table 9.1 on page 379.

To modify the default BGP preference value, include the `preference` statement, specifying a value from 0 through 4,294,967,295 ($2^{32} - 1$):

```
preference preference;
```

Configuring Routing Table Path Selection

By default, only the MEDs of routes that have the same peer ASs are compared. You can configure routing table path selection options to get different behaviors. To configure routing table path selection behavior, include the `path-selection` statement:

```
[edit protocols bgp]
path-selection (cisco-non-deterministic | always-compare-
med);
```

Routing table path selection can be configured in one of two ways:

- Using the same nondeterministic behavior as does the Cisco IOS software (`cisco-non-deterministic`). This behavior has two effects:
    - The active path is always first. All nonactive, but eligible, paths follow the active path and are maintained in the order in which they were received, with the most recent path first. Ineligible paths remain at the end of the list.
    - When a new path is added to the routing table, path comparisons are made without removing from consideration those paths that should never be selected because those paths lose the MED tie-breaking rule.

These two effects cause the system to only sometimes compare the MEDs between paths that it should otherwise compare. Because of this, it is recommended that you not configure nondeterministic behavior.

- Always comparing MEDs whether the peer ASs of the compared routes are the same (`always-compare-med`).

Configuring BGP to Select Multiple BGP Paths

You can configure BGP to select multiple nonmultihop EBGP or IBGP paths as active paths. Selecting multiple paths allows BGP peerings to load-balance traffic across an AS confederation boundary. The JUNOS BGP multipath supports the following:

- Load balancing across multiple links between two routers belonging to different ASs
- Load balancing across a common subnet or multiple subnets to different routers belonging to the same peer AS
- Load balancing across multiple links between two routers belonging to different external confederation peers
- Load balancing across a common subnet or multiple subnets to different routers belonging to external confederation peers

To configure a BGP multipath, include the `multipath` statement:

```
multipath;
```

Configuring a Local AS

You can configure BGP with a different local AS number for each EBGP session, which allows BGP to configure a local AS for each EBGP session. Configuring a local AS simulates a virtual AS for the router. The AS paths for the routes from that EBGP peer have the configured `local-as` prepended before the peer AS for that session.

To configure a local AS, include the `local-as` statement:

```
local-as autonomous-system <private>;
```

If you include the `private` keyword, the local AS is not prepended before the peer AS. This means that the AS paths do not show details of such a configuration.

Removing Private AS Numbers from AS Paths

By default, when BGP advertises AS paths to remote systems, it includes all AS numbers, including private AS numbers. Configuring the software so that it removes private AS numbers from AS paths is useful when all the following circumstances are true:

- A remote AS for which you provide connectivity is multihomed, but only to the local AS.
- The remote AS does not have an officially allocated AS number.
- It is not appropriate to make the remote AS a confederation member AS of the local AS.

To have the local system strip private AS numbers from the AS path, include the `remove-private` statement:

```
remove-private;
```

The AS numbers are stripped from the AS path starting at the left end of the AS path (the end where AS paths have been most recently added). This operation takes place after any confederation member ASs have already been removed from the AS path, if applicable.

The software is preconfigured with knowledge of the set of AS numbers that is considered private, a range that is defined in the IANA assigned numbers document. The set of AS numbers reserved as private are in the range 64,512 through 65,534, inclusive.

Enabling MBGP

Multiprotocol BGP (MBGP) is an extension to BGP that enables BGP to carry routing information for multiple network layers and address families. MBGP can carry the unicast routes used for multicast routing separately from the routes used for unicast IP forwarding.

To enable MBGP, you configure BGP to carry network layer reachability information (NLRI) for address families other than unicast IPv4 by including the `family inet` statement:

```
family inet {
  (any | multicast | unicast) {
    prefix-limit {
      maximum number;
      teardown <percentage> <idle-timeout (forever |
        minutes)>;
    }
    rib-group group-name;
  }
}
```

By default, BGP peers carry only unicast routes used for unicast forwarding purposes. To configure BGP peers to carry only multicast routes, specify the `multicast` option. To configure BGP peers to carry both unicast and multicast routes, specify the `any` option.

When MBGP is configured, BGP installs the MBGP routes into different routing tables. Each routing table is identified by the protocol family or address family identifier (AFI) and a subaddress family indicator (SAFI). The JUNOS software supports AFI IPv4 and IPv6 and SAFI 1 for unicast routes, AFI IPv4 and IPv6 and SAFI 2 for multicast sources, and AFI IPv4 and IPv6 and SAFI 3 for both unicast and multicast prefixes. If BGP receives a prefix (NLRI) with SAFI 1, it places this route into the `inet` routing table. It places NLRIs with SAFI 2 into the `inet.2` routing table and those with SAFI 3 into both the `inet.0` and `inet.2` routing tables.

If peers do not support MBGP, you cannot export routes from the `inet.2` routing table to them, only routes in the `inet.0` routing table. Routes in the `inet.2` routing table can be sent only to MBGP peers, because they are sent with a SAFI that identifies them as routes to multicast sources. The `inet.2` routing table should be a subset of the routes that you have in the `inet.0` routing table, because it is unlikely that you would have a route to a multicast source to which you could not send unicast traffic.

The `inet.2` routing table is used to keep the unicast routes that are used for multicast reverse-path-forwarding checks. An `inet.2` routing table is automatically located when you configure MBGP (by setting NLRI to `any`). The additional reachability information learned by MBGP from the NRLI multicast updates is placed in the `inet.2` routing table.

When you enable multiprotocol BGP, you can limit the number of prefixes received on a BGP peering and log rate-limited messages when the number of injected prefixes exceeds a set limit. You can also tear down the peering when the number of prefixes exceeds the limit. To configure a maximum number of prefixes, include the `prefix-limit` statement:

```
prefix-limit {
  maximum number;
  teardown <percentage> <idle-timeout (forever |
    minutes)>;
}
```

When you set the maximum number of prefixes, a message is logged when that number is reached.

If you include the teardown statement, the session is torn down when the maximum number of prefixes is reached. If you specify a percentage, messages are logged when the number of prefixes reaches that percentage. After the session is torn down, it is reestablished in a short time (unless you include the idle-timeout statement). Then the session can be kept down for a specified amount of time, or forever. If you specify forever, the session is reestablished only after you issue a clear bgp neighbor command.

When a BGP session receives a unicast or multicast NLRI, it installs the route in the appropriate routing table (inet.0 for unicast and inet.2 for multicast). To add unicast prefixes to both the unicast and multicast routing tables, you can configure BGP routing table groups. This is useful if you cannot perform multicast NLRI negotiation. To configure BGP routing table groups, include the rib-group statement:

```
rib-group group-name;
```

Configuring BGP Routing Policy

All routing protocols use the JUNOS software routing table to store the routes they learn and to determine which routes they should advertise in their protocol packets. Routing policy allows you to control which routes the routing protocols store in and retrieve from the routing table.

See Chapter 8, "Routing Policy and Firewall Filters," on page 301.

You define routing policy at the [edit policy-options] hierarchy level. To apply policies you have defined for BGP, include the import and export statements within the BGP configuration.

You can apply BGP policies as follows:

- BGP global import and export statements—Include these statements at the [edit protocols bgp] hierarchy level.
- Group import and export statements—Include these statements at the [edit protocols bgp group *group-name*] hierarchy level. A group-level import or export statement overrides a global BGP import or export statement.
- Peer import statements—Include these statements at the [edit protocols bgp group *group-name* neighbor *address*] hierarchy level. A peer-level import statement overrides a group import statement.

To apply policy to routes being imported into the routing table from BGP, include the `import` statement, listing the names of one or more policies to be evaluated:

```
import [ policy-names ];
```

To apply policy to routes being exported from the routing table into BGP, include the `export` statement, listing the names of one or more policies to be evaluated:

```
export [ policy-names ];
```

If you specify more than one policy, they are evaluated in the order specified, from first to last, and the first matching filter is applied to the route. If, on importing, no match is found, BGP places into the routing table only those routes that were learned from BGP routers. If, on exporting, no routes match the filters, the routing table exports into BGP only the routes that it learned from BGP.

By default, BGP stores the route information it receives from update messages in the JUNOS routing table, and the routing table exports only active routes into BGP, which BGP then advertises to its peers. To have the routing table export to BGP all routes learned by BGP even if the JUNOS software did not select them to be active routes, include the `advertise-inactive` statement:

```
advertise-inactive;
```

BGP stores the route information it receives from update messages in the routing table, and the routing table exports active routes from the routing table into BGP. BGP then advertises the exported routes to its peers. By default, the exchange of route information between BGP and the routing table occurs immediately after the routes are received. This immediate exchange of route information might cause instabilities in the network reachability information. To guard against this, you can delay the time between when BGP and the routing table exchange route information. To configure a delay between when the routing table receives route information and when it exports that information to BGP, include the `out-delay` statement:

```
out-delay seconds;
```

By default, the routing table retains some of the route information learned from BGP. To have the routing table retain all or none of this information, include the `keep` statement:

```
keep (all | none);
```

The routing table can retain the route information learned from BGP in one of the following ways:

- Default (omit the `keep` statement)—Keep all route information that was learned from BGP except for routes whose AS path is looped and the loop includes the local AS.
- `keep all`—Keep all route information that was learned from BGP.
- `keep none`—Discard routes that were received from a peer and that were rejected by import policy or other sanity checking, such as AS path or next hop. When you configure `keep none` for the BGP session and the inbound policy changes, the JUNOS software forces readvertisement of the full set of routes advertised by the peer.

Configuring BGP to Log System Log Messages

Whenever a BGP peer makes a state transition, you can configure BGP so that it generates a system log (syslog) message by including the `log-updown` statement:

```
log-updown;
```

Describing the BGP Router Configuration

To configure a plain text string to describe the BGP router configuration, include the `description` statement:

```
description description-text;
```

Tracing BGP Protocol Traffic

To trace BGP protocol traffic, specify BGP-specific options by including the `traceoptions` statement:

```
[edit protocols bgp]
traceoptions {
  file name <replace> <size size> <files number> <no-
      stamp> <(world-readable | no-world-readable)>;
  flag flag <flag-modifier> <disable>;
}
```

For more information about tracing and global tracing options, see the JUNOS technical documentation.

You can specify the following BGP-specific options in the BGP `traceoptions` statement:

- `aspath`—AS path regular expression operations
- `damping`—Damping operations
- `keepalive`—BGP keepalive messages
- `open`—BGP open packets
- `packets`—All BGP protocol packets
- `update`—Update packets

IS-IS

The Intermediate System-to-Intermediate System (IS-IS) protocol is an IGP that uses link-state information to make routing decisions.This protocol originally was developed for routing International Organization for Standardization (ISO) Connectionless Network Protocol (CLNP) packets.

An IS-IS network is a single AS, also called a *routing domain*, that consists of *end systems* and *intermediate systems*. End systems are network entities that send and receive packets. Intermediate systems send and receive packets and relay (forward) packets. (Intermediate system is the Open System Interconnection [OSI] term for a router.) ISO packets are called network *protocol data units* (*PDUs*).

In IS-IS, a single AS can be divided into smaller groups called *areas*. Routing between areas is organized hierarchically, allowing a domain to be administratively divided into smaller areas. This organization is accomplished by configuring *Level 1* and *Level 2* intermediate systems. Level 1 systems route within an area, and when the destination is outside an area, they route toward a Level 2 system. Level 2 intermediate systems route between areas and toward other ASs.

IS-IS uses ISO network addresses. Each address identifies a point of connection to the network, such as a router interface, and is called a *network service access point* (*NSAP*). An end system can have multiple NSAP addresses, in which case the addresses differ only by the last byte (called the *n-selector*). Each NSAP represents a service that is available at that node. In addition to having multiple services, a single node can belong to multiple areas.

Each network entity also has a special network address called a *network entity title* (*NET*). Structurally, an NET is identical to an NSAP address but has an n-selector of 00. Most end systems and intermediate systems have one NET. Intermediate systems that participate in multiple areas can have multiple NETs.

The following ISO addresses illustrate the IS-IS address format:

```
49.0001.00a0.c96b.c490.00
49.0001.2081.9716.9018.00
```

The first portion of the address is the area number, which is a variable number from 1 through 13 bytes. The first byte of the area number (49) is the authority and format indicator (AFI). The next bytes are the assigned domain (area) identifier, which can be from 0 through 12 bytes. In the examples above, the area identifier is 0001.

The next six bytes form the system identifier (sysid), which can be any six bytes that are unique throughout the entire domain. The system identifier commonly is the Media Access Control (MAC) address (as in the first example, `00a0.c96b.c490`) or the IP address expressed in binary-coded decimal (BCD) (as in the second example, `2081.9716.9018`, which corresponds to IP address `208.197.169.18`). The last byte (`00`) is the n-selector.

To provide help with IS-IS debugging, the JUNOS software supports dynamic mapping of ISO sysids to the hostname. Each system can be configured with a host name, which allows the sysid-to-hostname mapping to be carried in a dynamic hostname type length value (TLV) in IS-IS LSP packets. This permits ISs in the routing domain to learn about the ISO sysid of a particular IS.

To help provide traffic engineering and MPLS with information about network topology and loading, extensions have been added to the JUNOS implementation of IS-IS. Specifically, IS-IS supports new TLVs that specify link attributes. These TLVs are included in the IS-IS link-state PDUs. The link-attribute information is used to populate the traffic engineering database (TED), which is used by the Constrained Shortest-Path First (CSPF) algorithm to compute the paths that MPLS LSPs will take. This path information is used by RSVP to set up LSPs and reserve bandwidth for them.

In IS-IS, you can configure shortcuts, which allow IS-IS to use an LSP as the next hop as if it were a logical interface from the ingress router to the egress router. When used in this way, LSPs are no different than ATM and Frame Relay VCs, except that LSPs carry only IPv4 traffic.

Table 9.4 lists the IS-IS standards and protocol extensions supported by the JUNOS software.

Table 9.4 *IS-IS Standards Supported by the JUNOS Software*

Standard	Title
ISO/IEC 10589	*Information technology, Telecommunications and information exchange between systems, Intermediate system to intermediate system intradomain routing information exchange protocol for use in conjunction with the protocol for providing the connectionless-mode network service (ISO 8473)*
RFC 1195	*Use of OSI IS-IS for Routing in TCP/IP and Dual Environments*
RFC 2763	*Dynamic Hostname Exchange Mechanism for IS-IS*
RFC 2966	*Domain-wide Prefix Distribution with Two-Level IS-IS*
RFC 2973	*IS-IS Mesh Groups*
draft-ietf-isis-wg-snp-checksum-02.txt	*Optional Checksums for IS-IS*
draft-draft-isis-traffic-traffic-02	*IS-IS Extensions for Traffic Engineering*

IS-IS Packets

IS-IS uses the following PDUs to exchange protocol information:

- IS-IS hello (IIH) PDUs—Broadcast to discover the identity of neighboring IS-IS systems and to determine whether the neighbors are Level 1 or Level 2 intermediate systems.
- Link-state PDUs (LSPs)—Contain information about the state of adjacencies to neighboring IS-IS systems. LSPs are flooded periodically throughout an area.
- Complete sequence number PDUs (CSNPs)—Contain a complete list of all LSPs in the IS-IS database. CSNPs are sent periodically on all links, and the receiving systems use the information in the CSNP to update and synchronize their LSP databases. The desig-

nated router multicasts CSNPs on broadcast links in place of sending explicit acknowledgments for each LSP.

- Partial sequence number PDUs (PSNPs)—Multicast by a receiver when it detects that it is missing an LSP; that is, when its LSP database is out of date. The receiver sends a PSNP to the system that transmitted the CSNP, effectively requesting that the missing LSP be transmitted. That router, in turn, forwards the missing LSP to the requesting router.

Configuring IS-IS

To configure IS-IS, include the following statements in the configuration. For IS-IS to run on the router, you must enable IS-IS on the router, configure a network entity title (NET) on one of the router's interfaces (preferably the loopback interface, `lo0`), and configure the ISO family on all interfaces on which you want IS-IS to run. When you enable IS-IS, Level 1 and Level 2 are enabled by default. In the `address` statement, *`address`* is the NET.

```
[edit]
interfaces {
  lo0 {
    unit logical-unit-number {
      family iso {
        address address;
      }
    }
  }
  type-fpc/pic/port {
    unit logical-unit-number {
      family iso;
    }
  }
}
protocols {
  isis {
    disable;
    authentication-key key;
    authentication-type authentication;
    export [ policy-names ];
    ignore-attached-bit;
    label-switched-path name level level metric metric;
    level level-number {
      authentication-key key;
      authentication-type authentication;
      external-preference preference;
```

```
      preference preference;
      wide-metrics-only;
    }
    lsp-lifetime seconds;
    multicast-topology;
    no-authentication-check;
    reference-bandwidth reference-bandwidth;
    rib-group group-name;
    overload <timeout seconds>;
    traffic-engineering {
      disable;
      shortcuts;
    }
    traceoptions {
      file name <replace> <size size> <files number> <no-
        stamp>
        <(world-readable | no-world-readable)>;
      flag flag <flag-modifier> <disable>;
    }
    interface interface-name {
      authentication-key key;
      authentication-type authentication;
      disable;
      checksum;
      csnp-interval (seconds | disable);
      hello-authentication-key key;
      hello-authentication-type authentication;
      lsp-interval milliseconds;
      mesh-group (value | blocked);
      passive;
      level level-number {
        authentication-key key;
        authentication-type authentication;
        disable;
        hello-authentication-key key;
        hello-authentication-type authentication;
        hello-interval seconds;
        hold-time seconds;
        metric metric;
        multicast-metric metric;
        passive;
        priority number;
        te-metric metric;
      }
    }
  }
}
```

Configuring IS-IS Authentication

All IS-IS protocol exchanges can be authenticated to guarantee that only trusted routers participate in the AS's routing. By default, IS-IS authentication is disabled on the router. To configure IS-IS authentication, define an authentication password and specify the authentication type. You can configure one of the following authentication methods:

- Simple authentication—Uses a text password that is included in the transmitted packet. The receiving router uses an authentication key (password) to verify the packet. Simple authentication is included for compatibility with existing IS-IS implementations. However, it is recommended that you do *not* use this authentication method because it is insecure (the text can be "sniffed").

- HMAC-MD5 authentication—Uses an iterated cryptographic hash function. The receiving router uses an authentication key (password) to verify the packet. HMAC-MD5 authentication is defined in RFC 2104. Note that this RFC presents only a proposal for using HMAC-MD5 with IS-IS; it is currently not a standard.

To configure more fine-grained authentication hello packets, see "Configuring IS-IS Levels on an Interface," on page 426.

To enable authentication and specify an authentication method, include the `authentication-type` statement, specifying the `simple` or `md5` authentication type:

```
authentication-type authentication;
```

To configure a password, include the `authentication-key` statement. The authentication password for all routers in a domain must be the same. The password can contain up to 255 characters. If you include spaces, enclose all characters in quotation marks (" ").

```
authentication-key key;
```

When using the JUNOS IS-IS software with another implementation of IS-IS, the other implementation must be configured to use the same password for the domain, the area, and all interfaces that are shared with a JUNOS implementation.

To configure IS-IS to generate authenticated packets, but not to check the authentication on received packets, include the `no-authentication-check` statement:

```
[edit protocols isis]
no-authentication-check;
```

Configuring Interface-Specific Properties

To configure interface-specific IS-IS properties, include the `interface` statement:

```
[edit protocols isis]
interface interface-name {
  authentication-key key;
  authentication-type authentication;
  disable;
  checksum;
  csnp-interval (seconds | disable);
  hello-authentication-key key;
  hello-authentication-type authentication;
  lsp-interval milliseconds;
  mesh-group (value | blocked);
  passive;
  level level-number {
    authentication-key key;
    authentication-type authentication;
    disable;
    hello-authentication-type authentication;
    hello-authentication-key key;
    hello-interval seconds;
    hold-time seconds;
    metric metric;
    passive;
    priority number;
    te-metric metric;
  }
}
```

Configuring the CSNP Interval

By default, IS-IS sends CSN packets periodically. If the router is the designated router on a LAN, IS-IS sends CSN packets every 10 seconds. If the router is on a point-to-point interface, it sends CSN packets every 5 seconds. You might want to modify the default interval to protect against LSP flooding. To modify the CSNP interval, include the `csnp-interval` statement. The time can range from 1 through 65,535 seconds.

```
[edit protocols isis interface interface-name]
csnp-interval seconds;
```

To configure the interface not to send any CSN packets, specify the `disable` option:

```
[edit protocols isis interface interface-name]
csnp-interval disable;
```

Configuring Mesh Groups

A *mesh group* is a set of routers that are fully connected; that is, they have a fully meshed topology. When LSP packets are being flooded throughout an area, each router within a mesh group receives only a single copy of an LSP packet instead of receiving one copy from each neighbor, thus minimizing the overhead associated with the flooding of LSP packets. To create a mesh group and designate that an interface is part of the group, assign a mesh-group number to all the router interfaces in the group:

```
[edit protocols isis interface interface-name]
mesh-group value;
```

To prevent an interface in the mesh group from flooding LSPs, configure blocking on that interface:

```
[edit protocols isis interface interface-name]
mesh-group blocked;
```

Modifying the Interface Metric

All IS-IS interfaces have a cost, which is a routing metric used in the IS-IS link-state calculation. Routes with lower total path metrics are preferred over those with higher path metrics. When several equal-cost routes to a destination exist, traffic is distributed equally among them. The cost of a route is described by a single dimensionless metric that is determined using the following formula:

```
cost = reference-bandwidth/bandwidth
```

`reference-bandwidth` is the reference bandwidth. If the reference bandwidth is not configured, all interfaces have a default metric of 10 (with the exception of the `lo0` interface, which has a default metric of 0).

To modify the reference bandwidth, include the `reference-bandwidth` statement at the `[edit protocols isis]` hierarchy level:

```
[edit protocols isis]
reference-bandwidth reference-bandwidth;
```

For example, if you set the reference bandwidth to 1 Gbps (that is, `reference-bandwidth` is set to 1,000,000,000), a 100-Mbps interface has a default metric of 10.

Configuring Route Preferences

Route preferences are used to select which route is installed in the forwarding table when several protocols calculate routes to the same destination. The route with the lowest preference value is selected.

For more information about route preferences, see Table 9.1 on page 379.

By default, Level 1 IS-IS internal routes have a preference value of 15, Level 2 IS-IS internal routes have a preference of 18, Level 1 IS-IS external routes have a preference of 160, and Level 2 external routes have a preference of 165. To change the preference values, include the `preference` statement (for internal routes) or the `external-preference` statement (for external routes). The preference value can range from 0 through 255.

```
[edit protocols isis level level-number]
external-preference preference;
preference preference;
```

Configuring IS-IS Levels on an Interface

You can administratively divide a single AS into smaller groups called *areas*. There are two types of areas: Level 1 areas and Level 2 areas. Routers in Level 1 areas route within the area and, when the destination is outside the area, toward a Level 2 router. Routers in Level 2 areas route between areas and toward other ASs. You configure each router interface to be in an area. Any interface can be in any area. You can configure one Level 1 routing process and one Level 2 routing process on each interface, and you can configure the two levels differently. To configure an area, include the `level` statement:

```
[edit protocols isis interface interface-name]
level level-number {
    authentication-key key;
    authentication-type authentication;
    disable;
    hello-authentication-key key;
    hello-authentication-type authentication;
    hello-interval seconds;
    hold-time seconds;
    metric metric;
    passive;
    priority number;
    te-metric metric;
}
```

By default, IS-IS is enabled for Level 1 and Level 2 areas on all enabled interfaces on which the `iso` protocol family is enabled (at the `[edit interfaces interface unit logical-unit-number]` hierarchy level). To disable IS-IS at any particular level on an interface, include the `disable` statement:

```
[edit protocols isis interface interface-name level level-
number]
disable;
```

Enabling IS-IS on an interface (by including the `interface` statement at the `[edit protocols isis]` hierarchy level), disabling it (by including the `disable` statement), and not actually having IS-IS run on an interface (by including the `passive` statement) are mutually exclusive states.

By default, IS-IS must be configured on an interface or a level for direct interface addresses to be advertised into that level. To advertise the direct interface addresses without actually running IS-IS on that interface or level, include the `passive` statement:

```
passive;
```

You can configure authentication for all IS-IS hello packets for an interface and, to achieve a more fine-grained authentication, you can configure authentication for a given IS-IS level on that interface. If you configure a point-to-point link and if you enable both levels, the hello packets are sent with the password configured for Level 1. By default, hello authentication is not configured on an interface. However, if IS-IS authentication is configured, the hello packets are authenticated using the IS-IS authentication type and password. To configure IS-IS hello packet authentication, you must define an authentication password and specify the authentication type. To enable hello authentication for an interface or level, include the `hello-authentication-type` statement:

```
[edit protocols isis interface interface-name] or
[edit protocols isis interface interface-name level level-
number]
hello-authentication-type authentication;
```

Routers send hello packets at a fixed interval on all interfaces to establish and maintain neighbor relationships. This interval is advertised in the hello interval field in the hello packet. By default, a designated intersystem (DIS) router sends hello packets every 3 seconds, and a non-DIS router sends hello packets every 9 seconds. To modify how often the router sends hello packets out of an interface, include the `hello-interval` statement:

```
[edit protocols isis interface interface-name level level-
number]
hello-interval seconds;
```

The hold time is how long a neighbor should consider this router to be operative without receiving another hello packet. If the neighbor does not receive a hello packet from this router within the hold time, it marks the router as being unavailable. The default hold-time value is three times the default hello interval: 9 seconds for a DIS router and 27 seconds for a non-DIS router. To modify the hold-time value on the local router, include the `hold-time` statement:

```
[edit protocols isis interface interface-name level level-
number]
hold-time seconds;
```

All IS-IS routes have a cost, which is a routing metric used in the IS-IS link-state calculation. The cost is an arbitrary, dimensionless integer that can range from 1 through 63, or from 1 through $2^{24} - 1$ (16,777,215) if you are using wide metrics. The default metric value is 10 (with the exception of the `lo0` interface, which has a default metric of 0). To modify the default value, include the `metric` statement:

```
[edit protocols isis interface interface-name level level-
number]
metric metric;
```

When traffic engineering is enabled on the router, you can configure an IS-IS metric that is used exclusively for traffic engineering. The traffic engineering metric is used for information injected into the traffic engineering database (TED). Its value does not affect normal IS-IS forwarding. To modify the default value, include the `te-metric` statement:

```
[edit protocols isis interface interface-name level level-
number]
te-metric metric;
```

A router advertises its priority to become a designated router in its hello packets. On all multiaccess networks, IS-IS uses the advertised priorities to elect a designated router for the network. This router is responsible for sending network link-state advertisements, which describe all the routers attached to the network. These advertisements are flooded throughout a single area. The priority value is meaningful only on a multiaccess network. It has no meaning on a point-to-point interface. A router's priority for becoming the designated router is indicated by an arbitrary number from 0 through 127; routers with a higher value are more likely to become the designated router. By default, routers have a priority value of 64. To modify the interface's priority value, include the `priority` statement:

```
[edit protocols isis interface interface-name level level-
number]
priority number;
```

Modifying the LSP Interval

By default, the router sends one link-state PDU (LSP) packet out an interface every 100 milliseconds. To modify this interval, include the `lsp-interval` statement. To disable the transmission of all LSP packets, set the interval to 0.

```
[edit protocols isis interface interface-name]
lsp-interval milliseconds;
```

Modifying the LSP Lifetime

By default, link-state PDUs (LSPs) are maintained in network databases for 1,200 seconds (20 minutes) before being considered invalid. This length of time, called the *LSP lifetime*, normally is sufficient to guarantee that LSPs never expire. To modify the LSP lifetime, include the `lsp-lifetime` statement. The time can range from 350 to 65,535 seconds. The LSP refresh interval is derived from the LSP lifetime and is equal to the lifetime minus 317 seconds.

```
[edit protocols isis]
lsp-lifetime seconds;
```

Advertising Label-Switched Paths into IS-IS

You can advertise label-switched paths into IS-IS as point-to-point links, and the label-switched paths can be used in SPF calculations. The advertisement contains a local address (the `from` address of the label-switched path), a remote address (the `to` address of the label-switched path), and a metric with a precedence that either uses the label-switched path metric defined under IS-IS, uses the label-switched path metric configured for the label-switched path under MPLS, or, if you do not configure any of the above, uses the default IS-IS metric of 10. To advertise label-switched paths, include the `label-switched-path` statement, with a specified `level` and `metric`:

```
[edit protocols isis]
label-switched-path name level level metric metric;
```

See Chapter 11, "MPLS Applications," on page 519.

Before a label-switched path can be announced as a link and used in SPF calculations, you must configure a label-switched path in both directions between two label-switched routers.

Configuring the Router to Appear Overloaded

You can configure the local router so that it appears to be overloaded. You might want to do this when you want the router to participate in IS-IS routing, but do not want it to be used for transit traffic. (Note that traffic to immediately attached interfaces continues to transit the router.) To mark the router as overloaded, include the `overload` statement:

```
[edit protocols isis]
overload;
```

To specify the number of seconds at which overload is reset, include the `timeout` option when specifying the `overload` statement. The time can range from 60 through 1,800 seconds.

```
[edit protocols isis]
overload timeout seconds;
```

IS-IS and Multipoint Configurations

IS-IS does not support multipoint configurations. Therefore, when configuring Frame Relay or ATM networks, you must configure them as collections of point-to-point links, not as multipoint clouds.

Configuring IS-IS Traffic Engineering Attributes

You can configure various attributes related to IS-IS traffic engineering Normally, IS-IS metrics can have values up to 63, and IS-IS generates two TLVs, one for an IS-IS adjacency and the second for an IP prefix. To allow IS-IS to support traffic engineering, a second pair of TLVs has been added to IS-IS, one for IP prefixes and the second for IS-IS adjacency and traffic engineering information. With these TLVs, IS-IS metrics can have values up to $2^{24} - 1$ (16,777,215). By default, the JUNOS software allows a maximum metric value of 63 and generates both pairs of TLVs. To configure IS-IS to generate only the new pair of TLVs and thus to allow the wider range of metric values, include the `wide-metrics-only` statement. By default, the JUNOS software supports the sending and receiving of wide metrics.

```
[edit protocols isis]
wide-metrics-only;
```

See Chapter 11, "MPLS Applications," on page 519.

IS-IS always performs SPF calculations to determine next hops. For prefixes reachable through a particular next hop, IS-IS places that next hop for that prefix in the `inet.0` routing table. In addition, for routers running MPLS, IS-IS also installs the prefix in the `inet.3` routing table. The `inet.3` table, which is present on the ingress router, contains the host address of each MPLS label-switched path's egress router. BGP uses this routing table to resolve next-hop addresses. If you enable IS-IS traffic engineering shortcuts, and if there is a label-switched path to a point along the path to that prefix, IS-IS installs the prefix in the `inet.3` routing table and uses the label-switched path as a next hop. The net result is that for BGP egress routers for which there is no label-switched path, BGP automatically uses a label-switched path along the path to reach the egress router. To configure IS-IS so that it uses label-switched paths as shortcuts when installing information in the `inet.3` routing table, include the `shortcuts` statement. Because the `inet.3` routing table is present only on ingress routers, you can configure label-switched path shortcuts only on these routers.

```
[edit protocols isis]
traffic-engineering {
  shortcuts;
}
```

By default, IS-IS supports traffic engineering by exchanging basic information with the traffic engineering database (TED). To disable this support, and to disable IS-IS shortcuts if they are configured, include the `disable` statement:

```
[edit protocols isis]
traffic-engineering {
  disable;
}
```

Configuring IS-IS Multicast Extensions

Most multicast routing protocols perform a reverse-path forwarding (RPF) check on the source of multicast data packets. If a packet comes in on the interface that is used to send data to the source, the packet is accepted and forwarded to one or more downstream interfaces. Otherwise, the packet is discarded and a notification is sent to the multicast routing protocol running on the interface. In certain instances, the unicast routing table used for the RPF check is also the table used for forwarding unicast data packets. Thus, unicast and multicast routing are congruent. In cases in which it is preferred that multicast routing be independent of unicast routing, the multicast routing protocols are configured to perform the RPF check using an alternate unicast routing table, `inet.2`. You can configure IS-IS to calculate an alternate multicast topology in addition to the normal unicast topology, and add the corresponding routes to the `inet.2` routing table. The IS-IS interface metrics for the multicast topology can be configured independently of the unicast metrics. You can also selectively disable interfaces from participating in the multicast topology while continuing to participate in the regular unicast topology. This lets you exercise control over the paths that multicast data takes through a network so that it is independent of unicast data paths.

To enable support for multicast extensions, include the `multicast-topology` statement:

```
[edit protocols isis]
multicast-topology;
```

To set the multicast metric on a level, include the `multicast-metric` statement:

```
[edit protocols isis interface interface-name level level-
number]
multicast-metric metric;
```

Disabling IS-IS on the Router

To disable IS-IS on the router without removing the IS-IS configuration statements from the configuration, include the `disable` statement:

```
[edit protocols]
isis {
  disable;
}
```

Configuring IS-IS Routing Policy

For IS-IS, you can apply routing policies that affect how routing protocol process (`rpd`) exports routes into IS-IS. You should not apply routing policies that affect how routes are imported into the routing table; doing so with a link-state protocol could easily lead to an inconsistent topology database. To apply routing policies, include the `export` statement:

```
[edit protocols isis]
export [ policy-names ];
```

Tracing IS-IS Protocol Traffic

To trace IS-IS protocol traffic, include the `traceoptions` statement:

```
[edit protocols isis]
traceoptions {
  file name <replace> <size size> <files number> <no-
      stamp>
    <(world-readable | no-world-readable)>;
  flag flag <flag-modifier> <disable>;
}
```

You can specify the following IS-IS–specific options:

- `all`—All IS-IS information
- `csn`—Complete sequence number PDU (CSNP) packets
- `error`—Errored packets
- `general`—General events
- `hello`—Hello packets
- `lsp`—Link-state PDU (LSP) packets
- `lsp-generation`—Link-state PDU generation packets
- `normal`—Normal events
- `packets`—All IS-IS protocol packets
- `policy`—Policy processing
- `psn`—Partial sequence number PDU (PSNP) packets
- `route`—Routing information
- `spf`—Shortest-path-first (SPF) calculations
- `state`—State transitions
- `task`—Routing protocol task processing
- `timer`—Routing protocol timer processing

For more information about tracing and global tracing options, see the JUNOS technical documentation.

You can optionally specify one or more of the following flag modifiers:

- `detail`—Detailed trace information
- `receive`—Packets being received
- `send`—Packets being transmitted

OSPF

The Open Shortest Path First (OSPF) protocol is an IGP that routes packets within a single AS. OSPF uses link-state information to make routing decisions, making route calculations using the shortest-path-first (SPF) algorithm (also referred to as the Dijkstra algorithm). Each router running OSPF floods link-state advertisements (LSAs) throughout the AS that contain information about that router's attached interfaces and routing metrics. Each router takes the information in these link-state advertisements and creates a complete routing table for the network.

The JUNOS software supports OSPF Version 2, including virtual links, stub areas, and authentication. It does not support type-of-service (ToS) routing.

In OSPF, a single AS can be divided into smaller groups called *areas*. This reduces the number of LSAs and other OSPF overhead traffic sent on the network, and it reduces the size of the topological database that each router must maintain. An *area* is a set of networks and hosts within an AS that have been administratively grouped together. Juniper Networks recommends that you configure an area as a collection of contiguous IP subnetted networks. Routers that are wholly within an area are called *internal routers*. All interfaces on internal routers are directly connected to networks within the area. The topology of an area is hidden from the rest of the AS, thus significantly reducing routing traffic in the AS. Also, routing within the area is determined only by the area's topology, providing the area with some protection from bad routing data. All routers within an area have identical topological databases.

Routers that belong to more than one area are called *area border routers*. They maintain a separate topological database for each area to which they are connected.

An OSPF *backbone area* consists of all networks in area ID `0.0.0.0`, their attached routers, and all area border routers. The backbone itself does not have any area border routers. The backbone distributes routing information between areas. The backbone is simply another area, so the terminology and rules of areas apply: a router that is directly connected to the backbone is an internal router on the backbone, and the backbone's topology is hidden from the other areas in the AS. The routers that make up the backbone must be physically contiguous. If they are not, you must configure *virtual links* to create the appearance of backbone connectivity. You can create virtual links between any two area border routers that have an interface to a common nonbackbone area. OSPF treats two routers joined by a virtual link as if they were connected to an unnumbered point-to-point network.

Routers that exchange routing information with routers in other ASs are called *AS boundary routers*. They advertise externally learned routes throughout the AS. Any router in the AS—an internal router, an area border router, or a backbone router—can be an AS boundary router. Every router within the AS knows the path to the AS boundary routers.

Stub areas are areas through which or into which AS external advertisements are not flooded. You might want to create stub areas when much of the topological database consists of AS external advertisements. Doing so reduces the size of the topological databases and therefore the amount of memory required on the internal routers in the stub area. When an area border router is configured for a stub area, the router automatically advertises a default route in place of the external routes that are not being advertised within the stub area so that routers in the stub area can reach destinations outside the area. The following restrictions apply to stub areas: you cannot create a virtual link through a stub area, and a stub area cannot contain an AS boundary router.

An OSPF stub area has no external routes in it, so you cannot redistribute from another protocol into a stub area. A not-so-stubby area (NSSA) allows external routes to be flooded within the area. These routes are then leaked into other areas. However, external routes from other areas still do not enter the NSSA.

Transit areas are used to pass traffic from one adjacent area to the backbone (or to another area if the backbone is more than two hops away from an area). The traffic does not originate in, nor is it destined for, the transit area.

When OSPF exports route information from external ASs, it includes a cost, or *external metric*, in the route. There are two types of external metric: Type 1 and Type 2. Type 1 external metrics are equivalent to the link-state metric; that is, the cost of the route used in the internal AS. Type 2 external metrics are greater than the cost of any path internal to the AS.

Each multiaccess network has a *designated router*, which originates network link advertisements on behalf of the network and establishes adjacencies with all routers on the network, thus participating in the synchronizing of the link-state databases. The OSPF hello protocol elects a designated router for the network based on the priorities advertised by all the routers. In general, when an interface first becomes functional, it checks whether the network currently has a designated router. If there is one, the router accepts that designated router regardless of its own router priority. Otherwise, if the router has the highest priority on the network, it becomes the designated router. If router priorities tie, the router with the highest router ID (which is typically the router's IP address) is chosen as the designated router.

See Chapter 11, "MPLS Applications," on page 519.

To help provide traffic engineering and MPLS with information about network topology and loading, extensions have been added to the JUNOS implementation of OSPF. Specifically, OSPF generates opaque LSAs, which carry traffic engineering parameters. These parameters are used to populate the traffic engineering database (TED), which is used by the Constrained Shortest-Path First (CSPF) algorithm to compute the paths that MPLS LSPs take. This path information is used by RSVP to set up LSPs and reserve bandwidth for them. The JUNOS software also supports an LSP as the next hop as if it were a logical interface from the ingress router to the egress router. When used in this way, LSPs are no different than ATM and Frame Relay VCs, except that LSPs carry only IPv4 traffic.

Table 9.5 lists the OSPF standards and protocol extensions supported by the JUNOS software.

Table 9.5 *OSPF Standards Supported by JUNOS Software*

Standard	Title
RFC 2328	*OSPF Version 2*
RFC 1587	*The OSPF NSSA Option*
RFC 2370	*The OSPF Opaque LSA Option*
draft-katz-yeung-ospf-traffic-06.txt	*Traffic Engineering Extension to OSPF*

OSPF Routing Algorithm

OSPF uses the shortest-path-first (SPF) algorithm, also referred to as the Dijkstra algorithm, to determine the route to reach each destination. All routers in an area run this algorithm in parallel, storing the results in their individual topological databases. Routers with interfaces to multiple areas run multiple copies of the algorithm. This section provides a brief summary of how the SPF algorithm works.

When a router starts, it initializes OSPF and waits for indications from lower-level protocols that the router interfaces are functional. The router then uses the OSPF hello protocol to acquire neighbors, doing this by sending hello packets to its neighbors and receiving their hello packets.

On broadcast or nonbroadcast multiaccess networks (physical networks that support the attachment of more than two routers), the OSPF hello protocol elects a designated router for the network. This router is responsible for sending LSAs that describe the network, which reduces the amount of network traffic and the size of the routers' topological databases.

The router then attempts to form *adjacencies* with some of its newly acquired neighbors. (On multiaccess networks, only the designated router and backup designated router form adjacencies with other routers.) Adjacencies determine the distribution of routing protocol packets: routing protocol packets are sent and received only on adjacencies, and topological database updates are sent only along adjacencies. When adjacencies have been established, pairs of adjacent routers synchronize their topological databases.

A router sends LSA packets to advertise its state periodically and when the router's state changes. These packets include information about the router's adjacencies, which allows detection of nonoperational routers.

Using a reliable algorithm, the router floods LSAs throughout the area, which ensures that all routers in an area have exactly the same topological database. Each router uses the information in its topological database to calculate a shortest-path tree, with itself as the root. The router then uses this tree to route network traffic.

The description of the SPF algorithm up to this point has explained how the algorithm works within a single area (*intra-area routing*). For internal routers to be able to route to destinations outside the area (*interarea routing*), the area border routers must inject additional routing information into the area. Because the area border routers are connected to the backbone, they have access to complete topological data about the backbone. They use this information to calculate paths to all destinations outside its area and then advertise these paths to the area's internal routers.

AS boundary routers flood information about external ASs throughout the AS, except to stub areas. Area border routers are responsible for advertising the paths to all AS boundary routers.

OSPF Packets

All OSPF packets have a common 24-byte header that contains all information necessary to determine whether OSPF should accept the packet. The header consists of the following fields:

- Version number—The current OSPF version number is 2.
- Type—Type of OSPF packet.
- Packet length—Length of the packet, in bytes, including the header.
- Router ID—IP address of the router from which the packet originated.
- Area ID—Identifier of the area in which the packet is traveling. Each OSPF packet is associated with a single area. Packets traveling over a virtual link are labeled with the backbone area ID, `0.0.0.0`. You configure the area ID with the `area` statements.
- Checksum—Fletcher checksum.
- Authentication type—Authentication scheme to use for the packet. You configure the authentication type with the `authentication-type` statement.
- Authentication—The authentication information itself.

Routers periodically send hello packets on all interfaces, including virtual links, to establish and maintain neighbor relationships. Hello packets are multicast on physical networks that have a multicast or broadcast capability, which enables dynamic discovery of neighboring routers. (On nonbroadcast networks, dynamic neighbor discovery is not possible, so you must configure all neighbors statically using the `neighbor` statement.)

Hello packets consist of the OSPF header plus the following fields:

- Network mask—Network mask associated with the interface.
- Hello interval—How often the router sends hello packets. All routers on a shared network must use the same hello interval. You configure this interval with the `hello-interval` statement.
- Options—Optional capabilities of the router.
- Router priority—The router's priority to become the designated router. You can configure this value with the `priority` statement.
- Router dead interval—How long the router waits without receiving any OSPF packets from a router before declaring that router to be down. All routers on a shared network must use the same router dead interval. You can configure this value with the `dead-interval` statement.
- Designated router—IP address of the designated router.
- Backup designated router—IP address of the backup designated router.
- Neighbor—IP addresses of the routers from which valid hello packets have been received within the time specified by the router dead interval.

When initializing an adjacency, OSPF exchanges database description packets, which describe the contents of the topological database. These packets consist of the OSPF header, this packet's sequence number, and the link-state advertisement's header.

When a router detects that portions of its topological database are out of date, it sends a link-state request packet to a neighbor requesting a precise instance of the database. These packets consist of the OSPF header plus fields that uniquely identify the database information that the router is seeking.

Link-state update packets carry one or more LSAs one hop farther from their origin. The router multicasts (floods) these packets on physical networks that support multicast or broadcast mode. The router acknowledges all link-state update packets and, if retransmission is necessary, sends the retransmitted advertisements unicast.

Link-state update packets consist of the OSPF header plus the following fields:

- Number of advertisements—Number of LSAs included in this packet
- Link-state advertisements—The LSAs themselves

The router sends link-state acknowledgment packets in response to link-state update packets to verify that the update packets have been received successfully. A single acknowledgment packet can include responses to multiple update packets. Link-state acknowledgment packets consist of the OSPF header plus the LSA header.

Link-state request, link-state update, and link-state acknowledgment packets are used to reliably flood LSA packets. OSPF sends the following types of LSAs:

- Router link advertisements—Sent by all routers to describe the state and cost of the router's links to the area. These LSAs are flooded throughout a single area only.
- Network link advertisements—Sent by designated routers to describe all the routers attached to the network. These LSAs are flooded throughout a single area only.
- Summary link advertisements—Sent by area border routers to describe the routes that they know about in other areas. There are two types of summary link advertisements: those used when the destination is an IP network, and those used when the destination is an AS boundary router. Summary link advertisements describe interarea routes; that is, routes to destinations outside the area but within the AS. These LSAs are flooded throughout the advertisement's associated areas.
- AS external link advertisement—Sent by AS boundary routers to describe external routes that they know about. These LSAs are flooded throughout the AS (except for stub areas).

Each LSA type describes a portion of the OSPF routing domain. All LSAs are flooded throughout the AS. Each LSA packet begins with a common 20-byte header.

Configuring OSPF

For OSPF to run on the router, you must configure a backbone area on at least one interface.

```
[edit protocols]
ospf {
  disable;
  domain-id domain-id;
  export [ policy-names ];
  external-preference preference;
  overload {
    timeout seconds;
  }
  preference preference;
  rib-group group-name;
  reference-bandwidth reference-bandwidth;
  traffic-engineering {
    no-topology;
    shortcuts;
  }
  traceoptions {
    file name <replace> <size size> <files number> <no-
        stamp>
      <(world-readable | no-world-readable)>;
    flag flag <flag-modifier> <disable>;
  }
  area area-id {
    area-range network/mask-length <restrict>;
    authentication-type authentication;
    interface interface-name {
      disable;
      authentication-key key <key-id identifier>;
      dead-interval seconds;
      hello-interval seconds;
      interface-type type;
      metric metric;
      neighbor address <eligible>;
      passive;
      poll-interval seconds;
      priority number;
      retransmit-interval seconds;
      transit-delay seconds;
      transmit-interval seconds;
    }
    label-switched-path name metric metric;
    nssa {
      area-range network/mask-length <restrict>;
      default-lsa {
        default-metric metric;
```

```
            metric-type type;
          }
          (no-summaries | summaries)
        }
        stub <default-metric metric> <summaries | no-
          summaries>;
        virtual-link neighbor-id router-id transit-area area-
          id {
          disable;
          authentication-key key <key-id identifier>;
          dead-interval seconds;
          hello-interval seconds;
          retransmit-interval seconds;
          transit-delay seconds;
        }
      }
    }
```

Configuring the Backbone Area and Other Areas

You can group routers in a single AS into areas to reduce the amount of LSA traffic on the network and to reduce the size of the topological databases that OSPF routers must maintain. If you do this, the AS must contain a single backbone area and optionally can contain any number of nonbackbone areas. The routers that make up the backbone must be physically contiguous. If they are not, you must configure virtual links to create the appearance of connectivity. You also can configure stub areas, which are areas through which AS external advertisements are not flooded, and NSSAs, which allow external routes to be flooded within an area.

You must create a backbone area if your network consists of multiple areas. An area border router must have at least one interface in the backbone area, or it must have a virtual link to a router in the backbone area. The backbone comprises all area border routers and all routers that are not included in any other area. You configure all these routers by including the following `area` statement:

```
[edit protocols ospf]
area 0.0.0.0;
```

Each OSPF area consists of routers configured with the same area number. To configure a router to be in an area, include the `area` statement. The area number can be any number except `0.0.0.0`, which is reserved for the backbone area.

```
[edit protocols ospf]
area area-id;
```

Stub areas are areas into which OSPF does not flood AS external advertisements. You might want to configure stub areas when much of the topological database consists of AS external advertisements and you want to minimize the size of the topological databases on an area's routers. You must include the `stub` statement when configuring all routers that are in the stub area. You cannot configure an area as being both a stub area and an NSSA. To configure a stub area, include the `stub` statement:

```
[edit protocols ospf area area-id]
stub <default-metric metric> <(no-summaries | summaries)>;
```

To inject a default route with a specified metric value into the area, include the `default-metric` option and a metric value. The default route matches any destination that is not explicitly reachable from within the area. To have the stub areas not advertise summary routes into the stub area, include the `no-summaries` option. Only the default route is advertised, and only if you include the `default-metric` option. The default route injected into the NSSA area is a Type 3 LSA.

An OSPF stub area has no external routes in it, so you cannot redistribute from another protocol into a stub area. An NSSA allows external routes to be flooded within the area. These routes are then leaked into other areas. However, external routes from other areas still do not enter the NSSA. You cannot configure an area to be both a stub area and an NSSA. To configure an NSSA, include the `nssa` statement:

```
[edit protocols ospf area area-id]
nssa {
  area-range network/mask-length <restrict>;
  default-lsa {
    default-metric metric;
    metric-type type;
  }
  (no-summaries | summaries)
}
```

By default, a default route is not advertised. To advertise a default route with the specified metric within the area, include the `default-metric` statement. You can configure this option only on area border routers.

To prevent area border routers from advertising summary routes into an NSSA, include the `no-summaries` statement. If you include the `default-metric option` in addition to the `no-summaries` statement, only the default route is advertised. The default route is a Type 3 LSA injected into the NSSA. To flood summary (Type 7) LSAs into the NSSA area, include the `summaries` statement.

To aggregate external routes learned within the area when a route is advertised to other areas, include one or more `area-range` statements. If you also include the `restrict` option, the aggregate is not advertised, effectively creating a route filter. All external routes learned within the area that do not fall into the range of one of the prefixes are advertised individually to other areas.

If any router on the backbone is not physically connected to the backbone itself, you must establish a virtual connection, or virtual link, between that router and the backbone. You can establish virtual links between area border routers only. For the virtual link to work, you also must configure a virtual link to the backbone area on the remote area border router (the router at the other end of the virtual link). To configure a virtual link, include the `virtual-link` statement when configuring the backbone area (area 0):

```
[edit protocols ospf area 0.0.0.0]
virtual-link neighbor-id router-id transit-area area-id;
```

Specify the IP address of the router at the other end of the virtual link. This router must be an area border router that is physically connected to the backbone. Also, specify the number of the area through which the virtual link transits.

Configuring OSPF on Router Interfaces

To enable OSPF on the router, you must configure OSPF on at least one of the router's interfaces. How you configure an interface depends on whether the interface is connected to a broadcast or point-to-point network, a point-to-multipoint network, or a nonbroadcast, multiaccess (NBMA) network.

When you configure OSPF on an interface, you must also include the `family inet` statement at the `[edit interfaces` *`interface-name`* `unit` *`logical-unit-number`*`]` hierarchy level.

If the interface on which you are configuring OSPF supports broadcast mode (such as a LAN), or if the interface supports point-to-point mode (such as a PPP interface or a point-to-point logical interface on Frame Relay), include the following form of the `interface` statement, specifying the IP address or name of the interface:

```
[edit protocols ospf area area-id]
interface interface-name;
```

When you configure OSPF on an NBMA network, such as a multipoint ATM or Frame Relay logical interface, OSPF operates by default in point-to-multipoint mode. In this mode, OSPF treats the network as a set of point-to-point links. Because there is no autodiscovery mechanism, each neighbor must be configured. To configure OSPF in point-to-multipoint mode, include the following statements, specifying the IP address or name of the interface. To configure multiple neighbors, include a `neighbor` statement for each neighbor.

```
[edit protocols ospf area 0.0.0.0]
interface interface-name {
  neighbor address;
}
```

When configuring OSPF on an NBMA network, you can use nonbroadcast mode rather than point-to-multipoint mode. Using this mode offers no advantages over point-to-multipoint mode, but it has more disadvantages than point-to-multipoint mode. Nevertheless, you might occasionally find it necessary to configure nonbroadcast mode to interoperate with other equipment. Nonbroadcast mode treats the NBMA network as a partially connected LAN, electing designated and backup designated routers. All routers must have a direct connection to both the designated and backup designated routers, or unpredictable results occur. To configure nonbroadcast mode, include the following statements, specifying the IP address of the interface. To configure multiple neighbors, include a `neighbor` statement for each neighbor.

```
[edit protocols ospf area 0]
interface interface-name {
  interface-type nbma;
  neighbor address <eligible>;
  poll-interval seconds;
}
```

OSPF routers normally discover their neighbors dynamically by listening to the broadcast or multicast hello packets on the network. Because an NBMA network does not support broadcast (or multicast), the router cannot discover its neighbors dynamically, so you must configure all the neighbors statically. Do this by including the `neighbor` statement and specifying the IP address of each neighboring router in the *`address`* option. To configure multiple neighbors, include multiple `neighbor` statements. If the neighbor is allowed to become the designated router, include the `eligible` keyword.

By default, the router sends hello packets out the interface every 120 seconds before it establishes adjacency with a neighbor. To modify the interval, include the `poll-interval` statement.

Configuring OSPF Authentication

All OSPF protocol exchanges can be authenticated to guarantee that only trusted routers participate in the AS's routing. By default, OSPF authentication is disabled. You can configure one of the following authentication methods. Each area must use the same method.

- Simple authentication—Uses a text password that is included in the transmitted packet. The receiving router uses an authentication key (password) to verify the packet.
- MD5 algorithm—Creates an encoded checksum that is included in the transmitted packet. The receiving router uses an authentication key (password) to verify the packet. For MD5 authentication to work, both the receiving and transmitting routers must have the same MD5 key. Define an MD5 key for each interface. If MD5 is enabled on an interface, that interface accepts routing updates only if MD5 authentication succeeded; otherwise, updates are rejected. The key ID for MD5 authentication is hard-coded to 1. If you use equipment from other vendors, you must configure the key ID for that equipment to 1 to interoperate with the access path.

To enable authentication and specify an authentication method, include the `authentication-type` statement. *`authentication`* can be `none`, `simple`, or `md5`.

```
[edit protocols ospf area area-id]
authentication-type authentication;
```

To configure a key (password) on each interface, include the `authentication-key` statement. The key (password) can be 1 to 8 characters long. Characters can include any text strings. If you include spaces, enclose all characters in quotation marks (" "). The key identifier, which is required for MD5 authentication, specifies the identifier associated with the MD5 key. You can define multiple keys, each with a different key identifier. OSPF uses the key with the highest number.

```
[edit protocols ospf area area-id interface interface-
name]
authentication-key key key-id identifier;
```

Configuring the Priority for Becoming the Designated Router

A router advertises its priority to become a designated router in its hello packets. On all multiaccess networks, the OSPF hello protocol uses the advertised priorities to elect a designated router for the network. This router is responsible for sending network link advertisements, which describe all the routers attached to the network. These advertisements are flooded throughout a single area. At least one router on each logical IP network or subnet must be eligible to be the designated router.

A router's priority for becoming the designated router is indicated by an arbitrary number from 0 through 255, with a higher value indicating a greater likelihood of becoming the designated router. By default, routers have a priority value of 128. A value of 1 means that the router has the least chance of becoming a designated router. A value of 0 marks the router as ineligible to become the designated router. To modify the router's priority value, include the `priority` statement:

```
[edit protocols ospf area area-id interface interface-
name]
priority number;
```

Configuring Route Summarization

Area border routers send summary link advertisements to describe the routes to other areas. To minimize the number of these advertisements that are flooded, you can configure the router to coalesce, or summarize, a range of IP addresses and send reachability information about these addresses in a single link-state advertisement. To summarize a range of IP addresses, include the `area-range` statement. To summarize multiple ranges, include multiple `area-range` statements.

```
[edit protocols ospf area area-id]
area-range network/mask-length <restrict >;
```

All routes that match the specified area range are filtered at the area boundary, and the summary is advertised in their place. If you specify the `restrict` option, the routes are filtered, but no summary is advertised.

Modifying the Interface Metric

All OSPF interfaces have a cost, which is a routing metric that is used in the OSPF link-state calculation. Routes with lower total path metrics are preferred over those with higher path metrics. When several equal-cost routes to a destination exist, traffic is distributed equally among them. The cost of a route is described by a single dimensionless metric that is determined using the following formula:

```
cost = reference-bandwidth/bandwidth
```

`reference-bandwidth` is the reference bandwidth. Its default value is 100 Mbps (which you specify as 100,000,000), which gives a metric of 1 for any bandwidth that is 100 Mbps or greater.

To modify the metric for routes advertised from an interface, include the `metric` statement:

```
[edit protocols ospf area area-id interface interface-
name]
metric metric;
```

To modify the reference bandwidth, include the `reference-bandwidth` statement:

```
[edit protocols ospf]
reference-bandwidth reference-bandwidth;
```

For example, if you set the reference bandwidth to 1 Gbps (that is, *`reference-bandwidth`* is set to 1,000,000,000), a 100-Mbps interface has a default metric of 10.

By default, the loopback interface (`lo0`) metric is 0. No bandwidth is associated with the loopback interface.

Configuring Route Preferences

Route preferences are used to select which route is installed in the forwarding table when several protocols calculate routes to the same destination. The route with the lowest preference value is selected. By default, internal OSPF routes have a preference value of 10, and external OSPF routes have a value of 150. To change the preference values, include the `preference` statement (for internal routes) or the `external-preference` statement (for external routes). The preference value can range from 0 through 255.

For more information about route preferences, see Table 9.1 on page 379.

```
[edit protocols ospf]
external-preference preference;
preference preference;
```

Configuring OSPF Timers

OSPF routers constantly track the status of their neighbors, sending and receiving hello packets that indicate that the neighbor still is functioning, and sending and receiving LSA and acknowledgment packets. OSPF sends packets and expects to receive packets at specified intervals.

Routers send hello packets at a fixed interval on all interfaces, including virtual links, to establish and maintain neighbor relationships. This interval, which must be the same on all routers on a shared network, is advertised in the hello interval field in the hello packet. By default, the router sends hello packets every 10 seconds. To modify how often the router sends hello packets out of an interface, include the `hello-interval` statement:

```
[edit protocols ospf area area-id interface interface-name] or
[edit protocols ospf area area-id virtual-link]
hello-interval seconds
```

On nonbroadcast networks, the router sends hello packets every 120 seconds until active neighbors are detected by default. This interval is long enough to minimize the bandwidth required on slow WAN links. After the router detects an active neighbor, the hello packet interval changes from the time specified in the `poll-interval` statement to the time specified in the `hello-interval` statement. To modify the hello interval on nonbroadcast networks, include the `poll-interval` statement.

```
[edit protocols ospf area area-id interface interface-name]
poll-interval seconds;
```

The transmit interval specifies how often OSPF LSA packets are transmitted on an interface. This interval determines the maximum packet transmission rate on an interface, which affects network stability. Because packets are built at the instant of transmission, only the latest information is sent even if the transmission is delayed. The default transmit interval is 30 milliseconds. To modify the interval, include the `transmit-interval` statement:

```
[edit protocols ospf area area-id interface interface-
name]
transmit-interval milliseconds;
```

When a router sends LSAs to its neighbors, the router expects to receive an acknowledgment packet from the neighbor within a certain amount of time. If the router does not receive an acknowledgment, it retransmits the advertisement. By default, the router waits 5 seconds for an acknowledgment before retransmitting the LSA. To modify this interval, include the `retransmit-interval` statement:

```
[edit protocols ospf area area-id interface interface-
name] or
[edit protocols ospf area area-id virtual-link]
retransmit-interval seconds;
```

If a router does not receive a hello packet from a neighbor within a fixed amount of time, the router modifies its topological database to indicate that the neighbor is nonoperational. The time that the router waits is called the *router dead interval*. By default, this interval is 40 seconds (four times the default hello interval). To modify the router dead interval, include the `dead-interval` statement. This interval must be the same for all routers on a shared network.

```
[edit protocols ospf area area-id interface interface-
name] or
[edit protocols ospf area area-id virtual-link]
dead-interval seconds;
```

Before a link-state update packet is propagated out of an interface, the router must increase the age of the packet. If you have a very slow link (for example, one with an average propagation delay of multiple seconds), the age of the packet must be increased by a similar amount. Doing this ensures that you do not receive a packet back that is younger than the original copy. The default transit delay is 1 second. You should never have to modify the default value. However, if you need to specify the approximate transit delay to use to age update packets, include the `transit-delay` statement:

```
[edit protocols ospf area area-id interface interface-
name] or
[edit protocols ospf area area-id virtual-link]
transit-delay seconds;
```

Advertising Interface Addresses without Running OSPF

By default, OSPF must be configured on an interface for direct interface addresses to be advertised as interior routes. To advertise the direct interface addresses without actually running OSPF on that interface, include the `passive` statement:

```
[edit protocols ospf interface interface-name]
passive;
```

Point-to-point interfaces are different than multipoint in that only one OSPF adjacency is possible. (A LAN, for instance, can have multiple addresses and can run OSPF on each subnet simultaneously.) As such, when you configure a numbered point-to-point interface to OSPF by name, multiple OSPF interfaces are created. One, which is unnumbered, is the one on which the protocol is run. An additional OSPF interface is created for each address configured on the interface, if any, which is automatically marked as passive.

Enabling OSPF on an interface (by including the `interface` statement at the `[edit protocols ospf]` hierarchy level), disabling it (by including the `disable` statement), and not actually having OSPF run on an interface (by including the `passive` statement) are mutually exclusive states.

Advertising Label-Switched Paths into OSPF

You can advertise label-switched paths (LSPs) into OSPF as point-to-point links so that all participating routers can take the LSP into account when performing SPF calculations. The advertisement contains a local address (the `from` address of the label-switched path), a remote address (the `to` address of the label-switched path), and a metric with the following precedence:

1. Use the label-switched path metric defined under OSPF.
2. Use the label-switched path metric configured for the label-switched path under MPLS.

3. If you do not configure any of the above, use the default OSPF metric of 1.

To advertise label-switched paths, include the `label-switched-path` statement, with a specified `name` and `metric`:

```
[edit protocols ospf area area-id]
label-switched-path name metric metric;
```

For more information, see Chapter 11, "MPLS Applications," on page 519.

For a label-switched path that is announced into OSPF to be used in SPF calculations, a reverse link must exist (that is, a link from the egress router of the label-switched path to the ingress router). To establish a reverse link, configure a label-switched path in the reverse direction and announce it into OSPF.

Configuring the Router to Appear Overloaded

You can configure the local router so that it appears to be overloaded. You might do this when you want the router to participate in OSPF routing, but do not want it to be used for transit traffic. (Note that traffic to immediately attached interfaces continues to transit the router.) You configure or disable overload mode in OSPF with or without a timeout. Without a timeout, overload mode is set until it is explicitly deleted from the configuration. With a timeout, overload mode is set if the time elapsed since the OSPF instance started is less than the specified timeout. A timer is started for the difference between the timeout and the time elapsed since the instance started. When the timer expires, overload mode is cleared. In overload mode, the router LSA is originated with all the transit router links (except stub) set to a metric of `0xFFFF`. The stub router links are advertised with the actual cost of the interfaces corresponding to the stub. This causes the transit traffic to avoid the overloaded router and take paths around the router. However, the overloaded router's own links are still accessible.

To mark the router as overloaded, include the `overload` statement:

```
[edit protocols ospf]
overload;
```

To specify the number of seconds at which overload is reset, include the `timeout` statement. The time can range from 60 through 1,800 seconds.

```
[edit protocols ospf overload]
timeout seconds;
```

Enabling OSPF Traffic Engineering Support

When traffic engineering is enabled on the router, you can enable OSPF's traffic engineering support, which allows OSPF to generate LSAs that carry traffic engineering parameters. These parameters are used to create the traffic engineering database (TED), which is used by CSPF to compute MPLS label-switched paths (LSPs). By default, the traffic engineering support is disabled. To enable it, include the `traffic-engineering` statement:

For more information, see Chapter 11, "MPLS Applications," on page 519.

```
[edit protocols ospf]
traffic-engineering {
  no-topology;
  shortcuts;
}
```

Configuring OSPF Routing Policy

For OSPF, you can apply routing policies that affect how the routing table exports routes into OSPF. To do this, include the `export` statement at the `[edit protocols ospf]` hierarchy level:

For more information on routing policy, see Chapter 8, "Routing Policy and Firewall Filters," on page 301.

```
[edit protocols ospf]
export [ policy-names ];
```

For OSPF, you should not apply routing policies that affect how routes are imported into the routing table; doing so with a link-state protocol could easily lead to an inconsistent topology database.

Configuring OSPF Routing Table Groups

To install routes learned from OSPF routing instances into routing tables in the OSPF routing table group, include the `rib-group` statement:

```
[edit protocols ospf]
rib-group group-name;
```

Trace OSPF Protocol Traffic

To trace OSPF protocol traffic, specify OSPF-specific options by including the `traceoptions` statement:

```
[edit protocols ospf]
traceoptions {
  file name <replace> <size size> <files number> <no-
      stamp>
    <(world-readable | no-world-readable)>;
  flag flag <flag-modifier> <disable>;
}
```

You can specify the following OSPF-specific flags in the OSPF `traceoptions` statement:

For more information about tracing and global tracing options, see the JUNOS technical documentation.

- `all`—All OSPF information
- `database-description`—All database description packets
- `error`—OSPF errored packets
- `event`—OSPF state transitions
- `flooding`—Link-state flooding packets
- `general`—General events
- `hello`—Hello packets
- `lsa-ack`—Link-state acknowledgment packets
- `lsa-request`—Link-state request packets
- `lsa-update`—Link-state updates packets
- `normal`—Normal events
- `packets`—All OSPF packets
- `packet-dump`—Contents of selected packet types
- `policy`—Policy processing
- `spf`—Shortest-path-first (SPF) calculations
- `state`—State transitions
- `task`—Routing protocol task processing
- `timer`—Routing protocol timer processing

RIP

The Routing Information Protocol (RIP) is an interior gateway protocol (IGP) that uses the Bellman-Ford, or *distance-vector*, algorithm to determine the best route to a destination. RIP uses the hop count as the metric. RIP allows hosts and routers to exchange information for computing routes through an IP-based network. RIP is intended to be used as an IGP in reasonably homogeneous networks of moderate size.

The JUNOS software supports RIP Versions 1 and 2. It does not support RIP on multipoint interfaces. RIP Version 1 packets contain the minimal information necessary to route packets through a network. However, this version of RIP does not support authentication or subnetting. RIP uses UDP port 520.

RIP has the following architectural limitations:

- The longest network path cannot exceed 15 hops (assuming that each network, or hop, has a cost of 1).
- RIP depends on counting to infinity to resolve certain unusual situations. When the network consists of several hundred routers, and when a routing loop has formed, the amount of time and network bandwidth required to resolve a next hop might be great.
- RIP uses only a fixed metric to select a route. Other IGPs use additional parameters, such as measured delay, reliability, and load.

Table 9.6 lists the RIP standards supported by the JUNOS software.

Table 9.6 *RIP Standards Supported by JUNOS Software*

Standard	Title
RFC 1058	*Routing Information Protocol*
RFC 2082	*RIP-2 MD-5 Authentication*
RFC 2453	*RIP Version 2*

RIP Packets

RIP packets contain the following fields:

- Command—Indicates whether the packet is a request or response message. Request messages seek information for the router's routing table. Response messages are sent periodically and also when a request message is received. Periodic response messages are called *update messages*. Update messages contain the command and version fields and 25 destinations (by default), each of which includes the destination IP address and the metric to reach that destination.

- Version number—Version of RIP that the originating router is running.
- Address family identifier—Address family used by the originating router. The family is always IP.
- Address—IP address included in the packet.
- Metric—Value of the metric advertised for the address.
- Mask—Mask associated with the IP address (RIP Version 2 only).
- Next hop—IP address of the next-hop router (RIP Version 2 only).

Configuring RIP

To have a router exchange routes with other routers, you must configure RIP groups and neighbors. RIP routes received from routers not configured as RIP neighbors are ignored. Likewise, RIP routes are advertised only to routers configured as RIP neighbors. All other RIP configuration statements are optional. This minimum configuration defines one neighbor. Include one `neighbor` statement for each interface on which you want to receive routes. The local router imports all routes by default from this neighbor and does not advertise routes. The router can receive both Version 1 and Version 2 update messages, with 25 route entries per message.

```
[edit protocols]
rip {
  authentication-key password;
  authentication-type type;
  (check-zero | no-check-zero);
  import [ policy-names ];
  message-size number;
  metric-in metric;
  receive receive-options;
  rib-group group-name;
  send send-options;
  traceoptions {
    file name <replace> <size size> <files number> <no-
        stamp>
      <(world-readable | no-world-readable)>;
    flag flag <flag-modifier> <disable>;
  }
  group group-name {
    export [ policy-names ];
```

```
      metric-out metric
      preference number;
      neighbor interface-name {
        authentication-key password;
        authentication-type type;
        import [ policy-names ];
        message-size number;
        metric-in metric;
        receive receive-options;
        send send-options;
      }
    }
  }
  interfaces {
    interface-name {
      unit logical-unit-number {
        family inet;
      }
    }
  }
```

Defining RIP Global Properties

To define RIP global properties, which apply to all RIP neighbors, include one or more of the following statements:

```
[edit protocols rip]
authentication-key password;
authentication-type type;
(check-zero | no-check-zero);
import [ policy-names ];
message-size number;
metric-in metric;
receive receive-options;
rib-group group-name;
send send-options;
```

Defining RIP Neighbor Properties

To define neighbor-specific properties, include one or more of the following statements:

```
[edit protocols rip group group-name]
neighbor neighbor-name {
  authentication-key password;
  authentication-type type;
  (check-zero | no-check-zero);
  import [ policy-names ];
  message-size number;
  metric-in metric;
  receive receive-options;
  send send-options;
}
```

Configuring Authentication

You can configure the router to authenticate RIP route queries. By default, authentication is disabled. You can use simple authentication, which uses a text password that is included in the transmitted packet (the receiving router uses an authentication key [password] to verify the packet), or MD5 authentication, which creates an encoded checksum that is included in the transmitted packet (the receiving router uses an authentication key [password] to verify the packet's MD5 checksum).

To enable authentication and specify an authentication method and password, include the `authentication-key` and `authentication-type` statements. The password can be up to 16 contiguous characters and can include any text strings.

```
[edit protocols rip] or
[edit protocols rip group group-name]
authentication-key password;
authentication-type type;
```

Modifying the Incoming Metric

By default, RIP imports routes from the neighbors configured with the `neighbor` statement. These routes include those learned from RIP as well as those learned from other protocols. By default, routes that RIP imports from its neighbors have a metric of 1 added to the current route metric. To change the default metric to be added to incoming routes, include the `metric-in` statement. *`metric`* can be a value from 1 through 16.

```
[edit protocols rip] or
[edit protocols rip group group-name]
metric-in metric;
```

Configuring the Number of Route Entries in an Update Message

By default, RIP includes 25 route entries in each update message. To change the number of route entries in an update message, include the `message-size` statement. To ensure interoperability with routers from other vendors, do not change the default number of route entries in a RIP update message.

```
[edit protocols rip] or
[edit protocols rip group group-name]
message-size number;
```

Accepting Packets Whose Reserved Fields Are Nonzero

Some of the reserved fields in RIP Version 1 packets must be zero, while in RIP Version 2 packets most of these reserved fields can contain nonzero values. By default, RIP discards Version 1 packets that have nonzero values in the reserved fields and Version 2 packets that have nonzero values in the fields that must be zero. This default behavior implements the RIP Version 1 and Version 2 specifications. If you are receiving RIP Version 1 packets with nonzero values in the reserved fields or RIP Version 2 packets with nonzero values in the fields that must be zero, you can configure RIP to receive these packets in spite of the fact that they are being sent in violation of the specifications in RFC 1058 and RFC 2453. To receive packets whose reserved fields are nonzero, include the `no-check-zero` statement:

```
[edit protocols rip]or
[edit protocols rip group group-name]
no-check-zero;
```

Configuring Update Messages

You can configure whether the RIP update messages conform to RIP Version 1 only, to RIP Version 2 only, or to both versions. You can also disable the sending or receiving of update messages. To configure the sending and receiving of update messages, include the `receive` and `send` statements:

```
[edit protocols rip] or
[edit protocols rip group group-name]
receive receive-options;
send send-options;
```

Configuring Routing Table Groups

You can install routes learned through RIP into multiple routing tables by configuring a routing table group. RIP routes are installed into each routing table that belongs to that routing table group. To configure a routing table group for RIP routes, include the `rib-group` statement:

```
[edit protocols rip]
rib-group group-name;
```

Applying Import Policy

To filter routes being imported by the local router from its neighbors, include the `import` statement and list the names of one or more policies to be evaluated. If you specify more than one policy, they are evaluated in order (first to last) and the first matching policy is applied to the route. If no match is found, the local router does not import any routes.

For more information about routing policy, see Chapter 8, "Routing Policy and Firewall Filters," on page 301.

```
[edit protocols rip]
import [ policy-names ];
```

Configuring Group-Specific Properties

You can group together neighbors that share the same export policy and export metric defaults. You configure group-specific RIP properties by including the `group` statement. Each group must contain at least one neighbor. You should create a group for each export policy.

```
[edit protocols rip]
group group-name {
  export [ policy-names ];
  preference number;
  metric-out metric;
  neighbor neighbor-options;
}
```

For more information about routing policy, see Chapter 8, "Routing Policy and Firewall Filters," on page 301.

By default, RIP does not export routes it has learned to its neighbors. To have RIP export routes, apply one or more export policies. To apply export policies and to filter routes being exported from the local router to its neighbors, include the `export` statement and list the name of the policy to be evaluated. You can define one or more export policies. If no routes match the policies, the local router does not export any routes to its neighbors. Export policies override any metric values determined through calculations involving the `metric-in` and `metric-out` values.

For more information about preferences, see Table 9.1 on page 379.

By default, the JUNOS software assigns a preference of 100 to routes that originate from RIP. When the JUNOS software determines a route's preference to become the active route, the software selects the route with the lowest preference and installs this route into the forwarding table. To modify the default RIP preference value, include the `preference` statement. *`preference`* can be a value from 0 to 4,294,967,295 ($2^{32} - 1$).

If you have included the `export` statement, RIP exports routes it has learned to the neighbors configured with the `neighbor` statement.

If a route being exported was learned from a member of the same RIP group, the metric associated with that route (unless modified by an export policy) is the normal RIP metric. For example, a RIP route with a metric of 5 learned from a neighbor configured with a `metric-in` value of 2 is advertised with a combined metric of 7 when advertised to RIP neighbors in the same group. However, if this route was learned from a RIP neighbor in a different group or from a different protocol, the route is advertised with the metric value configured for that group with the `metric-out` statement. The default value for `metric-out` is 1. To increase the metric for routes advertised outside a group, include the `metric-out` statement.

Tracing RIP Protocol Traffic

To trace RIP protocol traffic, specify RIP-specific options by including the `traceoptions` statement:

```
[edit protocols rip]
traceoptions {
  file name <replace> <size size> <files number> <no-
      stamp>
    <(world-readable | no-world-readable)>;
  flag flag <flag-modifier> <disable>;
}
```

For more information about tracing and global tracing options, see the JUNOS technical documentation.

You can specify the following RIP-specific options in the RIP `traceoptions` statement:

- `auth`—RIP authentication
- `error`—RIP errors
- `expiration`—RIP route expiration processing
- `holddown`—RIP hold-down processing
- `packets`—All RIP packets
- `request`—RIP information packets
- `trigger`—RIP triggered updates
- `update`—RIP update packets

Multicast Protocols Overview

IP Version 4 (IPv4) has three fundamental types of addresses: unicast, broadcast, and multicast. A *unicast address* is used to send a packet to a single destination. A *broadcast address* is used to send a datagram to an entire subnetwork. A *multicast address* is used to send a datagram to a set of hosts that can be on different subnetworks and that are configured as members of a multicast group.

A multicast datagram is delivered to destination group members with the same best-effort reliability as a standard unicast IP datagram. This means that multicast datagrams are not guaranteed to reach all members of a group or to arrive in the same order in which they were transmitted. The only difference between a multicast IP packet and a unicast IP packet is the presence of a group address in the IP header destination address field. Multicast addresses use the Class D address format.

Individual hosts can join or leave a multicast group at any time. There are no restrictions on the physical location or the number of members in a multicast group. A host can be a member of more than one multicast group at any given time and does not have to belong to a group to send packets to members of a group.

Routers use a group membership protocol to learn about the presence of group members on directly attached subnetworks. When a host joins a multicast group, it transmits a group membership protocol message for the group or groups that it wants to receive and sets its IP process and network interface card to receive frames addressed to the multicast group.

The Internet multicast backbone (MBone) is an interconnected set of subnetworks and routers that support the delivery of IP multicast traffic. The MBone is a virtual network that is layered on top of sections of the physical Internet. The MBone is composed of islands of multicast routing capability that are connected to other islands by virtual point-to-point links called *tunnels*. The tunnels allow multicast traffic to pass undisturbed through the parts of the Internet that are not multicast-capable. Because the MBone and the Internet have different topologies, multicast routers execute a separate routing protocol to decide how to forward multicast packets.

Multicast host group addresses are defined to be the IP addresses whose high-order four bits are `1110`, giving an address range from `224.0.0.0` through `239.255.255.255`, or simply, `224.0.0.0/4`. (These addresses also are referred to as Class D addresses.)

The Internet Assigned Numbers Authority (IANA) maintains a list of registered IP multicast groups. The base address `224.0.0.0` is reserved and cannot be assigned to any group. The block of multicast addresses from `224.0.0.1` through `224.0.0.255` is reserved for local wire use. Groups in this range are assigned for various uses, including routing protocols and local discovery mechanisms.

The range `239.0.0.0` through `239.255.255.255` is reserved for administratively scoped addresses. Because packets addressed to administratively scoped multicast addresses do not cross configured administrative boundaries, and because administratively scoped multicast addresses are locally assigned, these addresses do not need to be unique across administrative boundaries.

PIM

Protocol-Independent Multicast (PIM) is used to efficiently route to multicast groups that might span wide-area and interdomain internetworks. It is referred to as "protocol independent" because it is not dependent on any particular unicast routing protocol. The software supports both sparse mode and dense mode. In sparse mode, routers must join and leave multicast groups explicitly. Upstream routers do not forward multicast traffic to this router unless this router has sent an explicit request (using a join message) to receive multicast traffic. When a host joins a multicast group, its first-hop router sends a join message upstream toward the rendezvous point (RP) for the group. The RP serves as the root of the shared multicast delivery tree and is responsible for forwarding multicast data from different sources toward the receivers. Multicast traffic is forwarded out a PIM interface only if the interface has received a join message from a downstream router or if group members are directly connected to the interface. Sparse-mode routers periodically send join messages toward the RP to join a shared tree and directly toward the source if they prefer to join the source tree. The routers also send periodic prune messages toward the RP when they move from the shared tree onto the source-based tree.

Table 9.7 lists the PIM standards and drafts supported by the JUNOS software.

Table 9.7 *PIM Standards Supported by JUNOS Software*

Standard	Title
RFC 2362	*Protocol Independent Multicast-Sparse Mode (PIM-SM): Protocol Specification*
IETF draft draft-ietf-pim-v2-dm-03.txt	*Protocol Independent Multicast Version 2 Dense Mode Specification*
IETF draft-ietf-mboned-anycast-rp-08.txt	*Anycast RP Mechanism Using PIM and MSDP*

PIM Packet Formats

All PIM Version 2 packets have a common 4-byte header that consists of the following fields:

- Version number—The PIM version number, which is 2
- Type—Type of PIM message
- Reserved—Set to 0 on transmission and ignored on receipt
- Checksum—Standard IP checksum

PIM uses encoded unicast addresses, which consist of the following fields:

- Address family—PIM address family
- Encoding type—Type of encoding used for the address family
- Unicast address—Unicast address represented by the address family and encoding type

Routers periodically send hello messages on all interfaces, including virtual links, to establish and maintain neighbor relationships. These messages consist of the PIM header plus the following fields:

- Option type—Type of option
- Option length—Length of the option field
- Option value—Value of the option. It can be one of the following:
    - Hold time—Amount of time a receiver must keep the neighbor reachable

- LAN prune delay—Time before pruning the propagation delay on multiaccess networks
- DR priority—Designated router election priority
- Generation ID—Interface on which hello messages are sent

Designated routers periodically send register messages to the RP or PIM multicast border router when the RP or border router needs to transmit a multicast packet. These messages consist of the PIM header plus the following fields:

- Border bit
- Null register bit
- Multicast data packet

The RP sends register-stop messages to the sender of register messages. These messages consist of the PIM header plus the following fields:

- Group address—Group address from the multicast data packet in the register
- Source address—Source address from the multicast data packet in the register

Routers send join/prune messages toward upstream sources and RPs. These messages consist of the PIM header plus the following fields:

- Unicast upstream neighbor address—Address of the RPF or upstream neighbor
- Hold time—Amount of time a receiver must keep the join/prune state alive
- Number of groups—Number of multicast group sets contained in the message
- Multicast group address
- Number of joined sources
- Join source address
- Number of pruned sources
- Prune source addresses

PIM uses assert messages to resolve forwarded conflicts between routers on a link. They are sent when a multicast data packet is received on an interface that the router would normally use to forward the packet. These messages consist of the PIM header plus the following fields:

- Group address—Group address for which the router wants to resolve the forwarding conflict
- Source address—Source address for which the router wants to resolve the forwarding conflict
- Metric preference—Preference value assigned by the unicast routing protocol that provided the route to the RP
- Metric—Route's metric from the unicast routing table

Configuring PIM

For PIM to operate on the router, you must configure it. By default, PIM operates in dense mode.

```
[edit protocols]
pim {
  disable;
  dense-groups {
    addresses;
  }
  import [ policy-name ];
  rib-group group-name;
  traceoptions {
    file name <replace> <size size> <files number> <no-
        stamp>
      <(world-readable | no-world-readable)>;
    flag flag <flag-modifier> <disable>;
  }
  interface interface-name {
    disable;
    hello-interval seconds;
    mode (dense | sparse | sparse-dense);
    priority number;
    version version;
  }
  rp {
    auto-rp (announce | discovery | mapping);
    bootstrap-import pim-import;
    bootstrap-export pim-export;
    bootstrap-priority number;
```

```
            local {
              disable;
              address address;
              group-ranges {
                destination-mask;
              }
              hold-time seconds;
              priority number;
            }
            static {
              address address {
                version version;
                group-ranges {
                  destination-mask;
                }
              }
            }
          }
        }
```

To enable PIM routing and associate it with PIM, a routing table group that imports and exports routes into the specified routing table group, include the following statements:

```
[edit protocols]
pim {
  rib-group group-name;
  interface interface-name;
}
```

You cannot configure both PIM and DVMRP on the same interface. However, you can configure PIM on the same interface if you configure DVMRP in unicast-routing mode.

Configuring Dense, Sparse, or Sparse-Dense Mode

By default, PIM interfaces operate in dense mode on all interfaces. To configure PIM to operate in sparse mode on an interface, include the `mode sparse` statement:

```
[edit protocols pim interface interface-name]
mode sparse;
```

To explicitly configure PIM to operate in dense mode on an interface, include the `mode dense` statement:

```
[edit protocols pim interface interface-name]
mode dense;
```

Sparse-dense mode is a mode in which some groups are forwarded using dense mode and some are forwarded using sparse mode. To configure PIM to operate in sparse-dense mode on an interface, include the `mode sparse-dense` statement to enable the mode and the `dense-groups` statement to specify which groups are operating in dense mode:

```
[edit protocols pim]
dense-groups {
  addresses;
}
interface interface-name {
  mode sparse-dense;
}
```

Configuring the Priority to Be Elected the Designated Router

By default, a PIM interface has the lowest likelihood of being elected to be the designated router. The default priority is 1. Configure a larger number to increase the interface's likelihood of being elected to be the designated router. To modify the likelihood, include the `priority` statement:

```
[edit protocols pim interface interface-name]
priority number;
```

Changing the PIM Version

All systems on a subnet must run the same version of PIM. By default, the JUNOS software uses PIM Version 2. To configure PIM Version 1, include the `version` statement:

```
[edit protocols pim interface interface-name]
version 1;
```

Modifying the Hello Interval

Routers send hello packets at a fixed interval on all interfaces to establish and maintain neighbor relationships. This interval is advertised in the hello interval field in the hello packet. By default, a designated intersystem (DIS) router sends hello packets every 3 seconds, and a non-DIS router sends hello packets every 9 seconds. To modify how often the router sends hello packets out of an interface, include the `hello-interval` statement:

```
[edit protocols pim interface interface-name]
hello-interval seconds;
```

Modifying the PIM Hold-Time Period

The PIM hold-time period is when the rendezvous point is considered to be down. The default hold-time period is 35 seconds. To modify the hold-time value for a rendezvous point, include the `hold-time` statement. The hold-time range is 1 to 255 seconds.

```
[edit protocols pim rp local]
hold-time seconds;
```

Configuring the Router's Properties for Becoming a Candidate RP

Each multicast group has a shared tree through which receivers learn about new multicast sources and new receivers learn about all multicast sources. The rendezvous point (RP) is the root of this shared tree. To configure this router's properties for becoming a candidate RP, include the `rp` statement:

```
[edit protocols pim]
rp {
  auto-rp (announce | discovery | mapping);
  bootstrap-import pim-import;
  bootstrap-export pim-export;
  bootstrap-priority number;
  local {
    disable;
    address address;
    group-ranges {
      destination-mask;
    }
    hold-time seconds;
    priority number;
  }
  static {
    address address {
      version version;
      group-ranges {
        destination-mask;
      }
    }
  }
}
```

To determine which router is the RP, all routers within a PIM domain collect bootstrap messages. (A PIM domain is a contiguous set of routers that all implement PIM and are configured to operate within a common boundary.) The domain's bootstrap router originates bootstrap messages, and these messages are sent hop by hop within the domain. The routers use bootstrap messages to distribute RP information dynamically and to elect a bootstrap router when necessary. By default, the router has a bootstrap priority of 0, which means the router can never be the bootstrap router. To modify this priority, include the `bootstrap-priority` statement. The router with the highest priority value is elected to be the bootstrap router. In the case of a tie, the router with the highest IP address is elected to be the bootstrap router.

The global multicast address space can be divided into multiple administrative domains. PIM sparse mode supports this concept and is commonly deployed within administrative domains. Naturally, some control information must remain within an administrative domain, yet PIM control information (bootstrap messages) is multicast. To filter PIM bootstrap router messages at administrative boundaries, include the following statements:

```
[edit protocols pim rp]
bootstrap-import pim-import;
bootstrap-export pim-export;
```

To configure the router's RP properties, include the `local` statement.

To specify the local RP address, include the `address` statement.

The router's priority value for becoming the RP is included in the bootstrap messages that the router sends. The bootstrap router uses the priority value to try to limit the number of candidate RPs it includes in the bootstrap message for a particular group range. After the set of candidate RPs is distributed, each router determines algorithmically the RP from the candidate RP set using a well-known hash function. By default, the priority value is set to 0, which means that the bootstrap router can override the group range being advertised by the candidate RP. To modify the router's priority, include the `priority` statement. The priority can be a number in the range 0 through 255.

By default, a router running PIM is eligible to be the RP for all groups (`224.0.0.0/4`). To limit the groups for which this router can be the RP, include the `group-ranges` statement.

For candidate RPs, the hold time is used by the bootstrap router to time out RPs. If the bootstrap router does not receive a candidate RP advertisement from an RP within the hold time, it removes that router from its list of candidate RPs. The default hold time is 150 seconds. To modify the hold-time value for the local RP, include the `hold-time` statement.

To configure static RPs, include the `static` statement. The default static RP address is `224.0.0.0/4`. To configure other addresses, include one or more `address` statements. For each static RP address, you can optionally specify the PIM version and the groups for which this address can be the RP. The default PIM version is Version 1. The RP that you select for a particular group must be consistent across all routers in a multicast domain.

When PIM is operating in sparse or sparse-dense mode, you can configure how the router handles automatic RP announcement and discovery. You can configure the router to advertise that it is eligible to be the RP, to learn which systems are RPs, and to run the RP election algorithm. However, you must first configure the two multicast groups, `224.0.1.39` and `224.0.1.40`, as dense groups (the router must be running in sparse-dense mode), or configure a static RP for those two groups. To configure automatic RP features, include the `auto-rp` statement. The `announce` option configures the router to listen only for mapping packets and also to advertise itself if it is an RP. The `discovery` option configures the router to listen only for mapping packets. The `mapping` option configures the router to announce, listens for and generates mapping packets, and announces that the router is eligible to be an RP. The RP that you select for a particular group must be consistent across all routers in a multicast domain. The router joins the auto-RP groups on the configured interfaces and on the loopback interface, `lo0.0`. For auto-RP to work correctly, you must configure an IP address on the loopback interface. You can use the loopback address `127.0.0.1`.

Configuring a PIM Routing Policy

You can restrict multicast traffic from certain source addresses by creating a routing policy and then applying it to PIM. The routing policy prevents a join from making it back to a source, so that multicast traffic never flows across the internetwork.

For more information, see Chapter 8, "Routing Policy and Firewall Filters," on page 301.

To apply one or more policies to routes being imported into the routing table from PIM, include the `import` statement:

```
[edit protocols pim]
import [ policy-names ];
```

Tracing PIM Protocol Traffic

To trace PIM protocol traffic, specify PIM-specific options by including the `traceoptions` statement:

```
[edit protocols pim]
traceoptions {
  file name <replace> <size size> <files number> <no-stamp>
    <(world-readable | no-world-readable)>;
  flag flag <flag-modifier> <disable>;
}
```

For more information about tracing and global tracing options, see the JUNOS technical documentation.

You can specify the following PIM-specific options in the PIM `traceoptions` statement:

- `assert`—Assert messages
- `bootstrap`—Bootstrap messages
- `cache`—Packets in the PIM routing cache
- `graft`—Graft and graft acknowledgment messages
- `hello`—Hello packets
- `join`—Join messages
- `packets`—All PIM packets
- `prune`—Prune messages
- `register`—Register and register-stop messages
- `rp`—Candidate RP advertisements

DVMRP

The Distance Vector Multicast Routing Protocol (DVMRP) provides connectionless datagram delivery to a group of hosts across an internetwork. DVMRP is a distributed protocol that dynamically generates IP multicast delivery trees using a technique called reverse-path multicasting (RPM) to forward multicast traffic to downstream interfaces. These mechanisms allow the formation of shortest-path trees, which are used to reach all group members from each network source of multicast traffic. DVMRP is designed to be used as an IGP within a multicast domain. Because not all IP routers support native multicast routing, DVMRP includes direct support for tunneling IP multicast datagrams through routers. The IP multicast datagrams are encapsulated in unicast IP packets and addressed to the routers that do support native multicast routing. DVMRP treats tunnel interfaces and physical network interfaces the same. DVMRP routers dynamically discover their neighbors by sending neighbor probe messages periodically to an IP multicast group address that is reserved for all DVMRP routers. Table 9.8 lists the DVMRP standard supported by the JUNOS software.

Table 9.8 *DVMRP Standard Supported by JUNOS Software*

Standard	Title
IETF draft draft-ietf-idmr-dvmrp-v3-10.txt	*Distance Vector Multicast Routing Protocol*

DVMRP Packet Formats

All DVMRP packets have a common 4-byte header that consists of the following fields:

- Type—IGMP packet type, which is always 0x13
- Code—DVMRP packet type
- Checksum—Standard IP checksum
- Minor version—DVMRP minor version, which is always 0xFF
- Major version—DVMRP major version, which is always 3

When a DVMRP router is configured to run on an interface, it multicasts probe messages to inform other DVMRP routers that it is operational. These messages allow the routers to locate each other and to determine their capabilities, and they provide a keepalive function. Probe messages consist of the DVMRP header plus the following fields:

- Capabilities—Router capabilities
- Generation ID—Indication of the age of prune information
- Neighbor addresses—Addresses of neighbors as determined from prune messages

Route report messages contain routing information that is used to determine the reverse path neighbor back to the source of the multicast traffic. These messages consist of the DVMRP header plus the following fields:

- Mask—Mask value of the source network
- Source network—Source network addresses
- Metric—Metric associated with the route

When the routers at the leaves of the multicast tree begin to receive unwanted multicast traffic, they send prune messages upstream toward the source. These messages consist of the DVMRP header plus the following fields:

- Source host address—IP address of the source of the datagram that triggered the prune
- Group address—IP address of the destination group of the datagram that triggered the prune
- Prune lifetime—Number of seconds the upstream neighbor should keep the prune active
- Source network mask—Network mask of the route to which this prune applies

After a multicast delivery tree has been pruned back, DVMRP sends graft messages to join new receivers onto the multicast tree. These messages consist of the DVMRP header plus the following fields:

- Source host address—IP address of the source host or network to graft
- Group address—IP address of the destination group to graft
- Source network mask—Network mask of the route to which this graft applies

DVMRP sends graft acknowledgment packets to ensure that the information in graft messages is correct. These messages consist of the DVMRP header plus the following fields:

- Source host address—IP address of the source host received in the graft message

- Group address—IP address of the destination group received in the graft message
- Source network mask—Network mask of the route to which this graft applies

Configuring DVMRP

For DVMRP to operate on an interface, you must configure it by including the following statements:

```
[edit protocols]
dvmrp {
  disable;
  export [ policy-names ];
  import [ policy-names ];
  interface interface-name {
    disable;
    hello-interval seconds;
    metric metric;
    mode (forwarding | unicast-routing);
  }
  rib-group group-name2;
  traceoptions {
    file name <replace> <size size> <files number> <no-
      stamp> <(world-readable | no-world-readable)>;
    flag flag <flag-modifier> <disable>;
  }
}
routing-options {
  interface-routes {
    rib-group group-name1;
  }
  rib-groups {
    group-name1 {
      import-rib [ inet.0 inet.2 ];
    }
    group-name2 {
      import-rib inet.2;
      export-rib inet.2;
    }
  }
}
```

If you have configured PIM on an interface, you can configure DVMRP in unicast-routing mode only. You cannot configure PIM and DVMRP in forwarding mode at the same time.

Modifying the DVMRP Hold-Time Period

The DVMRP hold-time period is the amount of time a neighbor should consider the sending router (this router) to be operative (up). The default hold-time period is 35 seconds. To modify the hold-time value for the local router, include the `hold-time` statement. The hold-time period can range from 1 through 255 seconds.

```
[edit protocols dvmrp interface interface-name]
hold-time seconds;
```

Modifying the Metric Value

For each source network reported, a route metric is associated with the unicast route being reported. The metric is the sum of the interface metrics between the router originating the report and the source network. A metric of 32 marks the source network as unreachable, thus limiting the breadth of the DVMRP network and placing an upper bound on the DVMRP convergence time. By default, a metric value of 1 is associated with each DVMRP route. To modify the metric value, include the `metric` statement. The metric can range from 1 through 31.

```
[edit protocols dvmrp interface interface-name]
metric metric;
```

Disabling DVMRP on an Interface

To disable DVMRP on an interface, include the `disable` statement:

```
[edit protocols dvmrp interface interface-name]
disable;
```

Configuring DVMRP Routing Policy

To apply policies to routes being imported into the routing table from DVMRP, include the `import` statement, listing the names of one or more policy filters to be evaluated. If you specify more than one policy, they are evaluated in the order specified, from first to last, and the first matching policy is applied to the route. If no match is found, DVMRP shares with the routing table only those routes that were learned from DVMRP routers.

```
[edit protocols dvmrp]
import [ policy-names ];
```

For more information about routing policy, see Chapter 8, "Routing Policy and Firewall Filters," on page 301.

To apply policies to routes being exported from the routing table into DVMRP, include the `export` statement, listing the names of one or more policies to be evaluated. If you specify more than one policy, they are evaluated in the order specified, from first to last, and the first matching policy is applied to the route. If no match is found, the routing table exports into DVMRP only the routes that it learned from DVMRP and direct routes.

```
[edit protocols dvmrp]
export [ policy-names ];
```

Configuring DVMRP Routing Modes

You can configure DVMRP for either forwarding or unicast-routing modes. In forwarding mode, DVMRP operates its protocol normally (for example, it does the routing as well as multicast data forwarding). In unicast routing mode, you can use DVMRP for unicast routing only; the actual forwarding of multicast data is done by enabling PIM on that interface.

The default mode is forwarding. To configure DVMRP for unicast routing, include the `mode unicast-routing` statement:

```
[edit protocols dvmrp interface interface-name]
mode unicast-routing;
```

Tracing DVMRP Protocol Traffic

To trace DVMRP protocol traffic, specify DVMRP-specific options by including the `traceoptions` statement:

```
[edit protocols dvmrp]
traceoptions {
  file name <replace> <size size> <files number> <no-
      stamp>
    <(world-readable | no-world-readable)>;
  flag flag <flag-modifier> <disable>;
}
```

For more information about tracing and global tracing options, see the JUNOS technical documentation.

You can specify the following DVMRP-specific options in the DVMRP `traceoptions` statement:

- `all`—All DVMRP information
- `general`—General events
- `graft`—Graft messages
- `neighbor`—Neighbor probe messages
- `normal`—Normal events
- `packets`—All DVMRP packets
- `poison`—Poison-route-reverse packets

- `policy`—Policy processing
- `probe`—Probe packets
- `prune`—Prune messages
- `report`—DVMRP route report packets
- `route`—Routing information
- `state`—State transitions
- `task`—Routing protocol task processing
- `timer`—Routing protocol timer processing

IGMP

Internet Group Management Protocol (IGMP) manages the membership of hosts and routers in multicast groups. IP hosts use IGMP to report their multicast group memberships to any immediately neighboring multicast routers. Multicast routers use IGMP to learn, for each of their attached physical networks, which groups have members. IGMP is also used as the transport for several related multicast protocols (for example, DVMRP and PIM Version 1).

IGMP is an integral part of IP and must be enabled on all routers and hosts that want to receive IP multicasts.

For each attached network, a multicast router can be either a querier or a nonquerier. The querier router periodically sends general query messages to solicit group membership information. Hosts on the network that are members of a multicast group send report messages. When a host leaves a group, it sends a leave group message.

IGMP Version 3 supports inclusion lists, which provide the ability to specify which sources can send to a multicast group. This type of multicast group is called a source specific multicast (SSM), and its multicast address is `232.0.0.0/8`. Exclusion mode works in a way opposite to inclusion lists, allowing any source but the ones listed to send to the SSM group.

IGMP Version 3 supports source filtering. For example, a router can specify particular routers from which it does, or does not, receive traffic. With IGMP Version 3, a multicast router can learn which sources are of interest to neighboring routers.

IGMP Version 3 interoperates with Versions 1 and 2 of the protocol. However, to remain compatible with older IGMP hosts and routers, IGMP Version 3 routers must also implement Versions 1 and 2 of the protocol. The following membership report record types are supported for IGMP Version 3: mode is allowed, allow new sources, and block old sources. Table 9.9 lists the IGMP standards supported by the JUNOS software.

Table 9.9 *IGMP Standards Supported by JUNOS Software*

Standard	Title
RFC 1112	*Host Extensions for IP Multicasting* (defines IGMP Version 1)
RFC 2236	*Internet Group Management Protocol, Version 2*
IETF draft draft-ietf-idmr-igmp-v3-07.txt	*Internet Group Management Protocol, Version 3*

IGMP Packets

IGMP Version 3 messages are encapsulated in IPv4 datagrams, with an IP protocol number of 2.

Routers send IGMP Version 3 membership query messages to query the multicast reception state of neighboring interfaces. They contain the following fields:

- Maximum response code—Maximum time before sending a responding report
- Checksum—Standard IP checksum
- Group address—Set to zero when sending a general query and to the IP multicast address being queried when sending a group-specific or group-and-source-specific query
- Suppress router-side processing flag
- Querier's robustness variable
- Querier's query interval code
- Number of sources—Number of source addresses the query contains
- Source address—IP unicast source addresses

Routers send IGMP Version 3 membership report messages to report to neighboring routers the current multicast reception state, or changes in the multicast reception state, of their interfaces. These messages contain the following fields:

- Checksum—Standard IP checksum
- Number of group records—Number of group records the report contains
- Group record—The record itself

IGMP Version 3 also supports the following message types: IGMP Version 1 membership report messages, IGMP Version 2 membership report messages, and IGMP Version 3 leave group messages.

Configuring IGMP

IGMP is automatically enabled on all broadcast interfaces when you configure PIM or DVMRP. You can configure it explicitly by including the following statements:

```
[edit protocols]
igmp {
  interface interface-name {
    disable;
    static {
      group group {
        source source;
      }
    }
    version version;
  }
  query-interval seconds;
  query-last-member-interval seconds;
  query-response-interval seconds;
  robust-count number;
  traceoptions {
    file name <replace> <size size> <files number> <no-
        stamp>
      <(world-readable | no-world-readable)>;
    flag flag <flag-modifier> <disable>;
  }
}
```

IGMP Version 3 supports SSM groups. By default, the SSM group multicast address is limited to the IP address range `232.0.0.0` to `232.255.255.255`. To configure additional SSM groups, include the following statements:

```
[edit]
routing-options {
  multicast {
    ssm-groups {
      address;
    }
  }
}
```

Modifying the IGMP Host-Query Message Interval

The IGMP querier router periodically sends general host-query messages. These messages solicit group membership information and are sent to the all-systems multicast group address, `224.0.0.1`. By default, host-query messages are sent every 125 seconds. You might want to change this interface to tune the number of IGMP messages sent on the subnet. To modify this interval, include the `query-interval` statement. The interval can range from 1 through 1,024 seconds.

```
[edit protocols igmp]
query-interval seconds;
```

Modifying the IGMP Query Response Interval

The query response interval is the maximum amount of time that can elapse between when the querier router sends a host-query message and when it receives a response from a host. Varying this interval allows you to tune the burstiness of IGMP messages on the subnet. By default, the query response interval is 10 seconds. To modify this interval, include the `query-response-interval` statement. The interval can range from 1 through 1,024 seconds and must be less than the host-query message interval.

```
[edit protocols igmp]
query-response-interval seconds;
```

Modifying the Last-Member Query Interval

The last-member query interval is the maximum amount of time between group-specific query messages, including those sent in response to leave-group messages. You might lower this interval to reduce the amount of time it takes a router to detect the loss of the last member of a group. The default last-member query interval is 1 second. To modify this interval, include the `query-last-member-interval` statement. The interval can range from 1 through 1,024 seconds.

```
[edit protocols igmp]
query-last-member-interval seconds;
```

Modifying the Robustness Variable

The IGMP robustness variable provides fine-tuning to allow for expected packet loss on a subnet. The value of the robustness variable is used in calculating the following IGMP message intervals:

- Group member interval—Amount of time that must pass before a multicast router decides there are no more members of a group on a network. This interval is calculated as follows: `(robustness variable x query interval) + (1 x query response interval)`.
- Other querier present interval—Amount of time that must pass before a multicast router decides that there is no longer another multicast router that is the querier. This interval is calculated as follows: `(robustness variable x query interval) + (0.5 x query response interval)`.
- Last member query count—Number of group-specific queries sent before the router assumes the group has no local members. The default number is the value of the robustness variable.

By default, the robustness variable is set to 2. You might want to increase this value if you expect a subnet to be lossy. To change the value of the robustness variable, include the `robust-count` statement. The number can range from 2 through 10.

```
[edit protocols igmp]
robust-count number;
```

Changing the IGMP Version

By default, the JUNOS software runs IGMP Version 2. To change to Version 3, include the `version` statement:

```
[edit protocols igmp interface interface-name]
version 3;
```

When routers are running different versions of IGMP, they negotiate the lowest common version of IGMP that is supported by hosts on their subnet and operate in that version.

If you already configured the router to use IGMP Version 1 and then configure it to use IGMP Version 2, the router continues to use Version 1 from one to six minutes, then switches to Version 2.

Enabling IGMP Static Group Membership

You can create IGMP static group membership to test multicast forwarding without a receiver host. When you enable IGMP static group membership, data is forwarded to an interface without receiving membership reports from host members. To configure IGMP static membership, include the `static` statement. Then specify the group, or the group and its sources. Specify a unique address for each group.

```
[edit protocols igmp interface interface-name]
static {
  group group {
    source source;
  }
}
```

Disabling IGMP

To disable IGMP on an interface, include the `disable` statement:

```
[edit protocols igmp interface interface-name]
disable;
```

Tracing IGMP Protocol Traffic

To trace IGMP protocol traffic, specify IGMP-specific options by including the `traceoptions` statement:

```
[edit protocols igmp]
traceoptions {
  file name <replace> <size size> <files number> <no-
      stamp>
    <(world-readable | no-world-readable)>;
  flag flag <flag-modifier> <disable>;
}
```

You can specify the following IGMP-specific options in the IGMP `flag` statement:

For more information about tracing and global tracing options, see the JUNOS technical documentation.

- `leave`—Leave-group messages (for IGMP Version 2 only)
- `mtrace`—mtrace packets
- `packets`—All IGMP packets
- `query`—IGMP membership query messages, including general and group-specific queries
- `report`—Membership report messages

To trace the paths of multicast packets, use the `mtrace` command.

SAP and SDP

Session announcements are handled by two protocols, Session Announcement Protocol (SAP) and Session Description Protocol (SDP). These two protocols display multicast session names and correlate the names with multicast traffic. SDP is a session directory protocol that is used for multimedia sessions. As such, it assists in advertising multimedia conference sessions and in communicating setup information to participants who want to join the session. SDP simply formats the session description; it does not incorporate a transport protocol. SDP is commonly used by a client to announce a conference session by periodically multicasting an announcement packet to a well-known multicast address and port using SAP. SAP is a session directory announcement protocol that is used by SDP as its transport protocol. Table 9.10 lists the SAP and SDP standards supported by the JUNOS software.

Table 9.10 *SAP and SDP Standards Supported by JUNOS Software*

Standard	Title
RFC 2327	*SDP: Session Description Protocol*
RFC 2974	*Session Announcement Protocol*

SAP and SDP Packets

SAP data packets are UDP packets that consist of a SAP header and a text payload. The packets contain the following fields:

- Version number—SAP version number, which is 1
- Address type—Indicates whether the originating source field contains a 32-bit IPv4 address or a 128-bit IPv6 address
- Message type—Indicates whether the packet is a session announcement or a session deletion packet
- Encryption bit—Indicates whether the payload is encrypted
- Compressed bit—Indicates whether the payload is compressed using the zlib compression algorithm
- Authentication length—Length of authentication data in the packet
- Authentication data—Authentication data including a digital signature of the packet
- Message identifier hash—Used in combination with the originating source to provide a globally unique identifier indicating the precise version of this announcement
- Originating source—IP address of the message's original source
- Payload type field—Type of data in the packet
- Payload—Packet data

Configuring SAP and SDP

You must explicitly enable SDP and SAP to enable the receipt of session announcements. By default, SAP always listens to the address and port `224.2.127.254:9875` for session advertisements. To add other addresses and ports, specify other address and port numbers. Sessions learned by SDP time out after 60 minutes.

```
[edit protocols]
sap {
  disable;
  listen <address> <port port>;
}
```

MSDP

Multicast Source Discovery Protocol (MSDP) is used to interconnect multicast routing domains. It is typically run on the same router as the PIM sparse-mode rendezvous point (RP). Each MSDP router establishes adjacencies with internal and external MSDP peers similar to BGP. These peer routers inform each other about active sources within the domain. When they detect active sources, the routers can send PIM sparse-mode explicit join messages to the active source. The peer with the higher IP address passively listens to a well-known port number and waits for the side with the lower IP address to establish a TCP connection. When a PIM sparse-mode RP that is running MSDP becomes aware of a new local source, it sends source-active TLVs to its MSDP peers. When a source-active TLV is received, a check is done to make sure that this peer is toward the originating RP. If not, the source-active TLV is dropped. The MSDP peers that receive source-active TLVs can be constrained by BGP reachability information. If the AS path of the network layer reachability information (NLRI) contains the receiving peer's AS number prepended second to last, the sending peer is using the receiving peer as a next hop for this source. If the split-horizon information is not being received, the peer can be pruned from the source-active TLV distribution list. Table 9.11 lists the MSDP standards supported by the JUNOS software.

Table 9.11 *MSDP Standards Supported by JUNOS Software*

Standard	Title
Internet draft draft-ietf-msdp-spec-13.txt	*Multicast Source Discovery Protocol (MSDP)*
Internet draft draft-ietf-msdp-mib-06.txt	*Multicast Source Discovery Protocol MIB*
Internet draft draft-ietf-mboned-anycast-rp-05.txt	*Anycast RP Mechanism using PIM and MSDP*

MSDP Packets

MSDP messages are encoded in a type-length-value (TLV) format that contains the following fields:

- Type—Format of the value field
- Length—Length of the complete TLV message
- Value—Actual information in the TLV message

When an RP in a PIM-SM domain first learns of a new sender, for example, by way of PIM register messages, it constructs a source-active message and sends it to its MSDP peers. Each MSDP peer forwards the message away from the RP address, thereby announcing the new sender to all its peers. In the MSDP TLV, the value field in the source-active message consists of the following fields:

- Entry count—Number of peer entries in this TLV
- RP address—Address of the RP in the domain in which the source has become active
- Sprefix length—Route prefix length associated with source address
- Group address—Group address to which the active source has sent data
- Source address—IP address of the active source

Source-active request messages are used to request source-active state from an MSDP peer. If an RP in a domain receives a PIM join message for a group, it can send a source-active request message for the group to learn all its active source. In the MSDP TLV, the value field in the source-active request message consists of the group address field, which is the group address the MSDP peer is requesting.

Source-active response messages are sent in response to source-active request messages. They have the same format as the source-active message.

A keepalive message is sent to an MSDP peer if no MSDP messages have been sent to the peer within the specified keepalive period. These messages are necessary to keep the MSDP connection operation. Keepalive messages consist of only the type and length fields.

A notification message is sent when an MSDP peer detects an error condition. In the MSDP TLV, the value field consists of the following fields:

- Open bit—Indicates whether to close the MSDP connection
- Error code—Type of error notification
- Error subcode—Additional information about the error
- Data—The error message or messages

Configuring MSDP

For MSDP to operate on an interface, configure it by including the following statements:

```
[edit protocols ]
msdp {
  disable;
  export [ policy-names ];
  import [ policy-names ];
  local-address address;
  rib-group group-name;
  traceoptions {
    file name <replace> <size size> <files number> <no-
        stamp>
      <(world-readable | no-world-readable)>;
    flag flag <flag-modifier> <disable>;
  }
  peer address {
    disable;
    export [ policy-names ];
    import [ policy-names ];
    local-address address;
    traceoptions {
      file name <replace> <size size> <files number> <no-
        stamp>
        <(world-readable | no-world-readable)>;
      flag flag <flag-modifier> <disable>;
    }
  }
  group group-name {
    disable;
    export [ policy-names ];
    import [ policy-names ];
    local-address address;
    mode <(mesh-group | standard)>;
    traceoptions {
      file name <replace> <size size> <files number> <no-
        stamp>
        <(world-readable | no-world-readable)>;
      flag flag <flag-modifier> <disable>;
    }
    peer address {
      disable;
      export [ policy-names ];
```

```
          import [ policy-names ];
          local-address address;
          traceoptions {
            file name <replace> <size size> <files number> <no-
                stamp>
              <(world-readable | no-world-readable)>;
            flag flag <flag-modifier> <disable>;
          }
        }
      }
    }
```

Configuring MSDP Peers

An MSDP router must know which routers are its peers. You define the peer relationships explicitly by configuring the neighboring routers that are the MSDP peers of the local router. After peer relationships are established, the MSDP peers exchange messages to advertise active multicast sources. You must configure at least one peer for MSDP to function. To configure MSDP peers, include the `peer` statement:

```
[edit msdp] or
[edit msdp group group-name]
peer address {
  export [ policy-names ];
  import [ policy-names ];
  local-address address;
  traceoptions {
    file name <replace> <size size> <files number> <no-
        stamp>
      <(world-readable | no-world-readable)>;
    flag flag <flag-modifier> <disable>;
  }
}
```

Configuring MSDP Groups

An MSDP router must know which routers are its peers (neighbors). You define the peer relationships explicitly by configuring the neighboring routers that are the MSDP peers of the local router. After peer relationships are established, the MSDP peers exchange messages to advertise active multicast sources. You can arrange peers into different groups. Each group must contain at least one peer. Arranging peers into groups is useful if you want to block sources from some peers and accept them from others, or set tracing options on one group and not others. To configure MSDP groups, include one or more of the following statements:

```
[edit protocols msdp]
group group-name {
  disable;
  export [ policy-names ];
  import [ policy-names ];
  local-address address;
  mode <(mesh-group | standard)>;
  traceoptions {
    file name <replace> <size size> <files number> <no-
        stamp>
      <(world-readable | no-world-readable)>;
    traceflag flag <flag-modifier> <disable>;
  }
  peer address; {
    disable;
    export [ policy-names ];
    import [ policy-names ];
    local-address address;
    traceoptions {
      file name <replace> <size size> <files number> <no-
          stamp>
        <(world-readable | no-world-readable)>;
      flag flag <flag-modifier> <disable>;
  }
}
```

Configuring MSDP Mesh Groups

MSDP mesh groups are groups of peers configured in a full-mesh topology that limit the flooding of source-active messages to neighboring peers. Every mesh group member must have a peer connection with every other mesh group member. When a source-active message is received from a mesh group member, the source-active message is always accepted but is not flooded to other members of the same mesh group. However, the source-active message is flooded to non-mesh group peers or members of other mesh groups. By default, standard flooding rules apply if `mesh-group` is not specified. To configure an MSDP mesh group, define a peer group and set the `mode` to `mesh-group`:

```
[edit protocols msdp]
group group-name {
  mode mesh-group;
  local-address address;
  peer address;
}
```

When configuring MSDP mesh groups, you must configure all members the same. If you do not configure a full mesh, excessive flooding of source-active messages can occur.

Figure 9.3 illustrates source-active message flooding between different mesh groups and peers within the same mesh group. Table 9.12 explains how flooding is handled by peers in this configuration.

Figure 9.3 *Source-Active Message Flooding*

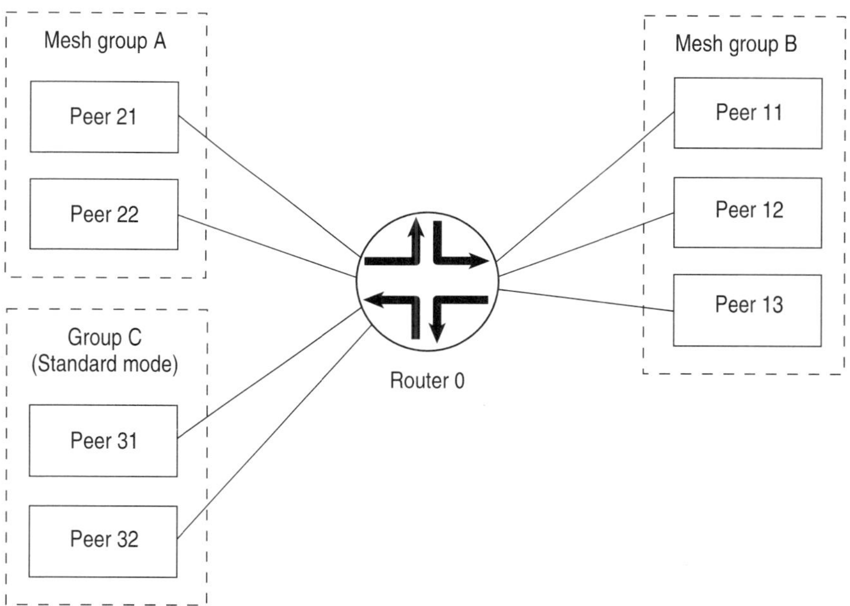

Table 9.12 *Source-Active Message Flooding Explanation*

Source-Active Message Received from	Source-Active Message Flooded to	Source-Active Message not Flooded to
Peer 21	Peer 11, Peer 12, Peer 13, Peer 31, Peer 32	Peer 22
Peer 11	Peer 21, Peer 22, Peer 31, Peer 32	Peer 12, Peer 13
Peer 31	Peer 21, Peer 22, Peer 11, Peer 12, Peer 13, Peer 32	

Configuring MSDP Routing Policy

You can configure routing policy globally for all MSDP peers (at the `[edit protocols msdp]` hierarchy level), for all peers in a group (at the `[edit protocols msdp group *group-name*]` level), or for an individual peer (at the `[edit protocols msdp peer *address*]` or the `[edit protocols msdp group *group-name* peer *address*]` level). If you configure routing policy at the group level, each individual peer in a group inherits the group's routing policy.

To apply policies to routes being imported into the routing table from MSDP, include the `import` statement, listing the names of one or more policy filters to be evaluated. If you specify more than one policy, they are evaluated in the order specified, from first to last, and the first matching policy is applied to the route. If no match is found, MSDP shares with the routing table only those routes that were learned from MSDP routers.

```
import [ policy-names ];
```

For more information about routing policy, see Chapter 8, "Routing Policy and Firewall Filters," on page 301.

To apply policies to routes being exported from the routing table into MSDP, include the `export` statement, listing the names of one or more policies to be evaluated. If you specify more than one policy, they are evaluated in the order specified, from first to last, and the first matching policy is applied to the route. If no match is found, the routing table exports into MSDP only the routes that it learned from MSDP and direct routes.

```
export [ policy-names ];
```

Configuring Multiple Rendezvous Points in a Domain

You can configure multiple rendezvous points (RPs) in a shared-tree PIM sparse-mode domain. You need to configure an MSDP local address to enable the RPs in the domain to maintain a consistent view of the active sources.

To configure a router to act as an RP in a domain with other RPs, do the following for each router in the domain that will act as an RP:

- Create the router ID by configuring a unique IP address on the loopback interface and setting the preferred address flag.
- Configure a nonunique unicast address on the loopback interface.
- Use the nonunique unicast address to configure the PIM to be the local rendezvous point.
- Configure MSDP with the unique address (router ID) as the local address of the peer.

Disabling MSDP

To disable MSDP on the router, include the `disable` statement:

```
[edit msdp] or
[edit msdp group group-name]
disable;
```

Tracing MSDP Protocol Traffic

To trace MSDP protocol traffic, specify MSDP-specific options by including the `traceoptions` statement:

```
traceoptions {
  file name <replace> <size size> <files number> <no-
      stamp>
    <(world-readable | no-world-readable)>;
  flag flag <flag-modifier> <disable>;
}
```

For more information about tracing and global tracing options, see the JUNOS technical documentation.

You can specify the following MSDP-specific options in the `flag` statement:

- `keepalive`—Keepalive messages
- `packets`—All MSDP packets
- `route`—MSDP changes to the routing table
- `sa`—Source-active packets
- `sa-request`—Source-active request packets
- `sa-response`—Source-active response packets

Multicast Scoping

Multicast scoping is a technique that can be used to limit multicast traffic by configuring it to an administratively defined topological region. Major objectives of scoping are to relieve stress on scarce resources, such as bandwidth, and to improve privacy or scaling properties. IP multicast implementations can achieve some level of scoping by using the time-to-live (TTL) field in the IP header. However, TTL scoping has proven difficult to implement reliably, and the resulting schemes often are complex and difficult to understand.

Administratively scoped IP multicast provides clearer and simpler semantics for multicast scoping. The key properties of administratively scoped IP multicast are that packets addressed to administratively scoped multicast addresses do not cross configured administrative boundaries, and administratively scoped multicast addresses are locally assigned, and hence are not required to be unique across administrative boundaries. The administratively scoped IPv4 multicast address space is the range `239.0.0.0` through `239.255.255.255`. The structure of the IPv4 administratively scoped multicast space is based loosely on the IPv6 addressing architecture as described in RFC 1884.

There are two well-known scopes:

- IPv4 local scope—This scope comprises addresses in the range `239.255.0.0/16`. The local scope is the minimal enclosing scope, and hence is not further divisible. Although the exact extent of a local scope is site-dependent, locally scoped regions must not span any other scope boundary and must be contained completely within or be equal to any larger scope. If scope regions overlap in an area, the area of overlap must be within the local scope.
- IPv4 organization local scope—This scope comprises `239.192.0.0/14`. It is the space from which an organization should allocate subranges when defining scopes for private use.

The ranges `239.0.0.0/10`, `239.64.0.0/10`, and `239.128.0.0/10` are unassigned and available for expansion of this space. Two other scope classes already exist in IPv4 multicast space: the statically assigned link-local scope, which is `224.0.0.0/24`, and the static global scope allocations, which contain various addresses.

Table 9.13 lists the multicast scoping standard supported by the JUNOS software.

Table 9.13 *Multicast Scoping Standard Supported by JUNOS Software*

Standard	Title
RFC 2365	*Administratively Scoped IP Multicast*

Configuring Multicast Scoping

To configure multicast scoping, include the following statements:

```
[edit]
routing-options {
  multicast {
    scope scope-name {
      interface interface-name;
      prefix prefix-range;
    }
  }
}
```

CHAPTER

10

IPv6

Internet Protocol Version 6 (IPv6) is the new version of the Internet Protocol (IP). The Internet Protocol allows numerous nodes on different networks to interoperate seamlessly. Internet Protocol Version 4 (IPv4) is currently used in intranets and private networks, as well as the Internet. IPv6 is the successor to IPv4 and is based for the most part on IPv4. IPv6 builds on the functionality of IPv4, providing improvements to addressing, configuration and maintenance, and security. IPv6 offers the following benefits:

- Expanded addressing capabilities—IPv6 provides a larger address space. IPv4 addresses consist of 32 bits, while IPv6 addresses consist of 128 bits, thus increasing the address space by approximately 10^{29} unique addresses.
- Header format simplification—IPv6 packet header format designed to be efficient. IPv6 standardizes the size of the packet header to 40 bytes, divided into 8 fields.
- Improved support for extensions and options—Extension headers carry Internet-layer information and have a standard size and structure.
- Flow labeling capability—Flow labels provide consistent handling of packets belonging to the same flow.
- Improved privacy and security—IPv6 supports extensions for authentication and data integrity, which enhances privacy and security.

Table 10.1 lists the IPv6 standards and protocol extensions supported by the JUNOS software.

Table 10.1 *IPv6 Standards Supported by JUNOS Software*

Standard	Title
RFC 2460	*Internet Protocol, Version 6 (IPv6)*
RFC 2464	*Transmission of IPv6 Packets over Ethernet Networks*
RFC 2373	*IP Version 6 Addressing Architecture*
RFC 2472	*IP Version 6 over PPP*
RFC 2461	*Neighbor Discovery for IP Version 6 (IPv6)*
RFC 1157	*A Simple Network Management Protocol (SNMP)*
RFC 1213	*Management Information Base for Network Management of TCP/IP-Based Internets: MIB-II*

Table 10.1 *IPv6 Standards Supported by JUNOS Software*

Standard	Title
RFC 1215	*A Convention for Defining Traps for Use with SNMP*
RFC 1195	*Use of OSI IS-IS for Routing in TCP/IP and Dual Environments*
RFC 1771	*A Border Gateway Protocol 4 (BGP-4)*
RFC 1772	*Application of the Border Gateway Protocol in the Internet*
RFC 1901	*Introduction to Community-based SNMPv2*
RFC 1902	*Structure of Management Information for Version 2 of the Simple Network Management Protocol (SNMPv2)*
RFC 1905	*Protocol Operations for Version 2 of the Simple Network Management Protocol (SNMPv2)*
RFC 1965	*Autonomous System Confederations for BGP*
RFC 1966	*BGP Route Reflection: An Alternative to Full-Mesh IBGP*
RFC 1997	*BGP Communities Attribute*
RFC 2080	*RIPng for IPv6*
RFC 2081	*RIPng Protocol Applicability Statement*
RFC 2270	*Using a Dedicated AS for Sites Homed to a Single Provider*
RFC 2283	*Multiprotocol Extensions for BGP-4*
RFC 2385	*Protection of BGP Sessions via the TCP MD5 Signature Option*
RFC 2439	*BGP Route Flap Damping*
RFC 2545	*Use of BGP-4 Multiprotocol Extensions for IPv6 Interdomain Routing*
RFC 2578	*Structure of Management Information Version 2 (SMIv2)*
RFC 2763	*Dynamic Hostname Exchange Mechanism for IS-IS*
RFC 2893	*Transition Mechanisms for IPv6 Hosts and Routers*
Internet Draft draft-ietf-isis-ipv6-02.txt	*Routing IPv6 with IS-IS*
Internet Draft draft-ietf-idr-cap-neg-01.txt	*Capabilities Negotiation with BGP4*
Internet Draft draft-ramachandra-bgp-ext-communities-09.txt	*BGP Extended Communities Attribute*
ISO/IEC 10589	*Information technology, Telecommunications and information exchange between systems, Intermediate system to intermediate system intradomain routing information exchange protocol for use in conjunction with the protocol for providing the connectionless-mode network service (ISO 8473)*

IPv6 Packet Headers and Addressing

IPv6 packet headers contain many of the fields found in IPv4 packet headers; some of these fields have been modified from IPv4. The 40-byte IPv6 header fields are described in Table 10.2.

Table 10.2 *IPv6 Packet Header Fields*

Field	Description
Traffic class	Class-of-service (CoS) priority of the packet. Previously the type-of-service (ToS) field in IPv4. However, the semantics of this field (for example, DiffServ code points) are identical to IPv4.
Destination address	Final destination node address for the packet.
Flow label	Packet flows requiring a specific CoS. The flow label identifies all packets belonging to a specific flow, and routers can identify these packets and handle them in a similar fashion.
Hop limit	Maximum number of hops allowed. Same as the IPv4 time-to-live (TTL) field.
Next header	Next extension header to examine. Same as the IPv4 protocol field.
Payload length	Length of the IPv6 payload. Same as the IPv4 total length field.
Source address	Address of the source node sending the packet.
Version	Version of the Internet Protocol.

Extension headers are used to encode optional Internet-layer information. They are placed between the IPv6 header and the upper layer header in a packet. Extension headers are chained together using the next header field in the IPv6 header. The next header field indicates to the router which extension header to expect next. If there are no more extension headers, the next header field indicates the upper layer header (TCP header, UDP header, ICMPv6 header, an encapsulated IP packet, or other items).

IPv6 introduces a new 128-bit addressing model. This creates a much larger address space than IPv4 addresses, which are made up of 32 bits. IPv6 addresses also contain a scope field that categorizes what types of applications are suitable for the address.

IPv6 addresses consist of eight groups of 16-bit hexadecimal values separated by colons (:). The IPv6 address format is as follows:

```
aaaa:aaaa:aaaa:aaaa:aaaa:aaaa:aaaa:aaaa
```

aaaa is a 16-bit hexadecimal value, and *a* is a 4-bit hexadecimal value. Following is an example of an actual IPv6 address:

```
3FFE:0000:0000:0001:0200:F8FF:FE75:50DF
```

Leading zeros can be omitted, as shown:

```
3FFE:0:0:1:200:F8FF:FE75:50DF
```

Sixteen-bit groups of zeros can be compressed to "::", as shown here, but only once per address:

```
3FFE::1:200:F8FF:FE75:50DF
```

There are three types of IPv6 addresses:

- Unicast—For a single interface.
- Multicast—For a set of interfaces on the same physical medium. A packet is sent to all the interfaces associated with the address. IPv6 uses multicast addresses to serve the role of IPv4 broadcast addresses.
- Anycast—For a set of interfaces on different physical medium. A packet is sent to only one of the interfaces associated with this address, not to all the interfaces. There is no equivalent IPv4 address type.

IPv6 addresses have *scope*, which identifies the application suitable for the address. Unicast and multicast addresses support scoping. Unicast addresses support two types of scope: *global* scope and *local* scope. There are two types of local scope: *link-local* addresses and *site-local* addresses. Link-local unicast addresses are used within a single network link. The first 10 bits of the prefix identifies the address as a link-local address. Link-local addresses cannot be used outside a network link. Site-local unicast addresses are used within a site or intranet. A site consists of multiple network links, and site-local addresses identify nodes inside the intranet. Site-local addresses cannot be used outside the site. Multicast addresses support 16 different types of scope, including node, link, site, organization, and global scope. A 4-bit field in the prefix identifies the scope.

Unicast addresses identify a single interface. The address consists of *n* bits for the prefix, and 128–*n* bits for the interface ID.

Multicast addresses identify a set of interfaces. The address consists of the first 8 bits of all ones, a 4-bit flags field, a 4-bit scope field, and 112-bit group ID. The first octet of ones identifies the address as a multicast address. The flags field identifies whether the multicast address is a well-known address or whether it is a transient multicast address. The scope field identifies the scope of the multicast address. The 112-bit group ID identifies the multicast group.

Similar to multicast addresses, anycast addresses identify a set of interfaces. However, packets are sent to only one of the interfaces, not all interfaces. Anycast addresses are allocated from the normal unicast address space and cannot be distinguished from a unicast address in format. Therefore, each member of an anycast group must be configured to recognize certain addresses as anycast addresses.

Configuring IPv6

In general, you configure IPv6 on a Juniper Networks router the same way you configure IPv4. This section highlights the differences between IPv6 and IPv4 configuration and discusses IPv6-specific configuration.

Configuring Interfaces

For the interfaces on a router to support IPv6, you must configure them, specifying properties such as the interface location (that is, in which slot the FPC is installed and in which location on the FPC the PIC is installed), the interface type (such as SONET or ATM), encapsulation, interface-specific properties, and an IPv6 address. For IPv6, you must use IPv6 addresses and specify the `inet6` family in the interface configuration. Also, IPv6 interfaces support autogeneration of link-local addresses.

For the interface to support IPv6, you must configure the interface family type of `inet6`. To configure the logical interface's protocol family, include the `family` statement, specifying the `inet6` option. In the `address` statement, specify an 128-bit IPv6 address for the interface.

```
[edit interfaces interface-name unit logical-unit-number]
family inet6 {
  mtu size;
  address address {
    destination address;
    eui-64;
    primary;
    preferred;
  }
}
```

The router generates a link-local address for each interface that has `family inet6` configured on it. This address contains a 64-bit interface identifier. If you are configuring a non-link-local address on an interface, you can incorporate this interface identifier into the final address. To use the interface identifier in the address, include the `eui-64` statement. The configured IPv6 address must be 64 bits or fewer.

```
[edit interfaces interface-name unit logical-unit-number
family inet6 address address]
eui64;
```

Configuring Firewall Filters

Configuring firewall filters for IPv6 addresses is similar to configuring them for IPv4 addresses. To configure firewall filters for IPv6 addresses, include statements at the `[edit firewall family inet6]` hierarchy level.

See Chapter 8, "Routing Policy and Firewall Filters," on page 301.

When you specify the match condition, you define the fields that the IPv6 packet must match. These fields include the IPv6 source and destination address fields. You can also filter on the following IPv6-specific match conditions: next header field and traffic class. The JUNOS software does not filter on IPv6 extension headers.

Configuring Routing Policy

To configure a routing policy, see Chapter 8, "Routing Policy and Firewall Filters," on page 301.

You configure IPv6 routing policies the same way you configure IPv4 routing policies. In the `route-filter` statement, you can specify an IPv6 prefix or an IPv4 prefix. The JUNOS software automatically creates a route filter of the correct type. In the `route-filter` statement, you can specify a 128-bit IPv6 prefix or an IPv4 prefix. The router interprets the prefix and creates an IPv6 or IPv4 route filter, as appropriate. All the `route-filter` statements within a policy term must be of the same address family. You cannot specify both IPv6 and IPv4 prefixes within the same policy term.

Creating IPv6 Routing Tables

The JUNOS software can maintain one or more routing tables, allowing the software to store route information learned from different protocols separately. For example, it is common for the routing software to maintain unicast routes and multicast routes in different routing tables. You also might have policy considerations that would lead you to create separate routing tables to manage the propagation of routing information. The JUNOS software uses the default IPv6 routing table, which is `inet6.0` for unicast routes.

For more information about routing tables, see "Creating Routing Tables," on page 380.

To configure an IPv6 routing table, include the `rib` statement, specifying the name of an IPv6 routing table. The protocol family must be `inet6` for the IPv6 address family. The number represents the instance of the routing table. For example, the primary instance is 0.

```
[edit routing-options]
rib inet6.0 {
  martians {
    destination-prefix match-type <allow>;
  }
  static {
    defaults {
      static-options;
    }
    rib-group group-name;
    route destination-prefix {
      next-hop;
      qualified-next-hop address {
```

```
                metric metric;
                preference preference;
            }
            static-options;
        }
    }
}
```

Configuring IPv6 Routing Protocols

For IPv6, the JUNOS software supports the following routing protocols: IS-IS, BGP, RIPng, and Neighbor Discovery. The IS-IS for IPv6 and IPv4 are identical. There are minor differences in how to configure BGP for IPv6 and IPv4, which are discussed in this section. RIPng is the IPv6 version of RIP, and Neighbor Discovery replaces the router discovery (RDISC), address resolution protocol (ARP), and ICMPv4 redirect IPv4 protocols.

Configuring BGP for IPv6

For IPv6, there are minor differences in how to configure BGP. For BGP to run on an IPv6 router, you must define the local AS number, configure at least one group, and include information about at least one IPv6 peer in the group. For the peer, specify its IPv6 address and AS number.

For information about configuring BGP, see "Configuring BGP," on page 398.

Each router running BGP must have a BGP identifier. This identifier is included in the BGP identifier field of open messages, which are sent between two BGP peers when establishing a BGP session. Explicitly assigning a BGP identifier is optional. If you do not assign one, the IPv4 address of the first interface encountered in the router is used.

You can export both IPv6 and IPv4 prefixes over an IPv4 connection where both sides are configured with an IPv4 interface. For this case, the BGP neighbors are IPv4 prefixes. The IPv4-compatible IPv6 prefixes are configured on the interfaces to preclude configuring static routes on them. Keep the following in mind when exporting IPv6 BGP prefixes:

- BGP derives next-hop prefixes using the IPv4-compatible IPv6 prefix. For example, the IPv4 next-hop prefix `10.19.1.1` translates to the IPv6 next-hop prefix `::10.19.1.1` (hexadecimal format `::a13:101`). There must be an active route to the IPv4-compatible IPv6 next hop to export IPv6 BGP prefixes.

- An IPv6 connection must be configured over the link, either an IPv6 tunnel or a dual-stack configuration.
- When configuring IPv4-compatible IPv6 prefixes, use a mask that is longer than 96 bits.
- If you want to use normal IPv6 prefixes, configure a static route.

Configuring RIPng

The Routing Information Protocol Next-Generation (RIPng) is an interior gateway protocol (IGP) that uses a distance-vector algorithm to determine the best route to a destination, using the hop count as the metric. RIPng is a routing protocol that exchanges routing information used to compute routes and is intended for IPv6-based networks.

The JUNOS software implementation of RIPng is similar to RIP Version 2. However, RIPng does not need to implement authentication on packets, and there is no support for multiple instances or routing table groups. RIPng is a UDP-based protocol and uses UDP port 521.

RIPng has the following architectural limitations:

- The longest network path cannot exceed 15 hops (assuming that each network, or hop, has a cost of 1).
- RIPng depends on counting to infinity to resolve certain unusual situations. When the network consists of several hundred routers, and when a routing loop has formed, the amount of time and network bandwidth required to resolve a next hop might be great.
- RIPng uses only a fixed metric to select a route. Other IGPs use additional parameters, such as measured delay, reliability, and load.

Table 10.3 lists the RIPng standards supported by the JUNOS software.

Table 10.3 *RIPng Standards Supported by JUNOS Software*

Standard	Title
RFC 2080	*RIPng for IPv6*
RFC 2081	*RIPng Protocol Applicability Statement*

A RIPng packet header contains the following fields:

- Command—Indicates whether the packet is a request or response message. Request messages seek information for the router's routing table. Response messages are sent periodically or when a request message is received. Periodic response messages are called *update messages*. Update messages contain the command and version fields and a set of destinations and metrics.
- Version number—Version of RIPng that the originating router is running. This is currently set to Version 1.

The rest of the RIPng packet contains a list of routing table entries that contain the following fields:

- Destination prefix—128-bit IPv6 address prefix for the destination.
- Prefix length—Number of significant bits in the prefix.
- Metric—Value of the metric advertised for the address.
- Route tag—A route attribute that must be advertised and redistributed with the route. Primarily, the route tag distinguishes external RIPng routes from internal RIPng routes, in cases where routes must be redistributed across an EGP.

For a router to accept RIPng routes, you must configure at least one RIPng group and the associated neighbor. Routes received from routers that are not configured as neighbors are ignored. Include one `neighbor` statement for each interface on which you want to receive routes. The local router imports all routes by default from this neighbor and does not advertise routes.

```
[edit protocols]
ripng {
group group-name {
neighbor interface-name;
}
}
```

To define RIPng global properties, which apply to all RIPng neighbors, include one or more of the following statements:

```
[edit protocols ripng]
import [ policy-names ];
metric-in metric;
receive receive-options;
send send-options;
```

To define neighbor-specific properties, include one or more of the following statements:

```
[edit protocols ripng group group-name]
neighbor neighbor-name {
  import [ policy-names ];
  metric-in metric;
  receive receive-options;
  send send-options;
}
```

By default, RIPng imports routes from the neighbors configured with the `neighbor` statement. These routes include those learned from RIPng as well as those learned from other protocols. By default, routes that RIPng imports from its neighbors have a metric of 1 added to the current route metric. To modify the default metric to be added to incoming routes, include the `metric-in` statement. *`metric`* can be a value from 1 through 15. A value of 16 indicates infinity, or unreachable.

```
[edit protocols ripng] or
[edit protocols ripng group group-name]
metric-in metric;
```

By default, sending and receiving update messages is enabled. To disable the sending and receiving of update messages, include the `receive` and `send` statements, specifying the `none` option:

```
[edit protocols ripng] or
[edit protocols ripng group group-name]
receive none;
send none;
```

To filter routes being imported by the local router from its neighbors, include the `import` statement and list the names of one or more policies to be evaluated. If you specify more than one policy, they are evaluated in order (first to last), and the first matching policy is applied to the route. If no match is found, the local router does not import any routes.

```
[edit protocols ripng] or
[edit protocols ripng group group-name]
import [ policy-names ];
```

You can group together neighbors that share the same export policy and export metric defaults. You configure group-specific RIPng properties by including the `group` statement. Each group must contain at least one neighbor. Create a group for each export policy that you have.

```
[edit protocols ripng]
group group-name {
  export [ policy-names ];
  metric-out metric;
  neighbor {
    neighbor-options;
  }
  preference number;
}
```

By default, RIPng does not export routes it has learned to its neighbors. To have RIPng export routes, apply one or more export policies. To apply export policies and to filter routes being exported from the local router to its neighbors, include the `export` statement and list the name of the policy to be evaluated:

```
[edit protocols ripng group group-name] or
[edit protocols ripng group group-name neighbor neighbor-
name]
export [ policy-names ];
```

You can define one or more export policies. If no routes match the policies, the local router does not export any routes to its neighbors. Export policies override any metric values determined through calculations involving the `metric-in` and `metric-out` values.

By default, the JUNOS software assigns a preference of 100 to routes that originate from RIPng. When the JUNOS software determines a route's preference to become the active route, the software selects the route with the lowest preference and installs this route into the forwarding table. To modify the default RIPng preference value, include the `preference` statement. *`preference`* can be a value from 0 to 4,294,967,295 ($2^{32} - 1$).

```
[edit protocols ripng group group-name]
preference preference;
```

If you configure an export policy, RIPng exports routes it has learned to the neighbors configured with the `neighbor` statement. If a route being exported was learned from a member of the same RIPng group, the metric associated with that route (unless modified by an export policy) is the normal RIPng metric. For example, a RIPng route with a metric of 5 learned from a neighbor configured with a `metric-in` value of 2 is advertised with a combined metric of 7 when advertised to RIPng neighbors in the same group. However, if this route was learned from a RIPng neighbor in a different group or from a different protocol, the route is advertised with the metric value configured for that group with the `metric-out` statement. The default value for `metric-out` is 1. To modify the metric for routes advertised outside a group, include the `metric-out` statement:

```
[edit protocols ripng group group-name]
metric-out metric;
```

To trace RIPng protocol traffic, you can specify options in the global `traceoptions` statement at the `[edit routing-options]` hierarchy level, and you can specify RIPng-specific options by including the `traceoptions` statement at the `[edit protocols ripng]` hierarchy level:

```
[edit protocols ripng]
traceoptions {
  file name <replace> <size size> <files number> <no-
      stamp>
    <(world-readable | no-world-readable)>;
  flag flag <flag-modifier> <disable>;
}
```

For more information about tracing and global tracing options, see the JUNOS technical documentation.

You can specify the following RIPng-specific options in the RIPng `traceoptions` statement:

- `all`—All RIPng information
- `error`—RIPng errors
- `expiration`—RIPng route expiration processing
- `general`—General events
- `holddown`—RIPng hold-down processing
- `normal`—Normal events
- `packets`—All RIPng packets

- `policy`—Policy processing
- `request`—RIPng information packets
- `route`—Routing information
- `state`—State transitions
- `task`—Routing protocol task processing
- `timer`—Routing protocol timer processing
- `trigger`—RIPng triggered updates
- `update`—RIPng update packets

Configuring Neighbor Discovery

Neighbor discovery allows different nodes on the same link to advertise their existence to their neighbors and to learn about the existence of their neighbors. A router periodically multicasts a router advertisement from each of its multicast interfaces, announcing its availability. Hosts listen for these advertisements for address autoconfiguration and discovery of link-local addresses of the neighboring routers. When a host starts, it multicasts a router solicitation to ask for immediate advertisements. The router discovery messages do not constitute a routing protocol. They enable hosts to discover the existence of neighboring routers, but are not used to determine which router is best to reach a particular destination.

Neighbor discovery is defined in RFC 2461, *Neighbor Discovery for IP Version 6.*

Neighbor discovery uses the following Internet Control Message Protocol Version 6 (ICMPv6) messages: router solicitation, router advertisement, neighbor solicitation, neighbor advertisement, and redirect.

To configure neighbor discovery, include the following statements. You configure router advertisement on a per-interface basis.

```
[edit protocols]
router-advertisement {
  interface interface-name {
    current-hop-limit number;
    default-lifetime seconds;
    (managed-configuration | no-managed-configuration);
    max-advertisement-interval seconds;
    min-advertisement-interval seconds;
    (other-stateful-configuration | no-other-stateful-
      configuration);
    prefix prefix {
      (autonomous | no-autonomous);
      (on-link | no-on-link);
```

```
        preferred-lifetime seconds;
        valid-lifetime seconds;
      }
      reachable-time milliseconds;
      retransmit-timer milliseconds;
      traceoptions {
        file name <replace> <size size> <files number> <no-
            stamp>
          <(world-readable | no-world-readable)>;
        flag flag <detail> <disable>;
      }
    }
  }
```

To configure the router to send router advertisement messages, include at least the following statements in the configuration. All other router advertisement configuration statements are optional.

```
[edit protocols]
router-advertisement {
  interface interface-name {
    prefix prefix;
  }
}
```

The current hop limit field in the router advertisement messages indicates the default value placed in the hop count field of the IP header for outgoing packets. The default hop limit is 64. To modify the default, include the `current-hop-limit` statement:

```
[edit protocols router-advertisement interface interface-
name]
current-hop-limit number;
```

The default lifetime in router advertisement messages indicates the lifetime associated with the default router. By default, the router lifetime is three times the maximum advertisement interval. To modify the default lifetime timer, include the `default-lifetime` statement:

```
[edit protocols router-advertisement interface interface-
name]
default-lifetime seconds;
```

You can set the managed configuration and other statement configuration fields in the router advertisement message to enable stateful autoconfiguration on a host. Setting the managed configuration field enables the host to use a stateful autoconfiguration protocol for address autoconfiguration, along with any stateless autoconfiguration already configured. Setting the other stateful configuration field enables autoconfiguration of other nonaddress-related information. By default, stateful autoconfiguration is disabled. To set the managed configuration field and enable address autoconfiguration, include the `managed-configuration` statement:

```
[edit protocols router-advertisement interface interface-
name]
managed-configuration;
```

To set the other stateful configuration field and enable autoconfiguration of other types of information, include the `other-stateful-configuration` statement:

```
[edit protocols router-advertisement interface interface-
name]
other-stateful-configuration;
```

The router sends router advertisements on each interface configured to transmit messages. The advertisements include route information and indicate to network hosts that the router still is operational. The router sends these messages periodically, with a time range defined by minimum and maximum values. By default, the maximum advertisement interval is 600 seconds, and the minimum advertisement interval is one-third the maximum interval, or 200 seconds. To modify the defaults, include the `min-advertisement-interval` and `max-advertisement-interval` statements:

```
[edit protocols router-advertisement interface interface-
name]
min-advertisement-interval seconds;
max-advertisement-interval seconds;
```

After receiving a reachability confirmation from a neighbor, a node considers that neighbor reachable for a certain amount of time without receiving another confirmation. This mechanism is used for neighbor unreachability detection, to find link failures to a target node. By default, the reachable time period is 0 milliseconds. To modify the default, include the `reachable-time` statement:

```
[edit protocols router-advertisement interface interface-
name]
reachable-time milliseconds;
```

The retransmit timer determines the retransmission frequency of neighbor solicitation messages. This timer is used to detect when a neighbor has become unreachable and to resolve addresses. By default, the retransmit timer is 0 milliseconds. To modify the default, include the `retransmit-timer` statement:

```
[edit protocols router-advertisement interface interface-
name]
retransmit-timer milliseconds;
```

Router advertisement messages carry prefixes and information about them. A prefix is *onlink* when it is assigned to an interface on a specified link. The prefixes specify whether they are onlink or not onlink. A node considers a prefix to be onlink if it is represented by one of the link's prefixes, a neighboring router specifies the address as the target of a redirect message, a neighbor advertisement message is received for the (target) address, or any neighbor discovery message is received from the address. These prefixes are also used for address autoconfiguration. The information about the prefixes specifies the lifetime of the prefixes, whether the prefix is autonomous, and whether the prefix is onlink.

By default, prefixes are onlink, which means you can specify them in the router advertisement messages as onlink so that they are used for onlink determination. To set prefixes as not onlink, include the `no-on-link` statement:

```
[edit protocols router-advertisement interface interface-
name prefix prefix]
no-on-link;
```

By default, prefixes are autonomous, which means you can specify them in the router advertisement messages as autonomous. To specify prefixes as not autonomous, include the `no-autonomous` statement:

```
[edit protocols router-advertisement interface interface-
name prefix prefix]
no-autonomous;
```

The preferred lifetime for the prefixes in the router advertisement messages specifies how long that the prefix generated by stateless autoconfiguration remains preferred. By default, the preferred lifetime is set to 604,800 seconds. To modify the preferred lifetime, include the preferred-lifetime statement. If you set the preferred lifetime to 0xFFFFFFFF, the lifetime is infinite. The preferred lifetime value must never exceed the valid lifetime value.

```
[edit protocols router-advertisement interface interface-
name prefix prefix]
preferred-lifetime seconds;
```

The valid lifetime for the prefixes in the router advertisement messages specifies how long the prefix remains valid for onlink determination. By default, the valid lifetime is set to 2,592,000 seconds. To modify the valid lifetime, include the valid-lifetime statement. If you set the valid lifetime to 0xFFFFFFFF, the lifetime is infinite. The valid lifetime value must never be smaller than the preferred lifetime value.

```
[edit protocols router-advertisement interface interface-
name prefix prefix]
valid-lifetime seconds;
```

To trace router advertisement traffic, specify router advertisement options by including the following traceoptions statement:

```
[edit protocols router-advertisement]
traceoptions {
  file name <replace> <size size> <files number> <no-
      stamp>
    <(world-readable | no-world-readable)>;
  flag flag <flag-modifier> <disable>;
}
```

For more information about tracing and global tracing options, see the JUNOS technical documentation.

You can specify the following router advertisement-specific options in the BGP traceoptions statement:

- error—Router advertisement errors
- expiration—Router advertisement route expiration processing
- holddown—Router advertisement hold-down processing
- packets—All router advertisement packets
- request—Router advertisement information packets such as request, poll, and poll entry packets
- trigger—Router advertisement triggered updates
- update—Router advertisement update packets

IPv4-to-IPv6 Transition Mechanisms

Implementing IPv6 requires a transition mechanism to allow interoperability between IPv6 nodes (both routers and hosts) and IPv4 nodes. The transition mechanism is the key factor in the successful deployment of IPv6. Because millions of IPv4 nodes already exist, upgrading every node to IPv6 at the same time is not feasible. As a result, the transition from IPv4 to IPv6 happens gradually, allowing nodes to be upgraded independently and without disruption to other nodes. While a gradual upgrade occurs, compatibility between IPv6 and IPv4 nodes becomes a requirement. Otherwise, an IPv6 node would not be able to communicate with an IPv4 node.

Transition mechanisms allow IPv6 and IPv4 nodes to coexist together in the same network and makes gradual upgrading possible. Two transition mechanisms are supported by the JUNOS software:

- Dual IP layer operation—Allows a node to support both IPv6 and IPv4 Internet protocols. This mechanism is also known as dual stack.
- Configured tunnels—Allows IPv6 packets to be encapsulated into IPv4 headers and sent across an IPv4 infrastructure.

Dual IP Layer

Dual IP layer is a transition mechanism in which a node (router or host) supports both IPv6 and IPv4 simultaneously. Dual IP layer support indicates a node's capability to send and receive both IPv6 and IPv4 packets. This transition mechanism involves no data encapsulation (such as tunneling). A node that has dual IP layer capabilities can interoperate with IPv6 nodes and IPv4 nodes directly.

A node that supports dual IP layer can disable one of the IP layers. If a dual IP layer node disables the IPv6 layer, the node acts as an IPv4 node only. If that node disables the IPv4 layer, that node acts as an IPv6 node only.

You can configure a dual IP layer node with either an IPv6 address or an IPv4 address. A dual IP layer node can acquire its IPv6 address through an IPv6 mechanism (such as stateless address autoconfiguration) and its IPv4 address through an IPv4 mechanism (such as Dynamic Host Control Protocol [DHCP]).

The Domain Naming System (DNS) uses resource records and resolver libraries to map between IP addresses and hostnames. IPv4 uses record type A, whereas IPv6 uses record type AAAA. Dual IP layer nodes provide resolver libraries that can handle the new record types.

When a query locates an AAAA record holding an IPv6 address and an A record holding an IPv4 address, the resolver library sends back one of the following types of address to the application making the query: IPv4 address, IPv6 address, or both. If the library sends back an IPv4 address, the application making the query uses IPv4 to communicate with the node. If the library sends back an IPv6 address, the application making the query uses IPv6 to communicate with the node. If the library sends back both IPv6 and IPv4 addresses, the application must choose based on ordering of the addresses sent by the resolver library. If an IPv6 address is the first in the order, the application chooses IPv6. If an IPv4 address is first in the order, the application chooses IPv4.

Configured Tunnels

IPv6-over-IPv4 tunnels are defined in RFC 2893, *Transition Mechanisms for IPv6 Hosts and Routers.*

If a Tunnel Services PIC is installed in the router, you can configure IPv6 over IPv4 tunnels. The JUNOS Internet software supports the IP over IP (IP-IP) and Generic Route Encapsulation (GRE) tunnel encapsulations. A configured tunnel is a point-to-point connection across an existing IPv4 network infrastructure. IPv6 packets are encapsulated in IPv4 headers and sent across the IPv4 infrastructure through the configured tunnel. You manually configure configured tunnels on each end point. A configured tunnel cannot go through a network address translation (NAT) at any point along the way to the destination.

To configure a tunnel using IP-IP encapsulation, include the following statements:

```
[edit interfaces]
ip-fpc/pic/port {
  unit logical-unit-number {
    tunnel {
      source address;
      destination address;
    }
    family inet6 {
      address address;
    }
  }
```

```
}
```

To configure a tunnel using GRE encapsulation, include the following statements:

```
[edit interfaces]
gr-fpc/pic/port {
  unit logical-unit-number {
    tunnel {
      source address;
      destination address;
    }
    family inet6 {
      address address;
    }
  }
}
```

You can configure multiple logical units for each interface. You can configure only one tunnel per unit. Each tunnel interface must be a point-to-point interface. Point to point is the default interface connection type, so you do not need to include the `point-to-point` statement at the `[edit interfaces` *`interface-name`* `unit` *`logical-unit-number`*`]` hierarchy level. You must specify the configured tunnel's destination and source addresses. The remaining statements are optional. You must configure `inet6` address family on the logical interface to create a configured tunnel. Configured tunnels are bidirectional.

Chapter 11

MPLS Applications

Traffic engineering has become an extremely important tool for ISPs as they struggle to keep pace with the ever-increasing volume of Internet traffic. The approach of Juniper Networks and the IETF to traffic engineering are MPLS applications that provide a traffic engineering solution based on the Multiprotocol Label Switching (MPLS), Resource Reservation Protocol (RSVP), and Label Distribution Protocol (LDP).

Traffic Engineering

The task of mapping traffic flows onto an existing physical topology is called *traffic engineering*. Traffic engineering provides the capability to move traffic flow away from the shortest path selected by the interior gateway protocol (IGP) and onto a potentially less congested physical path across a network.

Traffic engineering provides the capabilities to do the following:

- Route primary paths around known bottlenecks or points of congestion in the network.
- Provide precise control over how traffic is rerouted when the primary path is faced with single or multiple failures.
- Provide more efficient use of available aggregate bandwidth and long-haul fiber by ensuring that subsets of the network do not become overutilized while other subsets of the network along potential alternate paths are underutilized.
- Maximize operational efficiency.
- Enhance the traffic-oriented performance characteristics of the network by minimizing packet loss, minimizing prolonged periods of congestion, and maximizing throughput.
- Enhance statistically bound performance characteristics of the network (such as loss ratio, delay variation, and transfer delay) required to support a multiservices Internet.

Traffic Engineering Components

In the JUNOS software, traffic engineering is implemented with Multiprotocol Label Switching (MPLS) and the Resource Reservation Protocol (RSVP). Traffic engineering consists of four functional components: the packet forwarding, information distribution, path selection, and signaling.

The packet forwarding component of the JUNOS traffic engineering architecture is MPLS, which is responsible for directing a flow of IP packets along a predetermined path across a network. This path is called a *label-switched path (LSP)*. LSPs are simplex; that is, the traffic flows in one direction from the head-end (ingress) router to a tail-end (egress) router. Duplex traffic requires two LSPs: one LSP to carry traffic in each direction. An LSP is created by the concatenation of one or more label-switched hops, allowing a packet to be forwarded from one router to another across the MPLS domain.

When an ingress router receives an IP packet, it adds an MPLS header to the packet and forwards it to the next router in the LSP. The labeled packet is forwarded along the LSP by each router until it reaches the egress of the LSP, at which point the MPLS header is removed and the packet is forwarded based on Layer 3 information such as the IP destination address. The key purpose in this scheme is that the physical path of the LSP not be limited to what the IGP would choose as the shortest path to reach the destination IP address.

The packet forwarding process at each router is based on the concept of *label swapping*. This concept is similar to what occurs at each ATM switch in a PVC. Each MPLS packet carries a 4-byte encapsulation header that contains a 20-bit, fixed-length label field. When a packet containing a label arrives at a router, the router examines the label and uses it as an index into its MPLS forwarding table. Each entry in the forwarding table contains an interface-inbound label pair mapped to a set of forwarding information that is applied to all packets arriving on the specific interface with the same inbound label.

Traffic engineering consists of detailed knowledge about the network topology as well as dynamic information about network loading. The information distribution component is implemented by defining relatively simple extensions to the IGPs so that link attributes are included as part of each router's link-state advertisement. IS-IS extensions include the definition of new type-length values (TLVs), whereas OSPF extensions are implemented with opaque link-state advertisements (LSAs). The standard flooding algorithm used by the link-state IGPs ensures that link attributes are distributed to all routers in the routing domain. Some of the traffic engineering extensions to be added to the IGP LSA include maximum link bandwidth, maximum reserved link bandwidth, current bandwidth reservation, and link coloring.

Each router maintains network link attributes and topology information in a specialized traffic engineering database (TED). The TED is used exclusively for calculating explicit paths for the placement of LSPs across the physical topology. A separate database is maintained so that the subsequent traffic engineering computation is independent of the IGP and the IGP's link-state database. Meanwhile, the IGP continues its operation without modification, performing the traditional shortest-path calculation based on information contained in the router's link-state database.

After network link attributes and topology information are flooded by the IGP and placed in the TED, each ingress router uses the TED to calculate the paths for its own set of LSPs across the routing domain. The path for each LSP can be represented by either a strict or loose explicit route. An explicit route is a preconfigured sequence of routers that should be part of the physical path of the LSP. If the ingress router specifies all the routers in the LSP, the LSP is said to be identified by a *strict* explicit route. If the ingress router specifies only some of the routers in the LSP, the LSP is described as a *loose* explicit route. Support for strict and loose explicit routes allows the path selection process to be given broad latitude whenever possible, but to be constrained when necessary.

The ingress router determines the physical path for each LSP by applying a Constrained Shortest-Path First (CSPF) algorithm to the information in the TED. CSPF is a shortest-path-first algorithm that has been modified to take into account specific restrictions when calculating the shortest path across the network. Input into the CSPF algorithm includes the following:

- Topology link-state information learned from the IGP and maintained in the TED.
- Attributes associated with the state of network resources (such as total link bandwidth, reserved link bandwidth, available link bandwidth, and link color) that are carried by IGP extensions and stored in the TED.

- Administrative attributes required to support traffic traversing the proposed LSP (such as bandwidth requirements, maximum hop count, and administrative policy requirements) that are obtained from user configuration.

As CSPF considers each candidate node and link for a new LSP, it either accepts or rejects a specific path component based on resource availability or whether selecting the component violates user policy constraints. The output of the CSPF calculation is an explicit route consisting of a sequence of router addresses that provides the shortest path through the network that meets the constraints. This explicit route is then passed to the signaling component, which establishes forwarding state in the routers along the LSP.

An LSP is not known to be workable until it is actually established by the signaling component. The signaling component, which is responsible for establishing LSP state and distributing labels, relies on a number of extensions to the RSVP:

- Explicit Route Object—Allows an RSVP path message to traverse an explicit sequence of routers that is independent of conventional shortest-path IP routing. The explicit route can be either strict or loose.
- Label Request Object—Permits the RSVP path message to request that intermediate routers provide a label binding for the LSP that it is establishing.
- Label Object—Allows RSVP to support the distribution of labels without having to change its existing mechanisms. Because the RSVP resv message follows the reverse path of the RSVP path message, the label object supports the distribution of labels from downstream nodes to upstream nodes.

MPLS

In the traditional Layer 3 forwarding paradigm, as a packet travels from one router to the next, an independent forwarding decision is made at each hop. In an MPLS environment, the analysis of the packet header is performed just once, when a packet enters the MPLS cloud. The packet then is assigned to a stream, which is identified by a *label*, which is a short (20-bit), fixed-length value at the front of the packet. Labels are used as lookup indexes into the label forwarding table. For each label, this table stores forwarding information.

Traffic engineering allows you to control the path that data packets follow, bypassing the standard routing model, which uses routing tables. Traffic engineering moves flows from congested links to alternate links that would not be selected by the automatically computed destination-based shortest path. With traffic engineering, you can do the following:

- Make more efficient use of expensive long-haul fibers.
- Control how traffic is rerouted in the face of single or multiple failures.
- Classify critical and regular traffic on a per-path basis.

The core of the traffic engineering design is based on building LSPs among routers. An LSP is connection-oriented, like a virtual circuit in Frame Relay or ATM. LSPs are not reliable: Packets entering an LSP do not have delivery guarantees, although preferential treatment is possible. LSPs also are similar to unidirectional tunnels in that packets entering a path are encapsulated in an envelope and switched across the entire path without being touched by intermediate nodes.

Table 11.1 lists the MPLS standards and protocol extensions supported by the JUNOS software.

Table 11.1 *MPLS Standards and Protocol Extensions Supported by JUNOS Software*

Standard	Title
RFC 3031	*Multiprotocol Label Switching Architecture*
RFC 3032	*MPLS Label Stack Encoding*
RFC 2702	*Requirements for Traffic Engineering over MPLS*
IETF draft draft-ietf-isis-traffic-02.txt	*IS-IS Extensions for Traffic Engineering*
IETF draft-katz-yeung-ospf-traffic-04.txt	*Traffic Engineering Extensions to OSPF*
IETF draft-ietf-mpls-icmp-02.txt	*ICMP Extensions for Multiprotocol Label Switching*
RFC 3031	*Multiprotocol Label Switching Architecture*

MPLS supports the following link-layer protocols, which are all supported in the JUNOS MPLS implementation:

- PPP—Protocol ID 0x0281, NCP protocol ID 0x8281.

- Ethernet/Cisco HDLC—Ethernet type 0x8847.
- ATM—SNAP-encoded Ethernet type 0x8847. Support is included for both point-to-point mode or NBMA mode. Support is not included for encoding MPLS labels as part of ATM VPI/VCI.

The JUNOS software supports a proprietary MIB for MPLS objects; see the JUNOS technical documentation: Network Management and MPLS.

- Frame Relay—SNAP-encoded, Ethernet type 0x8847. Support is not included for encoding MPLS labels as part of Frame Relay DLCI.
- GRE Tunnel—Ethernet type 0x8847.

Types of LSPs

There are three types of LSPs:

- Static LSPs—For static paths, you must manually assign labels on all routers involved (ingress, transit, and egress). No signaling protocol is needed. This procedure is similar to configuring static routes on individual routers. Like static routes, there is no error reporting, no liveliness detection, and no statistics reporting.
- LDP-signaled LSPs.
- RSVP-signaled LSPs—For signaled paths, RSVP is used to set up the path and dynamically assign labels. (RSVP signaling messages are used to set up signaled paths.) You configure only the ingress router. The transit and egress routers accept signaling information from the ingress router, and they set up and maintain the LSP cooperatively. Any errors encountered while establishing an LSP are reported to the ingress router for diagnostics. For signaled LSPs to work, a version of RSVP that supports tunnel extensions must be enabled on all routers. There are two types of RSVP-signaled LSPs:
  - Explicit-path LSPs—All intermediate hops of the LSP are manually configured. The intermediate hops can be strict, loose, or any combination of the two. Explicit path LSPs provide you with complete control over how the path is set up. They are similar to static LSPs but require much less configuration.

- Constrained-path LSPs—The intermediate hops of the LSP are automatically computed by the software. The computation takes into account information provided by the topology information from the IS-IS or OSPF link-state routing protocol, the current network resource utilization determined by RSVP, and the resource requirements and constraints of the LSP. For signaled constrained-path LSPs to work, either the IS-IS or OSPF protocol and the IS-IS or OSPF traffic engineering extensions must be enabled on all routers.

For constrained-path LSPs, the LSP computation is confined to one IGP area and cannot cross any AS boundary. This prevents an AS from extending its IGP into another AS. Explicit-path LSPs, however, can cross as many AS boundaries as necessary. Because intermediate hops are manually specified, the LSP has no dependency on the IGP topology or a local forwarding table.

Flexible LSP Calculation and Configuration

The JUNOS software supports a number of different ways to route and configure an LSP:

- You can calculate the full path for the LSP offline and individually configure each router in the LSP with the necessary static forwarding state. This is analogous to how some ISPs currently configure their IP-over-ATM core networks.
- You can calculate the full path for the LSP offline and statically configure the ingress router with the full path. The ingress router then uses RSVP as a dynamic signaling protocol to install a forwarding state in each router along the LSP.
- You can rely on constraint-based routing to perform dynamic online LSP calculation. You configure the constraints for each LSP, and then the network itself determines the path that best meets those constraints. Specifically, the ingress router calculates the entire LSP based on the constraints and then initiates signaling across the network.
- You can calculate a partial path for an LSP offline and statically configure the ingress router with a subset of the routers in the path and then permit online calculation to determine the complete path.

- You can configure the ingress router with no constraints whatsoever. In this case, normal IGP shortest-path routing is used to determine the path of the LSP. This configuration does not provide any value in terms of traffic engineering. However, it is easy and might be useful in situations when services such as Virtual Private Networks (VPNs) are needed.

In all these cases, you can specify any number of LSPs as backups for the primary LSP, thus allowing you to combine more than one configuration approach.

MPLS provides a mechanism for engineering network traffic patterns that is independent of routing tables. MPLS assigns short labels to network packets that describe how to forward them through the network. MPLS is independent of any routing protocol and can be used for unicast packets.

Labels

Packets traveling along an LSP are identified by a *label*, a 20-bit, unsigned integer in the range 0 through 1,048,575. The labels are assigned as follows:

- 0 through 15—Reserved and have special semantics.
- 16 through 1,023 and 10,000 through 99,999—Unused and unassigned by the software, a feature that is specific to the JUNOS software. You can use labels to manually configure static LSPs and to ensure that there are no conflicts with labels that are dynamically assigned by the software.
- 1,024 through 9,999—Reserved for future applications.
- 100,000 through 1,048,575—Automatically negotiated, assigned, released, and reused by the software. Typically, per-router labels are assigned in the 100,000-799,999 range, and per-interface labels are assigned in the 800,000-1,048,575 range.

Some of the reserved labels in the 0 through 15 range have well-defined meanings:

For more details, see RFC 3032, *MPLS Label Stack Encoding*.

- 0, IPv4 Explicit Null Label—This value is valid only when it is the sole label entry (no label stacking). It indicates that the label must be popped on receipt. Forwarding continues based on the IPv4 packet.

- 1, Router Alert Label—When a packet is received with a top label value of 1, it is delivered to the local software module for processing.
- 2, IPv6 Explicit Null Label—This value is valid only when it is the sole label entry (no label stacking). It indicates that the label must be popped on receipt. Forwarding continues based on the IPv6 packet.
- 3, Implicit Null Label—This label is used in the control protocol (LDP, RSVP) only to request label popping by the downstream router. It never actually appears in the encapsulation. Labels with a value of 3 should not be used in the data packet as real labels. No payload type (IPv4 or IPv6) is implied with this label.

Special labels are commonly used between the egress and penultimate routers of an LSP. If the LSP is configured to carry IPv4 packets only, the egress router might signal the penultimate router to use 0 as a final hop label. If the LSP is configured to carry IPv6 packets only, the egress router might signal the penultimate router to use 2 as a final hop label.

Label values are allocated per router only. The display output shows only the label (for example, `01024`).

Labels for multicast packets are independent of those for unicast packets. Currently, the JUNOS software does not support multicast labels.

Labels are assigned by downstream routers relative to the flow of packets. A router receiving labeled packets (the next-hop router) is responsible for assigning incoming labels. A received packet containing a label that is unrecognized (unassigned) is dropped. For unrecognized labels, the router does not attempt to unwrap the label to analyze the network layer header, nor does it generate an ICMP destination unreachable message.

A packet can carry a number of labels, organized as a last-in, first-out stack. This is referred to as a *label stack*. At a particular router, the decision as to how to forward a labeled packet is based exclusively on the label at the top of the stack.

Figure 11.1 shows the encoding of a single label. The encoding appears after data link layer headers, but before any network layer header.

Figure 11.1 *Label Encoding*

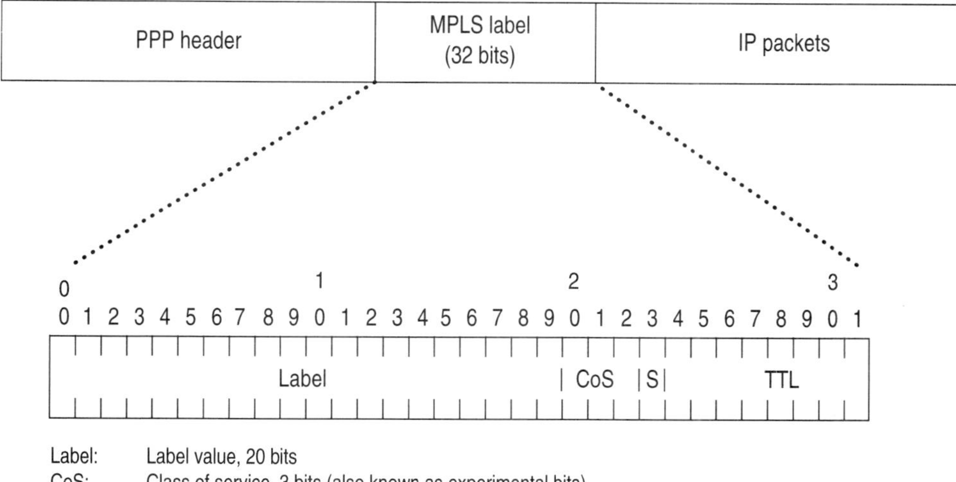

Label: Label value, 20 bits
CoS: Class of service, 3 bits (also known as experimental bits)
S: Bottom of stack, 1 bit
TTL: Time to live, 8 bits

The router supports the following label operations:

- Push—Add a new label to the top of the packet. For IPv4 packets, the new label is the first label. The TTL, S, and CoS fields are derived from the IP packet header. If a push operation is performed on an existing MPLS packet, the packet has two or more labels. This is called *label stacking*. The top label must have its S field set to 0 and might derive CoS and TTL from lower levels. The new top label in a label stack always initializes its TTL to 255, regardless of the TTL value of lower labels.
- Pop—Remove the label from the beginning of the packet. When the label is removed, the TTL is copied from the label into the IP packet header, and the underlying IP packet is forwarded as a native IP packet. In the case of multiple labels in a packet (label stacking), removing the top label yields another MPLS packet. The new top label might derive CoS and TTL from a previous top label. The popped TTL value from the previous top label is not written back to the new top label.

- Swap—Replaces the label at the top of the label stack with a new label. The S and CoS bits are copied from the previous label, and the TTL value is copied and decremented (unless the `no-decrement-ttl` or `no-propagate-ttl` statements are configured). A transit router supports a label stack of any depth.
- Multiple push—Add multiple labels (up to three) on top of existing packets. This is equivalent to doing a push operation multiple times.
- Swap and push—Replace the existing top of the label stack with a new label, followed by pushing another new label on top.

Routers in an LSP

Each router in an LSP performs one of the following functions:

- Ingress router—At the beginning of an LSP, this router encapsulates IP packets with an MPLS Layer 2 frame and forwards it to the next router in the path. Each LSP can have only one ingress router.
- Egress router—At the end of an LSP, this router removes the MPLS encapsulation, thus transforming it from an MPLS packet to an IP packet, and forwards the packet to its final destination using information in the IP forwarding table. Each LSP can have only one egress router. The ingress and egress routers in an LSP cannot be the same router.
- Transit router—Any intermediate router in the LSP between the ingress and egress routers. A transit router forwards received MPLS packets to the next router in the MPLS path. An LSP can contain zero or more transit routers, up to a maximum of 253 transit routers in a single LSP.

A single router can be part of multiple LSPs. It can be the ingress or egress router for one or more LSPs, and it also can be a transit router in one or more LSPs. The functions that each router supports depend on your network design.

How a Packet Travels along an LSP

When an IP packet enters an LSP, the ingress router examines the packet and assigns it a label based on its destination, placing the label in the packet's header. The label transforms the packet from one that is forwarded based on its IP routing information to one that is forwarded based on information associated with the label.

The packet then is forwarded to the next router in the LSP. This router and all subsequent routers in the LSP do not examine any of the IP routing information in the labeled packet. Rather, they use the label to look up information in their label forwarding table. Then, they replace the old label with a new label and forward the packet to the next router in the path.

When the packet reaches the egress router, the label is removed, and the packet again becomes a native IP packet and is again forwarded based on its IP routing information.

Constrained-Path LSP Computation

The Constrained Shortest-Path First (CSPF) algorithm is an advanced form of the Shortest-Path First (SPF) algorithm used in OSPF and IS-IS route computations. CSPF is used in computing paths for LSPs that are subject to multiple constraints. When computing paths, CSPF considers not only the topology of the network, but also the attributes of the LSP and the links, and it attempts to minimize congestion by intelligently balancing the network load.

The constraints that CSPF considers include the following:

- LSP attributes
    - Bandwidth requirements
    - Hop limitations
    - Administrative groups (that is, link color requirements)
    - Priority (setup and hold)
    - Explicit route (strict or loose)

- Link attributes
  - Reservable bandwidth of the links (static bandwidth minus the currently reserved bandwidth)
  - Administrative groups (that is, link colors assigned to the link)

The data that CSPF considers comes from the following:

- Traffic Engineering Database (TED)—Provides CSPF with up-to-date topology information, the current reservable bandwidth of links, and the link colors. For the CSPF algorithm to perform its computations, a link-state IGP (such as OSPF or IS-IS) with special extensions is needed. For CSPF to be effective, the link-state IGP on all routers must support the special extensions. While building the topology database, the extended IGP must take into consideration the current LSPs and must flood the route information everywhere. Because changes in the reserved link bandwidth and link color cause database updates, an extended IGP tends to flood more frequently than a normal IGP. See Figure 11.2 for a diagram of the relationships between these components.
- Currently active LSPs—Includes all the LSPs that should originate from the router and their current operational status (up, down, or timeout).

Figure 11.2 *CSPF Computation Process*

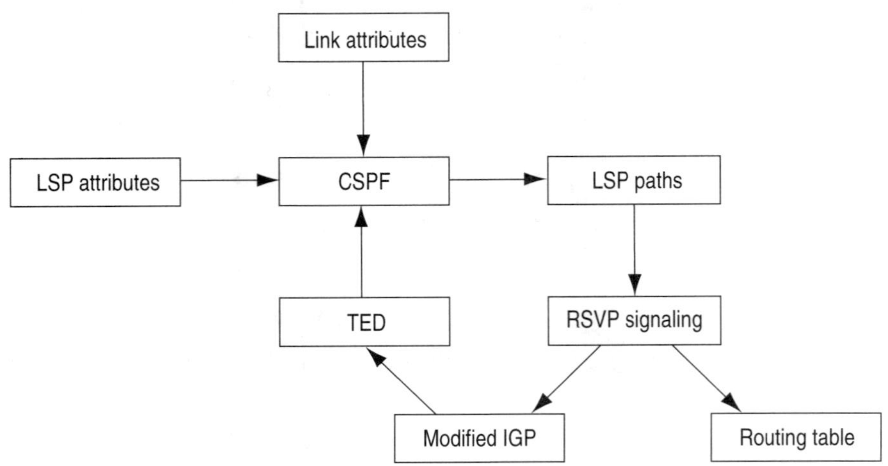

Fate Sharing

Fate sharing allows you to create a database of information that CSPF uses to compute one or more backup paths to use in case the primary path becomes unstable. The database describes the relationships between elements of the network, such as routers and links. You can specify one or more elements within a group.

For more information about fate sharing, see the JUNOS technical documentation: *Routing and Routing Protocols*.

Through fate sharing, you can configure backup paths that minimize the number of shared links and fiber paths with the primary paths as much as possible, to ensure that, if a fiber is cut, the minimum amount of data is lost and that a path still exists to the destination.

For a backup path to work optimally, it must not share links or physical fiber paths with the primary path. This ensures that a single point of failure will not affect the primary and backup paths at the same time.

IGP Shortcuts

Link-state protocols, such as OSPF and IS-IS, use the SPF algorithm to compute the shortest-path tree to all nodes in the network. The results of such computations can be represented by the destination node, next-hop address, and output interface, where the output interface is a physical interface. LSPs can be used to augment the SPF algorithm. On the node performing the calculations, LSPs appear to be logical interfaces directly connected to remote nodes in the network. If you configure the IGP to treat LSPs the same as a physical interface and to use the LSPs as a potential output interface, the SPF computation results are represented by the destination node and output LSP, effectively using the LSP as a shortcut through the network to the destination.

As an illustration, begin with a typical SPF tree as shown in Figure 11.3. If an LSP connects Router A to Router D and if IGP shortcuts are enabled on Router A, you might have the SPF tree shown in Figure 11.4.

Figure 11.3 *Typical SPF Tree, Sourced from Router A*

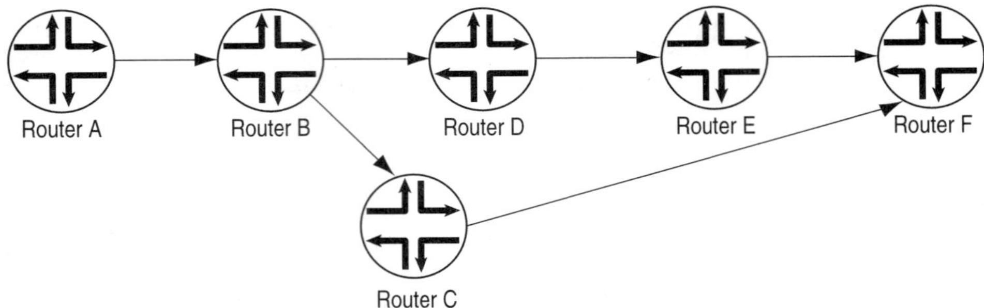

Figure 11.4 *Modified SPF Tree, Using LSP A–D as a Shortcut*

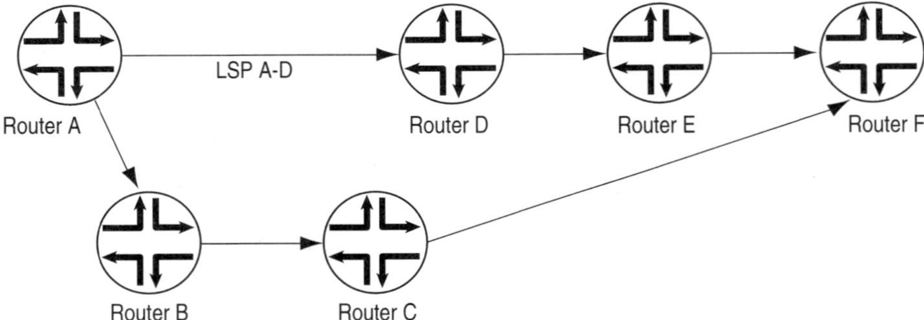

Router D is now reachable through LSP A–D. When computing the shortest path to reach Router D, Router A has two choices:

- Use IGP path A–B–D
- Use LSP A–D

To decide between the two choices, Router A compares the IGP metrics for path A–B–D with the LSP metrics for LSP A–D. If the IGP metric is lower, path A–B–D is chosen (see Figure 11.3). If the LSP metric is lower, LSP A–D is used (see Figure 11.4). If both metrics are equal, Router A might share the load between the two paths.

Routers E and F are also reachable through LSP A–D because they are downstream from Router D in the SPF tree.

Assuming that another LSP connects Router A to Router E, you might have the SPF tree shown in Figure 11.5.

Figure 11.5 *Modified SPF Tree, Using Both LSP A–D and LSP A–E as Shortcuts*

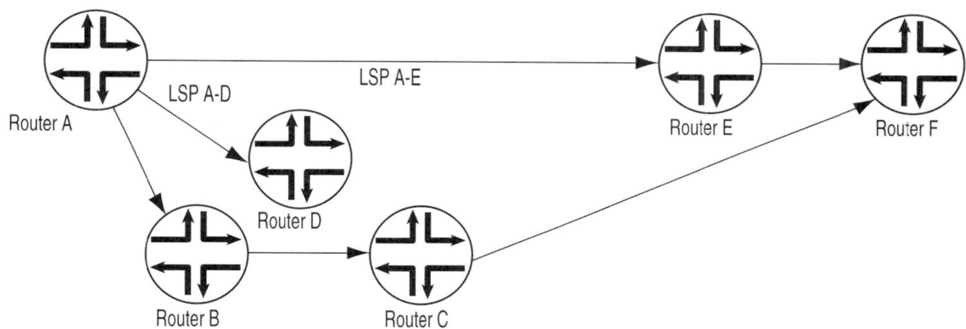

For information about enabling IGP shortcuts for IS-IS and OSPF, see Chapter 9, "Routing and Routing Protocols," on page 373.

IGP shortcuts are supported for both IS-IS and OSPF. A link-state protocol is required for IGP shortcuts. Shortcuts are disabled by default. You can enable IGP shortcuts on a per-router basis; you do not need to enable shortcuts globally. A router's shortcut computation does not depend on another router performing similar computations, and shortcuts performed by other routers are irrelevant.

Advertising LSPs into IGPs

IGP shortcuts allow an ingress router of an LSP to use the LSP in its SPF computation. However, other routers on the network do not know of the existence of that LSP, so they cannot use it. This can lead to less than optimal traffic engineering. As an example, consider the network shown in Figure 11.6.

Figure 11.6 *SPF Computations with Advertised LSPs*

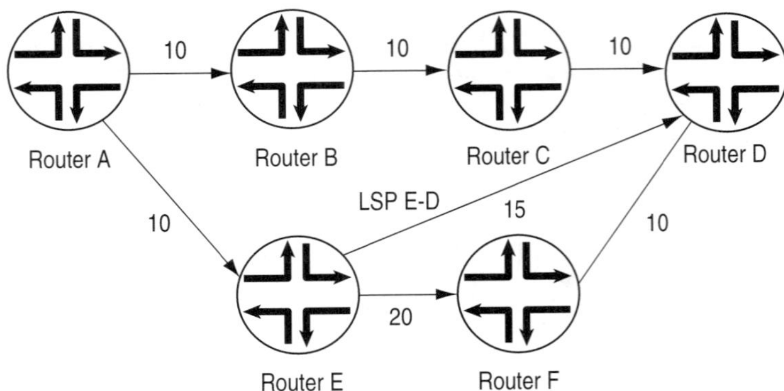

Assume that Router A is computing a path to Router D. The link between Router E and Router F has metric 20; all other links have metric 10. Here, the path chosen by Router A is A–B–C–D, which has a metric of 30, instead of A–E–F–D, which has a metric of 40.

If Router E has an LSP to Router D with a metric of 15, you want traffic from Router A to Router D to use the path A–E–D, which has a metric of 25, instead of the path A–B–C–D. However, because Router A does not know about the LSP between Router E and Router D, it cannot route traffic through this path.

For all routers on the network to know about the LSP between Router E and Router D, you need to advertise it. This advertisement announces the LSP as a unidirectional, point-to-point link in the link-state database, and all routers can compute paths using the LSP. The link-state database maintains information about the AS topology and contains information about the router's local state (for example, the router's usable interfaces and reachable neighbors). In Figure 11.6, Router A sees the link from Router E to Router D and routes traffic along this lower-metric path.

Because an LSP is announced as a unidirectional link, you might need to configure a reverse LSP (one that starts at the egress router and ends at the ingress router) so that the SPF bidirectional check succeeds. As a step in the SPF computation, IS-IS considers a link from Router E to Router D. Before IS-IS uses any link, it verifies that there is a link from Router D to Router E (there is bidirectional connectivity between router E and D). Otherwise, the SPF computation does not use an announced LSP.

IP and MPLS Packets on Aggregated Interfaces

You can send IP and MPLS packets over aggregated interfaces. To the IP or MPLS session, there is a single LSP composed of the aggregated interfaces. Packets sent to an LSP that is part of an aggregated interface are redistributed over the aggregated member interfaces.

To configure aggregated Ethernet and aggregated SONET interfaces, see Chapter 6, "Interfaces and Class of Service," on page 185.

Sending IP and MPLS packets over aggregated interfaces has the following benefits:

- Bandwidth aggregation—You can increase the number of MPLS packet flows sent over each connection. In MPLS, a set of packets sharing the same label is considered a part of the same flow.
- Link redundancy—If a link or a line card failure affects an aggregate member link, the traffic flowing across that link is immediately forwarded across one of the remaining links.

MPLS Applications for Traffic Engineering

In the JUNOS implementation of MPLS, establishing an LSP installs on the ingress router a host route (a 32-bit mask) toward the egress router. The address of the host route is the destination address of the LSP. By default, the route has a preference value of 7, a value that is higher than all routes except direct interface and static routes. The 32-bit mask ensures that the route is more specific (that is, a longer match) than all other subnet routes. The host routes can be used to traffic-engineer BGP destinations only, or both IGP and BGP destinations.

You can configure MPLS to control the paths that traffic takes to destinations outside an AS. Both IBGP and EBGP take advantage of the LSP host routes without requiring extra configuration. BGP compares the BGP next-hop address with the LSP host route. If a match is found, the packets for the BGP route are label-switched over the LSP. If multiple BGP routes share the same next-hop address, all the BGP routes are mapped to the same LSP route, regardless of which BGP peer the routes are learned from. If the BGP next-hop address does not match an LSP host route, BGP routes continue to be forwarded based on the IGP routes within the routing domain. In general, when both an LSP route and an IGP route exist for the same BGP next-hop address, the one with the highest preference is chosen.

Figure 11.7 shows an MPLS topology that illustrates how MPLS and LSPs work. This topology consists of a single domain with four routers. The two routers at the edges of the domain, Router 1 and Router 4, are running EBGP to communicate with peers outside the domain and IBGP to communicate between themselves. For intradomain communication, all four routers are running an IGP. Finally, an LSP tunnel exists from Router 1 to Router 4.

Figure 11.7 *MPLS Application Topology*

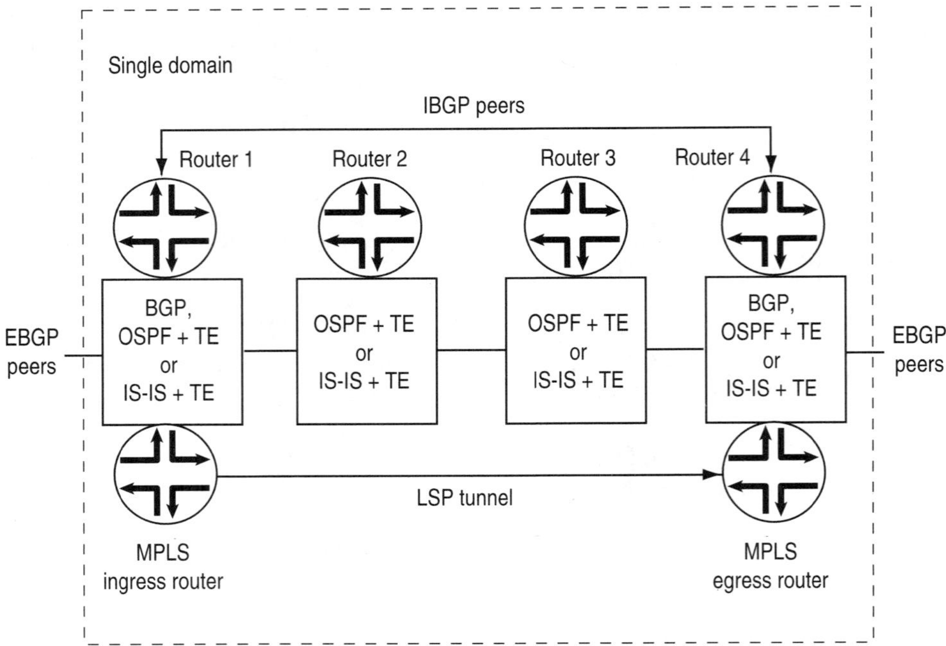

When BGP on Router 1 receives prefixes from Router 4, it must determine how to reach a BGP next-hop address. Typically, when traffic engineering is not enabled, BGP uses IGP routes to determine how to reach next-hop addresses. (See the left side of Figure 11.8.) However, when traffic engineering is enabled, if the BGP next hop matches the LSP tunnel end point (that is, the MPLS egress router), those prefixes enter the LSP tunnel. If the BGP next hop does not match an LSP tunnel end point, those prefixes are sent following the IGP's shortest path (see Figure 11.8).

You can configure MPLS to control the paths that traffic takes to destinations within an AS. When traffic engineering is for IGP destinations only, the MPLS host routes are installed in the `inet.3` routing table (see Figure 11.9 on page 541), separate from the routes learned from other routing protocols. Not all `inet.3` routes are downloaded into the forwarding table. Packets directly addressed to the egress router do not follow the LSP, which prevents routes learned from LSPs from overriding routes learned from IGPs or other sources.

Figure 11.8 *How BGP Determines How to Reach Next-Hop Addresses*

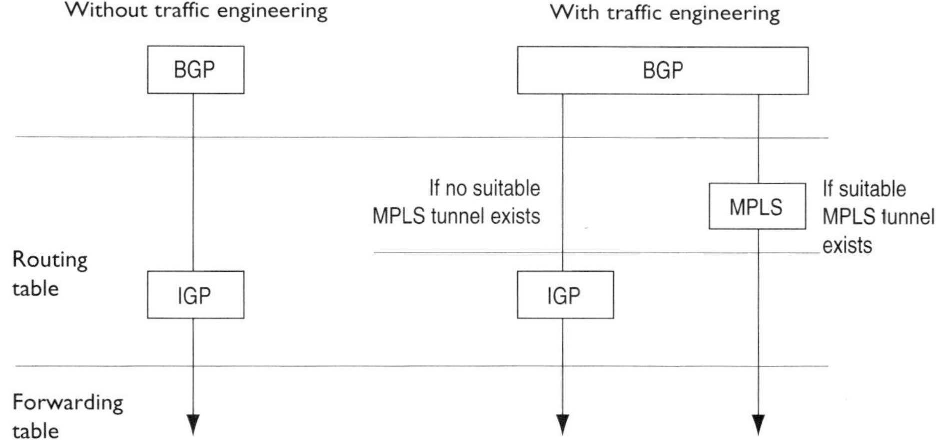

Traffic within a domain, including BGP control traffic between BGP peers, is not affected by LSPs. MPLS affects interdomain transit traffic only; that is, it affects only those BGP prefixes that are learned from an external domain. MPLS does not disrupt intradomain traffic, so IS-IS or OSPF routes remain undisturbed. If you issue a `ping` or `traceroute` command to any destination within the domain, the `ping` or `traceroute` packets follow the IGP path. However, if you issue a `ping` or `traceroute` command from Router 1 in Figure 11.8 (the LSP ingress router) to a destination outside the domain, the packets use the LSP tunnel.

When traffic engineering for IGP and BGP destinations is enabled, the MPLS host routes are installed in the `inet.0` table (see Figure 11.9) and downloaded into the forwarding table. Any traffic destined to the egress router could enter the LSP. In effect, it moves all the routes in `inet.3` into `inet.0`, thus emptying the `inet.3` table.

RSVP packets automatically avoid all MPLS LSPs, including those established by RSVP or LDP. This prevents placing one RSVP session into another LSP, or in other words, nesting one LSP into another.

If more than one LSP tunnel to a BGP next hop exists, the prefixes learned from the BGP next hop are randomly divided among the LSP tunnels. To control which LSP BGP uses to forward data for a given prefix, use the `install-nexthop` statement in the export policy applied to the forwarding table.

MPLS and Routing Tables

The IGPs and BGP store their routing information in the `inet.0` routing table, which is the primary IP routing table. If `traffic-engineering bgp` is configured, thereby allowing only BGP to use MPLS paths for forwarding traffic, MPLS path information is stored in a separate routing table, `inet.3`. Only BGP accesses the `inet.3` routing table. BGP uses both `inet.0` and `inet.3` to resolve next-hop addresses. If `traffic-engineering bgp-igp` is configured, thereby allowing the IGPs to use MPLS paths for forwarding traffic, MPLS path information is stored in the `inet.0` routing table. (Figure 11.9 and Figure 11.10 illustrate the routing tables in the two traffic engineering configurations.)

The `inet.3` routing table contains the host address of each LSP's egress router. This routing table is used on ingress routers to route packets to the destination egress router. BGP uses the `inet.3` routing table on the ingress router to help in resolving next-hop addresses.

MPLS also maintains an MPLS path routing table (`mpls.0`), which contains a list of the next label-switched router in each LSP. This routing table is used on transit routers to route packets to the next router along an LSP.

Figure 11.9 *MPLS Routing and Forwarding Tables When Traffic-Engineering BGP Is Configured*

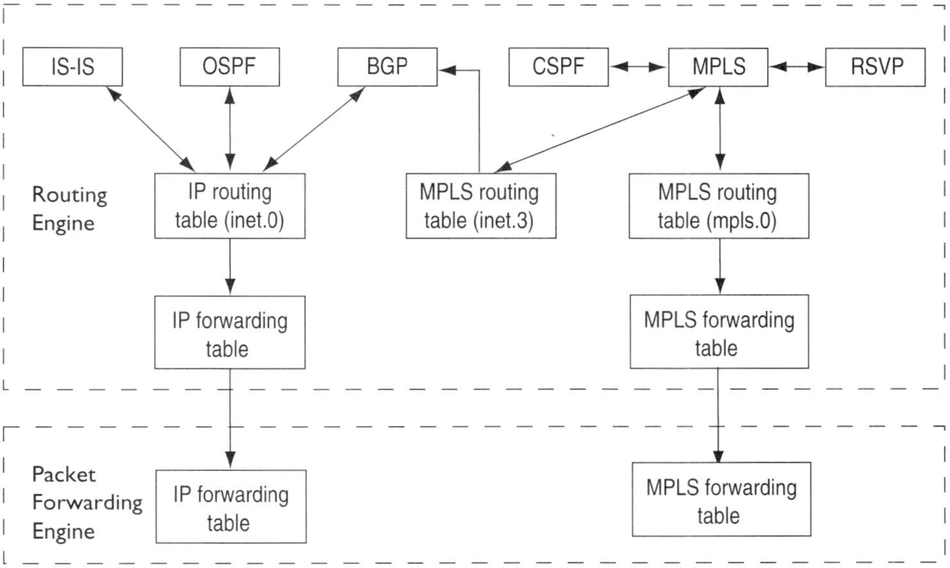

Typically, the egress router in an LSP does not consult the `mpls.0` routing table. (This router does not need to consult `mpls.0` because the penultimate router in the LSP either changes the packet's label to a value of 0 or pops the label.) In either case, the egress router forwards it as an IPv4 packet, consulting the IP routing table, `inet.0`, to determine how to forward the packet.

When a transit or egress router receives an MPLS packet, information in the MPLS forwarding table is used to determine the next transit router in the LSP or to determine that this router is the egress router.

When BGP resolves a next-hop prefix, it examines both the `inet.0` and `inet.3` routing tables, seeking the next hop with the highest preference. If it finds a next-hop entry with an equal preference in both routing tables, BGP prefers the entry in the `inet.3` routing table.

Figure 11.10 *MPLS Routing and Forwarding Tables When Traffic-Engineering BGP-IGP Is Configured*

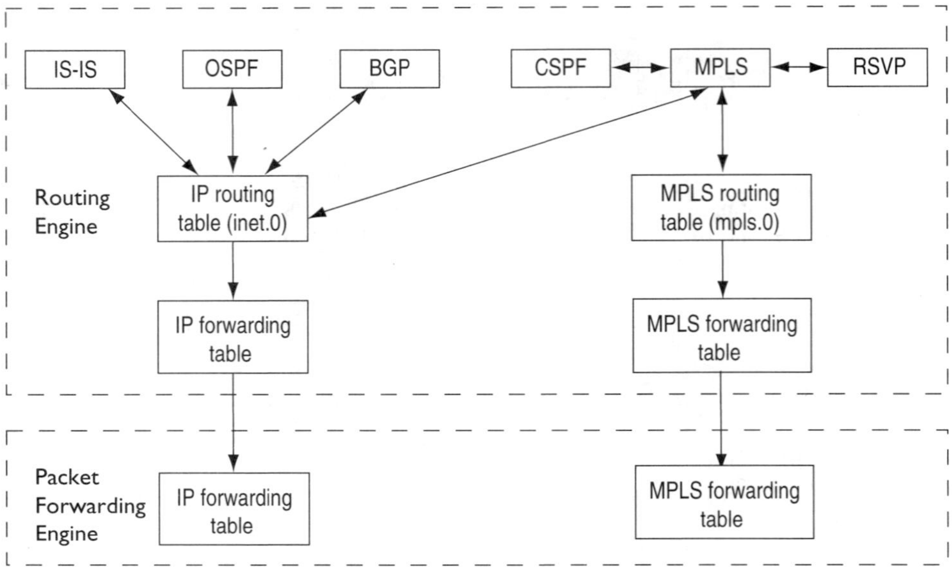

Generally, BGP selects next-hop entries in the `inet.3` routing table, because their preferences are always lower than OSPF and IS-IS next-hop preferences. When you configure LSPs, you can override the default preference for MPLS LSPs, which might alter the next-hop selection process.

When BGP selects a next-hop entry from the `inet.3` routing table, it installs that LSP into the forwarding table in the Packet Forwarding Engine, which causes packets destined for that next hop to enter and travel along the LSP. If the LSP is removed or fails, the path is removed from the `inet.3` routing table and from the forwarding table, and BGP reverts to using a next hop from the `inet.0` routing table.

MPLS and Traffic Protection

Typically, when an LSP fails, the router immediately upstream from the failure signals the outage to the ingress router. The ingress router calculates a new path to the egress router, establishes the new LSP, and then directs the traffic from the failed path to the new path. This rerouting process can be time consuming and prone to failure. For example, the outage signals to the ingress router might get lost, or the new path might take too long to come up, resulting in significant packet drops. The JUNOS software provides two complementary mechanisms for protecting against LSP failures:

- Standby secondary paths—You can configure primary and secondary paths. You configure secondary paths with the `standby` statement. To activate traffic protection, you need to configure these standby paths only on the ingress router. If the primary path fails, the ingress router immediately reroutes traffic from the failed path to the standby path, thereby eliminating the need to calculate a new route and signal a new path.
- Fast reroute—You configure fast reroute on an LSP to minimize the effect of a failure in the LSP. Fast reroute enables a router upstream from the failure to route around the failure quickly to the router downstream of the failure. The upstream router then signals the outage to the ingress router, thereby maintaining connectivity before a new LSP is established.

When standby secondary path and fast reroute are both configured on the LSP, full traffic protection is enabled. When a failure occurs in an LSP, the router upstream of the failure routes traffic around the failure and notifies the ingress router of the failure. This rerouting keeps the traffic flowing while waiting for the notification to be processed at the ingress router. After receiving the failure notification, the ingress router immediately reroutes the traffic from the patched primary path to the more optimal standby path.

Per-Prefix Load Balancing

When there are multiple equal cost tunnels to a destination, load balancing can be controlled for each path. Load balancing is proportional to the configured bandwidth per LSP. If an LSP has a larger bandwidth associated with it, that LSP carries a larger number of prefixes. If you configure the bandwidth, the prefixes automatically adjust themselves.

Automatic Bandwidth Allocation

An MPLS tunnel can automatically adjust its bandwidth allocation based on the volume of traffic flowing through the tunnel. You can configure an LSP with minimal bandwidth, and the LSP's bandwidth allocation is dynamically adjusted based on current traffic patterns. The bandwidth adjustments do not interrupt traffic flow through the tunnel.

You set a sampling interval on an LSP configured with automatic bandwidth allocation. The average bandwidth, is monitored during this interval. At the end of the interval, an attempt is made to signal a new path for the LSP with the bandwidth allocation set to the maximum average value for the preceding sampling interval. If the new path is successfully established and the original path is removed, the LSP is switched over to the new path. If a new path is not created, the LSP continues to use its current path until the end of the next sampling interval, when another attempt is made to establish a new path. You can set both the minimum and maximum bandwidth values for the LSP.

Configuring MPLS-Signaled LSPs

For more information about LDP-signaled LSPs, see "LDP," on page 594.

To configure MPLS-signaled LSPs, create an LSP that runs from the ingress router to the egress router. To create the LSP, configure only the ingress router; you do not have to configure any other routers. You can configure the LSP so that the JUNOS software makes all forwarding decisions, or you can configure some or all routers in the path. The LSP is set up by RSVP, through RSVP signaling messages. The JUNOS software automatically negotiates, assigns, releases, and reuses labels. Automatically assigned labels have a value from 1,024 through 1,048,575.

Configuring the Ingress Router for MPLS-Signaled LSPs

To configure signaled LSPs, you first create one or more named paths on the ingress router. For each path, you can specify some or all transit routers in the path, or you can leave it empty. Each path name can contain up to 32 characters and can include letters, digits, periods, and hyphens. The name must be unique within the ingress router. After a named path is created, you can configure primary and secondary LSPs using the named path. You can specify the same named path on any number of LSPs. To create an empty path, include the `path` statement but do not specify a name. Here, any path between the ingress and egress routers is accepted. In actuality, the path used tends to be the same path as is followed by destination-based, best-effort traffic.

```
[edit protocols mpls]
path path-name;
```

To create a path in which you specify some or all transit routers in the path, include the following form of the `path` statement:

```
[edit protocols mpls]
path path-name {
  (address | host-name ) <strict | loose>;
}
```

Specify one or more transit router addresses in order, starting with the ingress router (optional) or the first transit router, and continuing sequentially along the path up to the egress router (optional) or the router immediately before the egress router. For each router address, you specify the type, which can be one of the following:

- `strict`—(Default) The route taken from the previous router to this router is a direct path and cannot include any other routers. You must ensure that the router immediately preceding the router you are configuring has a direct connection to that router.
- `loose`—The route taken from the previous router to this router need not be a direct path and can include other routers and can be received on any interface.

The second step in configuring signaled LSPs is to create one or more LSPs and define the properties associated with the LSP on the ingress router. To configure an LSP, include the `label-switched-path` statement:

```
[edit protocols mpls]
label-switched-path lsp-path-name {
  disable;
  to address;
  from address;
  adaptive;
  admin-group {
    exclude group-names;
    include group-names;
  }
  auto-bandwidth {
    adjust-interval seconds;
    adjust-threshold percent;
    maximum-bandwidth bps;
    minimum-bandwidth bps;
    monitor-bandwidth;
  }
  bandwidth bps;
  class-of-service cos-value;
  fast-reroute {
    fast-reroute bps;
    exclude group-names;
    hop-limit number;
    include group-names;
  }
  hop-limit number;
  ldp-tunneling;
  metric number;
  no-cspf;
  no-decrement-ttl;
  optimize-timer seconds;
  preference preference;
  priority setup-priority hold-priority;
  (random | least-fill | most-fill);
  (record | no-record);
  retry-limit number;
  retry-timer seconds;
  standby;
  primary path-name {
    adaptive;
    admin-group {
      exclude group-names;
      include group-names;
    }
    bandwidth bps;
```

```
      class-of-service cos-value;
      hop-limit number;
      no-cspf;
      optimize-timer seconds;
      preference preference;
      priority setup-priority hold-priority;
      (record | no-record);
      standby;
    }
    secondary path-name {
      adaptive;
      admin-group {
        exclude group-names;
        include group-names;
      }
      bandwidth bps;
      class-of-service cos-value;
      hop-limit number;
      no-cspf;
      optimize-timer seconds;
      preference preference;
      priority setup-priority hold-priority;
      (record | no-record);
      standby;
    }
  }
```

Each LSP must have a name, *lsp-path-name*, which can be up to 32 characters long and can contain letters, digits, periods (.), and hyphens (-). The name must be unique within the ingress router. For ease of management and identification, configure unique names across the entire domain.

Configuring the Ingress and Egress Router Addresses

Specify the address of the egress router by including the `to` statement. When you are setting up an LSP, the `to` statement is the only required statement. All other statements are optional.

```
[edit protocols mpls label-switched-path lsp-path-name]
to address;
```

After the LSP is established, the address of the egress router is installed as a host route in the routing table. Then, this route can be used by BGP to forward traffic. To have the software send BGP traffic over an LSP, the address of the egress router is the same as the address of the BGP next hop. You can specify the egress router's address as any one of the router's interface addresses or as the BGP router ID. If you specify a different address, even if the address is on the same router, BGP traffic is not sent over the LSP.

The local router always is considered to be the ingress router, which is the beginning of the LSP. The software automatically determines the proper outgoing interface and IP address to use to reach the next router in an LSP. By default, the router ID is chosen as the address of the ingress router. To override the automatic selection of the source address, specify a source address in the `from` statement. The outgoing interface used by the LSP is not affected by the source address that you configure.

```
[edit protocols mpls label-switched-path lsp-path-name]
from address;
```

Configuring the Primary and Secondary LSPs

By default, an LSP routes itself hop by hop toward the egress router. The LSP tends to follow the shortest path as dictated by the local routing table, usually taking the same path as destination-based, best-effort traffic. These paths are "soft" in nature because they automatically reroute themselves whenever a change occurs in a routing table or in the status of a node or link. To configure the path so that it follows a particular route, create a named path using the `path` statement. Then apply the named path by including the `primary` or `secondary` statement. A named path can be referenced by any number of LSPs.

```
[edit protocols mpls label-switched-path lsp-path-name]
primary path-name {
  ...
}
secondary path-name {
  ...
}
```

The `primary` statement creates the primary path, which is the LSP's preferred path. The `secondary` statement creates an alternative path. If the primary path can no longer reach the egress router, the alternative path is used.

For more information about retry times, see "Configuring Path Connection Retry Information," on page 555.

When the software switches from the primary to a secondary path, it continuously attempts to revert to the primary path, switching back to it when it is again reachable, but no sooner than the retry time specified in the `retry-timer` statement.

You can configure zero or one primary path. If you do not configure a primary path, the first secondary path that is established is selected as the path. You can configure zero or more secondary paths. All secondary paths are equal, and the software tries them in the order that they are listed in the configuration. The software does not attempt to switch among secondary paths. If the current secondary path is not available, the next one is tried. To create a set of equal paths, specify secondary paths without specifying a primary path. If you do not specify any named paths, or if the path you specify is empty, the software makes all the routing decisions necessary to reach the egress router.

Configuring Fast Reroute

Fast reroute provides a mechanism for automatically rerouting traffic on an LSP if a node or link in an LSP fails, thus reducing the loss of packets traveling over the LSP. Fast rerouting is accomplished by precomputing and preestablishing a number of detours along the LSP. Figure 11.11 illustrates an LSP from Router A to Router F, showing some of the detours that are established for the LSP. Each detour is established by an upstream node with the intent of avoiding the link toward the immediate downstream node and the immediate downstream node itself. Each detour might traverse through one or more label-switched routers that are not shown in the figure.

Figure 11.11 *Detours Established for an LSP Using Fast Reroute*

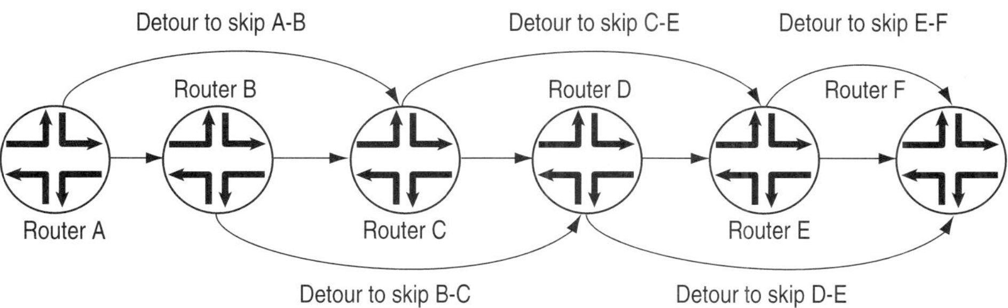

If a node detects either that a downstream link has failed (using a link-layer–specific liveness detection mechanism) or that a downstream node has failed (for example, using the RSVP neighbor hello protocol), the node quickly splices the traffic onto the detour and, at the same time, signals the ingress router about the link or node failure. Figure 11.12 illustrates the detour taken when the link between

Router B and Router C fails. If the network topology is not rich enough, some of the detours might not succeed. For example, the detour from Router A to Router C in Figure 11.12 cannot traverse link A-B and Router B. If such a path is not possible, the detour is not established.

Figure 11.12 *Detour after the Link from Router B to Router C Fails*

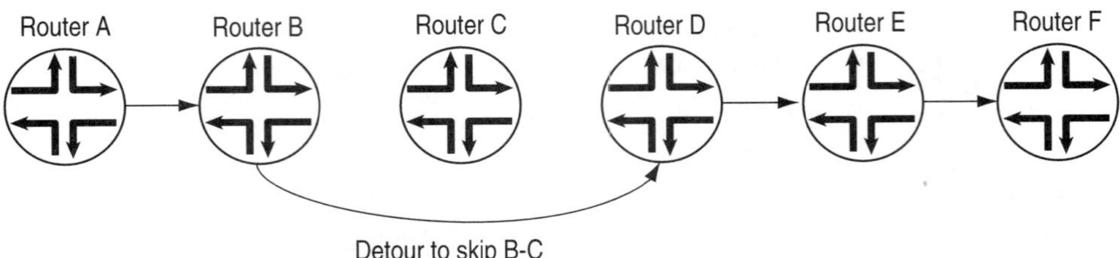

The time required for a fast-rerouting detour to take effect depends on two independent time intervals:

- Amount of time to detect a link or node failure—This time interval depends on the link layer in use and the nature of the failure. For example, failure detection on an SDH/SONET link typically is much faster than on a Gigabit Ethernet link, and both are much faster than detection of a router failure.
- Amount of time required to splice the traffic onto the detour—This time interval is primarily the CPU time required to update the routing table and then to update the forwarding table. The amount of time depends on the current CPU load and how busy the other routing protocols are that are sharing the CPU.

Fast reroute is a short-term patch to reduce packet loss. Because detour computation might not reserve adequate bandwidth, the detours might introduce congestion on the alternate links. The ingress router is the only router that is fully aware of LSP policy constraints and, therefore, is the only router able to come up with adequate long-term alternate paths.

Fast reroute protects traffic against any single point of failure between the ingress and egress routers. If there are multiple failures along an LSP, it is possible that fast reroute itself might fail. Also, fast reroute does not protect against failure of the ingress or egress routers.

Detours are created using RSVP and, like all RSVP sessions, they require extra state and overhead in the network. For this reason, each node establishes at most one detour for each LSP that has fast reroute enabled. Creating more than one detour for each LSP increases the overhead but serves no practical purpose.

To reduce network overhead further, each detour attempts to merge back into the LSP as soon as possible after the failed node or link. If you can consider an LSP that travels through *N* router nodes, it is possible to create *N* – 1 detours. For instance, in Figure 11.13, the detour tries to merge back into the LSP at Router D instead of at Router E or Router F. Merging back into the LSP makes the detour scalability problem more manageable. If topology limitations prevent the detour from quickly merging back into the LSP, detours merge with other detours automatically.

Figure 11.13 *Detours Merging into Other Detours*

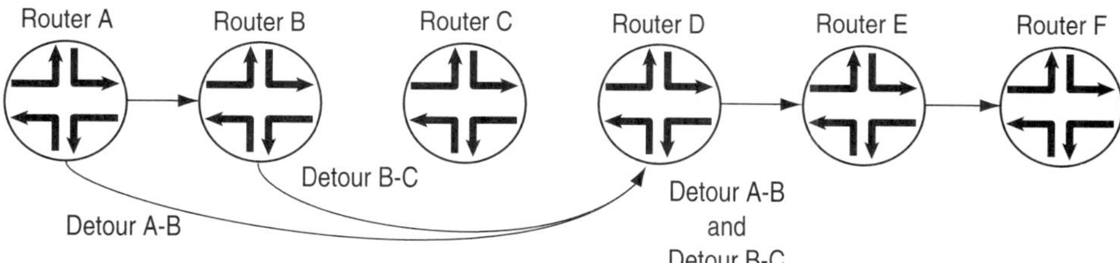

A router on which MPLS is enabled (referred to as a *label-switched router*) uses certain procedures to determine which LSP to select when the router receives path messages from different interfaces with identical SESSION and SENDER_TEMPLATE objects. When this occurs, the label-switched router needs to merge the path states. The router on which MPLS is enabled uses the following procedure to determine when and how to merge path states:

1. When all the path messages do not include a `FAST_REROUTE` or a `DETOUR` object, or when the label-switched router is the egress of the LSP, no merging is required. The messages are processed according to RSVP-TE.

2. Otherwise, the label-switched router *must* record the path state in addition to the incoming interface. If the path messages do not share the same outgoing interface and next-hop label-switched router, the label-switched router considers them to be independent LSPs and does not merge them.

3. For all the path messages that share the same outgoing interface and next-hop label-switched router, the label-switched router uses the following procedure to select the final LSP:

   a. If only one LSP originates from this node, select it as the final LSP.

   b. If only one LSP contains a `FAST_REROUTE` object, select it as the final LSP.

   c. If there are several LSPs and some of them have a `DETOUR` object, eliminate those containing a `DETOUR` object from the final LSP selection process.

   d. If several final LSP candidates remain (that is, there are still both `DETOUR` and protected LSPs), select the LSPs with `FAST_REROUTE` objects.

   e. If none of the LSPs has `FAST_REROUTE` objects, select the ones without `DETOUR` objects. If all the LSPs have `DETOUR` objects, select them all.

   f. Of the remaining LSP candidates, eliminate from consideration those that traverse nodes that other LSPs avoid.

   g. If several candidate LSPs still remain, select the one with the shortest explicit route object (ERO) path length. If more than one LSP has the same path length, select one randomly.

4. When the final LSP has been identified, the label-switched router must transmit only the path messages that correspond to this LSP. All other LSPs are considered merged at this node.

Computing and setting up detours are done independently at each node. On a node, if an LSP has fast reroute enabled and if a downstream link or node can be identified, the router performs a CSPF computation using the information in the local TED. For this reason, detours rely on the IGP's supporting traffic engineering extensions. Without the TED, detours cannot be established.

Detour computations might not succeed the first time. If a computation fails, the router recomputes detours approximately once every refresh interval until the computation succeeds.

To enable fast reroute on an LSP, include the `fast-reroute` statement on the ingress router:

```
[edit protocols mpls label-switched-path lsp-path-name]
fast-reroute {
  bandwidth bps;
  (exclude group-names | no-exclude);
  hop-limit number;
  (include group-names | no-include);
}
```

You do not need to configure fast reroute on the LSP's transit and egress routers. When fast reroute is enabled, the ingress router signals all the downstream routers that fast reroute is enabled on the LSP, and each downstream router does its best to set up detours for the LSP. If a downstream router does not support fast reroute, it ignores the request to set up detours and continues to support the LSP. A router that does not support fast reroute causes some of the detours to fail but otherwise has no impact on the LSP.

By default, no bandwidth is reserved for the rerouted path. To allocate bandwidth for the rerouted path, include the `bandwidth` statement. The bandwidth does not need to be identical to that allocated for the LSP.

Hop-limit constraints define how many more routers a detour is allowed to traverse compared to the LSP itself. By default, the hop limit is set to 6. For example, if an LSP traverses four routers, any detour for the LSP can be up to 10 (that is, 4 + 6) router hops, including the ingress and egress routers.

For more information about administrative group constraints, see "Configuring Administrative Groups," on page 562.

By default, a detour inherits the same administrative (coloring) group constraints as its parent LSP when CSPF is determining the alternate path. Administrative groups, also known as link coloring or resource class, are manually assigned attributes that describe the "color" of links, such that links with the same color conceptually belong to the same class. If you specify the `include` statement when configuring the parent LSP, all links traversed by the alternate session must have at least one color found in the list of groups. If you specify the `exclude` statement when configuring the parent LSP, none of the links must have a color found in the list of groups.

Associating Addresses with an LSP

By default, a host route toward the egress router is installed in the inet.3 routing table. (The host route address is the one you configure in the to statement.) Installing the host route allows BGP to perform next-hop resolution. It also prevents the host route from interfering with prefixes learned from dynamic routing protocols and stored in the inet.0 routing table.

Unlike the routes in the inet.0 table, routes in the inet.3 table are not copied to the Packet Forwarding Engine, and hence they cause no changes in the system forwarding table directly. You cannot ping or traceroute through these routes. The only use for inet.3 is to permit BGP to perform next-hop resolution. To examine the inet.3 table, use the show route table inet.3 command.

To inject additional routes into the inet.3 routing table, include the install statement:

```
[edit protocols mpls label-switched-path lsp-path-name]
install {
  destination/mask <active>;
}
```

The specified routes are installed as aliases into the routing table when the LSP is established. Installing additional routes allows BGP to resolve next hops within the specified prefix and to direct additional traffic for these next hops to a particular LSP.

Including the active option with the install statement installs the specified prefix into the inet.0 routing table, which is the primary forwarding table. The result is a route that is installed in the forwarding table any time the LSP is established, which means you can ping or traceroute the route. Use this option with care, because this type of prefix is very similar to a static route.

You use alias routes for routers that have multiple addresses being used as BGP next hops or for routers that are not MPLS-capable. In either of these cases, the LSP can be configured to another MPLS-capable system within the local domain, which then acts as a "border" router. The LSP then terminates on the border router and, from that router, Layer 3 forwarding takes the packet to the true next-hop router.

In the case of an interconnect, the domain's border router can act as the proxy router and can advertise the prefix for the interconnect if the border router is not setting the BGP next hop to itself.

In the case of a POP that has routers that do not support MPLS, one router (for example, a core router) that supports MPLS can act as a proxy for the entire POP and can inject a set of prefixes that cover the POP. Thus, all routers within the POP can advertise themselves as IBGP next hops, and traffic can follow the LSP to reach the core router. This means that normal IGP routing would prevail within the POP.

For BGP next-hop resolution, it makes no difference whether a route is in the `inet.0` or `inet.3` routing table; the route with the best match (longest mask) is chosen. Among multiple best-match routes, the one with the highest preference value is chosen.

Configuring Path Connection Retry Information

The ingress router might make many attempts to connect and reconnect to the egress router using the primary path. You can control how often the ingress router tries to establish a connection using the primary path and how long it waits between retry attempts.

The retry timer configures how long the ingress router waits before trying to connect again to the egress router using the primary path. The default retry time is 30 seconds. The time can be from 1 through 600 seconds. To modify this value, include the `retry-timer` statement:

```
[edit protocols mpls label-switched-path lsp-path-name]
retry-timer seconds;
```

By default, no limit is set to the number of times an ingress router attempts to establish or reestablish a connection to the egress router using the primary path. To limit the number of attempts, include the `retry-limit` statement:

```
[edit protocols mpls label-switched-path lsp-path-name]
retry-limit number;
```

The limit can be a value up to 10,000. When the retry limit is exceeded, no more attempts are made to establish a path connection. At this point, intervention is required to restart the primary path.

If you set a retry limit, it is reset to 1 each time a successful primary path is created.

Configuring the Dynamic and Static LSP Metrics

If you do not configure a specific metric, an LSP uses dynamic metrics by default, attempting to track the IGP metric toward the same destination (the `to` address of the LSP). IGP metrics considered include OSPF, IS-IS, RIP, and static routes. BGP and other RSVP and LDP routes are excluded. For example, if the OSPF metric toward a router is 20, all LSPs toward that router automatically inherit metric 20. If the OSPF toward a router later changes to a different value, all LSP metrics change accordingly. If there are no IGP routes toward the router, the LSP raises its metric to 65,535. Note that in this case, the LSP metric is completely determined by the IGP; it bears no relationship to the actual path the LSP is currently traversing. If LSP reroutes (such as through reoptimization), its metric does not change, and thus it remains transparent to users.

Using dynamic metrics is the default behavior; no configuration is required. To manually assign a fixed metric value to an LSP, include the `metric` statement:

```
[edit protocols mpls label-switched-path lsp-name]
metric number;
```

The LSP metric is used in several situations:

- When there are parallel LSPs with the same egress router, the metrics are compared to see which LSP has the lowest metric value (the lowest cost) and, therefore, the preferred path to the destination. If the metrics are the same, the traffic is shared.

  Adjusting the metric values can force traffic to prefer some LSPs over others, regardless of the underlying IGP metric.

- When an IGP shortcut is enabled, an IGP route might be installed in the routing table with an LSP as the next hop if the LSP is on the shortest path to the destination. In this case, the LSP metric is added to the other IGP metrics to determine the total path metric. For example, if an LSP whose ingress router is X and egress router is Y is on the shortest path to destination Z, the LSP metric is added to the metric for the IGP route from Y to Z to determine the total cost of the path. If several LSPs are potential next hops, the total metrics of the paths are compared to determine which path is preferred (that is, has the lowest total metric). As another example, IGP paths and LSPs leading to the same destination can be compared using the metric value to determine the preferred path.

Adjusting the LSP metric can force traffic to prefer LSPs, to prefer the IGP path, or to share the load among them.

- If router X and Y are BGP peers with an LSP between them, the LSP metric represents the total cost to reach Y from X. If for any reason the LSP reroutes, the underlying path cost might change significantly, but X's cost to reach Y remains the same (the LSP metric), which allows X to report through BGP MED a stable metric to downstream neighbors. As long as Y remains reachable through the LSP, no changes are visible to downstream BGP neighbors.

Configuring CSPF Tie-Breaking

When selecting a path for an LSP, CSPF uses a tie-breaking process if there are several equal-cost paths. To configure a random tie-breaking rule for CSPF to use to choose among equal-cost paths, include the `random` statement:

For information about how CSPF selects a path, see "Constrained-Path LSP Computation," on page 531.

```
[edit protocols mpls path label-switched-path lsp-path-
name]
random;
```

To prefer the path with the least-utilized links, include the `least-fill` statement:

```
[edit protocols mpls path label-switched-path lsp-path-
name]
least-fill;
```

To prefer the path with the most-utilized links, include the `most-fill` statement:

```
[edit protocols mpls path label-switched-path lsp-path-
name]
most-fill;
```

Configuring Load Balancing LSPs without CSPF

An LSP tends to load-balance its placement by randomly selecting one of the equal-cost next hops and using it exclusively. The random selection is made independently at each transit router and is made by comparing IGP metrics alone. No consideration is given to bandwidth or congestion levels.

Disabling Normal TTL Decrementing

By default, the TTL field value in the packet header is decremented by 1 for every hop the packet traverses in the LSP, thereby preventing loops. If the TTL field value reaches 0, packets are dropped, and an ICMP error packet might be sent to the originating router.

If normal TTL decrementing is disabled, the TTL field of IP packets entering LSPs is decremented by only 1 when transiting the LSP, making the LSP appear as a one-hop router to diagnostic tools, such as `traceroute`. This is done by the ingress router, which pushes a label on IP packets with the TTL field in the label initialized to 255. The label's TTL field value is decremented by 1 for every hop the MPLS packet traverses in the LSP. On the penultimate hop of the LSP, the router pops the label but does not write the label's TTL field value to the IP packet's TTL field. Instead, when the IP packet reaches the egress router, the IP packet's TTL field value is decremented by 1.

When you use `traceroute` to diagnose problems with an LSP, `traceroute` sees the ingress router, although the egress router performs the TTL decrementing. Note that this assumes that `traceroute` is initiated outside the LSP. The behavior of `traceroute` is different if it is initiated from the ingress router of the LSP. In this case, the egress router would be the first router to respond to `traceroute`.

You can disable normal TTL decrementing in an LSP so that the TTL field value does not reach 0 before the packet reaches its destination, thus preventing the packet from being dropped. You can also disable normal TTL decrementing to make the MPLS cloud appear as a single hop, thereby hiding the network topology.

There are two ways to disable TTL decrementing:

- On the ingress of the LSP, if you include the `no-decrement-ttl` statement, the ingress router negotiates with all downstream routers using a proprietary RSVP object, to ensure that all routers are in agreement. If negotiation succeeds, the entire LSP behaves as one hop to transit IP traffic.

  ```
  [edit protocols mpls label-switched-path lsp-path-
  name]
  no-decrement-ttl;
  ```

Note that the RSVP object is proprietary to the JUNOS software and might not work with other software. This potential incompatibility applies only to RSVP-signaled LSPs, not to LDP-signaled LSPs. When you include the `no-decrement-ttl` statement, hiding the TTL can be enforced on a per-LSP basis.

- On the router, you can include the `no-propagate-ttl` statement. This statement applies to all LSPs, regardless of whether they are RSVP-signaled or LDP-signaled. When set, all future LSPs traversing through this router behave as a single hop to IP packets. LSPs established before you configure this statement are not affected.

```
[edit protocols mpls]
no-propagate-ttl;
```

If you include the `no-propagate-ttl` statement, make sure that all routers are configured consistently within an MPLS domain; otherwise, the IP packet TTL might increase while in transit within LSPs. This can happen, for example, when the ingress router has `no-propagate-ttl` configured but the penultimate router does not, so the penultimate router writes the MPLS TTL value (which starts from the ingress router as 255) into the IP packet.

The operation of the `no-propagate-ttl` statement is more interoperable with other vendors' equipment. However, you must ensure that all routers are configured identically.

Allocating Bandwidth Automatically

An MPLS tunnel can automatically adjust its bandwidth allocation based on the volume of traffic flowing through the tunnel. You can configure an LSP with minimal bandwidth, and then MPLS can dynamically adjust the LSP's bandwidth allocation based on current traffic patterns. The bandwidth adjustments do not interrupt traffic flow through the tunnel.

At the end of a specified time interval, the current maximum average bandwidth usage is compared to the allocated bandwidth for the LSP. If the LSP needs more bandwidth, an attempt is made to set up a new path where bandwidth is equal to the current maximum average usage. If the attempt is successful, the LSP's traffic is routed through the new path, and the old path is removed. If the attempt fails, the LSP continues to use its current path.

You might not be able to use automatic bandwidth allocation to adjust the bandwidth of fast-reroute LSPs. Because the LSPs use fixed filter (FF) reservation style, when a new path is signaled, the bandwidth might be double-counted. This can prevent a fast-reroute LSP from ever adjusting its bandwidth when automatic bandwidth allocation is enabled.

To enable automatic bandwidth allocation, first configure MPLS statistics by including the following statements. In the `interval` statement, configure the interval for calculating the average bandwidth usage. This setting applies to all LSPs configured on the router.

```
[edit]
protocols {
  mpls {
    statistics {
      file filename;
      interval seconds;
      auto-bandwidth;
    }
  }
}
```

Then, configure automatic bandwidth by including the following statements. You can maintain the LSP's bandwidth between minimum and maximum bounds by specifying values for the `minimum-bandwidth` and `maximum-bandwidth` statements. Specify the bandwidth reallocation interval in seconds using the `adjust-interval` statement.

```
[edit protocols mpls label-switched-path label-switched-
path-name]
auto-bandwidth {
  adjust-interval seconds;
  minimum-bandwidth bps;
  maximum-bandwidth bps;
}
```

You can specify how sensitive the automatic bandwidth adjustment for an LSP is to changes in bandwidth utilization. The threshold is used to trigger automatic bandwidth adjustments. When configured, the LSP adjust bandwidth for the current interval is compared to the LSP's current bandwidth. If the percentage difference in bandwidth is greater than or equal to the specified `adjust-threshold` percentage, the LSP's bandwidth is adjusted to the adjust bandwidth. To adjust the bandwidth threshold, include the following statements:

```
[edit protocols mpls label-switched-path label-switched-
path-name]
auto-bandwidth {
  adjust-threshold percent;
}
```

You can switch to a passive bandwidth utilization monitoring mode. In this mode, no automatic bandwidth adjustments are made, but the maximum average bandwidth utilization is continuously monitored and recorded. To switch to passive bandwidth utilization monitoring mode, include the `monitor-bandwidth` statement:

```
[edit protocols mpls label-switched-path label-switched-
path-name]
auto-bandwidth {
  monitor-bandwidth;
}
```

If you have configured an LSP with primary and secondary paths, the automatic bandwidth allocation statistics are carried over to the secondary path if the primary path fails. For example, consider a primary path whose adjustment interval is half complete and whose maximum average bandwidth usage is currently calculated as 50 Mbps. If the primary path suddenly fails, the time remaining for the next adjustment and the maximum average bandwidth usage are carried over to the secondary path.

Disabling Constrained-Path LSP Computation

See "Enabling OSPF Traffic Engineering Support," on page 453, and "Configuring IS-IS Traffic Engineering Attributes," on page 430.

If the IGP is a link-state protocol that supports extensions to allow the current bandwidth reservation on each router's link to be reported, constrained path LSPs are computed by default.

The JUNOS implementations of IS-IS and OSPF include the extensions that support constrained-path LSP computation. In IS-IS, these extensions are enabled by default. (To disable this support, include the `disable` statement at the `[edit protocols isis traffic-engineering]` hierarchy level.) In OSPF, to enable this support, include the `traffic-engineering` statement.

Constrained-path LSP computation works as follows: LSPs advertise their link information in the IGP's link-state packets. These packets are flooded throughout the network and hence provide information to all nodes. This link information is placed into the TED and provides each ingress router with LSP topology information and recent LSP bandwidth reservation information. When computing complete paths for LSPs, the ingress router uses the information in the TED, along with the requirements you configure for the LSP, including bandwidth (configured with the `bandwidth` statement), hop limit (configured with the `hop-limit` statement), and the address of the egress router (configured with the `to` statement).

Constrained-path LSPs have a greater chance of being established quickly and successfully because the LSP computation takes into account the current bandwidth reservation and because constrained-path LSPs reroute themselves away from node failures and congestion.

See "Optimizing Signaled LSPs," on page 569.

When constrained-path LSP computation is enabled, you can configure the LSP so that it is periodically reoptimized.

For more information about the retry timer, see "Configuring Path Connection Retry Information," on page 555.

When an LSP is being established or when an existing LSP fails, the constrained-path LSP computation is repeated periodically at the interval specified by the retry timer until the LSP is set up successfully. When the LSP is set up, no recomputation is done.

By default, constrained-path LSP computation is enabled. You might want to disable constrained-path LSP computation when all nodes do not support the necessary traffic engineering extensions. To disable constrained-path LSP computation, include the `no-cspf` statement:

```
[edit protocols mpls label-switched-path lsp-path-name]
or [edit protocols mpls label-switched-path lsp-path-name
(primary | secondary)]
no-cspf;
```

Configuring Administrative Groups

Administrative groups, also known as link coloring or resource class, are manually assigned attributes that describe the "color" of links, such that links with the same color conceptually belong to the same class. You can use administrative groups to implement a variety of policy-based LSP setups. Administrative groups are meaningful only when constrained-path LSP computation is enabled. To configure administrative groups, follow these steps:

1. Configure a table of group names:

```
[edit protocols mpls]
admin-groups{
  group-name group-value;
}
```

   You can assign up to 32 names and values in the range 0 through 31, which define a series of names and their corresponding values. The administrative names and values must be identical across all routers within a single domain.

2. Define multiple levels of service quality:

```
[edit]
protocols {
  mpls {
    admin-groups {
      best-effort 1;
      copper 2;
      silver 3;
      gold 4;
      violet 5;
    }
  }
}
```

3. Define administrative groups for an interface. These groups identify the administrative groups to which an interface belongs. You can assign multiple groups to an interface.

```
[edit]
protocols {
  mpls {
    interface interface name {
      admin-group [ group-name group-name... ];
    }
  }
}
```

   If you do not include the `admin-group` statement, an interface does not belong to any group.

   IGPs use the group information to build link-state packets, which are then flooded throughout the network, providing information to all nodes in the network. At any router, the IGP topology, as well as administrative groups of all the links, is available.

4. Configure an administrative group constraint for each LSP or for each primary or secondary LSP path:

```
[edit]
protocols {
  mpls {
    label-switched-path lsp-path-name {
      to address;
      ...
      primary path-name {
        admin-group {
          exclude [ group-name group-name ... ];
          include [ group-name group-name ... ];
        }
      }
      secondary path-name {
        admin-group {
          exclude [ group-name group-name ... ];
          include [ group-name group-name ... ];
        }
            admin-group {
          exclude [ group-name group-name ... ];
          include [ group-name group-name ... ];
        }
      }
    }
  }
}
```

If you omit the `include` or `exclude` statements, the path computation proceeds unchanged using constrained-path LSP computation. If you configure an `exclude` list, all chosen links must not have a color in the `exclude` list. If you configure an `include` list, all chosen links must have at least one color in the `include` list. Links that have no color are automatically disqualified by any `include` or `exclude` list.

Configuring the LSP Preference

You can configure multiple LSPs between the same pair of ingress and egress routers, for example, if you want to balance the load among the LSPs because all LSPs, by default, have the same preference level. To prefer one LSP over another, set different preference levels for individual LSPs. The LSP with the lowest preference value is used. The default preference of all LSPs is 7, which is lower (more preferred) than all learned routes except for direct interface routes. To change the default preference value, include the `preference` statement:

```
preference preference;
```

Configuring Whether to Record Path Routes

The JUNOS implementation of RSVP supports the record route object, which allows an LSP to actively record the routers through which it transits. You can use this information for troubleshooting and to prevent routing loops. By default, path route information is recorded. To disable recording, include the `no-record` statement:

```
no-record;
```

Configuring the MPLS CoS Value

When IP traffic enters an LSP tunnel, the ingress router marks all packets with a class-of-service (CoS) value, which is used to place the traffic into a transmission priority queue. On the router, for SDH/SONET and T3 interfaces, each interface has four transmit queues. The CoS value is encoded as part of the MPLS header and remains in the packets until the MPLS header is removed when the packets exit from the egress router. The routers within the LSP use the CoS value set at the ingress router.

See Chapter 6, "Interfaces and Class of Service," on page 185.

MPLS class of service works in conjunction with the router's general CoS functionality. If you do not configure any CoS features, the default general CoS settings are used. For MPLS class of service, you might want to prioritize how the transmit queues are serviced by configuring weighted round-robin and to configure congestion avoidance using Random Early Detection (RED).

When traffic enters an LSP tunnel, the CoS bits in the MPLS header are set in one of two ways. In the first way, the number of the output queue into which the packet was buffered and the packet loss priority (PLP) bit are written into the MPLS header and are used as the packet's CoS value. This behavior is the default, and no configuration is required.

In the second way, you set a fixed CoS value on all packets entering the LSP tunnel. This means that all packets entering the LSP receive the same class of service. To do this, include the `class-of-service` statement:

```
class-of-service cos-value;
```

The CoS value can be a decimal number from 0 through 7. This number corresponds to a 3-bit binary number. The high-order two bits of the CoS value select which transmit queue to use on the outbound interface card. The low-order bit of the CoS value is treated as the PLP bit and is used to select the RED drop profile to use on the output queue. If the low-order bit is 0, the non-PLP drop profile is used, and if the low-order bit is 1, the PLP drop profile is used. It is generally expected that RED will more aggressively drop packets that have the PLP bit set.

Table 11.2 summarizes how MPLS CoS values correspond to the transmit queue and PLP bit. Note that in MPLS, the mapping between the CoS bit value and the output queue is hard-coded. You cannot configure the mapping for MPLS; you can configure it only for IPv4 traffic flows.

Table 11.2 *MPLS CoS Values*

MPLS CoS Value	Bits	Transmit Queue	PLP Bit
0	000	0	Not set
1	001	0	Set
2	010	1	Not set
3	011	1	Set
4	100	2	Not set
5	101	2	Set
6	110	3	Not set
7	111	3	Set

Because the CoS value is part of the MPLS header, the value is associated with the packets only as they travel through the LSP tunnel. The value is not copied back to the IP header when the packets exit from the LSP tunnel.

Configuring an LSP to Be Adaptive

An LSP occasionally might need to reroute itself. Reasons include the following:

- Continuous reoptimization process is configured with the `optimize-timer` statement.
- The current path has connectivity problems.

- The LSP is preempted by another LSP configured with the `priority` statement and is forced to reroute.
- The explicit-path information for an active LSP is modified, or the LSP's bandwidth is increased.

You can configure an LSP to be *adaptive* when it is attempting to reroute itself. When it is adaptive, the LSP holds onto existing resources until the new path is successfully established and traffic has been cut over to the new LSP. To retain its resources, an adaptive LSP does the following:

- Maintains existing paths and allocated bandwidths—This ensures that the existing path is not torn down prematurely and allows the current traffic to continue flowing while the new path is being set up.
- Avoids double-counting for links that share the new and old paths—Double-counting occurs when an intermediate router does not recognize that the new and old paths belong to the same LSP and counts them as two separate LSPs, requiring separate bandwidth allocations. If some links are close to saturation, double-counting might cause the setup of the new path to fail.

By default, adaptive behavior is disabled. You can include the `adaptive` statement in two different hierarchy levels. If you include the following form of the `adaptive` statement, adaptive behavior is enabled on all primary and secondary paths of the LSP. This means both the primary and secondary paths share the same bandwidth on common links.

```
[edit protocols mpls label-switched-path lsp-path-name]
adaptive;
```

If you include the following form of `adaptive` statement, adaptive behavior is enabled only on the path on which it is specified. Double-counting of bandwidth occurs between different paths.

```
[edit protocols mpls label-switched-path lsp-path-name
(primary | secondary)]
adaptive;
```

Configuring Priority and Preemption

When there is insufficient bandwidth to establish a more important LSP, you might want to tear down a less important existing LSP to free up the bandwidth. You do this by preempting the existing LSP. Whether an LSP can be preempted is determined by two properties associated with the LSP:

- Setup priority—Determines whether a new LSP that preempts an existing LSP can be established. For preemption to occur, the setup priority of the new LSP must be higher than that of the existing LSP. Also, the act of preempting the existing LSP must produce sufficient bandwidth to support the new LSP. That is, preemption occurs only if the new LSP can be set up successfully.
- Hold priority—Determines the degree to which an LSP holds onto its session reservation after the LSP has been set up successfully. When the hold priority is high, the existing LSP is less likely to give up its reservation and hence it is unlikely that the LSP can be preempted.

You cannot configure an LSP with a high setup priority and a low hold priority because permanent preemption loops might result if two LSPs are allowed to preempt each other. You must configure the hold priority to be higher than or equal to the setup priority.

The setup priority also defines the relative importance of LSPs on the same ingress router. When the software starts, when a new LSP is established, or during fault recovery, the setup priority determines the order in which LSPs are serviced. Higher priority LSPs tend to be established first and hence enjoy more optimal path selection.

To configure the LSP's preemption properties, include the `priority` statement at the `[edit protocols mpls]`, `[edit protocols mpls label-switched-path` *`lsp-path-name`*`]`, or `[edit protocols mpls label-switched-path` *`lsp-path-name`* `(primary | secondary)]` hierarchy level:

```
priority setup-priority hold-priority;
```

Both *`setup-priority`* and *`hold-priority`* can be a value from 0 through 7. The value 0 corresponds to the highest priority, and the value 7 to the lowest. By default, an LSP has a setup priority of 7 (that is, it cannot preempt any other LSPs) and a hold priority of 0 (that is, other LSPs cannot preempt it). These defaults are such that preemption does not happen. When you are configuring these values, the setup priority should always be less than or equal to the hold priority.

Optimizing Signaled LSPs

After an LSP has been established, topology or resource changes might, over time, make the path less than optimal. A subsequent recomputation might be able to determine a more optimal path.

If reoptimization is enabled, an LSP can be rerouted through different paths by constrained-path recomputations. However, if reoptimization is disabled, the LSP has a fixed path and cannot take advantage of newly available network resources. The LSP is fixed until the next topology change breaks the LSP and forces a recomputation.

Reoptimization is not related to failover. A new path is always computed when topology failures occur that disrupt an established path.

Because of the potential system overhead involved, you need to control carefully the frequency of reoptimization. Network stability might suffer when reoptimization is enabled. By default, `optimize-timer` is set to 0 (that is, it is disabled).

Configuring LSP optimization is meaningful only when constrained-path LSP computation is enabled, which is the default behavior. See "Disabling Constrained-Path LSP Computation," on page 561.

To enable path reoptimization, include the `optimize-timer` statement:

```
optimize-timer seconds;
```

After reoptimization is run, the result is accepted only if it meets the following criteria:

1. The new path is not higher in IGP metric. (The metric for the old path is updated during computation, so if a recent link metric changed somewhere along the old path, it is accounted for.)
2. If the new path has the same IGP metric, it is not more hops away.
3. The new path does not cause preemption. (This is enforced to reduce the ripple effect of preemption causing more preemption.)
4. The new path does not worsen congestion overall. This is done by comparing the percentage of available bandwidth on each link traversed by the new and old paths, starting from the most congested links.

When all the above conditions are met, then:

5. If the new path has a lower IGP metric, it is accepted.
6. If the new path has an equal IGP metric and lower hop count, it is accepted.

7. If you choose `least-fill` as a load-balancing algorithm and if the new path reduces congestion by at least 10 percent aggregated over all links it traversed, it is accepted. For `random` or `most-fill` algorithms, this rule does not apply.
8. Otherwise, the new path is rejected.

To disable items 2, 3, 4, and 6 above, enter the `clear mpls optimize-aggressive` command or include the `optimize-aggressive` statement to make the reoptimization process more aggressive. Not only does aggressive optimization tend to reroute more often, but it also limits the reoptimization algorithm to be based on the IGP metric only.

```
[edit protocols mpls]
optimize-aggressive;
```

Configuring the Path Bandwidth and Maximum Path Length

Each LSP has a bandwidth value. This value is included in the sender's Tspec field in RSVP path setup messages. To specify a bandwidth value, include the `bandwidth` statement. Specify the bandwidth value in bits per second, with a higher value configuring a greater user traffic volume. The default bandwidth is 0 bits per second.

```
bandwidth bps;
```

A nonzero bandwidth requires transit routers to reserve capacity along the outbound links for the path. This is done using RSVP's reservation scheme. Any failure in bandwidth reservation (such as failures at RSVP policy control or admission control) might cause the LSP setup to fail.

By default, each LSP can traverse a maximum of 255 hops, including the ingress and egress routers. To modify this value, include the `hop-limit` statement. The number of hops can be from 2 through 255. (A path with two hops consists of the ingress and egress routers only.)

```
hop-limit number;
```

Configuring the Standby State

By default, secondary paths are set up only as needed. To have the system maintain a secondary path in a hot-standby state indefinitely, include the `standby` statement:

```
standby;
```

The hot-standby state is meaningful only on secondary paths.

Maintaining a path in a hot-standby state enables swift cutover to the secondary path when downstream routers on the current active path indicate connectivity problems. The hot-standby state has two advantages:

- It eliminates the call-setup delay during network topology changes. Call setup can suffer from significant delays when network failures trigger large numbers of LSP reroutes at the same time.
- A cutover to the secondary path can be made before RSVP learns that an LSP is down. There can be significant delays between the time the first failure is detected by protocol machinery (which can be an interface down, a neighbor becoming unreachable, a route becoming unreachable, or a transient routing loop being detected) and the time an LSP actually fails (which requires a timeout of soft-state information between adjacent RSVP routers). When topology failures occur, hot-standby secondary paths can usually achieve the smallest cutover delays with minimal disruptions to user traffic.

When the primary path is considered to be stable again, traffic is automatically switched from the standby secondary path back to the primary path. The switch is performed no faster than twice the retry-timer interval and only if the primary path exhibits stability throughout the entire switch interval.

The drawback of the hot-standby state is that more state information must be maintained by all the routers along the path, which imposes additional overhead on each of the routers.

Configuring the LSP Hold Time

When an LSP changes from being up to being down, or from down to up, this transition takes effect immediately in the router software and hardware. However, when advertising LSPs into IS-IS, you might want to damp LSP transitions, thereby not advertising the transition until a certain period of time has transpired (known as the hold time). In this case, if the LSP goes from up to down, the LSP is not advertised as being down until it has remained down for the hold-time period. Transitions from down to up are advertised into IS-IS immediately. Note that LSP damping only affects IS-IS advertisements of the LSP; other routing software and hardware react immediately to LSP transitions.

To damp LSP transitions, include the `advertisement-hold-time` statement. The time can be a value from 0 through 65,535 seconds. The default is 5 seconds.

```
[edit protocols mpls]
advertise-hold-time seconds;
```

Configuring LDP Tunneling

To correctly identify an LDP session associated with an RSVP LSP, ensure that the RSVP LSP end point address is the same as the transport address of the LDP peer.

Using Fate Sharing to Configure Alternate Backup Paths

You can create a database of information that CSPF uses to compute one or more backup paths to use in case the primary path becomes unstable. The database describes the relationships between elements of the network, such as routers and links. Because these network elements share the same fate, this relationship is called *fate sharing*.

You can configure backup paths that minimize the number of shared links and fiber paths with the primary paths as much as possible to ensure that, if a fiber is cut, the minimum amount of data is lost and a path still exists to the destination.

For a backup path to work optimally, it must not share links or physical fiber paths with the primary path. This ensures that a single point of failure will not affect the primary and backup paths at the same time.

To configure fate sharing, include the `fate-sharing` statement:

```
[edit routing-options]
fate-sharing {
  group group-name {
    cost value;
    from address <to address>;
  }
}
```

Each fate-sharing group must have a name, which can be up to 32 characters long and can contain letters, digits, periods (.), and hyphens (-). You can define up to 512 groups.

Fate-sharing groups contain three types of objects:

- Point-to-point links—Identified by the IP addresses at each end of the link. Unnumbered point-to-point links are typically identified by borrowing IP addresses from other interfaces. Order is not important; the statements `from 1.2.3.4 to 1.2.3.5` and `from 1.2.3.5 to 1.2.3.4` have the same meaning.
- Nonpoint-to-point links—Include links on a LAN interface (such as Gigabit Ethernet interfaces) or NBMA interfaces (such as ATM or Frame Relay). You identify these links by their individual interface address.
- A router node—Identified by its configured router ID.

All objects in a group share certain similarities. For example, you can define a group for all fibers sharing the same fiber conduit, all optical channels that share the same fiber, all links that connect to the same LAN switch, all equipment sharing the same power source, and so on. All objects are treated as `/32` host addresses.

For a group to be meaningful, it should contain at least two objects. You can configure groups with zero or one object, but they are ignored during processing.

An object can be in any number of groups, and a group can contain any number of objects. Each group has a configurable cost attributed to it, which represents the level of impact this group has on CSPF computations. The higher the cost, the less likely a backup path shares with the primary path any objects in the group. The cost is directly comparable to traffic engineering metrics. By default, the cost is 1. Changing the fate-sharing database does not affect existing established LSPs until the next reoptimization of CSPF. The fate-sharing database does influence fast-reroute computations.

When CSPF computes the primary paths of an LSP (or secondary paths when the primary path is not active), it ignores the fate-sharing information. You always want to find the best possible path (least IGP cost) for the primary path.

When CSPF computes a secondary path of an LSP while that LSP's primary path is active, the following occurs:

1. CSPF identifies all fate-sharing groups that are associated with the primary path. CSPF does this by identifying all links and nodes that the primary path traverses and compiling group lists that contain at least one of the links or nodes. CSPF ignores the ingress and egress nodes in the search.
2. CSPF checks each link in the TED against the compiled group list. If the link is a member of a group, the cost of the link is increased by the cost of the group. If a link is a member of multiple groups, all group costs are added together.
3. CSPF performs the check for every node in the TED, except the ingress and egress node. Again, a node can belong to multiple groups, so costs are additive.
4. The router performs regular CSPF computation with the adjusted topology.

Enabling RSVP

For all routers that should participate in signaled LSPs, you must enable RSVP because it is used to set up LSPs. To do this, include the following statements in the configuration. In general, we recommend that you enable RSVP on all router interfaces, except for those on the AS border.

```
[edit]
interfaces {
  interface-name {
    unit logical-unit-number {
      family mpls;
    }
  }
}
protocols {
  mpls {
    interface all;
  }
  rsvp {
    interface all;
  }
}
```

Configuring MPLS over GRE Tunnels

See "Configuring Tunnel Interfaces," on page 262.

MPLS LSPs can use GRE tunnels to cross routing areas, ASs, and ISPs. Bridging MPLS LSPs over an intervening IP domain is possible without disrupting the outlying MPLS domain. LSPs can reach any destination that the GRE tunnels can reach. MPLS applications can be deployed without requiring all transit nodes to support MPLS, or requiring all transit nodes to support the same label distribution protocols (LDP or RSVP). If you use CSPF, you must configure OSPF or IS-IS through the GRE tunnel. Traffic engineering is not supported over GRE tunnels; for example, you cannot reserve bandwidth or set priority or preemption.

Configuring Static LSPs

To configure static LSPs, configure the ingress router and each router along the path up to and including the egress router.

For the ingress router, configure which packets to tag (based on the packet's IP destination address), the next router in the LSP, and the tag to apply to the packet. Manually assigned labels can have values in the range 16 through 1,023. Optionally, you can apply preference and CoS values to the packets.

For the intermediate routers in the path, configure the next router in the path and the tag to apply to the packet. Again, you can optionally apply preference and CoS values to the packets.

For the egress router, you generally just remove the label and continue forwarding the packet to the next hop. However, if the previous router removed the label, the egress router examines the packet's IP header and forwards the packet toward its IP destination.

The ingress router checks the IP address in the incoming packet's destination address field and, if it finds a match in the routing table, applies the label associated with that address to the packets. The label has forwarding information associated with it, including the address of the next-hop router and the route preference and CoS values.

To configure static LSPs on the ingress router, include the `static-path` statement:

```
[edit protocols mpls]
static-path inet {
  prefix {
    next-hop (address | interface-name | address/
      interface-name)
    push out-label;
    class-of-service value;
    preference preference;
  }
}
```

Specify the criteria to use to analyze an incoming packet. The `inet` option creates an LSP that handles IPv4 packets. All static MPLS routes created using the `inet` option are installed in the default IPv4 routing table (`inet.0`), and the creating protocol is identified as `static`. This is no different from creating static IPv4 routes at the `[edit routing-options static]` hierarchy level. In the *`prefix`* option, configure the IP destination address to check when analyzing incoming packets. If the address matches, the specified label, *`out-label`*, is assigned to the packet and the packet enters an LSP. Each prefix that you specify is installed as a static route in the routing table. You can specify one or more *`prefix`* statements at the `[edit protocols mpls static-path]` hierarchy level.

In the `next-hop` statement, specify the IP address of the next hop to the destination as the IP address of the next hop, the interface name (for point-to-point interfaces only), or as *`address/interface-name`* to specify an IP address on an operational interface. When the next hop is on a directly attached interface, the route is installed in the routing table. You cannot configure a LAN or point-to-multipoint (NMBA) interface as a next-hop interface.

Finally, specify the label properties applied to the packet in the LSP. In the `push` statement, specify one label itself. The label is a 20-bit integer, so it can be a number in the range 0 through 1,048,575 ($2^{20} - 1$). Dynamic MPLS assigns the labels 100,000 through 1,048,575, so if your network uses both static and dynamic MPLS, Juniper Networks recommends that you use labels 16 through 1,023 and 10,000 through 99,999 only for static MPLS. (Labels 0 through 15 are reserved and require special semantics. Labels 1,024 through 9,999 are reserved for future applications.) Also specify the preference of this route and the CoS value to apply to the packet.

To determine whether a static ingress route is installed, use the `show route table inet.0 protocol static` command. The following is a sample output. The `push` keyword identifies that a label is to be added in front of IP packet.

```
10.0.0.0/8      *[Static/5] 00:01:48
                > to 11.1.1.1 via so-0/0/0, push 123
```

Intermediate and egress routers perform similar functions—they modify the label that has been applied to a packet. An intermediate router can change the label. An egress router removes the label (if the packet still contains a label) and continues forwarding the packet to its destination. To configure static MPLS on intermediate and egress routers, include the `interface` statement. You can include any number of `label-map` statements in the configuration.

```
[edit protocols mpls]
interface interface-name {
  label-map in-label {
    (next-hop <address; interface-name>) | (reject |
      discard);
    (pop | (swap <out-label>);
    class-of-service value;
    preference preference;
    type type;
  }
}
```

Specify the criteria to use to analyze the labeled packet. Two criteria are used: the interface on which the packet was received (specified in the opening `interface` statement itself) and the packet's label (specified in the `label-map` statement).

In the `next-hop` statement, configure the IP address of the next hop to the destination, specified as the IP address of the next hop, the interface name (for point-to-point interfaces only), or *`address/interface-name`* to specify an IP address on an operational interface. When the specified next hop is on a directly attached interface, this route is installed in the routing table. You cannot configure a LAN or point-to-multipoint (NBMA) interface as a next-hop interface.

Configure one of the following operations to perform on the labeled packet:

- For egress routers, remove the packet's label altogether (`pop`).
- For intermediate routers only, exchange the label for another label (`swap` *`out-label`*).

- Discard the packet, sending an ICMP unreachable message to the packet's originator (`reject`).
- Discard the packet without sending an ICMP unreachable message to the packet's originator (`discard`).

Configure label properties to apply to the packet, all of which are optional:

- Type of traffic in the LSP. Currently, the type can be IPv4 only (`type inet`), which is the default.
- Preference value for this route (`preference` *`preference`*).
- For intermediate routers only, the CoS value to apply to the packet (`class-of-service` *`cos-value`*).

The static routes are installed in the default MPLS routing table, `mpls.0`, and the creating protocol is identified as `static`. To verify that a static route is properly installed, use the `show route table mpls.0 protocol static` command. The following is an example of the output:

```
123
*[Static/5] 00:00:38
> to 12.2.2.2 via so-5/0/0.0, swap 456
```

Configuring Explicit-Path LSPs

If you disable constrained-path LSP computation, as described in "Disabling Constrained-Path LSP Computation," on page 561, you must configure LSPs manually. Experimenting with particular explicit paths can familiarize you with MPLS.

When explicit-path LSPs are configured, the LSP is established along the path you specified. If the path is topologically not feasible, either because the network is partitioned or insufficient resources are available along some parts of the path, the LSP fails. No alternative paths can be used. If the setup succeeds, the LSP stays on the defined path indefinitely.

Using explicit-path LSPs has the following drawbacks:

- More configuration effort is required.
- Configured path information cannot take into account dynamic network bandwidth reservation, so the LSPs tend to fail when resources become depleted.

- When an explicit-path LSP fails, you might need to manually repair it.

Because of these limitations, Juniper Networks recommends that you use explicit-path LSPs only in controlled situations, such as to enforce an optimized LSP placement strategy resulting from computations with an offline simulation software package.

To configure an explicit path LSP, follow these steps:

See "Configuring the Ingress Router for MPLS-Signaled LSPs," on page 545.

1. Configure the path information in a named path. To configure complete path information, specify every router hop between the ingress and egress routers, preferably using the `strict` attribute. To configure incomplete path information, specify only a subset of router hops, using the `loose` attribute in places where the path is incomplete.

   For incomplete paths, the MPLS routers complete the path by querying the local routing table. This query is done on a hop-by-hop basis, and each router can determine only enough information to reach the next explicit hop. It might be necessary to traverse a number of routers in order to reach the next (loose) explicit hop.

   Configuring incomplete path information creates portions of the path that are dependent on the current routing table, and this portion of the path can reroute itself as the topology changes. Therefore, an explicit-path LSP that contains incomplete path information is not completely fixed. These types of LSPs have only a limited capability to repair themselves, and they tend to create loops or flaps depending on the contents of the local routing table.

See "Configuring the Primary and Secondary LSPs," on page 548.

2. To configure the LSP and point it to the named path, use either the `primary` or `secondary` statement.

See "Disabling Constrained-Path LSP Computation," on page 561.

3. Disable constrained-path LSP computation by including the `no-cspf` statement either as part of the LSP or as part of a `primary` or `secondary` statement.
4. Configure any other LSP properties.

Configuring Miscellaneous MPLS Properties

This section discusses additional MPLS properties that are not directly related to creating LSPs.

Popping the Label on the Ultimate-Hop Router

You can control the label value advertised on the egress router of an LSP. The default advertised label is label 3 (implicit null label). If label 3 is advertised, the penultimate-hop router removes the label and sends the packet to the egress router. By enabling ultimate-hop popping, label 0 (IPv4 Explicit Null Label) is advertised. Ultimate hop-popping ensures that any packets traversing an MPLS network include a label.

To configure MPLS to pop the label on the ultimate hop, include the `explicit-null` statement:

```
[edit protocols ldp]
explicit-null;
```

Juniper Networks routers queue packets based on the incoming label. Routers from other vendors might queue packets differently. Keep this in mind when working with networks containing routers from multiple vendors.

Configuring Traffic Engineering for LSPs

Establishing an LSP installs a host route (a 32-bit mask) in the ingress router toward the egress router. The address of the host route is the destination address of the LSP. By default, only BGP can use LSPs in its route calculations. On the ingress router, to enable both BGP and the IGPs to use an LSP in forwarding traffic destined for the egress router of that LSP, include the `traffic-engineering` statement with the `bgp-igp` option:

```
[edit protocol mpls]
traffic-engineering bgp-igp;
```

To install the ingress routes in both the `inet.0` and `inet.3` routing tables, which are used to support VPNs, include the traffic engineering statement with the `bgp-igp-both-ribs` option:

```
[edit protocol mpls]
traffic-engineering bgp-igp-both-ribs;
```

Configuring MPLS to Gather Statistics

To configure MPLS so that it periodically gathers traffic statistics about all MPLS sessions, including transit sessions, include the statistics statement:

```
[edit protocol mpls]
statistics {
  file filename <size size files number>;
  interval seconds;
  auto-bandwidth;
}
```

The default interval is 300 seconds.

The statistics are placed in a file, with one entry per LSP. During the specified interval, the following information is recorded in this file:

- Number of packets, number of bytes, packets per second, and bytes per second transmitted by each LSP.
- Percent of bandwidth transmitted over a given LSP in relation to the bandwidth percentage configured for that LSP. Note that if no bandwidth is configured for an LSP, 0 percent is recorded in the percentage column.

At the end of each periodic report, a summary shows the current time, total number of sessions, number of sessions read, number of sessions ignored, and read errors, if any. Ignored sessions are typically those not in the up state or those with a reserved (0 through 15) incoming label (typically the egress point of an LSP). The reason for a read error appears on the same line as the entry for the LSP on which the error occurred. Gathering statistics is an unreliable process; occasional read errors might affect their accuracy.

Controlling MPLS System Log Messages and SNMP Traps

For more information about the MPLS SNMP traps and the proprietary MPLS MIB, see the JUNOS technical documentation: *MPLS*.

Whenever an LSP makes a transition from up to down, or down to up, and whenever an LSP switches from one active path to another, the ingress router generates a system log message and sends an SNMP trap.

To disable the generation of system log messages and SNMP traps, include the following statements. For scalability reasons, only the ingress router generates SNMP traps. By default, MPLS issues traps for all configured LSPs. If you have many LSPs, the number of traps can become quite large.

```
[edit protocols mpls]
log-updown {
  no-syslog;
  no-trap;
}
```

Tracing MPLS Protocol Packets and Operations

To trace MPLS protocol packets and operations, include the traceoptions statement:

```
[edit protocol mpls]
traceoptions {
  file filename <replace> <size size> <files number>
      <no-stamp>
    <(world-readable | no-world-readable)>;
  flag flag <flag-modifier> <disable>;
}
```

For more information about tracing and global tracing options, see the JUNOS technical documentation.

You can specify the following MPLS-specific flags:

- connection—All circuit cross-connect (CCC) activity
- connection-detail—Detailed CCC activity
- cspf—CSPF computations
- cspf-link—Links visited during CSPF computations
- cspf-node—Nodes visited during CSPF computations
- error—MPLS error conditions
- state—All LSP state transitions

RSVP

The Resource Reservation Protocol (RSVP) is a resource reservation setup protocol that is used by both network hosts and routers. Hosts use RSVP to request a specific quality of service (QoS) from the network for particular application flows. Routers use RSVP to deliver QoS requests to all routers along the data path. RSVP also can maintain and refresh states for a requested QoS application flow.

RSVP treats an application flow as a simplex connection. That is, the QoS request travels only in one direction—from the sender to the receiver. RSVP is a transport layer protocol that uses IP as its network layer. However, RSVP does not transport application flows. Rather, it is more of an Internet control protocol, similar to ICMP, IGMP, IS-IS, or OSPF. RSVP runs as a separate software process in the JUNOS Internet software and is not in the packet forwarding path.

RSVP is not a routing protocol, but rather is designed to operate with current and future unicast and multicast routing protocols. The routing protocols are responsible for choosing the routes to use to forward packets, and RSVP consults local routing tables to obtain routes. RSVP is responsible only for ensuring the QoS of packets traveling along a data path.

The receiver in an application flow is responsible for requesting the preferred QoS from the sender. To do this, the receiver issues an RSVP QoS request on behalf of the local application. The request propagates to all routers in reverse direction of the data paths toward the sender. In this process, RSVP requests might be merged, resulting in a protocol that scales well when there are a large number of receivers.

Because the number of receivers in an application flow is likely to change, and the flow of delivery paths might change during the life of an application flow, RSVP takes a soft-state approach in its design, creating and removing the protocol states in routers and hosts incrementally over time. RSVP sends periodic refresh messages to maintain its state and to recover from occasional lost messages. In the absence of refresh messages, the RSVP states automatically time out and are deleted.

The JUNOS implementation of RSVP supports RSVP Version 1. The software includes support for all mandatory objects and RSVP message types, and supports message integrity and node authentications through the integrity object.

The primary purpose of the JUNOS RSVP software is to support dynamic signaling within MPLS LSPs. Supporting resource reservations over the Internet is only a secondary purpose of the JUNOS implementation. Because of this, the RSVP software does not support IP multicasting sessions or traffic control (it cannot make resource reservations for real-time video or audio sessions).

With regard to the protocol mechanism, packet processing, and RSVP objects supported, the JUNOS implementation of the software is interoperable with other RSVP implementations.

Table 11.3 lists the RSVP standards and protocol extensions supported by the JUNOS software.

Table 11.3 *RSVP Standards Supported by JUNOS Software*

Standard	Title
RFC 2205	*Resource Reservation Protocol (RSVP), Version 1, Functional Specification*
RFC 2209	*Resource Reservation Protocol (RSVP), Version 1, Message Processing Rules*
RFC 2210	*The Use of RSVP with IETF Integrated Services*
RFC 2211	*Specification of the Controlled-Load Network Element Service*
RFC 2215	*General Characterization Parameters for Integrated Service Network Elements*
RFC 2216	*Network Element Service Specification Template*
RFC 2747	*RSVP Cryptographic Authentication*
Internet draft draft-ietf-mpls-rsvp-lsp-tunnel-05.txt	*Extensions to RSVP for LSP Tunnels*
Internet draft draft-ietf-rsvp-refresh-reduct-05.txt	*RSVP Refresh Reduction Extensions*

RSVP creates independent sessions to handle each data flow. A session is identified by a combination of the destination address, an optional destination port, and a protocol. Within a session, there can be one or more senders. Each sender is identified by a combination of its source address and source port. An out-of-band mechanism, such as a session announcement protocol or human communication, is used to communicate the session identifier to all senders and receivers.

A typical RSVP session involves the following sequence of events:

1. A potential sender starts sending RSVP path messages to the session address.
2. A receiver, wanting to join the session, registers itself if necessary. For example, a receiver in a multicast application would register itself with IGMP.
3. The receiver receives the path messages.
4. The receiver sends appropriate resv messages toward the sender. These messages carry a flow descriptor, which is used by routers along the path to make reservations in their link-layer media.
5. The sender receives the resv message, and then it starts sending application data.

This sequence of events is not necessarily strictly synchronized. For example, receivers can register themselves before receiving path messages from the sender, and application data can flow before the sender receives resv messages. Application data that is delivered before the actual reservation contained in the resv message typically is treated as best effort, nonreal-time traffic with no QoS guarantee.

RSVP uses several types of messages to establish and remove paths for data flows, to establish and remove reservation information, to confirm the establishment of reservations, and to report errors as specified in Table 11.4.

A reservation request includes options for specifying the reservation style. The reservation styles define how reservations for different senders within the same session are treated and how senders are selected. Two options specify how reservations for different senders within the same session are treated:

- Distinct reservation—Each receiver establishes its own reservation with each upstream sender.
- Shared reservation—All receivers make a single reservation that is shared among many senders.

Table 11.4 *RSVP Message Types*

Message Type	Description
Path	Transmitted downstream by each sender host, along the routes provided by the unicast and multicast routing protocols. Path messages follow the exact paths of application data, creating path states in the routers along the way, thus enabling routers to learn the previous hop and next-hop node for the session. Path messages are sent periodically to refresh path states. The refresh interval is controlled by a variable called the *refresh time*, which is the periodical refresh timer expressed in seconds. A path state times out if a router does not receive a specified number of consecutive path messages. This number is specified by a variable called *keep-multiplier*. Path states are kept for ((*keep-multiplier* + 0.5) * 1.5 * *refresh-time*) seconds.
Resv	Each receiver host sends reservation request (resv) messages upstream toward senders and sender applications. Resv messages must follow exactly the reverse path of path messages. Resv messages create and maintain a reservation state in each router along the way. Resv messages are sent periodically to refresh reservation states. The refresh interval is controlled by the same refresh time variable, and reservation states are kept for ((*keep-multiplier* + 0.5) * 1.5 * *refresh-time*) seconds.
PathTear	PathTear messages remove (tear down) path states as well as dependent reservation states in any routers along a path. PathTear messages follow the same path as path messages. A PathTear typically is initiated by a sender application or by a router when its path state times out. PathTear messages are not required, but they enhance network performance because they release network resources quickly. If PathTear messages are lost or not generated, path states eventually time out when they are not refreshed, and then the resources associated with the path are released.
ResvTear	ResvTear messages remove reservation states along a path. These messages travel upstream toward senders of the session. In a sense, ResvTear messages are the reverse of resv messages. ResvTear messages typically are initiated by a receiver application or by a router when its reservation state times out. ResvTear messages are not required, but they enhance network performance because they release network resources quickly. If ResvTear messages are lost or not generated, reservation states eventually time out when they are not refreshed, and then the resources associated with the reservation are released.
PathErr	When path errors occur (usually because of parameter problems in a path message), the router sends a unicast PathErr message to the sender that issued the path message. Using PathErr messages is advisory; these messages do not alter any path state along the way.
ResvErr	When a reservation request fails, a ResvErr error message is delivered to all the receivers involved. Using ResvErr messages is advisory; these messages do not alter any reservation state along the way.

Table 11.4 *RSVP Message Types*

Message Type	Description
ResvConfirm	Receivers can request confirmation of a reservation request, and this confirmation is sent with ResvConfirm message. Because of the complex RSVP flow-merging rules, a confirmation message does not necessarily provide end-to-end confirmation of the entire path. Therefore, ResvConfirm messages are an indication of potential success only, with no guarantees.
	RSVP is a resource reservation setup protocol that is designed to interact with integrated services on the Internet.

Two options specify how senders are selected:

- Explicit sender—List all selected senders.
- Wildcard sender—Select all senders, which then participate in the session.

The following reservation styles, formed by a combination of these four options, currently are defined:

- Fixed filter (FF)—This reservation style consists of distinct reservations among explicit senders. Examples of applications that use fixed-filter style reservations are video applications and unicast applications, which both require flows that have a separate reservation for each sender.
- Wildcard filter (WF)—This reservation style consists of shared reservations among wildcard senders. This type of reservation reserves bandwidth for any and all senders, and propagates upstream toward all senders, automatically extending to new senders as they appear. A sample application for wildcard filter reservations is an audio application in which each sender transmits a distinct data stream. Typically, only a few senders are transmitting at any one time. Such a flow does not require a separate reservation for each sender; a single reservation is sufficient.
- Shared explicit (SE)—This reservation style consists of shared reservations among explicit senders. This type of reservation reserves bandwidth for a limited group of senders. A sample application is an audio application similar to that described for wildcard filter reservations.

Enabling RSVP

To enable RSVP, include the following statements. To enable RSVP on all interfaces, specify `all` for *`interface-name`*:

```
[edit]
protocols {
  rsvp {
    interface interface-name;
  }
}
```

Configuring RSVP Aggregation

The resource requirements—processing, bandwidth, and memory—for running RSVP on a router increase proportionally with the number of sessions. Handling large numbers of refresh messages transmitted between RSVP neighbors is crucial for supporting large numbers of sessions. Path and Resv messages typically represent the majority of refreshes.

If topology failures occur, every node adjacent to the failure might notify all affected sender and receiver nodes. These notification messages are either tear or error messages, and they typically represent a flood that ripples out from the original failure point.

Aggregation provides a mechanism for reducing message flooding and network overload. It also enhances the efficiency and reliability in delivering RSVP tear or error messages. Note that RSVP aggregation is called *bundle message* in the Internet draft *RSVP Refresh Reduction Extensions*.

By default, aggregation is disabled on all interfaces. For interoperability with other routers, you might need to keep aggregation disabled. However, we recommend that you enable aggregation between Juniper Networks routers to improve scalability. If you have several thousand MPLS LSPs, you must enable aggregation to ensure stable operation. To enable aggregation, include the `aggregate` statement:

```
[edit protocols rsvp interface interface-name]
aggregate;
```

Configuring the RSVP Hello Interval

RSVP hello packets enable RSVP nodes to detect the loss of a neighboring node's RSVP state information. (Losses typically occur when the neighboring router restarts or the link fails.) In standard RSVP, such detection occurs as a consequence of RSVP's soft-state model. However, detection typically requires several minutes to time out the soft state. RSVP hello packets detect the neighboring node's state changes much more quickly, usually within 10 to 20 seconds.

Between hello-capable neighbors, hello packets are sent unicast toward each other. A loss of (2 * `keep-multiplier +1`) consecutive hello packets causes the neighbor's state to go down, and all RSVP sessions to and from that neighbor are declared to be down.

JUNOS RSVP hello packets are optional and are backward compatible with RSVP implementations that do not support hello packets. For neighbors that do not support hello packets, RSVP uses the soft-state timeout for loss detection.

If all neighboring nodes support hello packets, you can reduce the refresh overhead (by increasing the value set in the `refresh-time` statement) without adversely affecting the node or link failure detection time. Also, the network can scale to a larger number of sessions because the refresh operations consume less CPU and bandwidth.

For information about setting the refresh overhead, see "Configuring RSVP Timers," on page 591.

By default, RSVP sends hello packets every 3 seconds. To modify how often RSVP sends hello packets, include the `hello-interval` statement:

```
[edit protocols rsvp interface interface-name]
hello-interval seconds;
```

Configuring RSVP Authentication

All RSVP protocol exchanges can be authenticated to guarantee that only trusted neighbors participate in setting up reservations. RSVP authentication uses an HMAC-MD5 message-based digest. This scheme produces a message digest based on a secret authentication key and the message contents. (The message contents also include a sequence number.) The computed digest is transmitted with RSVP messages. After you have configured authentication, all received and transmitted RSVP messages with all neighbors are authenticated on this interface.

MD5 authentication also provides protection against forgery and message modification. However, it does not provide confidentiality because all messages are sent in clear text, and it does not prevent replay attacks.

By default, authentication is disabled. To enable authentication, configure a key on each interface by including the `authentication-key` statement:

```
[edit protocols rsvp interface interface-name]
authentication-key key;
```

Reserving Bandwidth on an Interface

For each interface on which RSVP is enabled, by default, RSVP permits all the interface's bandwidth (100 percent) to be used for RSVP reservations.

Oversubscription on an interface occurs when the aggregate demand of all RSVP sessions is allowed to exceed physical capacity of the link. You can use oversubscription to take advantage of the statistical nature of traffic patterns and to permit higher utilization of links. In particular, you can use oversubscription in places where peak utilizations of traffic do not coincide in time.

Undersubscription on an interface occurs when the total demand of all RSVP sessions is always less than the physical capacity of the link. You can use undersubscription to bound utilization of links and reduce congestion.

You can modify the link bandwidth used for RSVP reservations, either decreasing it below 100 percent or oversubscribing the interface. To do this, include the `subscription` statement:

```
[edit protocols rsvp interface interface-name]
subscription percentage;
```

`percentage` is the percentage of the interface's bandwidth that RSVP allows to be used for reservations. It can be a value from 0 through

65,000 percent. If you specify a value greater than 100, you are over-subscribing the interface.

You can use the subscription factor to shut down new RSVP sessions on a per-interface basis. If you set the percentage to 0, no new sessions (including those with zero bandwidth requirements) are permitted on the interface. Existing RSVP sessions are not affected by changing the subscription factor. To clear an existing session, issue the `clear rsvp session` command.

Configuring RSVP Timers

RSVP uses two interrelated timing parameters:

- Refresh time—Controls the interval between the successive generation of refresh messages. Refresh messages include Path and Resv messages. Refresh messages are sent periodically so that reservation states in neighboring nodes do not time out. Each node chooses a value for the refresh timer independently. Each Path and Resv message carries the refresh timer value, and the receiving node extracts this value from the messages.
- Keep multiplier—A locally configured small integer in the range 1 through 255.

To determine the lifetime of a reservation state, use the following formula:

```
lifetime = (keep-multiplier + 0.5) * 1.5 * refresh-time
```

In the worst case, `(keep-multiplier - 1)` successive refresh messages must be lost before a reservation state is deleted.

By default, the refresh timer value is 30 seconds. To modify this value, include the `refresh-time` statement:

```
[edit protocols rsvp]
refresh-time seconds;
```

The default value of the keep multiplier is 3. To modify this value, include the `keep-multiplier` statement:

```
[edit protocols rsvp]
keep-multiplier number;
```

Preempting RSVP Sessions

Whenever bandwidth is insufficient to handle all RSVP sessions, you can control the preemption of RSVP sessions. By default, an RSVP session is preempted only by a new higher-priority session.

To always preempt a session when the bandwidth is insufficient, include the `preemption aggressive` statement:

```
[edit protocols rsvp]
preemption aggressive;
```

To disable RSVP session preemption, include the `preemption disabled` statement:

```
[edit protocols rsvp]
preemption disabled;
```

To return to the default (that is, preempt a session only for a new higher-priority session), include the `preemption normal` statement:

```
[edit protocols rsvp]
preemption normal;
```

Tracing RSVP Protocol Traffic

To trace RSVP protocol traffic, include the `traceoptions` statement at the `[edit protocols rsvp]` hierarchy level:

```
[edit protocols rsvp]
traceoptions {
  file filename <replace> <size size> <files number>
<no-stamp>
    <(world-readable | no-world-readable)>;
  flag flag <flag-modifier> <disable>;
}
```

You can specify the following RSVP-specific flags in the RSVP `traceoptions` statement:

For more information about tracing and global tracing options, see the JUNOS technical documentation.

- `all`—All tracing operations
- `error`—All detected error conditions
- `packets`—All RSVP messages
- `path`—Path messages

- `pathtear`—PathTear messages
- `resv`—Resv messages
- `resvtear`—ResvTear messages
- `route`—Routing table changes in RSVP
- `state`—Session state transitions

Configuring RSVP and MPLS

The primary purpose of the JUNOS RSVP software is to support dynamic signaling within LSPs. When you enable both MPLS and RSVP on a router, MPLS becomes a client of RSVP. No additional configuration is required to bind MPLS and RSVP.

You can configure MPLS to set up signaled paths using the `label-switched-path` statement. Each LSP translates into a request for RSVP to initiate an RSVP session. This request is passed through the internal interface between label switching and RSVP. After examining the request information, checking RSVP states, and checking the local routing tables, RSVP initiates one session for each LSP. The session is sourced from the local router and is destined to the target of the LSP.

When an RSVP session is successfully created, the LSP is set up along the paths created by the RSVP session. If the RSVP session is unsuccessful, RSVP notifies MPLS of its status. It is up to MPLS to try to initiate backup paths or to continue retrying the initial path.

To pass label-switching signaling information, RSVP supports four additional objects: label request object, label object, explicit route object, and record route object. For an LSP to be set up successfully, all routers along the path must support MPLS, RSVP, and these four objects. Of the four objects, record route object is not mandatory.

To configure MPLS and make it a client of RSVP, do the following:

- Enable MPLS on all routers that are to participate in label switching (that is, on all routers that might be part of an LSP).
- Enable RSVP on all routers and on all router interfaces that form the LSP.
- Configure the routers that are to be the beginning of the LSP.

LDP

The Label Distribution Protocol (LDP) is a protocol for distributing labels in nontraffic-engineered applications. LDP allows routers to establish LSPs through a network by mapping network-layer routing information directly to data link layer-switched paths.

LDP is described in *Label Distribution Protocol (LDP)—Version 1 Functional Specification,* Internet draft draft-ietf-mpls-ldp-06.txt.

These LSPs might have an end point at a directly attached neighbor (comparable to IP hop-by-hop forwarding), or they might have an end point at a network egress node, enabling switching through all intermediary nodes. LSPs established by LDP can also traverse traffic-engineered LSPs created by RSVP.

LDP associates a set of destinations (route prefixes and router addresses) with each data link LSP. This set of destinations is called the forwarding equivalence class (FEC). These destinations all share a common data LSP path egress and a common unicast routing path. Each router chooses the label advertised by the next hop for the FEC and splices it to the label it advertises to all other routers. This forms a tree of LSPs that converge on the egress router.

See Chapter 12, "Layer 2 and Layer 3 VPNs," on page 613.

You can implement Virtual Private Networks (VPNs) using MPLS for tunneling. This allows the use of overlapping address spaces by different VPNs. Some MPLS-based approaches to VPNs support only LDP for signaling. With the JUNOS implementation of LDP, and Juniper Networks routers at the core of a network, you can implement edge devices that support VPNs using LDP signaling for MPLS.

The JUNOS implementation of LDP supports LDP Version 1. The JUNOS software supports a simple mechanism for tunneling between routers in an IGP, to eliminate the required distribution of external routes within the core. The JUNOS software allows an MPLS tunnel next hop to all egress routers in the network, with only an IGP running in the core to distribute routes to egress routers. Edge routers run BGP but do not distribute external routes to the core. Instead, the recursive route lookup at the edge resolves to an LSP switched to the egress router. No external routes are necessary.

You must configure LDP for each interface on which you want LDP to run. LDP creates LSP trees rooted at each egress router for the router ID address that is the subsequent BGP next hop. The ingress point is at every router running LDP. This process provides an `inet.3` route to every egress router. If BGP is running, it attempts to resolve next hops by using the `inet.3` table first, which binds most, if not all, of the BGP routes to MPLS tunnel next hops.

Two adjacent routers running LDP become neighbors. If the two routers are connected by more than one interface, they become neighbors on each interface. When LDP routers become neighbors, they establish an LDP session to exchange label information. If per-router labels are in use on both routers, only one LDP session is established between them, even if they are neighbors on multiple interfaces. For this reason, an LDP session is not related to a particular interface.

For LDP to run on an interface, MPLS must be enabled on a logical interface on that interface.

LDP operates in conjunction with a unicast routing protocol. LDP installs LSPs only when both LDP and the routing protocol are enabled. For this reason, you must enable both LDP and the routing protocol on the same set of interfaces. If this is not done, LSPs might not be established between each egress router and all ingress routers, which might result in loss of BGP-routed traffic.

You can apply policy filters to labels received from and distributed to other routers through LDP. Policy filters provide you with a mechanism to control the establishment of LSPs.

If you are using RSVP for traffic engineering, you can run LDP simultaneously to eliminate the distribution of external routes in the core. The LSPs established by LDP are tunneled through the LSPs established by RSVP. LDP effectively treats the traffic-engineered LSPs as single hops.

When you configure the router to run LDP across RSVP-established LSPs, LDP automatically establishes sessions with the router at the other end of the LSP. LDP control packets are routed hop-by-hop, rather than carried through the LSP. This allows you to use simplex (one-way) traffic-engineered LSPs. Traffic in the opposite direction flows through LDP-established LSPs that follow unicast routing rather than through traffic-engineered tunnels.

Figure 11.14 depicts an LDP LSP being tunneled through an RSVP LSP. The shaded inner oval represents the RSVP domain, while the outer oval depicts the LDP domain. RSVP establishes an LSP through routers B, C, D, and E, with the sequence of labels L3, L4. LDP establishes an LSP through Routers A, B, E, F, and G, with the sequence of labels L1, L2, L5. LDP views the RSVP LSP between routers B and E as a single hop.

For more details about label operations, see "Labels," on page 527.

When the packet arrives at Router A, it enters the LSP established by LDP, and a label (L1) is pushed onto the packet. When the packet arrives at Router B, the label (L1) is swapped with another label (L2). Because the packet is entering the traffic-engineered LSP established by RSVP, a second label (L3) is pushed onto the packet.

This outer label (L3) is swapped with a new label (L4) at the intermediate router (Router C) within the RSVP LSP tunnel, and when the penultimate router (Router D) is reached, the top label is popped. Router E swaps the label (L2) with a new label (L5), and the penultimate router for the LDP-established LSP (Router F) pops the last label.

Figure 11.14 *Swap and Push Label Operation when Tunneling LDP LSPs through RSVP LSPs*

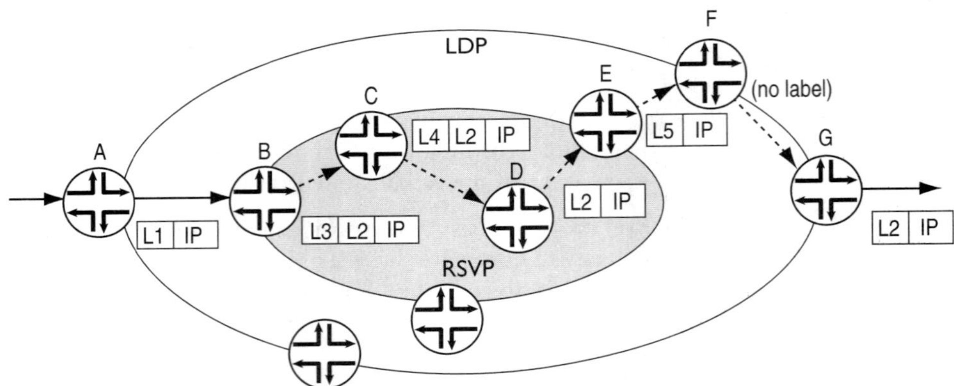

Figure 11.15 depicts double push label operation (L1L2), which is used when the ingress router (Router A) of the LDP and the RSVP are the same router. Note that Router D is the penultimate hop for the LDP-established LSP, so L2 is popped from the packet by Router D.

You cannot use RIP as an IGP for shortcuts.

The IGP shortcut computation imposes some restrictions on the network topology allowed. All the routers in the traffic-engineered core and in the surrounding LDP cloud must belong to the same OSPF area or IS-IS level. Using multiple areas or levels prevents the IGP shortcut computation from finding an RSVP LSP next hop. As a result, you cannot use a label from a remote LDP session for this router.

Figure 11.15 *Double Push Label Operation when Tunneling LDP LSPs through RSVP LSPs*

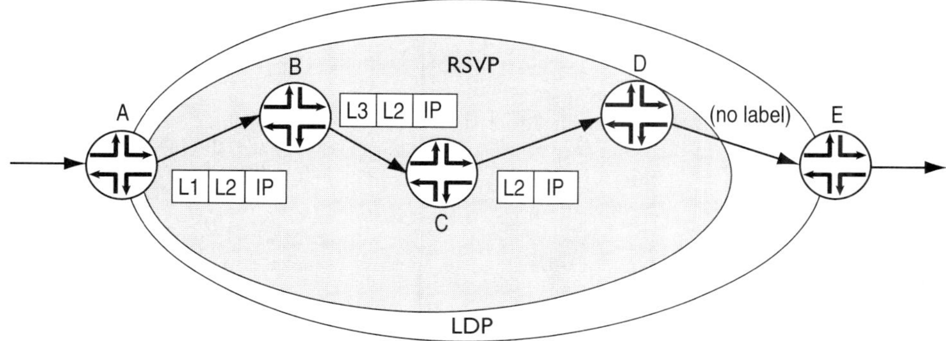

If all the routers do not belong to the same area or level, traffic engineering shortcuts must be explicitly enabled in the IGP.

LDP uses several types of messages to establish and remove mappings and to report errors. All LDP messages have a common structure that uses a type-length-value (TLV) encoding scheme (see Table 11.5).

Table 11.5 *LDP Message Types*

Message Type	Description
Discovery	Announces and maintains the presence of a router in a network. Routers indicate their presence in a network by sending the hello message periodically. This hello message is transmitted as a UDP packet to the LDP port at the group multicast address for all routers on the subnet.
Session	Establishes, maintains, and terminates sessions between LDP peers. When a router establishes a session with another router learned through the hello message, it uses the LDP initialization procedure over TCP transport. When the initialization procedure completes successfully, the two routers are LDP peers and can exchange advertisement messages.
Advertisement	Creates, changes, and deletes label mappings for forwarding equivalence classes (FECs). Requesting a label or advertising a label mapping to a peer is a decision made by the local router. In general, the router requests a label mapping from a neighboring router when it needs one and advertises a label mapping to a neighboring router when it wants the neighbor to use a label.

Table 11.5 *LDP Message Types*

Message Type	Description
Notification	Provides advisory information and signal error information. LDP sends notification messages to report errors and other events of interest. There are two kinds of LDP notification messages: ■ Error notifications signal fatal errors. If a router receives an error notification from a peer for an LDP session, it terminates the LDP session by closing the TCP transport connection for the session and discarding all label mappings learned through the session. ■ Advisory notifications pass a router information about the LDP session or the status of some previous message received from the peer.

Enabling LDP

To enable LDP on all interfaces, include the following statement in the configuration file. To enable LDP on a specific interface, specify an interface name in the `interface` statement. All other LDP configuration statements are optional.

```
[edit]
protocols {
  ldp {
    interface all;
  }
}
```

Configuring the LDP Hello Interval

LDP hello messages enable LDP nodes to discover one another and to detect the failure of a neighbor or of the link to the neighbor. Hello messages are sent periodically on all interfaces where LDP is enabled. By default, LDP sends hello messages every 5 seconds. To modify how often LDP sends hello packets, include the `hello-interval` statement:

```
[edit protocols ldp interface interface-name]
hello-interval seconds;
```

Configuring the LDP Hold Time

The hold time determines how long an LDP node should wait for a hello message before declaring a neighbor to be down. This value is sent as part of a hello message so that each LDP node tells its neighbors how long to wait. The values sent by each neighbor do not have to match. The hold time should be at least three times the hello interval. The default is 15 seconds. To modify the hold time, include the `hold-time` statement:

```
[edit protocols ldp interface interface-name]
hold-time seconds;
```

Configuring the LDP Keepalive Interval

The keepalive interval determines how often a message is sent over the session to ensure that the keepalive timeout is not exceeded. If no other LDP traffic is sent over the session in this much time, a keepalive message is sent. The default is 10 seconds. To modify the keepalive interval, include the `keepalive-interval` statement:

```
[edit protocols ldp interface interface-name]
keepalive-interval seconds;
```

Configuring the LDP Keepalive Timeout

After an LDP session is established, messages must be exchanged periodically to ensure that the session is still working. The keepalive timeout defines the amount of time that the neighbor LDP node waits before deciding that the session has failed. This value is usually set to at least three times the keepalive interval. The default is 30 seconds. To modify the keepalive interval, include the `keepalive-timeout` statement:

```
[edit protocols ldp interface interface-name]
keepalive-timeout seconds;
```

Configuring LDP Route Preferences

When several protocols calculate routes to the same destination, route preferences are used to select which route is installed in the forwarding table. The route with the lowest preference value is selected. The preference value can be a number in the range 0 through 255. By default, LDP routes have a preference value of 9. To modify the route preferences, include the `preference` statement:

```
[edit protocols ldp]
preference preference;
```

Popping the LDP Ultimate-Hop Router

You can control the label value advertised on the egress router of an LSP. The default advertised label is label 3 (implicit null label). If label 3 is advertised, the penultimate hop router removes the label and sends the packet to the egress router. By enabling ultimate-hop popping, label 0 (IPv4 explicit null label) is advertised. Ultimate-hop popping ensures that any packets traversing an MPLS network include a label. To configure ultimate-hop popping, include the `explicit-null` statement:

```
[edit protocols ldp]
explicit-null;
```

Juniper Networks routers queue packets based on the incoming label. Routers from other vendors might queue packets differently. Keep this in mind when working with networks containing routers from multiple vendors.

Filtering Inbound and Outbound LDP Labels

You can filter received LDP label bindings, applying policies to accept or deny bindings advertised by neighboring routers. To configure received label-filtering, include the `import` statement:

```
[edit protocols ldp]
import [ policy-names ];
```

See Chapter 8, "Routing Policy and Firewall Filters," on page 301.

The named policy (configured at the `[edit policy-options]` hierarchy level) is applied to all label bindings received from all LDP neighbors. All filtering is done using `from` statements. Table 11.6 lists the only operators that apply when filtering LDP labels.

Table 11.6 *from Operators for LDP Received Label Filtering*

from Operator	Matches
`interface`	Bindings received from a neighbor that is adjacent over the specified interface
`neighbor`	Bindings received from the specified LDP router ID
`next hop`	Bindings received from a neighbor advertising the specified interface address
`route-filter`	Bindings with the specified prefix

You can configure export policies to filter LDP outbound labels. You can filter outbound label bindings by applying routing policies to block bindings from being advertised to neighboring routers. To configure outbound label-filtering, include the `export` statement:

```
[edit protocols ldp]
export [ policy-names ];
```

The named export policy (configured at the `[edit policy-options]` hierarchy level) is applied to all label bindings transmitted to all LDP neighbors. The only `from` operator that applies to LDP outbound label-filtering is `route-filter`, which matches bindings with the specified prefix. Table 11.7 lists the only `to` operators that apply to outbound label filtering.

Table 11.7 *to Operators for LDP Outbound Label Filtering*

to Operator	Matches
`interface`	Bindings sent to a neighbor that is adjacent over the specified interface
`neighbor`	Bindings sent to the specified LDP router ID
`next hop`	Bindings sent to a neighbor advertising the specified interface address

If a binding is filtered, the binding is not advertised to the neighboring router, but it can be installed as part of an LSP on the local router. You can apply policies in LDP to block the establishment of LSPs but not to control their routing. The path an LSP follows is determined by unicast routing, not by LDP.

However, when there are multiple equal-cost paths to the destination through different neighbors, you can use LDP filtering to exclude some of the possible next hops from consideration. Otherwise, LDP randomly chooses one of the possible next hops.

LDP sessions are not bound to interfaces or interface addresses. LDP advertises only per-router (not per-interface) labels. If multiple parallel links exist between two routers, only one LDP session is established, and it is not bound to a single interface.

Do not use the `next-hop` and `interface` operators when a router has multiple adjacencies to the same neighbor.

Filtered labels are marked in the database:

```
user@host> show ldp database
Input label database, 10.10.255.1:0-10.10.255.3:0
Label Prefix
100007 10.10.255.2/32
3 10.10.255.3/32
Output label database, 10.10.255.1:0-10.10.255.3:0
Label Prefix
3 10.10.255.1/32
100001 10.10.255.6/32 (Filtered)
```

Enabling LDP over LSPs Established by RSVP

See "Enabling LDP," on page 598.

You can run LDP over LSPs established by RSVP, effectively tunneling the LSP established by LDP through the one established by RSVP. To do so, you must enable LDP on the `lo0.0` interface. Additionally, you must configure the LSPs over which you want LDP to operate by including the `ldp-tunneling` statement:

```
[edit protocols mpls]
label-switched-path lsp-path-name {
  from source;
  to destination;
  ldp-tunneling;
}
```

Configuring the Transport Address Used by LDP

You can control the transport address used by LDP. The transport address is the address used for the TCP session over which LDP is running. To configure transport address control, include the `transport-address` statement:

```
[edit protocols ldp] or
[edit protocols ldp interface interface-name]
transport-address ( loopback | interface );
```

If you specify `loopback`, the address of the loopback interface is used as the transport address. If you specify `interface`, the interface address is used as the transport address for any LDP sessions to neighbors reachable over that interface.

You cannot use the `interface` option when there are multiple parallel links to the same LDP neighbor, because the LDP specification requires that the same transport address be advertised on all interfaces to the same neighbor. If LDP detects multiple parallel links to the same neighbor, it disables interfaces to that neighbor one by one until the condition is cleared, either by disconnecting the neighbor on an interface or by configuring the address of the loopback interface.

Configuring LDP Egress Policy

You can control the set of prefixes that are advertised into LDP and cause the router to be the egress router for those prefixes. By default, only the loopback address is advertised into LDP. To configure the set of prefixes from the routing table to be advertised into LDP, include the `egress-policy` statement:

```
[edit protocols ldp]
egress-policy policy-name;
```

See Chapter 8, "Routing Policy and Firewall Filters," on page 301.

Juniper Networks routers queue packets based on the incoming label. Routers from other vendors might queue packets differently. Keep this in mind when working with networks containing routers from multiple vendors.

The named policy (configured at the `[edit policy-options]` hierarchy level) is applied to all routes in the routing table. Those routes that match the policy are advertised into LDP. You can control the set of neighbors to which those prefixes are advertised using the `export` statement. Only `from` operators are considered; you can use any valid `from` operator.

Configuring FEC Deaggregation

When an LDP egress router advertises multiple prefixes, the prefixes are bound to a single label and aggregated into a single forwarding equivalence class (FEC). By default, LDP maintains this aggregation as the advertisement traverses the network.

By default, because an LSP cannot be split across multiple next hops and all the prefixes are bound into a single LSP, you cannot load-balance across equal-cost paths. It also allows the resulting multiple LSPs to be distributed across multiple equal-cost paths and distributes LSPs across the multiple next hops on the egress segments but installs only one next hop per LSP.

To change the default to load-balance across equal-cost paths, deaggregate FECs. Deaggregating FECs causes each prefix to be bound to a separate label and become a separate LSP.

To configure deaggregated FECs, include the `deaggregate` statement. You can configure deaggregated FECs globally only, for all LDP sessions.

```
[edit protocols ldp]
deaggregate;
```

Configuring LDP to Use the IGP Route Metric

To use the IGP route metric for the LDP routes instead of the default LDP route metric, which is 1, include the `track-igp-metric` statement. Note that whenever you change the metric used, the LDP connection is reset.

```
[edit protocols ldp]
track-igp-metric;
```

Tracing LDP Protocol Traffic

To trace LDP protocol traffic, include the `traceoptions` statement:

```
[edit protocols ldp]
traceoptions {
  file filename <replace> <size size> <files number> <no-
      stamp>
    <(world-readable | no-world-readable)>;
  flag flag <flag-modifier> <disable>;
}
```

You can specify the following LDP-specific flags in the LDP `traceoptions` statement:

- `address`—Address and address withdrawal messages
- `binding`—Label-binding operations
- `error`—Error conditions
- `event`—Protocol events
- `initialization`—Initialization messages
- `label`—Label request, label map, label withdrawal, and label release messages
- `notification`—Notification messages
- `packet`—address, address withdrawal, initialization, label request, label map, label withdrawal, label release, notification, and periodic messages; equivalent to setting the `address`, `initialization`, `label`, `notification`, and `periodic` flags
- `packet-dump`—Contents of the messages selected with the message operation flags
- `path`—Label-switched paths
- `periodic`—Hello and keepalive messages
- `state` —Protocol state transitions

Circuit Cross-Connect

Circuit cross-connect (CCC) allows you to configure transparent connections between two circuits, where a circuit can be a Frame Relay DLCI, an ATM VC, a PPP interface, a Cisco HDLC interface, or an MPLS LSP. When CCC is enabled, packets from the source circuit are delivered to the destination circuit with, at most, the Layer 2 address being changed. No other processing—such as header checksums, TTL decrementing, or protocol processing—is done.

CCC circuits fall into two categories: logical interfaces, which include DLCIs, VCs, VLAN IDs, PPP, and Cisco HDLC interfaces; and LSPs. The two circuit categories provide three types of cross-connect:

- Layer 2 switching—Cross-connects between logical interfaces provide what is essentially Layer 2 switching. The interfaces that you connect must be of the same type.
- MPLS tunneling—Cross-connects between interfaces and LSPs allow you to connect two distant interface circuits of the same type by creating MPLS tunnels that use LSPs as the conduit.
- LSP stitching—Cross-connects between LSPs provide a way to "stitch" together two label-switched paths, including paths that fall in two different TED areas.

For Layer 2 switching and MPLS tunneling, the cross-connect is bidirectional, so packets received on the first interface are transmitted out the second interface, and those received on the second interface are transmitted out the first. For LSP stitching, the cross-connect is unidirectional.

For CCC connections that connect interfaces, the interfaces must be of the same type; that is, ATM to ATM, Frame Relay to Frame Relay, PPP to PPP, or Cisco HDLC to Cisco HDLC.

Configuring Layer 2 Switching Cross-Connects

Layer 2 switching cross-connects join logical interfaces to form what is essentially Layer 2 switching. The interfaces that you connect must be of the same type. You can configure Layer 2 switching cross-connects on PPP, Cisco HDLC, Frame Relay, Ethernet, and ATM circuits. In a single cross-connect, only like interfaces can be connected.

To configure Layer 2 switching cross-connects, you must define the CCC encapsulation for Layer 2 cross-connects, define the connection between the two circuits, and configure MPLS.

To configure the CCC encapsulation on the router for PPP or Cisco HDLC circuits, specify the encapsulation in the `encapsulation` statement. This statement configures the entire physical device. For these circuits to work, you must configure a logical interface unit 0.

```
[edit]
interfaces {
  type-fpc/pic/port {
    encapsulation (ppp-ccc | cisco-hdlc-ccc);
    unit 0;
  }
}
```

For Ethernet circuits, specify the encapsulation in the `encapsulation` statement. This statement configures the entire physical device. For these circuits to work, you must configure a logical interface—unit 0. Note that only the four-port Fast Ethernet PICs support the `ethernet-ccc` encapsulation type.

```
[edit]
interfaces {
  fe-fpc/pic/port {
    encapsulation ethernet-ccc;
    unit 0;
  }
}
```

For ATM circuits, specify the encapsulation when configuring the VC. Configure each VC as a circuit or a regular logical interface.

```
[edit]
interfaces {
  at-fpc/pic/port {
    atm-options {
      vpi vpi-identifier maximum-vcs maximum-vcs;
    }
    unit logical-unit-number {
      point-to-point;
      encapsulation atm-ccc-vc-mux;
      vci vpi-identifier.vci-identifier;
    }
  }
}
```

For Frame Relay circuits, specify the encapsulation when configuring the DLCI. Configure each DLCI as a circuit or a regular logical interface. The DLCI for regular interfaces must be in the range 1 through 511. For CCC interfaces, it must be in the range 512 through 1,022.

```
[edit]
interfaces {
  interface-switch frame-relay-ccc;
  type-fpc/pic/port {
    unit logical-unit-number {
      point-to-point;
      encapsulation frame-relay-ccc;
      dlci dlci-identifier;
    }
  }
}
```

To configure Layer 2 switching cross-connects, define the connection between the two circuits. The connection joins the interface that comes from the circuit's source to the interface that leads to the circuit's destination. When you specify the interface names, include the logical portion of the name, which corresponds to the logical unit number. The cross-connect is bidirectional, so packets received on the first interface are transmitted out the second interface, and those received on the second interface are transmitted out the first.

```
[edit protocols]
connections {
  interface-switch connection-name {
    interface interface-name.unit-number;
    interface interface-name.unit-number;
  }
}
```

For Layer 2 switching cross-connects to work, you must configure MPLS. The following is a minimal MPLS configuration:

```
[edit protocols]
mpls {
  interface (interface-name | all);
}
```

Configuring MPLS LSP Tunnel Cross-Connects

MPLS tunnel cross-connects between interfaces and LSPs allow you to connect two distant interface circuits of the same type by creating MPLS tunnels that use LSPs as the conduit. You can configure LSP tunnel cross-connects on PPP, Cisco HDLC, Frame Relay, and ATM circuits. In a single cross-connect, only like interfaces can be connected.

When you use MPLS tunnel cross-connects, if you use the default MTU size, IS-IS does not form adjacencies across the tunnel. For the tunnel cross-connects to work, the MTU size on the edge routers must be smaller than the LSP's MTU. Use the following calculation to determine the maximum IS-IS MTU size:

IS-IS MTU = MPLS MTU – 4 bytes – link-layer overhead

The link-layer overhead varies, depending on the encapsulation:

- ATM—8 bytes
- Frame Relay—2 bytes

- HDLC—4 bytes
- PPP—4 bytes
- VLAN—4 bytes

See Chapter 6, "Interfaces and Class of Service," on page 185.

Juniper Networks recommend that you simply set the MTU to 1,497 bytes, which is small enough so that IS-IS works properly.

To modify the MTU, include the `mtu` statement when configuring the logical interface family, at the `[edit interfaces` *`interface-name`* `unit` *`logical-unit-number`* `encapsulation` *`family`*`]` hierarchy level.

To configure LSP tunnel cross-connects, you must configure the CCC encapsulation on the ingress and egress routers. You cannot configure families on CCC interfaces; that is, you cannot include the family statement at the `[edit interfaces` *`interface-name`* `unit` *`logical-unit-number`*`]` hierarchy level.

For PPP or Cisco HDLC circuits, specify the encapsulation in the `encapsulation` statement. This statement configures the entire physical device. For these circuits to work, you must configure a logical interface unit 0.

```
[edit]
interfaces {
  type-fpc/pic/port {
    encapsulation (ppp-ccc | cisco-hdlc-ccc);
    unit 0;
  }
}
```

For ATM circuits, specify the encapsulation when configuring the VC. For each VC, you configure whether it is a circuit or a regular logical interface.

```
[edit]
interfaces {
  at-fpc/pic/port {
    atm-options {
      vpi vpi-identifier maximum-vcs maximum-vcs;
    }
    unit logical-unit-number {
      point-to-point;
      encapsulation atm-ccc-vc-mux;
      vci vpi-identifier.vci-identifier;
    }
  }
}
```

For Frame Relay circuits, specify the encapsulation when configuring the DLCI. For each DLCI, you configure whether it is a circuit or a regular logical interface. The DLCI for regular interfaces must be in the range 1 through 511. For CCC interfaces, it must be in the range 512 through 1,022.

```
[edit}
interfaces {
  interface-switch frame-relay-ccc;
  type-fpc/pic/port {
    unit logical-unit-number {
      point-to-point;
      encapsulation frame-relay-ccc;
      dlci dlci-identifier;
    }
  }
}
```

To configure LSP tunnel cross-connects, define the connection between the two circuits on the ingress and egress routers. The connection joins the interface or LSP that comes from the circuit's source to the interface or LSP that leads to the circuit's destination. When you specify the interface name, include the logical portion of the name, which corresponds to the logical unit number. For the cross-connect to be bidirectional, you must configure cross-connects on two routers.

```
[edit protocols]
connections {
  remote-interface-switch connection-name {
    interface interface-name.unit-number;
    transmit-lsp label-switched-path;
    receive-lsp label-switched-path;
  }
}
```

Configuring LSP Stitching Cross-Connects

LSP stitching cross-connects "stitch" together LSPs to join two LSPs. For example, they stitch together LSPs that fall in two different TED areas. You can use LSP stitching to create a seamless LSP for LSPs carrying any kind of traffic.

To configure LSP stitching cross-connects, you configure the two LSPs that you are stitching together on the two ingress routers. Then, on the interdomain router, you define the connection between the two LSPs. The connection joins the LSP that comes from the connection's source to the LSP that leads to the connection's destination.

```
[edit protocols]
connections {
  lsp-switch connection-name {
    transmit-lsp label-switched-path;
    receive-lsp label-switched-path;
  }
}
```

CHAPTER

12

Layer 2 and Layer 3 VPNs

A Virtual Private Network (VPN) is a set of sites that share common routing information and whose connectivity is controlled by a collection of policies. The sites that make up a VPN are connected over a service provider's existing Internet backbone. In a Layer 2 VPN, routing operations are controlled and performed on the customer's routers, typically on the customer edge (CE) routers, whereas in a Layer 3 VPN, they are handled on the service provider's routers.

VPN Concepts

A VPN consists of two topological areas, the provider's network and the customer's network. The provider's network, which runs across the public Internet infrastructure, consists of routers that provide VPN services to a customer's network as well as routers that provide other services. The customer's network is commonly located at multiple physical sites. The provider's network acts to connect the various customer sites in what appears to the customer and the provider to be a private network. To ensure that VPNs remain private and isolated from other VPNs and from the public Internet, the provider's network maintains policies that keep routing information from different VPNs separate. A provider can service multiple VPNs as long as its policies keep routes from different VPNs separate. Similarly, a site can belong to multiple VPNs as long as it keeps routes from the different VPNs separate.

Table 12.1 lists the VPN standards supported by the JUNOS software.

Table 12.1 *VPN Standards Supported by JUNOS Software*

Standard	Title
Internet Draft draft-kompella-ppvpn-l2vpn-00.txt	*MPLS-based Layer 2 VPNs*
RFC 2547	*BGP/MPLS VPNs*
Internet Draft draft-rosen-rfc2547bis	*BGP/MPLS VPNs*
RFC 2283	*Multiprotocol Extensions for BGP4*

VPNs contain the following types of network devices (see Figure 12.1 on page 616):

- Provider edge (PE) routers—Routers in the provider's network that connect to CE devices located at customer sites. PE routers support VPN and label functionality. (The label functionality can be provided either by RSVP or LDP.) Within a single VPN, pairs of PE routers are connected through a tunnel, which can be either an MPLS LSP or an LDP tunnel.
- Provider (P) routers—Routers within the core of the provider's network that are not connected to any routers at a customer site but that are part of the tunnel between pairs of PE routers. Provider routers support MPLS LSP or LDP functionality but do not need to support VPN functionality.
- Customer edge (CE) devices—Routers or switches located at the customer's site that connect to the provider's network. CE devices are typically IP routers.

VPN functionality is provided by the PE routers; the provider and CE routers have no special configuration requirements for VPNs.

Because VPNs connect private networks—which can use either public addresses or private addresses, as defined in RFC 1918—over the public Internet infrastructure, when the private networks use private addresses, the addresses might overlap with the addresses of another private network. To avoid overlapping private addresses, you can configure the network devices to use public addresses instead of private addresses. However, this is a large and complex undertaking. The solution provided in RFC 2547bis uses the existing private network numbers to create a new address that is unambiguous. The new address is part of the VPN-IPv4 address family, which is a BGP address family added as an extension to the BGP protocol. In VPN-IPv4 addresses, a value that identifies the VPN, called a *route distinguisher,* is prefixed to the private IPv4 address, providing an address that uniquely identifies a private IPv4 address.

Figure 12.1 *VPN Router Components*

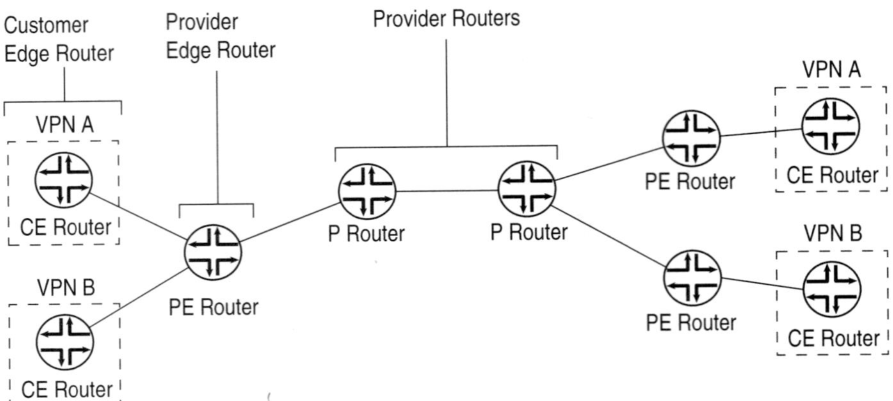

Only the PE routers need to support the VPN-IPv4 address extension to BGP. When an ingress PE router receives an IPv4 route from a device within a VPN, it converts it into a VPN-IPv4 route by prefixing the route distinguisher to the route. The VPN-IPv4 addresses are used only for routes exchanged between PE routers. When an egress PE router receives a VPN-IPv4 route, it converts it back to an IPv4 route, by removing the route distinguisher, before announcing the route to its connected CE routers.

VPN-IPv4 addresses have the following format:

- Route distinguisher—8-byte value that identifies the VPN. The route distinguisher consists of the following fields:
  - Type field (2 bytes)—Determines the length of the other two fields. If the value in the type field is 0, the administrator (Adm) field is 4 bytes, and the assigned number (AN) field is 2 bytes. If the value in the type field is 1, the administrator (Adm) field is 2 bytes, and the assigned number (AN) field is 4 bytes.
  - Administrator field—Identifies an assigned number authority.

    For a type field value of 0, the administrator field contains an IPv4 address. RFC 2547bis recommends that you use the router's IP address (the address you configure in the `router-id` statement), which is a nonprivate address.

For a type field value of 1, the administrator field contains an AS number. RFC 2547bis recommends that you use an IANA-assigned, nonprivate AS number, preferably the ISP's or customer's own AS number.

- Assigned number field—Number assigned by the service provider. For a type field value of 0, the assigned number field is 2 bytes long. For a type field value of 1, the assigned number field is 4 bytes.

- IPv4 address—4-byte address of a device within the VPN.

To separate a VPN's routes from routes in the public Internet or those in other VPNs, the PE router creates a separate routing table for each VPN, called a VPN Routing and Forwarding (VRF) table. The PE router creates one VRF table for each VPN that has a connection to a CE router. Any customer or site that belongs to the VPN can access only the routes in the VRF tables for that VPN. Each VRF table is populated from routes received from directly connected CE sites associated with that VRF and from routes received from other PE routers that passed BGP community filtering and are in the same VPN. Each PE router also maintains one global routing table (`inet.0`) to reach other routers in and outside the provider's core network. Each customer connection (that is, logical interface) is associated with one VRF table. Only the VRF table associated with a customer site is consulted for packets from that site. You can configure the router so that if a next hop to a destination is not found in the VRF table, the router performs a lookup in the global routing table, which is used for Internet access.

The JUNOS software uses the following routing tables for VPNs:

- `bgp.l3vpn.0`—Stores all VPN-IPv4 unicast routes received from other PE routers. (This table does not store routes received from directly connected CE routers.) This table is present only on PE routers.

  When a PE router receives a route from another PE router, it places the route into its `bgp.l3vpn.0` routing table. The route is resolved using the information in the `inet.3` routing table. The resultant route is converted into IPv4 format and redistributed to all *`routing-instance-name`*`.inet.0` routing tables on the PE router if it matches the VRF import policy.

The `bgp.l3vpn.0` table is also used to resolve routes over the MPLS tunnels that connect the PE routers. These routes are stored in the `inet.3` routing table. PE-PE router connectivity must exist in `inet.3` (not just in `inet.0`) for VPN routes to be resolved properly.

To determine whether to add a route to the `bgp.l3vpn.0` routing table, the JUNOS software checks it against the VRF import policies for all the VPNs configured on the PE router. If the VPN-IPv4 route matches one of the policies, it is added to the `bgp.l3vpn.0` table. To display the routes in the `bgp.l3vpn.0` routing table, use the `show route table bgp.l3vpn.0` command.

- *`routing-instance-name`*`.inet.0`—Stores all unicast IPv4 routes received from directly connected CE routers in a routing instance (that is, in a single VPN) and all explicitly configured static routes in the routing instance. This is the VRF table and is present only on PE routers. For example, for a routing instance named `VPN-A`, the routing table for that instance is named `VPN-A.inet.0`.

  When a CE router advertises to a PE router, the PE router places the route into the corresponding *`routing-instance-name`*`.inet.0` routing table and advertises the route to other PE routers if it passes a VRF export policy. Among other things, this policy tags the route with the route distinguisher (route target) that corresponds to the VPN site to which the CE belongs. A label is also allocated and distributed with the route. The `bgp.l3vpn.0` routing table is not involved in this process.

  The *`routing-instance-name`*`.inet.0` table also stores routes announced by a remote PE router that match the VRF import policy for that VPN. The remote PE router redistributes these routes from its `bgp.l3vpn.0` table.

  Routes are not redistributed from the *`routing-instance-name`*`.inet.0` table to the `bgp.l3vpn.0` table; they are directly advertised to other PE routers.

For each *routing-instance-name*.inet.0 routing table, one forwarding table is maintained in the router's Packet Forwarding Engine. This table is maintained in addition to the forwarding tables that correspond to the router's inet.0 and mpls.0 routing tables. As with the inet.0 and mpls.0 routing tables, the best routes from the *routing-instance-name*.inet.0 routing table are placed into the forwarding table. To display the routes in the *routing-instance-name*.inet.0 table, use the show route table *routing-instance-name*.inet.0 command.

- inet.3—Stores all MPLS routes learned from LDP and RSVP signaling done for VPN traffic. The routing table stores the MPLS routes only if the traffic-engineering bgp-igp option is not enabled.

  For VPN routes to be resolved properly, the inet.3 table must contain routes to all the PE routers in the VPN. To display the routes in the inet.3 table, use the show route inet.3 command.

  Note that IGP shortcuts do not work in VPN environments and should not be configured. IGP shortcuts move routes in inet.3 to inet.0. VPN IBGP (family inet-vpn) relies on next hops that are in the inet.3 table; thus, IGP shortcuts are incompatible with VPNs.

- inet.0—Stores routes learned by the IBGP sessions between the PE routers. To provide Internet access to the VPN sites, configure the *routing-instance-name*.inet.0 routing table to contain a default route to the inet.0 routing table.

  To display the routes in the inet.0 table, use the show route inet.0 command.

The following routing policies, which are defined in VRF import and export statements, are specific to VRF tables:

- Import policy—Applied to VPN-IPv4 routes learned from another PE router to determine whether the route should be added to the PE router's bgp.l3vpn.0 routing table. Each routing instance on a PE router has a VRF import policy.

- Export policy—Applied to VPN-IPv4 routes that are announced to other PE routers. The VPN-IPv4 routes are IPv4 routes that have been announced by locally connected CE routers.

VPN route processing differs from normal BGP route processing in one way. In BGP, routes are accepted if they are not explicitly rejected by import policy. However, because many more VPN routes are expected, the JUNOS software does not accept (and hence store) VPN routes unless the route matches at least one VRF import policy. If no VRF import explicitly accepts the route, it is discarded and not even stored in the `bgp.l3vpn.0` table. As a result, if a VPN change occurs on a PE router—such as adding a new VRF table or changing a VRF import policy—the PE router sends a BGP route refresh message to the other PE routers (or to the route reflector if this is part of the VPN topology) to retrieve all VPN routes so that they can be reevaluated to determine whether they should be kept or discarded.

Within a VPN, the distribution of VPN-IPv4 routes occurs between the PE and CE routers and between the PE routers.

A CE router announces its routes to the directly connected PE router. The announced routes are in IPv4 format. The PE router places the routes into the VRF table for the VPN. In the JUNOS software, this is the *`routing-instance-name`*`.inet.0` routing table, where *`routing-instance-name`* is the configured name of the VPN. The connection between the CE and PE routers can be a remote connection (a WAN connection) or a direct connection (such as a Frame Relay or Ethernet connection). CE routers can communicate with PE routers using OSPF, RIP, BGP, or static routes.

When one PE router receives routes advertised from a directly connected CE router, it checks the received route against the VRF export policy for that VPN. If it matches, the route is converted to VPN-IPv4 format (that is, the route distinguisher [route target] is added to the route). The PE router then announces the route in VPN-IPv4 format to the remote PE routers. The routes are distributed using IBGP sessions, which are configured in the provider's core network. If the route does not match, it is not exported to other PE routers but can still be used locally for routing, for example, if two CE routers in the same VPN are directly connected to the same PE router. The remote PE router places the route into its `bgp.l3vpn.0` table if the route passes the import policy on the IBGP session between the PE routers. At the same time, it checks the route against the VRF import policy for the VPN. If it matches, the route distinguisher is removed from the route, and it is placed into the VRF table (the *`routing-instance-name`*`.inet.0` table) in IPv4 format.

The remote PE router announces the routes in its VRF tables, which are in IPv4 format, to its directly connected CE routers. PE routers can communicate with CE routers using OSPF, RIP, BGP, or static routes.

The PE routers in the provider's core network are the only routers that are configured to support VPNs and hence are the only routers that know about the existence of the VPNs. From the point of view of VPN functionality, the provider routers in the core—those provider routers that are not directly connected to CE routers—are merely routers along the tunnel between the ingress and egress PE routers. The tunnels can be either LDP or MPLS. Any provider routers along the tunnel must support the protocol used for the tunnel, either LDP or MPLS. When PE-router-to-PE-router forwarding is tunneled over MPLS LSPs, the MPLS packets have a two-level label stack (see Figure 12.2):

- Outer label—Label assigned to the address of the BGP next hop by the IGP next hop
- Inner label—Label that the BGP next hop assigned for the packet's destination address

Figure 12.2 *Using MPLS LSPs to Tunnel between PE Routers*

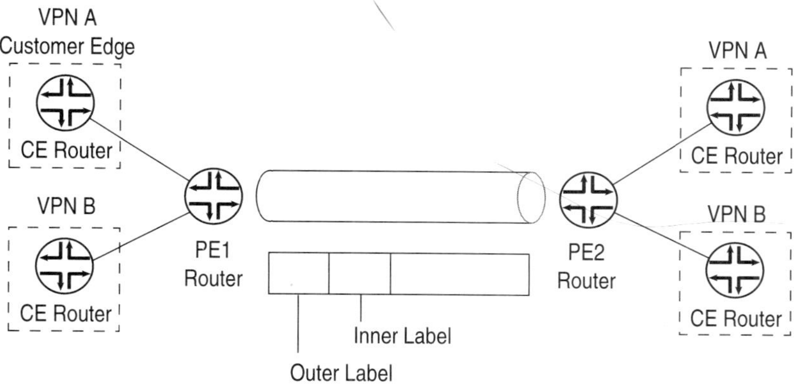

Figure 12.3 illustrates how the labels are assigned and removed:

1. When CE Router X forwards a packet to Router PE1 with a destination of CE Router Y, the PE router identifies the BGP next hop to Router Y and assigns a label that corresponds to the BGP next hop and identifies the destination CE router. This label is the inner label.
2. Router PE1 then identifies the IGP route to the BGP next hop and assigns a second label that corresponds to the LSP of the BGP next hop. This label is the outer label.
3. The inner label remains the same as the packet traverses the LSP tunnel. The outer label is swapped at each hop along the LSP and is then popped by the penultimate hop router (the third provider router).
4. Router PE2 pops the inner label from the route and forwards the packet to Router Y.

Figure 12.3 *Label Stack*

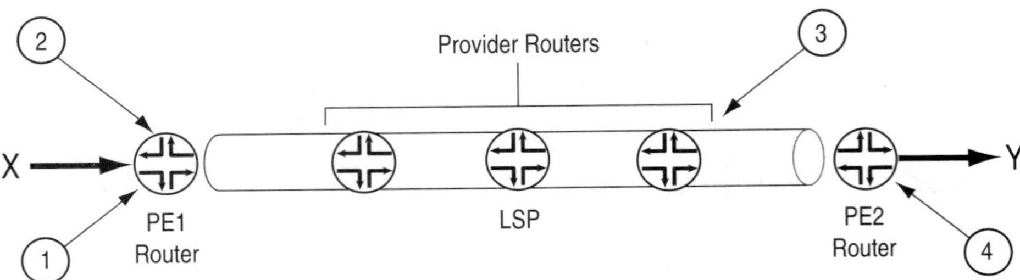

To implement Layer 3 VPNs in the JUNOS software, you configure one routing instance for each VPN. You configure the routing instances on PE routers only. Each VPN routing instance consists of the following components:

- VRF table—On each PE router, you configure one VRF table for each VPN.
- Set of interfaces that use the VRF table—The logical interface to each directly connected CE router must be associated with a VRF table. You can associate more than one interface with the same VRF table if more than one CE router in a VPN is directly connected to the PE router.

- Policy rules—These control the import of routes into and the export of routes from the VRF table.
- One or more routing protocols that install routes from CE routers into the VRF table—You can use the BGP, OSPF, and RIP routing protocols, and you can use static routes.

Configuring Layer 2 VPNs

To configure Layer 2 VPN functionality, you must enable Layer 2 VPN support on the PE router. You must also configure PE routers to distribute routing information to the other PE routers in the VPN and configure the circuits between the PE routers and the CE routers. Each Layer 2 VPN is configured under a routing instance of type `l2vpn`. An `l2vpn` routing instance can transparently carry Layer 3 traffic across the service provider's network. As with other routing instances, all logical interfaces belonging to a Layer 2 VPN routing instance are listed under that instance. The configuration of the CE routers is not relevant to the service provider. The CE routers need to provide only the appropriate Layer 2 circuits to send traffic to the PE router.

To configure Layer 2 VPNs, you include the following statements:

```
[edit routing-instances routing-instance-name]
description text;
instance-type l2vpn;
interface interface-name;
route-distinguisher (as-number:id | ip-address:id);
vrf-export [ policy-names ];
vrf-import [ policy-names ];
protocols {
  l2vpn {
    encapsulation-type type
    traceoptions {
      file filename <replace> <size size> <files number>
        <nostamp>;
      flag flag <flag-modifier> <disable>;
    }
    site site-name {
      site-identifier identifier;
      interface interface-name {
        remote-site-id remote-site-id;
      }
    }
  }
}
```

In addition, you must configure MPLS LSPs between the PE routers, IBGP sessions between the PE routers, and an IGP on the PE and provider routers.

By default, Layer 2 VPNs are disabled.

For Layer 2 VPNs to function, you configure MPLS LSPs between the PE routers using either the LDP or RSVP.

To use LDP to configure the MPLS LSPs, perform the following steps on the PE and provider routers:

1. Configure LDP on the interfaces in the core of the service provider's network. You need to configure LDP only on the interfaces between PE routers or between PE and provider routers. You can think of these as the "core-facing" interfaces.

```
[edit protocols]
ldp {
  interface interface-name;
}
```

2. Configure the MPLS address family on the interfaces on which you enable LDP (that is, on the interfaces you configured in Step 1):

```
[edit interfaces]
interface-name {
  unit logical-unit-number {
    family mpls;
  }
}
```

3. Configure OSPF or IS-IS on each PE and provider router. You configure these protocols at the master instance of the routing protocol, not within the routing instance used for the VPN.

   To configure OSPF, include the `ospf` statement. At a minimum, you must configure a backbone area on at least one of the router's interfaces.

```
[edit protocols]
ospf {
  area 0.0.0.0 {
    interface interface-name;
  }
}
```

To configure IS-IS, include the `isis` statement and configure the loopback interface and ISO family. At a minimum, you must enable IS-IS on the router, configure a network entity title (NET) on one of the router's interfaces (preferably the loopback interface, `lo0`), and configure the ISO family on all interfaces on which you want IS-IS to run. When you enable IS-IS, Level 1 and Level 2 are enabled by default. The following is the minimum IS-IS configuration. In the `address` statement, *`address`* is the NET.

```
[edit]
interfaces {
  lo0 {
    unit logical-unit-number {
      family iso {
        address address;
      }
    }
  }
  type-fpc/pic/port {
    unit logical-unit-number {
      family iso;
    }
  }
}
protocols {
  isis {
    interface all;
  }
}
```

To configure the MPLS LSPs using RSVP, perform the following steps:

1. On each PE router, configure traffic engineering. To do this, you must configure an IGP that supports traffic engineering (either IS-IS or OSPF) and enable traffic engineering support for that protocol. For IS-IS, traffic engineering support is enabled by default. To enable OSPF traffic engineering support, include the `traffic-engineering` statement:

   ```
   [edit protocols ospf]
   traffic-engineering;
   ```

2. On each PE and provider router, enable RSVP on the router interfaces that participate in the LSP. On the PE router, these are the interfaces that are the ingress and egress points to the LSP. On the provider router, these are the interfaces that connect the LSP between the PE routers. To configure RSVP on the PE and provider routers, include one `interface` statement for each interface on which you are enabling RSVP.

   ```
   [edit rsvp]
   interface interface-name;
   ```

3. On each PE router, configure an MPLS LSP to the PE router that is the LSP's egress point by including the `label-switched-path` and `interface` statements. In the `to` statement, specify the address of the LSP's egress point, which is an address on the remote PE router. In the `interface` statement, specify the name of the interface (both the physical and logical portions). Include one `interface` statement for the interface associated with the LSP.

   ```
   [edit mpls]
   label-switched-path path-name {
     to ip-address;
   }
   interface interface-name;
   ```

   You must also configure `family mpls` and `family inet` when configuring the logical interface:

   ```
   [edit interfaces interface-name unit logical-unit-
   number]
   family inet;
   family mpls;
   ```

4. On all provider routers that participate in the LSP, enable MPLS by including one `interface` statement for each connection to the LSP:

   ```
   [edit mpls]
   interface interface-name;
   ```

5. Enable MPLS on the interface between the PE and CE routers by including the `interface` statement. Doing this allows the PE router to assign an MPLS label to traffic entering the LSP or to remove the label from traffic exiting the LSP.

   ```
   [edit mpls]
   interface interface-name;
   ```

To allow the PE and provider routers to exchange routing information, you must either configure an IGP on all these routers or you must configure static routes. You configure the IGP on the master instance of the routing protocol process (`rpd`) (that is, at the `[edit protocols]` hierarchy level), not within the routing instance used for the Layer 2 VPN (that is, not at the `[edit routing-instances]` hierarchy level). When you configure the PE router, do not configure any summarization of the PE router's loopback addresses at the area boundary. Each PE router's loopback address should appear as a separate route.

You must configure an IBGP session between PE routers to allow these routers to exchange information about Layer 2 VPNs, particularly information about sites connected to Layer 2 VPNs. The PE routers rely on this information to determine which labels to use for traffic destined for remote sites. To enable an IBGP session between the PE routers, include the `family l2vpn` statement when configuring IBGP in the master instance to indicate that the IBGP session is for the Layer 2 VPN:

```
[edit protocols]
bgp {
  group group-name {
    type internal;
    local-address ip-address;
    family l2vpn {
      unicast;
    }
    neighbor ip-address;
  }
}
```

The IP address in the `local-address` statement is the same as the address configured in the `to` statement at the `[edit protocols mpls label-switched-path lsp-path-name]` hierarchy level on the remote PE router. The IBGP session uses this address as the source in the peering session. The IP address in the `neighbor` statement is the loopback address of the neighboring PE router. If you are using RSVP signaling, this IP address is the same address you specify in the `to` statement at the `[edit mpls label-switched-path]` hierarchy level when you configure the MPLS LSP.

To configure routing instances for Layer 2 VPNs, include the `routing-instances` statement. You configure Layer 2 VPN routing instances only on the PE routers. The `instance-type`, `interface`, `route-distinguisher`, `vrf-export`, and `vrf-import` statements are required for the Layer 2 VPN to function.

```
[edit]
routing-instances {
  routing-instance-name {
    description text;
    instance-type l2vpn;
    interface interface-name;
    route-distinguisher (as-number:id | ip-address:id);
    vrf-export [ policy-names ]
    vrf-import [ policy-names ]
  }
}
```

To provide a textual description for the routing instance, include the `description` statement. To enable Layer 2 VPN routing on a PE router, include the `instance-type` statement, specifying the instance type as `l2vpn`.

On each PE router, you must configure the interfaces over which the Layer 2 VPN traffic travels between PE and CE routers by including the `interface` statement. You should specify both the physical and logical portions of the interface name, in the format *`physical.logical`*. If you do not specify the logical portion of the interface name, `0` is set by default. A logical interface can be associated with only one routing instance.

You need to specify a circuit cross-connect (CCC) encapsulation type for each PE-router-to-CE-router interface running a Layer 2 VPN. This encapsulation type should match the encapsulation type configured under the routing instance. To configure the CCC encapsulation type, include the following statements:

```
[edit]
interfaces {
  interface name {
    encapsulation-type ccc-encapsulation-type;
    unit unit number {
      encapsulation ccc-encapsulation-type;
    }
  }
}
```

You can run both standard Frame Relay and CCC Frame Relay on the same device. If you specify Frame Relay encapsulation (`frame-relay-ccc`) for the interface, you should also configure the encapsulation at the `[edit interfaces` *`interface name`* `unit` *`unit-number`*`]` hierarchy level as `frame-relay-ccc`. Otherwise, the logical interface unit defaults to standard Frame Relay. The CCC encapsulation type can be `atm-aal5-ccc`, `atm-cell-ccc`, `cisco-hdlc-ccc`, `ethernet-vlan-ccc`, `frame-relay-ccc`, or `ppp-ccc`.

To configure different encapsulation types at different Layer 2 VPN sites, you need to use one of the following encapsulation types: `atm-aal5-tcc`, `atm-cell-tcc`, `cisco-hdlc-tcc`, `frame-relay-tcc`, or `ppp-tcc`.

Each routing instance that you configure on a PE router must have a unique route distinguisher associated with it. The route distinguisher is used to place bounds around a VPN so that the same IP address prefixes can be used in different VPNs without overlapping. To configure a route distinguisher on a PE router, include the `route-distinguisher` statement. The route distinguisher is a 6-byte value that you can specify in one of the following formats:

- *`as-number`*:*`number`*, where *`as-number`* is an AS number (a 2-byte value), and *`number`* is any 4-byte value. The AS number can be in the range 1 through 65,535. We recommend that you use an IANA assigned, nonprivate AS number, preferably the ISP's own or the customer's own AS number.
- *`ip-address`*:*`number`*, where *`ip-address`* is an IP address (a 4-byte value), and *`number`* is any 2-byte value. The IP address can be any globally unique unicast address. We recommend that you use the address that you configure in the `router-id` statement, which is a nonprivate address in your assigned prefix range.

For each local site, the PE router advertises a set of VPN labels to the other PE routers servicing the Layer 2 VPN. The VPN labels comprise a single block of contiguous labels; however, to allow for reprovisioning, more than one such block can be advertised. Each label block consists of a label base, a range (the size of the block), and a remote site ID that identifies the sequence of remote sites that connect to the local site using this label block (the remote site ID is the first site identifier in the sequence). The encapsulation type is also advertised along with the label block.

All the Layer 2 circuits provisioned for a local site are listed as the set of logical interfaces (using the `interface` statement) within the `site` statement. On each PE router, you must configure each site that has a circuit to the PE router by including the `site` statement:

```
[edit routing-instances routing-instance-name protocols
l2vpn]
site site-name {
  site-identifier identifier;
  interface interface-name {
    remote-site-id remote-site-id;
  }
}
```

The encapsulation type you configure at each Layer 2 VPN site varies depending on which Layer 2 protocol you choose to configure. You need to use the same protocol at each Layer 2 VPN site if you configure `ethernet-vlan` as the encapsulation type. You do *not* need to use the same protocol at each Layer 2 VPN site if you configure an encapsulation type of `atm-aal5`, `atm-cell`, `cisco-hdlc`, `frame-relay`, or `ppp`. If you configure different protocols at your Layer 2 VPN sites, you need to configure a different type of CCC encapsulation. To configure the Layer 2 protocol accepted by the PE router, specify the encapsulation type by including the `encapsulation-type` statement at the `[edit routing-instances` *`routing-instance-name`* `protocols l2vpn]` hierarchy level.

To trace Layer 2 VPN protocol traffic, include the `traceoptions` statement:

```
[edit routing-instances routing-instance-name protocols
l2vpn]
traceoptions {
  file filename <replace> <size size> <files number>
    <nostamp>;
  flag flag <flag-modifier> <disable>;
}
```

You can specify the following Layer 2-specific flags in the Layer 2 VPN `traceoptions` statement:

- `all`—All Layer 2 VPN options
- `connections`—Layer 2 VPN connections (events and state changes)
- `error`—Error conditions

- `nlri`—Layer 2 VPN advertisements received or sent using BGP
- `route`—Routing information
- `topology`—Layer 2 VPN topology changes caused by reconfiguration or advertisements received from other PE routers using BGP

Configuring Layer 3 VPNs

To configure Layer 3 VPN functionality, you must enable VPN support on the PE router. You must also configure any P routers that service the VPN, and you must configure the CE routers so that their routes are distributed into the VPN. To configure Layer 3 VPNs, you include statements. In addition, you must enable a signaling protocol, IBGP sessions between the PE routers, and an IGP on the PE and provider routers.

```
[edit routing-instances]
routing-instance-name {
  description text;
  interface interface-name;
  instance-type vrf;
  route-distinguisher ( as-number:number | ip-
    address:number );
  vrf-import [ policy-names ];
  vrf-export [ policy-names ];
  vrf-table-label;
  protocols {
    bgp {
      bgp configuration
    }
    ospf {
      ospf configuration
    }
    rip {
      rip configuration
    }
  }
  routing-options {
    autonomous-system autonomous-system <loops number>;
    forwarding-table {
      export [ policy-names ];
    }
    interface-routes {
      rib-group group-name;
    }
    martians {
      destination-prefix match-type <allow>;
```

```
    }
    maximum-routes route-limit <log-only | threshold
value>;
    options {
      syslog (level level | upto level);
    }
    rib routing-table {
      static {
        defaults {
          static-options;
        }
        route destination-prefix {
          next-hop;
          static-options;
          }
        }
      }
      martians {
        destination-prefix match-type <allow>;
      }
      static {
        defaults {
          static-options;
        }
        route destination-prefix {
          policy [ policy-names ];
          static-options;
        }
      }
    }
    router-id address;
    static {
      defaults {
        static-options;
      }
      route destination-prefix {
        policy [ policy-names ];
        static-options;
      }
    }
  }
}
```

By default, Layer 3 VPNs are disabled. For Layer 3 VPNs to function, you enable a signaling protocol on the PE routers using either LDP or RSVP.

To use LDP for VPN signaling, perform the following steps on the PE and provider routers:

1. Configure LDP on the interfaces in the core of the service provider's network by including the `ldp` statement. You need to configure LDP only on the interfaces between PE routers or between PE and provider routers. You can think of these as the "core-facing" interfaces. You do not need to configure LDP on the interface between the PE and CE routers.

   ```
   [edit protocols]
   ldp {
     interface interface-name;
   }
   ```

2. Configure the MPLS address family on the interfaces on which you enable LDP (that is, on the interfaces you configured in Step 1):

   ```
   [edit]
   interfaces {
     interface-name {
       unit logical-unit-number {
         family mpls;
       }
     }
   }
   ```

3. Configure OSPF or IS-IS on each PE and provider router. You configure these protocols at the master instance of the routing protocol, not within the routing instance used for the VPN:

   To configure OSPF, include the `ospf` statement. At a minimum, you must configure a backbone area on at least one of the router's interfaces.

   ```
   [edit protocols]
   ospf {
     area 0.0.0.0 {
       interface interface-name;
     }
   }
   ```

To configure IS-IS, include the `isis` statement and configure the loopback interface and ISO family at the `[edit interfaces]` hierarchy level. At a minimum, you must enable IS-IS on the router, configure a network entity title (NET) on one of the router's interfaces (preferably the loopback interface, `lo0`), and configure the ISO family on all interfaces on which you want IS-IS to run. When you enable IS-IS, Level 1 and Level 2 are enabled by default. The following is the minimum IS-IS configuration. In the `address` statement, *`address`* is the NET.

```
[edit]
interfaces {
  lo0 {
    unit logical-unit-number {
      family iso {
        address address;
      }
    }
  }
  type-fpc/pic/port {
    unit logical-unit-number {
      family iso;
    }
  }
}
protocols {
  isis {
    interface all;
  }
}
```

To use RSVP for VPN signaling, perform the following steps:

1. On each PE router, configure traffic engineering. To do this, you must configure an IGP that supports traffic engineering (either IS-IS or OSPF) and enable traffic engineering support for that protocol. For IS-IS, traffic engineering support is enabled by default. To enable OSPF traffic engineering support, include the `traffic-engineering` statement:

   ```
   [edit protocols ospf]
   traffic-engineering {
     no-topology;
     shortcuts;
   }
   ```

2. On each PE and provider router, enable RSVP on the router interfaces that participate in the label-switched path (LSP). On the PE router, these are the interfaces that are the ingress and egress points to the LSP. On the provider router, these are the interfaces that connect the LSP between the PE routers. Do not enable RSVP on the interface between the PE and the CE routers, because this interface is not part of the LSP. To configure RSVP on the PE and provider routers, include one `interface` statement for each interface on which you are enabling RSVP:

   ```
   [edit rsvp]
   interface interface-name;
   ```

3. On each PE router, configure an MPLS LSP to the PE router that is the LSP's egress point by including the `label-switched-path` and `interface` statements. In the `to` statement, specify the address of the LSP's egress point, which is an address on the remote PE router. In the `interface` statement, specify the name of the interface (both the physical and logical portions). Include one `interface` statement for the interface associated with the LSP.

   ```
   [edit mpls]
   label-switched-path path-name {
     to ip-address;
   }
   interface interface-name;
   ```

   You must also configure `family mpls` and `family inet` when configuring the logical interface:

   ```
   [edit interfaces interface-name unit logical-unit-
   number]
   family inet;
   family mpls;
   ```

4. On all provider routers that participate in the LSP, enable MPLS by including one `interface` statement for each connection to the LSP:

   ```
   [edit mpls]
   interface interface-name;
   ```

5. Enable MPLS on the interface between the PE and CE routers by including the `interface` statement. Doing this allows the PE router to assign an MPLS label to traffic entering the LSP or to remove the label from traffic exiting the LSP.

```
[edit mpls]
interface interface-name;
```

To allow the PE and provider routers to exchange routing information, you must either configure an IGP on all these routers, or you must configure static routes. You configure the IGP on the master instance of the routing protocol process (`rpd`) (that is, at the `[edit protocols]` hierarchy level), not within the routing instance used for the VPN (that is, not at the `[edit routing-instances]` hierarchy level). When you configure the PE router, do not configure any summarization of the PE router's loopback addresses at the area boundary. Each PE router's loopback address should appear as a separate route. You must configure an IBGP session between PE routers to allow the PE routers to exchange information about routes originating and terminating in the VPN. To do this, include the `family inet-vpn` statement when configuring IBGP to indicate that the IBGP session is for the VPN:

```
[edit protocols]
bgp {
  group group-name {
    type internal;
    local-address ip-address;
    family inet-vpn {
      unicast;
    }
    neighbor ip-address;
  }
}
```

The IP address in the `local-address` statement is the address of the loopback interface (`lo0`) on the local PE router. The IBGP session for VPNs runs through the loopback address. (You must also configure the `lo0` interface at the `[edit interfaces]` hierarchy level.) The IP address in the `neighbor` statement is the loopback address of the neighboring PE router. If you are using RSVP signaling, this IP address is the same address you specify in the `to` statement at the `[edit mpls label-switched-path]` hierarchy level when you configure the MPLS LSP.

To configure routing instances for VPNs, include the `routing-instances` statement. You configure VPN routing instances only on PE routers. The `instance-type`, `interface`, `route-distinguisher`, `vrf-export`, and `vrf-import` statements are required for the Layer 2 VPN to function.

```
[edit]
routing-instances {
  routing-instance-name {
    description text;
    instance-type vrf;
    interface interface-name;
    route-distinguisher ( as-number:number | ip-
      address:number );
    vrf-import [ policy-names ];
    vrf-export [ policy-names ];
    vrf-table-label;
  }
}
```

To provide a textual description for the routing instance, include the `description` statement. To enable Layer 2 VPN routing on a PE router, include the `instance-type` statement, specifying the instance type as `vrf`.

On each PE router, include the `interface` statement to configure an interface over which the VPN traffic travels between the PE and CE routers. You should specify both the physical and logical portions of the interface name, in the format *physical.logical*. A logical interface can be associated with only one routing instance. When you configure this same interface at the `[edit interfaces]` hierarchy level, you must also configure `family inet` and `family mpls` when configuring the logical interface:

```
[edit interfaces interface-name unit logical-unit-number]
family inet;
family mpls;
```

Each routing instance that you configure on a PE router must have a unique route distinguisher associated with it. The route distinguisher is used to place bounds around a VPN so that the same IP address prefixes can be used in different VPNs without overlapping. To configure a route distinguisher on a PE router, include the `route-distinguisher` statement. The route distinguisher is a 6-byte value that you can specify in one of the following formats:

- *as-number:number*, where *as-number* is an AS number (a 2-byte value), and *number* is any 4-byte value. The AS number can be in the range 1 through 65,535. We recommend that you use an IANA assigned, nonprivate AS number, preferably the ISP's own or the customer's own AS number.
- *ip-address:number*, where *ip-address* is an IP address (a 4-byte value), and *number* is any 2-byte value. The IP address can be any globally unique unicast address. We recommend that you use the address that you configure in the `router-id` statement, which is a nonprivate address in your assigned prefix range.

Configuring Policy for the PE Router's VRF Table

On each PE router, you must define policies that define how routes are imported into and exported from the router's VRF table. In these policies, you must define the route target, and you can optionally define the route origin.

In the import and export policies for the PE router's VRF table, you must define the route target, which defines which VPN the route is part of. To do this, include the `target` option in the `community` statement:

```
[edit policy-options]
community name members target:community-id;
```

In the import and export policies for the PE router's VRF table, you can optionally define the route origin (otherwise known as the site of origin), which identifies the set of routes learned from a particular CE site. To do this, include the `origin` option in the `community` statement:

```
[edit policy-options]
community name members origin:community-id;
```

name is the name of the community. *community-id* is the identifier of the community. You specify it in one of the following formats:

- *as-number:number*, where *as-number* is an AS number (a 2-byte value), and *number* is a 4-byte community identifier. The AS number can be in the range 1 through 65,535. We recommend that you use an IANA assigned, nonprivate AS number, preferably the ISP's own or the customer's own AS number. The community identifier can be a number in the range 0 through $2^{32} - 1$.

- *ip-address:number*, where *ip-address* is an IPv4 address (a 4-byte value), and *number* is a 2-byte community identifier. The IP address can be any globally unique unicast address. We recommend that you use the address that you configure in the `router-id` statement, which is a nonprivate address in your assigned prefix range. The community identifier can be a number in the range 1 through 65,535.

Each VPN must have a policy that defines how routes are imported into the PE router's VRF table. The import policy is applied to routes received from other PE routers in the VPN. The policy must evaluate all routes received over the IBGP session with the other PE router. If the routes match the conditions, the route is installed in the PE router's *routing-instance-name*`.inet.0` VRF table. The import policy must contain a second term that rejects all other routes. Unless the import policy contains only a `then reject` statement, it must include a reference to a community. Otherwise, when you try to commit the configuration, the commit fails. You can configure multiple import policies.

To configure an import policy for the PE router's VRF table, follow these steps:

1. To define the import policy, include the `policy-statement` statement. For all PE routers, the import policy must always include the following, at a minimum. This policy evaluates all routes received over the IBGP session with the other PE router. If the routes match the conditions in the `from` statement, the route is installed in the PE router's *routing-instance-name*`.inet.0` VRF table. The second term in the policy rejects all other routes.

```
[edit]
policy-options {
  policy-statement import-policy-name {
    term import-term-name {
      from {
        protocol bgp;
        community community-id;
      }
      then accept;
    }
    term term-name {
      then reject;
    }
  }
}
```

2. To apply the import policy, include the `vrf-import` statement:

```
[edit routing-instances routing-instance-name]
vrf-import [ import-policy-names ];
```

Each VPN must have a policy that defines how routes are exported from the PE router's VRF table. The export policy is applied to routes sent to other PE routers in the VPN. The export policy must evaluate all routes received over the routing protocol session with the CE router. (This session can use either the BGP, OSPF, or RIP routing protocol or static routes.) If the routes match the conditions, the specified community target (which is the route target) is added to them, and they are exported to the remote PE routers. The export policy must contain a second term that rejects all other routes. Export policies defined within the VPN routing instance are the only export policies that apply to the VRF table. Any export policy that you define on the IBGP session between the PE routers has no effect on the VRF table. You can configure multiple export policies.

To configure an export policy for the PE router's VRF table, follow these steps:

1. To define the export policy, include the `policy-statement` statement. For all PE routers, the export policy must distribute VPN routes to and from the connected CE routers in accordance with the type of routing protocol that you configure between the CE and PE routers within the routing instance. The export policy must always include the following, at a minimum. The first term evaluates all routes received over the routing protocol session with the CE router. (This session can use either the BGP, OSPF, or RIP routing protocol or static routes.) If the routes match the conditions in the `from` statement, the community target specified in the `then community add` statement is added to them, and they are exported to the remote PE routers. The second term in the policy rejects all other routes.

```
[edit]
policy-options {
  policy-statement export-policy-name {
    term export-term-name {
      from protocol (bgp | ospf | rip | static);
      then {
        community add community-id;
        accept;
      }
    }
```

```
      term term-name {
        then reject;
      }
    }
  }
```

2. To apply the policy, include the `vrf-export` statement:

```
[edit routing-instances routing-instance-name]
vrf-export [ export-policy-names ];
```

Configuring VPN Routing between the PE and CE Routers

For the PE router to distribute VPN-related routes to and from connected CE routers, you must configure routing within the VPN routing instance. You can configure a routing protocol—either BGP, OSPF, or RIP—or you can configure static routing. For the connection to each CE router, you can configure only one type of routing.

To configure BGP as the routing protocol between the PE and the CE router, include the `protocols bgp` statement:

```
[edit routing-instances routing-instance-name]
protocols {
  bgp {
    group group-name {
      peer-as as-number;
      neighbor ip-address;
    }
  }
}
```

To configure OSPF to distribute VPN-related routes between the PE and CE routers, configure an OSPF domain ID for each distinct OSPF domain. Routes from an OSPF domain need to have an OSPF domain ID when they are distributed in BGP as VPN-IPv4 routes in VPNs with multiple OSPF domains. In a VPN connecting multiple OSPF domains, there is a possibility that the routes from one of the domains could overlap with the routes of a different domain. Configuring a unique OSPF domain ID for each domain ensures that the routes for each domain remain separate. When a PE router receives a route with a different OSPF domain ID, it redistributes the route as a type 5 link-state advertisement (LSA). If the OSPF domain IDs match and the route is a summary route, it is distributed as a type 3 LSA (type 5 LSAs are passed as type 5 LSAs). Each VRF table in a PE router associated with an OSPF instance must be configured with the same OSPF domain ID.

You can set a VPN tag for the OSPF external routes generated by the provider edge (PE) router. By default, this tag is automatically calculated and needs no configuration. To configure the domain VPN tag for Type 5 LSAs, include the `domain-vpn-tag number` statement at the `[edit routing-instances routing-instance-name protocols ospf]` hierarchy level; the range is 1 through 4,294,967,295. If you set VPN tags manually, you must set the same value for all PE routers in that VPN.

To configure OSPF as the routing protocol between the PE and the CE router, include the `ospf` statement:

```
[edit routing-instances routing-instance-name protocols]
ospf {
  area area {
    interface interface-name;
  }
  domain-id domain-id;
  domain-vpn-tag number;
}
```

For a Layer 3 VPN, you can configure RIP on the PE router to learn the routes of the CE router or to propagate the routes of the PE router to the CE router. RIP routes learned from neighbors configured under any `routing-instance` hierarchy level are added to the routing instance's inet table (*`instance_name`*`.inet.0`). To configure RIP as the routing protocol between the PE and the CE router, include the `rip` statement:

```
[edit routing-instances routing-instance-name protocols]
rip {
  group group-name {
    neighbor interface-name;
  }
}
```

To install routes learned from a RIP routing instance to multiple routing tables, include the `rib-group` statement:

```
[edit protocols rip] or
[edit routing-instances routing-instance-name protocols
rip]
protocols rip {
  rib-group inet routing-table-group-name;
  group group-name {
    neighbor interface-name;
  }
}
```

The first routing table name specified in the `import-rib` statement at the `[edit routing-options rib table1.inet.0 static]` hierarchy level must be the name of the routing table you are configuring.

To configure a static route between the PE and the CE router, include the `static` statement:

```
[edit routing-instances routing-instance-name routing-
options]
static {
  route destination-prefix {
    next-hop;
    static-options;
  }
}
```

To limit the number of prefixes installed into routing tables, include the `maximum-routes` statement. Route limits apply only to dynamic routing protocols and are not applicable to static or interface routes.

```
[edit routing-instances routing-instance-name routing-
options]
maximum-routes route-limit <log-only | threshold value>;
```

Route limits can be advisory (set with the `log-only` option) or mandatory. An advisory limit triggers only warnings. The log messages are rate-limited to once every 30 seconds. A mandatory limit, in addition to triggering a warning message, rejects any additional routes after the threshold is reached. The threshold value is a percentage of the route limit at which warning messages are logged.

Configuring Layer 3 VPN Tunnel Interfaces

To configure a Layer 3 VPN as the tunnel end point of a generic routing encapsulation (GRE) tunnel interface, you need to specify which routing table to search on the router, indicated by the destination IP address, so that the appropriate routing table can be searched for the routing prefix, because identical routing prefixes can appear in different routing tables. To configure a Layer 3 VPN as the tunnel end point of a tunnel interface, include the `routing-instance` statement:

```
[edit interfaces interface-name unit unit-number tunnel {
routing-instance {
  destination routing-instance-name;
}
```

You must also configure the GRE tunnel interface at the `[edit routing-instance routing-instance-name]` hierarchy level. Otherwise, any prefix mentioned under `family inet` of that tunnel interface is placed in the default `inet` routing table.

To configure an encrypted tunnel interface for a Layer 3 VPN, you configure ES tunnel interfaces on the PE and CE routers, and you configure Internet Protocol Security (IPSec) on these routers. To configure these routers as tunnel end points of an ES tunnel interface, configure a tunnel on the ES interface:

```
[edit]
interfaces {
  interface-name {
    unit unit-number {
      family mpls;
      tunnel {
        source address;
        destination address;
      }
    }
  }
}
```

Then associate the ES interface on the appropriate routing instance:

```
[edit routing-instances]
routing-instance-name {
  interface interface-name;
}
```

CHAPTER

13

Monitoring Commands

System Management

Table 13.1 *System Management Monitoring Commands*

Information to Monitor	Command	Example

Versions of software running on the router.	`show version`	`user@host>` **`show version brief`**
		`Model: m160`
		`JUNOS Base OS boot [5.4R1]`
		`JUNOS Base OS Software Suite [5.4R1]`
		`JUNOS Kernel Software Suite [5.4R1]`
		`JUNOS Routing Software Suite [5.4R1]`
		`JUNOS Packet Forwarding Engine Support [5.4R1]`
		`JUNOS Crypto Software Suite [5.4R1]`
		`Juniper Networks Online Documentation Files [5.4R1]`

JUNOS software extensions.	`show system software`	`user@host>` **`show system software`**
		`Information for jbase:`
		`Comment:`
		`JUNOS Base OS Software Suite [5.4R1]`
		`...`

Current time and how long the router has been operational.	`show system uptime`	`user@host>` **`show system uptime`**
		`Current time:      1998-10-13 19:45:47 UTC`
		`System booted:     1998-10-12 20:51:41 UTC (22:54:06 ago)`
		`Protocols started: 1998-10-13 19:33:45 UTC (00:12:02 ago)`
		`Last configured:   1998-10-13 19:33:45 UTC (00:12:02 ago) by abc`
		`12:45PM  up 22:54, 2 users, load averages: 0.07, 0.02, 0.01`

Current running system configuration.	`show configuration`	`user@host>` **`show configuration`**
		`system {`
		`    host-name my-host;`
		`    domain-name juniper.net;`
		`    backup-router 192.1.1.254;`
		`    time-zone America/Los_Angeles;`
		`...`

Table 13.1 *System Management Monitoring Commands*

Information to Monitor	Command	Example

Verify the syntax of a configuration file.	test configuration	user@host> **test configuration terminal**
		[Type ^D to end input]
		system {
		  host-name my-name;
		  ok computer;
		  login;
		}
		terminal:3:(8) syntax error: ok
		  [edit system]
		    'ok computer;'
		      syntax error
		terminal:4:(11) statement must contain additional statements: ;
		  [edit system login]
		    'login ;'
		      statement must contain additional statements
		configuration syntax failed

Users currently logged in to the router.	show system users	user@host> **show system users** 7:30PM up 4 days, 2:26, 2 users, load averages: 0.07, 0.02, 0.01 USER TTY FROM LOGIN@ IDLE WHAT root d0 - Fri05PM 4days -csh (csh) boojum p0 berry.juniper.net 7:30PM - cli

Login permissions for the current user.	show cli authorization	root@host> **show cli authorization**
		Current user: 'root' login: 'boojum' class '(root)'
		Permissions:
		  admin -- Can view user accounts
		  admin-control-- Can modify user accounts
		  clear -- Can clear learned network information
		  configure -- Can enter configuration mode
		...

Table 13.1 *System Management Monitoring Commands*

Information to Monitor	Command	Example

Log files and their contents and recent user logins.	`show log`	`user@host>` **`show log`**
		`total 57518`
		`-rw-r--r--  1 root  bin     211663 Oct  1 19:44 dcd`
		`-rw-r--r--  1 root  bin     999947 Oct  1 19:41 dcd.0`
		`-rw-r--r--  1 root  bin     999994 Oct  1 17:48 dcd.1`
		`-rw-r--r--  1 root  bin     238815 Oct  1 19:44 rpd`
		`-rw-r--r--  1 root  bin    1049098 Oct  1 18:00 rpd.0`
		`-rw-r--r--  1 root  bin    1061095 Oct  1 12:13 rpd.1`
		`-rw-r--r--  1 root  bin    1052026 Oct  1 06:08 rpd.2`

Monitor the contents of log files.	`monitor`	`user@host>` **`monitor start system-log`**
		`*** system-log***`
		`Jul 20 15:07:34 hang sshd[5845]: log: Generating 768 bit RSA key.`
		`Jul 20 15:07:35 hang sshd[5845]: log: RSA key generation complete.`
		`Jul 20 15:07:35 hang sshd[5845]: log: Connection from 204.69.248.180`
		`port 912`
		`Jul 20 15:07:37 hang sshd[5845]: log: RSA authentication for root`
		`accepted.`
		`Jul 20 15:07:37 hang sshd[5845]: log: ROOT LOGIN as 'root' from`
		`trip.jcmax.com`
		`Jul 20 15:07:37 hang sshd[5847]: log: executing remote command as root:`
		`scp -t /`
		`tmp`
		`Jul 20 15:07:37 hang sshd[5845]: log: Closing connection to`
		`204.69.248.180`

Recent CLI history.	`show cli history`	`user@host>` **`show cli history`**
		`  11:14:14 -- show arp`
		`  11:22:10 -- show cli authorization`
		`  11:27:12 -- show cli history`

Check host reachability and network connectivity.	`ping`	`user@host>` **`ping boojum`**
		`PING boojum.juniper.net (192.156.169.254): 56 data bytes`
		`64 bytes from 192.156.169.254: icmp_seq=0 ttl=253 time=1.028 ms`
		`64 bytes from 192.156.169.254: icmp_seq=5 ttl=253 time=1.044 ms`
		`^C [abort]`

Table 13.1 *System Management Monitoring Commands*

Information to Monitor	Command	Example
Check the reachability of a remote ATM node.	ping atm	user@host> **ping atm vci 0.128 interface at-**5/3/0 53 byte oam cell received on (vpi=0 vci=128): seq=1 53 byte oam cell received on (vpi=0 vci=128): seq=2 ^C[abort] --- atmping statistics --- 2 cells transmitted, 2cells received, 0% cell loss
Check the reachability of a remote VPN node.	ping vpn-interface	user@vpnhost> **ping vpn-interface fe-1/1/0.1 192.168.197.94 local 192.168.197.93 count 3** PING 192.168.197.94 (192.168.197.94): 56 data bytes 64 bytes from 192.168.197.94: icmp_seq=0 ttl=255 time=0.866 ms 64 bytes from 192.168.197.94: icmp_seq=1 ttl=255 time=0.728 ms 64 bytes from 192.168.197.94: icmp_seq=2 ttl=255 time=0.753 ms --- 192.168.197.94 ping statistics --- 3 packets transmitted, 3 packets received, 0% packet loss round-trip min/avg/max/stddev = 0.728/0.782/0.866/0.060 ms
Determine the route to a network system.	traceroute	user@host> **traceroute venus** traceroute to venus.juniper.net (192.156.169.254), 30 hops max, 40 byte packets 1 alice (192.168.1.254) 2.370 ms 2.853 ms 0.367 ms 2 snark (192.168.255.250) 0.778 ms 2.937 ms 0.446 ms 3 boojum (192.156.169.254) 7.737 ms 89.905 ms 0.834 ms

Table 13.1 *System Management Monitoring Commands*

Information to Monitor	Command	Example

Network connection information.	`show system connections`	`user@host>` **`show system connections`**
		`Active Internet connections (including servers)`
		`Proto Recv-Q Send-Q  Local Address          Foreign Address`
		`(state)`
		`tcp         0      2  192.168.4.16.513       208.197.169.254.894`
		`ESTABLISHED`
		`tcp         0      0  192.168.4.16.513       208.197.169.195.945`
		`ESTABLISHED`
		`tcp         0      0  *.23                   *.*`
		`LISTEN`
		`tcp         0      0  *.22                   *.*`
		`LISTEN`
		`tcp         0      0  *.513                  *.*`
		`LISTEN`
		`tcp 0   0 *.514    *.*                  LISTEN`
		`tcp 0   0 *.21     *.*                  LISTEN`
		`udp 0   0 192.168.4.16.1634208.197.169.249.2049`
		`udp 0   0 192.168.4.16.1627208.197.169.254.2049`
		`udp 0   0 192.168.4.16.1371208.197.169.195.2049`

Open secure shell connections between the local router and a remote system.	`ssh`	`user@host>` **`ssh berry`**
		`Host key not found from the list of known hosts.`
		`Are you sure you want to continue connecting (yes/no)? yes`
		`Host ‘berry’ added to the list of known hosts.`
		`boojun@berry’s password:`
		`Last login: Sun Jun 21 10:43:42 1998 from junos-router`
		`% ...`
		`% exit`
		`user@host>`

Table 13.1 *System Management Monitoring Commands*

Information to Monitor	Command	Example
Open a telnet session to a remote system.	telnet	user@host> **telnet 192.154.1.254** Trying 192.154.169.254... Connected to berry.juniper.net. Escape character is '^]'. ttypa login: <Control>] telnet> quit Connection closed. user@host>
NTP peers and their state.	show ntp associations	user@host> **show ntp associations** remote refid st t when poll reach delay offset disp == ====== *wolfe-gw.junipe tick.ucla.edu 2 u 43 64 377 1.86 0.319 0.08
NTP peer variables.	show ntp status	user@host> **show ntp status** status=06f4 leap_none, sync_ntp, 15 events, event_peer/strat_chg system="FreeBSD", leap=00, stratum=4, rootdelay=7.90, rootdispersion=22.99, peer=23732, refid=olive-oyl.juniper.net, reftime=b97c36cf.bed61000 Wed, Aug 12 1998 15:44:15.745, poll=7, clock=b97c3715.ba307000 Wed, Aug 12 1998 15:45:25.727, phase=-0.283, freq=-23633.96, error=0.695

Table 13.1 *System Management Monitoring Commands*

Information to Monitor	Command	Example

FPC information	`show pfe fpc`	user@host> **show pfe fpc 1**
		FPC 1 status:
		  Slot: Present
		  State: Online
		  Last State Change: 2000-01-10 18:12:27 UTC
		  Uptime: 1d 03:31
		  Failures: 0
		  Pending: 0
		
		PFE listener statistics:
		...
		PFE IPC statistics:
		...
		PFE socket-buffer mbuf depth:
		...
		PFE socket-buffer bytes pending transmit:
		...

Packet Forwarding Engine information.	`show pfe terse`	user@host> **show pfe terse**
		Slot Type Slot State Flags Uptime
		  0 SFM Present Online 0x0bf 01:25:42
		  2 SFM Present Online 0x0bf 01:25:40
		  0 FPC Present Online 0x102 01:25:57
		  1 FPC Present Online 0x102 01:25:55
		  2 FPC Present Online 0x102 01:25:53

Packet Forwarding Engine next-hop information.	`show pfe next-hop`	user@host> **show pfe next-hop** SFM 0 Nexthop Info: ID Type Interface Protocol Encap Next Hop Addr MTU ...

Table 13.1 *System Management Monitoring Commands*

Information to Monitor	Command	Example

SCB information	show pfe scb	user@host> **show pfe scb**
		SCB status:
		  Slot: Present
		  State: Online
		  Last State Change: 1999-02-05 11:02:36 UTC
		  Uptime: 1d 02:31
		  Failures: 0
		  Pending: 0
		PFE listener statistics:
		...
		PFE IPC statistics:
		...

SFM information	show pfe sfm	user@host> **show pfe sfm 1**
		SFM 1 status:
		  Slot: Offline
		  State: Init
		  Last State Change: 2000-03-01 07:45:55 UTC
		  Downtime: 17:47:29
		  Failures: 167
		  Pending: 0
		PFE listener statistics:
		...
		PFE IPC statistics:
		...

Table 13.1 *System Management Monitoring Commands*

Information to Monitor	Command	Example

System memory and buffer usage information.	`show system buffers`	`user@host>` **`show system buffers`**
		`        853 mbufs in use:`
		`        2 mbufs allocated to packet headers`
		`        37 mbufs allocated to protocol control blocks`
		`        28 mbufs allocated to socket names and addresses`
		`        2 mbufs allocated to socket send data`
		`        400 mbufs allocated to pfe refill data`
		`        384 mbufs allocated to fxp data`
		`784/944 mbuf clusters in use`
		`1994 Kbytes allocated to network (83% in use)`
		`0 requests for memory denied`
		`0 requests for memory delayed`
		`0 calls to protocol drain routines`

Software processes running on the router.	`show system processes`	`user@host>` **`show system processes brief`**
		`last pid:   543;  load averages:  0.00,  0.00,  0.00    18:29:47`
		`37 processes:  1 running, 36 sleeping`
		
		`Mem: 25M Active, 3976K Inact, 19M Wired, 8346K Buf, 202M Free`
		`Swap: 528M Total, 64K Used, 528M Free`

Systemwide protocol-related statistics.	`show system statistics`	`user@host>` **`show system statistics`**
		`ip: ...`
		`icmp: ...`
		`tcp: ...`
		`udp: ...`
		`igmp: ...`
		`arp: ...`
		`clnl: ...`
		`esis: ...`

Table 13.1 *System Management Monitoring Commands*

Information to Monitor	Command	Example
Statistics about amount of free disk space in the router's file systems.	`show system storage`	user@host> **show system storage** Filesystem 1K-blocks Used Avail Capacity Mon /dev/wd1s1a 65687 28888 31545 48% / devfs 16 16 0 100% dut devfs 16 16 0 100% /d/
Routing, routing protocol, and interface tasks that are currently running.	`show task`	user@host> **show task summary** Pri Task Name Pro Port So Flags 10 IF 15 LABEL 15 ISO 15 INET 7 20 Aggregate 20 RT 30 ICMP 1 9 39 ISIS I/O 12 40 IS-IS 10 40 BGP RT Background <LowPrio> 40 BGP.0.0.0.0+179 179 15 <Accept LowPrio> 50 BGP_69.192.168.201.234+179 179 17 <LowPrio> 50 BGP_70.192.168.201.233+179 179 16 <LowPrio> 50 BGP_Group_69_153 <LowPrio> 50 BGP_Group_70_153 <LowPrio> 50 ASPaths 60 KRT 255 1 60 Redirect 70 MGMT.local 14 <LowPrio> 70 MGMT_Listen./var/run/rpd_mgmt 13 <Accept LowPrio> 70 SNMP Subagent./var/run/sub_rpd.sock 8 <LowPrio>

Table 13.1 *System Management Monitoring Commands*

Information to Monitor	Command	Example

State and checksum value for files in a file system.	`show system audit`	`user@host>` **`show system audit root-only`**
		`#          user: root`
		`#       machine: my-host`
		`#          tree: /`
		`date: Fri Feb 11 21:21:46 2000`
		
		`# .`
		`/set type=file uid=0 gid=0 mode=0755 nlink=1`
		`.                type=dir nlink=23 size=1024 time=950252640.0`
		`    .cshrc       uid=3 gid=7 mode=0644 size=177 time=939182975.0 \`
		`                 md5digest=f414e06fea6bd646244b98e13d6e6226`
		`    .kernel.jkernel.backup \`
		`                 mode=0744 size=1934552 time=944688902.0 \`
		`                 md5digest=2c343cf0bd9fea8f04f78604feed7aa4`
		`...`

Hostname lookup using DNS.	`show host`	`user@host>` **`show host snark`**
		`snark.boojum.net has address 192.168.1.254`
		`user@host> show host 192.168.1.254`
		`Name: snark.boojum.net`
		`Address: 192.168.1.254`
		`Aliases:`

Contents of the ARP table.	`show arp`	`user@host>` **`show arp`**
		`MAC Address       Address       Name               Flags`
		`00:00:0c:06:2c:0d 192.168.1.2   firewall.my.net`

Zero the contents of the ARP table.	`clear arp`	`user@host>` **`clear arp`** `user@host>`

Restart a JUNOS software process.	`restart`	`user@host>` **`restart interfaces`**
		`interfaces process terminated`
		`interfaces process restarted`
		`user@host>`

Table 13.1 *System Management Monitoring Commands*

Information to Monitor	Command	Example

Install software bundles or packages onto the router.	`request system software add`	`user@host>` **`request system software add 5.4R1-signed.tgz`**
		`Initializing...`
		`Using /packages/jbase-5.4R1`
		`...`

Remove software bundles or packages from the router.	`request system software delete`	`user@host>` **`request system software delete 5.4R1-signed.tgz`**
Roll back to previously installed version.	`request system software rollback`	`user@host>` **`request system software rollback`**

Check candidate software compatibility against the current configuration.	`request system software validate`	`user@host>` **`request system software validate 5.3R1.tgz`**
		`Checking compatibility with configuration`
		`Initializing...`
		`Using /packages/jbase-5.4R1`
		`...`

Stop the routing software.	`request system halt`	`user@host>` **`request system halt`**
		`Halt the system ? [yes,no] (no) yes`
		`*** FINAL System shutdown message from root@lab8 ***`
		`System going down IMMEDIATELY`
		`Terminated`
		`...`
		`syncing disks... 11 8 done`
		`The operating system has halted.`
		`Please press any key to reboot.`

Table 13.1 *System Management Monitoring Commands*

Information to Monitor	Command	Example
Reboot the routing software.	request system reboot	user@host> **request system reboot** Reboot the system ? [yes,no] (no) user@host> user@host> request system reboot at 2300 message "Maintenance time!" Reboot the system ? [yes,no] (no) yes shutdown: [pid 186] *** System shutdown message from root@berry.network.net *** System going down at 23:00
Display pending system halts or reboots.	show system reboot	user@host> **show system reboot** reboot requested by root at Wed Feb 10 17:40:46 1999 [process id 17885]
Clear a pending system halt or reboot.	clear system reboot	user@host> **clear system reboot** reboot requested by root at Sat Dec 12 19:37:34 1998 [process id 17855] Terminating...
Back up the file systems on the router.	request system snapshot	user@host> **request system snapshot** umount: /altroot: not currently mounted Copying / to /altroot.. (this may take a few minutes) umount: /altconfig: not currently mounted Copying /config to /altconfig.. (this may take a few minutes) The following filesystems were archived: / /config
Copy a file to another location on the router or to another system on the network.	file copy	user@host> **copy /var/tmp/rpd.core.4 berry:/c/junipero/tmp** ...transferring.file...... | 0 KB | 0.3 kB/s | ETA: 00:00:00 | 100%
List files and directories on the router.	file list	user@host> **file list /var/tmp** dcd.core rpd.core snmpd.core

Table 13.1 *System Management Monitoring Commands*

Information to Monitor	Command	Example
Rename a file on the router.	`file rename`	user@host> **file rename /var/tmp/dcd.core /var/tmp/dcd.core.990413** user@host> **file list /var/tmp** dcd.core.990413 rpd.core snmpd.core
Display the contents of a file.	`file show`	user@host> **file show /var/log/messages** Apr 13 21:00:08 romney /kernel: so-1/1/2: loopback suspected; going to standby. Apr 13 21:00:40 romney /kernel: so-1/1/2: loopback suspected; going to standby. Apr 13 21:02:48 romney last message repeated 4 times Apr 13 21:07:04 romney last message repeated 8 times Apr 13 21:07:13 romney /kernel: so-1/1/0: Clearing SONET alarm(s) RDI-P Apr 13 21:07:29 romney /kernel: so-1/1/0: Asserting SONET alarm(s) RDI-P Apr 13 21:07:36 romney /kernel: so-1/1/2: loopback suspected; going to standby. Apr 13 21:08:08 romney /kernel: so-1/1/2: loopback suspected; going to standby. ...
Delete a file on the router.	`file delete`	user@host> **file delete /var/tmp/snmpd.core** user@host> file list /var/tmp dcd.core rpd.core
Send messages to users currently logged in to the router.	`request message`	user@host> **request message message "Maintenance window in 10 minutes" user boojum** Message from user@host on ttyp0 at 20:27 ... Maintenance window in 10 minutes EOF
Display boot messages.	`show system boot-messages`	user@host> **show system boot-messages** Copyright (c) 1992-1998 FreeBSD Inc. Copyright (c) 1996-2000 Juniper Networks, Inc. All rights reserved. ...

Table 13.1 *System Management Monitoring Commands*

<table>
<tr><th>Information to Monitor</th><th>Command</th><th>Example</th></tr>
<tr><td>Collect system information before contacting customer support.</td><td><code>request support information</code></td><td><code>user@host> request support information | save filename</code>
<code>Wrote 1143 lines of output to ‘filename’</code>
<code>user@host></code></td></tr>
</table>

SNMP

Table 13.2 *SNMP Monitoring Commands*

<table>
<tr><th>Information to Monitor</th><th>Command</th><th>Example</th></tr>
<tr><td>Statistics about SNMP packets sent and received</td><td><code>show snmp statistics</code></td><td><code>user@host> show snmp statistics</code>
<code>SNMP statistics:</code>
<code> Input:</code>
<code>   Packets: 8, Bad versions: 0, Bad community names: 0,</code>
<code>   Bad community uses: 0, ASN parse errors: 0,</code>
<code>   Too bigs: 0, No such names: 0, Bad values: 0,</code>
<code>   Read onlys: 0, General errors: 0,</code>
<code>   Total request varbinds: 8, Total set varbinds: 0,</code>
<code>   Get requests: 0, Get nexts: 8, Set requests: 0,</code>
<code>   Get responses: 0, Traps: 0,</code>
<code>   Silent drops: 0, Proxy drops 0</code>
<code> Output:</code>
<code>   Packets: 2298, Too bigs: 0, No such names: 0,</code>
<code>   Bad values: 0, General errors: 0,</code>
<code>   Get requests: 0, Get nexts: 0, Set requests: 0,</code>
<code>   Get responses: 8, Traps: 2290</code></td></tr>
</table>

Table 13.2 *SNMP Monitoring Commands*

<table>
<tr><th>Information to Monitor</th><th>Command</th><th>Example</th></tr>
<tr><td>Zero SNMP statistics.</td><td>clear snmp statistics</td><td>user@host> clear snmp statistics
user@host> show snmp statistics
SNMP statistics:
Input:
Packets: 0, Bad versions: 0, Bad community names: 0,
Bad community uses: 0, ASN parse errors: 0,
Too bigs: 0, No such names: 0, Bad values: 0,
Read onlys: 0, General errors: 0,
Total request varbinds: 0, Total set varbinds: 0,
Get requests: 0, Get nexts: 0, Set requests: 0,
Get responses: 0, Traps: 0,
Silent drops: 0, Proxy drops 0
Output:
Packets: 0, Too bigs: 0, No such names: 0,
Bad values: 0, General errors: 0,
Get requests: 0, Get nexts: 0, Set requests: 0,
Get responses: 0, Traps: 0</td></tr>
<tr><td>Information about rmon alarms and events.</td><td>show snmp rmon</td><td>user@host> show snmp rmon
Alarm
Index State Variable name
1 falling threshold crossed ifInOctets.1
Event
Index Type Last Event
1 log and trap 2002-01-30 01:13:01 PST</td></tr>
</table>

Chassis

These commands obtain information from the chassis software process, which runs when the router is up and running. If the SCB, SSB, SFM, or FEB is not running, no information about chassis components is available through the CLI.

Table 13.3 *Chassis Monitoring Commands*

Information to Monitor	Command	Example

Chassis alarm status	`show chassis alarms`	`user@host>` **`show chassis alarms`**
		`3 alarms are currently active`
		`Alarm time Class Description`
		`2000-02-07 10:12:22 UTC Major fxp0: ethernet link down`
		`2000-02-07 10:11:54 UTC Minor YELLOW ALARM - PEM 1 Removed`
		`2000-02-07 10:11:03 UTC Minor YELLOW ALARM - Lower Fan Tray Removed`

Chassis clock-source configuration	`request chassis pcg`	`user@host>` **`request chassis pcg slot offline`**

Information currently on the craft display	`show chassis craft-interface`	`user@sheep>` **`show chassis craft-interface`**
		
		`Red alarm:     LED off, relay off`
		`Yellow alarm:  LED on, relay on`
		`Host OK LED:   On`
		`Host fail LED: Off`
		
		`FPCs     0  1  2  3`
		`-------------------`
		`Green    .  *  *  .`
		`Red      .  .  .  .`
		
		`LCD screen:\LCD Screen:`
		`     +--------------------+`
		`     |sheep               |`
		`     |1 Alarm active      |`
		`     |Y: FERF             |`
		`     |                    |`
		`     +--------------------+`

Table 13.3 *Chassis Monitoring Commands*

<table>
<tr><th>Information to Monitor</th><th>Command</th><th>Example</th></tr>
<tr><td>Environmental information</td><td><code>show chassis environment</code></td><td><pre>user@m5-host> show chassis environment
Class Item   Status   Measurement

Power Power Supply A   OK
      Power Supply B   OK

Temp FPC Slot 0   OK   32 degrees C / 89 degrees
F
      FEB   OK   31 degrees C / 87 degrees
F
      PS Intake   OK   26 degrees C / 78 degrees
F
      PS Exhaust   OK   31 degrees C / 87 degrees
F

Fans Left Fan 1   OK   Spinning at normal speed
      Left Fan 2   OK   Spinning at normal speed
      Left Fan 3   OK   Spinning at normal speed
      Left Fan 4   OK   Spinning at normal speed

Misc Craft Interface   OK</pre></td></tr>
<tr><td>Firmware version</td><td><code>show chassis firmware</code></td><td><pre>user@m40-host> show chassis firmware
Part   Type   Version
System control board   ROM   Juniper ROM Monitor Version
2.0i126Copyri
                        O/S   Version 2.0i1 by root on Thu
Jul 23 00:51
FPC 5   ROM   Juniper ROM Monitor Version
2.0i49Copyrig
                        O/S   Version 2.0i1 by root on Thu
Jul 23 00:59</pre></td></tr>
</table>

Table 13.3 *Chassis Monitoring Commands*

Information to Monitor	Command	Example
FPC and PIC status	`show chassis fpc`	user@m20-host> **show chassis fpc** FPC status: Temp CPU Utilization (%) Memory Utilization (%) Slot State (C) Total Interrupt DRAM (MB) Heap Buffer 0 Empty 0 0 0 0 0 0 1 Online 38 0 0 8 0 4 2 Online 35 0 0 8 0 3 3 Empty 0 0 0 0 0 0
Control FPC operation.	`request chassis fpc`	user@m40ehost> request chassis fpc slot 0 offline
Control PIC operation.	`request chassis pic`	user@m20host> request chassis pic 0 4 offline
Hardware inventory	`show chassis hardware`	user@m10-host> **show chassis hardware** Hardware inventory: Item Version Part number Serial number Description Chassis 1122 M10 Midplane REV 1.1 710-001950 S/N AC6626 Power supply A Rev 01 740-002497 S/N LC36095 AC Power supply B Rev 01 740-002497 S/N LC36100 AC Display REV 1.2 710-001995 S/N AC6656 Host 18000005dfb3fb01 teknor FEB REV 01 710-001948 S/N AC6632 Internet Processor II FPC 0 PIC 0 REV 08 750-001072 S/N AB2485 1x G/E, 1000 BASE-SX PIC 1 REV 01 750-000613 S/N AA1048 1x OC-12 SONET, SMIR FPC 1

Table 13.3 *Chassis Monitoring Commands*

Information to Monitor	Command	Example

MAC address	show chassis mac-addresses	user@host> **show chassis mac-addresses**
		MAC address information
		  Public base address 0:90:69:0:4:0
		  Public count 1008
		  Private base address 0:90:69:0:7:f0
		  Private count 16

Routing Engine information	show chassis routing-engine	user@m10-host> **show chassis routing-engine**
		Routing Engine status:
		    Temperature 29 degrees C / 84 degrees F
		    DRAM 768 Mbytes
		    CPU utilization:
		      User 0 percent
		      Background 0 percent
		      Kernel 0 percent
		      Interrupt 0 percent
		      Idle 100 percent
		    Start time 2000-08-23 19:53:31 PDT
		    Uptime 4 days, 21 hours, 53 minutes,
		38 seconds
		    Load averages: 1 minute 5 minute 15 minute
		                                       0.12 0.03 0.01

Control the Routing Engine.	request chassis routing-engine master	user@M20-host> **request chassis routing-engine master acquire** warning: Traffic will be interrupted while the PFE is re-initialized warning: The other routing engine's file system could be corrupted Reset other routing engine and become master ? [yes,no] (no) root@m20-host-0> **request chassis routing-engine master switch** warning: Traffic will be interrupted while the PFE is re-initialized Toggle mastership between Routing Engines ? [yes,no] (no) yes Resolving mastership... Complete. The other Routing Engine becomes the master. root@m20-host-0>

Table 13.3 *Chassis Monitoring Commands*

Information to Monitor	Command	Example
System board information	show chassis feb show chassis scb show chassis sfm show chassis ssb	user@m160-host> **show chassis sfm** SFM status: Temp CPU Utilization (%) Memory Utilization (%) Slot State (C) Total Interrupt DRAM (MB) Heap Buffer 0 Online 39 0 0 64 0 6 1 Online 43 0 0 64 0 6 2 Empty 0 0 0 0 0 0 3 Empty 0 0 0 0 0 0
Control SFM operation.	request chassis sfm	user@host> **request chassis sfm slot 7 offline**
Control SFM and SSB mastership.	request chassis sfm master switch request chassis ssb master switch	user@host> **request chassis sfm master switch** warning: Traffic will be interrupted while the PFE is re-initialized Toggle mastership between system forwarding module? [yes,no] (no) yes Switch initiated, use "show chassis sfm" to verify

Table 13.3 *Chassis Monitoring Commands*

Information to Monitor	Command	Example
Display a message on the router's craft interface.	`set chassis display message`	user@sheep> **set chassis display message "NOC contact Dusty (888) 526-1234"** message sent user@sheep> **show chassis craft-interface** Red alarm: LED off, relay off Yellow alarm: LED off, relay off Host OK LED: On Host fail LED: Off FPCs 0 1 2 3 4 5 6 7 ------------------------------- Green . . * . . * * . Red . . . . LCD screen: +--------------------+ |NOC contact Dusty | |(888) 526-1234 | | | | | +--------------------+

Accounting Options

Table 13.4 *Accounting Options Monitoring Commands*

Information to Monitor	Command	Example

Display accounting statistics.	`show accounting profile`	`user@host>` **`show accounting profile filter_profile`**
		`Profile filter_profile`
		`Sampling interval: 1 minute(s),  Profile Usage Count: 0`
		`File accounting_profile_stats: maximum size 1048576, maximum number 5, bytes written 822`
		`Transfer Interval: 15 minute(s),  Next Scheduled Transfer: 2001-06-17-18:00:46`
		`Column Labels:`
		`  profile-layout`
		`  epoch-timestamp`
		`  interfaces`
		`  filter-name`
		`  counter-name`
		`  packet-count`
		`  byte-count`
		`Filter Name                 Next Scheduled Collection`
		`myfiltero                         2001-06-03-04:32:59`

Display records.	`show accounting records`	`user@host>` **`show accounting records filter_profile`**
		`Timestamp: 2000-10-03-00:30:41, Filter Name: ap_filter,`
		`Interfaces: fxp0.0`
		`    Counter Name: c1`
		`              2440   Packets`
		`            223509   Bytes`

Interfaces

With the `show interfaces` and `clear interfaces` commands, you can use wildcard characters when specifying interface names (in the *`interface-name`* option) to refer to groups of interface names without having to type each name individually. Table 13.5 lists the available wildcard characters. You must enclose all wildcard characters except the asterisk in quotation marks (" ").

Table 13.5 *Wildcard Characters for Specifying Interface Names*

Wildcard Character	Description
`* (asterisk)`	Match any string of characters in that position in the interface name. For example, `so*` matches all SONET/SDH interfaces.
"[*character* <*character*...>]"	Match one or more individual characters in that position in the interface name. For example, "`so-[03]`"* matches all SONET/SDH interfaces in slots 0 and 3.
"[!*character* <*character*...>]"	Match all characters except the ones included in the brackets. For example, "`so-[!03]`"* matches all SONET/SDH interfaces except for those in slots 0 and 3.
"[*character1*-*character2*]"	Match a range of characters. For example, `so-"[0-3]"*` matches all SONET/SDH interfaces in slots 0, 1, 2, and 3.
"[!*character1*-*character2*]"	Match all characters that are not in the specified range of characters. For example, `so-"[!0-3]"*` matches all SONET/SDH interfaces in slots 4, 5, 6, and 7.

Table 13.6 *Interfaces Monitoring Commands*

Information to Monitor	Command	Example

General interface information	show interfaces	user@host> **show interfaces fe-5/0/0**
		Physical interface: fe-5/0/0, Enabled, Physical link is Up
		  Interface index: 37, SNMP ifIndex: 14
		  Link-level type: Ethernet, MTU: 1514, Source filtering: Disabled
		  Speed: 100mbps Loopback: Disabled, Flow control: Enabled,
		  Ingress Rate Limit: 20mbs
		  Device flags : Present Running
		  Interface flags: SNMP-Traps
		  Link flags : None
		  Current address: 00:90:69:0c:0e:76, Hardware address: 00:90:69:0c:0e:76
		  Input rate : 0 bps (0 pps), Output rate: 0 bps (0 pps)
		  Active alarms : None
		  Active defects : None
		  Logical interface fe-5/0/0.0 (Index 511) (SNMP ifIndex 15)
		    Flags: SNMP-Traps, Encapsulation: ENET2
		    Protocol inet, MTU: 1500
		      Addresses, Flags: Is-Preferred Is-Primary
		        Destination: 29.0.1/24, Local: 29.0.1.1, Broadcast: 29.0.1.255

Summary interface information	show interfaces terse	user@host> **show interfaces ml-1/0/0 terse**
		Interface Admin Link Proto Local Remote
		ml-1/0/0 up up
		ml-1/0/0.1 up up inet 10.20.30.40 --> 10.20.30.50
		ml-1/0/0.2 up up inet 10.0.0.2 --> 10.0.0.1
		                iso
		                mpls
		ml-1/0/0.10 up up inet 128.1.1.3 --> 128.1.1.2
		                iso

Table 13.6 *Interfaces Monitoring Commands*

Information to Monitor	Command	Example
Configured interface descriptions	`show interfaces descriptions`	user@host> **show interfaces descriptions** Interface Admin Link Description so-3/2/0 up up interface-1 so-3/2/0.0 up up interface-2 so-3/2/1 up up interface-3 so-3/2/2.0 up up interface-4
Routing information for each interface	`show interfaces routing`	user@host> **show interfaces routing brief** Interface State Addresses so-5/0/3.0 Down ISO enabled so-5/0/2.0 Up MPLS enabled ISO enabled INET 192.168.2.120 INET enabled ...
Media-specific interface information	`show interfaces media`	user@host> **show interfaces media at-5/1/0** Physical interface: at-5/1/0, Enabled, Physical link is Up Interface index: 21, SNMP ifIndex: 9 Link-level type: ATM-PVC, MTU: 4482, Clocking: Internal, SONET mode Speed: OC12, Loopback: None, Payload scrambler: Enabled Device flags : Present Running Link flags : None OAM F5 cell statistics: Output: Loop 797, RDI 0 Input: Loop 797, RDI 0, AIS 0 Input rate : 448 bps (1 pps), Output rate: 432 bps (1 pps) Active alarms : None Active defects : None SONET errors: BIP-B1: 10, BIP-B2: 140, REI-L: 380, BIP-B3: 31, REI-P: 220

Table 13.6 *Interfaces Monitoring Commands*

Information to Monitor	Command	Example

Interface statistics	`show interfaces statistics`	`user@host>` **`show interfaces e1-1/1/0 statistics`**
		`Physical interface: e1-1/1/0, Enabled, Physical link is Up`
		`  Interface index: 30, SNMP ifIndex: 130`
		`  Link-level type: PPP, MTU: 4474, Clocking: Internal`
		`  Speed: E1, Loopback: None, FCS: 16, Framing: G704`
		`  Device flags    : Present Running`
		`  Interface flags: Point-To-Point SNMP-Traps`
		`  Link flags      : Keepalives`
		`  Statistics last cleared: Never`
		`  Input rate      : 0 bps (0 pps), Output rate: 0 bps (0 pps)`
		`  Input errors    : 0, Output errors : 0`
		`  Active alarms   : None`
		`  Active defects  : None`

Zero interface statistics	`clear interfaces statistics`	`user@host>` **`clear interfaces statistics all`** `user@host>`

Filters or policers installed	`show interfaces (filters | policers)`	`user@host>` **`show interfaces policers so-2/1/0`**
		`Interface        Admin Link Proto Input Policer         Output`
		`Policer`
		`so-2/1/0         up    down`
		`so-2/1/0.0       up    down inet  so-2/1/0.0-in-policer so-2/1/`
		`0.0-out-policer`
		`                            iso`
		`                            inet6`

Table 13.6 *Interfaces Monitoring Commands*

Information to Monitor	Command	Example

Interface statistics	`monitor interface`	`user@host>` **`monitor interface so-0/0/0`**
		`router1                     Seconds: 19`
		`Time: 15:46:29`
		
		`Interface: so-0/0/0, Enabled, Link is Up`
		`Encapsulation: PPP, Keepalives, Speed: OC48`
		`Traffic statistics: ...`
		`Encapsulation statistics: ...`
		`Error statistics: ...`
		`Active alarms : None`
		`Active defects: None`
		`SONET error counts/seconds: ...`
		`SONET statistics: ...`
		`Received SONET overhead: ...`
		`Transmitted SONET overhead: ...`
		
		`Next='n', Quit='q' or ESC, Freeze='f', Thaw='t', Clear='c',`
		`Interface='i'`

Perform a tcpdump	`monitor traffic`	`user@host>` **`monitor traffic interface fxp0`**
		`listening on fxp0.0`
		`18:17:28.800650  In server.home.net.723 > host1-`
		`0.lab.home.net.log`
		`18:17:28.800733 Out host2-0.lab.home.net.login >`
		`server.home.net.7`
		`18:17:28.817813  In host30.lab.home.net.syslog > host40.home0`
		`18:17:28.817846  In host30.lab.home.net.syslog > host40.home0`
		`18:17:28.819174  In host30.lab.home.net.syslog > host40.home0`
		`...`

Automatic Protection Switching information	`show aps`	`user@host>` **`show aps`**
		`Interface   Group          Circuit  Intf State`
		`t3-1/2/0:0 king           Working  enabled, up`
		`t3-1/3/0:0 king           Protect  disabled, up`

Table 13.6 *Interfaces Monitoring Commands*

Information to Monitor	Command	Example

Start bit error rate test	`test interface bert-start`	user@host> **test interface t3-5/2/0 bert-start**
		user@host> **show interfaces t3-5/2/0 extensive**
		...
		 DSU configuration:
		   Compatibility mode: None, Scrambling: Disabled, Subrate:
		Disabled
		   FEAC loopback: Inactive, Response: Disabled, Count: 0
		   BERT time period: 10 seconds, Elapsed: 10 seconds (completed)
		   Algorithm: 2^3 - 1, Pseudorandom (1), Error rate: 10e-0
		   Bit count : 5656, Overflows: 0
		   Error bit count: 811, Overflows: 0
		   LOS status: OK, LOS count: 1, LOS seconds: 9
		...

Stop bit error rate test	`test interface bert-stop`	user@host> **test interface t3-5/2/0 bert-stop**
Transmit over FDL to initiate or terminate a far-end line loopback	`test interface feac-loop-initiate`	user@host> **test interface t3-5/2/0 fdl-line-loop ansi**
Transmit over FDL to initiate or terminate a far-end payload loopback	`test interface fdl-payload-loop`	user@host> **test interface t3-5/2/0 fdl-payload-loop ansi**
Transmit the line loopback activate code word sequence on the interface's FEAC channel	`test interface feac-loop-initiate`	user@host> **test interface t3-5/2/0 feac-loop-initiate**
Transmit the line loopback deactivate code word sequence on the interface's FEAC channel	`test interface feac-loop-terminate`	user@host> **test interface t3-5/2/0 feac-loop-terminate**

Table 13.6 *Interfaces Monitoring Commands*

Information to Monitor	Command	Example
VRRP groups	show vrrp	user@backup-router> **show vrrp brief** Interface Unit Group Type Address Int state VR state Timer ge-5/2/0 0 10 lcl 192.168.29.10 up backup D 7.133 vip 192.168.29.55 mas 192.168.29.254
Zero VRRP group statistics	clear vrrp	user@backup-router> **clear vrrp statistics all**
ILMI messages	show ilmi	user@host> **show ilmi all** Physical interface: at-6/2/1, VCI: 0.16 Peer IP address: 192.168.4.24, Peer interface name: 1C4 Physical interface: at-6/3/0, VCI: 0.16 Peer IP address: 192.168.7.6, Peer interface name: 2C3 Physical interface: at-6/4/0, VCI: 0.16 Peer IP address: 192.168.9.10, Peer interface name: 1C2
ILMI statistics	show ilmi statistics	user@host> **show ilmi statistics** ILMI statistics: Input: Packets: 0, Bad versions: 0, Bad community names: 0, Bad community uses: 0, ASN parse errors: 0, Too bigs: 0, No such names: 0, Bad values: 0, Read onlys: 0, General errors: 0, Total request varbinds: 0, Total set varbinds: 0, Get requests: 0, Get nexts: 0, Set requests: 0, Get responses: 0, Traps: 0, Silent drops: 0, Proxy drops 0 Output: Packets: 0, Too bigs: 0, No such names: 0, Bad values: 0, General errors: 0, Get requests: 0, Get nexts: 0, Set requests: 0, Get responses: 0, Traps: 0
Zero ILMI statistics	clear ilmi statistics	user@host> **clear ilmi statistics**

Firewall Filters

Table 13.7 *Firewall Filters Monitoring Commands*

Information to Monitor	Command	Example
Counters for firewall filters	`show firewall filter`	user@host> **show firewall filter hello1** Filter/Counter Packet count Byte count ip-option-filter rr-count 27 3348 ts-count 0 0 ssrr-count 0 0 lsrr-count 0 0 ra-count 11654 2493120
Clear firewall filter counters	`clear firewall`	user@host> **clear firewall filter hello1**
Firewall filter log information	`show firewall log`	user@host> **show firewall log** Time Filter A Interface Pro Source address Destination address 16:08:04 pfe A so-1/1/0.0 ICM 123.168.10.65 123.168.10.66:24373 16:08:03 pfe A so-1/1/0.0 ICM 123.168.10.65 123.168.10.66:29531 16:08:02 pfe A so-1/1/0.0 ICM 123.168.10.65 123.168.10.66:27265 16:08:01 pfe A so-1/1/0.0 OSP 123.168.10.65 212.0.0.5:48 16:08:01 pfe A so-1/1/0.0 ICM 123.168.10.65 123.168.10.66:43943 16:08:00 pfe A so-1/1/0.0 ICM 123.168.10.65 123.168.10.66:58572 16:07:59 pfe A so-1/1/0.0 ICM 123.168.10.65 123.168.10.66:56307 16:07:58 pfe A so-1/1/0.0 ICM 123.168.10.65 123.168.10.66:60185 16:07:57 pfe A so-1/1/0.0 ICM 123.168.10.65 123.168.10.66:1600 16:07:56 pfe A so-1/1/0.0 ICM 123.168.10.65 123.168.10.66:6502 16:07:55 pfe A so-1/1/0.0 ICM 123.168.10.65 123.168.10.66:17548 16:07:54 pfe A so-1/1/0.0 ICM 123.168.10.65 123.168.10.66:5298 16:07:53 pfe A so-1/1/0.0 ICM 123.168.10.65 123.168.10.66:24536

Forwarding Options

Table 13.8 *Forwarding Options Monitoring Commands*

Information to Monitor	Command	Example

Show statistics collected by the UDP forwarding process	`show helper statistics`	`user@host> `**`show helper statistics`**
		`domain:`
		`  Received packets: 63`
		`  Forwarded packets: 61`
		`  Dropped packets: 2`
		`    Due to no interface in fud database: 0`
		`    Due to an error during packet read: 1`
		`    Due to an error during packet send: 1`
		`tftp:`
		`  Received packets: 5`
		`  Forwarded packets: 5`
		`  Dropped packets: 0`
		`    Due to no interface in fud database: 0`
		`    Due to an error during packet read: 0`
		`    Due to an error during packet send: 0`

Zero statistic counters in the UDP forwarding process	`clear helper statistics`	`user@host>`**`clear helper statistics`**
		`user@host>`**`show helper statistics`**
		`domain:`
		`  Received packets: 0`
		`  Forwarded packets: 0`
		`  Dropped packets: 0`
		`    Due to no interface in fud database: 0`
		`    Due to an error during packet read: 0`
		`    Due to an error during packet send: 0`
		`tftp:`
		`  Received packets: 0`
		`  Forwarded packets: 0`
		`  Dropped packets: 0`
		`    Due to no interface in fud database: 0`
		`    Due to an error during packet read: 0`
		`    Due to an error during packet send: 0`

Table 13.8 *Forwarding Options Monitoring Commands*

Information to Monitor	Command	Example
Restart the UDP forwarding process	`restart helper`	`user@host>` **`restart helper`** `Forwarding UDP daemon started, pid 9261`

Class of Service

Table 13.9 *Class-of-Service Monitoring Commands*

Information to Monitor	Command	Example

Interface queue information	`show interfaces queue`	`user@host>` **`show interfaces queue so-0/2/3 forwarding-class expedited-forwarding`**
		`Physical interface: so-0/2/3, Enabled, Physical link is Up`
		`  Interface index: 32, SNMP ifIndex: 60`
		`Forwarding Class: expedited-forwarding, Queue: 1`
		`  Queued:`
		`    Packets              :        0        0 pps`
		`    Bytes                :        0        0 bps`
		`  Transmitted:`
		`    Packets              :        0        0 pps`
		`    Bytes                :        0        0 bps`
		`    Tail-dropped packets :        0        0 pps`
		`    RED-dropped packets  :        0        0 pps`
		`     Low, non-TCP        :        0        0 pps`
		`     Low, TCP            :        0        0 pps`
		`     High, non-TCP       :        0        0 pps`
		`     High, TCP           :        0        0 pps`
		`    RED-dropped bytes    :        0        0 bps`
		`     Low, non-TCP        :        0        0 bps`
		`     Low, TCP            :        0        0 bps`
		`     High, non-TCP       :        0        0 bps`
		`     High, TCP           :        0        0 bps`

Table 13.9 *Class-of-Service Monitoring Commands*

<table>
<tr><th>Information to Monitor</th><th>Command</th><th>Example</th></tr>
<tr><td>Queue statistics summary per interface</td><td><code>show interfaces extensive</code></td><td><pre>
user@host> show interfaces extensive ge-0/0/0
Physical interface: ge-0/0/0, Enabled, Physical link is Up
...
 Queue counters: Queued packets Transmitted packets   Dropped packets
   0 best-effort   103   103   0
   1 expedited-fo   616679163   588733189   0
   2 assured-forw   2648825387   2528227577   120446880
   3 network-cont   27284126   26134172   1149954
...
  PFE configuration:
    Destination slot: 0, PLP byte: 1 (0x00)
    CoS transmit queue   Bandwidth   Buffer   Priority   Limit
                            %   bps   %   bytes
    0 best-effort   95   0 95   0   low   none
    1 expedited-forwarding   0   0   0   0   low   none
    2 assured-forwarding   0   0   0   0   low   none
    3 network-control   5   0   5   0   low   none
</pre></td></tr>
<tr><td>Complete CoS configuration</td><td><code>show class-of-service</code></td><td><pre>
user@host> show class-of-service
class-of-service {
...
}
</pre></td></tr>
</table>

Table 13.9 *Class-of-Service Monitoring Commands*

Information to Monitor	Command	Example

Mapping of code-point value to forwarding class and loss priority	`show class-of-service classifier`	<pre>user@host> **show class-of-service classifier type ieee-802.1**
		Classifier: ieee802.1-default, Code point type: ieee-802.1, Index: 3
		Code Point Forwarding Class Loss priority
		  000 best-effort low
		  001 best-effort high
		  010 expedited-forwarding low
		  011 expedited-forwarding high
		  100 assured-forwarding low
		  101 assured-forwarding high
		  110 network-control low
		  111 network-control high
		
		Classifier: users-ieee802.1, Code point type: ieee-802.1
		  Code point Forwarding class Loss priority
		  100 expedited-forwarding low</pre>

Code-point aliases	`show class-of-service code-point-aliases`	<pre>user@host> **show class-of-service code-point-aliases exp**
		Code point type: exp
		  Alias Bit pattern
		  af11 100
		  af12 101
		  be 000
		  be1 001
		  cs6 110
		  cs7 111
		  ef 010
		  ef1 011
		  nc1 110
		  nc2 111</pre>

Table 13.9 *Class-of-Service Monitoring Commands*

<table>
<tr><th>Information to Monitor</th><th>Command</th><th>Example</th></tr>
<tr><td>Random Early Detection (RED) profiles</td><td><code>show class-of-service drop-profile</code></td><td><pre>
user@host> show class-of-service drop-profile
Drop profile: <default-drop-profile>, Type: discrete, Index: 1
  Fill level   Drop probability
         100   100
Drop profile: user-drop-profile, Type: interpolated, Index: 2989
  Fill level   Drop probability
           0   0
           1   1
           2   2
           4   4
           5   5
           6   6
           8   8
          10   10
          12   15
          14   20
          15   23
          ... 64 entries total
...
</pre></td></tr>
<tr><td>Forwarding class to queue mapping</td><td><code>show class-of-service forwarding-class</code></td><td><pre>
user@host> show class-of-service forwarding-class
Forwarding class   Queue
  my-forwarding-class   0
  his-forwarding-class   1
  her-forwarding-class   2
  the-forwarding-class   3
</pre></td></tr>
<tr><td>CoS configuration on interfaces</td><td><code>show class-of-service interface</code></td><td><pre>
user@host> show class-of-service interface so-0/2/3
 Physical interface: so-0/2/3, c: 32
  Scheduler map: my-scheduler-map, Index: 17638

  Logical interface: so-0/2/3.0, Index: 15
   Object   Name   Type   Index
   Rewrite   my-dscp-rewrite   dscp   3753
   Classifier   my-dscp-classifier   dscp   62436
</pre></td></tr>
</table>

Table 13.9 *Class-of-Service Monitoring Commands*

Information to Monitor	Command	Example
Rewrite rules	show class-of-service rewrite-rule	user@host> **show class-of-service rewrite-rule type dscp** Rewrite rule: dscp-default, Code point type: dscp Forwarding class Loss priority Code point gold high 000000 silver low 110000 silver high 111000 bronze low 001010 bronze high 001100 lead high 101110
Scheduler-to-forwarding-class mapping	show class-of-service scheduler-map	user@host> **show class-of-service scheduler-map** Scheduler map: dd-scheduler-map, Index: 84 Scheduler: aa-scheduler, Index: 8721, Forwarding class: aa-forwarding-class Transmit rate: 30 percent, Rate Limit: none, Maximum buffer delay: 39 ms, Priority: high Drop profiles: Loss priority Protocol Index Name Low non-TCP 8724 aa-drop-profile Low TCP 9874 bb-drop-profile High non-TCP 8833 cc-drop-profile High TCP 8484 dd-drop-profile

Table 13.9 *Class-of-Service Monitoring Commands*

Information to Monitor	Command	Example

Classifiers	show class-of-service forwarding-table classifier	user@host> **show class-of-service forwarding-table classifier**
		`Classifier table index: 62436, # entries: 64, Table type: DSCP`
		
		`Entry #   Code point   Queue #   PLP`
		`   0        000000        0       0`
		`   1        000001        0       0`
		`   2        000010        0       0`
		`   3        000011        0       0`
		`   4        000100        0       0`
		`   5        000101        0       0`
		`   6        000110        0       0`
		`   7        000111        0       0`
		`   8        001000        0       0`
		`   9        001001        0       0`
		`  10        001010        1       1`
		`  11        001011        0       0`
		`...`

Classifier information for logical interfaces	show class-of-service forwarding-table classifier mapping	user@host> **show class-of-service forwarding-table classifier mapping**
		`                             Table index/`
		`Interface        Index       Q num        Table type`
		`so-5/0/0.0          10       62436        DSCP`
		`so-0/1/0.0          11       62436        DSCP`
		`so-0/2/0.0          12           1        Fixed`
		`so-0/2/1.0          13       62436        DSCP`
		`so-0/2/1.0          13       62437        IEEE 802.1`
		`so-0/2/2.0          14       62436        DSCP`
		`so-0/2/2.0          14       62438        IPv4 precedence`

Table 13.9 *Class-of-Service Monitoring Commands*

Information to Monitor	Command	Example

Scheduler information for physical interfaces	show class-of-service forwarding-table scheduler-map	user@host> **show class-of-service forwarding-table scheduler-map**
		Interface: so-5/0/0 (Index: 9, Map index: 17638, Num of queues: 2):
		  Entry 0 (Scheduler index: 6090, Queue #: 0):
		    Tx rate: 0 Kb (30%), Max buffer delay: 39 bytes (0%)
		    High priority is set
		    PLP high: 25393, PLP low: 24627, TCP PLP high: 25393, TCP PLP low:8742
		    Policy is exact
		  Entry 1 (Scheduler index: 38372, Queue #: 1):
		    Traffic chunk: Max = 0 bytes, Min = 0 bytes
		    Tx rate: 0 Kb (40%), Max buffer delay: 68 bytes (0%)
		    High priority is set
		    PLP high: 25393, PLP low: 24627, TCP PLP high: 25393, TCP PLP low: 8742
		...

Random Early Detection (RED) forwarding table profiles	show class-of-service forwarding-table drop-profile	user@host> **show class-of-service forwarding-table drop-profile**
		RED drop profile index: 4, # entries: 1
		                                    Drop
		Entry Fullness(%) Probability(%)
		  0 100 100
		
		RED drop profile index: 8742, # entries: 3
		                                    Drop
		Entry Fullness(%) Probability(%)
		  0 10 10
		  1 20 20
		  2 30 30
		...

Rewrite rules	show class-of-service forwarding-table rewrite-rule	user@host> **show class-of-service forwarding-table rewrite-rule** Rewrite table index: 3753, # entries: 4, Table type: DSCP Q# Low bits State High bits State 0 000111 Enabled 001010 Enabled 2 000000 Disabled 001100 Enabled 1 101110 Enabled 110111 Enabled 3 110000 Enabled 111000 Enabled

Table 13.9 *Class-of-Service Monitoring Commands*

Information to Monitor	Command	Example

Interface rewrite rules on logical interfaces	`show class-of-service forwarding-table rewrite-rule mapping`	`user@host>` **`show class-of-service forwarding-table rewrite-rule mapping`**
		`Interface      Index   Table index  Type`
		`so-5/0/0.0        10          3753  DSCP`
		`so-0/1/0.0        11          3753  DSCP`
		`so-0/2/0.0        12          3753  DSCP`
		`so-0/2/1.0        13          3753  DSCP`
		`so-0/2/2.0        14          3753  DSCP`
		`so-0/2/3.0        15          3753  DSCP`

Protocol-Independent Routing

Table 13.10 *Protocol-Independent Routing Monitoring Commands*

Information to Monitor	Command	Example

Information about the entries in the routing tables.	`show route`	`user@host>` **`show route brief`**
		`inet.0: 14 destinations, 14 routes (13 active, 0 holddown, 1 hidden)`
		`+ = Active Route, - = Last Active, * = Both`
		
		`0.0.0.0/0          *[Static/5] 00:00:08`
		`                    > to 111.222.5.254 via fxp0.0`
		`1.0.0.1/32         *[Direct/0] 00:00:09`
		`                    > via at-5/3/0.0`
		`1.0.0.2/32         *[Local/0] 00:00:09`
		`                     Local`
		`...`

Routes transmitted by a particular routing protocol.	`show route advertising-protocol`	`user@host>` **`show route advertising-protocol bgp 111.222.1.3`**
		`inet.0: 46498 destinations, 46498 routes (46496 active, 0 holddown, 2 hidden)`
		`Prefix             Next hop           MED        Lclpref    AS path`
		`15.0.0.1/32        111.222.1.1                          69 IGP`

Table 13.10 *Protocol-Independent Routing Monitoring Commands*

Information to Monitor	Command	Example

Routes containing a specified AS path.	`show route aspath-regex`	`user@host>` **`show route aspath-regex 65477`**
		`inet.0: 46411 destinations, 46411 routes (46409 active, 0 holddown, 2 hidden)`
		`+ = Active Route, - = Last Active, * = Both`
		
		`111.222.1.0/25     *[BGP/170] 00:08:48, localpref 100, from`
		`111.222.2.24`
		`                   AS Path: [65477] ({65488 65535}) IGP`
		`                     to 111.222.18.225 via fpa0.0(111.222.18.233)`
		`111.222.1.128/25   *[IS-IS/15] 09:15:37, metric 37, tag 1`
		`                     to 111.222.18.225 via fpa0.0(111.222.18.233)`
		`                    [BGP/170] 00:08:48, localpref 100, from`
		`111.222.2.24`
		`                   AS Path: [65477] ({65488 65535}) IGP`
		`                     to 111.222.18.225 via fpa0.0(111.222.18.233)`
		`...`

Best route to the specified address or range of addresses.	`show route best`	`user@host>` **`show route best 111.222/24`**
		
		`inet.0: 12 destinations, 12 routes (11 active, 0 holddown, 1 hidden)`
		`+ = Active Route, - = Last Active, * = Both`
		
		`0.0.0.0/0          *[Static/5] 00:09:41`
		`                    > to 111.222.5.254 via so-2/0/1`

Table 13.10 *Protocol-Independent Routing Monitoring Commands*

Information to Monitor	Command	Example
Routes containing members of a BGP community.	`show route community`	user@host> **show route community 234:80** inet.0: 46511 destinations, 46511 routes (46509 active, 0 holddown, 2 hidden) + = Active Route, - = Last Active, * = Both 4.0.0.0/8 *[BGP/170] 03:33:07, localpref 100, from 131.103.20.49 AS Path: {666} 234 2548 1 IGP to 192.156.169.1 via 192.156.169.14(so-0/0/0) 6.0.0.0/8 *[BGP/170] 03:33:07, localpref 100, from 131.103.20.49 AS Path: {666} 234 2548 568 721 Incomplete to 192.156.169.1 via 192.156.169.14(so-0/0/0) ... inet.1: 728 destinations, 728 routes (545 active, 0 holddown, 183 hidden) + = Active Route, - = Last Active, * = Both ... inet.2: 7367 destinations, 7360 routes (7307 active, 53 holddown, 0 hidden) + = Active Route, - = Last Active, * = Both ...

Table 13.10 *Protocol-Independent Routing Monitoring Commands*

<table>
<tr><th>Information to Monitor</th><th>Command</th><th>Example</th></tr>
<tr><td>Routes that have been damped.</td><td><code>show route damping</code></td><td><pre>user@host> show route damping detail
inet.0: 21 destinations, 21 routes (15 active, 0 holddown, 6
hidden)
    + = Active Route, - = Last Active, * = Both

    1.1.1.0/24 (1 entry, 0 announced)
           BGP   Preference: /-101
                  Nexthop: 10.12.1.2 via en0.0, selected
                  State: <Hidden Ext>
                  Local AS: 911 Peer AS: 922
                  Age: 11:50
                  Task: BGP_922.10.12.1.2+179
                  AS path: 922 I
                  Localpref: 100
                  Router ID: 111.222.1.46
                  Merit (last update/now): 4833/2796
                  Default damping parameters used
                  Last update: 00:11:50
                  First update: 01:01:43
                  Flaps: 10
                  Suppressed. Reusable in: 00:28:40
                  Preference will be: 170
...</pre></td></tr>
<tr><td>Routes that exactly match the specified address or range of addresses.</td><td><code>show route exact</code></td><td><pre>user@host> show route exact 24.226.160.0/19

inet.0: 53294 destinations, 53294 routes (53293 active, 0
holddown, 1 hidden)
+ = Active Route, - = Last Active, * = Both

24.226.160.0/19   *[BGP/170] 00:31:04, MED 0, localpref 100,
from 208.197.169.14
                    AS path: 2914 701 3493 11290 I
                     > to 111.222.5.254 via fxp0.0</pre></td></tr>
</table>

Table 13.10 *Protocol-Independent Routing Monitoring Commands*

Information to Monitor	Command	Example

Routes that are currently inactive.	`show route inactive`	`user@host>` **`show route inactive`**
		`inet.0: 12 destinations, 12 routes (11 active, 0 holddown, 1 hidden)`
		`+ = Active Route, - = Last Active, * = Both`
		
		`127.0.0.1/32        [Direct/0] 19:40:17`
		`                    > via lo0.0`

Routing instance information.	`show route instance`	`user@host>` **`show route instance summary`**
		`Instance            Type          Primary rib       Active/`
		`holddown/hidden`
		`yellow-vpn          vrf           yellow-vp.inet.0  5/0/0`
		`pink-vpn            vrf           pink-vpn.inet.0   4/0/0`
		`green-vpn           vrf           green-vpn.inet.0  6/0/0`
		`blue-vpn            vrf           blue-vpn.inet.0   5/0/0`
		`master              forwarding    inet.0            29/0/1`

Table 13.10 *Protocol-Independent Routing Monitoring Commands*

Information to Monitor	Command	Example
Routes that form a label-switched path.	`show route label-switched-path`	user@host> **show route label-switched-path sf-to-ny** inet.0: 29 destinations, 29 routes (29 active, 0 holddown, 0 hidden) + = Active Route, - = Last Active, * = Both 1.1.1.1/32 [MPLS/7] 00:00:06, metric 0 > to 111.222.1.9 via s0-0/0/0, label-switched-path sf-to-ny 3.3.3.3/32 *[MPLS/7] 00:00:06, metric 0 > to 111.222.1.9 via s0-0/0/0, label-switched-path sf-to-ny inet.3: 3 destinations, 3 routes (3 active, 0 holddown, 0 hidden) + = Active Route, - = Last Active, * = Both 2.2.2.2/32 *[MPLS/7] 00:00:06, metric 0 > to 111.222.1.9 via s0-0/0/0, label-switched-path sf-to-ny 111.222.1.9/32 [MPLS/7] 00:00:06, metric 0 > to 111.222.1.9 via s0-0/0/0, label-switched-path sf-to-ny iso.0: 1 destinations, 1 routes (1 active, 0 holddown, 0 hidden) + = Active Route, - = Last Active, * = Both mpls.0: 2 destinations, 2 routes (2 active, 0 holddown, 0 hidden) + = Active Route, - = Last Active, * = Both
Routes that contain the specified next hop.	`show route next-hop`	user@host> **show route next-hop 111.222.5.254** inet.0: 12 destinations, 12 routes (11 active, 0 holddown, 1 hidden) + = Active Route, - = Last Active, * = Both 0.0.0.0/0 *[Static/5] 00:43:39 > to 111.222.5.254 via fxp0.0

Table 13.10 *Protocol-Independent Routing Monitoring Commands*

Information to Monitor	Command	Example
Routes exiting the router through the specified interface.	`show route output`	user@host> **show route output interface t3-5/2/1** inet.0: 12 destinations, 12 routes (11 active, 0 holddown, 1 hidden) + = Active Route, - = Last Active, * = Both 13.13.13.13/32 *[Direct/0] 00:44:55 > via t3-5/2/1.0 iso.0: 1 destinations, 1 routes (1 active, 0 holddown, 0 hidden) + = Active Route, - = Last Active, * = Both
Routes learned by the specified protocol.	`show route protocol`	user@host> **show route protocol direct** inet.0: 35 destinations, 35 routes (34 active, 0 holddown, 1 hidden) + = Active Route, - = Last Active, * = Both 127.0.0.1/32 [Direct/0] 14:36:24 > via lo0.0 111.222.5.0/24 *[Direct/0] 14:36:24 > via fxp0.0 111.222.8.16/28 *[Direct/0] 14:36:24 > via at-5/3/0.0 ... iso.0: 1 destinations, 1 routes (1 active, 0 holddown, 0 hidden) + = Active Route, - = Last Active, * = Both 47.0005.80ff.f800.0000.0108.0001.1921.6800.5081.00/160 *[Direct/0] 14:36:24 > via lo0.0

Table 13.10 *Protocol-Independent Routing Monitoring Commands*

Information to Monitor	Command	Example

Routes in a range of destination prefixes.	`show route range`	`user@host>` **`show route range`**
		`inet.0: 27 destinations, 27 routes (26 active, 0 holddown, 1 hidden)`
		`+ = Active Route, - = Last Active, * = Both`
		
		`0.0.0.0/0          *[Static/5] 06:03:18`
		`                    Discard`
		`10.255.245.87/32   *[Direct/0] 06:03:19`
		`                   > via lo0.0`
		`123.16.1.0/24      *[Static/5] 06:03:18`
		`                   > to 111.222.4.254 via fxp0.0`
		`123.16.14.0/24     *[Static/5] 06:03:18`
		`                   > to 111.222.4.254 via fxp0.0`
		`...`

Table 13.10 *Protocol-Independent Routing Monitoring Commands*

<table>
<tr><th>Information to Monitor</th><th>Command</th><th>Example</th></tr>
<tr><td>Routes received by a particular routing protocol.</td><td>show route receive-protocol</td><td>user@host> show route receive-protocol bgp 10.255.245.63 extensive

inet.0: 244 destinations, 244 routes (243 active, 0 holddown, 1 hidden)
Prefix Nexthop MED Lclpref AS path
1.1.1.0/24 (1 entry, 1 announced)
Nexthop: 10.0.50.3
Localpref: 100
AS path: I <Originator>
Cluster list: 10.2.3.1
Originator ID: 10.255.245.45
165.3.0.0/16 (1 entry, 1 announced)
Nexthop: 111.222.5.254
Localpref: 100
AS path: I <Originator>
Cluster list: 10.2.3.1
Originator ID: 10.255.245.68
165.4.0.0/16 (1 entry, 1 announced)
Nexthop: 111.222.5.254
Localpref: 100
AS path: I <Originator>
Cluster list: 10.2.3.1
Originator ID: 10.255.245.45
195.1.2.0/24 (1 entry, 1 announced)
Nexthop: 111.222.5.254
Localpref: 100
AS path: I <Originator>
Cluster list: 10.2.3.1
Originator ID: 10.255.245.68

inet.2: 63 destinations, 63 routes (63 active, 0 holddown, 0 hidden)
Prefix Nexthop MED Lclpref AS path

inet.3: 10 destinations, 10 routes (10 active, 0 holddown, 0</td></tr>
</table>

Table 13.10 *Protocol-Independent Routing Monitoring Commands*

Information to Monitor	Command	Example
		hidden) Prefix Nexthop MED Lclpref AS path iso.0: 1 destinations, 1 routes (1 active, 0 holddown, 0 hidden) Prefix Nexthop MED Lclpref AS path mpls.0: 48 destinations, 48 routes (48 active, 0 holddown, 0 hidden)
Entries in the next-hop resolution database.	`show route resolution`	user@host> **show route resolution detail** Table inet.0 Nodes 111590 0.0.0.0/0 Originating RIB: inet.0 Metric: 0 Forwarding nexthops: 0 Next hop type: Discard 1.0.0.0/8 Originating RIB: inet.0 Metric: 2 Indirect nexthops: 1 Protocol nexthop: 10.255.14.181 Metric: 2 Indirect nexthop: 84cc770 104 Indirect path forwarding nexthops: 1 Nexthop: 10.19.2.2 via t1-0/2/0.0 10.255.14.181/32 Originating RIB: inet.0 Metric: 2 Forwarding nexthops: 1 Nexthop: 10.19.2.2 via t1-0/2/0.0 Has inactive paths with indirect nexthops: Indirect nexthops: 1 Protocol nexthop: 10.255.14.175 Metric: 4 Indirect nexthop: 84cc6e8 103 Indirect path forwarding nexthops: 1 Nexthop: 10.19.4.2 via t3-0/3/0.0 10.255.14.175/32 Originating RIB: inet.0 Metric: 4 Forwarding nexthops: 1 Nexthop: 10.19.4.2 via t3-0/3/0.0 ...

Table 13.10 *Protocol-Independent Routing Monitoring Commands*

Information to Monitor	Command	Example

Routes learned from the specified source.	show route source-gateway	user@host> **show route source-gateway 131.103.20.49**
		inet.0: 46035 destinations, 46035 routes (46033 active, 0 holddown, 2 hidden)
		+ = Active Route, - = Last Active, * = Both
		
		4.0.0.0/8 *[BGP/170] 04:43:40, from 131.103.20.49
		                    AS Path: {666} 234 2548 1 IGP
		                      to 192.156.169.1 via 192.156.169.14(de0.0)
		6.0.0.0/8 *[BGP/170] 04:43:40, from 131.103.20.49
		                    AS Path: {666} 234 2548 568 721 Incomplete
		                      to 192.156.169.1 via 192.156.169.14(de0.0)
		...

Statistics about routes in all routing tables.	show route summary	user@host> **show route summary**
		inet.0: 66452 destinations, 66452 routes (66452 active, 0 holddown, 0 hidden)
		              Direct: 3 routes, 3 active
		               Local: 2 routes, 2 active
		                 BGP: 84654 routes, 64536 active
		               IS-IS: 1904 routes, 1903 active
		
		inet.3: 1 destinations, 1 routes (1 active, 0 holddown, 0 hidden)
		              Static: 1 routes, 1 active
		
		iso.0: 1 destinations, 1 routes (1 active, 0 holddown, 0 hidden)
		              Direct: 1 routes, 1 active

Table 13.10 *Protocol-Independent Routing Monitoring Commands*

Information to Monitor	Command	Example
Routes in a particular routing table.	show route table	user@host> **show route table inet.0** inet.0: 12 destinations, 12 routes (11 active, 0 holddown, 1 hidden) + = Active Route, - = Last Active, * = Both 0.0.0.0/0 *[Static/5] 00:51:57 > to 111.222.5.254 via fxp0.0 1.0.0.1/32 *[Direct/0] 00:51:58 > via at-5/3/0.0 1.0.0.2/32 *[Local/0] 00:51:58 Local ...
High-level summary of routing table information.	show route terse	user@host> **show route terse** inet.0: 12 destinations, 12 routes (11 active, 0 holddown, 1 hidden) + = Active Route, - = Last Active, * = Both A Destination P Prf Metric 1 Metric 2 Next hop AS path * 0.0.0.0/0 S 5 >111.222.5.254 * 1.0.0.1/32 D 0 >at-5/3/0.0 * 1.0.0.2/32 L 0 Local ...
Information about the entries in the kernel's forwarding table.	show route forwarding-table	user@host> **show route forwarding-table** Internet: Destination Type RtRef Nexthop Type Index NhRef Netif ... 123.456.0.0/18 user 0 111.222.5.254 ucst 19 55371 fxp0.0 123.457.0.0/18 user 0 111.222.5.254 ucst 19 55371 fxp0.0 123.123.0.0/17 user 0 111.222.5.254 ucst 19 55371 fxp0.0 ...

Table 13.10 *Protocol-Independent Routing Monitoring Commands*

Information to Monitor	Command	Example
Clear a route entry from the kernel's forwarding table.	`clear route forwarding-table`	user@host> **clear route forwarding-table 123.456.0.0** user@host> show route forwarding-table Internet: Destination Type RtRef Nexthop Type Index NhRef Netif ... 123.457.0.0/18 user 0 111.222.5.254 ucst 19 55371 fxp0.0 123.123.0.0/17 user 0 111.222.5.254 ucst 19 55371 fxp0.0 ...
Information about martian addresses.	`show route martians`	user@host> **show route martians** inet.0: 0.0.0.0/0 Match: Exact, Advertise: <none> 0.0.0.0/8 Match: <none>, Advertise: <none> 127.0.0.0/8 Match: <none>, Advertise: Restrict 128.0.0.0/16 Match: <none>, Advertise: Restrict 191.255.0.0/16 Match: <none>, Advertise: Restrict 192.0.0.0/24 Match: <none>, Advertise: Restrict 223.255.255.0/24 Match: <none>, Advertise: Restrict 240.0.0.0/4 Match: <none>, Advertise: Restrict inet.1: 0.0.0.0/0 Match: Exact, Advertise: <none> 0.0.0.0/8 Match: <none>, Advertise: <none> 127.0.0.0/8 Match: <none>, Advertise: Restrict 128.0.0.0/16 Match: <none>, Advertise: Restrict ...
AS paths.	`show as-path`	user@host> **show as-path** Total AS paths: 24744 Path: 234 234 3561 6503 278 3596 I Refs: 2 ASes: 6 Segments: 1 Overhead: 64 Path: 267 234 3561 4926 4926 4926 10834 5648 I <ASLoop> Refs: 2 ASes: 8 Segments: 1 Overhead: 64 ...

Routing Policy

Table 13.11 *Routing Policy*

Information to Monitor	Command	Example

Configured routing policies	show policy	user@host> **show policy**
		Configured policies:
		test-statics
		> show policy test-statics
		Policy test-statics:
		    from
		        3.0.0.0/8 accept
		        3.1.0.0/16 accept
		    then reject

Test import and export policies	test policy	user@host> **test policy test-statics 3.0.0.1/8**
		inet.0: 44 destinations, 44 routes (44 active, 0 holddown, 0 hidden)
		Prefixes passing policy:
		
		3.0.0.0/8 *[BGP/170] 16:22:46, localpref 100, from 10.255.255.41
		                   AS Path: 50888 I
		                    > to 10.11.4.32 via en0.2, label-switched-path 12
		3.3.3.1/32 *[IS-IS/18] 2d 00:21:46, metric 0, tag 2
		                    > to 10.0.4.7 via fxp0.0
		3.3.3.2/32 *[IS-IS/18] 2d 00:21:46, metric 0, tag 2
		                    > to 10.0.4.7 via fxp0.0
		3.3.3.3/32 *[IS-IS/18] 2d 00:21:46, metric 0, tag 2
		                    > to 10.0.4.7 via fxp0.0
		3.3.3.4/32 *[IS-IS/18] 2d 00:21:46, metric 0, tag 2
		                    > to 10.0.4.7 via fxp0.0
		Policy test-statics: 5 prefixes accepted, 0 prefixes rejected

Table 13.11 *Routing Policy*

Information to Monitor	Command	Example

Configured BGP damping parameters that can be used in policy filters.	`show policy damping`	`user@host>` **`show policy damping`**
		`Default damping information:`
		`  Halflife: 15 minutes`
		`  Reuse merit: 750 Suppress/cutoff merit: 3000`
		`  Maximum suppress time: 60 minutes`
		`  Computed values:`
		`    Merit ceiling: 12110`
		`    Maximum decay: 6193`

Routes that have been damped	`show route inactive`	`user@host>` **`show route inactive`**
		`inet.0: 12 destinations, 12 routes (11 active, 0 holddown, 1 hidden)`
		`+ = Active Route, - = Last Active, * = Both`
		
		`127.0.0.1/32        [Direct/0] 19:40:17`
		`                    > via lo0.0`

IS-IS

Table 13.12 *IS-IS Monitoring Commands*

<table>
<tr><th>Information to Monitor</th><th>Command</th><th>Example</th></tr>
<tr><td>Status of IS-IS interfaces</td><td><code>show isis interface</code></td><td><pre>
user@host> show isis interface
IS-IS interface database:
Interface L CirID Level 1 DR   Level 2 DR   L1/L2 Metric
fxp0.0 3   0x2 Disabled   Disabled   10/10
fxp1.0 3   0x3 mpls6.03   mpls6.03   10/10
lo0.0 0   0x1 Passive   Passive   0/0
sr0.0 3   0x1 Point to point Point to point   10/10
sr1.0 3   0x1 Point to point Point to point   10/10
</pre></td></tr>
<tr><td>Hostname mapping</td><td><code>show isis hostname</code></td><td><pre>
user@host> show isis hostname
IS-IS hostname database:
   System Id   Hostname
Type
   1921.6800.4201 isis1
Dynamic
   1921.6800.4202 isis2
Static
   1921.6800.4203 isis3
Dynamic
</pre></td></tr>
<tr><td>Database entries</td><td><code>show isis database</code></td><td><pre>
user@host> show isis database
IS-IS level 1 link-state database:
LSP ID   Sequence Checksum Lifetime (secs)
crater.00-00   0x12   0x84dd   1139
  1 LSPs
IS-IS level 2 link-state database:
LSP ID   Sequence Checksum Lifetime (secs)
crater.00-00   0x19   0xe92c   1134
badlands.00-00   0x16   0x1454   985
carlsbad.00-00   0x33   0x220b   1015
ranier.00-00   0x2e   0xfc31   1007
1921.6800.5066.00-00   0x11   0x7313   566
1921.6800.5067.00-00   0x14   0xd9d4   939
  6 LSPs
</pre></td></tr>
</table>

Table 13.12 *IS-IS Monitoring Commands*

Information to Monitor	Command	Example
Remove database entries	`clear isis database`	user@host> **clear isis statistics** user@host> **show isis statistics** IS-IS level 1 link-state database: LSP ID Sequence Checksum Lifetime (secs) IS-IS level 2 link-state database: LSP ID Sequence Checksum Lifetime (secs)
IS-IS routing table entries	`show isis route`	user@host> **show ospf route** IS-IS routing table Current version: L1: 89 L2: 158 Prefix L Version Metric Type Interface Via 10.1.1.1/32 2 158 20 int so-1/0/0.0 router-d ge-2/1/0.0 router-d 10.10.20.16/29 2 158 20 int ge-4/2/0.0 router-b 10.10.20.24/29 2 158 20 int so-1/0/0.0 router-d ge-2/1/0.0 router-d 10.10.20.102/32 2 158 10 int ge-4/2/0.0 router-b 10.10.20.103/32 2 158 20 int so-1/0/0.0 router-d
Adjacent routers	`show isis adjacency`	user@host> **show isis adjacency brief** IS-IS adjacency database: Interface System L State Hold (secs) SNPA so-1/0/0.0 karakul 3 Up 26 so-1/1/3.0 1921.6800.5080 3 Up 23 so-5/0/0.0 1921.6800.5080 3 Up 19
Clear adjacent routers	`clear ospf adjacency`	user@host> **clear ospf adjacency** user@host> **show ospf adjacency** IS-IS adjacency database: Interface System L State Hold (secs) SNPA so-1/0/0.0 karakul 3 Initializing 26 so-1/1/3.0 1921.6800.5080 3 Up 24 so-5/0/0.0 1921.6800.5080 3 Up 21

Table 13.12 *IS-IS Monitoring Commands*

Information to Monitor	Command	Example
SPF calculations	`show isis spf`	user@host> **show isis spf brief**

```
user@host> show isis spf brief
IS-IS level 1 SPF results:

IS-IS level 2 SPF results:
Node                   Metric Interface Via                SNPA
badlands.00                23 so-1/2/0.0 1921.6800.5067
                              so-1/0/0.0 1921.6800.5067
                              so-1/1/0.0 1921.6800.5067
                              so-1/3/0.0 1921.6800.5067
carlsbad.00                13 so-1/2/0.0 1921.6800.5067
                              so-1/0/0.0 1921.6800.5067
                              so-1/1/0.0 1921.6800.5067
                              so-1/3/0.0 1921.6800.5067
1921.6800.5064.00          13 so-1/2/0.0 1921.6800.5067
                              so-1/0/0.0 1921.6800.5067
                              so-1/1/0.0 1921.6800.5067
                              so-1/3/0.0 1921.6800.5067
1921.6800.5067.00          10 so-1/2/0.0 1921.6800.5067
                              so-1/0/0.0 1921.6800.5067
                              so-1/1/0.0 1921.6800.5067
                              so-1/3/0.0 1921.6800.5067
1921.6800.5066.00          10 so-2/2/0.0 1921.6800.5066
                              so-2/0/0.0 1921.6800.5066
                              so-2/1/0.0 1921.6800.5066
                              so-2/3/0.0 1921.6800.5066
  5 nodes
```

Table 13.12 *IS-IS Monitoring Commands*

<table>
<tr><th>Information to Monitor</th><th>Command</th><th>Example</th></tr>
<tr><td>General IS-IS statistics</td><td><code>show isis statistics</code></td><td><pre>
user@host> show isis statistics
IS-IS statistics for merino:

PDU type   Received Processed   Drops   Sent   Rexmit
LSP   12227   12227   0   8184   683
IIH   113808   113808   0   115817   0
CSNP   198868   198868   0   198934   0
PSNP   6985   6979   6   8274   0
Unknown   0   0   0   0   0
Totals   331888   331882   6   331209   683

Total packets received: 331888 Sent: 331892

SNP queue length: 0 Drops: 0
LSP queue length: 0 Drops: 0

SPF runs: 1014
Fragments rebuilt: 1038
LSP regenerations: 425
Purges initiated: 0
</pre></td></tr>
<tr><td>Clear IS-IS statistics</td><td><code>clear isis statistics</code></td><td><pre>
user@host> clear isis statistics
user@host> show isis statistics
</pre></td></tr>
</table>

OSPF

Table 13.13 *OSPF Monitoring Commands*

Information to Monitor	Command	Example
Status of OSPF interfaces	show ospf interface	user@host> **show ospf interface brief** Intf State Area DR ID BDR ID Nbrs at-5/1/0.0 PtToPt 0.0.0.0 0.0.0.0 0.0.0.0 1 ge-2/3/0.0 DR 0.0.0.0 192.168.4.16 192.168.4.15 1 user@host> **show ospf interface detail** Interface State Area DR ID BDR ID Nbrs ge-1/0/0.0 DR 0.0.0.0 10.10.20.103 10.10.20.102 1 Type LAN, address 10.10.20.18, mask 255.255.255.248, MTU 1500, cost 1 DR addr 10.10.20.18, BDR addr 10.10.20.17, adj count 1 Hello 10, Dead 40, ReXmit 5, Not Stub
Link-state database entries	show ospf database	user@host> **show ospf database brief** OSPF link state database, area 0.0.0.0 Type ID Adv Rtr Seq Age Cksum Len Router 10.250.240.8 10.250.240.8 0x800001fc 2388 0x3684 36 Router 10.250.240.17 10.250.240.17 0x80000217 1835 0x444c 36 Network 192.168.254.230 10.250.240.8 0x800001cc 117 0xab67 40 Summary 10.1.2.0 10.250.240.17 0x80000216 1535 0x1729 28 Summary 10.1.3.34 10.250.240.8 0x8000013a 2217 0x842f 28 Summary 10.1.3.34 10.250.240.35 0x800001a3 800 0x0f20 28

Table 13.13 *OSPF Monitoring Commands*

<table>
<tr><th>Information to Monitor</th><th>Command</th><th>Example</th></tr>
<tr><td>Remove link-state database entries</td><td>clear ospf database</td><td><pre>
user@host> clear ospf statistics
user@host> show ospf statistics
user@host>
</pre></td></tr>
<tr><td>OSPF routing table entries</td><td>show ospf route</td><td><pre>
user@host> show ospf route
Prefix   Route/Path Type   Metric Next hop i/f
Next hop addr
1.1.1.0/24   Ext2   Network   0   fxp0.0
10.10.0.16
1.1.1.1/32   Intra   AS BR   1   fxp0.0
10.10.0.16
user@host> show ospf route detail
Prefix   Route/Path Type   Metric Next hop i/f
Next hop addr
1.1.1.0/24   Ext2   Network   0   fxp0.0
10.10.0.16
  area 0.0.0.0, options 0x0, origin 1.1.1.1
1.1.1.1/32   Intra   AS BR   1   fxp0.0
10.10.0.16
  area 0.0.0.0, options 0x0, origin 1.1.1.1
</pre></td></tr>
<tr><td>Adjacent routers</td><td>show ospf neighbor</td><td><pre>
user@host> show ospf neighbor brief
  Address   Intf   State   ID
Pri Dead
192.168.254.225 fxp3.0   2Way   10.250.240.32
128   36
192.168.254.230 fxp3.0   Full   10.250.240.8
128   38
user@host> show ospf neighbor detail
  Address   Intf   State   ID
Pri Dead
192.168.254.225 fxp3.0   2Way   10.250.240.32
128   35
  area 0.0.0.0, opt 0x2, DR 192.168.254.230, BDR 192.168.254.229
  Up 1w5d 18:09:18
</pre></td></tr>
</table>

Table 13.13 *OSPF Monitoring Commands*

Information to Monitor	Command	Example
Clear adjacent routers	`clear ospf neighbor`	`user@host>` **`clear ospf neighbor`** `user@host>` **`show ospf neighbor`** `user@host>`

SPF log	`show ospf log`	`user@host>` **`show ospf log`**
		`When              Type          Elapsed`
		`1w4d 17:25:58     Stub          0.000017`
		`1w4d 17:25:58     SPF           0.000070`
		`1w4d 17:25:58     Stub          0.000019`
		`1w4d 17:25:58     Interarea     0.000054`
		`1w4d 17:25:58     External      0.000005`
		`1w4d 17:25:58     Cleanup       0.000203`
		`1w4d 17:25:58       Total       0.000537`

OSPF statistics	`show ospf statistics`	`user@host>` **`show ospf statistics`**
		`Packet type            Total                Last 5 seconds`
		`                   Sent      Received        Sent     Received`
		`     Hello       505739        990495           4            5`
		`       DbD           20            26           0            0`
		`     LSReq            6             5           0            0`
		`  LSUpdate        27060         15319           0            0`
		`     LSAck        10923         52470           0            0`
		
		`LSAs retransmitted: 16, last 5 seconds: 0`
		
		`Receive errors:`
		`  862 no interface found`
		`  115923 no virtual link found`

Table 13.13 *OSPF Monitoring Commands*

Information to Monitor	Command	Example

Clear OSPF statistics	`clear ospf statistics`	`user@host> clear ospf statistics`
		`user@host> show ospf statistics`
		`user@host> show ospf statistics`
		`Packet type Total Last 5 seconds`
		`Sent Received Sent Received`
		`Hello o 0 o 0`
		`DbD 0 0 0 0`
		`LSReq 0 0 0 0`
		`LSUpdate 0 0 0 0`
		`LSAck 0 0 0 0`
		
		`LSAs retransmitted: o, last 5 seconds: 0`
		
		`Receive errors:`
		`0 no interface found`
		`0 no virtual link found`

BGP

Table 13.14 *BGP Monitoring Commands*

<table>
<tr><th>Information to Monitor</th><th>Command</th><th>Example</th></tr>
<tr><td>Entries in the BGP neighbor database</td><td>show bgp neighbor</td><td>user@host> show bgp neighbor
Peer: 10.168.1.222+2691 AS 1   Local: 10.168.1.220+179 AS 1
  Type: Internal State: Established   Flags: <>
  Last State: OpenConfirm   Last Event: RecvKeepAlive
  Last Error: None
  Options: <Preference LocalAddress HoldTime>
        Local Address: 10.168.1.220   Holdtime: 90
Preference: 170
  Number of flaps: 0
  Peer ID: 10.168.1.222 Local ID: 10.168.1.220 Active Holdtime:
90
  NLRI advertised by peer: unicast
  NLRI for this session: unicast
  Table inet.0 Bit: 1
    Send state: in sync
    Active Prefixes: 100
    Received Prefixes: 100
    Suppressed due to damping: 0
  Table inet.2 Bit: 10000
    Send state: not advertising
    Active Prefixes: 0
    Received Prefixes: 0
    Suppressed due to damping: 0
  Last traffic (seconds):   Received 22   Sent 5 Checked 5
  Input messages: Total 13425   Updates 1   Octets
255318
  Output messages: Total 13423   Updates 0   Octets
255055
  Output Queue[0]: 0
  Output Queue[1]: 0</td></tr>
<tr><td>Remove entries from the neighbor database</td><td>clear bgp neighbor</td><td>user@host> clear bgp neighbor
user@host></td></tr>
</table>

Table 13.14 *BGP Monitoring Commands*

Information to Monitor	Command	Example

Entries in the BGP group database	show bgp group	user@host> **show bgp group**
		Group Type: External Local AS: 65004
		  Name: pe-pe
		  Export: [match-all]
		  Options: <Multihop Confed>
		  Total peers: 1 Established: 0
		  11.134.0.3+179
		
		Group Type: External Local AS: 65004
		  Name: pe-ce
		  Export: [gr-export]
		  Total peers: 1 Established: 1
		  10.145.0.5+179
		  Route Queue Timer: unset Route Queue: empty

BGP summary information	show bgp summary	user@host> **show bgp summary** Groups: 1 Peers: 1 Down Peers: 0 Table Tot Paths Act Paths Suppressed History Damp State Pending inet.0 100 100 0 0 0 0 inet.2 0 0 0 0 0 0 Peer AS InPkt OutPkt OutQ Flaps Last Up/Dwn State|#Active/Received/Damped... 10.168.1.222 1 13433 13430 0 0 4d 15:55:10 100/100/0 0/0/0
Remove damping information	clear bgp damping	user@host> **clear bgp damping** user@host>

Generic IP Multicast Information

Table 13.15 *Generic Multicast Information Monitoring Commands*

Information to Monitor	Command	Example
Entries in the multicast forwarding cache	`show multicast route`	See below

```
user@host> show multicast route detail
Group            Source prefix      Act Pru InIf  NHid  AgeOut  Packets
Session
224.0.1.1        128.112.0.0    /12 I   P   4     0     0            0
Network
 Cloned from:    0.0.0.0        /0
    Source:      128.112.136.5
224.0.1.32       160.0.0.0      /3  I   P   4     0     0            0
mtrace
 Cloned from:    0.0.0.0        /0
    Source:      171.68.27.126
224.2.123.4      136.0.0.0      /5  I   P   4     0     0            0
Multimed
 Cloned from:    0.0.0.0        /0
    Source:      137.132.50.14
224.2.127.1      129.0.0.0      /8  I   P   4     0     0            0
Multimed
 Cloned from:    0.0.0.0        /0
    Source:      129.79.17.70
224.2.127.254    128.0.0.0      /11 A   F   4     42    122          6
SAPv1 An
 Cloned from:    0.0.0.0        /0
    Source:      128.9.160.109
224.2.127.254    128.32.0.0     /11 A   F   4     42    428          2
SAPv1 An
 Cloned from:    0.0.0.0        /0
    Source:      128.32.131.169
```

Table 13.15 *Generic Multicast Information Monitoring Commands*

Information to Monitor	Command	Example
Entries in the multicast next-hop table	`show multicast nexthops`	user@host> **show multicast nexthops brief** ID Refcount KRefcount Downstream interface 11 2 1 local so-1/1/0.0 33 4 2 so-0/0/0.0 so-3/1/0.0 t3-4/2/0.0 ge-6/3/0.0 39 8 4 so-0/0/0.0 at-2/1/0.0 at-2/1/0.1 so-3/1/0.0 t3-4/2/0.0 ge-6/3/0.0
Multicast reverse-path-forwarding calculations	`show multicast rpf`	user@host> **show multicast rpf brief** Source prefix Protocol RPF interface RPF neighbor 0.0.0.0 /0 DVMRP ipip.0 192.168.1.1 0.0.0.0 /2 Cloned ipip.0 192.168.1.1 0.0.0.0 /3 Cloned ipip.0 192.168.1.1 127.0.0.1 /32 Direct lo0.0 user@host> **show multicast rpf detail** Source prefix Protocol RPF interface RPF neighbor 0.0.0.0 /0 DVMRP ipip.0 192.168.1.1 0.0.0.0 /2 Cloned ipip.0 192.168.1.1 Cloned from: 0.0.0.0 /0 DVMRP ipip.0 192.168.1.1 0.0.0.0 /3 Cloned ipip.0 192.168.1.1 Cloned from:

Table 13.15 *Generic Multicast Information Monitoring Commands*

Information to Monitor	Command	Example
Announced multicast sessions	`show multicast sessions`	user@host> **show multicast sessions** Bird test Colorado/UCSD Networks Class Colorado/UCSD wb LBL - Deb test LabWeb - The Spectro-Microscopy Collaboratory NASA - Shuttle Mission STS-95 NASA TV - Broadcast from NASA HQ NLANR Techs Conf. MPEG1 (IP/TV) SPT Meeting(private) Titanic Trailor UC Berkeley MIG seminar UW CS&E Colloquium test1@fsu-acns

Table 13.15 *Generic Multicast Information Monitoring Commands*

<table>
<tr><th>Information to Monitor</th><th>Command</th><th>Example</th></tr>
<tr><td>Multicast statistics</td><td><code>show multicast statistics</code></td><td><pre>
user@host> show multicast statistics
Interface   Protocol   Resolve   Resolve   Resolve Resolve
                               primary secondary   no route errors
local   0   0   0   0

fxp0.0   PIM-dense   100   100   0   0

fxp1.0   PIM-dense   62   62   0   0

ipip.0   DVMRP   6309   6309   3   0

Interface   Protocol   Interface IfMismatch IfMismatch
                            mismatches   no route   errors
local   0   0   0
fxp0.0   PIM-dense   0   0   0
fxp1.0   PIM-dense   0   0   0
ipip.0   DVMRP   0   0   0

Resolve requests on interfaces not enabled for multicast 0
Interface Mismatches on interfaces not enabled for multicast 0
</pre></td></tr>
<tr><td>Clear multicast statistics</td><td><code>clear multicast statistics</code></td><td><pre>
user@host> clear multicast statistics
user@host> show multicast statistics
user@host>
</pre></td></tr>
</table>

Table 13.15 *Generic Multicast Information Monitoring Commands*

Information to Monitor	Command	Example
Most active multicast groups	show multicast usage	user@host> **show multicast usage** Group Sources Packets Bytes 224.225.1.1 1 1 0 224.225.1.2 1 1 0 224.225.1.3 1 1 0 224.225.1.4 1 1 0 224.225.1.5 1 1 0 Prefix /len Groups Packets Bytes 10.6.0.1 /32 489 489 0 10.255.245.35 /32 2 0 0 user@host> **show multicast usage detail** Group Sources Packets Bytes 224.225.1.1 1 1 0 Source: 10.6.0.1 /32 Packets: 1 Bytes: 0 224.225.1.2 1 1 0 Source: 10.6.0.1 /32 Packets: 1 Bytes: 0 224.225.1.3 1 1 0 Source: 10.6.0.1 /32 Packets: 1 Bytes: 0 224.225.1.4 1 1 0 Source: 10.6.0.1 /32 Packets: 1 Bytes: 0 224.225.1.5 1 1 0 Source: 10.6.0.1 /32 Packets: 1 Bytes: 0
Trace information about a multicast path from a source to a receiver.	mtrace	user@host> **mtrace 192.168.1.74** mtrace: WARNING: no multicast group specified, so no statistics printed Mtrace from 192.168.1.74 to 192.168.1.5 via group 0.0.0.0 Querying full reverse path... * * 0 router1.juniper.net (192.168.1.5) -1 router2.juniper.net (192.168.1.6) PIM thresh^ 1 -2 router3.juniper.net (192.168.1.69) PIM thresh^ 1 -3 router3.juniper.net (192.168.1.74) Round trip time 2 ms; total ttl of 2 required.

PIM

Table 13.16 *PIM Monitoring Commands*

<table>
<tr><th>Information to Monitor</th><th>Command</th><th>Example</th></tr>
<tr><td>Bootstrap router</td><td><code>show pim bootstrap</code></td><td><pre>
user@host> show pim bootstrap
BSR   Pri Local address   Pri State   Timeout
10.10.20.103   3 10.10.20.101   0 InEligible   119
</pre></td></tr>
<tr><td>PIM groups</td><td><code>show pim join</code></td><td><pre>
user@host> show pim join brief
Group   Source   RP   Flags
224.0.1.39   10.10.20.103   dense
    Upstream interface: so-2/0/0.0
224.0.1.40   10.10.20.103   dense
    Upstream interface: so-2/0/0.0
224.1.1.1   0.0.0.0   10.10.20.103
sparse,rptree,wildcard
    Upstream interface: so-2/0/0.0
224.1.1.1   10.10.20.17   sparse
    Upstream interface: so-2/0/0.0
224.1.1.1   10.30.1.1   sparse
    Upstream interface: so-1/0/0.0
224.1.1.2   0.0.0.0   10.10.20.103
sparse,rptree,wildcard
    Upstream interface: so-2/0/0.0
224.1.1.2   10.10.20.17   sparse
    Upstream interface: so-2/0/0.0
224.1.1.2   10.30.1.1   sparse
    Upstream interface: o-1/0/0.0
</pre></td></tr>
<tr><td>Clear PIM join and prune states</td><td><code>clear pim join</code></td><td><pre>
user@host> clear pim join
user@host> show pim join
user@host>
</pre></td></tr>
</table>

Table 13.16 *PIM Monitoring Commands*

Information to Monitor	Command	Example

Status of interfaces on which PIM is configured	`show pim interfaces`	`user@host>` **`show pim interfaces`**
		`Name Stat Mode V State Priority DR address Neighbors`
		`lo0.0 Up SparseDense 2 DR 1 10.10.20.101 0`
		`at-1/0/0.0 Up SparseDense 1 P2P 1`
		`so-1/1/0.0 Up SparseDense 1 P2P 1`
		`ge-2/0/0.0 Up SparseDense 2 DR 3 10.10.20.1 3`
		`ge-3/0/0.0 Up SparseDense 2 NotDR 1 10.10.30.11 2`
		`so-5/0/0.0 Down SparseDense 1 P2P 0`
		`so-5/0/1.0 Up SparseDense 1 P2P 1`
		`so-5/0/2.0 Down SparseDense 1 P2P 0`
		`pe-6/3/0.32769 Up Sparse 2 P2P 0`

Table 13.16 *PIM Monitoring Commands*

Information to Monitor	Command	Example
PIM neighbors	`show pim neighbors`	user@host> **show pim neighbors** Interface DR priority Neighbor addr V Mode Holdtime Timeout at-1/0/0.0 none 10.10.30.3 1 SparseDense 105 99 so-1/1/0.0 none 10.10.40.7 1 SparseDense 105 82 ge-2/0/0.0 1 10.10.20.3 2 Unknown 105 93 ge-2/0/0.0 1 10.10.20.4 2 Unknown 105 101 ge-2/0/0.0 1 10.10.20.5 2 Unknown 105 88 ge-3/0/0.0 1 10.10.20.10 2 Unknown 105 78 ge-3/0/0.0 1 10.10.20.11 2 Unknown 105 100 so-5/1/0.0 none 10.10.50.6 1 SparseDense 105 79

Table 13.16 *PIM Monitoring Commands*

Information to Monitor	Command	Example
Rendezvous points	show pim rps	user@host> **show pim rps brief** RP address Type Holdtime Timeout Active groups Group prefixes 204.69.248.224 auto-rp 180 124 6 224.0.0.0/4 user@host> **show pim rps detail** RP: 204.69.248.224 Learned from 204.69.248.1 via: auto-rp Time Active: 00:00:12 Holdtime: 180 with 168 remaining Group Ranges: 224.0.0.0/4 Active groups using RP: 224.1.127.255 224.2.127.253 224.2.127.254 total 3 groups active

Table 13.16 *PIM Monitoring Commands*

Information to Monitor	Command	Example

PIM source RFP state	`show pim source`	`user@host> show pim source`
		`RPF Address      Prefix/length      Upstream interface`
		`Neighbor address`
		`10.10.10.101     10.10.10.101    /32 local              Local`
		`10.10.10.103     10.10.10.103    /32 so-0/1/0.0`
		`10.10.20.10`
		`10.10.20.121     10.10.20.0      /24 ge-0/0/0.0         Direct`
		`10.10.30.55      10.10.30.0      /24 so-0/1/0.0`
		`10.10.20.10`
		`10.10.30.87      10.10.30.0      /24 so-0/1/0.0`
		`10.10.20.10`
		`10.10.30.103     10.10.30.0      /24 so-0/1/0.0`
		`10.10.20.10`
		`10.10.40.79      10.10.40.0      /24 at-3/2/0.0`
		`10.11.20.17`
		`10.10.40.119     10.10.40.0      /24 at-3/2/0.0`
		`10.11.20.17`
		`10.10.50.13      10.10.50.0      /24 ge-6/3/0.0         Direct`
		`10.10.50.29      10.10.50.0      /24 ge-6/3/0.0         Direct`
		`10.10.50.47      10.10.50.0      /24 ge-6/3/0.0         Direct`
		`10.10.50.63      10.10.50.0      /24 ge-6/3/0.0         Direct`

PIM (*,*,RP) join and prune states	`show pim wildcard`	`user@host> show pim wildcard` `RP               Interface        Neighbor addr   Holdtime Timeout`

Table 13.16 *PIM Monitoring Commands*

Information to Monitor	Command	Example

PIM statistics	`show pim statistics`	`user@host>` **`show pim statistics`**
		`PIM statistics on all interfaces:`
		`PIM message type        Received       Sent  Rx errors`
		`Hello                          0          0          0`
		`Register                       0          0          0`
		`Register Stop                  0          0          0`
		`Join Prune                     0          0          0`
		`Bootstrap                      0          0          0`
		`Assert                         0          0          0`
		`Graft                          0          0          0`
		`Graft Ack                      0          0          0`
		`Candidate RP                   0          0          0`
		`V1 Query                    2102       4203          0`
		`V1 Register                    0          0          0`
		`V1 Register Stop               0          0          0`
		`V1 Join Prune              14153      13074          0`
		`V1 RP Reachability             0          0          0`
		`V1 Assert                      0          0          0`
		`V1 Graft                       0          0          0`
		`V1 Graft Ack                   0          0          0`

Table 13.16 *PIM Monitoring Commands*

Information to Monitor	Command	Example

PIM statistics summary for all interfaces		`Unknown type 0`
		`V1 Unknown type 0`
		`Unknown Version 0`
		`Neighbor unknown 0`
		`Bad Length 0`
		`Bad Checksum 0`
		`Bad Receive If 0`
		`Rx Intf disabled 1998`
		`Rx V1 Require V2 0`
		`Rx Register not RP 0`
		`RP Filtered Source 0`
		`Unknown Reg Stop 0`
		`Rx Join/Prune no state 1034`
		`Rx Graft/Graft Ack no state 0`
		`Rx Graft on upstream if 0`
		`Rx CRP not BSR 0`
		`Rx BSR when BSR 0`
		`Rx BSR not RPF if 0`
		`Rx unknown hello opt 0`
		`Rx data no state 0`
		`Rx RP no state 0`
		`Rx aggregate 0`
		`Rx malformed packet 0`
		`No RP 0`
		`No route upstream 0`
		`RP mismatch 0`
		`RPF neighbor unknown 0`

Clear PIM statistics	`clear pim statistics`	`user@host>` **`clear pim statistics`** `user@host>` **`show pim statistics`** `user@host>`

Table 13.16 *PIM Monitoring Commands*

Information to Monitor	Command	Example

Most active PIM groups	`show multicast usage`	`user@host>` **`show multicast usage`**
		`Group Sources Packets Bytes`
		`224.225.1.1 1 1 0`
		`224.225.1.2 1 1 0`
		`224.225.1.3 1 1 0`
		`224.225.1.4 1 1 0`
		`224.225.1.5 1 1 0`
		`Prefix /len Groups Packets Bytes`
		`10.6.0.1 /32 489 489 0`
		`10.255.245.35 /32 2 0 0`

DVMRP and PIM tunnels	`show multicast tunnels`	`user@host>` **`show multicast tunnels`**
		`Interface    Local address    Remote address  TTL`
		`ipip.0       204.69.248.187   192.168.1.1     64`

DVMRP

Table 13.17 *DVMRP Monitoring Commands*

Information to Monitor	Command	Example
DVMRP neighbors	show dvmrp neighbors	user@host> **show dvmrp neighbors** Neighbor Interface Version Flags Routes Timeout Transitions 192.168.1.1 ipip.0 3.255 PGM 3 28 1
DVMRP prefixes	show dvmrp prefix	user@host> **show dvmrp prefix detail** Prefix Next hop Age 0.0.0.0 /0 192.168.1.1 00:00:03 224.2.127.254: Prunes sent Grafts sent Cache lifetime Prune lifetime 0 0 0 0/ 0 224.2.127.254: Prunes sent Grafts sent Cache lifetime Prune lifetime 0 0 0 0/ 0 224.2.139.68: Prunes sent Grafts sent Cache lifetime Prune lifetime 2 2 0 0/ 7200 224.2.245.3: Prunes sent Grafts sent Cache lifetime Prune lifetime 2 2 0 0/ 7200
DVMRP prunes	show dvmrp prunes	user@host> **show dvmrp prunes** Group Source prefix Timeout Neighbor 224.0.1.1 128.112.0.0 /12 7077 192.168.1.1 224.0.1.32 160.0.0.0 /3 7087 192.168.1.1 224.2.123.4 136.0.0.0 /5 6955 192.168.1.1 224.2.127.1 129.0.0.0 /8 7046 192.168.1.1 224.2.135.86 128.102.128.0 /17 7071 192.168.1.1 224.2.135.86 129.0.0.0 /8 7074 192.168.1.1 224.2.135.86 130.0.0.0 /7 7071 192.168.1.1
DVMRP graft retransmission queue	show dvmrp grafts	user@host> **show dvmrp grafts** Group Source Expire Neighbor

Table 13.17 *DVMRP Monitoring Commands*

Information to Monitor	Command	Example

Status of interfaces on which DVMRP is configured	`show dvmrp interfaces`	`user@host>` **`show dvmrp interfaces`**
		`Interface State Leaf Metric Announce Mode`
		`fxp0.0    Up    N    1      4 Forwarding`
		`fxp1.0    Up    N    1      4 Forwarding`
		`fxp2.0    Up    N    1      3 Forwarding`
		`lo0.0     Up    Y    1      0 Unicast-routing`

Most active DVMRP groups	`show multicast usage`	`user@host>` **`show multicast usage`**
		`Group Sources Packets Bytes`
		`224.225.1.1 1 1 0`
		`224.225.1.2 1 1 0`
		`224.225.1.3 1 1 0`
		`224.225.1.4 1 1 0`
		`224.225.1.5 1 1 0`
		`Prefix /len Groups Packets Bytes`
		`10.6.0.1 /32 489 489 0`
		`10.255.245.35 /32 2 0 0`

DVMRP and PIM tunnels	`show multicast tunnels`	`user@host>` **`show multicast tunnels`**
		`Interface        Local address   Remote address  TTL`
		`ipip.0           204.69.248.187  192.168.1.1     64`

IGMP

Table 13.18 *IGMP Monitoring Commands*

<table>
<tr><th>Information to Monitor</th><th>Command</th><th>Example</th></tr>
<tr><td>IGMP group members</td><td><code>show igmp group</code></td><td><pre>user@host> show igmp group
Interface   Group   Last Reported   Timeout
ge-4/1/0.0   224.1.1.1   10.6.0.7   239
ge-4/1/0.0   224.1.1.2   10.6.0.7   252
ge-4/1/0.0   224.1.1.3   10.6.0.7   257
ge-5/3/0.0   224.3.3.1   10.9.0.5   138
ge-5/3/0.0   224.3.3.2   10.9.0.5   227
local   224.0.0.2   (null)   0
local   224.0.0.13   (null)   0
local   224.0.1.39   (null)   0
local   224.0.1.40   (null)   0</pre></td></tr>
<tr><td>IGMP group members by interface</td><td><code>show igmp interface</code></td><td><pre>user@host> show igmp interface
Interface   State Querier   Timeout Version Groups
ge-2/0/0.0   Down   0   2   0
ge-4/0/0.0   Up   10.3.0.9   199   2   0
ge-4/1/0.0   Up   10.6.0.1   None   2   3
ge-3/0/0.0   Down   0   2   0
ge-5/3/0.0   Up   10.9.0.1   None   2   2</pre></td></tr>
<tr><td>Clear IGMP group members</td><td><code>clear igmp membership</code></td><td><pre>user@host> clear igmp membership</pre></td></tr>
</table>

Table 13.18 *IGMP Monitoring Commands*

Information to Monitor	Command	Example
IGMP statistics	show igmp statistics	user@host> **show igmp statistics** IGMP statistics on all interfaces: IGMP message type Received Transmitted Rx errors Queries 986 18131 0 Report V1 0 0 0 DVMRP 19603 35171 0 PIM V1 18137 0 0 Cisco Trace 0 0 0 Report V2 6 0 0 Leave 0 0 0 Mtrace Response 0 0 0 Mtrace Request 0 0 0 Domain Wide Reports 0 0 0 IGMP statistics summary for all interfaces: Unknown type 0 Bad Length 0 Bad Checksum 0 Bad Receive If 0 Rx non-local 0
Clear IGMP statistics	clear igmp statistics	user@host> **clear igmp statistics** user@host> **show igmp statistics** user@host>

MSDP

Table 13.19 *MSDP Monitoring Commands*

Information to Monitor	Command	Example

MSDP peers	`show msdp`	`user@host>` **`show msdp`**
		`Peer address Local address State Last up/down Peer-Group`
		`10.255.245.34 10.255.245.39 Listen 00:05:07`
		`user@host>` **`show msdp detail`**
		`Peer: 10.255.245.34`
		`Local address: 10.255.245.39`
		`State: Listen`
		`Peer Connect Retries: 0`
		`State timer expires: 0`
		`Peer: 10.255.245.43`
		`Local address: 10.255.245.39`
		`State: Established`
		`Peer Connect Retries: 0`
		`State timer expires: 53`
		`Peer Times out: 2`

Clear MSDP source active cache	`clear msdp cache`	`user@host>` **`clear msdp statistics`**

Table 13.19 *MSDP Monitoring Commands*

Information to Monitor	Command	Example

MSDP statistics	`show msdp statistics`	`user@host>` **`show msdp statistics`**
		`Peer: 10.255.245.39`
		`Last State Change: 11:54:49 (00:24:59)`
		`Last message received from peer: 11:53:32 (00:26:16)`
		`RPF Failures: 0`
		`Remote Closes: 0`
		`Peer Timeouts: 0`
		`SA messages sent: 376`
		`SA messages received: 459`
		`SA request messages sent: 0`
		`SA request messages received: 0`
		`SA response messages sent: 0`
		`SA response messages received: 0`
		`Keepalive messages sent: 17`
		`Keepalive messages received: 19`
		`Unknown messages received: 0`
		`Error messages received: 0`

Clear MSDP statistics	`clear msdp statistics`	`user@host>` **`clear msdp statistics`** `user@host>` **`show msdp statistics`** `user@host>`
Test MSDP peers	`test msdp`	`user@host>` **`test msdp`**

Multicast Scoping

Table 13.20 *Multicast Scoping Monitoring Commands*

Information to Monitor	Command	Example
Administratively scoped addresses	`show multicast scope`	user@host> **show multicast scope** Resolve Scope name Group Prefix Interface Rejects "local" 239.255.0.0 /16 ipip.0 0

MPLS

Table 13.21 *MPLS Monitoring Commands*

Information to Monitor	Command	Example
Status of interfaces on which MPLS is running	`show mpls interface`	user@host> **show mpls interface** Interface State Administrative groups so-1/0/0.0 Up Blue Yellow Red
Configured named paths that are used in dynamic MPLS	`show mpls path`	user@host> **show mpls path** Path name Address Strict/loose address p1 123.456.55.6 Strict 123.456.1.6 Loose p2 191.456.1.4 Strict

Table 13.21 *MPLS Monitoring Commands*

Information to Monitor	Command	Example
Configured LSPs on this router, and all ingress, transit, and egress LSPs	`show mpls lsp`	user@host> **show mpls lsp brief** Ingress LSP: 0 label-switched paths Total 0 displayed, Up 0, Down 0 Egress RSVP: 0 sessions Total 0 displayed, Up 0, Down 0 Transit RSVP: 1 sessions To From State Rt Style Labelin Labelout LSPname 123.456.2.34 101.0.0.1 Up 1 1 FF 1024 0 sfo1 Total 1 displayed, Up 1, Down 0
Disconnect and restart dynamic LSPs that originate from this router	`clear mpls lsp`	user@host> **clear mpls lsp** user@host>
Configured MPLS administrative groups	`show mpls admin-groups`	user@host> **show mpls admin-groups** Group Bit index black 3 blue 2 gold 1 green 0

CSPF statistics	`show mpls cspf`	user@host> **show mpls cspf**
		CSPF statistics
		Queue length current maximum dequeued
		                     0 0 0
		
		Paths total successful no route sys error
		CSPFs
		                 0 0 0 0
		0
		
		Time (secs) total CSPFs avg per CSPF % of rpd
		               0.000000 0.000000 0.000000 0.0000

Table 13.21 *MPLS Monitoring Commands*

<table>
<tr><th>Information to Monitor</th><th>Command</th><th>Example</th></tr>
<tr><td>Entries in the TED database</td><td><code>show ted database</code></td><td><pre>
user@host> show ted database brief
TED database: 6 ISIS nodes 6 INET nodes
ID   Type Age(s) LnkIn LnkOut Protocol
cheviot.00(123.456.1.10)   Rtr   383   1   1 IS-IS(2)
IS-IS(1)
corriedale.00(123.456.1.11) Rtr   36   2   0 IS-IS(2)
IS-IS(1)
wolff.00(123.456.1.12)   Rtr   399   0   0 IS-IS(2)
IS-IS(1)
perendale.00(123.456.1.13)   Rtr   385   2   0 IS-IS(2)
IS-IS(1)
merino.00(123.456.1.14)   Rtr   379   1   3 IS-IS(2)
IS-IS(1)
romney.00(123.456.1.15)   Rtr   427   0   2 IS-IS(2)
IS-IS(1)
</pre></td></tr>
<tr><td>Protocols contributing to the TED</td><td><code>show ted protocol</code></td><td><pre>
user@host> show ted protocol
Protocol name   Credibility Self node
IS-IS(2)   2 (highest) corriedale.00(123.456.1.11)
IS-IS(1)   1   corriedale.00(123.456.1.11)
</pre></td></tr>
<tr><td>Current TED links</td><td><code>show ted link</code></td><td><pre>
user@host> show ted link brief
TED link:
ID   ->ID
LocalPath LocalBW
cheviot.00(123.456.1.10)   merino.00(123.456.1.14)
0 0bps
merino.00(123.456.1.14)   corriedale.00(123.456.1.11)
0 0bps
merino.00(123.456.1.14)   perendale.00(123.456.1.13)
0 0bps
merino.00(123.456.1.14)   cheviot.00(123.456.1.10)
0 0bps
romney.00(123.456.1.15)   corriedale.00(123.456.1.11)
0 0bps
romney.00(123.456.1.15)   perendale.00(123.456.1.13)
0 0bps
</pre></td></tr>
</table>

Table 13.21 *MPLS Monitoring Commands*

Information to Monitor	Command	Example
Configured circuit cross-connect information	show connections	(see below)

```
user@host> show connections all
CCC connections
  Legend for status (St)               Legend for connection types
  UN -- uninitialized                  if-sw:  interface switching
  NP -- not present                    rmt-if: remote interface
switching
  WE -- wrong encapsulation            lsp-sw: LSP switching
  DS -- disabled
  Dn -- down                           Legend for circuit types
  -> -- only outbound conn is up       intf -- interface
  <- -- only inbound  conn is up       tlsp -- transmit LSP
  Up -- operational                    rlsp -- receive LSP

Connection/Circuit                    Type    St   Time last up
# Up trans
intf-sw                               if-sw   Dn
  at-1/2/3.4                            intf  NP
  at-3/2/1.0                            intf  NP
pr-pr                                 lsp-sw  Dn
  from-proz                             rlsp  NP
  to-proz                               tlsp  Dn
rmt-intf-sw                           rmt-if  Dn
  so-5/3/1.0                            intf  NP
  here-catch!                           tlsp  Dn
  gimme-gimme-gimme                     rlsp  NP
```

RSVP

Table 13.22 *RSVP Monitoring Commands*

Information to Monitor	Command	Example
Status of interfaces on which RSVP is running	show rsvp interface	user@host> **show rsvp interface detail** RSVP interface: 1 active Update threshold 5% Active Subscr- Static Available Reserved Highest Interface State resv iption BW BW BW BW de0.0 Up 1 23% 10Mbps 989.992kbps 1.31Mbps 1.31Mbps PacketType Total Last 5 seconds Sent Received Sent Received Path 8288 0 1 0 PathErr 0 0 0 0 PathTear 0 0 0 0 Resv 0 3372 0 0 ResvErr 1685 0 0 0 ResvTear 0 0 0 0
Neighbors with which this router exchanges information	show rsvp neighbor	user@host> **show rsvp neighbor** RSVP neighbor: 2 learned Address Idle Up/Dn LastChange HelloInt HelloTx/Rx 192.168.207.203 0 3/2 13:01 3 366/349 192.168.207.207 0 1/0 22:49 3 448/448

Table 13.22 *RSVP Monitoring Commands*

Information to Monitor	Command	Example
Currently active RSVP sessions	`show rsvp session`	user@host> **show rsvp session brief** Ingress RSVP: 6 sessions To From State Rt Style Labelin Labelout LSPname 192.168.1.1 192.168.1.3 Dn 0 0 - - - test1 192.168.1.1 192.168.1.3 Dn 0 0 - - - test2 192.168.1.1 192.168.1.3 Dn 0 0 - - - test3 192.168.1.4 192.168.1.3 Up 2 1 FF - - sf-la 192.168.1.4 192.168.1.3 Up 3 1 FF - - test4 192.168.1.4 192.168.1.3 Dn 0 0 - - - k0 * indicates this router
Clear all RSVP sessions	`clear rsvp session`	user@host> **clear rsvp session** user@host> **show rsvp session brief** Ingress RSVP: 0 sessions To From State Rt Style Labelin Labelout LSPname

Table 13.22 *RSVP Monitoring Commands*

<table>
<tr><th>Information to Monitor</th><th>Command</th><th>Example</th></tr>
<tr><td>RSVP packet and error counters</td><td><code>show rsvp statistics</code></td><td><pre>
user@host> show rsvp statistics
PacketType   Total   Last 5 seconds
                    Sent   Received   Sent   Received
  Path   842   0   2   0
  PathErr   0   614   0   0
  PathTear   0   0   0   0
  Resv FF   0   282   0   4
  Resv WF   0   0   0   0
  Resv SE   0   0   0   0
  ResvErr   0   0   0   0
  ResvTear   0   0   0   0
  ResvConf   0   0   0   0

Errors   Total   Last 5 seconds
  Rcv pkt bad length   0   0
  Rcv pkt unknown type   0   0
  Rcv pkt bad version   0   0
  Rcv pkt bad cksum   0   0
  Rcv pkt bad format   0   0
  memory alloc fail   0   0
  no path info   0   0
  Resv style conflict   0   0
  Port conflict   0   0
  Resv no interface   0   0
  PathErr to client   614   0
  ResvErr to client   0   0
  Path timeout   0   0
  Resv timeout   0   0
</pre></td></tr>
<tr><td>Clear RSVP packet and error counters</td><td><code>clear rsvp statistics</code></td><td><pre>
user@host> clear rsvp statistics
</pre></td></tr>
<tr><td>RSVP version and configuration information</td><td><code>show rsvp version</code></td><td><pre>
user@host> show rsvp version
Resource ReSerVation Protocol, version 1. rfc2205
   RSVP protocol   = Enabled
   R (refresh timer)   = 30 seconds
   K (keep multiplier) = 3
</pre></td></tr>
</table>

LDP

Table 13.23 *LDP Monitoring Commands*

Information to Monitor	Command	Example
Entries in the LDP database	show ldp database	user@host> **show ldp database brief** Input label database, 10.255.245.222:0--10.255.245.221:0 Label Prefix 100018 10.255.245.222/32 3 10.255.245.221/32 100011 L2CKT FRAME RELAY VC 11 Output label database, 10.255.245.222:0--10.255.245.221:0 Label Prefix 100018 10.255.245.222/32 3 10.255.245.221/32 100011 L2CKT FRAME RELAY VC 1
Status of interfaces on which LDP is running	show ldp interface	user@host> **show ldp interface brief** Interface Label space ID Nbr count Next hello fxp0.0 10.10.255.6:0 2 3 mps0.0 10.10.255.6:0 0 0
LDP neighbor	show ldp neighbor	user@host> **show ldp neighbor brief** Address Interface Label space ID Hold Time 192.168.1.213 so-0/0/0 10.10.255.4:0 13 192.168.1.211 so-0/0/0 10.10.255.2:0 14
Clear LDP neighbors	clear ldp neighbor	user@host> **clear ldp neighbor** user@host> **show ldp neighbor brief** Address Interface Label space ID Hold Time

Table 13.23 *LDP Monitoring Commands*

<table>
<tr><th>Information to Monitor</th><th>Command</th><th>Example</th></tr>
<tr><td>Configured named paths that are used by LDP</td><td><code>show ldp path</code></td><td><pre>user@host> show ldp path brief
Output Session (label)   Input Session (label)
10.10.255.6:0(3)   (egress)
10.10.255.3:0(3)   .
10.10.255.4:0(3)   .
10.10.255.6:0(100000)   10.10.255.3:0(3)
10.10.255.4:0(100000)   .
10.10.255.3:0(100001)   10.10.255.6:0(3)
10.10.255.4:0(100001)   .
10.10.255.6:0(100002)   10.10.255.4:0(3)
10.10.255.3:0(100002)   .</pre></td></tr>
<tr><td>LDP routing table entries</td><td><code>show ldp route</code></td><td><pre>user@host>show ldp route brief
Destination   Next-hop intf   Next-hop address
 10.10.255.1/32   so-2/3/0
*10.10.255.3/32   so-1/0/0   10.10.1.3
*10.10.255.1/32   so-2/3/0
 10.10.255.4/32   so-0/0/0   192.168.1.213
*10.10.255.4/32   so-0/0/0   192.168.1.213
 10.10.255.6/32   so-0/0/0   192.168.1.215
*10.10.255.6/32   so-0/0/0   192.168.1.215
*10.10.255.2/32
 0.0.0.0/0   so-0/0/0   192.168.1.254
 10.10.255.3/32   so-1/0/0   10.10.1.3</pre></td></tr>
<tr><td>Currently active LDP sessions</td><td><code>show ldp session</code></td><td><pre>user@host> show ldp session brief
  Address   State   Connection   Hold Time
10.10.255.2   Operational Open   25
10.10.255.4   Operational Open   26</pre></td></tr>
</table>

Table 13.23 *LDP Monitoring Commands*

Information to Monitor	Command	Example
LDP statistics	`show ldp statistics`	user@host> **show ldp statistics**

```
Message type                 Total                      Last 5
seconds
                       Sent        Received            Sent
Received
Hello                  265          263                2
2
Initialization           2            2                0
0
Keepalive              112          111                1
0
Notification             0            0                0
0
Address                  2            2                0
0
Address withdraw         0            0                0
0
Label mapping            7            6                0
0
Label request            0            0                0
0
Label withdraw           2            0                0
0
Label release            0            2                0
0
Label abort              0            0                0
0
All UDP                265          263                2
2
All TCP                123          121                1
0

Event type                               Total        Last 5
seconds

Sessions opened                              2                 0
Sessions closed                              0                 0
Topology changes                            11                 0

No interface                                 0                 0
No session                                   0                 0
No adjacency                                 0                 0
```

Table 13.23 *LDP Monitoring Commands*

Information to Monitor	Command	Example

		`Unknown version 0 0`
		`Malformed PDU 0 0`
		`Malformed message 0 0`
		`Unknown message type 0 0`
		`Inappropriate message 0 0`
		`Malformed TLV 0 0`
		`Bad TLV value 0 0`
		`Missing TLV 0 0`
		`PDU too large 0 0`

Clear LDP statistics	`clear ldp statistics`	`user@host>` **`clear ldp statistics`**

Layer 2 VPNs

Table 13.24 *Layer 2 VPNs Monitoring Commands*

<table>
<tr><th>Information to Monitor</th><th>Command</th><th>Example</th></tr>
<tr><td>Entries in the BGP neighbor database</td><td><code>show bgp neighbor</code></td><td><pre>
user@host> show bgp neighbor bgp.l2.vpn.0
Peer: 192.168.16.1+1037 AS 65412 Local: 192.168.24.1+179 AS 65412
  Type: Internal   State: Established   Flags: <>
  Last State: OpenConfirm   Last Event: RecvKeepAlive
  Last Error: None
  Options: <Preference LocalAddress HoldTime AddressFamily Rib-
group Refresh>
  Address families configured: inet-unicast l2vpn
  Local Address: 192.168.24.1 Holdtime: 90 Preference: 170
  Number of flaps: 0
  Peer ID: 192.168.16.1   Local ID: 192.168.24.1   Active
Holdtime: 90
  Keepalive Interval: 30
  NLRI advertised by peer: inet-unicast inet-multicast l2vpn
  NLRI for this session: inet-unicast l2vpn
  Peer supports Refresh capability (2)
  Table inet.0 Bit: 10000
    Send state: in sync
    Active prefixes: 0
    Received prefixes: 0
    Suppressed due to damping: 0
  Table bgp.l2vpn.0 Bit: 30000
    Send state: in sync
    Active prefixes: 1
    Received prefixes: 1
    Suppressed due to damping: 0
  Table vpna.l2vpn.0 Bit: 50000
    Send state: in sync
    Active prefixes: 1
    Received prefixes: 1
</pre></td></tr>
</table>

Table 13.24 *Layer 2 VPNs Monitoring Commands*

Information to Monitor	Command	Example

BGP summary information	`show bgp summary`	`user@host>` **`show bgp summary`**
		`Groups: 1 Peers: 5 Down peers: 0`
		`Table          Tot Paths  Act Paths Suppressed    History Damp`
		`State`
		`Pending`
		`bgp.l2vpn.0            1          1          0          0`
		`0          0`
		`inet.0                 0          0          0          0`
		`0          0`
		`Peer                AS      InPkt     OutPkt    OutQ   Flaps Last`
		`Up/Dwn`
		`State|#Active/Received/Damped...`
		`10.255.245.35   65299         72         74       0       1`
		`19:00`
		`Establ`
		`  bgp.l2vpn.0: 1/1/0`
		`  frame-vpn.l2vpn.0: 1/1/0`
		`10.255.245.36   65299       2164       2423       0       4`
		`19:50`
		`Establ`
		`  bgp.l2vpn.0: 0/0/0`
		`  frame-vpn.l2vpn.0: 0/0/0`
		`...`

General interface information	`show interfaces terse`	`user@host>` **`run show interfaces terse |match so`**
		`so-0/0/0       up    up`
		`so-0/0/0.1     up    down inet  10.1.13.2/30`
		`                          iso`
		`so-0/0/0.2     up    down inet  10.1.23.2/30`
		`                          iso`
		`so-0/0/0.4     up    down inet  10.1.34.1/30`
		`                          iso`
		`so-0/0/0.5     up    up   inet  10.1.35.1/30`
		`                          iso`
		`...`

Table 13.24 *Layer 2 VPNs Monitoring Commands*

Information to Monitor	Command	Example

Layer 2 virtual circuit information	`show l2circuit connections`	user@host> **show l2circuit connections brief**
		Layer-2 Circuit Connections:
		
		Legend for connection status (St) Legend for interface status
		EI -- encapsulation invalid UP -- operational
		EM -- encapsulation mismatch Dn -- down
		OL -- no outgoing label NP -- no present
		Dn -- down DS -- disabled
		VC-Dn -- Virtual circuit Down WE -- wrong encapsulation
		UP -- operational UN -- uninitialized
		XX -- unknown
		
		Neighbor: 10.1.1.195
		    Interface Type St Time last up
		# Up trans
		  so-0/1/0.1 (vc 1) rmt Up Oct 8 15:44:19 2001
		1
		  so-0/1/0.2 (vc 2) rmt Up Oct 8 15:44:19 2001
		1

Layer 2 VPN information	`show l2vpn connections`	user@host> **show l2vpn connections**
		L2VPN Connections :
		Instance : vpna
		Local site: 2 (ce-2)
		offset: 1, range: 3, label-base: 32768
		    connection-site Type St Time last up #
		Up trans
		  3 (3) loc Up Jul 18 20:45:46 2001
		1
		    Local circuit: fe-0/0/0.1, Status: Up
		    Remote circuit: fe-0/0/3.0, Status: Up
		  1 rmt Up Jul 18 21:47:25 2001
		1
		    Local circuit: fe-0/0/0.0, Status: Up
		    Remote PE: 192.168.16.1
		    Incoming label: 32768, Outgoing label: 32769
		...

Table 13.24 *Layer 2 VPNs Monitoring Commands*

Information to Monitor	Command	Example
Routes transmitted by a particular routing protocol	show route advertising-protocol	user@host> **show route advertising-protocol bgp 192.168.24.1 detail** vpn-a.l2vpn.0: 3 destinations, 3 routes (3 active, 0 holddown, 0 hidden) Prefix Nexthop MED Lclpref AS path 192.168.16.1:1:1:1/96 (1 entry, 1 announced) BGP group int type Internal Route Distinguisher: 192.168.16.1:1 Label-base : 32768, range : 3 Nexthop: Self Localpref: 100 AS path: I • Communities: target:65412:100 Layer2-info: encaps:VLAN, control flags:0, mtu: 0
Information about the entries in the kernel's forwarding table	show route forwarding-table	user@host>**show route forwarding-table | find ccc** Routing table:: ccc MPLS: Interface.Label Type RtRef Nexthop Type Index NhRef Netif default perm 0 dscd 3 1 0 user 0 recv 5 2 1 user 0 recv 5 2 32769 user 0 ucst 45 1 fe-0/0/0.534 fe-0/0/0. (CCC) user 0 indr 44 2 10.0.16.2 Push 32768, Push 100004(top)fe-0/0/1.0

Table 13.24 *Layer 2 VPNs Monitoring Commands*

Information to Monitor	Command	Example

Routes received by a particular routing protocol	`show route receive-protocol`	user@host> **show route receive-protocol bgp 10.255.14.171 detail**
		
		inet.0: 68 destinations, 68 routes (67 active, 0 holddown, 1
		hidden)
		Prefix Nexthop MED Lclpref AS path
		
		inet.3: 4 destinations, 4 routes (4 active, 0 holddown, 0 hidden)
		Prefix Nexthop MED Lclpref AS path
		
		iso.0: 1 destinations, 1 routes (1 active, 0 holddown, 0 hidden)
		Prefix Nexthop MED Lclpref AS path
		
		mpls.0: 10 destinations, 10 routes (10 active, 0 holddown, 0
		hidden)
		Prefix Nexthop MED Lclpref AS path
		
		frame-vpn.l2vpn.0: 2 destinations, 2 routes (2 active, 0
		holddown, 0
		hidden)
		Prefix Nexthop MED Lclpref AS path
		10.255.245.35:1:5:1/96 (1 entry, 1 announced)
		     Route Distinguisher: 10.255.245.35:1
		     Label-base : 800000, range : 4, status-vector : 0x0
		     Nexthop: 10.255.245.35
		     Localpref: 100
		     AS path: I
		     Communities: target:65299:100 Layer2-info: encaps:FRAME
		RELAY, control
		flags:
		0, mtu: 0
		
		bgp.l2vpn.0: 1 destinations, 1 routes (1 active, 0 holddown, 0
		hidden)
		...

Table 13.24 *Layer 2 VPNs Monitoring Commands*

<table>
<tr><th>Information to Monitor</th><th>Command</th><th>Example</th></tr>
<tr><td>Routes in a particular routing table</td><td><code>show route table</code></td><td><pre>user@host>show route table vpn-a

vpn-a.l2vpn.0: 3 destinations, 3 routes (3 active, 0 holddown, 0
hidden)
+ = Active Route, - = Last Active, * = Both

192.168.16.1:1:1:1/96
                        *[VPN/7] 05:48:27
                          Discard
192.168.24.1:1:2:1/96
                        *[BGP/170] 00:02:53, localpref 100, from
192.168.24.1
                           AS path: I
                         > to 10.0.16.2 via fe-0/0/1.0, label-
switched-path am
192.168.24.1:1:3:1/96
                        *[BGP/170] 00:02:53, localpref 100, from
192.168.24.1
                           AS path: I
                         > to 10.0.16.2 via fe-0/0/1.0, label-
switched-path am</pre></td></tr>
</table>

Layer 3 VPNs

Table 13.25 *Layer 3 VPNs Monitoring Commands*

Information to Monitor	Command	Example
Entries in the BGP neighbor database	show bgp neighbor	user@host> **show bgp neighbor** Peer: 10.39.1.5+2135 AS 2 Local: 10.39.1.6+179 AS 1 Type: External State: Established Flags: <> Last State: OpenConfirm Last Event: RecvKeepAlive Last Error: None Export: [ospf-to-bgp stat-to-bgp] Options: <Preference LocalAddress HoldTime AddressFamily PeerAS Rib-group Refresh> Address families configured: inet-unicast Local Address: 10.39.1.6 Holdtime: 90 Preference: 170 Number of flaps: 0 Peer ID: 10.255.245.245 Local ID: 10.255.71.14 Active Holdtime: 90 Keepalive Interval: 30 NLRI advertised by peer: inet-unicast NLRI for this session: inet-unicast Peer supports Refresh capability (2) Table VPN-AB.inet.0 Bit: 30000 Send state: in sync Active prefixes: 1 Received prefixes: 1 Suppressed due to damping: 0 Last traffic (seconds): Received 26 Sent 25 Checked 25 Input messages: Total 22 Updates 8 Refreshes 0 Octets 714 Output messages: Total 23 Updates 8 Refreshes 0 Octets 737 Output Queue[2]: 0

Table 13.25 *Layer 3 VPNs Monitoring Commands*

Information to Monitor	Command	Example
BGP summary information	show bgp summary	user@host> **show bgp summary** Groups: 2 Peers: 2 Down peers: 0 Table Tot Paths Act Paths Suppressed History Damp State Pending bgp.l3vpn.0 2 2 0 0 0 0 Peer AS InPkt OutPkt OutQ Flaps Last Up/Dwn State|#Active/Received/Damped... 10.39.1.5 2 21 22 0 0 6:26 Establ VPN-AB.inet.0: 1/1/0 10.255.71.15 1 19 21 0 0 6:17 Establ bgp.l3vpn.0: 2/2/0 VPN-A.inet.0: 1/1/0 VPN-AB.inet.0: 2/2/0 VPN-B.inet.0: 1/1/0 d

Table 13.25 *Layer 3 VPNs Monitoring Commands*

<table>
<tr><th>Information to Monitor</th><th>Command</th><th>Example</th></tr>
<tr><td>Entries in the kernel's forwarding table</td><td><code>show route forwarding-table</code></td><td><pre>
user@host> show route forwarding-table vpn VPN-A
      Routing table:: VPN-A.inet
      Internet:
      Destination   Type RtRef Nexthop   Type Index
NhRef Netif
      default   perm   0   dscd   4
4
      10.39.10.20/30   intf   0 ff.3.0.21   ucst   40
1
      so-0/0/0.0
      10.39.10.21/32   intf   0 10.39.10.21   locl   36
1
      10.255.14.172/32   user   0   ucst   69
2
      so-0/0/0.0
      10.255.14.175/32   user   0   indr   81
3
                                                      Push
100004, Push
      100004(top) so-1/0/0.0
      224.0.0.0/4   perm   2   mdsc   5
3
      224.0.0.1/32   perm   0 224.0.0.1   mcst   1
8
      224.0.0.5/32   user   1 224.0.0.5   mcst   1
8
      255.255.255.255/32 perm   0   bcst   2
3
</pre></td></tr>
</table>

Table 13.25 *Layer 3 VPNs Monitoring Commands*

Information to Monitor	Command	Example
Routes transmitted by a particular routing protocol	`show route advertising-protocol`	user@host> **show route advertising-protocol bgp 10.255.14.171** VPN-A.inet.0: 6 destinations, 6 routes (6 active, 0 holddown, 0 hidden) Prefix Nexthop MED Lclpref AS path 10.255.14.172/32 Self 1 100 I VPN-B.inet.0: 6 destinations, 6 routes (6 active, 0 holddown, 0 hidden) Prefix Nexthop MED Lclpref AS path 10.255.14.181/32 Self 2 100 I
Route entries in the kernel's forwarding table	`show route forwarding-table`	user@host> **show route forwarding-table vpn VPN-A** Routing table:: VPN-A.inet Internet: Destination Type RtRef Nexthop Type Index NhRef Netif default perm 0 dscd 4 4 10.39.10.20/30 intf 0 ff.3.0.21 ucst 40 1 so-0/0/0.0 10.39.10.21/32 intf 0 10.39.10.21 locl 36 1 10.255.14.172/32 user 0 ucst 69 2 so-0/0/0.0 10.255.14.175/32 user 0 indr 81 3 Push 100004, Push 100004(top) so-1/0/0.0 224.0.0.0/4 perm 2 mdsc 5 3 224.0.0.1/32 perm 0 224.0.0.1 mcst 1 8 224.0.0.5/32 user 1 224.0.0.5 mcst 1 8 255.255.255.255/32 perm 0 bcst 2 3

Table 13.25 *Layer 3 VPNs Monitoring Commands*

<table>
<tr><th>Information to Monitor</th><th>Command</th><th>Example</th></tr>
<tr><td>Route instance information</td><td>show route instance</td><td>user@host> show route instance detail
yellow-vpn:
  Type: vrf   State: Active
  Interfaces:
    fe-1/0/3.0
  Route-distinguisher: 69:40
  Vrf-import: [yellow-vpn-import]
  Vrf-export: [yellow-vpn-export]
  Tables:
    yellow-vp.inet.0   : 5 routes (5 active, 0 holddown, 0
hidden)
pink-vpn:
  Type: vrf   State: Active
  Interfaces:
    fe-1/0/1.0
  Route-distinguisher: 69:30
  Vrf-import: [pink-vpn-import]
  Vrf-export: [pink-vpn-export]
  Tables:
    pink-vpn.inet.0   : 4 routes (4 active, 0 holddown, 0
hidden)</td></tr>
</table>

Table 13.25 *Layer 3 VPNs Monitoring Commands*

Information to Monitor	Command	Example

Routes learned by the specified protocol	`show route protocol`	`user@host>` **`show route protocol ospf`**
		`inet.0: 40 destinations, 40 routes (39 active, 0 holddown, 1 hidden)`
		`+ = Active Route, - = Last Active, * = Both`
		
		`10.39.1.4/30       *[OSPF/10] 00:05:18, metric 4`
		`                    > via t3-3/2/0.0`
		`10.39.1.8/30        [OSPF/10] 00:05:18, metric 2`
		`                    > via t3-3/2/0.0`
		`10.255.14.171/32   *[OSPF/10] 00:05:18, metric 4`
		`                    > via t3-3/2/0.0`
		`10.255.14.179/32   *[OSPF/10] 00:05:18, metric 2`
		`                    > via t3-3/2/0.0`
		`224.0.0.5/32       *[OSPF/10] 20:25:55, metric 1`
		
		`VPN-AB.inet.0: 5 destinations, 5 routes (5 active, 0 holddown, 0 hidden)`
		`+ = Active Route, - = Last Active, * = Both`
		
		`10.39.1.16/30       [OSPF/10] 00:05:43, metric 1`
		`                    > via so-0/2/2.0`
		`10.255.14.173/32   *[OSPF/10] 00:05:43, metric 1`
		`                    > via so-0/2/2.0`
		`224.0.0.5/32       *[OSPF/10] 20:26:20, metric 1`

Table 13.25 *Layer 3 VPNs Monitoring Commands*

<table>
<tr><th>Information to Monitor</th><th>Command</th><th>Example</th></tr>
<tr><td>Routes received by a particular routing protocol</td><td>show route receive-protocol</td><td><pre>
user@host> show route receive-protocol bgp 10.255.14.171
      inet.0: 33 destinations, 33 routes (32 active, 0 holddown,
1 hidden)
      Prefix   Nexthop   MED   Lclpref AS
path
      inet.3: 2 destinations, 2 routes (2 active, 0 holddown, 0
hidden)
      Prefix   Nexthop   MED   Lclpref AS
path
      VPN-A.inet.0: 6 destinations, 6 routes (6 active, 0
holddown, 0 hidden)
      Prefix   Nexthop   MED   Lclpref AS
path
      10.255.14.175/32   10.255.14.171   100 2
I
      10.255.14.179/32   10.255.14.171   2   100 I
      VPN-B.inet.0: 6 destinations, 6 routes (6 active, 0
holddown, 0 hidden)
      Prefix   Nexthop   MED   Lclpref AS
path
      10.255.14.175/32   10.255.14.171   100 2
I
      10.255.14.177/32   10.255.14.171   100 I
      iso.0: 1 destinations, 1 routes (1 active, 0 holddown, 0
hidden)
      Prefix   Nexthop   MED   Lclpref AS
path
      mpls.0: 9 destinations, 9 routes (9 active, 0 holddown, 0
hidden)
      Prefix   Nexthop   MED   Lclpref AS
path
      bgp.l3vpn.0: 3 destinations, 3 routes (3 active, 0
holddown, 0 hidden)
      Prefix   Nexthop   MED   Lclpref AS
path
      10.255.14.171:300:10.255.14.177/32
                          10.255.14.171   100 I
      10.255.14.171:100:10.255.14.179/32
                          10.255.14.171   2   100 I
      10.255.14.171:200:10.255.14.175/32
                          10.255.14.171   100 2
</pre></td></tr>
</table>

Table 13.25 *Layer 3 VPNs Monitoring Commands*

Information to Monitor	Command	Example

Routes in a particular routing table	`show route table`	`user@host> show route table bgp.l3vpn.0`
		`bgp.l3vpn.0: 2 destinations, 2 routes (2 active, 0 holddown, 0 hidden)`
		`+ = Active Route, - = Last Active, * = Both`
		`10.255.71.15:100:10.255.71.17/32`
		`*[BGP/170] 00:03:59, MED 1, localpref 100, from 10.255.71.15`
		`AS path: I`
		`> via so-2/1/0.0, Push 100020, Push 100011(top)`
		`10.255.71.15:200:10.255.71.18/32`
		`*[BGP/170] 00:03:59, MED 1, localpref 100, from 10.255.71.15`
		`AS path: I`
		`> via so-2/1/0.0, Push 100021, Push 100011(top)`

IP Security (IPSec)

Table 13.26 *IP Security (IPSec) Monitoring Commands*

Information to Monitor	Command	Example
IKE security association information	show ike security-associations	user@host> **show ike security-associations** Remote Address State Initiator cookie Responder cookie Exchange type 4.4.4.4 Matured 93870456fa000011 723a20713700003e Main
Clear IKE security associations	clear ike security-associations	user@host> **clear ike security-associations** user@host> **show ike security-associations** Remote Address State Initiator cookie Responder cookie Exchange type user@host>
IPSec security association information	show ipsec security-associations	user@host> **show ipsec security-associations detail** Security association: sa-dynamic, Interface family: Up Direction: inbound, SPI: 242379418, State: Installed Mode: tunnel, Type: dynamic Protocol: ESP, Authentication: hmac-md5-96, Encryption: None Soft lifetime: Expires in 22979 seconds Hard lifetime: Expires in 28739 seconds Direction: outbound, SPI: 368592771, State: Installed Mode: tunnel, Type: dynamic Protocol: ESP, Authentication: hmac-md5-96, Encryption: None Soft lifetime: Expires in 22979 seconds Hard lifetime: Expires in 28739 seconds

Table 13.26 *IP Security (IPSec) Monitoring Commands*

Information to Monitor	Command	Example
Clear IPSec security associations	`clear ipsec security-associations`	user@host> **clear ipsec security-associations** user@host> **show ipsec security-associations detail** Security association: sa-dynamic, Interface family: Up Direction: inbound, SPI: 1031597683, State: Installed Mode: tunnel, Type: dynamic Protocol: ESP, Authentication: hmac-md5-96, Encryption: None Soft lifetime: Expires in 23037 seconds Hard lifetime: Expires in 28797 seconds Direction: outbound, SPI: 1618419878, State: Installed Mode: tunnel, Type: dynamic Protocol: ESP, Authentication: hmac-md5-96, Encryption: None Soft lifetime: Expires in 23037 seconds Hard lifetime: Expires in 28797 seconds

CHAPTER

14

Sample JUNOS Configurations

This chapter provides several examples of JUNOS configurations that enable standard functionality, including interfaces, BGP, IS-IS, and Layer 3 VPNs.

ATM Interface Configuration

The following configuration consists of two routers connected through an ATM interface. Each interface has four VPIs, each of which has a maximum of 1,024 VCIs. Twenty logical units are defined on the ATM interface. Each of the logical units has a different VCI defined on it. The encapsulation is defined such that every five logical units have the same encapsulation. The OSPF and IS-IS routing protocols are also configured.

```
interfaces {
  at-1/3/0 {
    mtu 9192;
        atm-options {
            vpi 0 maximum-vcs 1016;
            vpi 1 maximum-vcs 1016;
            vpi 2 maximum-vcs 1016;
            vpi 3 maximum-vcs 1016;
        }
        unit 32 {
            encapsulation atm-cisco-nlpid;
            vci 0.32;
            family inet {
                mtu 9184;
                address 10.1.0.63/32 {
                    destination 10.1.0.64;
                }
            }
        }
        unit 33 {
            encapsulation atm-cisco-nlpid;
            vci 0.33;
            family inet {
                mtu 9184;
                address 10.1.0.65/32 {
                    destination 10.1.0.66;
                }
            }
        }
        unit 34 {
            encapsulation atm-cisco-nlpid;
            vci 0.34;
            family inet {
```

```
            mtu 9184;
            address 10.1.0.67/32 {
                destination 10.1.0.68;
            }
        }
    }
    unit 35 {
        encapsulation atm-cisco-nlpid;
        vci 0.35;
        family inet {
            mtu 9184;
            address 10.1.0.69/32 {
                destination 10.1.0.70;
            }
        }
    }
    unit 36 {
        encapsulation atm-cisco-nlpid;
        vci 0.36;
        family inet {
            mtu 9184;
            address 10.1.0.71/32 {
                destination 10.1.0.72;
            }
        }
    }
    unit 37 {
        encapsulation atm-nlpid;
        vci 1.32;
        family inet {
            mtu 9184;
            address 10.1.8.63/32 {
                destination 10.1.8.64;
            }
        }
    }
    unit 38 {
        encapsulation atm-nlpid;
        vci 1.33;
        family inet {
            mtu 9184;
            address 10.1.8.65/32 {
                destination 10.1.8.66;
            }
        }
    }
    unit 39 {
        encapsulation atm-nlpid;
        vci 1.34;
        family inet {
```

```
            mtu 9184;
            address 10.1.8.67/32 {
                destination 10.1.8.68;
            }
        }
    }
    unit 40 {
        encapsulation atm-nlpid;
        vci 1.35;
        family inet {
            mtu 9184;
            address 10.1.8.69/32 {
                destination 10.1.8.70;
            }
        }
    }
    unit 41 {
        encapsulation atm-nlpid;
        vci 1.36;
        family inet {
            mtu 9184;
            address 10.1.8.71/32 {
                destination 10.1.8.72;
            }
        }
    }
    unit 42 {
        encapsulation atm-snap;
        vci 2.32;
        family inet {
            mtu 9180;
            address 10.1.16.63/32 {
                destination 10.1.16.64;
            }
        }
        family iso;
    }
    unit 43 {
        encapsulation atm-snap;
        vci 2.33;
        family inet {
            mtu 9180;
            address 10.1.16.65/32 {
                destination 10.1.16.66;
            }
        }
        family iso;
    }
    unit 44 {
        encapsulation atm-snap;
```

```
        vci 2.34;
        family inet {
            mtu 9180;
            address 10.1.16.67/32 {
                destination 10.1.16.68;
            }
        }
        family iso;
    }
    unit 45 {
        encapsulation atm-snap;
        vci 2.35;
        family inet {
            mtu 9180;
            address 10.1.16.69/32 {
                destination 10.1.16.70;
            }
        }
        family iso;
    }
    unit 46 {
        encapsulation atm-snap;
        vci 2.36;
        family inet {
            mtu 9180;
            address 10.1.16.71/32 {
                destination 10.1.16.72;
            }
        }
        family iso;
    }
    unit 47 {
        encapsulation atm-vc-mux;
        vci 3.32;
        family inet {
            mtu 9184;
            address 10.1.24.63/32 {
                destination 10.1.24.64;
            }
        }
    }
    unit 48 {
        encapsulation atm-vc-mux;
        vci 3.33;
        family inet {
            mtu 9184;
            address 10.1.24.65/32 {
                destination 10.1.24.66;
            }
        }
```

```
                }
                unit 49 {
                    encapsulation atm-vc-mux;
                    vci 3.34;
                    family inet {
                        mtu 9184;
                        address 10.1.24.67/32 {
                            destination 10.1.24.68;
                        }
                    }
                }
                unit 50 {
                    encapsulation atm-vc-mux;
                    vci 3.35;
                    family inet {
                        mtu 9184;
                        address 10.1.24.69/32 {
                            destination 10.1.24.70;
                        }
                    }
                }
                unit 51 {
                    encapsulation atm-vc-mux;
                    vci 3.36;
                    family inet {
                        mtu 9184;
                        address 10.1.24.71/32 {
                            destination 10.1.24.72;
                        }
                    }
                }
            }
        }
        protocols {
            isis {
                interface lo0 {
                    level 1 metric 10;
                    level 2 metric 20;
                }
                interface at-1/3/0.42 {
                    level 1 metric 10;
                    level 2 metric 20;
                }
                interface at-1/3/0.43 {
                    level 1 metric 10;
                    level 2 metric 20;
                }
                interface at-1/3/0.44 {
                    level 1 metric 10;
                    level 2 metric 20;
```

```
            }
            interface at-1/3/0.45 {
                level 1 metric 10;
                level 2 metric 20;
            }
            interface at-1/3/0.46 {
                level 1 metric 10;
                level 2 metric 20;
            }
        }
        ospf {
            area 0.0.0.0 {
                interface lo0;
                interface at-1/3/0.32;
                interface at-1/3/0.33;
                interface at-1/3/0.34;
                interface at-1/3/0.35;
                interface at-1/3/0.36;
                interface at-1/3/0.37;
                interface at-1/3/0.38;
                interface at-1/3/0.39;
                interface at-1/3/0.40;
                interface at-1/3/0.41;
                interface at-1/3/0.47;
                interface at-1/3/0.48;
                interface at-1/3/0.49;
                interface at-1/3/0.50;
                interface at-1/3/0.51;
            }
        }
    }
```

BGP Configurations

The examples in this section use the topology shown in Figure 14.1.

Figure 14.1 *BGP Configuration Topology*

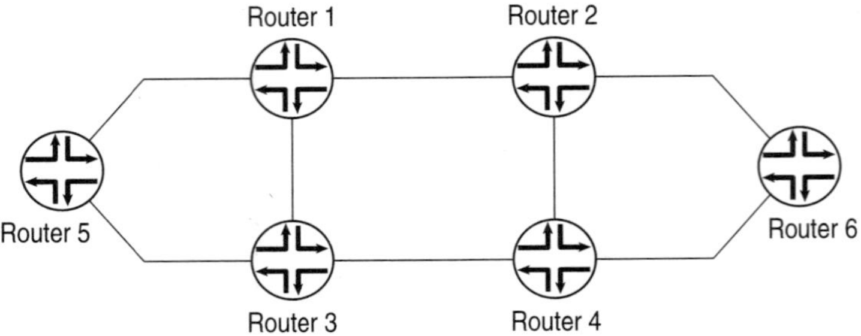

Table 14.1 lists the router loopback addresses. Table 14.2 lists the router interface addresses.

Table 14.1 *BGP Configuration: Router Loopback Addresses*

Router Number	Loopback Address (lo0)
R1	10.1.71.80
R2	10.1.71.82
R3	10.1.71.82
R4	10.1.71.85
R5	10.1.71.81
R6	10.1.71.84

Table 14.2 *BGP Configuration: Router Interface Addresses*

Interface Connects...	Interface Name	Interface IP Address
R1R2	at-1/1/0	192.168.100.25
R2R1	at-1/1/0	192.168.100.26
R1R3	at-1/3/0	192.168.100.65
R3R1	at-0/3/1	192.168.100.66
R3R4	so-1/3/0	192.168.100.89

Table 14.2 *BGP Configuration: Router Interface Addresses*

Interface Connects...	Interface Name	Interface IP Address
R4R3	so-1/2/0	192.168.100.90
R4R2	at-0/3/1	192.168.100.126
R2R4	at-0/3/1	192.168.100.125
R2R6	so-1/0/0	192.168.100.110
R6R2	so-0/3/2	192.168.100.109
R4R6	so-1/0/1	192.168.100.106
R6R4	so-0/3/1	192.168.100.105
R1R5	at-1/3/1	192.168.100.61
R5R1	at-1/0/0	192.168.100.62
R3R5	t3-1/2/0	192.168.100.130
R5R3	t3-0/2/1	192.168.100.129

Basic BGP Configuration

The basic BGP configuration for the six routers in the sample topology is similar. The following sample, for Router 1, shows the snippets of the configuration related to the basic BGP configuration:

```
routing-options {
    router-id 10.1.71.80;
    autonomous-system 69;
}
protocols {
    bgp {
        nlri any;
        group toR2 {
            type internal;
            local-address 10.1.71.80;
            peer-as 69;
            neighbor 10.1.71.83;
        }
        group toR5 {
            type external;
            peer-as 1;
            neighbor 192.168.100.62;
        }
    }
    isis {
```

```
                interface all {
                    level 1 disable;
                    level 2 metric 10;
                }
            }
            ospf {
                area 0.0.0.0 {
                    interface all {
                        metric 10;
                    }
                    interface fxp0.0 {
                        disable;
                    }
                }
            }
        }
```

BGP Routing Policy

The examples in this section use the ASs shown in Figure 14.2. AS 69 uses IS-IS as its IGP. EBGP peering is being configured between Router 5 and Router 1, and IBGP peering between Router 1 and Router 2.

Figure 14.2 *BGP Routing Policy Configuration*

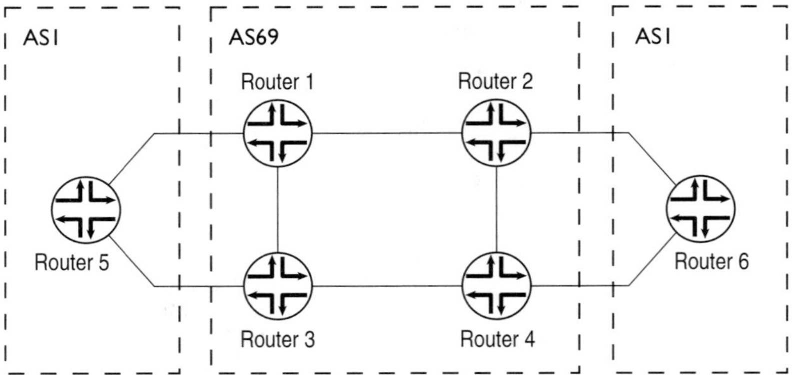

Router 5 Configuration

```
routing-options {
    router-id 10.1.71.81;
    autonomous-system 1;
}
protocols {
    bgp {
        nlri any;
        group toR1 {
            type external;
            export nts;
            peer-as 69;
            neighbor 192.168.100.61;
        }
    }
}
policy-options {
       policy-statement nts {
        from protocol static;
        then {
            metric 50;
            community add ntsR5;
            accept;
        }
    }
    community ntsR5 members 69:1000;
}
```

Router 1 Configuration

```
routing-options {
    router-id 10.1.71.80;
    autonomous-system 69;
}
protocols {
    bgp {
        nlri any;
        group toR2 {
            type internal;
            local-address 10.1.71.80;
            peer-as 69;
            neighbor 10.1.71.83;
        }
        group toR5 {
            type external;
            peer-as 1;
            neighbor 192.168.100.62;
        }
    }
    isis {
```

```
            interface all {
                level 1 disable;
                level 2 metric 10;
            }
        }
    }
```

Router 2 Configuration

```
routing-options {
    router-id 10.1.71.83;
    autonomous-system 69;
}
protocols {
    bgp {
        nlri any;
        group toR1 {
            type internal;
            local-address 10.1.71.83;
            peer-as 69;
            neighbor 10.1.71.80;
        }
    }
    isis {
        interface all {
            level 1 disable;
            level 2 metric 10;
        }
    }
}
```

Route Aggregation

Route aggregation allows routes to be grouped together and announced as a single route to other BGP speakers. Aggregate routes can be used to perform aggregation as well as to modify aggregation related path attributes, such as AGGREGATOR and ATOMIC_AGGREGATE.

The example in this section assumes the topology shown in Figure 14.3.

Figure 14.3 *BGP Route Aggregation Topology*

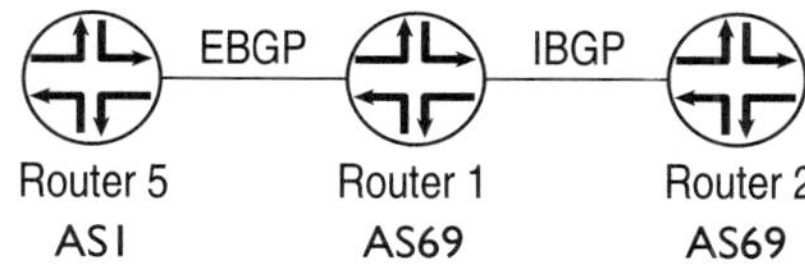

To enable route aggregation, specify the routes to aggregate with the `aggregate` statement and configure a BGP export policy to distribute the aggregate routes:

```
routing-options {
    aggregate {
        route 199.1.0.0/16;
    }
    router-id 10.1.71.80;
    autonomous-system 69;
}
protocols {
    bgp {
        nlri any;
        export redistribute-aggregate;
        group toR2 {
            type internal;
            local-address 10.1.71.80;
            peer-as 69;
            neighbor 10.1.71.83;
        }
        group toR5 {
            type external;
            peer-as 1;
            neighbor 192.168.100.62;
        }
    }
}
policy-options {
    policy-statement redistribute-aggregate {
        from protocol aggregate;
        then accept;
    }
}
```

Controlling Peering

The example in this section assumes the topology shown in Figure 14.4. The routers within AS 69—Router 1, Router 2, Router 3, and Router 4—are fully meshed. The interfaces on all these routers are configured with the same IGP metric.

Figure 14.4 *BGP Peering Topology*

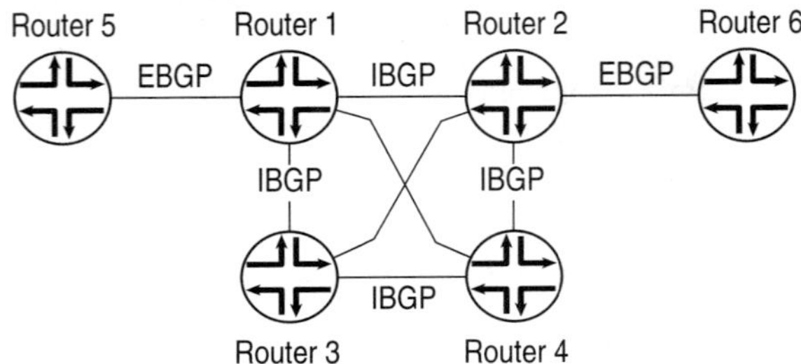

Router 1 Configuration

```
routing-options {
    router-id 10.1.71.80;
    autonomous-system 69;
}
protocols {
    bgp {
        keep all;
        nlri any;
        group int {
            type internal;
            local-address 10.1.71.80;
            peer-as 69;
            neighbor 10.1.71.77;
            neighbor 10.1.71.81;
            neighbor 10.1.71.78;
        }
        group extR5 {
            type external;
            peer-as 1;
            neighbor 192.168.100.66;
        }
    }
    isis {
        export redist-direct;
        interface all {
```

```
                level 1 disable;
                level 2 metric 10;
            }
            interface fxp0.0 {
                disable;
            }
        }
}
policy-options {
    policy-statement redist-direct {
        from protocol direct;
        then accept;
    }
}
```

Router 2 Configuration

```
routing-options {
    router-id 10.1.71.83;
    autonomous-system 1;
}
protocols {
    bgp {
        nlri any;
        group internal {
            type internal;
            local-address 10.1.71.83;
            peer-as 1;
            neighbor 10.1.71.80;
            neighbor 10.1.71.82;
            neighbor 10.1.71.85;
        }
        group toR6 {
            type external;
            peer-as 3356;
            neighbor 192.168.100.109;
        }
    }
    isis {
        interface all {
            level 1 disable;
            level 2 metric 10;
        }
    }
}
```

Router 3 Configuration

```
routing-options {
    router-id 10.1.71.82;
    autonomous-system 69;
}
protocols {
    bgp {
        group extR1 {
            type external;
            export redist-static;
            peer-as 69;
            neighbor 192.168.100.65;
        }
    }
    isis {
        interface all {
            level 1 disable;
            level 2 metric 10;
        }
    }
}
```

Router 4 Configuration

```
routing-options {
    router-id 10.1.71.85;
    autonomous-system 69;
}
protocols {
    bgp {
        nlri any;
        group internal {
            type internal;
            local-address 10.1.71.85;
            peer-as 1;
            neighbor 10.1.71.80;
            neighbor 10.1.71.83;
            neighbor 10.1.71.82;
        }
    }
    isis {
        interface all {
            level 1 disable;
            level 2 metric 10;
        }
    }
}
```

Router 5 Configuration

```
routing-options {
    router-id 10.1.71.81;
    autonomous-system 1;
}
protocols {
    bgp {
        keep all;
        nlri any;
        group int {
            type internal;
            local-address 10.1.71.81;
            peer-as 69;
            neighbor 10.1.71.80;
            neighbor 10.1.71.77;
            neighbor 10.1.71.78;
        }
    }
    isis {
        export redist-direct;
        interface all {
            level 1 disable;
            level 2 metric 10;
        }
        interface fxp0.0 {
            disable;
        }
    }
}
policy-options {
    policy-statement redist-direct {
        from protocol direct;
        then accept;
    }
}
```

Router 6 Configuration

```
routing-options {
    router-id 10.1.71.84;
    autonomous-system 3356;
}
protocols {
    bgp {
        nlri any;
        group toR2 {
            type external;
            export redist-static;
```

```
                peer-as 1;
                neighbor 192.168.100.110;
            }
        }
    }
    policy-options {
        policy-statement redist-static {
            from protocol static;
            then accept;
        }
    }
```

Route Flap Damping

The example in this section assumes the topology shown in Figure 14.5. The routers within AS 69—Router 1, Router 2, Router 3, and Router 4—are fully meshed. The interfaces on all these routers are configured with the same IGP metric.

Figure 14.5 *BGP Route Flap Damping Topology*

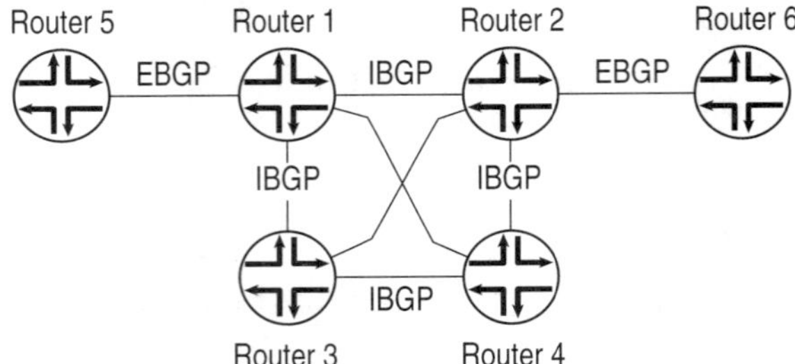

To configure route-flap damping on R1, include the `damping` statement when configuring BGP:

```
protocols {
    bgp {
        damping;
        nlri any;
        group internal {
            type internal;
            local-address 10.1.71.80;
            peer-as 1;
            neighbor 10.1.71.83;
            neighbor 10.1.71.82;
            neighbor 10.1.71.85;
        }
    }
}
```

Route Reflectors

The example in this section assumes the topology shown in Figure 14.6.

Figure 14.6 *BGP Route Reflector Topology*

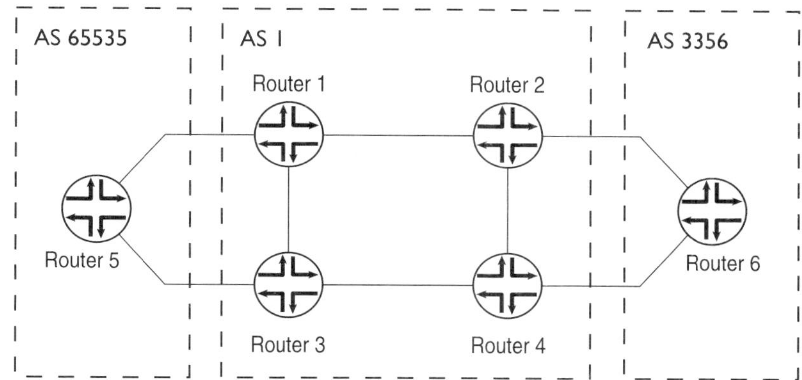

Single Route Reflector

In this example, Router 1 is the route reflector, and Router 3 and Router 4 are clients of Router 1, as shown in Figure 14.7.

Figure 14.7 *BGP Single Route Reflector Topology*

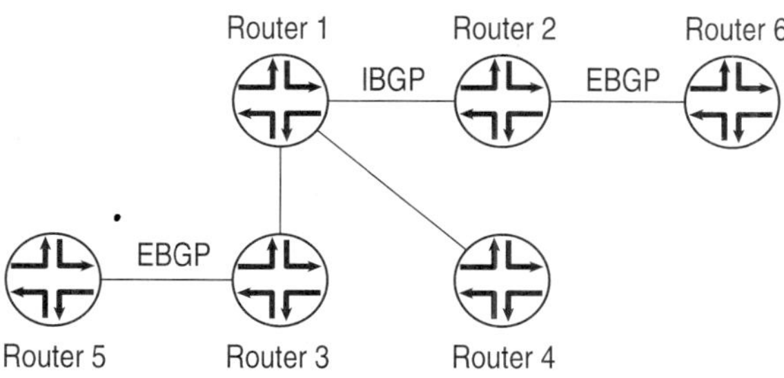

Router 1 Configuration

```
routing-options {
    autonomous-system 1;
}
protocols {
```

```
        bgp {
            local-address 10.1.71.80;
            group toR3R4 {
                type internal;
                cluster 1.2.3.4;
                peer-as 1;
                neighbor 10.1.71.85;
                neighbor 10.1.71.82;
            }
            group toR2 {
                type internal;
                peer-as 1;
                neighbor 10.1.71.83;
            }
        }
        isis {
            interface all {
                level 1 disable;
                level 2 metric 10;
            }
        }
    }
```

Router 3 Configuration

```
routing-options {
    autonomous-system 1;
}
protocols {
    bgp {
        group toR1 {
            type internal;
            local-address 10.1.71.82;
            peer-as 1;
            neighbor 10.1.71.80;
        }
        group toR5 {
            type external;
            peer-as 65535;
            neighbor 192.168.100.129;
        }
    }
    isis {
        interface all {
            level 1 disable;
            level 2 metric 10;
        }
    }
}
```

Router 4 Configuration

```
routing-options {
    autonomous-system 1;
}
protocols {
    bgp {
        group toR1 {
            type internal;
            local-address 10.1.71.85;
            peer-as 1;
            neighbor 10.1.71.80;
        }
    }
    isis {
        interface all {
            level 1 disable;
            level 2 metric 10;
        }
    }
}
```

Router 2 Configuration

```
routing-options {
    autonomous-system 1;
}
protocols {
    bgp {
        group toR1 {
            type internal;
            local-address 10.1.71.83;
            advertise-inactive;
            peer-as 1;
            neighbor 10.1.71.80;
        }
        group toR6 {
            type external;
            peer-as 3356;
            neighbor 192.168.100.109;
        }
    }
    isis {
        interface all {
            level 1 disable;
            level 2 metric 10;
        }
    }
}
```

Router 5 Configuration

```
routing-options {
    autonomous-system 65535;
}
protocols {
    bgp {
        group toR3 {
            type external;
            export redist-static;
            peer-as 1;
            neighbor 192.168.100.130;
        }
    }
}
policy-options {
    policy-statement redist-static {
        from protocol static;
        then accept;
    }
}
```

Router 6 Configuration

```
routing-options {
    autonomous-system 3356;
}
protocols {
    bgp {
        export redist-static;
        group toR2 {
            type external;
            export redist-static;
            peer-as 1;
            neighbor 192.168.100.110;
        }
    }
}
```

Router Reflection Cluster

In this configuration, Router 1 and Router 2 are route reflectors with a cluster ID of `1.2.3.4`. Router 1 is a client of Router 1, Router 3 is a client of Router 1, and Router 4 is a regular IBGP neighbor of Router 2 (see Figure 14.8).

Figure 14.8 *BGP Route Reflection Cluster Topology*

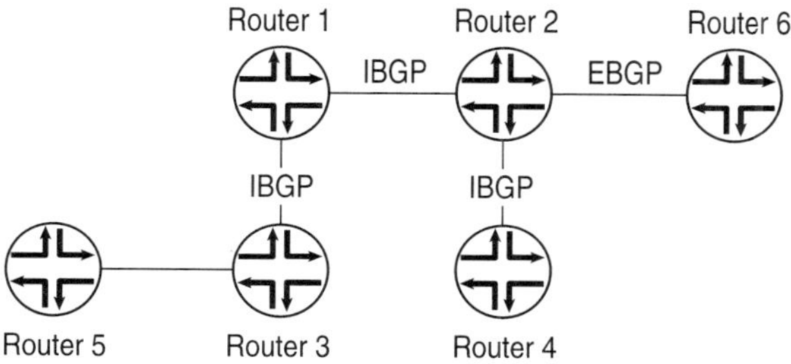

Router 1 Configuration

```
routing-options {
    autonomous-system 1;
}
protocols {
    bgp {
        local-address 10.1.71.80;
        keep all;
        nlri any;
        group toR2 {
            type internal;
            peer-as 1;
            neighbor 10.1.71.83;
        }
        group toR3 {
            type internal;
            cluster 1.2.3.4;
            peer-as 1;
            neighbor 10.1.71.82;
        }
    }
    isis {
        interface all {
            level 1 disable;
            level 2 metric 10;
        }
    }
}
```

Router 2 Configuration

```
routing-options {
    autonomous-system 1;
}
protocols {
    bgp {
        nlri any;
        group toR6 {
            type external;
            peer-as 3356;
            neighbor 192.168.100.109;
        }
        group toR1 {
            type internal;
            local-address 10.1.71.83;
            keep all;
            cluster 1.2.3.4;
            peer-as 1;
            neighbor 10.1.71.80;
        }
        group toR4 {
            type internal;
            local-address 10.1.71.83;
            peer-as 1;
            neighbor 10.1.71.85;
        }
    }
    isis {
        interface all {
            level 1 disable;
            level 2 metric 10;
        }
    }
}
```

Router 3 Configuration

```
routing-options {
    autonomous-system 1;
}
protocols {
    bgp {
        nlri any;
        group toR1 {
            type internal;
            local-address 10.1.71.82;
            peer-as 1;
            neighbor 10.1.71.80;
```

```
            }
            group toR5 {
                type external;
                peer-as 65535;
                neighbor 192.168.100.129;
            }
        }
        isis {
            interface all {
                level 1 disable;
                level 2 metric 10;
            }
        }
    }
```

Router 4 Configuration

```
routing-options {
    autonomous-system 1;
}
protocols {
    bgp {
        nlri any;
        export redist-static;
        group toR2 {
            type internal;
            local-address 10.1.71.85;
            peer-as 1;
            neighbor 10.1.71.83;
        }
    }
    isis {
        interface all {
            level 1 disable;
            level 2 metric 10;
        }
    }
}
policy-options {
    policy-statement redist-static {
        from protocol static;
        then accept;
    }
}
```

Router 5 Configuration

```
routing-options {
    autonomous-system 65535;
}
protocols {
    bgp {
        nlri any;
        group toR3 {
            type external;
            export redist-static;
            peer-as 1;
            neighbor 192.168.100.130;
        }
        group r {
            peer-as 70;
            neighbor 192.168.5.48 {
                multihop;
            }
        }
    }
    isis {
        disable;
        interface all {
            level 1 disable;
            level 2 metric 10;
        }
    }
}
policy-options {
    policy-statement redist-static {
        from protocol static;
        then accept;
    }
}
```

Router 6 Configuration

```
routing-options {
    autonomous-system 3356;
}
protocols {
    bgp {
        nlri any;
        export redist-static;
        group toR2 {
            type external;
            export redist-static;
            peer-as 1;
```

```
                neighbor 192.168.100.110;
            }
            group r {
                peer-as 10458;
                neighbor 208.197.169.14 {
                    multihop;
                }
            }
        }
    }
    policy-options {
        policy-statement redist-static {
            from protocol static;
            then accept;
        }
    }
```

Hierarchical Route Reflection

In this configuration, Router 2 and Router 4 are the route reflectors. Router 4 in cluster 1 is a client of Router 2, and Router 3 in cluster 2 is a client of Router 4 (see Figure 14.9).

Figure 14.9 *BGP Hierarchical Route Reflection Topology*

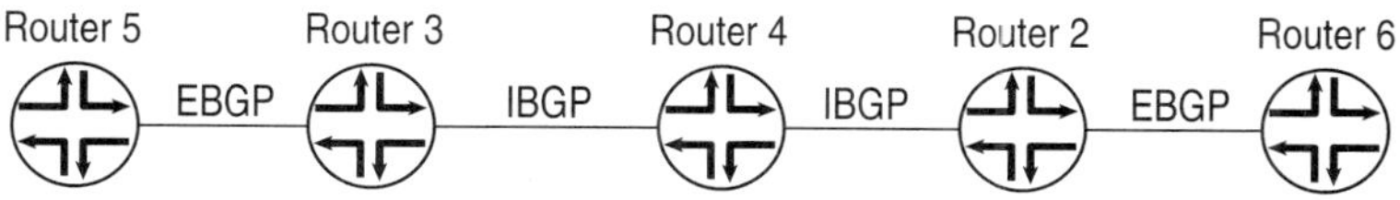

Router 2 Configuration

```
routing-options {
    autonomous-system 1;
}
protocols {
    bgp {
        nlri any;
        group toR6 {
            type external;
            peer-as 3356;
            neighbor 192.168.100.109;
        }
        group toR4 {
            type internal;
            local-address 10.1.71.83;
            cluster 1.2.3.4;
            peer-as 1;
```

```
                neighbor 10.1.71.85;
            }
        }
        isis {
            interface all {
                level 1 disable;
                level 2 metric 10;
            }
        }
    }
```

Router 4 Configuration

```
routing-options {
    autonomous-system 1;
}
protocols {
    bgp {
        local-address 10.1.71.85;
        nlri any;
        group toR3 {
            type internal;
            local-address 10.1.71.85;
            cluster 5.6.7.8;
            peer-as 1;
            neighbor 10.1.71.82;
        }
        group toR2 {
            type internal;
            local-address 10.1.71.85;
            peer-as 1;
            neighbor 10.1.71.83;
        }
    }
    isis {
        interface all {
            level 1 disable;
            level 2 metric 10;
        }
    }
}
```

Router 3 Configuration

```
routing-options {
    autonomous-system 1;
}
protocols {
```

```
        bgp {
            nlri any;
            group toR4 {
                type internal;
                local-address 10.1.71.82;
                peer-as 1;
                neighbor 10.1.71.85;
            }
            group toR5 {
                type external;
                peer-as 65535;
                neighbor 192.168.100.129;
            }
        }
        isis {
            interface all {
                level 1 disable;
                level 2 metric 10;
            }
        }
    }
```

Routing Loop Protection

This configuration uses clusters to provide protection from routing loops (see Figure 14.10). In this configuration, Router 1, Router 2, and Router 3 are the route reflectors. Router 4 is a client of Router 3 and has a cluster ID of `1.0.0.1`. Router 3 is a client of Router 1 and Router 2 and has a cluster ID of 1.0.0.2. IGP metrics are selected such that Router 2 prefers routes from Router 1 over Router 3.

Figure 14.10 *BGP Routing Loop Protection Topology*

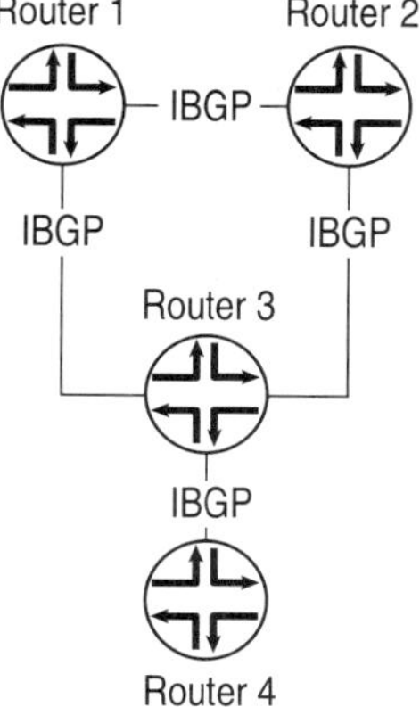

Router 1 Configuration

```
routing-options {
    autonomous-system 1;
}
protocols {
    bgp {
        local-address 10.1.71.80;
        nlri any;
        group toR3 {
            type internal;
            cluster 1.0.0.2;
            peer-as 1;
            neighbor 10.1.71.82;
        }
        group toR2 {
            type internal;
            peer-as 1;
            neighbor 10.1.71.83;
        }
    }
    isis {
        interface all {
            level 1 disable;
            level 2 metric 10;
        }
    }
}
```

Router 2 Configuration

```
routing-options {
    autonomous-system 1;
}
protocols {
    bgp {
        keep all;
        nlri any;
        group toR3 {
            type internal;
            local-address 10.1.71.83;
            cluster 1.0.0.2;
            peer-as 1;
            neighbor 10.1.71.82;
        }
        group toR1 {
            type internal;
            local-address 10.1.71.83;
            peer-as 1;
```

```
                neighbor 10.1.71.80;
            }
        }
        isis {
            interface all {
                level 1 disable;
                level 2 metric 10;
            }
        }
    }
```

Router 3 Configuration

```
routing-options {
    autonomous-system 1;
}
protocols {
    bgp {
        nlri any;
        group toR1R2 {
            type internal;
            local-address 10.1.71.82;
            peer-as 1;
            neighbor 10.1.71.83;
            neighbor 10.1.71.80;
        }
        group toR4 {
            type internal;
            local-address 10.1.71.82;
            cluster 1.0.0.1;
            peer-as 1;
            neighbor 10.1.71.85;
        }
    }
    isis {
        interface all {
            level 1 disable;
            level 2 metric 10;
        }
    }
}
```

Router 4 Configuration

```
routing-options {
    autonomous-system 1;
}
protocols {
    bgp {
        nlri any;
        export redist-static;
        group toR3 {
            type internal;
            local-address 10.1.71.85;
            peer-as 1;
            neighbor 10.1.71.82;
        }
    }
    isis {
        interface all {
            level 1 disable;
            level 2 metric 10;
        }
    }
}
```

Confederations

This example shows a router confederation between Router 1 and Router 2 (see Figure 14.11).

Figure 14.11 *BGP Confederation Topology*

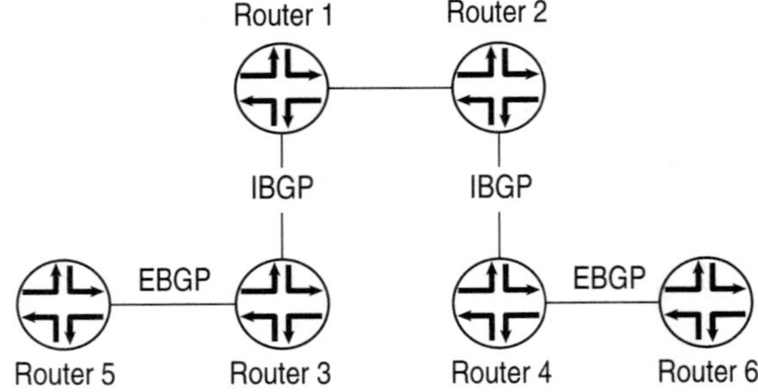

Router 1 Configuration

```
routing-options {
    router-id 10.1.71.80;
    autonomous-system 65000;
    confederation 32 members [ 65000 65001 ];
}
protocols {
    bgp {
        multihop {
            ttl 6;
        }
        keep all;
        nlri any;
        group extR2 {
            type external;
            local-address 10.1.71.80;
            peer-as 65001;
            neighbor 10.1.71.83;
        }
        group int {
            type internal;
            local-address 10.1.71.80;
            neighbor 10.1.71.82;
        }
    }
    isis {
        export redist-direct;
        interface all {
            level 1 disable;
            level 2 metric 10;
        }
        interface fxp0.0 {
            disable;
        }
    }
}
policy-options {
    policy-statement redist-direct {
        from protocol direct;
        then accept;
    }
}
```

Router 2 Configuration

```
routing-options {
    router-id 10.1.71.83;
    autonomous-system 65001;
    confederation 32 members [ 65000 65001 ];
}
protocols {
    bgp {
        multihop {
            ttl 6;
        }
        keep all;
        nlri any;
        group extR1 {
            type external;
            local-address 10.1.71.83;
            peer-as 65000;
            neighbor 10.1.71.80;
        }
        group int {
            type internal;
            local-address 10.1.71.83;
            neighbor 10.1.71.85;
        }
    }
    isis {
        export redist-direct;
        interface all {
            level 1 disable;
            level 2 metric 10;
        }
        interface fxp0.0 {
            disable;
        }
    }
}
policy-options {
    policy-statement redist-direct {
        from protocol direct;
        then accept;
    }
}
```

Router 3 Configuration

```
routing-options {
    router-id 10.1.71.82;
    autonomous-system 65000;
    confederation 32 members [ 65000 65001 ];
}
protocols {
    bgp {
        keep all;
        nlri any;
        group extR5 {
            type external;
            local-address 192.168.100.130;
            peer-as 65535;
            neighbor 192.168.100.129;
        }
        group int {
            type internal;
            multihop {
                ttl 6;
            }
            local-address 10.1.71.82;
            neighbor 10.1.71.80;
        }
    }
    isis {
        export redist-direct;
        interface all {
            level 1 disable;
            level 2 metric 10;
        }
        interface fxp0.0 {
            disable;
        }
    }
}
policy-options {
    policy-statement redist-direct {
        from protocol direct;
        then accept;
    }
}
```

Router 4 Configuration

```
routing-options {
    router-id 10.1.71.85;
    autonomous-system 65001;
    confederation 32 members [ 65000 65001 ];
}
protocols {
    bgp {
        keep all;
        nlri any;
        group extR6 {
            type external;
            local-address 192.168.100.106;
            peer-as 37;
            neighbor 192.168.100.105;
        }
        group int {
            type internal;
            multihop {
                ttl 6;
            }
            local-address 10.1.71.85;
            neighbor 10.1.71.83;
        }
    }
    isis {
        export redist-direct;
        interface all {
            level 1 disable;
            level 2 metric 10;
        }
        interface fxp0.0 {
            disable;
        }
    }
}
policy-options {
    policy-statement redist-direct {
        from protocol direct;
        then accept;
    }
}
```

Router 5 Configuration

```
routing-options {
    router-id 10.1.71.81;
    autonomous-system 65535;
}
protocols {
    bgp {
        group extR3 {
            type external;
            local-address 192.168.100.129;
            export redist-static;
            peer-as 32;
            neighbor 192.168.100.130;
        }
    }
}
policy-options {
    policy-statement redist-direct {
        from protocol direct;
        then accept;
    }
}
```

Router 6 Configuration

```
routing-options {
    router-id 10.1.71.84;
    autonomous-system 37;
}
protocols {
    bgp {
        keep all;
        group extR4 {
            type external;
            local-address 192.168.100.105;
            export redist-static;
            peer-as 32;
            neighbor 192.168.100.106;
        }
    }
}
policy-options {
    policy-statement redist-direct {
        from protocol direct;
        then accept;
    }
}
```

IS-IS Configurations

The examples in this section configure an IS-IS connection between two routers.

Basic Configuration

In this basic configuration, you set up an adjacency between two routers, set the metric for the link, and set up the IS to be a level 1 or level 2 system.

You must configure the interface, here, `so-1/0/0`, to be under `family iso`, and you must configure the ISO address on the loopback interface, `lo0`. In the protocols configuration, you specify the protocols as `isis` and include the interfaces you want. Disable `fxp0` so that no IS-IS packets are sent over it. Configure the level under the interface. An interface can belong to level 1 or level 2 or in both; here, the interface is in both levels. To configure the metric of the link, include the metric keyword, specifying the cost of using that link.

```
interfaces {
    so-1/0/0 {
        unit 0 {
            family inet {
                address 10.10.10.5/30;
            }
            family iso;
        }
    }
    fxp0 {
        unit 0 {
            family inet {
                address 192.168.5.239/24;
            }
        }
    }
    lo0 {
        unit 0 {
            family inet {
                address 127.0.0.1/32;
                address 10.255.245.239/32;
            }
            family iso {
                address
47.0005.80ff.f800.0000.0108.0001.0102.5524.5239.00;
            }
        }
```

```
    }
}

protocols {
    isis {
        interface so-1/0/0.0 {
            level 1 metric 10;
            level 2 metric 20;
        }
        interface fxp0.0 {
            disable;
        }
        interface lo0.0;
    }
}
```

To check whether the adjacencies actually are formed, use the `show isis adjacency` CLI command.

Export Static Routes

To export some static routes, you configure a routing policy. First, include some static routes in the configuration by configuring the routing options with the static route, specifying the next hop to use:

```
routing-options {
    static {
        /* corporate and alpha net */
        route 172.16.0.0/12 {
            next-hop 192.168.5.254;
            retain;
            no-readvertise;
        }
        /* old lab nets */
        route 192.168.0.0/18 {
            next-hop 192.168.5.254;
            retain;
            no-readvertise;
        }
        route 10.255.245.35/32 {
            discard;
            retain;
        }
    }
    router-id 10.255.245.236;
    autonomous-system 69;
}
```

Then configure a policy that accepts these static routes. Here, we have defined a policy named `redist-static` which accepts static routes by specifying the protocol to be static. We could in turn make the protocol to be EBGP or an IGP.

```
policy-options {
    policy-statement redist-static {
        from protocol static;
        then accept;
    }
}
```

Finally, export these routes through IS-IS by including this policy in the IS-IS configuration. Here, we are exporting the policy `redist-static` under `isis`, which in turn means export all static routes that you learned into IS-IS.

```
protocols {
    isis {
        export redist-static;
        interface so-0/2/3.0 {
            level 1 metric 10;
            level 2 metric 20;
        }
        interface fxp0.0 {
            disable;
        }
        interface lo0.0;
    }
}
```

Simple Authentication

Simple authentication allows two ISs to perform system-level authentication using a nonencrypted alphanumeric password (key). To configure this, include the `authentication-type` statement, specifying the `simple` option. Then set the authentication key with the `authentication-key` statement.

```
protocols {
    isis {
        export redist-static;
        authentication-key "$9$4QZiq36A01E9ABRSy8LDjH"; #
SECRET-DATA
        authentication-type simple; # SECRET-DATA
        interface so-0/2/3.0 {
```

```
                level 1 metric 10;
                level 2 metric 20;
            }
            interface fxp0.0 {
                disable;
            }
            interface lo0.0;
        }
    }
```

Interface-Level Hello Authentication

Interface-level hello authentication verifies the hello messages exchanged across interfaces. You configure this by adding the `hello-authentication-key` statement to the IS-IS authentication configuration:

```
protocols {
    isis {
        export redist-static;
        authentication-key "$9$4QZiq36A01E9ABRSy8LDjH"; #
SECRET-DATA
        authentication-type simple; # SECRET-DATA
        interface so-0/2/3.0 {
            hello-authentication-key
"$9$LdGNwgikPQ39mf39puhcs24"; # SECRET-DATA
            hello-authentication-type simple; # SECRET-DATA
            level 1 metric 10;
            level 2 metric 20;
        }
        interface fxp0.0 {
            disable;
        }
        interface lo0.0;
    }
}
```

Passive Interfaces

A passive interface is one that cannot be used for sending and receiving IS-IS packets. Here, interface `so-1/0/0` has been made passive. The `show isis interface` command shows this interface as passive.

```
protocols {
    isis {
        export redist-static;
        authentication-key "$9$vGHL-bZUHm5zjHfQn6007Nd"; #
```

```
SECRET-DATA
        authentication-type simple; # SECRET-DATA
        no-authentication-check;
        interface so-1/0/0.0 {
            hello-authentication-key
"$9$0zzSISeNds4JDwYJDkqzFylK"; # SECRET-DATA
            hello-authentication-type simple; # SECRET-DATA
            level 1 {
                metric 10;
                hello-authentication-key
"$9$4wZiq36CuBRVwoZjiPfREc"; # SECRET-DATA
                hello-authentication-type simple; # SECRET-
DATA
                passive;
            }
            level 2 metric 8;
        }
        interface fxp0.0 {
            disable;
        }
        interface lo0.0;
    }
}
```

Layer 3 VPN Configurations

These configurations illustrate a typical Layer 3 VPN scenario. Router 4, Router 8, and Router 9 belong to one VPN site named blue. Router 5, Router 6, and Router 7 belong to another VPN site named green. The PE-CE protocols could be BGP, static route (with the next hop configured toward the attached PE), or an IGP such as OSPF or RIP. The PE-PE connections are running MBGP. Labelled VPN routes are exchanged over the MBGP sessions that terminate on the PE routers.

The topology shown in Figure 14.12 is used in these configurations.

Figure 14.12 *Layer 3 VPN Topology*

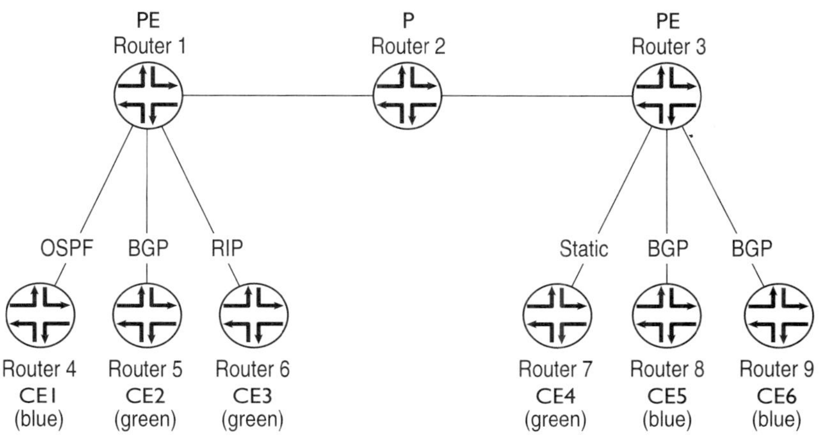

Router 1 Configuration

```
interfaces {
    fe-0/0/0 {
        description "to Router 1 fe-0/0/2";
        unit 0 {
            family inet {
                address 192.168.210.38/30;
            }
            family iso;
            family mpls;
        }
    }
    ge-0/2/0 {
        unit 0 {
            family inet {
                address 192.167.188.1/30;
            }
            family mpls;
        }
    }
    t1-0/3/0 {
        unit 0 {
            family inet {
                address 192.167.188.13/30;
            }
            family mpls;
        }
    }
```

```
        t1-0/3/1 {
            description "to Router 6 t1-0/2/1";
            unit 0 {
                family inet {
                    address 192.168.210.57/30;
                }
                family iso;
                family mpls;
            }
        }
    }
    routing-options {
        router-id 10.255.71.54;
        autonomous-system 69;
    }
    protocols {
        rsvp {
            interface all;
        }
        mpls {
            label-switched-path to_Router 3 {
                to 10.255.71.61;
            }
            interface ge-0/2/0.0;
            interface at-1/3/1.0;
            interface at-1/3/0.0;
            interface t1-0/3/0.0;
        }
        bgp {
            group from_Router 1_to_Router 3 {
                type internal;
                local-address 10.255.71.54;
                family inet {
                    any;
                }
                family inet-vpn {
                    any;
                }
                neighbor 10.255.71.61;
            }
        }
        ospf {
            traffic-engineering;
            area 0.0.0.0 {
                interface ge-0/2/0.0;
                interface lo0.0 {
                    passive;
                }
            }
        }
```

```
}
policy-options {
    policy-statement green-import {
        term a {
            from {
                protocol bgp;
                community green-comm;
            }
            then accept;
        }
        term b {
            then reject;
        }
    }
    policy-statement blue-import {
        term a {
            from {
                protocol bgp;
                community blue-comm;
            }
            then accept;
        }
        term b {
            then reject;
        }
    }
    policy-statement green-export {
        term a {
            from protocol [ bgp rip ];
            then {
                community add green-comm;
                accept;
            }
        }
        term b {
            then reject;
        }
    }
    policy-statement blue-export {
        term a {
            from protocol ospf;
            then {
                community add blue-comm;
                accept;
            }
        }
        term b {
            then reject;
        }
    }
```

```
        policy-statement rip-export {
            term a {
                from protocol bgp;
                then accept;
            }
            term b {
                then reject;
            }
        }
        policy-statement bgp-export {
            term a {
                from protocol [ bgp rip ];
                then accept;
            }
            term b {
                then reject;
            }
        }
        community blue-comm members target:69:2;
        community green-comm members target:69:1;
    }
    routing-instances {
        blue {
            instance-type vrf;
            interface at-1/3/1.0;
            route-distinguisher 10.255.71.54:200;
            vrf-import blue-import;
            vrf-export blue-export;
            protocols {
                ospf {
                    export blue-import;
                    area 1.1.1.1 {
                        interface at-1/3/1.0;
                    }
                }
            }
        }
        green {
            instance-type vrf;
            interface at-1/3/0.0;
            interface t1-0/3/0.0;
            route-distinguisher 10.255.71.54:100;
            vrf-import green-import;
            vrf-export green-export;
            protocols {
                bgp {
                    group to_Router5 {
                        type external;
                        export bgp-export;
                        peer-as 1;
```

```
                    neighbor 192.167.188.10;
                }
            }
            rip {
                group to_Router6 {
                    export rip-export;
                    neighbor t1-0/3/0.0;
                }
            }
        }
    }
}
```

Router 2 Configuration

```
interfaces {
    fe-0/0/2 {
        description "to Router 1 fe-0/0/2";
        unit 0 {
            family inet {
                address 192.168.210.37/30;
            }
            family iso;
            family mpls;
        }
    }
    fe-0/0/3 {
        description "to Router 3 fe-0/0/0";
        unit 0 {
            family inet {
                address 192.168.210.41/30;
            }
            family iso;
            family mpls;
        }
    }
}
routing-option {
    router-id 10.255.71.62;
    autonomous-system 69;
}
protocols {
    rsvp {
        interface all;
    }
    mpls {
        interface ge-0/3/0.0;
        interface ge-0/3/1.0;
    }
```

```
        ospf {
            traffic-engineering;
            area 0.0.0.0 {
                interface ge-0/3/0.0;
                interface ge-0/3/1.0;
                interface lo0.0 {
                    passive;
                }
            }
        }
    }
```

Router 3 Configuration

```
    interfaces {
        fe-0/0/0 {
            description "to Router 2 fe-0/0/3";
            unit 0 {
                family inet {
                    address 192.168.210.42/30;
                }
                family iso;
                family mpls;
            }
        }
      ...
    }
    routing-option {
        router-id 10.255.71.61;
        autonomous-system 69;
    }
    protocols {
        rsvp {
            interface all;
        }
        mpls {
            label-switched-path to_Router 1 {
                to 10.255.71.54;
            }
            interface ge-0/2/0.0;
            interface so-1/0/0.0;
            interface at-0/3/1.0;
            interface so-1/0/1.0;
        }
        bgp {
            group from_Router 3_to_Router 1 {
                type internal;
                local-address 10.255.71.61;
                family inet {
```

```
                any;
            }
            family inet-vpn {
                any;
            }
            neighbor 10.255.71.54;
        }
    }
    ospf {
        traffic-engineering;
        area 0.0.0.0 {
            interface ge-0/2/0.0;
            interface lo0.0 {
                passive;
            }
        }
    }
}
policy-options {
    policy-statement green-import {
        term a {
            from {
                protocol bgp;
                community green-comm;
            }
            then accept;
        }
        term b {
            then reject;
        }
    }
    policy-statement blue-import {
        term a {
            from {
                protocol bgp;
                community blue-comm;
            }
            then accept;
        }
        term b {
            then reject;
        }
    }
    policy-statement green-export {
        term a {
            from protocol static;
            then {
                community add green-comm;
                accept;
            }
```

```
            }
            term b {
                then reject;
            }
        }
        policy-statement blue-export {
            term a {
                from protocol bgp;
                then {
                    community add blue-comm;
                    accept;
                }
            }
            term b {
                then reject;
            }
        }
        community blue-comm members target:69:2;
        community green-comm members target:69:1;
    }
    routing-instances {
        blue {
            instance-type vrf;
            interface at-0/3/1.0;
            interface so-1/0/1.0;
            route-distinguisher 10.255.71.61:200;
            vrf-import blue-import;
            vrf-export blue-export;
            protocols {
                bgp {
                    group to_Router8_Router9 {
                        type external;
                        peer-as 1;
                        neighbor 192.167.188.26;
                        neighbor 192.167.188.30;
                    }
                }
            }
        }
        green {
            instance-type vrf;
            interface so-1/0/0.0;
            route-distinguisher 10.255.71.61:100;
            vrf-import green-import;
            vrf-export green-export;
            routing-options {
                static {
                    route 10.255.71.60/32 next-hop 192.167.188.22;
                    route 10.220.1.0/24 next-hop 192.167.188.22;
                }
```

```
        }
    }
}
```

Router 4 Configuration

```
protocols {
    mpls {
        interface at-1/0/0.0;
    }
    ospf {
        export export-vpn;
        area 1.1.1.1 {
            interface at-1/0/0.0;
        }
    }
}
policy-options {
    policy-statement export-vpn {
        term a {
            from {
                protocol direct;
                route-filter 10.255.71.55/32 exact;
            }
            then accept;
        }
        term b {
            from {
                protocol static;
                route-filter 10.220.1.0/24 exact;
            }
            then accept;
        }
        term c {
            then reject;
        }
    }
}
```

Router 5 Configuration

```
protocols {
    bgp {
        group to_Router1 {
            export export-vpn;
            peer-as 69;
            neighbor 192.167.188.9;
        }
```

```
    }
}
policy-options {
    policy-statement export-vpn {
        term a {
            from {
                protocol direct;
                route-filter 10.255.71.56/32 exact;
            }
            then accept;
        }
        term b {
            from {
                protocol static;
                route-filter 10.220.1.0/24 exact;
            }
            then accept;
        }
        term c {
            then reject;
        }
    }
}
```

Router 6 Configuration

```
protocols {
    rip {
        group to_Router1 {
            export export-vpn;
            neighbor t1-0/2/0.0;
        }
    }
}
policy-options {
    policy-statement export-vpn {
        term a {
            from {
                protocol direct;
                route-filter 10.255.71.57/32 exact;
            }
            then accept;
        }
        term b {
            from {
                protocol static;
                route-filter 10.220.1.0/24 exact;
            }
            then accept;
```

```
        }
        term c {
            then reject;
        }
    }
}
```

Router 7 Configuration

```
policy-options {
    policy-statement export-vpn {
        term a {
            from {
                protocol direct;
                route-filter 10.255.71.57/32 exact;
            }
            then accept;
        }
        term b {
            from {
                protocol static;
                route-filter 10.220.1.0/24 exact;
            }
            then accept;
        }
        term c {
            then reject;
        }
    }
}
```

Router 8 Configuration

```
protocols {
    bgp {
        group to-Router 3 {
            export export-vpn;
            peer-as 69;
            neighbor 192.167.188.25;
        }
    }
}
policy-options {
    policy-statement export-vpn {
        term a {
            from {
                protocol direct;
                route-filter 10.255.71.59/32 exact;
```

```
                }
                then accept;
            }
            term b {
                from {
                    protocol static;
                    route-filter 10.220.1.0/24 exact;
                }
                then accept;
            }
            term c {
                then reject;
            }
        }
    }
```

Router 9 Configuration

```
protocols {
    bgp {
        group to-Router 3 {
            export export-vpn;
            peer-as 69;
            neighbor 192.167.188.29;
        }
    }
}
policy-options {
    policy-statement export-vpn {
        term a {
            from {
                protocol direct;
                route-filter 10.255.71.58/32 exact;
            }
            then accept;
        }
        term b {
            from {
                protocol static;
                route-filter 10.220.1.0/24 exact;
            }
            then accept;
        }
        term c {
            then reject;
        }
    }
```

APPENDIX

Additional Resources

The information in this book has been largely cultivated from the Juniper Networks technical documentation, as well as field notes, quick reference cards, and Web sites.

Use this field guide as a quick reference either onsite or in review of basic requirements, specifications, and procedures. For complete details and more thorough discussions of software and hardware issues, consult the most current technical documentation.

The technical documentation is available at www.juniper.net. It is freely available in PDF and HTML formats. You can purchase printed copies at www.vervante.com/juniper.

If you are a registered customer with a service contract, consult the Juniper Networks Technical Assistance Center (JTAC) and Customer Service Center (CSC). For a description of available programs, see "Juniper Networks Technical Assistance Center (JTAC)" on page 5.

Another source of information is juniper-nsp, which is an open customer e-mail list for discussing Juniper Networks products and technology. To view the e-mail archives, see http://puck.nether.net/lists/juniper-nsp/. To subscribe to the list, see http://puck.nether.net/juniper-nsp/.

Throughout this book, the editors have tried to call out pertinent RFCs for additional reference and understanding. The three tables beginning with Table 2.1, "Supported Internet RFCs and Drafts" on page 19 list the RFCs and other standards documents supported by Juniper Networks platforms.

Juniper Networks conducts dozens of educational and training programs around the world. For a list of the most current classes and seminars, and to enroll, see www.juniper.net/education.

The Solutions & Technology section of www.juniper.net contains dozens of downloadable PDF and HTML versions of white papers, technology notes, and test papers on a variety of topics related to Juniper Networks platforms.

The following are additional sources of information related to the Juniper Networks product line and technology:

- For the T640 routing node, the T640 Internet Routing Node Installation Authorization Examination, offered through Juniper Networks Educational Services
- For additional information about router installation and setup
  - JUNOS software configuration getting started manual
  - Hardware guide and PIC guide for each router
- For additional information about the CLI, see the JUNOS software configuration getting started manual.
- For additional information about IPSec, see the JUNOS software configuration getting started manual.
- For additional information about CoS, see the JUNOS software configuration interfaces and class of service manual.
- For additional information about routing policy and firewall filters, see the JUNOS software configuration policy framework manual.
- For additional information about routing and routing protocols
  - JUNOS software configuration routing and routing protocols and multicast manuals
  - *Internetworking with TCP/IP*, Douglas E. Comer
  - *TCP/IP Illustrated*, W. Richard Stevens
  - Internet Engineering Task Force, www.ietf.org
  - North American Network Operators' Group, www.nanog.org
- For additional information about IPv6
  - JUNOS software configuration routing and routing protocols and multicast manuals
  - IPv6 Forum, http://www.ipv6forum.com/
  - 6Bone IPv6 Deployment Testbed, http://www.6bone.net/
- For additional information about MPLS, see the JUNOS software configuration MPLS applications manual.
- For additional information about VPNs, see the JUNOS software configuration VPN manual.

Glossary

A

active route Route chosen from all routes in the routing table to reach a destination. Active routes are installed into the forwarding table.

add/drop multiplexer *See ADM.*

Address Resolution Protocol *See ARP.*

adjacency Portion of the local routing information that pertains to the reachability of a single neighbor over a single circuit or interface.

ADM Add/drop multiplexer. SONET functionality that allows lower-level signals to be dropped from a high-speed optical connection.

aggregation Combination of groups of routes that have common addresses into a single entry in the routing table.

ANSI American National Standards Institute. The United States' representative to the ISO.

APS Automatic Protection Switching. Technology used by SONET ADMs to protect against circuit faults between the ADM and a router and to protect against failing routers.

area Routing subdomain that maintains detailed routing information about its own internal composition and that maintains routing information that allows it to reach other routing subdomains. In IS-IS, an area corresponds to a Level 1 subdomain.

In IS-IS and OSPF, a set of contiguous networks and hosts within an autonomous system that have been administratively grouped together.

area border router Router that belongs to more than one area. Used in OSPF.

ARP Address Resolution Protocol. Protocol for mapping IP addresses to MAC addresses.

AS Autonomous system. Set of routers under a single technical administration. Each AS normally uses a single interior gateway protocol (IGP) and metrics to propagate routing information within the set of routers. Also called *routing domain*.

AS boundary router In OSPF, routers that exchange routing information with routers in other ASs.

AS external link advertisements OSPF link-state advertisement sent by AS boundary routers to describe external routes that they know. These link-state advertisements are flooded throughout the AS (except for stub areas).

AS path In BGP, the route to a destination. The path consists of the AS numbers of all routers a packet must go through to reach a destination.

ASIC Application-specific integrated circuit. Specialized processors that perform specific functions on the router.

ATM Asynchronous Transfer Mode. A high-speed multiplexing and switching method utilizing fixed-length cells of 53 octets to support multiple types of traffic.

Automatic Protection Switching *See APS.*

autonomous system *See AS.*

autonomous system boundary router In OSPF, routers that exchange routing information with routers in other ASs.

autonomous system external link advertisements OSPF link-state advertisement sent by autonomous system boundary routers to describe external routes that they know. These link-state advertisements are flooded throughout the autonomous system (except for stub areas).

autonomous system path In BGP, the route to a destination. The path consists of the autonomous system numbers of all the routers a packet must pass through to reach a destination.

B

backbone area In OSPF, an area that consists of all networks in area ID 0.0.0.0, their attached routers, and all area border routers.

backplane On an M40 router, component of the Packet Forwarding Engine that distributes power, provides signal connectivity, manages shared memory on FPCs, and passes outgoing data cells to FPCs.

bandwidth The range of transmission frequencies a network can use, expressed as the difference between the highest and lowest frequencies of a transmission channel. In computer networks, greater bandwidth indicates faster data-transfer rate capacity.

BERT Bit error rate test. A test that can be run on a T3 interface to determine whether it is operating properly.

BGP Border Gateway Protocol. Exterior gateway protocol used to exchange routing information among routers in different autonomous systems.

bit error rate test *See BERT.*

Border Gateway Protocol *See BGP.*

broadcast Operation of sending network traffic from one network node to all other network nodes.

bundle Collection of software that makes up a JUNOS software release.

Control Board On a T640 routing node, provides control and monitoring functions for router components, working in conjunction with a Routing Engine.

CCC Circuit cross-connect. A JUNOS software feature that allows you to configure transparent connections between two circuits, where a circuit can be a Frame Relay DLCI, an ATM VC, a PPP interface, a Cisco HDLC interface, or an MPLS label-switched path (LSP).

CE device Customer edge device. Router or switch in the customer's network that is connected to a service provider's provider edge (PE) router and participates in a Layer 3 VPN.

CFM Cubic feet per minute. Measure of fan speed.

channel service unit *See CSU/DSU.*

CIDR Classless interdomain routing. A method of specifying Internet addresses in which you explicitly specify the bits of the address to represent the network address instead of determining this information from the first octet of the address.

CIP Connector Interface Panel. On an M160 or M40e router or a T640 routing node, the panel that contains connectors for the Routing Engines and alarm relay contacts.

circuit cross-connect *See CCC.*

class of service *See CoS.*

CLI Command-line interface. Interface provided for configuring and monitoring the routing protocol software.

client peer In a BGP route reflection, a member of a cluster that is not the route reflector. *See also nonclient peer.*

CLNP Connectionless Network Protocol. ISO-developed protocol for OSI connectionless network service. CLNP is the OSI equivalent of IP.

cluster In BGP, a set of routers that have been grouped together. A cluster consists of one system that acts as a route reflector, along with any number of client peers. The client peers receive their route information only from the route reflector system. Routers in a cluster do not need to be fully meshed.

community In BGP, a group of destinations that share a common property. Community information is included as one of the path attributes in BGP update messages.

confederation In BGP, a group of systems that appears to external autonomous systems to be a single autonomous system.

constrained path In traffic engineering, a path determined using RSVP signaling and constrained using CSPF. The ERO carried in the packets contains the constrained path information.

core The central backbone of the network.

CoS Class of service. A group of privileges and features assigned to a particular service.

CPE Customer premises equipment. Telephone or other service provider equipment located at a customer site.

craft interface Mechanisms used by a Communication Workers of America craftsperson to operate, administer, and maintain equipment or provision data communications. On a Juniper Networks router, the craft interface allows you to view status and troubleshooting information and perform system control functions.

CSNP Complete sequence number PDU. Packet that contains a complete list of all the LSPs in the IS-IS database.

CSPF Constrained Shortest Path First. An MPLS algorithm that has been modified to take into account specific restrictions when calculating the shortest path across the network.

CSU/DSU Channel service unit/data service unit. Channel service unit connects a digital phone line to a multiplexer or other digital signal device. Data service unit connects a DTE to a digital phone line.

customer edge device *See CE device.*

D

daemon Background process that performs operations on behalf of the system software and hardware. Daemons normally start when the system software is booted, and they run as long as the software is running. In the JUNOS software, daemons are also referred to as processes.

damping Method of reducing the number of update messages sent between BGP peers, thereby reducing the load on these peers without adversely affecting the route convergence time for stable routes.

data circuit-terminating equipment *See DCE.*

data-link connection identifier *See DLCI.*

data service unit *See CSU/DSU.*

Data Terminal Equipment *See DTE.*

dcd The JUNOS software interface process (daemon).

DCE Data circuit-terminating equipment. RS-232-C device, typically used for a modem or printer, or a network access and packet switching node.

default address Router address that is used as the source address on unnumbered interfaces.

denial of service *See DoS.*

designated router In OSPF, a router selected by other routers that is responsible for sending link-state advertisements that describe the network, which reduces the amount of network traffic and the size of the routers' topological databases.

destination prefix length Number of bits of the network address used for host portion of a CIDR IP address.

DHCP Dynamic Host Configuration Protocol. Allocates IP addresses dynamically so that they can be reused when they are no longer needed.

Dijkstra algorithm *See SPF.*

DIMM Dual-inline memory module. 168-pin memory module that supports 64-bit data transfer.

direct routes *See interface routes.*

DLCI Data-link connection identifier. Identifier for a Frame Relay virtual connection (also called a *logical interface*).

DoS Denial of service. System security breach in which network services become unavailable to users.

DRAM Dynamic random-access memory. Storage source on the router that can be accessed quickly by a process.

DSU Data service unit. A device used to connect a DTE to a digital phone line. Converts digital data from a router to voltages and encoding required by the phone line. *See also CSU/DSU.*

DTE Data Terminal Equipment. RS-232-C interface that a computer uses to exchange information with a serial device.

DVMRP Distance Vector Multicast Routing Protocol. Distributed multicast routing protocol that dynamically generates IP multicast delivery trees using a technique called reverse path multicasting (RPM) to forward multicast traffic to downstream interfaces.

Dynamic Host Configuration Protocol *See DHCP.*

E

EBGP External BGP. BGP configuration in which sessions are established between routers in different ASs.

edge router In MPLS, a router located at the beginning or end of a label-switching tunnel. When at the beginning of a tunnel, an edge router applies labels to new packets entering the tunnel. When at the end of a tunnel, the edge router removes labels from packets exiting the tunnel. *See also MPLS.*

EGP Exterior gateway protocol, such as BGP.

egress router In MPLS, last router in a label-switched path (LSP). *See also ingress router.*

EIA Electronic Industries Association. A United States trade group that represents manufacturers of electronics devices and sets standards and specifications.

EMI Electromagnetic interference. Any electromagnetic disturbance that interrupts, obstructs, or otherwise degrades or limits the effective performance of electronics or electrical equipment.

end system In IS-IS, network entity that sends and receives packets.

ERO Explicit route object. Extension to RSVP that allows an RSVP PATH message to traverse an explicit sequence of routers that is independent of conventional shortest-path IP routing.

explicit path *See signaled path.*

Explicit Route Object *See ERO.*

export To place routes from the routing table into a routing protocol.

external BGP *See EBGP.*

external metric A cost included in a route when OSPF exports route information from external autonomous systems. There are two types of external metrics: Type 1 and type 2. Type 1 external metrics are equivalent to the link-state metric; that is, the cost of the route, used in the internal autonomous system. Type 2 external metrics are greater than the cost of any path internal to the autonomous system.

F

fast reroute Mechanism for automatically rerouting traffic on an LSP if a node or link in an LSP fails, thus reducing the loss of packets traveling over the LSP.

FEAC Far-end alarm and control. T3 signal used to send alarm or status information from the far-end terminal back to the near-end terminal and to initiate T3 loopbacks at the far-end terminal from the near-end terminal.

FEB Forwarding Engine Board. In M5 and M10 routers, provides route lookup, filtering, and switching to the destination port.

flap damping *See damping.*

flapping *See route flapping.*

Flexible PIC Concentrator *See FPC.*

Forwarding Engine Board *See FEB.*

forwarding information base *See forwarding table.*

forwarding table JUNOS software forwarding information base (FIB). The JUNOS routing protocol process installs active routes from its routing tables into the Routing Engine forwarding table. The kernel copies this forwarding table into the Packet Forwarding Engine, which is responsible for determining which interface transmits the packets.

FPC Flexible PIC Concentrator. An interface concentrator on which PICs are mounted. An FPC inserts into a slot in a Juniper Networks router. *See also PIC.*

FRU Field-replaceable unit. Router component that customers can replace onsite.

G–H

group A collection of related BGP peers.

HDLC High-level data link control. An International Telecommunication Union (ITU) standard for a bit-oriented data link layer protocol on which most other bit-oriented protocols are based.

hold time Maximum number of seconds allowed to elapse between the time a BGP system receives successive keepalive or update messages from a peer.

host module On an M160 router, provides routing and system management functions of the router. Consists of the Routing Engine and Miscellaneous Control Subsystem (MCS).

I

IANA Internet Assigned Numbers Authority. Regulatory group that maintains all assigned and registered Internet numbers, such as IP and multicast addresses. *See also NIC.*

IBGP Internal BGP. BGP configuration in which sessions are established between routers in the same ASs.

ICMP Internet Control Message Protocol. Used in router discovery, ICMP allows router advertisements that enable a host to discover addresses of operating routers on the subnet.

IDE Integrated Drive Electronics. Type of hard disk on the Routing Engine.

IEC International Electrotechnical Commission. *See ISO.*

IEEE Institute of Electronic and Electrical Engineers. International professional society for electrical engineers.

IETF Internet Engineering Task Force. International community of network designers, operators, vendors, and researchers concerned with the evolution of the Internet architecture and the smooth operation of the Internet.

IGMP Internet Group Membership Protocol. Used with multicast protocols to determine whether group members are present.

IGP Interior gateway protocol, such as IS-IS, OSPF, and RIP.

import To install routes from the routing protocols into a routing table.

ingress router In MPLS, first router in a label-switched path (LSP). *See also egress router.*

inter-AS routing Routing of packets among different ASs. *See also EBGP.*

intercluster reflection In a BGP route reflection, the redistribution of routing information by a route reflector system to all nonclient peers (BGP peers not in the cluster). *See also route reflection.*

interface routes Routes that are in the routing table because an interface has been configured with an IP address. Also called *direct routes*.

intermediate system In IS-IS, network entity that sends and receives packets and that can also route packets.

internal BGP *See IBGP.*

intra-AS routing The routing of packets within a single AS. *See also IBGP.*

IP Internet Protocol. The protocol used for sending data from one point to another on the Internet.

IS-IS Intermediate System-to-Intermediate System protocol. Link-state, interior gateway routing protocol for IP networks that also uses the shortest-path first (SPF) algorithm to determine routes.

ISO International Organization for Standardization. Worldwide federation of standards bodies that promotes international standardization and publishes international agreements as International Standards.

ISP Internet service provider. Company that provides access to the Internet and related services.

ITU International Telecommunications Union (formerly known as the CCITT). Group supported by the United Nations that makes recommendations and coordinates the development of telecommunications standards for the entire world.

K

kernel forwarding table *See forwarding table.*

L

label In MPLS, 20-bit unsigned integer in the range 0 through 1,048,575 used to identify a packet traveling along an LSP.

label-switched path (LSP) Sequence of routers that cooperatively perform MPLS operations for a packet stream. The first router in an LSP is called the *ingress router*, and the last router in the path is called the *egress router*. An LSP is a point-to-point, half-duplex connection from the ingress router to the egress router. (The ingress and egress routers cannot be the same router.)

label switching *See MPLS.*

label-switching router *See LSR.*

link Communication path between two neighbors. A link is *up* when communication is possible between the two end points.

link-state PDU (LSP) Packets that contain information about the state of adjacencies to neighboring systems.

local preference Optional BGP path attribute carried in internal BGP update packets that indicates the degree of preference for an external route.

loose In the context of traffic engineering, a path that can use any route or any number of other intermediate (transit) points to reach the next address in the path.

LSP See *label-switched path* (LSP) and *link-state PDU* (LSP).

LSR Label-switching router. A router on which MPLS and RSVP are enabled and is thus capable of processing label-switched packets.

M

martian address Network address about which all information is ignored.

mask *See subnet mask.*

MBGP Multiprotocol BGP. An extension to BGP that allows you to connect multicast topologies within and between BGP ASs.

MBone Internet multicast backbone. An interconnected set of subnetworks and routers that support the delivery of IP multicast traffic. The MBone is a virtual network that is layered on top of sections of the physical Internet.

MCS Miscellaneous Control Subsystem. On an M160 router, provides control and monitoring functions for router components and SONET clocking for the router.

MED Multiple exit discriminator. Optional BGP path attribute consisting of a metric value that is used to determine the exit point to a destination when all other factors in determining the exit point are equal.

mesh Network topology in which devices are organized in a manageable, segmented manner with many, often redundant, interconnections between network nodes.

MIB Management Information Base. Definition of an object that can be managed by SNMP.

midplane Forms the rear of the PIC cage on M5 and M10 routers and the FPC card cage on M20 and M160 routers. Provides data transfer, power distribution, and signal connectivity.

Miscellaneous Control Subsystem *See MCS.*

MPLS Multiprotocol Label Switching. Mechanism for engineering network traffic patterns that functions by assigning to network packets short labels that describe how to forward them through the network. Also called *label switching. See also traffic engineering.*

MTBF Mean time between failure. Measure of hardware component reliability.

MTU Maximum transfer unit. Limit on segment size for a network.

multicast Operation of sending network traffic from one network node to multiple network nodes.

multiprotocol BGP *See MBGP.*

Multiprotocol Label Switching *See MPLS.*

N

neighbor Adjacent system reachable by traversing a single subnetwork. An immediately adjacent router. Also called a *peer.*

NET Network entity title. Network address defined by the ISO network architecture and used in CLNS-based networks.

network layer reachability information *See NLRI.*

network link advertisement An OSPF link-state advertisement flooded throughout a single area by designated routers to describe all routers attached to the network.

Network Time Protocol *See NTP.*

NIC Network Information Center. Internet authority responsible for assigning Internet-related numbers, such as IP addresses and autonomous system numbers. *See also IANA.*

NLRI Network layer reachability information. Information that is carried in BGP packets and is used by MBGP.

nonclient peer In a BGP route reflection, a BGP peer that is not a member of a cluster. *See also client peer.*

not-so-stubby area *See NSSA.*

NSAP Network service access point. Connection to a network that is identified by a network address.

n-selector Last byte of a nonclient peer address.

NSSA Not-so-stubby area. In OSPF, a type of stub area in which external routes can be flooded.

NTP Network Time Protocol. Protocol used to synchronize computer clock times on a network.

O

OC Optical Carrier. In SONET, Optical Carrier levels indicate the transmission rate of digital signals on optical fiber.

OSI Open System Interconnection. Standard reference model for how messages are transmitted between two points on a network.

OSPF Open Shortest Path First. A link-state IGP that makes routing decisions based on the shortest-path-first (SPF) algorithm (also referred to as the *Dijkstra algorithm*).

P

package A collection of files that make up a JUNOS software component.

Packet Forwarding Engine The architectural portion of the router that processes packets by forwarding them between input and output interfaces.

path attribute Information about a BGP route, such as the route origin, AS path, and next-hop router.

PCI Peripheral Component Interconnect. Standard, high-speed bus for connecting computer peripherals. Used on the Routing Engine.

PCMCIA Personal Computer Memory Card International Association. Industry group that promotes standards for credit card-size memory or I/O devices.

PDU Protocol data unit. IS-IS packets.

PE router Provider edge router. A router in the service provider's network that is connected to a customer edge (CE) device and that participates in a Virtual Private Network (VPN).

PEC Policing Equivalence Classes. In traffic policing, a set of packets that is treated the same by the packet classifier.

peer An immediately adjacent router with which a protocol relationship has been established. Also called a *neighbor.*

PFE *See Packet Forwarding Engine.*

Physical Interface Card *See PIC.*

PIC Physical Interface Card. A network interface–specific card that can be installed on an FPC in the router.

PIM Protocol Independent Multicast. A protocol-independent multicast routing protocol. PIM sparse mode routes to multicast groups that might span wide-area and interdomain internets. PIM dense mode is a flood-and-prune protocol.

PLP Packet loss priority.

policing Applying rate limits on bandwidth and burst size for traffic on a particular interface.

pop Removal of the last label, by a router, from a packet as it exits an MPLS domain.

PPP Point-to-Point Protocol. Link-layer protocol that provides multiprotocol encapsulation. It is used for link-layer and network-layer configuration.

preference Desirability of a route to become the active route. A route with a lower preference value is more likely to become the active route. The preference is an arbitrary value in the range 0 through 255 that the routing protocol process uses to rank routes received from different protocols, interfaces, or remote systems.

preferred address On an interface, the default local address used for packets sourced by the local router to destinations on the subnet.

primary address On an interface, the address used by default as the local address for broadcast and multicast packets sourced locally and sent out the interface.

primary interface Router interface that packets go out from when no interface name is specified and when the destination address does not imply a particular outgoing interface.

Protocol-Independent Multicast *See PIM.*

provider edge router *See PE router.*

provider router Router in the service provider's network that does not attach to a customer edge (CE) device.

PSNP Partial sequence number PDU. Packet that contains only a partial list of the LSPs in the IS-IS link-state database.

push Addition of a label or stack of labels, by a router, to a packet as it enters an MPLS domain.

Q

QoS Quality of service. Performance, such as transmission rates and error rates, of a communications channel or system.

quality of service *See QoS.*

R

RADIUS Remote Authentication Dial-In User Service. Authentication method for validating users who attempt to access the router using Telnet.

Random Early Detection *See RED.*

rate limiting *See policing.*

RED (Pronounced "red") Random Early Detection. Gradual drop profile for a given class that is used for congestion avoidance. RED tries to anticipate incipient congestion and reacts by dropping a small percentage of packets from the head of the queue to ensure that a queue never actually becomes congested.

Resource Reservation Protocol *See RSVP.*

RFC Request for Comments. Internet standard specifications published by the Internet Engineering Task Force.

RFI Radio frequency interference. Interference from high-frequency electromagnetic waves emanating from electronic devices.

RIP Routing Information Protocol. Distance-vector interior gateway protocol that makes routing decisions based on hop count.

route flapping Situation in which BGP systems send an excessive number of update messages to advertise network reachability information.

route identifier IP address of the router from which a BGP, IGP, or OSPF packet originated.

route reflection In BGP, configuring a group of routers into a cluster and having one system act as a route reflector, redistributing routes from outside the cluster to all routers in the cluster. Routers in a cluster do not need to be fully meshed.

router link advertisement OSPF link-state advertisement flooded throughout a single area by all routers to describe the state and cost of the router's links to the area.

routing domain *See AS.*

Routing Engine Architectural portion of the router that handles all routing protocol processes, as well as other software processes that control the router's interfaces, some of the chassis components, system management, and user access to the router.

routing table Common database of routes learned from one or more routing protocols. All routes are maintained by the JUNOS routing protocol process.

rpd JUNOS software routing protocol process (daemon). User-level background process responsible for starting, managing, and stopping the routing protocols on a Juniper Networks router.

RPM Reverse-path multicasting. Routing algorithm used by DVMRP to forward multicast traffic.

RSVP Resource Reservation Protocol. Resource reservation setup protocol designed to interact with integrated services on the Internet.

S

SAP Session Announcement Protocol. Used with multicast protocols to handle session conference announcements.

SCB System Control Board. On an M40 router, the part of the Packet Forwarding Engine that performs route lookups, monitors system components, and controls FPC resets.

SDH Synchronous Digital Hierarchy. CCITT variation of SONET standard.

SDP Session Description Protocol. Used with multicast protocols to handle session conference announcements.

SDRAM Synchronous Dynamic Random Access Memory.

secure shell *See SSH.*

SFM Switching and Forwarding Module. On an M160 router, a component of the Packet Forwarding Engine that provides route lookup, filtering, and switching to FPCs.

shortest-path-first algorithm *See SPF.*

signaled path In traffic engineering, an explicit path; that is, a path determined using RSVP signaling. The ERO carried in the packets contains the explicit path information.

simplex interface An interface that assumes that packets it receives from itself are the result of a software loopback process. The interface does not consider these packets when determining whether the interface is functional.

SNMP Simple Network Management Protocol. Protocol governing network management and the monitoring of network devices and their functions.

SONET Synchronous Optical Network. High-speed (up to 2.5 Gbps) synchronous network specification developed by Bellcore and designed to run on optical fiber. STS-1 is the basic building block of SONET. Approved as an international standard in 1988. *See also SDH.*

SPF Shortest-path first, an algorithm used by IS-IS and OSPF to make routing decisions based on the state of network links. Also called the *Dijkstra algorithm.*

SSB System and Switch Board. On an M20 router, Packet Forwarding Engine component that performs route lookups and component monitoring and monitors FPC operation.

SSH Secure shell. Software that provides a secured method of logging in to a remote network system.

SSRAM Synchronous Static Random Access Memory.

static LSP *See static path.*

static path In the context of traffic engineering, a static route that requires hop-by-hop manual configuration. No signaling is used to create or maintain the path. Also called a *static LSP.*

STM Synchronous Transport Module. CCITT specification for SONET at 155.52 Mbps.

strict In the context of traffic engineering, a route that must go directly to the next address in the path.

STS Synchronous Transport Signal. Synchronous Transport Signal level 1. Basic building block signal of SONET, operating at 51.84 Mbps. Faster SONET rates are defined as STS-*n*, where *n* is a multiple of 51.84 Mbps. *See also SONET.*

stub area In OSPF, an area through which, or into which, AS external advertisements are not flooded.

subnet mask Number of bits of the network address used for host portion of a Class A, Class B, or Class C IP address.

summary link advertisement OSPF link-statement advertisement flooded throughout the advertisement's associated areas by area border routers to describe the routes that they know about in other areas.

sysid System identifier. Portion of the ISO nonclient peer. The sysid can be any 6 bytes that are unique throughout a domain.

System and Switch Board *See SSB.*

T

TACACS+ Terminal Access Controller Access Control System Plus. Authentication method for validating users who attempt to access the router using telnet.

TCP Transmission Control Protocol. Works in conjunction with Internet Protocol (IP) to send data over the Internet. Divides a message into packets and tracks the packets from point of origin to destination.

ToS Type of service.

traffic engineering Process of selecting the paths chosen by data traffic in order to balance the traffic load on the various links, routers, and switches in the network. *See also MPLS.*

transit area In OSPF, an area used to pass traffic from one adjacent area to the backbone or to another area if the backbone is more than two hops away from an area.

transit router In MPLS, any intermediate router in the LSP between the ingress router and the egress router.

tunnel Private, secure path through an otherwise public network.

type of service *See ToS.*

U

unicast Operation of sending network traffic from one network node to another individual network node.

V

VCI Virtual circuit identifier. Identifier for an ATM virtual connection. Also called a *logical interface.*

virtual circuit identifier *See VCI.*

virtual link In OSPF, a link created between two routers that are part of the backbone but are not physically contiguous.

virtual path identifier Virtual circuit identifier. *See VCI.*

Virtual Router Redundancy Protocol *See VRRP.*

VPI *See VCI.*

VRRP Virtual Router Redundancy Protocol. On Fast Ethernet and Gigabit Ethernet interfaces, allows you to configure virtual default routers.

weighted round-robin *See WRR.*

WRR Weighted round-robin. Scheme used to decide the queue from which the next packet should be transmitted.

Index

B

C

D

E

I

P

Q

R

S